Broadcast Engineering & IT Conference 2022

Held at the 2022 NAB Show

Las Vegas, Nevada, USA
23-27 April 2022

ISBN: 978-1-7138-5345-9

Printed from e-media with permission by:

Curran Associates, Inc.
57 Morehouse Lane
Red Hook, NY 12571

Some format issues inherent in the e-media version may also appear in this print version.

National Association of Broadcasters (NAB)
1 M Street SE
Washington, D.C. 20003

Phone: (202) 429 5300

www.nab.org

Additional copies of this publication are available from:

Curran Associates, Inc.
57 Morehouse Lane
Red Hook, NY 12571 USA
Phone: 845-758-0400
Fax: 845-758-2633
Email: curran@proceedings.com
Web: www.proceedings.com

NAB
NATIONAL ASSOCIATION OF BROADCASTERS

Proceedings of the 2022 Broadcast Engineering and IT Conference

Table of Contents

Proceedings of the 2022 Broadcast Engineering and IT Conference

Table of Contents

ATSC 3.0 / Next Gen TV Applications

Broadcast Workflows

Cybersecurity in Broadcast Facilities

IP-Based Video Facilities

NAB
NATIONAL ASSOCIATION OF BROADCASTERS

Proceedings of the 2022 Broadcast Engineering and IT Conference

Table of Contents

New Radio Transmission Technologies

OTT 1: Emerging Developments

OTT 2: Open Caching and the Network Edge

NAB
NATIONAL ASSOCIATION OF BROADCASTERS

Proceedings of the 2022 Broadcast Engineering and IT Conference

Table of Contents

5G-MAG Reference Tools: Putting 5G in Action for Media

Daniel Silhavy
Fraunhofer FOKUS
Berlin, Germany
daniel.silhavy@fokus.fraunhofer.de

Klaus Kühnhammer
Bitstem GmbH
Hausleiten, Austria
klaus@bitstem.com

Johann Mika
Austrian Broadcasting Services
Vienna, Austria
johann.mika@ors.at

Thomas Stockhammer
Qualcomm
Munich, Germany
tsto@qti.qualcomm.com

Jordi J. Gimenez
5G-MAG
Geneve, Switzerland
gimenez@5g-mag.com

Abstract – Content providers are increasingly using the Internet to deliver media content to users. The same applies to users who are able to enjoy media on a wide variety of devices anywhere and at any time. The increasing consumption of high-quality mobile video over 5G networks demands highly scalable, sophisticated and robust delivery architectures, systems and protocols ready to cope with different traffic loads and meet requirements and expectations from content owners. 5G is an opportunity to provide the media industry with a set of different tools to operate an advanced media delivery platform. With this in mind, 5G-MAG kickstarted the 5G-MAG Reference Tools project to develop common open-source reference tools to support implementation and interoperability of 5G-based media technologies.

In this paper, we present the current architecture of the 5G-MAG Reference Tools implementing client components in the context of 3GPP Release 16 5G Media Streaming and 5G Broadcast. Moreover, we provide detailed insights on the first two target use-cases, (i) "LTE-based 5G Broadcast" and (ii) "broadband-broadcast seamless switching". An outlook on future work on targeting use cases such as "targeted ad-insertion" and "regional content insertion" is given. We also show how the tools serve as a reference or integration platform for traditional broadcast networks and services including a DVB-I service layer or the alignment with the service layer of ATSC3.0.

Introduction

The Internet is now fully accessible to the media industry, and this creates tremendous opportunities for new user service propositions, more personalized experiences, and a fast lane for innovation for service providers and content creators. Within this developing ecosystem the combination of fixed and wireless networks, as well as the global 5G introduction enables media content providers to have access to a universal, ubiquitous, and future-proof distribution platform allowing them to reach users everywhere, anytime and on any device - in particular the Gen-Z for which the smartphone is the primary device for communication and entertainment [1]. The Ericsson Mobility Reports forecasts that by 2027 5G networks will carry 62 percent of the world's smartphone traffic. Specifically, the delivery of video content is expected to account for 79 percent of the mobile data traffic in 2027 [2].

To support media and content providers in getting access to the powerful, but complex 5G distribution platform, simplifications, support, and abstraction to the workflows of media providers are needed. In the dynamic world of apps, software-centric solutions and agile developments, access to open-source tools to support prototyping, trials and possibly even deployments are of utmost relevance. 5G-MAG has taken on the duty and mandate to fill the role in bringing together the media and the 5G world to support deployment of media services on 5G systems.

As a particular effort to respond to the need of fast access to technology, the 5G-MAG Reference Tools project[1] has been established. The overall goal of the project is to provide an end-to-end platform enabling the implementation of media players as part of a 5G client; service layers and the testing of applications developed by other media-related organizations; hybrid scenarios and integration of third-party functions in the network.

In this paper, we present the current architecture of the 5G-MAG Reference Tools focusing on two main initial uses cases. We illustrate the general working principles of the 5G-MAG Reference Tools focusing on the main components "MBMS Modem", "MBMS Middleware" and the "Webinterface". We demonstrate how to use the 5G-MAG Reference Tools to receive a 5G broadcast (5G BC) signal in dedicated mode, i.e. using 100 % downlink capacity (also known as EnTV/FeMBMS in 3GPP Rel.14 and LTE-based 5G Terrestrial Broadcast in 3GPP Rel.16). The 5G broadcast signal contains File Delivery over Unidirectional Transport (FLUTE) encoded DASH and HLS resources (the common format is CMAF). These CMAF resources are processed and cached for DASH and/or HLS clients. Using web-based players such as dash.js and hls.js the files received via 5G broadcast can be played the same way as normal unicast broadband streams delivered via a CDN. This abstraction permits re-use of existing apps and services independent of the delivery mode. Making use of the direct integration of unicast and broadcast, we further enhance the implementation by dynamically and seamlessly switching between broadcast and broadband content, referred to as "broadband-broadcast seamless switching".

5G Media Delivery

General

3GPP is defining core elements of the 5G system, including those that constitute the 5G media distribution platform. Such standardization effort is leading to the support of different deployment and collaboration among service providers, media companies and network operators to enable the creation of new services and user experiences.

The first releases of 5G specifications, with Rel-16 completed in mid-2020, include the definition of the 5G Media Streaming architecture and LTE-based 5G Broadcast. 3GPP Rel-16 has been taken as the starting point for the implementation of the 5G-MAG Reference Tools. Standardization continues in Rel-17 and Rel-18 with several extensions to 5G media streaming, including edge capabilities, the introduction of 5G Multicast Broadcast Services (5MBS) and the evolution of LTE-based 5G Broadcast, among others.

5G Media Streaming

5G Media Streaming responds to the growing consumption of multimedia services, with video as its maximum exponent, and the need to open the 5G System capabilities to content providers. A range of collaboration models are enabled focused on improving QoE for end users, optimizing delivery across the network, monetizing traffic or monitoring QoS and consumption.

The 5G Media Streaming architecture and basic procedures are specified in 3GPP TS 26.501 and stage-3 specifications in TS 26.511 and TS 26.512 define a series of protocols, codecs and functionalities well aligned with current over-the-top distribution models and applications [3].
The main components of 5G Media Streaming are the following:

[1] https://www.5g-mag.com/reference-tools

- 5GMS Application Function (AF): provides management functions for the 5GMS system (control plane), including provisioning and configuration (offered to the service provider) and reporting (from the user equipment). Depending on the collaboration model, the 5GMS AF can be deployed within the mobile network or in an external data Network (e.g. in the domain of the service provider).
- 5GMS Application Server (AS): provides data and content functionalities (data plane) including ingest functionalities (towards service providers) and the delivery to the 5GMS clients.
- 5GMS Client, containing the Media Session Handler (MSH), which receives the configuration information from the AF and handles the relevant 5GMS features, and the Media Player which obtains media content from the AS.

LTE-Based 5G Broadcast

3GPP specified the first global broadcast standard to address 5G-enabled devices. LTE-based 5G broadcast, widely known as 5G Broadcast, allows linear TV and radio to be broadcast to compatible 3GPP-based devices like smartphones, tablets, home gateways and connected cars. Rel-16 extended the capabilities of MBMS to support dedicated broadcast networks for the transmission of linear television and radio services. Among others, the standard supports the following key features:

- Support of Free-to-Air (FTA) services
- Broadcast-only service for UEs with no MNO broadcast subscription
- Decoupling of content, MBMS service and MBMS transport functions
- Exposure of eMBMS service and transport capabilities to third parties.
- Single Frequency Network (SFN) deployments with Inter-Site Distance (ISD) significantly larger than a typical ISD associated with typical cellular deployments
- Support for Receive-Only Mode (ROM) services and devices

Rel-17 is currently addressing additional functionalities such as the support of UHF band frequencies (with 6/7/8 MHz carrier bandwidths) or the connection of LTE-based 5G Broadcast to 5G Media Streaming, so the latter serves as the entry point for service providers to the complete 5G media distribution platform.

The 5G-MAG Reference Tools

The 5G-MAG Reference Tools project was started in late 2021. Since then, a steadily growing developer community is committed to create common open-source reference tools to support implementation and interoperability of 5G Media technologies.

The initial focus of the project was the development of Rel-16 5G Media Streaming and LTE-based 5G Broadcast client components, server/headend and corresponding 5G unicast and broadcast radio emulators. For that reason, multiple software components have been implemented and made publicly available on Github[2]. The overall architecture of the 5G-MAG Reference Tools is depicted in Figure 1. The main components of the 5G-MAG Reference Tools are the **rt-mbms-modem (MBMS Modem)**, the **rt-mbms-mw (MBMS Middleware)** and the **rt-wui (Webinterface).**

[2] https://github.com/5G-MAG

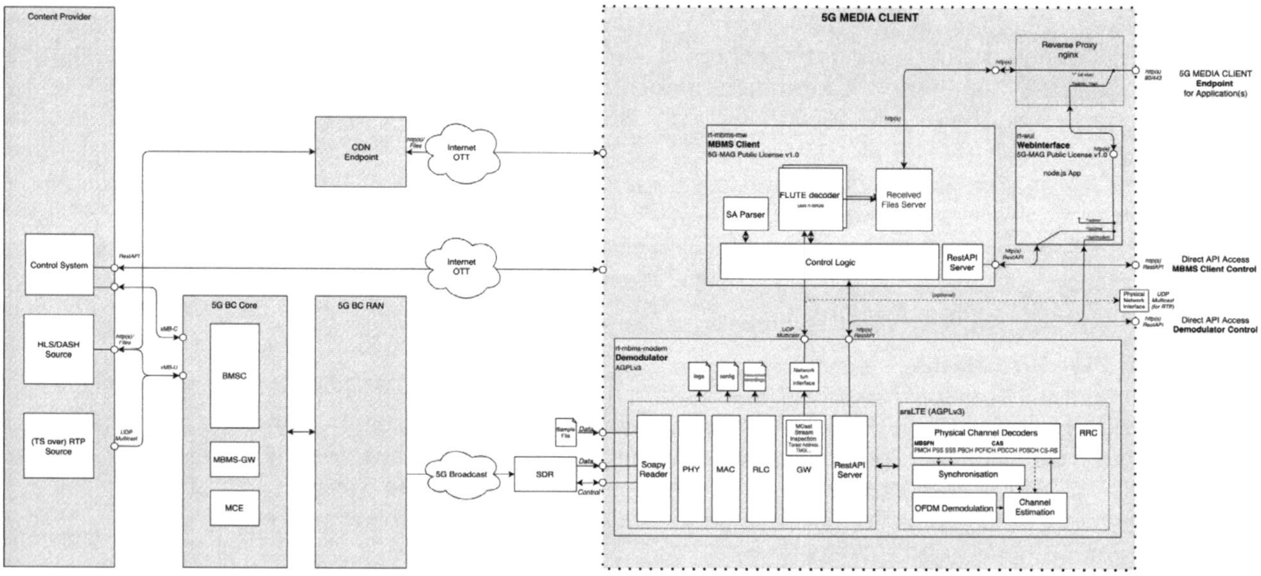

FIGURE 1: THE ARCHITECTURE OF THE 5G-MAG REFERENCE TOOLS

MBMS Modem

The MBMS Modem builds the lower part of the 5G-MAG Reference Tools. Its main task is to convert a 5G broadcast input signal to Multicast IP packets on the output. The MBMS Modem is implemented as a standalone C++ application which uses parts of the srsRAN[3] library.

The main components of the MBMS Modem are implemented as modules for a better structure and to easier improve specific parts:

- The Soapy Reader module processes the input signal that can either be received as I/Q raw data from a Software Defined Radio (SDR) or as a prerecorded sample file. The usage of sample files provides a convenient way to implement and test new features and to showcase specific functionality of the MBMS Modem.
- The Physical Layer module (PHY) is responsible for synchronization, OFDM demodulation, channel estimation, decoding of the physical control and user data channels. The Medium Access Control (MAC) module evaluates the Downlink Control Information (DCI) and the Control Format Indicator (CFI), as well as the System Information Block (SIB) and the Master Information Block (MIB). Moreover, a decoding of the Multicast Control Channel (MCCH) and Multicast Traffic Channel (MTCH) is performed. Additionally, the MBMS Modem uses the Radio Link Control (RLC) and Gateway (GW) module to output MTCH data on a tun network interface. The output of the MBMS Modem is a UDP multicast that can be further processed by the MBMS Middleware or directly be accessed by an external application or media player.

The MBMS Modem can be configured via a configuration file and writes important status messages to a log file. In addition, it exposes a RESTful API for dynamic configuration and querying status information.

MBMS Middleware

The MBMS Middleware presents the heart of the 5G-MAG Reference Tools. Its main task is to provide the best available content to the (internal or external) application at any time. If available, it combines content from (mobile) broadband, WiFi with the 5G BC content from the MBMS Modem using an

[3] https://github.com/srsran/srsRAN

advanced decision logic. The content is presented to the applications in form of an intelligent edge cache ready for pick up via http(s).

The MBMS Middleware uses the UDP multicast IP packets from the MBMS Modem. If the payload contains FLUTE encoded content (files, i.e. Service Announcement, DASH, HLS) the MBMS Middleware decodes the packets with its FLUTE/ALC decoder[4] into files. The MBMS Middleware includes a web-cache server and each service is available like an CDN publishing point including manifest and segment files.

Like the MBMS Modem, the MBMS Middleware can be configured via a configuration file and writes important status messages to a log file. In addition, it exposes a RESTful API for dynamic configuration and querying status information. The RESTful API is used by the Web-User Interface to query the location of the FLUTE decoded manifest and segment files.

Webinterface

The Webinterface provides a graphical interface with a control display. Its main purpose is to collect and display useful information from for the MBMS Modem and MBMS Middleware. For that reason, it uses the RESTful APIs provided by both processes. It also enables use cases where the 5G-MAG Reference Tools can be used for simple measurements (e.g., mobile measurements) or as a standalone device (e.g., set-top box, mobile phone/tablet showcase). The web-user interface consists of three tabs, one for each process. In addition, the Webinterface works as a media player using dash.js[5] and hls.js[6] as external dependencies for the playback of the FLUTE decoded DASH and HLS streams provided via the MBMS Middleware.

Use Case 1: LTE-Based 5G Broadcast

The first use case addressed by the 5G-MAG Reference tools focuses on the reception of an LTE-based 5G Broadcast. LTE-based 5G Broadcast can be used to:

- Distribute public and commercial linear TV and radio services, free-to-air or encrypted, to 3GPP-compatible devices such as smartphones, smart TVs, or car infotainment systems;
- Enable personalized media offers by delivering linear broadcast content alongside catch-up and on-demand using the same family of standards;
- Enable broadcast distribution of linear TV and radio services integrated into existing media applications with 3GPP-defined APIs.

A simplified illustration of the basic workflow for the processing of an LTE-based 5G broadcast in the 5G-MAG Reference Tools is depicted in Figure 2. The 5G broadcast or a sample file are processed by the MBMS Modem resulting in a UDP multicast output. In case the 5G broadcast contains an RTP stream the output of the MBMS modem can directly be played in a third-party media player such as VLC or ffplay. For FLUTE encoded DASH and HLS files the output of the MBMS Modem is further processed in the MBMS Middleware. The MBMS Middleware uses the Service Announcement (SA Parser) to set up a FLUTE decoder and saves the FLUTE decoded media files on a file server. Moreover, the MBMS Middleware modifies specific timing values in the DASH and HLS manifests to account for delays in the broadcast delivery. As a result, the client will not attempt to request files that have not yet been received. Once the media files have been cached in the MBMS Middleware they can be accessed by the Webinterface or any other DASH and HLS mediaplayer. The 5G-MAG Reference Tools use a Reverse nginx Proxy to perform an internal mapping of specific ports and routes to the standard ports used for http(80) and https (443). The Webinterface itself integrates dash.js and hls.js for playback of the DASH and HLS streams directly in the browser.

[4] https://github.com/5G-MAG/rt-libflute
[5] https://github.com/Dash-Industry-Forum/dash.js
[6] https://github.com/video-dev/hls.js/

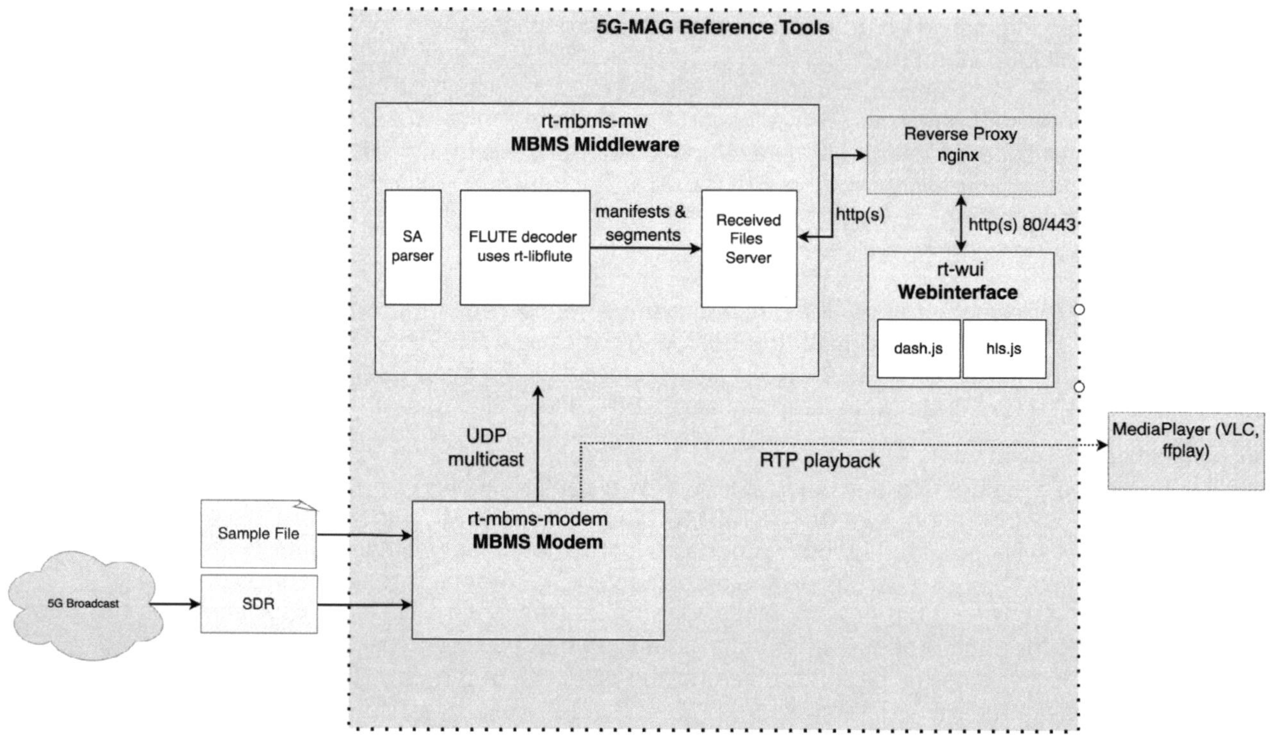

FIGURE 2: THE BASIC WORKFLOW OF LTE-BASED 5G BROADCASTING IN THE 5G-MAG REFERENCE TOOLS

Use Case 2: Broadband-Broadcast Seamless Switching

With seamless switching, universal service coverage can be provided by the complementarity of different networks and delivery mechanisms. In cases in which certain users are out of 5G broadcast coverage, the media playback is not disrupted, and the service continues to operate with unicast fallback from the 5G broadband network. In this way, quality of service conditions can be maintained at an exceptionally high level, and the user experience can be improved according to the needs of users and/or operators.

Technically, these requirements present two main challenges: push vs. pull availability of the data, and a time offset introduced by the added latency of 5G-Broadcast (5G-BC) incurred by the broadcast data acquisition mechanisms of the BC Core components and the lower broadcast layers in the RAN.

Playlists, video, and audio segments are collected from the content provider origin by the BC Core, and pushed through 5G-Broadcast to the clients, where they arrive with some delay. The clients can also pull all these files from a CDN individually but will receive different content for the playlists/manifests, as the delay means that the version received through 5G-BC will be older than the one loaded from the CDN.

To enable seamless switching of the video playback, the middleware must ensure that every audio and video segment has either been received through 5G-BC or can be fetched from the CDN in time for the player's request of this segment. This effectively precludes using the manifests from CDN directly, as the 5G-BC latency means they present segment availability too close to the live edge.

This becomes especially pertinent in cases where a client can receive a particular stream only from the CDN, and then either enters an area where this stream can also be received through 5G-BC; or when this stream becomes available through 5G-BC by scheduling or by a dynamic provisioning mechanism.

In the reference implementation of this use case, we demonstrate a simplified first approach for these challenges constrained to HLS streaming. For that reason, the architecture of the 5G-MAG Reference Tools is extended by additional components as illustrated in Figure 2. The handling of audio/video segments and playlists/manifests is split up into different components:

- The "Cache Management" component handles the segment data, which is stored when received through 5G-BC. A request from the player for a segment that has not yet been received triggers a cache miss, causing this segment to be immediately fetched from the CDN. In the current implementation, a 404 status is returned to the player's request, mimicking a request too close to the live edge and causing the player to retry with progressive intervals.
- The playlists/manifests are handled by "Playlist Management", which creates them dynamically when requested by the player. This component also receives playlists incoming on 5G-BC, and periodically requests playlists from CDN. From these two sources, the content of the playlists that are created and presented to the media player is determined: for 5G-BC playlists, it is assumed that the latest contained file should be available on 5G-BC, and hence can be presented as such to the player; whereas for CDN playlists, a configurable number of segments is stripped out of the playlist to offset the expected 5G-BC delay. For the mediaplayer itself it is not visible whether the manifests and segments originated from 5G-BC or from a CDN.

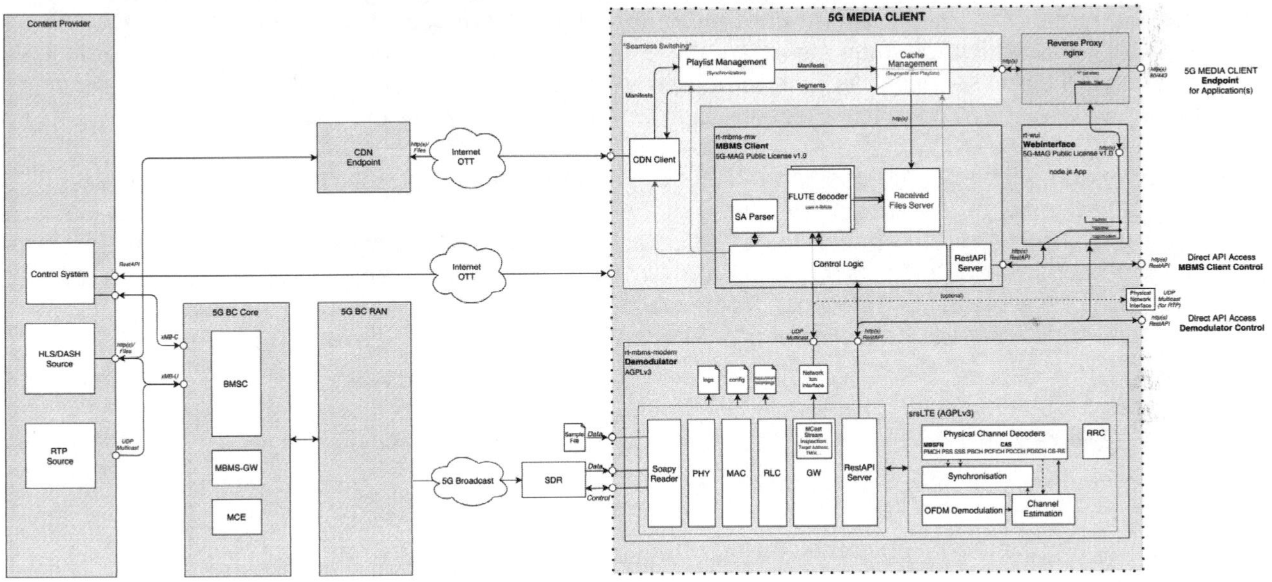

FIGURE 3: ENHANCED ARCHITECTURE OF THE 5G-MAG REFERENCE TOOLS TO SUPPORT BROADBAND-BROADCAST SEAMLESS SWITCHING

Conclusion

The global introduction of 5G and the trend to consume high-quality videos over mobile networks lead to a high demand for robust streaming service architectures on top of the complex 5G distribution platform. The 5G-MAG Reference Tools project has been established to provide an open-source end-to-end platform to support implementation and interoperability of 5G Media technologies.

In this paper we gave a detailed overview of the 5G-MAG Reference Tools focusing on two specific use cases "LTE-based 5G Broadcast" and "broadband-broadcast seamless switching". The implementation of the 5G-MAG Reference Tools is based on the Rel-16 3GPP 5G specifications for 5G Media Streaming and LTE-based 5G Broadcast. LTE-based 5G Broadcast can be used to distribute public and commercial linear TV and radio services, free-to-air or encrypted, to 3GPP-compatible devices such as smartphones, smart TVs, or car infotainment systems. With broadband-broadcast seamless switching, universal service coverage can be provided by the complementarity of different networks and delivery mechanisms. In cases in which certain users are out of 5G broadcast coverage, the media playback is not disrupted, and the service continues to operate with unicast fallback from the 5G broadband network.

The main components of the 5G-MAG Reference Tools are the rt-mbms-modem (MBMS Modem), the rt-mbms-mw (MBMS Middleware) and the rt-wui (Webinterface). For both use cases, "LTE-based 5G Broadcast" and "broadband-broadcast seamless switching" the broadcast signal is processed by the MBMS Modem and exposed as a UDP multicast to the MBMS Middleware. The MBMS Middleware decodes the FLUTE encoded DASH and HLS files and performs necessary manifest timing manipulations. Via an internal web server and a reverse proxy, the manifest files and the media segments are accessible by the Webinterface. The Webinterface uses open-source players such as dash.js and hls.js for playback of the media streams directly in browser-based environments. For "broadband-broadcast seamless switching" the 5G-MAG Reference Tools were extended by additional components to enable intelligent caching of files coming either from the 5G broadcast or via unicast directly from a CDN.

Future work will focus on further combining broadcast coverage and unicast connectivity. That way the seamless-switching use-case can also be used for other scenarios, like regional and local content insertions, content replacement, and on-demand or targeted advertising. While the developed tools focus on 5G-based distribution, they also may serve as a reference or integration platform for traditional broadcast networks and services. As an example, the integration of a DVB-I service layer is an ongoing effort. In addition, the developed tools closely align with the service layer of ATSC3.0.

In further development steps, the addition of Rel-16 5G Media Streaming functionalities will enable interaction between 5G broadcast and unicast together with overlaying services. As a result, the 5G-MAG Reference Tools further enhance the 5G media ecosystem and serve as foundation for validation, verification, demonstration, trials, and even commercial services. Moreover, the current Linux-based implementation of the 5G-MAG Reference Tools will be extended to support a multitude of devices such as smartphones, set-top boxes, car entertainment systems, wearables, and other Android-based platforms

How to Participate

The participation in the development of the 5G-MAG Reference Tools is open, i.e. not just limited to 5G-MAG members, quite the contrary we hope to attract researchers and independent developers into the community. More information can be found on: https://www.5g-mag.com/reference-tools

References

[1] 99Content, "Generation Z Statistics", https://99firms.com/blog/generation-z-statistics, *Last accessed on March 16th 2022*

[2] Ericsson, "Ericsson Mobility Report", November 2021, https://www.ericsson.com/4ad7e9/assets/local/reports-papers/mobility-report/documents/2021/ericsson-mobility-report-november-2021.pdf, *Last accessed on March 16th 2022*

[3] 3rd Generation Partnership Project, Technical Specification Group Services and System Aspects; 5G Media Streaming (5GMS); General description and architecture (Release 16) - TS 26.501, April 2021

ATSC 3.0, DVB-I and TV 3.0 Services Via 5G Broadcast – System Design and Reference Tools

Christophe Burdinat
Ateme
Velizy-Villacoublay, France
c.burdinat@ateme.com

Thomas Stockhammer
Qualcomm Incorporated
Munich, Germany
tsto@qti.qualcomm.com

Romain Bouqueau
Motion Spell GPAC
Paris, France
romain.bouqueau@motionspell.com

Mickaël Raulet
Ateme
Rennes, France
m.raulet@ateme.com

Abstract – 5G broadcast brings the promise of an independent or complementary linear TV experience, which can reuse existing terrestrial broadcast infrastructure to serve HD or 4K live contents to mobile devices, possibly independent of a mobile subscription. To benefit fully from this new capability, the design of a service layer is essential, including service discovery procedures and the delivery protocols over IP multicast. This paper examines the set of the different standardized service layers brought by 3GPP, ATSC and DVB which could target different regions, ecosystems or regulatory requirements. In order to support media service providers, a full ecosystem of tools is now emerging, including the Reference Tools from the 5G Media Action Group (5G-MAG) and the GPAC open-source solution. In this paper, we introduce the consolidated work from 3GPP and 5G-MAG to make this vision a reality, in terms of standardization and development of reference tools. We will detail how DVB-I services over 5G broadcast can now be experimented with commodity tools and commercial devices. We will also identify the potential synergies with ATSC 3.0 A/331 [1] and the possibilities for the Brazil's TV 3.0 project [2], for which ROUTE/DASH is the transport layer of choice and 5G Broadcast is a candidate for the physical layer.

Origination of 5G Broadcast

5G Broadcast is the result of continuous work at 3GPP since Release-9, which has been progressively enriched to allow terrestrial broadcast scenarios (Figure 1).

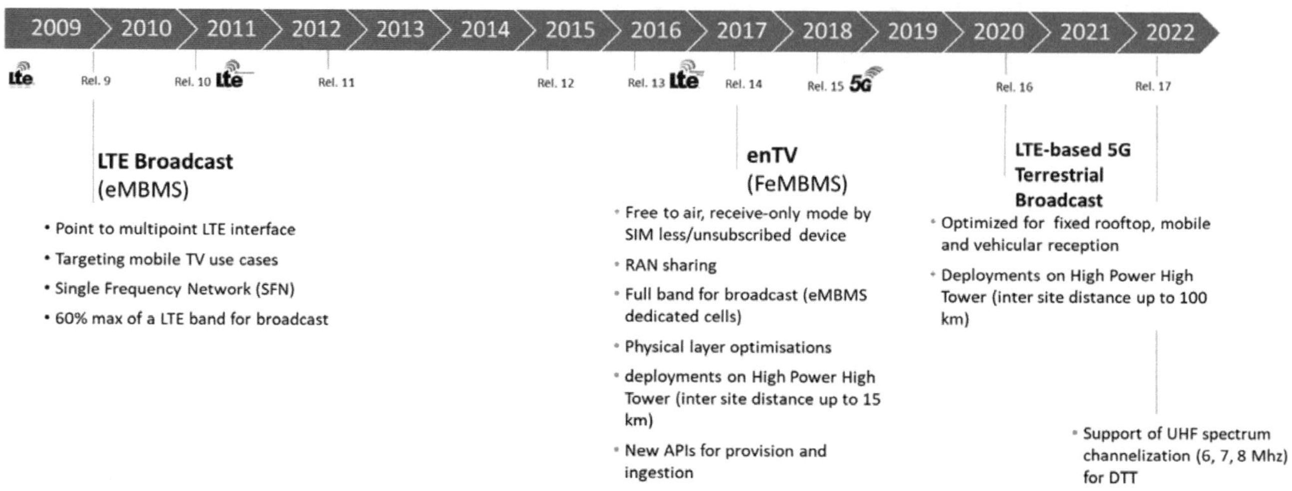

FIGURE 1: EMERGENCE OF 5G BROADCAST AT 3GPP.

The Evolved Multimedia Broadcast Multicast Services (eMBMS), also known as LTE-Broadcast, was introduced in Release-9 by 3GPP to offer a point-to-multipoint interface, using the LTE(4G) infrastructure. eMBMS was made possible with small changes to the LTE radio and core network protocols of LTE. While initially designed to target TV distribution to mobile receivers as an add-on mobile TV service in large pre-planned areas, this capacity was later included in the design of Public Safety LTE (PSLTE) and Internet of Things (IoT) systems. eMBMS transmissions are based on a Single Frequency Network (SFN) based Orthogonal frequency-division multiplexing (OFDM) waveform for which new dedicated physical, transport and logic channels were specified.

Before Release-14, eMBMS could only be deployable on Low Power Low Towers (LPLT) of mobile networks, sharing the capacity of a mobile frequency band with unicast transmissions, and serving only the subscribers of a given mobile operator.

Under the work item "enTV" (enhanced TV) in Release 14 and 16, 3GPP significantly enhanced the eMBMS capacity to address these limitations and implement key broadcast requirements:

- In pre-Release-14 eMBMS, only 60% of the subframes in a given frequency band could be allocated for broadcast services, the remaining being allocated to unicast transmissions. Release-14 enabled the full allocation of the dedicated band for eMBMS in so-called MBMS-dedicated cells.
- Contents can be delivered free-to-air, in receive-only mode, by SIMless/unsubscribed devices.
- RAN sharing, i.e. the ability for an eMBMS network to deliver in a same carrier the services of different operators.
- The physical layer of the radio signal becomes more efficient by removing the control region (first subframes) of LTE frames, used for the control of unicast transmissions and useless in an eMBMS dedicated cell.
- New numerologies and cyclic prefix durations to allow deployments in SFN on High Power High Tower (HPHT), with an Inter Site Distance (ISD) up to 15 km in Release 14, and up to 100 km in Release 16.
- Optimized for different reception conditions (fixed rooftop, mobile and vehicular reception).

This set of features addresses all the requirements of a 5G Broadcast System, formulated in [3] and are profiled by the European Telecommunications Standards Institute (ETSI) in TS 103 720 [4] for 5G dedicated broadcast networks. This profile is referred to as LTE-Based 5G Terrestrial Broadcast.

While many organizations are considering 5G Broadcast, the EBU studied the frequencies planning of 5G networks [5], including compatibility between 5G Broadcast and other Digital Terrestrial Television (DTT) technologies in the UHF spectrum. As 5G Broadcast is delivered within 3, 5, 10, or 20 MHz mobile bands, an additional adaptation is necessary to use 6, 7 or 8 MHz UHF bandwidths to fit with the spectrum channelization allocated to DTT. With this last enhancement, targeted this year in Release 17 [6], the 5G Broadcast standard becomes mature enough for commercial deployments, which is in line with the emergence of a full ecosystem of tools.

A Collection of Transport and Service Layers

5G Broadcast, allowing the distribution of IP multicast streams, must be associated with a service layer, specifying the discovery and announcement procedures and the protocol stacks on top of IP multicast. Associated procedures for reporting or loss recovery may be added. While traditional broadcast is relying on MPEG2 transport streams, the industry has shifted to a full IP-based broadcasting standard, facilitating the implementation of targeted advertisements and the delivery of hybrid services, whose components are delivered over broadcast and/or broadband. As HTTP adaptive streaming protocols are used to deliver all broadband streaming IP content [6][7], one of the main objectives of such a service layer for IP multicast is to specify how to deliver DASH/HLS streaming services to serve the native DASH/HLS players widely supported on connected devices.

The 3GPP service layer for eMBMS [8] offers the Download Delivery Method. Based on the FLUTE protocol [9], it allows delivery of files over multicast. Initially designed to deliver non-real-time content, it was adapted to support the delivery of live ABR services such as DASH or HLS. In Release-14, another method was proposed: the Transparent Delivery Method, in which any IP packet streams can be forwarded over eMBMS/5G Broadcast. This method was included to permit the distribution of any IP multicast services without restrictions, to support the transport of external content formats specified by broadcasting organizations such as ATSC or DVB. In other words, the Transparent Delivery Method opens 5G Broadcast to the usage of other service layers external to 3GPP, in particular the ATSC 3.0 transport layer [1] and the DVB-I service layer [10][11] (Figure 2). This flexibility may facilitate deployments targeted to different regions, ecosystems or regulatory requirements.

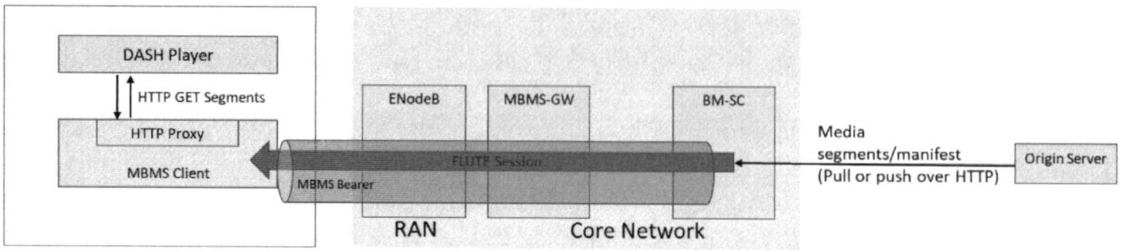

Dash service delivery with the 3GPP Download Delivery Method

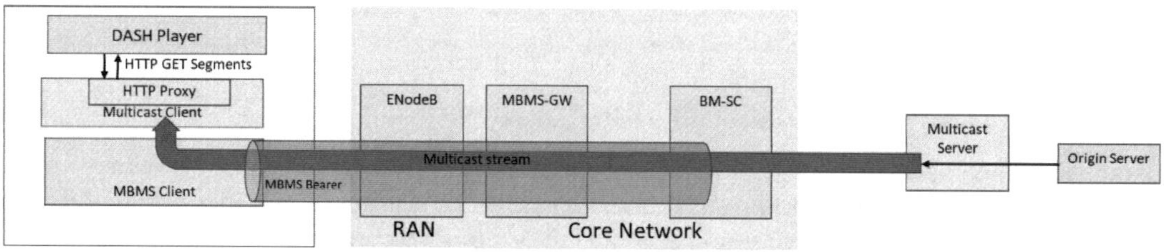

Dash service delivery with the 3GPP Transparent Delivery Method

FIGURE 2: MEDIA PLANE FOR THE DELIVERY OVER 5G BROADCAST WITH THE 3GPP SERVICE LAYER OR AN EXTERNAL SERVICE LAYER

When using the transparent delivery mode, the MBMS client function within the User Equipment (UE) only covers the access to the multicast IP streams transported by the MBMS Bearers (Logical channels for LTE-Broadcast transmissions) and those streams are decoded by an external multicast client function.

ATSC 3.0 Transport Layer

ATSC 3.0 adopted two protocols to transport TV over IP: the MPEG Multimedia Transport (MMT) [12] and the Real-Time Object Delivery over Unidirectional Transport (ROUTE) protocol [13]. MMT, designed by Moving Pictures Expert Group (MPEG), inherits some features from MPEG2-TS, adapted for delivery over IP. ROUTE is an evolution of FLUTE, finely tuned to deliver DASH live content over IP multicast and addressing limitations of the 3GPP service layer, in particular:

- FLUTE requires the transmission inline of a File Delivery Table (FDT), describing the FLUTE session content, by associating a file URI to each transmitted object. This FDT is a small XML file which has to be repeated to guarantee its reception. When delivering a DASH service, each new media segment is delivered with an updated FDT instance, creating an overhead and an additional risk of losing a full media segment if the FDT is missed. ROUTE specifies an extended FDT format, providing mapping rules between the sequence of media segments and the sequence of Transport Object Identifier (TOI). The extended FDT just has to be signaled once to the receiver to allow decoding the full media segment sequence.
- FLUTE allows protection against loss with Application Layer Forward Error Correction (AL-FEC). The AL-FEC is applied separately on each transmitted file. Such a method is inefficient to protect the delivery of small files, such as audio or subtitle segments. ROUTE specifies a mechanism to apply AL-FEC to a collection of objects with various lengths, to increase time diversity and assure an equal Quality of Service (QoS).
- FLUTE inherits the use of the FEC building block [14] from ALC, which specifies algorithmically how objects to be delivered are split into blocks, symbols and IP packets. This algorithm requires prior knowledge of the object length. Consequently, FLUTE cannot start the delivery of an object which has not been fully generated. ROUTE offers the possibility to progressively

deliver an object without knowing its final size. When the media segment, following the fMP4 format (clause 6.6.5 of [15]) and is composed of a sequence of chunks, ROUTE allows the immediate delivery of those chunks, in a low latency manner, before the end of the segment generation.

ROUTE/DASH has been selected as the recommended transport layer for the TV 3.0 project.

DVB-I, an Access Independent Service Layer

The DVB-I specifications are designed by DVB to bring the standard of linear TV delivered over IP networks up to the user experience level for the traditional broadcast experience. This includes delivery over unmanaged networks such as an Over The Top (OTT) service and over managed network. DVB-I targets any IP devices, whatever the nature of the access network (satellite, fiber, cable, mobile…). The objective is to signal and distribute services in a standardized manner, without the need of a specific application, without the need for users to care whether the service is received from a broadcast or broadcast network.

DVB-I specifications include the following:

- DVB-I Service Discovery and Programme Metadata [10], defines how linear TV services over broadband with their network specific parameters are discovered and signaled through a set of HTTP requests. It also specifies how the Electronic Program Guide (EPG) is distributed and defines a method for national TV operators to offer a list of trusted/regulated services.
- DVB MPEG-DASH Profile for Transport of ISO BMFF Based DVB Services over IP Based Networks [16], which provides a MPEG-DASH profile for DVB-I.
- DVB multicast ABR (DVB-MABR) [11] specifies how ABR segment-based services such as DASH or HLS can be delivered over IP multicast, to design a system for linear media distribution that is both efficient and scalable to very large audiences.

DVB has achieved last year a promising study about the distribution of DVB-I services over 5G [17]. A high-level vision of DVB consists in adding the 5G delivery systems as new alternative pipes for DVB-I services.

At the end of a multicast transmission a DVB-I MABR gateway receives the segment delivered with DVB-MABR, and acts as a CDN edge by caching them towards the application. Each application includes a DVB-I client which implements the service discovery procedures, the support of DVB-DASH and the DVB profiles for audio video codecs.

The specification phase is now starting at DVB in a joint effort with the 5G Media Action Group (5G-MAG).

DVB-MABR proposes 2 multicast protocol stacks (Figure 3). The first is reusing the FLUTE protocol from the 3GPP service layer, and the second is reusing the ROUTE protocol from ATSC 3.0. The FLUTE protocol is slightly modified to support low latency delivery as well, by transporting the segment chunks as individual files.

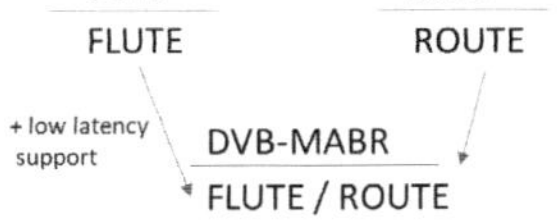

FIGURE 3: MULTICAST PROTOCOLS FOR THE 3GPP, ATSC AND DVB-I SERVICE LAYERS

Experimenting the Delivery of ATSC 3.0, DVB-I Services Over 5G Broadcast

The primary objective of our experimentation here is to validate the usage of various service/transport layers over 5G Broadcast as introduced in the previous section. We focus in particular on the usage of the ROUTE protocol to demonstrate the applicability of the ATSC 3.0 and DVB-I service layers over 5G Broadcast for various video codecs.

Implementing A Radio Broadcast Link

Specified in Release 14 and 16, with last improvements coming in Release-17, the 5G broadcast standard is too recent for being supported in commercially available handsets. Delivery over 5G Broadcast has nevertheless already been experimented successfully several times [18][19] using a Software Defined Radio (SDR) as a receiver [20]. To be able to experiment on handsets, we used LTE-Broadcast, providing a subset of 5G broadcast features (see first section), which is the only mobile broadcast transmission technology supported by commercial devices.

The core and radio network is provided by a AMARI callbox mini [21], serving a 10 meters coverage. Our tests are done with the LTE Band 7, using a bandwidth of 10 or 20 MHz. We allocate, by configuration, 50% of the subframes to LTE-Broadcast. A list of multicast streams, defined by their multicast IP address and destination port, is defined over pre-configured MBMS bearers for transmission over LTE-Broadcast. In laboratory conditions, we can use high values for the Modulation and Coding Scheme (MCS), for a spectral efficiency up to 3 b/Hz.

While the LTE-Broadcast feature is available on a large range of chipsets and devices, the feature is generally not activated by default and may require a firmware update. The experimentation is done with the OnePlus 9 [22] and the ASUS 'Smartphone for Snapdragon insiders' [23] smartphones, both supporting the activated LTE-Broadcast feature.

Accessing to the IP Multicast Streams from the Application

There are several APIs, to allow applications accessing the services delivered over LTE-Broadcast:

- 3GPP specifies the MBMS API [24], as an interface between the MBMS client and the applications. When using the 3GPP service layer, this specification specifies how the MBMS client can act as an HTTP proxy for the DASH/HLS services delivered with the Download Delivery Method.
- APIs covering the same functional scope are provided by the Enensys Cube Agent middleware [25] and the Qualcomm MSDC [26].
- For Mission Critical (MC) purposes and direct access to MBMS bearer contents, an integration API was specified by the Mission Critical Open Platform [27]. 3GPP also specified the MC MBMS API [28] for the same objective.
- The Android MBMS API [29], available since Android 9. This API requires that the Original Equipment Manufacturer (OEM) offers a middleware able to link this API to the modem internal API. It covers the functional scope of the MBMS API and the MC MBMS API. We do not expect any change on this Android API for the support of 5G Broadcast.

The ASUS smartphone supports the Android MBMS API. To trigger the reception of MBMS Bearers and access to their multicast streams, we leverage the Mission Critical functions of this API with the MbmsGroupCallSession, MBMSGroupCall, MbmsGroupCallSessionCallback classes. First, the MBMS Reception feature is activated and a callback indicates the name of the local network interface where the streams will be made available:

```
private MbmsGroupCallSessionCallback groupCallSessionCallback;
private MbmsGroupCallSession mbmsGroupCallSession;
private String mbmsInterfaceName;
/**
 * Activate MBMS reception
 */
public void enableMBMS() {

    groupCallSessionCallback = new MbmsGroupCallSessionCallback() {

        @Override
        public void onServiceInterfaceAvailable(@NonNull String interfaceName, int
index) {
            Log.e(TAG, "service interface for MBMS Reception " + interfaceName);
            mbmsInterfaceName = interfaceName;
        }

    };

    //Enabling MBMS reception
     mbmsGroupCallSession =
MbmsGroupCallSession.create(this.getApplicationContext(), 1,
this.getMainExecutor(), groupCallSessionCallback);

}
```

FIGURE 4: ACTIVATION OF THE MBMS CLIENT WITH THE ANDROID API

Then we can start the reception of a given MBMS bearer:

```
private GroupCall groupCall;

/**
 * Starting the reception of a MBMS bearer
 * @param tmgi the Temporary Multicast Group Identifier of the MBMS Bearer
 */
public void startReceptionMBMSBearer(long tmgi) {

    GroupCallCallback myCallBack = new GroupCallCallback() {

        @Override
        public void onGroupCallStateChanged(int state, int reason) {
            switch (state) {
                case  GroupCall.STATE_STARTED:
                    Log.i(TAG, "MBMS bearer reception is started");
                    break;

                case  GroupCall.STATE_STALLED:
                    Log.e(TAG, "onGroupCallStateChanged: stalled reason " +
reason);
                    break;

                case  GroupCall.STATE_STOPPED:
                    Log.e(TAG, "onGroupCallStateChanged: stopped reason " +
reason);
                    break;
```

```
            }
        }
    };

    //List of Service Area Identifiers and frequencies, may be left empty
    List<Integer> sais = new ArrayList<Integer>();
    List<Integer> frequencies = new ArrayList<Integer>();

    groupCall = mbmsGroupCallSession.startGroupCall(tmgi, sais, frequencies,
executor, myCallBack);
}
```

FIGURE 5: TRIGGERING THE RECEPTION OF AN MBMS BEARER

Finally, to access to the received multicast IP packets from this MBMS bearer, the application just has to join the multicast IP address on the local network interface returned in the first step:

```
/**
 * Access to the multicast IP packets
 * @param multicastAddress String representation of the multicast IP address to
join
 * @param destinationPort destination port
 * @throws Exception
 */
public void receive(String multicastAddress, int destinationPort) throws Exception
{
    NetworkInterface ni = NetworkInterface.getByName(mInterfaceName);

    //open a multicast socket
    MulticastSocket mSocket = new MulticastSocket(destinationPort);
    SocketAddress socketAddress =
                new InetSocketAddress(multicastAddress, destinationPort);

    //join the multicast group on a given network interface
    mSocket.joinGroup(socketAddress, ni);

    while (true) {
        byte[] buf = new byte[1500];
        DatagramPacket recv = new DatagramPacket(buf, buf.length);
        mSocket.receive(recv);

        //TODO process the received datagram
    }
}
```

FIGURE 6: ACCESS TO THE MULTICAST STREAMS

Multicasting a DASH Service With ROUTE

The ROUTE multicast server and client (Figure 2) are provided by the GPAC open-source solution [30]. GPAC is a multimedia framework focused on modularity and standards compliance. GPAC provides tools to process, inspect, package, stream, playback and interact with media content. It is well-known for its MP4Box tool, an mp4 file packager and HTTP streaming (DASH/HLS/CMAF) segmenter. GPAC also enables end users to build custom multimedia processing pipelines through its filter-based architecture. The project is distributed under LGPL v2.1+ license.

GPAC features in particular the ROUTE protocol. GPAC allows, by a single command line, to run a ROUTE session for the delivery of a given DASH or HLS source. The source can be a live service. GPAC offers a low latency mode, where the input media segments are not reassembled before being multicasted, so that the chunks are immediately delivered as soon as they are produced.

```
# gpac -i https://<hosting server>/<manifest path>.mpd dashin:forward=file -o
route://<multicast ip>:<port>[:llmode]
gpac -i https://source.//service.mpd dashin:forward=file -o
route://225.1.1.0:6000:llmode
```

FIGURE 7: GPAC COMMAND LINE TO START A ROUTE SSESSION

To decode and play a service delivered in a ROUTE session on an Android device, we can directly install the GPAC player, named MP4Client or Osmo4 and, from the menu, open the URL route://<multicast IP>:<port>.

A second option consists in using GPAC only as a ROUTE client, exposing the received segments as an HTTP proxy which could be requested by any DASH or HLS player. This option requires building directly GPAC from the github sources on the target Android devices. Then the ROUTE client can be launched from a Termux environment with the following command line:

```
gpac -i route://225.1.1.0:6000/:max_segs=40 dashin:forward=file @=file @
httpout:port=8081:rdirs=$PWD/tmp:reqlog='*':cors=auto -opt core:cache=$PWD/tmp_gpac
```

FIGURE 8: GPAC COMMAND LINE TO RECEIVE A ROUTE SESSION

In this example, the ROUTE session multicasted to 225.1.1.0:6000 is decoded, and its content (manifest and segments) is accessible to players under http://localhost:8081.

Our full setup is represented in Figure 9:

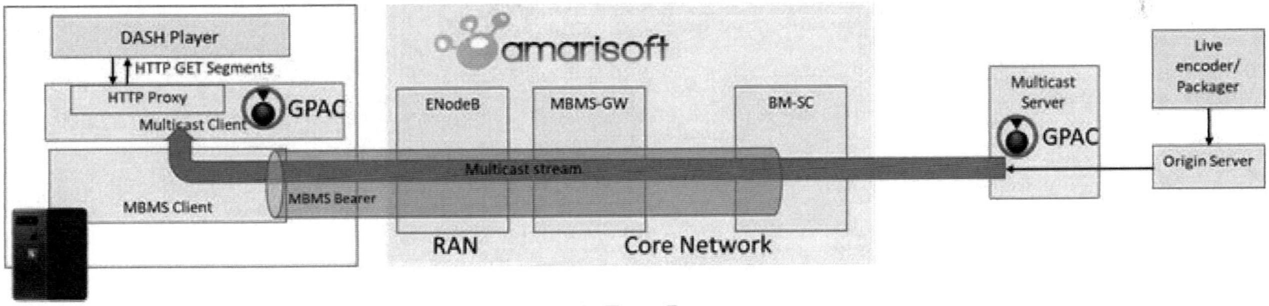

FIGURE 9: TEST PLATFORM

This setup allowed us to experiment the delivery with various players, including Dash.js - the reference client from the DASH Industry Forum [31], open-source players such as mpv media player [32], Exoplayer [33] or the GPAC player itself. A Titan Live encoder from Ateme, provided ISOBMFF packaging and CMAF Low-Latency encapsulation. The video chunks produced are pushed to an origin server, supporting HTTP chunked transfer encoding for low latency. In particular, we could experiment the delivery over ROUTE/5G Broadcast of H.266/Versatile Video Codec (VVC) linear contents.

This laboratory setup validates the usage of non-3GPP service/transport layers over 5G Broadcast. Follow-up experimentations will include latency evaluation and optimization of the end-to-end delivery chain. The GPAC open-source solution provides a stable and interoperable ROUTE implementation. Enhancements could be targeted to support additional features from the different service layers such as the different signaling/announcements procedure from ATSC 3.0 or DVB-I, the ability to perform file repair requests for loss recovery. The building and packaging chain may also be subject to improvements to facilitate deployments on mobile operating systems.

Emerging Reference Tools and Implementations

5G Media Action Group (5G-MAG) is a cross industry association to collaborate on the building of the 5G ecosystem for media production and distribution. The 5G-MAG Reference Tools development programme is now developing a set of common open-source reference tools to support the implementation and interoperability of 5G Media technologies.

The 5G-MAG Reference Tools [34] provide a platform, based on OBECA, to receive 5G Broadcast in dedicated mode, where 100% of a carrier is allocated to broadcast transmission. Based on the 3GPP service layer, the platform implements the delivery of hybrid services whose different components are available over broadcast and/or broadband, and the dynamic and seamless switch between those two delivery modes.

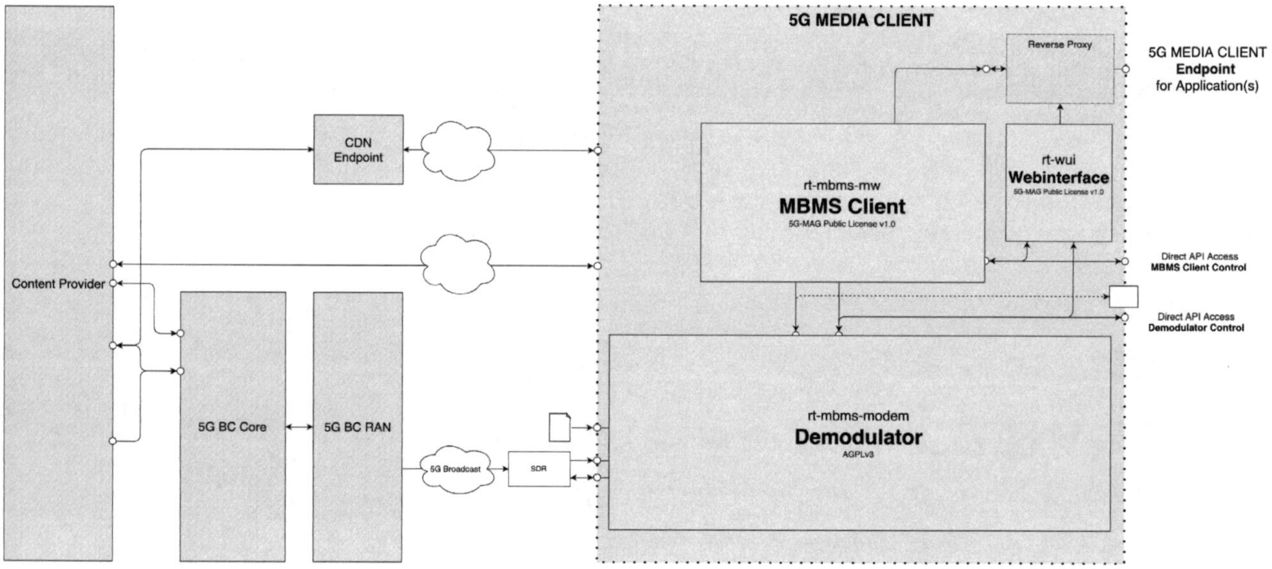

FIGURE 10: 5G-MAG REFERENCE TOOLS PLATFORM [34]

While the platform currently supports the 3GPP service layer, an extension is currently being implemented to include the support of the ROUTE protocol as well. The Reference Tools will also be enriched by a transmitter [35], providing a full set of open-source tools to experiment 5G Broadcast.

At the same time, the first proof-of-concepts of a TV signal sent from High-Power High Tower infrastructure in the UHF band, directly to a mobile device, without the need of any SIM card was completed and demonstrated at the Mobile World Congress in 2022. For details refer to [36] and [37].

Perspectives

TV 3.0

The SBTVD Forum (Sistema Brasileiro de TV Digital [2]) is the Brazilian organization responsible for development of digital television in Brazil, gathering more than eighty members, private and public, covering the complete ecosystem, including broadcasters, manufacturers, institutions, and universities. Over the years, SBTVD enabled the transition from analog to digital, releasing a number of specifications issued by the Brazilian Association of Technical Standards (ABNT). In July 2020, SBTVD issued a call for proposals aiming at extending the current digital television system to new use-cases and futuristic applications and distinguishing 6 system components: Over-the-air Physical Layer, Transport Layer, Video Coding, Audio Coding, Captions, and Application Coding (Figure 10). Among these applications, video formats such as 8K, HDR, AR/VR shall be supported and delivered over broadcast, or hybrid broadband/broadcast networks, based on IP-centric protocols.

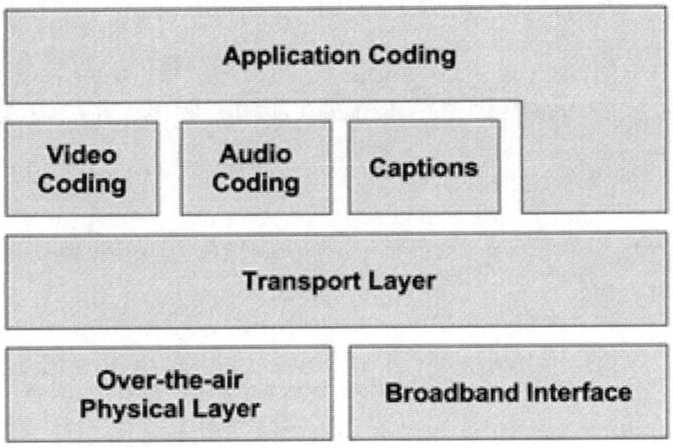

FIGURE 10: TV 3.0 ARCHITECTURE

After months of field and laboratory tests, the forum recommended the adoption of the ROUTE/DASH technology as the basis of the TV 3.0 transport layer, leaving the support of HLS as optional. For the Video Coding component, it adopted H266/VVC both for terrestrial broadcast and broadband while maintaining support for H.264 and H.265 for broadband. Tests for the selection of the Over-the-air physical layer are ongoing, for which 5G Broadcast is a candidate.

This is yet another large TV market after ATSC 3.0, DVB-I with multicast ABR and now TV 3.0 that has adopted ROUTE/DASH as the service layer of choice.

Conclusion

5G Broadcast has been designed in 3GPP Release-14 and 16. The coming enhancements in Release-17, allowing to reallocate directly the UHF spectrum for terrestrial broadcast to 5G Broadcast, bring the last piece to enable its commercialization. The combination of specifications and tools from the converging activities from 3GPP, ATSC, DVB and cross industry associations allows the emergence of a rich ecosystem from which various 5G Broadcast use cases can already be experimented. 5G-Broadcast, allowing any multicast IP-based transport layer, can be used to transport DVB-I or ATSC 3.0 services, facilitating its integration in regional ecosystems.

References

[1] Advanced Television Systems Committee (ATSC) Standard: "Signaling, Delivery, Synchronization, and Error Protection (A/331)"

[2] TV 3.0 Project, https://forumsbtvd.org.br/tv3_0/

[3] Third Generation Partnership Project (3GPP) TS 22.261, "Service requirements for the 5G system"

[4] European Telecommunications Standards Institute (ETSI) TS 103 720, "5G Broadcast System for linear TV and radio services; LTE-based 5G terrestrial broadcast system"

[5] European Broadcasting Union (EBU) Technical Report 064, "Compatibility between 5G Broadcast and other DTT systems in the sub-700 MHz band"

[6] ISO/IEC 23009-1:2014 "Information technology — Dynamic adaptive streaming over HTTP (DASH) — Part 1: Media presentation description and segment formats"

[7] IETF RFC 8216 HTTP Live Streaming

[8] Third Generation Partnership Project (3GPP) TS 26.346, "Multimedia Broadcast/Multicast Service (MBMS); Protocols and codec"

[9] IETF RFC 6726 FLUTE - File Delivery over Unidirectional Transport

[10] European Telecommunications Standards Institute (ETSI) TS 103 770, "Digital Video Broadcasting (DVB);Service Discovery and Programme Metadata for DVB-I"

[11] European Telecommunications Standards Institute (ETSI) TS 103 769 "Digital Video Broadcasting (DVB); Adaptive media streaming over IP multicast"

[12] ISO/IEC 23008-1:2017 "Information technology — High efficiency coding and media delivery in heterogeneous environments — Part 1: MPEG media transport (MMT)"

[13] IETF draft Real-time Transport Object delivery over Unidirectional Transport (ROUTE) https://datatracker.ietf.org/doc/draft-zia-route/

[14] IETF RFC 5052 Forward Error Correction (FEC) Building Block

[15] ISO/IEC 23000-19:2018 "Information technology — Multimedia application format (MPEG-A) — Part 19: Common media application format (CMAF) for segmented media"

[16] European Telecommunications Standards Institute (ETSI) TS 103 285, "Digital Video Broadcasting (DVB); MPEG-DASH Profile for Transport of ISO BMFF Based DVB Services over IP Based Networks"

[17] Digital Video Broadcasting (DVB) BlueBook C100, "Commercial Requirements for DVB-I over 5G"

[18] 5GVista Project, https://5gvista.co.uk/

[19] Österreichische Rundfunksender (ORS), https://www.ors.at/5g-broadcast/

[20] OBECA project https://github.com/Austrian-Broadcasting-Services/obeca-info

[21] Amarisoft mini call box datasheet https://www.amarisoft.com/app/uploads/2021/10/AMARI-Callbox-Mini.pdf

[22] Oneplus 9 https://www.oneplus.com/9

[23] ASUS smartphone for snapdragon insiders https://www.asus.com/Mobile/Phones/Snapdragon-Insiders/Smartphone-for-Snapdragon-Insiders/

[24] Third Generation Partnership Project (3GPP) TS 26.347, "Multimedia Broadcast/Multicast Service (MBMS); Application Programming Interface and URL"

[25] Enensys CubeAgent mobile https://www.enensys.com/products/enensys-cubeagent-mobile/

[26] Qualcomm Technologies LTE Broadcast SDK https://developer.qualcomm.com/software/lte-broadcast-sdk

[27] Mission Critical Open Platform (MCOP) https://www.mcopenplatform.org/

[28] Third Generation Partnership Project (3GPP) TS 26.479, "UE MBMS APIs for Mission Critical Services"

[29] Android MBMS API https://developer.android.com/reference/android/telephony/mbms/package-summary

[30] GPAC, Multimedia Open Source Project https://gpac.wp.imt.fr/

[31] Dash.js https://github.com/Dash-Industry-Forum/dash.js

[32] MPV player https://github.com/mpv-player

[33] Exoplayer, https://exoplayer.dev/

[34] 5G-MAG Reference Tools platform, https://github.com/5G-MAG/

[35] 5G-MAG Blog, https://www.5g-mag.com/post/1st-on-site-5g-mag-reference-tools-workshop-between-ors-and-upv

[36] First end-to-end live 5G Broadcast streaming to smartphones at MWC Barcelona 2022 with Qualcomm and Rohde & Schwarz, February 2022, https://www.rohde-schwarz.com/us/about/news-press/all-news/first-end-to-end-live-5g-broadcast-streaming-to-smartphones-at-mwc-barcelona-2022-with-qualcomm-and-rohde-schwarz-press-release-detailpage_229356-1180480.html

[37] 5G Broadcast the dawn of a new freedom, https://www.youtube.com/watch?v=ZKoigNQNDGU

Practicalities and Analysis of Using PTP Over 5G Systems with Dedicated Time Synchronization Support for Media Production

Ievgen Kostiukevych, Pavlo Kondratenko
European Broadcasting Union
Le Grand-Saconnex, Geneve, Switzerland
kostiukevych@ebu.ch, kondratenko@ebu.ch

Thorsten Lohmar, Mohamed Nabil Ibrahim
Ericsson GmbH, Eurolab
Herzogenrath, Aachen, Germany
thorsten.lohmar@ericsson.com, mohamed.nabil.ibrahim@ericsson.com

Thomas Kernen
NVIDIA
Zürich, Switzerland
tkernen@nvidia.com

Abstract – The 5G system is becoming more and more a multi-purpose wireless network. Several industry verticals have started using 5G networking technology for their purposes. 3GPP has defined a set of dedicated features relevant to one or more industry verticals. These new features make 5G more suitable for different media production scenarios, such as remote production or mobile studio scenarios, extending the local OB Van facilities and replacing the traditional RF cameras. 5G systems support bi-directional communication by nature, using Time Division Duplex (TDD) or Frequency Division Duplex (FDD). Further, the 5G radio network simultaneously shares the available spectrum with many devices by scheduling small radio resource units. However, some of these 5G systems concepts can become tricky to use for high-performance media over IP due to inherited jitter (due to scheduling and TDD), throughput variations, and path asymmetries (due to capacity allocation for uplink and downlink). Further, the time synchronization between media sources can be challenging in 5G environments due to varying latencies of the radio transmissions. The paper explores the possibility of using IEEE 1588 [1], Precision Time Protocol over a 5G system for media production applications. With 3GPP TS 23.501 Release 16, the 5G System specifications started to include dedicated time synchronization support [2]. Release 16 added specific time synchronization support for Time-Sensitive Networks (TSN), i.e., acting as a Time aware system. With 3GPP Release 17, the support for IEEE 1588 is extended with several additional features. It becomes possible to use PTP according to the SMPTE ST 2059-2 PTP Profile [3] reliably over 5G for media device synchronization. The paper describes lab sessions performed by the 5G RECORDS consortium members [4] testing the performance of PTP over 5G with and without the dedicated time synchronization support. The paper also describes the testing setup based on the open-sourced software used by the team and the methodology developed. The paper concludes on the performance and synchronization quality when using PTP over various 5G systems and analyzes the results from the lab trials.

This paper is excerpted from the Proceedings of the 2022 NAB Broadcast Engineering and Information Technology (BEIT) Conference, © 2022, National Association of Broadcasters, 1 M Street S.E., Washington, DC 20003 USA.

Intro/Use Case Reasoning and Explanation

Frequency and phase synchronization has been the basis for digital media formats and solutions since the earliest TDM-based implementations. This is due to the need to synchronize sampling frequencies in analog to digital (AD) and digital to analog conversion (DA) and the multiplexer and demultiplexer. While it remains essential with audio and video over IP solutions, an additional complication of packet-based networks needs to be considered. Because of non-constant bitrate and latency, there is a need for an "out of band" synchronization mechanism not based on the transmitting medium itself.

Nowadays, there are several reasons for having tight synchronization in media applications: genlock of the cameras in case of a multicamera setup to ensure frame sync at the origin, locking the sampling frequency of digital audio devices, using packet timestamping for stream synchronization in media over IP standards and protocols, and precise packet pacing in new high-performance video over IP standards like SMPTE ST 2110 [5]. All this leads to the need for accurate time synchronization in addition to frequency and phase synchronization.

The IEEE 1588 Precision Time Protocol [1] standard has become the go-to solution for synchronization in high-performance media over managed IP networks. But media over IP is not the first industry that adopted the IEEE 1588 standard. It has been used in the telecom industry for several synchronization use cases for many years. In particular, synchronizing the radio transmissions from multiple base stations (gNodeBs in 5G terminology) is a critical function within 5G communication. The importance of time synchronization for the 5G systems will be explored later.

While undoubtedly being an excellent time synchronization protocol, PTP is still vulnerable to the typical challenges of packet-based networks – jitter and path asymmetry. To mitigate the impact of jitter and path asymmetry, IEEE 1588 defines special types of clocks: Transparent Clock (TC) and Boundary Clock (BC) that can be implemented in network devices to help with PTP events message transmission through a network.

PTP is not limited to traditional wired networks and can operate over Layer 3 (IP) and Layer 2 (Ethernet). In any case, strictly managed networks are used. The 5G radio network simultaneously shares the available spectrum with many devices by scheduling small radio resources units. However, some of these 5G systems concepts can become tricky for time synchronization between media sources due to inherited jitter (due to scheduling and TDD), throughput variations, and path asymmetries (due to capacity allocation for uplink and downlink), and varying latencies of the radio transmissions. Therefore, at first glance, using a 5G network to transport PTP messages may seem counterintuitive.

Since 5G systems are becoming more ambiguous and widespread, making them a compelling choice for remote production and wireless mobile studios scenarios, extending the local OB Van facilities, and replacing the traditional RF cameras. The nature of the 5G systems can often make them tricky to use for high-performance media over IP due to the inherited jitter and path asymmetries mentioned above. The same challenges are present in wired networks. But while these challenges can be easily mitigated in wired networks, the wireless nature of 5G communications makes it more unpredictable. For example, the physical distance from the gNodeB (gNB) to the user equipment (UE) [2] can change dynamically, which does not happen in wired networks. If the time spent in transit through the 5G system can be measured, the PTP algorithm can compensate for it, just like it compensates for the time spent in a network device in the case of a Transparent Clock (TC). The principles of such measurements are described further in the paper. We will also explore the performance of such an approach.

For further reading on the challenges of IEEE 1588 and the Precision Time Protocol, as well as traditional approaches to mitigate them, the authors recommend referring to [6].

Time Synchronization in 3GPP

3GPP TS 23.501 Release 16 [2] introduced support for precise time synchronization, focusing initially on gPTP for TSN. The Time Synchronization feature was extended (and renamed from Time-sensitive networking (TSN) to time-sensitive communication (TSC)) in 3GPP TS 23.501 Release 17, also supporting SMPTE Profile [3] for the use of IEEE Std 1588 Precision Time Protocol in Professional Broadcast Applications ST 2059-2:2015. The 3GPP system can operate in three modes for time synchronization: PTP Relay (IEEE Std 802.1AS [7]), as a Boundary Clock, or as Transparent Clock for both PDU Session type Ethernet and IP.

PDU Session type Ethernet means that the 5G system identified UEs based on Ethernet addresses and carries Ethernet frames over the 5G system. PDU Session type IP means that the 5G system identifies the UE based on IP addresses, and IP packets are carried over the 5G system.
The 5G system operates as an end-to-end transparent clock in this paper. The critical functions of the 5G system are depicted in Figure 1.

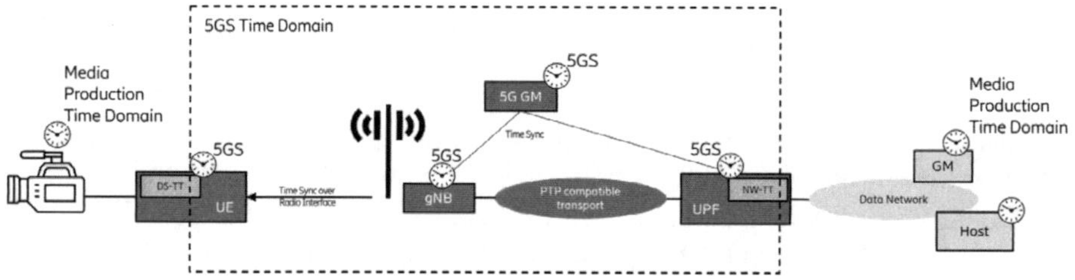

FIGURE 1: TIMING ARCHITECTURE

The network and the device side TSC Translator functions (DS-TT and NW-TT) [2] handle the PTP specific message processing, i.e., inserting an ingress timestamp when a PTP message enters the 5G system and calculating the residence time when the PTP message is leaving the 5G system. The residence time is added to the correction field within the PTP message. When the 5G system operates as an E2E transparent clock for the Media Production Time Domain, the PTP SYNC and the PTP DelayReq messages are processed by the DS-TT and the NW-TT functions.

The NW-TT function within the User Plane Function (UPF) [2] and the DS-TT function within the UE must be precisely synchronized to the same time domain to determine the residence time. The 5G system (5GS) clock is used as the time domain. The NW-TT function in the UPF and the Radio Network (gNBs) can receive precise time information using PTP or other means. The UE receives precise time information via the radio interface. The information from System Information Block 9 (SIB-9) or the Radio Resource Control is used for this purpose.

Measurement Setup

5G Testbed Description

Ericsson developed the Ultra-reliable low-latency communication (URLLC) test network to focus on 3GPP Release 16 radio functions for time-critical communication. The network includes features primarily from Release 16 but also from Release 17 [17][18][19].

The testbed operates within Frequency Range 2, i.e., at 28GHz (mmWave) and with a 200MHz bandwidth. It is configured with a 1:1 TDD pattern, which means the scheduler can split radio resources equally between the uplink and the downlink. The subcarrier spacing is set to 120KHz, resulting in a time slot duration of 0.125ms. This configuration will result in low latency because the UE gets a slot for transmission every short period of time. The testbed network can provide a consistent RTT of ~2ms.

For PTP support, the URLLC testbed acts as an end-to-end transparent clock. This PTP clock was added in Release 17 to support time synchronization for media production use-cases as defined by SMPTE ST 2059-2:2015.

PTP Setup

The measurement setup consisted of several elements:

- A Tektronix SPG8000A PTP Grandmaster locked to GPS reference clock
- Two Intel NUC8i7HVB PCs
- Two NVIDIA ConnectX-6 DX (CX6) network interface cards (NIC) with Pulse Per Second (PPS) interface [8] (only one was used in the measurement)
- An NVIDIA ConnectX-5 DX (CX5) [9] network interface card (NIC)
- Two Akitio Node Light Thunderbolt 3 to PCIe Gen3 x4 expansion chassis hosting the NVIDIA NICs
- An NVIDIA SN2010 Ethernet switch
- A Siglent SDS 1104X-E digital oscilloscope

The Tektronix SPG8000A was used as the main PTP clock providing grandmaster capabilities to the system. The standard SMPTE ST 2059-2:2015 PTP profile was used, except for the communication method set to Unicast. The SPG8000A was locked to GPS using a rooftop antenna. The reference output of SPG8000A was connected to the oscilloscope using a 50 Ohm cable and was configured for PPS out.

The NVIDIA SN2010 switch was used in a non-PTP aware state and therefore was simply forwarding the IP packets. The QoS was not enabled on the switch. 1000BASE-T Copper RJ-45 SFPs from FS were used in the switch.

Intel NUCs running Ubuntu 20.04 with NVIDIA NICs were used as PTP clients and iperf endpoints. The ptp4l library from linuxptp version 3.1.1 suite was used as PTP client [10] with the following baseline configuration:

```
[global]
verbose                     1
slaveOnly                   1
priority1                   16
priority2                   16
domainNumber                127
logging_level               6
time_stamping               hardware
twoStepFlag                 1
logAnnounceInterval         -2
logSyncInterval             -3
logMinDelayReqInterval      -3
announceReceiptTimeout      6
syncReceiptTimeout          6
delay_mechanism             E2E
hybrid_e2e                  0
net_sync_monitor            0
summary_interval            0
clock_servo                 linreg
```

```
tx_timestamp_timeout          30
#dscp_event                   46
#dscp_general                 46
#pi_proportional_const        0.0
#pi_integral_const            0.5
#pi_proportional_scale        0.85
#pi_proportional_exponent     -0.3
#pi_proportional_norm_max     0.5
#pi_integral_scale            0.5
#pi_integral_exponent         0.5
#pi_integral_norm_max         1.3
#delay_filter                 moving_average
#delay_filter_length          133
#delayAsymmetry               1000
[unicast_master_table]
table_id                      1
logQueryInterval              2
UDPv4                         172.20.2.1
[enp62s0f1]
unicast_master_table          1
```

The parameters that begin with "#" were uncommented and changed accordingly depending on the experiment and the type of clock servo used (linear regression and PI with and without advanced tweaks).

For precise iperf measurements, the system clocks of Intel NUCs were also synchronized to PTP through built-in NICs with PTP-capable Intel I210-AT Ethernet controllers [11]and using the phc2sys library. All NTP clients and services were disabled to avoid interfering with the PTP time transfer function.

The NVIDIA/Mellanox OFED driver version 5.5-1.0.3.2 was used with the real-time clock, and ports timestamping explicitly enabled and recommended kernel configuration applied [12][13].
The PPS output on ConnectX6 DX PPS was enabled for the appropriate built-in clock and set to a 1-second interval using testptp.c library compiled for the kernel used [14]. The PPS output of the NIC was connected to an oscilloscope with a 50 Ohm cable.

The second NUC with ConnectX-5 NIC was used exclusively as the second iperf endpoint.
Figure 2 shows the logical diagram of the setup used.

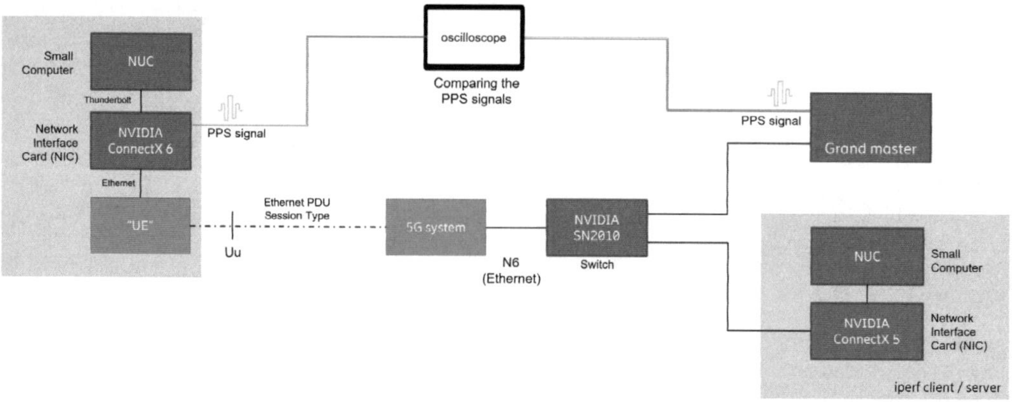

FIGURE 2: MEASUREMENT SETUP

Results Analysis

The results provided in this section are from two sources. First are the logs from the PTP client. Each data point designates a root mean square (RMS) of the time offset during a one second period for the PTP operations. The second data source compares two PPS signals: one coming from the Tektronix SPG8000A PTP grandmaster clock and the second coming from the NVIDIA ConnectX-6 DX PPS network interface card, whose clock was synchronized over a 5G network via PTP to the clock of the same SPG8000A grandmaster. Unfortunately, in the second case, the number of measurements is generally between 10 to 20. The team only had resources to manually take the measurements from the oscilloscope, which took time and only allowed to take a limited number of measurements.

Test 1: Measurements Without Timing Assistance or PTP Client's Parameters Tweaking

This was the test to set the baseline. This is the PTP accuracy that one can get from a 5G network with similar properties to the testbed used without tweaking the parameters of the PTP client and without getting information regarding the residence time of PTP packets traversing the 5G network.

The general parameters of the test are as follows:

- Residence time provided: No
- PTP servo used: Linear regression
- Advanced servo parameters tweaking in PTP client: No
- Number of data points: 1577

The main results are the following:

- Average PTP accuracy: 116653 ns (~117 µs)
- Median PTP accuracy: 116036 ns (~117 µs)

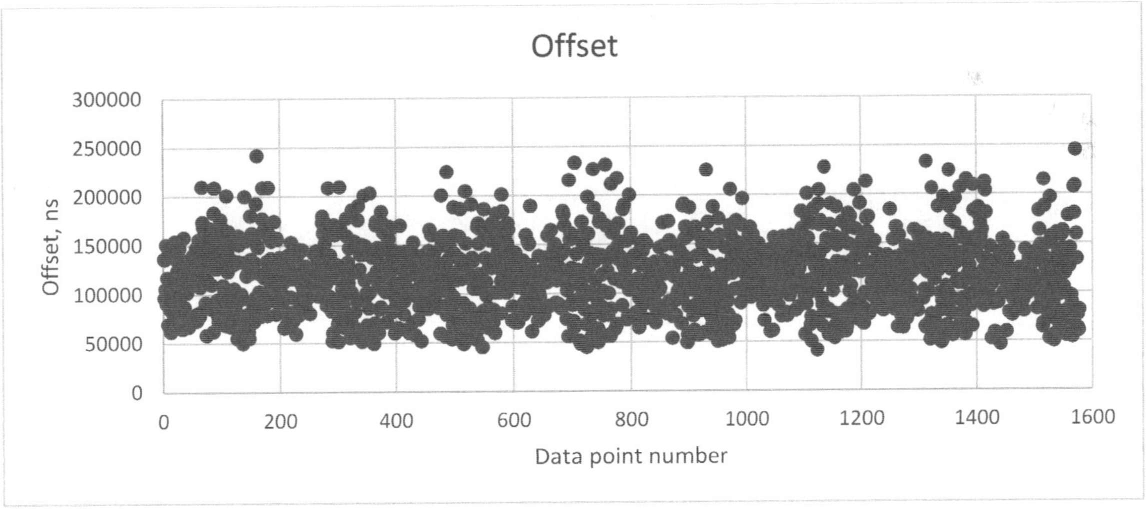

FIGURE 3: TIME OFFSET BETWEEN THE LOCAL CLOCK AND THE GRANDMASTER CLOCK FOR TEST 1

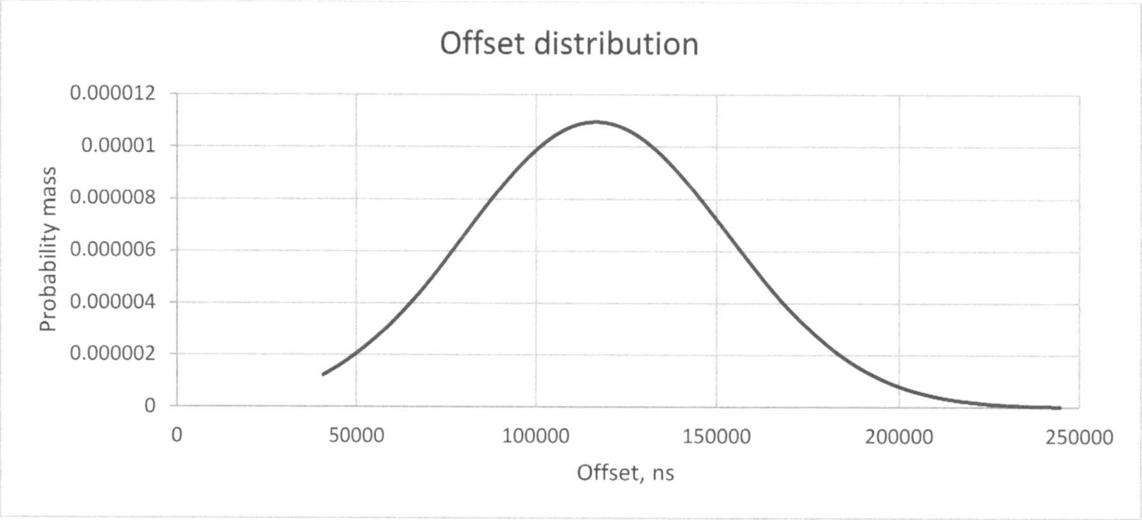

FIGURE 4: TIME OFFSET DISTRIBUTION FOR TEST 1

PPS measurements results:

- Number of data points: 12
- Average offset: 152 µs

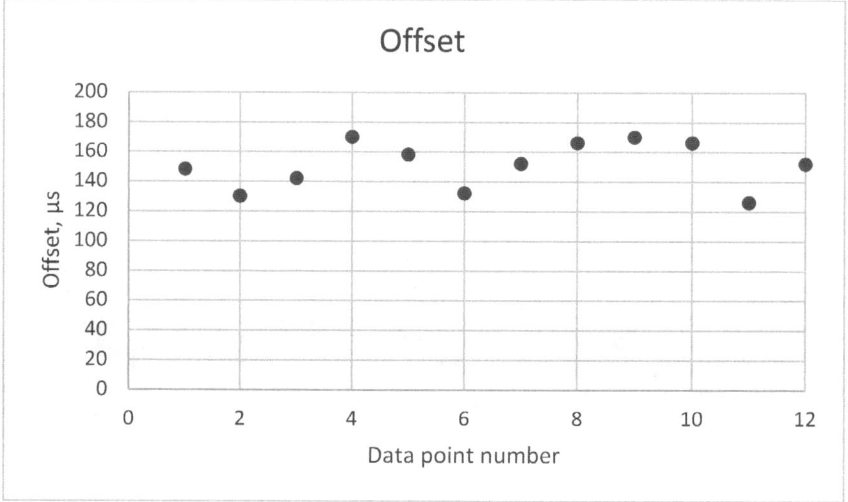

FIGURE 5: PPS OFFSET BETWEEN THE LOCAL CLOCK AND THE GRANDMASTER CLOCK FOR TEST 1.

Test 2: Measurements with Timing Assistance and PTP Client's Parameters Tweaking
This was the test with the best results. This is the PTP accuracy that one can get from a 5G network with similar properties to the testbed used by tweaking the advanced PI servo parameters of the PTP client and, most importantly, using the feature where the residence time of PTP packets traversing the 5G network is provided to PTP endpoints via the correction field of the PTP packets.

The general parameters of the test are as follows:

- Residence time provided: Yes
- PTP servo used: PI

- Advanced servo parameters tweaking in PTP client: Yes
- Number of data points: 932

The main results are the following:

- Average PTP accuracy: 3451 ns (~3,5 µs)
- Median PTP accuracy: 2832 ns (~2,8 µs)

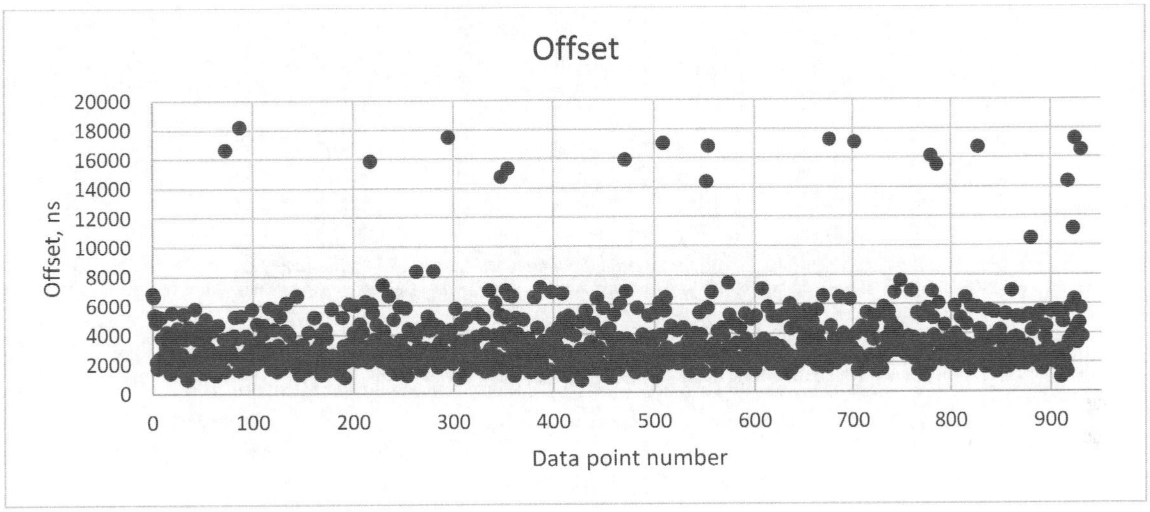

FIGURE 6: TIME OFFSET BETWEEN THE LOCAL CLOCK AND THE GRANDMASTER CLOCK FOR TEST 2.

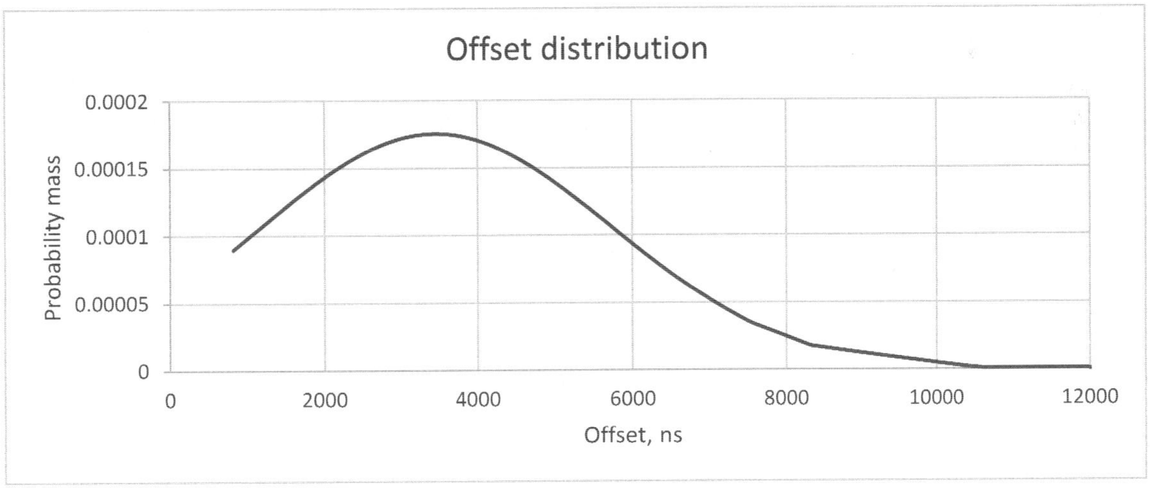

FIGURE 7: TIME OFFSET DISTRIBUTION FOR TEST 2

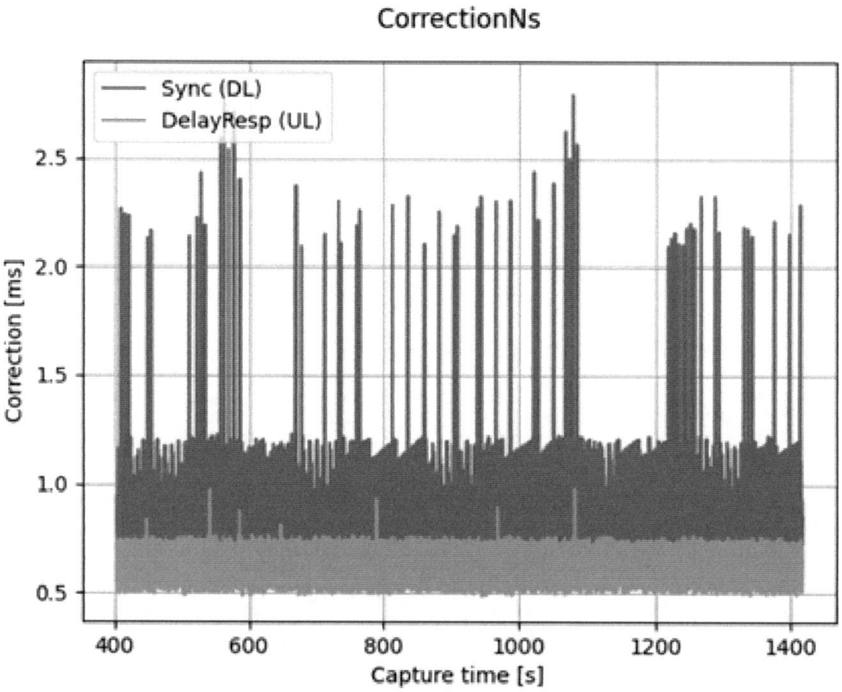

FIGURE 8: RESIDENCE TIME REPORTED BY THE TESTBED IN CORRECTION FIELDS OVER TIME FOR TEST 2

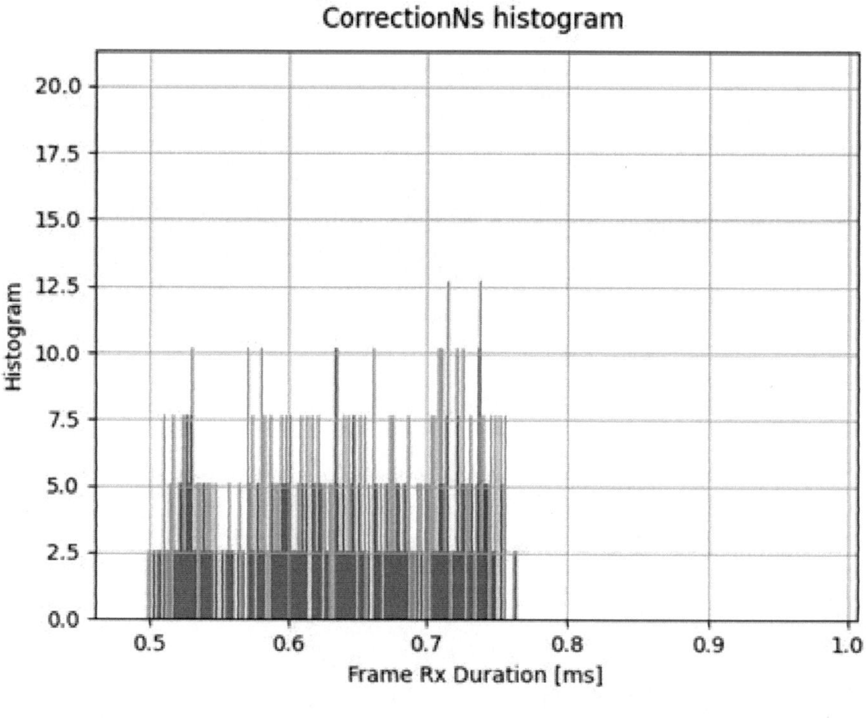

FIGURE 9: HISTOGRAM OF RESIDENCE TIME REPORTED BY THE TESTBED IN CORRECTION FIELDS FOR TEST 2

PPS measurements results:

- Number of data points: 20
- Average offset: 4,066 µs

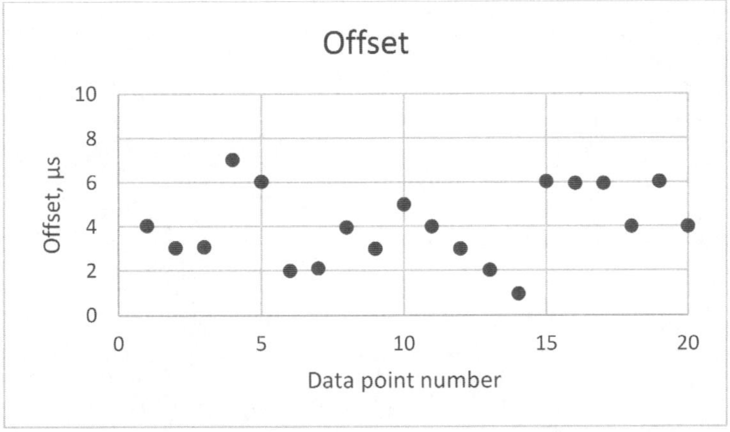

FIGURE 10: PPS OFFSET BETWEEN THE LOCAL CLOCK AND THE GRANDMASTER CLOCK FOR TEST 2

Test 3: Measurements with Timing Assistance but No PTP Client's Parameters Tweaking

This test was performed to see how much difference the PTP client's servo and advanced parameters tweaking make.

The general parameters of the test are as follows:

- Residence time provided: Yes
- PTP servo used: Linear regression
- Advanced servo parameters tweaking in PTP client: No
- Number of data points: 449

The main results are the following:

- Average PTP accuracy: 3633 ns (~3,6 µs)
- Median PTP accuracy: 3106 ns (~3,1 µs)

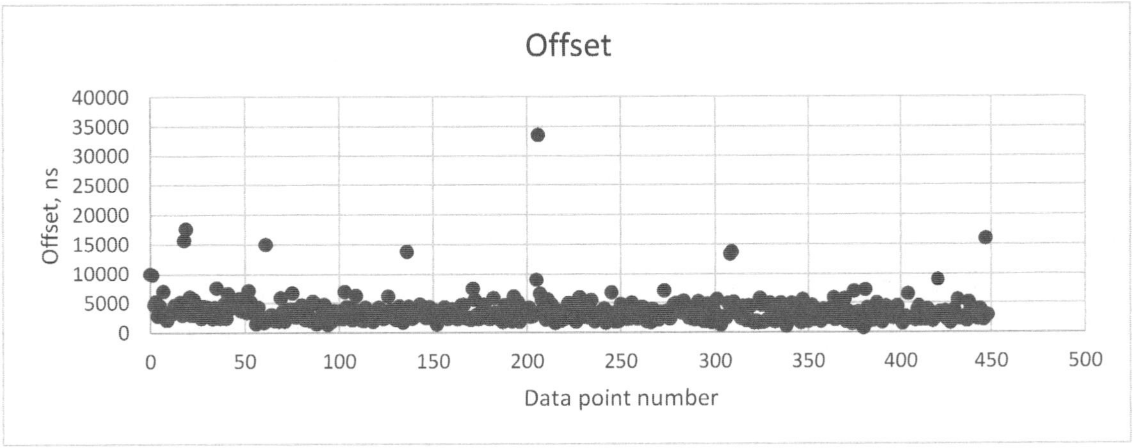

FIGURE 11: TIME OFFSET BETWEEN THE LOCAL CLOCK AND THE GRANDMASTER CLOCK FOR TEST 3

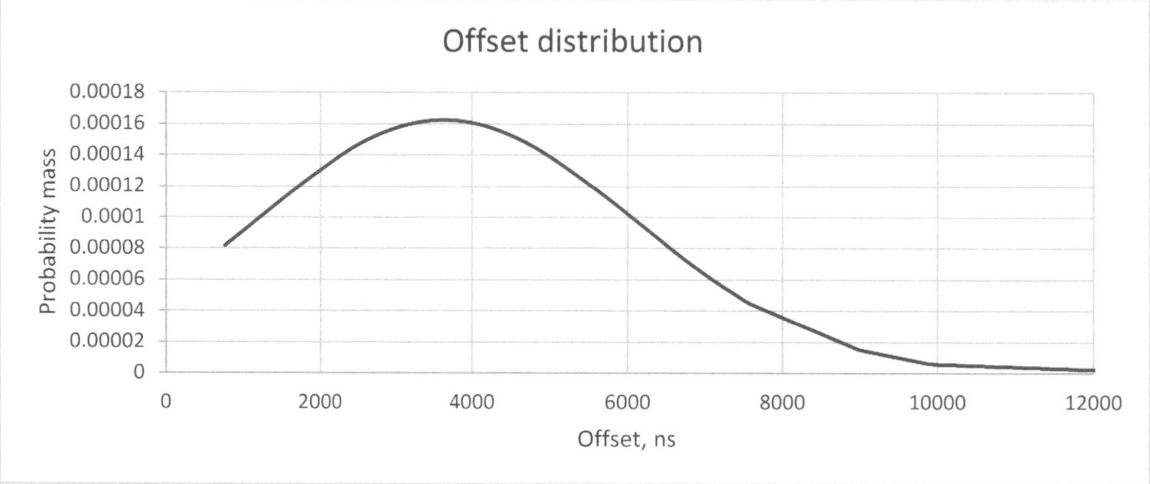

FIGURE 12: TIME OFFSET DISTRIBUTION FOR TEST 3

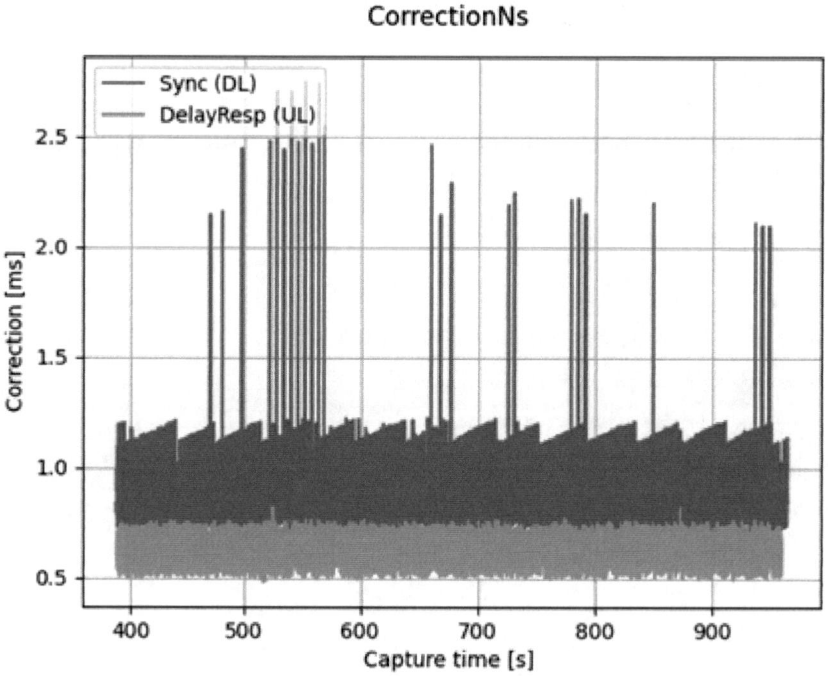

FIGURE 13: RESIDENCE TIME REPORTED BY THE TESTBED IN CORRECTION FIELDS OVER TIME

PPS measurements results:

- Number of data points: 10
- Average offset: 4,756 μs

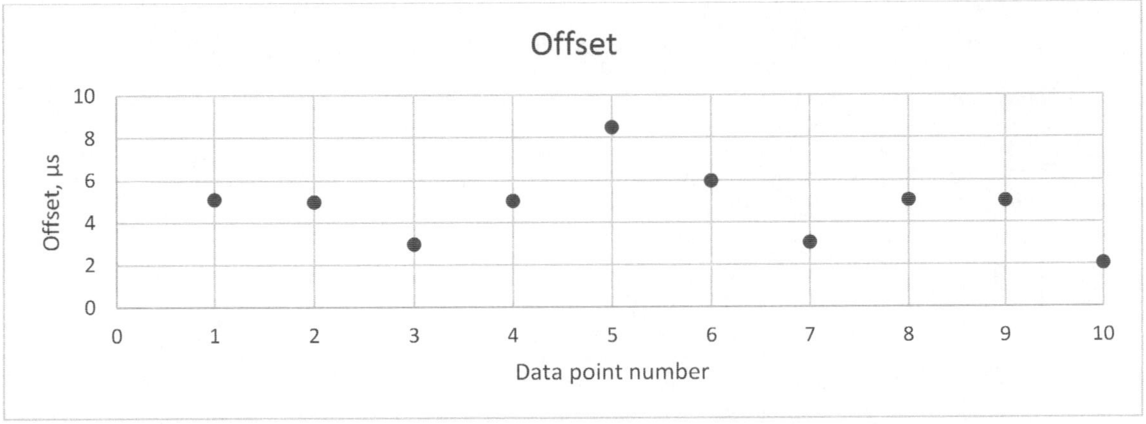

FIGURE 14: PPS OFFSET BETWEEN THE LOCAL CLOCK AND THE GRANDMASTER CLOCK FOR TEST 3

Test 4: Measurements Under Load - In the Presence of Network Congestion

This test was performed to see if the PTP accuracy is degraded if the 5G network is loaded significantly. 150 Mbps of uplink traffic and 120 Mbps of downlink traffic were generated.

The general parameters of the test are as follows:

- Residence time provided: Yes
- PTP servo used: Linear regression
- Advanced servo parameters tweaking in PTP client: No
- Number of data points: 737

The main results are the following:

- Average PTP accuracy: 23358 ns (~23,4 µs)
- Median PTP accuracy: 23350 ns (~23,4 µs)

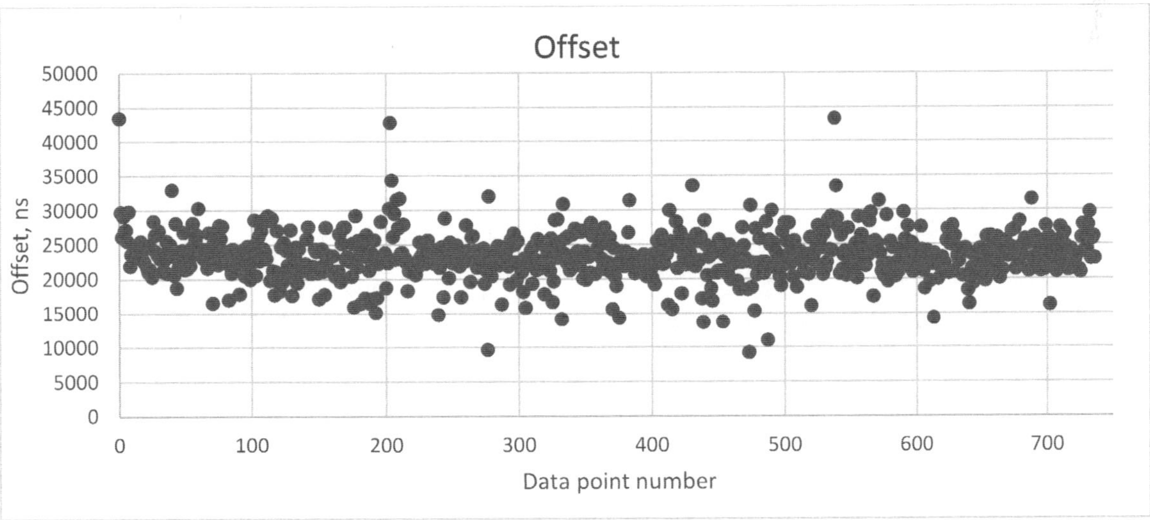

FIGURE 15: TIME OFFSET BETWEEN THE LOCAL CLOCK AND THE GRANDMASTER CLOCK FOR TEST 4

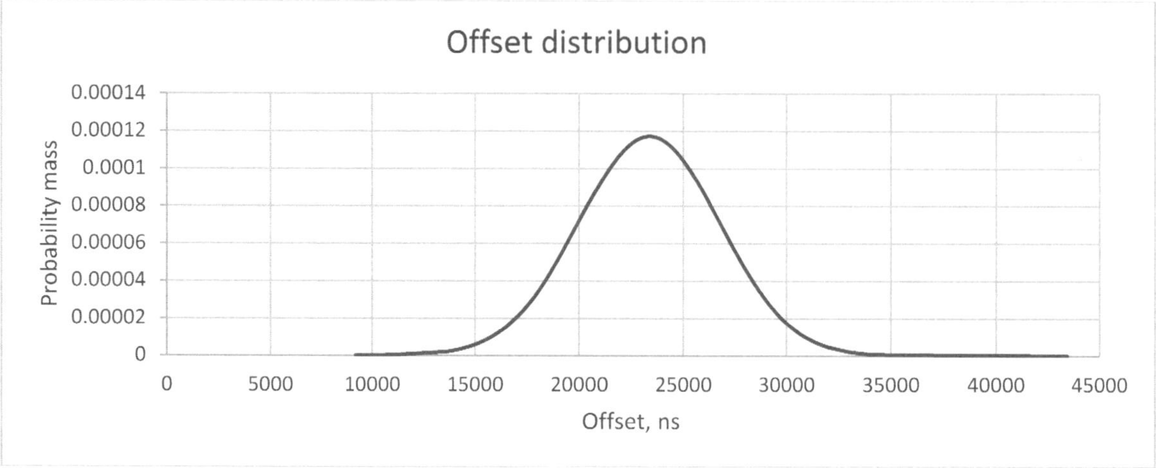

FIGURE 16: TIME OFFSET DISTRIBUTION FOR TEST 4

PPS measurements results.

- Number of data points: 10
- Average offset: 13,56 µs

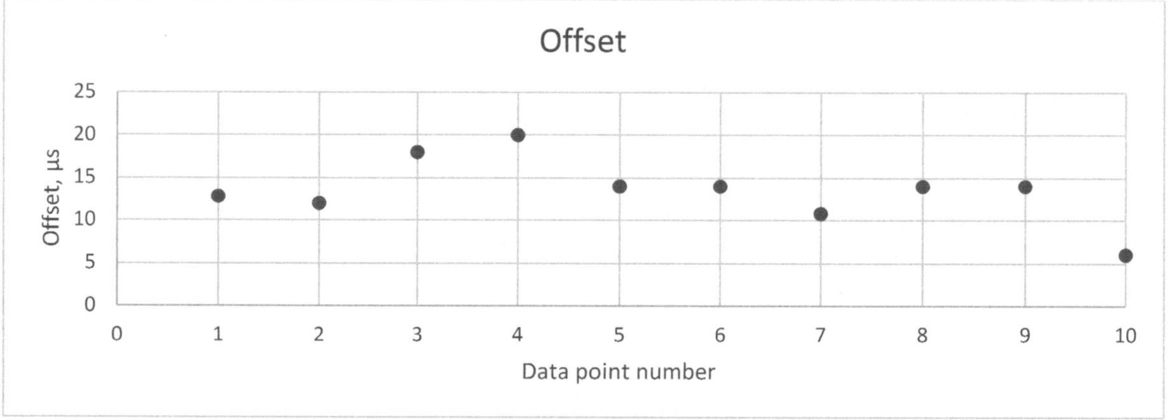

FIGURE 17: PPS OFFSET BETWEEN THE LOCAL CLOCK AND THE GRANDMASTER CLOCK FOR TEST 3

Conclusions

The paper presented evaluation results for potential options for synchronizing different Media Production devices over a 5G wireless like with a wired network connected PTP grandmaster. 3GPP introduced with Release 16 a feature that the 5G system can behave like a Time-Aware System according to TSN. With Release 17, 3GPP added additional PTP functionalities, such as enabling the 5G system to act as a Transparent Clock. This paper first presented an evaluation setup for systematically evaluating the time synchronization precision between a wireless device and a wired PTP Grandmaster. The paper presented results, focusing on the technical feasibility of precise time synchronization over a wireless link. The evaluation showed that a synchronization accuracy of less than 4 µs can be achieved with residence time measured and reported by the 5G system compared to ~120-150 µs achieved with the TSN features disabled. The accuracy difference between the linear regression servo and the PI servo with additional tweaks was neglectable. Therefore, a more hassle-free linreg servo can be used whenever available without any performance degradation. These results prove the possibility of using such a system for conventional media production over 5G, where the genlock or sampling references are generated locally by a media device receiving the timing information from a network via PTP. While this accuracy may theoretically be sufficient for high-performance uncompressed media over IP solutions like the ST 2110, and it can theoretically be evaluated if it is enough for the precise packet pacing required by the ST 2110-21 [15], it is unlikely that high-performance uncompressed video will be transported over a 5G network due to available spectrum being a too scared resource. However, the results look promising for potential use for compressed solutions like the ST 2110-22 [16], something that may be tested in future iterations of this work.

References

[1] IEEE Std 1588 - "IEEE Standard for a Precision Clock Synchronization Protocol for Networked Measurement and Control Systems", Edition 2019

[2] 3GPP TS 23.501: Technical Specification #: 23.501 "System architecture for the 5G System (5GS)"

[3] SMPTE ST 2059-2:2015 - SMPTE Standard - SMPTE Profile for Use of IEEE-1588 Precision Time Protocol in Professional Broadcast Applications, Edition 2015.

[4] 5G-RECORDS consortium, part of Horizon 2020, https://www.5g-records.eu/

[5] SMPTE ST 2110 - SMPTE Suite of Standards - Professional Media Over Managed IP Networks

[6] Ferrant J.L., Gilson M., Jobert S., Mayer M., Montini L., Ouellette M., Rodrigues S., Ruffini S., Synchronous Ethernet and IEEE 1588 in Telecoms, Wiley, 2013

[7] IEEE Std 802.1AS-2020: "IEEE Standard for Local and metropolitan area networks--Timing and Synchronization for Time-Sensitive Applications"

[8] NVIDIA ConnextX-6 User Manual and Datasheet, https://docs.nvidia.com/networking/display/connectx6en

[9] NVIDIA ConnextX-6 User Manual and Datasheet, https://docs.nvidia.com/networking/display/connectx5en

[10] linuxptp Github, https://github.com/richardcochran/linuxptp

[11] Intel I210-AT datasheet, https://ark.intel.com/content/www/us/en/ark/products/64400/intel-ethernet-controller-i210at.html

[12] “NVIDIA Rivermax PTP Best Practice Guidelines”, NVIDIA, 2021

[13] “NVIDIA Rivermax Linux Performance Tuning Guide”, https://support.mellanox.com/s/article/rivermax-linux-performance-tuning-guide--1-x

[14] How To Test 1PPS on Mellanox Adapters, https://support.mellanox.com/s/article/How-To-Test-1PPS-on-Mellanox-Adapters

[15] SMPTE ST 2110-21:2017 - SMPTE Standard - Professional Media Over Managed IP Networks: Traffic Shaping and Delivery Timing for Video, Edition 2017

[16] SMPTE ST 2110-22:2019 - SMPTE Standard - Professional Media Over Managed IP Networks: Constant Bit-Rate Compressed Video, Edition 2019

[17] Godor I., et al., A Look Inside 5G Standards to Support Time Synchronization for Smart Manufacturing, IEEE Communications Standards Magazine, vol. 4, no. 3, pp. 14-21, September 2020, DOI: 10.1109/MCOMSTD.001.2000010, https://ieeexplore.ieee.org/document/9204594

[18] Dhruvin P., et al., Time error analysis of 5G time synchronization solutions for time aware industrial networks, IEEE International Symposium on Precision Clock Synchronization for Measurement, Control and Communication, ISPCS, October 2021, IEEE Xplore, https://ieeexplore.ieee.org/document/9615318

[19] Mahmood A., et al., Time Synchronization in 5G Wireless Edge: Requirements and Solutions for Critical-MTC, IEEE Communications Magazine, vol. 57, issue 12, December 2019, DOI: 10.1109/MCOM.001.1900379, https://ieeexplore.ieee.org/document/8930825

A Cloud-Capable Synchronized Transport Architecture for FM and HD Radio Broadcasting

Philipp Schmid
Nautel Limited
Halifax, Nova Scotia, Canada
pschmid@nautel.com

Abstract – Radio broadcast infrastructure and deployment architecture is continually evolving to provide a reliable and secure on-air broadcast service embracing state-of-the-art technology in the broadcast plant to deliver new FM and HD Radio services efficiently. Can a software-based air-chain deployment be coupled with a broadcast transmitter? Can we leverage server and virtualization technology developed for cloud applications? Can we make use of IT standard resiliency and security improvements to better manage centralized air-chains back to the studio and content generation? Today's broadcast architecture using purpose-built embedded devices often deployed at the transmitter site does not interface well to a mission-critical data center lacking a transport stream with sufficient synchronization and security provisions.

An integrated FM and HD Radio transport architecture that allows for a location- and platform-agnostic air-chain architecture bonding all broadcast services into a single transport stream that ends at the transmitter exciter and originates from software-based air-chains (SAC) is presented and demonstrated. Software based air-chain services (ACS) can be cloned, virtualized, or containerized allowing for a common implementation regardless of the underlying host platform, whether this is a physical on-site server, an on-premises data center, or even cloud services like Amazon Web Services (AWS). To maintain consistent timing across the entire air-chain, all air-chain services are synchronized to the high-quality crystal in the broadcast transmitter all the way back to the air-chain ingest in the cloud, on-premises, or local server without the requirement for GPS synchronization.

This architecture definitively solves the FM-HD1 time alignment problem challenging the industry today. Critical to the architecture is a network protocol, based on established MPX and E2X industry standards, along with a synchronous buffer management algorithm that provides a superior level of redundancy and resiliency via multiple concurrent synchronous air-chains that always keep the transmitter on-air. Maximum network reliability through multiple TCP paths can be achieved. Adopting an IT standard client-server paradigm allows broadcasters to adopt state of the art security practices and authentication between transmitter and air-chain services. This shows that this architecture is not only cloud-capable but also suitable for on-premises deployments leading to a flexible, simpler, more secure, and more efficient conversion to HD Radio broadcasting on a modern digital capable broadcast transmitter adopting this architecture.

Why Software Air-Chains? Why the Cloud?

"What makes servers so special?" asked Greg Shay, CTO at The Telos Alliance [1]. His answer was succinctly "The fact that they are not special." If we can define a platform-agnostic architecture based on commodity servers that can prove to be reliable, secure and meets all industry requirements that works in the most challenging use case, the cloud, a milestone proof-point has been achieved. Certainly, the architecture will also work in a more controlled on-premises use case across a studio transmitter link (STL) and it most certainly will handle today's use case with much of the air-chain purpose-built equipment residing at the transmitter site. It does not mean use of the cloud has to be embraced today or even tomorrow but allows for recognition and planning for future possibilities in the cloud today. This new broadcast architecture can be realized today because it is built on industry standard protocols like digital composite MPX for the FM and E2X for the HD Radio broadcast. All air-chain components and building blocks, like the Xperi-supplied Gen4 encoder and exgine modulator, are field-proven and are available today without modification and continue to guarantee HD Radio receiver interoperability through a common air interface implementation; the blocks just have to be recombined under a new architecture paradigm that is location- and platform-agnostic so "non-special servers" may be utilized, whether physical or virtual.

Increasingly, broadcasters are centralizing studios and content distribution across their fleet of stations or affiliated partner stations. The goal is to effectively manage their network by simplifying broadcast transmission sites and keeping complicated system components subject to change in a centrally managed location. Ideally, the implementation is based on non-special industry standard servers or virtualization environments, such that an organization's IT department can service this mission critical infrastructure. Many organizations consider the cloud the ultimate centralized location no matter if it's a corporately managed data center or 3rd party service provider like Amazon Web Services (AWS), Microsoft Azure, or others. Even smaller broadcasters can benefit from shared centralization through simplified management and access to a pool of IT and technical experts with easy and flexible upgrades to HD Radio[1] broadcasting. Software-based air-chain services managed on physical or virtual servers are easily installed, cloned, scaled and provisioned. Nautel's vision is to create a broadcast transmitter that connects to one or more redundant, software-based air-chains that keep the transmitter on-air all the time.

The security concerns mentioned in this paper are of utmost importance for any network paths across the public internet and to the cloud. Demonstrating a solid defense strategy on the public internet also leads to best practices for systems entirely on a corporate wide area network (WAN) that allows you to protect the inner keep of your broadcast defense, the broadcast transmitter. Multiple software air-chains provide an additional layer of security via their expendability through cloning and backup with platform-agnostic deployments across standard server platforms. Cloud and on-premises based studio disaster recovery solutions exist today that are complementary to the multiple software air-chain solution presented here. On the other hand, should your broadcast transmitter or control interface become compromised, an emergency trip to turn off the transmitter with potentially length downtime or backup audio may be required. A backup transmitter may not help if both are sharing the same network resources. Nautel's goal, again, is to use the cloud as a proof-point with wider applicability for all broadcast use cases through best practices.

Fully implementing this vision today is challenging given the lack of an integrated FM and HD Radio transport stream. Bonding all broadcast content into a single data stream at point of ingest at the centralized studio or creation node enables backup air-chains for both FM and HD Radio. Integrated analog FM to HD Radio time alignment is a key aspect required for the broadcast plant to ensure a seamless listening experience when the receiver blends from analog FM to the digital main audio simulcast. The architecture presented herein addresses this requirement without the need of an off-air monitor that reactively adjusts audio delays across the two audio streams as is commonly used today. It is demonstrated that this new architecture never requires any audio delay adjustment over time or any air-chain interruptions including changeovers to hot standby air-chain connections. This important industry challenge is intrinsically solved in this architecture without the need for tight GPS-based

---

[1] HD Radio™ is a proprietary trademark of DTS, an Xperi affiliated company. The author is not affiliated with, and this text is not endorsed by DTS.

10 MHz timing tolerances that are challenging to maintain in a cloud-based environment. Seamless time-aligned transmitter cloud connectivity can be achieved no matter the global location of the serving data center.

HD Radio Broadcast Systems Architecture Evolution

To fully understand the limitations of today's HD Radio broadcast architecture, we should review its evolution due to technology advancements and changing requirements since the FCC authorized the use of In-Band On Channel (IBOC) for HD Radio in 2002.

2nd Generation: Early IBOC Adoption

The first commercially available HD Radio architecture topology dubbed Gen2 following an earlier proof of concept 1st generation was made available to early adopters in 2003 for AM and 2004 for FM stations. A simplified architecture topology is shown in Figure 1 depicting functional components in blue rectangles that may be grouped into purpose-built boxes indicated by the dotted black lines. The main audio originates at the studio and is delivered to the transmitter site via a studio-to-transmitter Link (STL), which could be analog audio/MPX, digital audio/MPX, or a switched network connection. This audio is delivered to an audio processor at the transmitter site that often is configured to provide the broadcast transmitter with an analog MPX signal, but other options are possible.

Without an HD Radio signal, the MPX would drive a typical FM exciter and transmitter. In the early days, HD Radio was implemented with the least impact on the FM air-chain. The audio was split at the transmitter site minimizing STL changes, and a second audio processor was used for the HD1 audio that was then fed into an external audio synchronization unit (EASU) and then into the In-Band On Channel (IBOC) exciter. In many cases the IBOC exciter drove a separate digital-only transmitter to either be space or high-level combined with an FM transmitter. Shown in Figure 1 is a low-level combined transmitter that amplifies both the FM and IBOC signal.

The standalone IBOC exciter box was responsible for two functions; encoding the HD1 audio in what later is termed the exporter and modulating the IBOC signal that would later become the exciter engine (exgine). The IBOC exciter required a companion box that is the heartbeat of the entire synchronous air-chain of this generation. Based on a GPS reference, it resamples the incoming HD1 audio to a perfect 44.1 kHz sample rate.

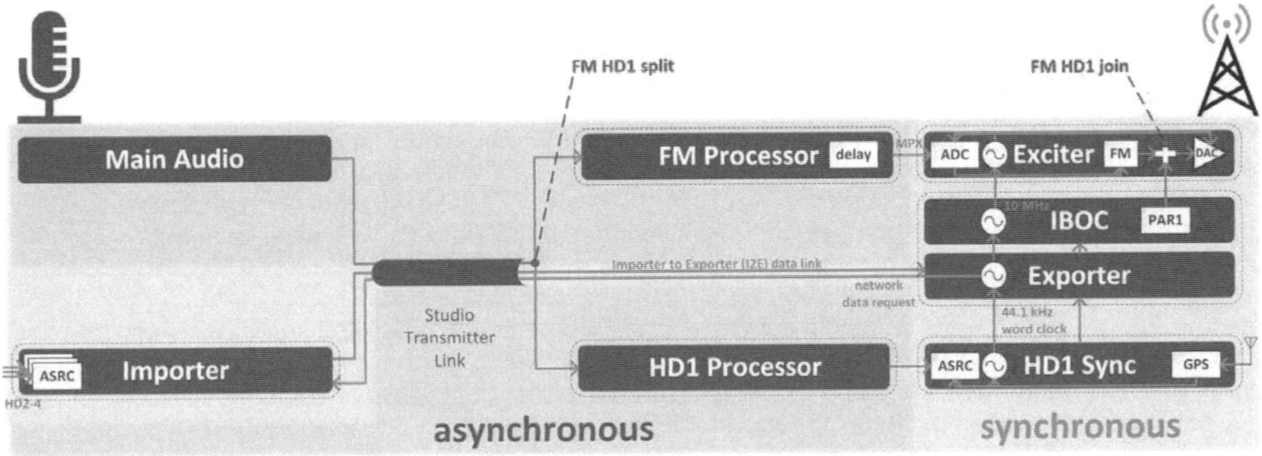

FIGURE 1: 2ND GENERATION BROADCAST ARCHITECTURE PLACES AN IBOC-ONLY EXCITER MODULATOR WITH THE TRANSMITTER. FM MODULATION IS INDEPENDENT AND THE IMPORTER WAS INTRODUCED LATER FOR SUB-CHANNELS.

In the context of this discussion a synchronous air-chain is any portion of the overall air-chain where all digital samples are fractionally related to each other. In this architecture the GPS module is the root of the clock distribution tree branching out via orange lines shown Figure 1. A synchronous air-chain can span a single or multiple components, provided synchronization exists between all components. For example, the 44.1 kHz word clock drives the exporter encoding rate shown as an oscillator. This oscillator may be a hardware oscillator or a software numerically controlled oscillator (NCO). In either case, operating sample rates are locked in a synchronous air-chain clock tree as shown in Table 1. Note other exciter sample rates are also possible; the ones shown are only exemplary from an early exciter generation.

	Ratio	Sample Rate	
GPS produces a 1 pulse per second		1	Hz
This drives a 10 MHz voltage-controlled crystal	$\frac{10e6\ cycles}{1\ PPS}$	10	MHz
This drives a 44.1 kHz word clock	$\frac{44100\ samples}{10e6\ cycles}$	44.1	kHz
This generates L1 frames (65536 audio samples)	$\frac{1\ L1\ frame}{65536\ samples}$	0.67291	Hz
This generates 512 IBOC symbols of 2160 IQ samples	$\frac{1105920\ IQ\ Samples}{1\ L1\ frame}$	744187.5	Hz
The 10 MHz drives the exciter MPX ADC sample rate	$\frac{1\ MPX\ Samples}{2\ IQ\ Samples}$	372093.75	Hz
The 10 MHz drives a direct-to-channel exciter DAC	$\frac{640\ DAC\ Samples}{1\ IQ\ Sample}$	476.28	MHz

TABLE 1: IBOC SYNCHRONOUS SAMPLE RATES

The key aspect of a synchronous air-chain is that one can obtain any of the intermediate sample rates through precise fractions. Because of this tight fractional relationship, all parts of the air-chain are akin to a fine watchmaker and precision gears and crystals for exact timing. This architecture following the audio flow pushes synchronization from the 44.1 kHz GPS disciplined audio rate out to the transmitter exciter, which ultimately drives the transmitter frequency. This synchronous air-chain can also control delays within the chain by managing the input and output rates of the air-chain.

However, the problem emerges once we recognize the FM and HD1 audio is split outside the synchronous air-chain, which means that portion of the air-chain cannot guarantee fixed throughput delay. This can lead to on-air time differences in the FM and HD1 simulcast as highlighted in later sections. In this architecture the asynchronous branches are constrained to the transmitter site and as long as the audio processors can provide consistent delay the FM-HD1 diversity delay alignment was not a big issue in this architecture. HD Radio has also not achieved critical receiver penetration at that time potentially masking this problem.

The importer was introduced to handle the encoding of HD2 through HD4, and it demonstrated that it is in fact possible to extend a synchronous audio chain all the way back to the studio using the importer 2 exporter (I2E) protocol. Network data requests instruct the encoders to provide additional audio data at precisely the rate required by the exporter data multiplexer and since no time alignment exists for the sub-channels, additional buffering was introduced to ensure a reliable connection to the transmitter site. This extension of the audio chain requires bi-directional communication across the STL and prevents the fan-out of sub-channel to multiple transmitters as they must run at precisely the rate of the exporter encoder.

3rd Generation: Exgine Modulator

Available as early as 2006, the main improvement of the 3rd generation broadcast architecture was the introduction of the exgine IBOC modulator that could now be integrated into the broadcast exciter directly, offering better synchronization internally either through a 10 MHz signal or other clock rates (see Figure 3). While the exporter can still be setup at the transmitter site beside the exgine, this separation from the exporter encoder allows the exporter now to be moved across an IP-enabled STL to the studio. A further improvement was the integration of the synchronization unit right into the exporter aiding synchronization at the studio side.

A big driver for this architecture was:

a) to perform all audio encoding at the studio and reduce STL bandwidth and
b) keep mission-critical equipment at the studio for easier maintenance; only an embedded exgine needed to remain at the transmitter site.

To facilitate this separation, a new network exporter 2 exciter (E2X) protocol was introduced that could feed the exgine with either UDP or TCP/IP packets allowing for unidirectional or bidirectional IP STLs. A key advantage of this topology is that with the exporter being the root of the clock tree, multiple transmitter branches could be synchronized for a translator or single frequency network (SFN) provided identical content is to be transmitted on-air.

The exciter can be synchronized either through a GPS unit or through a clock packet stream embedded within the E2X packet stream. While the HD portion of the air-chain is synchronous, the analog FM audio now traverses a potential lengthy asynchronous path creating the potential for FM to HD1 misalignment. Early on it became apparent that the network jitter imposed on the E2X clock packet stream posed a significant challenge to exciter synchronization and a reliable HD transport (RHDT) protocol was devised to create a constant bandwidth E2X stream to allow E2X clock packets to traverse the network with reduced network jitter over bandwidth constraint STLs [2]. Even with this improvement, it is challenging to achieve the tight FM to HD1 time alignment specifications required by NRSC-5 of 68 μs [3].

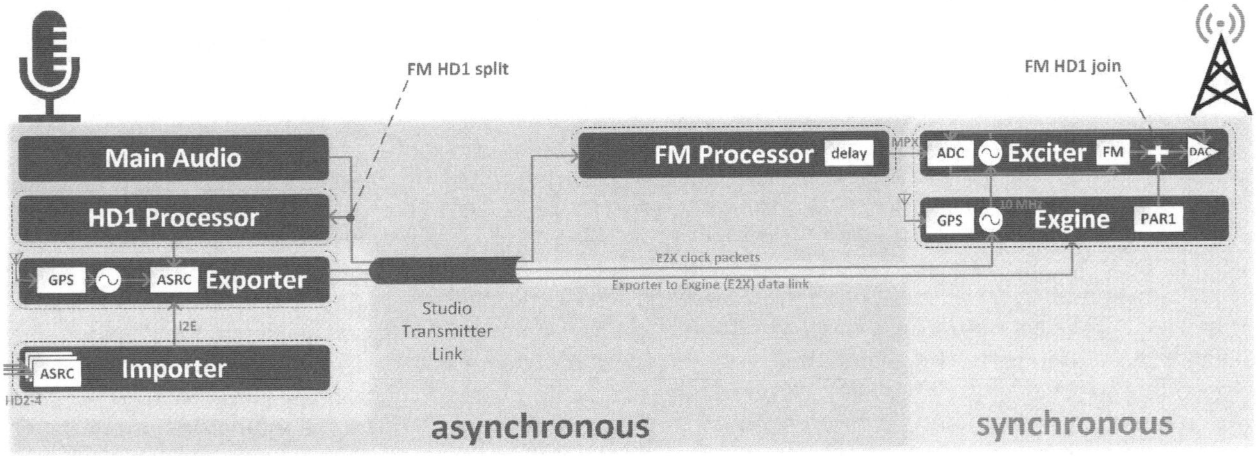

FIGURE 2: THE 3RD GENERATION BROADCAST ARCHITECTURE EMBEDS THE EXGINE MODULATOR RIGHT INTO THE TRANSMITTER EXCITER AND ALLOWS THE EXPORTER TO BE MOVED TO THE STUDIO USING A NEW E2X PROTOCOL. THIS WIDENS THE DIFFERING FM AND HD1 PATHS ACROSS AN STL CREATING FM-HD1 ALIGNMENT CHALLENGES.

4th Generation: Hybrid Peak-to-Average Power Reduction

This generation is defined by several key improvements as shown in Figure 3: Hybrid PAR, a combined importer/exporter, dual output FM+HD audio processors, and delay correction receivers.

Hybrid peak-to-average power reduction (PAR) in the exciter was introduced that takes into account the vector addition of FM and IBOC [4] when reducing signal peaks to allow the transmitter to produce a higher output power. Two implementations of hybrid PAR are available today: HD PowerBoost that maintains PAR within the exciter core implementation and PAR2 coupled with the exgine which now also requires the FM signal brought back into the exgine card. A new synchronization challenge emerged in that a batch of IBOC symbols had to be precisely aligned with the corresponding FM rather than sample by sample.

A combined importer/exporter solution allows collapsing two boxes into one, but functionally is equivalent to the two separate boxes. The I2E protocol is no longer required and the synchronization between the encoded HD1 and sub channels is much tighter since the synchronous air-chain distance has been greatly reduced. Subchannels can be encoded right within the Gen4 exporter, or alternatively, the encoder can be placed at a remote location via remote capture clients (RCC) that can be distributed either as software modules or discrete purpose-built encoder boxes are on the market today. The RCC encodes the audio precisely to the data rate required for the on-air broadcast and serves as an effective transport solution across an STL either to the studio or a 3rd party leasing a sub channel. Note that the sub-channel audio needs to be processed prior to audio encoding not shown in Figure 3 for the sake of clarity.

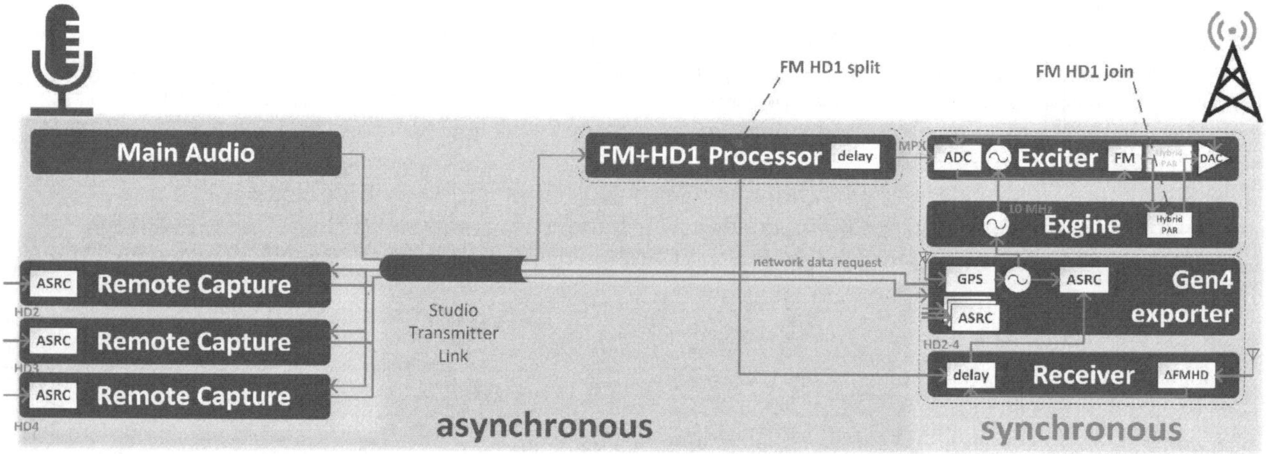

FIGURE 3: THE 4TH GENERATION BROADCAST ARCHITECTURE RECOMMENDS A COMBINED IMPORTER AND EXPORTER TO BE PLACED AT THE TRANSMITTER SITE UNDER GPS SYNCHRONIZATION TO MINIMIZE FM-HD1 PATHS FROM SPLIT IN AN EXTERNAL AUDIO PROCESSOR TO JOIN IN THE TRANSMITTER. A DELAY CORRECTING RECEIVER IS NEEDED TO CORRECT FOR START-UP DELAYS AND DRIFT. REMOTE CAPTURE CLIENTS REDUCE BANDWIDTH ACROSS THE STL.

A dual-output audio processor applies the same base audio processing to both the FM and HD1. It then applies FM-specific processing, like stereo generation, pre-emphasis and composite clipping and limiting to the composite MPX signal only. A dual-output processor has been found necessary to achieve the best possible FM to HD1 blend experience for the listener. Since many commercial stations want to maintain best possible audio processing and loudness control, often the main audio processor is at the transmitter site right beside the transmitter to be able to feed it either with analog or digital MPX. This now necessitates the Gen4 exporter also to be after the audio processor in the air chain at the transmitter site. Having the main FM+HD1 audio processor beside the transmitter exciter means the FM HD1 split to join has been minimized and can be more effectively controlled through common external clocking across all components.

However, all HD Radio generations have maintained the same feed-forward synchronization architecture from exporter to transmitter, splitting the FM and HD1 audio paths over synchronous and asynchronous air-chain portions leading to potential FM to HD1 time misalignment. To address this shortcoming, reactive feedback receivers were developed that measure the FM-HD1 delay and control a delay line to compensate. This delay line can be placed on either the analog or digital audio path provided the unit is told which path it is on to apply the correct delay direction. Often the delay is placed on the digital path by adding additional buffering on the FM to balance the two paths. This way we can continue to feed the transmitter exciter with MPX that is not delay corrected. However, care must be taken should one decide to control the MPX via a dynamic delay buffer since any delay affects the 19 kHz MPX pilot phase and poses a risk to analog FM receivers to switch back to mono reception if lock of the pilot is lost. Until the impact of MPX delay variation is better understood, Nautel recommends employing static MPX delays only.

The Problem of FM and HD1 Time Alignment

As many HD Radio listeners are aware, once an HD Radio receiver is tuned to a station it quickly acquires the analog FM carrier then blends to the HD1 simulcast audio. The blend function ramps down one set of audio then ramps the other audio up over a period of 1 to 2 seconds. If the two audio streams are grossly misaligned whole words may either be dropped or repeated during a transition from FM to HD1, which can become excessively annoying when listening to a station on the fringe of coverage. Listeners have brought back cars to the dealership thinking their radio was broken when in fact the station was misaligned.

Rough alignment can be achieved audibly by tuning some receiver models into "split mode" with the FM audio on speaker and HD1 audio on the other speaker. Human perception of the delay difference typically is limited to around 10 ms, which can address gross misalignment, but falls short of the stringent 3 sample NRSC-5 spec [3] which translates to 68 μs at a 44.1 kHz sample rate. The justification for this stringent specification lies in the audio comb filtering effect during the blend transition. We can model this effect as a Finite Impulse Response (FIR) filter as shown Equation (1), where x[n] represents the analog audio that is ramping down and x'[n] represents the almost identical audio on the HD1 that is ramping up. The z parameter represents an integer sample delay for any delay offset between the FM and HD1 audio. We can now compute the filter's frequency response shown in Figure 4 based on a variable delay difference (3, 12, 50 and 300 samples are shown) given where in the blend we are. The effect is most pronounced at the midpoint of the blend where both copies of the audio have similar amplitude.

$$y[n] = R_{down} * x[n] + R_{up} * x'[n]\, z^{-delay} \qquad (1)$$

From Figure 4 we can see that the filter introduces deep notches that are dependent on the delay factor. While within the NRSC-5 specification of 3 samples, we only see a single notch centered at 7.35 kHz. Should the blend transition occur with the main audio content at that time solely around 7 kHz, the listener would observe a temporary drop in audio level. Typical audio content is well below this frequency; only higher frequencies are impacted briefly.

As the delay increases, lower audio frequencies are impacted with 12 samples centered around 1.8 kHz with a notch bandwidth of 2 kHz. As frequencies are not equally impacted, instead of an audio drop, the listener may experience a wide range of audio artifacts during the blend transition. The process may even make typically inaudible watermarking audible during this time, exacerbating the observed artifacts. As the delay increases to 50 samples, more and more frequencies are notched out. By the time 300 samples (or 6.8 ms) is reached, close to the human ear's perception limit, the entire audio bandwidth is impacted. However, one observation to note is that the notches become increasingly frequency-selective, meaning that only crisp tones within the audio content are affected. While a misaligned blend of that magnitude does affect the blend transition, the effect is that it is less likely to affect large portions of the audio leading to a moderate degree of audio artifacts.

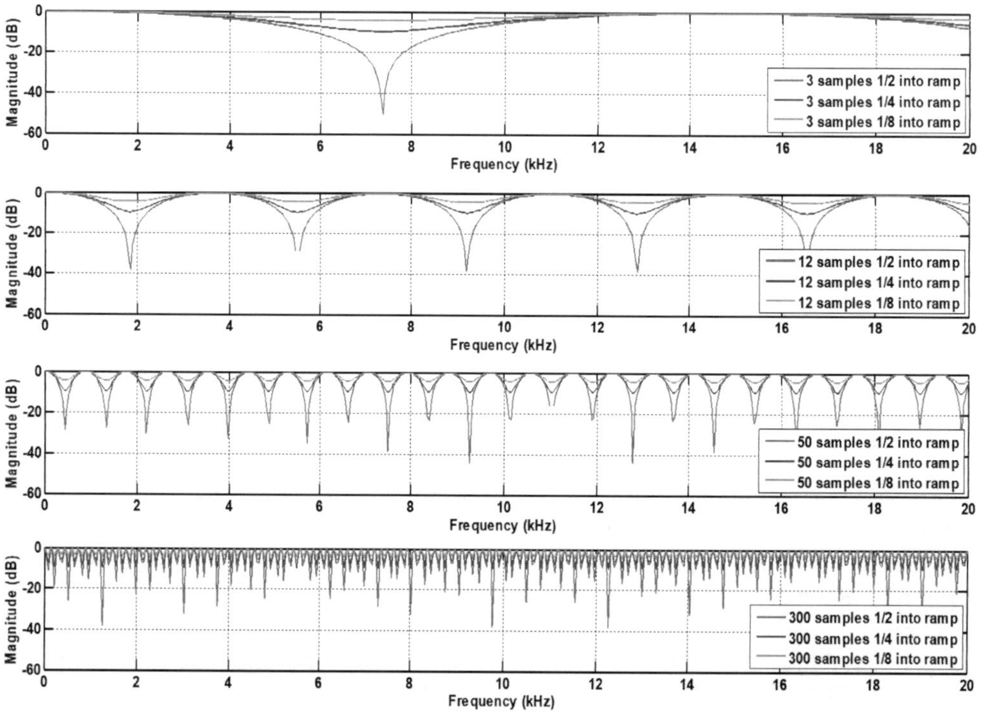

FIGURE 4: COMB FILTER EFFECT ON AUDIO DURING FM/HD1 BLEND UNDER INCREASING DELAY. LESS THAN 3 SAMPLES PRESENTS REASONABLE AUDIO PASS BAND, 12 SAMPLES IMPACTS KEY AUDIO FREQUENCY RANGES, 50 AND 300 SAMPLES IMPACT THE ENTIRE AUDIO BANDWIDTH BUT NOTCHES ARE MORE FREQUENCY SELECTIVE FOR SUBJECTIVELY LOWER BLEND IMPAIRMENT.

Typical station implementations often experience a delay drift rather than static delay offsets due to a complex broadcast plant. Various audio or network paths get switched in and out or reference clocks are not adequately synchronized leaving audio synchronizers undisciplined. Figure 5 shows typical time alignment drifts observed a 3rd generation topology across an STL with dual parallel FM and HD1 paths. Without a 10 MHz reference (see top plot of Figure 5) the alignment can vary wildly over the course of a few hours traversing the ideal ±3 sample window, entering a region of large artifacts and crossing into regions of moderate artifacts. While offering a large improvement, even with a solid 10 MHz reference at both the studio and the transmitter (see bottom plot of Figure 5), it is challenging to achieve the ±3 sample window across diverse STL paths.

The industry has developed off-air receivers capable of reactively measuring the FM-HD1 delay error and matching the delay across the two audio streams in variable delay buffers; Figure 5 was captured using a Justin 808 receiver by Inovonics Broadcast. HD Radio exporters exist today that can reactively correct for the diversity delay using off-air receivers and consistently keep the delay on-track. Reactive receivers are great at correcting any audio offsets that occur when re-starting any part of the air-chain. However, an underlying delay slip will be compensated by continually adjusting your broadcast audio, impacting audio quality and possibly hiding underlying systemic issues that should be addressed. Of course, reactive receivers are location limited to the geographical coverage of the broadcast signal.

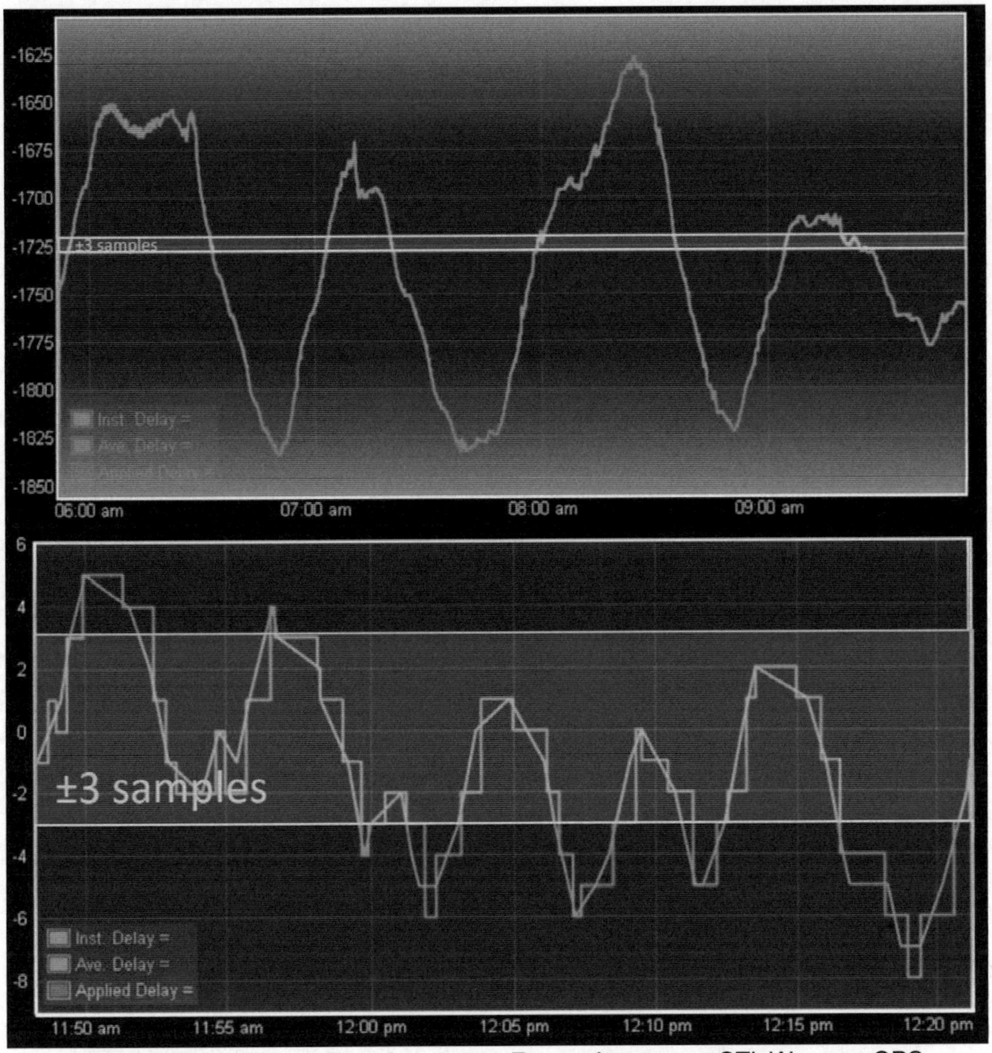

FIGURE 5: TOP: TYPICAL TIME ALIGNMENT ERROR ACROSS AN STL WITHOUT GPS.
BOTTOM: WITH GPS SYNCHRONIZATION [5].
TARGET RANGE ADDED FOR BOTH. CO-LOCATING LEGACY BROADCAST EQUIPMENT AT THE TRANSMITTER SITE IS RECOMMENDED FOR BETTER TIME SYNCHRONIZATION.

Caution must be exercised when using reactive receivers in a broadcast plant, as an increasing number of automotive receivers now have built-in reactive delay compensation. Effectively, this cascades two reactive delay adjustment loops along with a dynamically changing broadcast plant. This can lead to instabilities of obtaining a solid diversity delay correction within the automotive receiver forcing the receiver to turn off HD Radio entirely. If a broadcast plant delay is not fixed and stable, there is a risk of the HD transmission being rejected by an increasing number of receivers. The NRSC is formulating a set of specifications that limit the maximum rate adjustment a reactive receiver can apply to a broadcast to minimally impact automotive receivers. The conclusion that NRSC's time and level alignment guide [5] draws is the only solution to avoid reactive correction given today's 3rd and 4th generation equipment is to locate all the crucial HD air-chain components including the main audio processor at the transmitter site.

All HD Radio generations have maintained the same feed forward synchronization architecture from exporter to transmitter, splitting the FM and HD1 audio paths over synchronous and asynchronous air chain portions and leading to potential FM to HD1 time misalignment. A synchronous air chain from split to join is the definitive solution.

The Solution: Synchronous Air-Chain from Split to Join

The lengthy discussion regarding previous generations was necessary to understand the key aspects of this new architecture. For all previous generations, the FM-HD1 path, from split prior to audio processing to join in the exciter, crosses synchronous and asynchronous portions of the audio chain. The only way to guarantee FM-HD1 delay is to encompass the entire path from FM-HD1 split to join in a synchronous air-chain as shown in Figure 6, where only the external audio feeds remain asynchronous.

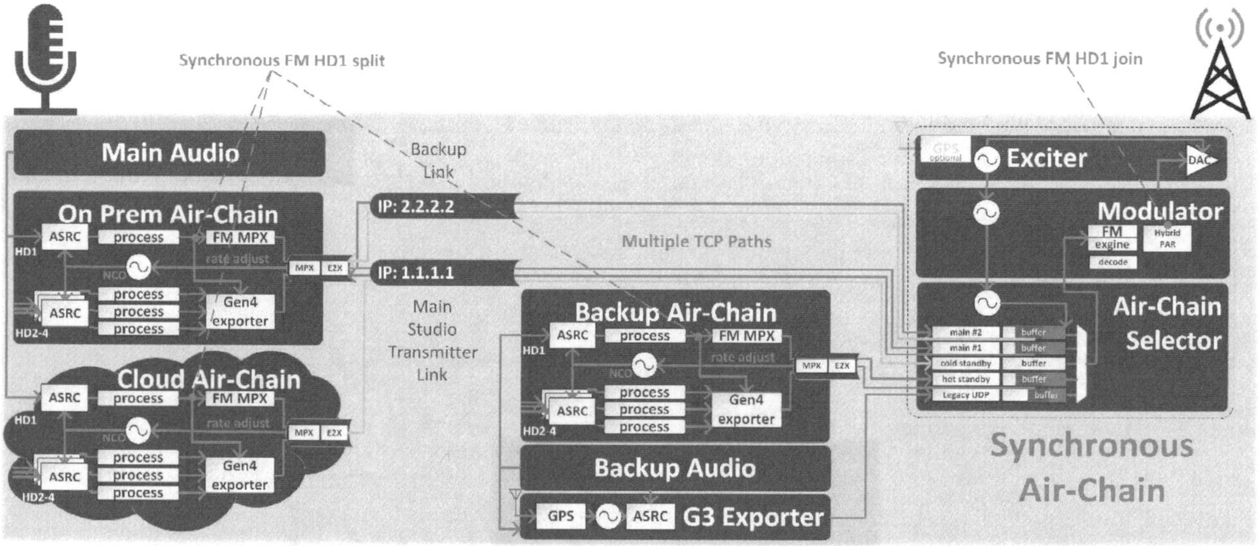

FIGURE 6: SYNCHRONOUS AIR-CHAIN FROM SPLIT TO JOIN WITHOUT ANY ASYNCHRONOUS PATHS. ALL AIR-CHAINS ARE SYNCHRONIZED TO THE HIGH-QUALITY TRANSMITTER CRYSTAL OPERATING ON AN IDENTICAL TIME BASE BY CONTROLLING ALL MAIN AND SECONDARY AUDIO INPUT ASYNCHRONOUS SAMPLE RATE CONVERTERS. THE ACTIVE AIR-CHAIN IS SELECTED BY THE AIR-CHAIN SELECTOR.

This new architecture introduces a further evolution of the Gen4 exporter by coupling it with synchronous audio processing for all HD channels, as well as, analog FM including stereo generation, RDS injection, and composite limiting all in hardware agnostic software modules, termed the Air-chain Services (ACS). The audio processor has several audio input options at arbitrary sample rates, some of which are highly asynchronous, like Internet Icecast connections to an external server with deep buffering and synchronization requirements. It is immaterial to this architecture how the audio arrives at the processor; the key is that the processor sample rate converts the incoming FM-HD1 main audio prior to splitting the audio paths after a common processing stage.

The processor and the exporter are operating in lock step on 2,048 audio sample batch sizes at a sample rate of 44.1 kHz. In turn, 4,096 audio samples produce precisely 1 E2X packet every ~92.8 ms. In parallel, the audio processor produces MPX samples at a sample rate of 4x44.1 kHz = 176.4 kHz, producing a batch of 16,384 MPX samples for every 4,096 audio samples and every coupled E2X data packet. This allows for definition of a synchronous transport protocol that transmits both E2X and MPX interleaved through a transport pipe like TCP/IP, where samples are strictly locked and cannot pass each other in transit; the same can be achieved using sequence numbers embedded into a protocol but TCP/IP already handles that. Standardizing upon this integrated E2X plus MPX transport protocol will lead to an interoperable ecosystem of products both on the encoding side as well as the transmitter exciter/modulation side, as it is now a single, integrated content flow that carries the entire broadcast signal.

The location of the exgine has not changed, it is still integrated with the transmitter as before. However, the FM audio chain has changed significantly, as now the entire FM content is also carried via the modified E2X protocol that also includes the MPX signal. This allows the flexibility to move the FM modulation process from the transmitter exciter to the exgine itself. The FM modulation process has been greatly simplified as all the MPX generation has been pushed upstream to the audio processor. Now the FM modulation corresponding to a batch of IBOC symbols modulated within the Xperi standard exgine core can be computed on a parallel path in conjunction with the IBOC modulation in a mini synchronous air-chain flow that follows the same principles taught so far on a smaller scale. A massive advantage of the proposed architecture is that it allows a higher degree of sophistication for a variety of main and backup inputs described below. The air-chain selector now provides multiple inputs with synchronized buffers across multiple air-chain inputs.

Table 2 provides an overview of the presented architectures in terms of impact on the studio, the studio transmitter link and transmitter site.

	Gen2	*Gen3*	*Gen4*	*Sync Air-Chain*
Transmitter Site Equipment	5 boxes	2 or 3 with external GPS	4 including delay receiver	1 transmitter plus optional backup audio
STL Bandwidth	**1.6 – 4.6 Mbps**	**1.7 Mbps**	**1.6 – 4.6 Mbps**	**0.8-3.0 Mbps**
FM Bandwidth	1.0 - 1.5 Mbps	1.0-1.5 Mbps	1.0 - 1.5 Mbps	2.8 Mbps 600 kbps (compressed)
HD Bandwidth	3-4.5 Mbps (discrete audio) <60 kbps (importer at studio)	~200 kbps	3-4.5 Mbps (discrete audio) <60 kbps (remote capture client)	~200 kbps
Studio Impact	low	high	medium	high
Content flow	forward	forward	forward	forward
Session connection flow	forward	forward	forward	reverse
Sync flow	forward	forward	forward	reverse
Authentication flow	none	none	none	reverse

TABLE 2: HD RADIO BROADCAST ARCHITECTURE COMPARISON

Buffer Synchronization with Air-Chain Feedback

Unlike previous generations, this architecture supports multiple concurrent air-chains and relies on a set of synchronized input buffers; one per air-chain. This means all air-chains must be clock synchronous. This architecture allows the transmitters high quality crystal to form the root of the entire clock tree rather than a potentially remote exporter clock that could introduce transmitter frequency offsets. The transmitter is already required to have a high-quality crystal to guarantee correct carrier frequency and modulation parameters as defined in 47CFR73.1545 and 47CFR73.1570. By keeping the transmitter crystal constant in an open loop configuration, we make the digital broadcast more robust as receivers are not subjected to swings in the transmitter frequency and OFDM constellation rotations that arises from sudden changes in the transmitter frequency control [6]. Additional GPS synchronization can still be used to control the transmitter crystal but is no longer required to keep the FMHD1 delay aligned.

As stated previously, in a synchronous air-chain the input and output sample rates need to be controlled to be lockstep, but intermediate processing stages enjoy a great degree of flexibility. All air-chains have the same output, the transmitter crystal driving the direct-to-channel DAC. All air-chains may have different inputs over possibly large geographic separation. The key innovation in this air-chain is that the common main audio ASRC located in each of the air-chains can be controlled to govern the chain's throughput delay and align buffer levels to within IBOC L1 frame boundaries. We can now synchronize all air chains together onto a common transmitter time base.

The buffer levels of any air-chain not currently on air can safely be adjusted without any negative impact to the on-air broadcast or affecting the FM-HD1 delay, provided one adjusts the FM and HD1 equally. This means any air-chain that is brought online can pre-charge its buffers prior to becoming active and start reasonably close to a desired target level (see Figure 7). The buffer levels are then continually monitored thereafter.

The air-chains implement a numerically controlled oscillator (NCO) to govern the processing rate of the audio processor. In simplified terms, the air-chain starts a stopwatch based on the underlying platform's time base and counts the number of input samples from that starting point in time. Given the core processing rate is at 44.1 kHz the air-chain compares how many samples have been processed against the number of samples that should have been processed. If the actual number is less than the target number, additional samples will be processed. The initial estimate based on the platform time base will most likely be wrong at first. Even if the time base is GPS, IEEE1588 or NTP synchronized, there is no guarantee the transmitter crystal, while very precise, is perfectly time synchronized.

There is no transmit buffering at the transmit side and all packets are immediately transferred to the exgine, the buffer levels of all air-chains can be monitored at the exgine. The buffer levels will change erratically depending on network jitter and can also be subject to slow-downs due to network congestion. The buffer is averaged over minutes before reporting the average buffer level. The error between the averaged buffer level and the target level becomes an input to a proportional, integral, derivative (PID) control loop commonly used in control theory.

It turns out that only the P and I terms are required for an effective control loop. The P term allows the control loop to react to large errors, such as an initial offset to the target level. The I term provides a long-term average estimate of the air-chain platform's frequency error which can be displayed in terms of parts per million (PPM). This frequency error is only valid after hours of steady-state operation. The PID loop produces as an output a correction of the air-chain platform's time base in terms of additional (or fewer) 44.1 kHz audio samples that are transmitted over the network. Figure 7 shows how the control loop can obtain a desired target buffer level of 24 packets (1.5 IBOC L1 frames) from an initial starting point of 32 packets that were initially pre-charged too high to demonstrate the control loop's ability to govern the buffer level.

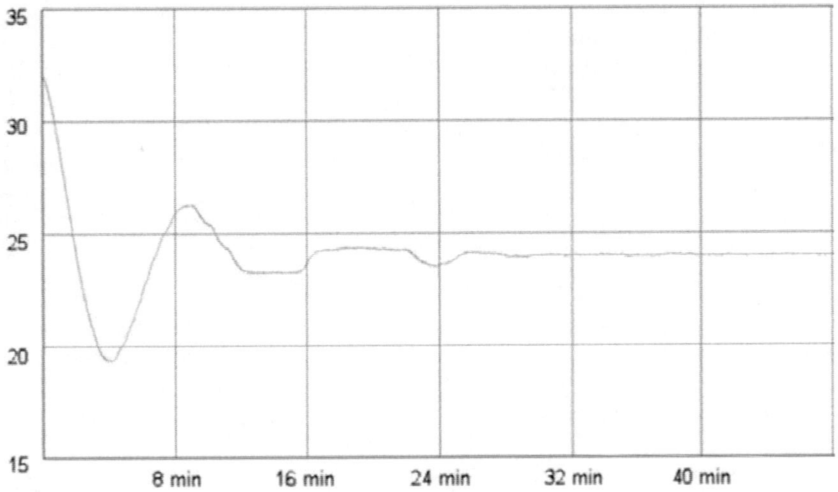

FIGURE 7: AIR CHAIN SELECTOR BUFFER LEVELS SYNCHRONIZED VIA PI FEEDBACK LOOP TO SETTLE ON A TARGET BUFFER LEVEL OF 24 PACKETS STARTING FROM AN INITIAL HIGH PRE-CHARGE OF 32 PACKETS. STEADY STATE AIR CHAIN PLATFORM TIME FREQUENCY OFFSET CAN BE ESTIMATED WITH RESIDUAL ADJUSTMENTS LONG TERM.

A typical implementation would pre-charge close to the target to avoid excessive control loop variation. The natural frequency of the control loop shown is around 10 minutes but may be subject to further tweaking and adjustment given a specific networking environment. Note the step function centered around integer packet numbers when a predominant number of buffer level reads center around the same integer buffer level; the I term will eventually push it to the correct level.

Figure 8 presents the results of an experiment, where 2 air-chains were configured, one on a local HDMultiCast+ server and another on AWS server in the Ohio data center with the transmitter located at Nautel. The on-premises HDMultiCast+ air-chain was pre-charged to a buffer level of 14, while the AWS air-chain was pre-charged with a buffer level of 32. The air-chain integrated Omnia 9 Enterprise OS audio processing module also provides a rate estimation of what it considers its input rate.

On startup, both the transmitter-based estimation and the audio processor estimation exhibit large errors that are induced by the control loop slewing to the desired target buffer level; no significant audio artefacts were noted on either the FM or HD audio. After about 30 minutes, the buffer levels had stabilized producing a frequency offset error of around 35 ppm for the on-premises server and close to 0 ppm for the AWS air-chain after approximately 10 hours of run time. Carrying a reliable, short-term accurate, time base into a virtual environment is a challenge as experienced using VirtualBox on a desktop platform. It appears AWS has effectively solved this challenge; other data centers may not have solved this challenge yet. It is interesting to note that the 1.6 Hz frequency offset reported by the audio processor represents a 36.2 ppm frequency error, very close to the 35.3 ppm transmitter-based estimate. However, both transmitter-based ppm readings fluctuated +-5 ppm due to residual network jitter. The transmitter crystal was running open loop without any GPS discipline demonstrating that GPS is now optional at the transmitter site.

All buffers are pre-charged such that the buffer read operation perfectly aligns with IBOC L1 frame boundaries and are kept in lockstep thereafter. By making the buffer a minimum of 1 L1 frame consisting of 16 packets we can perform a hitless transfer from one air-chain to another air-chain depending on the content switched to. Today the layer 5 audio framing within separate Gen4 exporters is not guaranteed to be perfectly aligned on L1 boundaries, so a 2-3 L1 frame IBOC drop is forced on a changeover causing a 3 to 4s silence on the secondary channels. This drop may be eliminated in the future if layer 5 frames can be aligned in the exporter.

FIGURE 7: INITIAL STARTUP (TOP) WITH ON PREMISES AIR-CHAIN STARTING AT 14 PACKETS AND THE ACTIVE CLOUD BASED AIR-CHAIN STARTING AT 28 PACKETS (LEFT). IMPERCEPTIBLE AUDIO PROCESSOR ASRC ADJUSTMENT (RIGHT) PULLS BOTH BUFFERS TO A TARGET OF 24 PACKETS. ONLY THE LONG-TERM FREQUENCY OFFSET REMAINS WITH THE TRANSMITTER ESTIMATE MATCHING THE PROCESSOR OFFSET (BOTTOM).

A New Transport Protocol Building on Existing Standards

The application layer protocol, from the session management, transport layer and network layer, must be specified; options exist at each level. An initial framework is presented here for consideration of standardization to allow for eventual vendor interoperability.

Application Layer links MPX and E2X

For the presented synchronization architecture to work, all that the application layer is required to provide is a linking between the analog MPX packet content and the E2X packet content that corresponds to the same 4,096 input audio samples at 44.1 kHz. The packet and sample stream must be ordered and transferred without errored or lost packets, a responsibility of the transport layer.

An initial version of the transfer protocol interleaves an E2X packet with 16,384 16-bit MPX samples at 4 x 44.1 kHz = 176.4 kHz sample rate across a TCP/IP pipe for the forward data direction. A new packet for buffer level feedback control is also introduced to adjust the air-chain NCO by a specific number of audio samples. In the future, multiple profiles can be defined to allow enabling MPX or E2X and the substitution of either component with alternate definitions. For example, MPX could be carried as an encoded MPX stream to reduce bandwidth in another profile. The proprietary E2X protocol defined initially by iBiquity, now Xperi, may be substituted by conveying the IBOC constellations occupying the same time slice in a carrier bitmap if an open protocol definition based on the NRSC-5 [7] specification is required.

Session and Presentation Layer Provides Authentication Options

Beyond the MPX and E2X sample transfer, it is recommended that profiles be added for authentication to the protocol. One profile can be based on a private and public key exchange between the transmitter and the air-chain service. The private key resides on the transmitter behind a solid firewall implementation and is never shared publicly and can be uniquely node-locked to the transmitter hardware. The public key needs to be installed on each instance of the air-chain service and can either be floating re-using the same key across all air-chains or can also be uniquely locked to the underlying air-chain platform. In this way, the air-chain service software module can be made available for download publicly or even directly from the transmitter. The private and public key generation will be performed by a trusted body and installed on the air-chain service separately from the installation. One can consider this a basic 2 factor authentication method, where the software module is installed from and linked to the transmitter while the keys are installed by an alternate means. In this way, a level of trust is established between the transmitter and air-chain service.

Only authentication is required by the application, encryption is not required considering the data content will be broadcast publicly on-air within 10 seconds. However, a man-in-the-middle attack must be prevented, where an intermediary node may hijack the current session and become an imposter. Encryption methods, like SSL, can solve this problem as the encryption and decryption requires synchronized state on both the sender and transmitter. To avoid the overhead of encoding the entire data flow, which is not required, a running checksum can be injected based on a hashing function like SHA-512 that takes both the private and public key into consideration. A malicious actor would now have to become a man-in-the-middle and learn the running state of the hashing function requiring the air-chain platform to become compromised. Should an air-chain platform or session become compromised by a malicious actor, it can be shut down at the transmitter, then address the attack vector, switch to an uncompromised backup air-chain, re-download the air-chain service or revert to a safe restore point, update the keys and bring the main air-chain back online.

Note that public key infrastructure suffers from a certificate management challenge of how to generate and manage the issued keys. Alternate authentication methods are emerging based on certificateless blockchain technology [8] that may be considered for a future authentication profile.

TCP Transport Defends Against Layer 4 Denial of Service Attacks

Broadcasters are in a feed-forward data flow mindset that follows the broadcast paradigm often with a low latency and multicast requirement reaching multiple targets; sometimes even across uni-directional links. It comes as no surprise that previous HD Radio generations placed the TCP server at the downstream device following the data flow. The legacy TCP/IP E2X mode has the downstream exgine listening for an upstream connection from the exporter, the TCP/IP I2E link has the downstream exporter listening for the upstream importer, the downstream importer is listening for connections from the upstream remote capture clients. The Legacy User Datagram Protocol (UDP) protocol also creates a listening UDP socket for incoming connections. Other broadcast streaming protocols like AES67 for PCM audio, Real Time Protocol (RTP), and SMPTE2110 for TV applications, are all based on UDP to allow for IP multicasting. They all introduce open listening ports. It is tempting to add transmitter site firewall port re-directs to allow remote content delivery or transmitter control...don't.

A public listening network socket is a serious attack vector, even if or especially when, re-directing through a firewall:

- **Listening UDP sockets** are vulnerable to **UDP flood attacks**, which "is a type of denial-of-service attack in which a large number of User Datagram Protocol (UDP) packets are sent to a targeted server with the aim of overwhelming that device's ability to process and respond. The firewall protecting the targeted server can also become exhausted as a result of UDP flooding, resulting in a denial-of-service to legitimate traffic." [9]
- **Listening TCP sockets** are vulnerable to **SYN flood attacks**, which "is a type of denial-of-service (DDoS) attack which aims to make a server unavailable to legitimate traffic by consuming all available server resources. By repeatedly sending initial connection request (SYN) packets, the attacker is able to overwhelm all available ports on a targeted server machine, causing the targeted device to respond to legitimate traffic sluggishly or not at all." [10]

It is proposed that the client-server architecture be flipped by making the upstream air-chain service the TCP/IP server and never establishing any listening socket shielding the transmitter from attack. By reaching out to an air-chain server, the transmitter can easily traverse a firewall, without compromising the firewall by opening port redirects or dropping other security guards. Using Network Address Translation (NAT) and IP Masquerading the IP address of the transmitter is never revealed outside the firewall eliminating another potential attack vector. Not only does it solve the firewall traversal problem, one can now reach out to a known location even across the public Internet; session management will authenticate the remote server identity.

A key security aspect of this new architecture is that by making the transmitter the root of your broadcast tree, your transmitter can survive an attack even if you lose an air chain branch. If an air chain is compromised or denied service, drop it and switch to another air chain. Your broadcast continues to be safe.

Lower layer attacks like layer 3 ICMP flood attacks or Smurf attacks must be handled by the firewall and network implementation or the ISP using industry standard practices. Of course, flipping the client-server makes it the responsibility of the air-chain service to guard against denial-of-service attacks. When implementing a cloud solution, this needs to be considered. Fortunately, leading cloud service providers offer DDOS solutions, like AWS Shield or Azure DDOS protection. Load balancers may also be used to limit access to your main air-chain.

Main and Backup Air-Chains for Resilient Broadcast Routing

The objective of the network protocol is to transfer audio broadcast content from ingest to transmission. Considering all audio paths from the main air-chain to the various backup air-chains part of our network topology, several different connection types are supported:

Multiple TCP Paths

Last-mile STLs are often the most unreliable link in the broadcast chain. Multiple TCP paths allows for simultaneous utilization of two or more STL paths for improved resiliency to network failure with hitless failover. Depending on the configured IP routing, the entire path from transmitter to ACS can be made redundant.

The connections labelled main #1 and main #2 in Figure 6 originate from the same On Prem Air-chain and terminate at the same transmitter and carry identical content. Using the described synchronous buffer architecture that aligns packet sequence numbers on read, these two connections may be treated as multiple TCP paths providing hitless failover from one STL link to another on complete link loss. This link diversity is like bit splicing in other protocols. Multiple TCP paths have to be accounted for in the air-chain service synchronization as only one buffer can control the air-chain service. The air-chain service can simply ignore all synchronization requests except for the first or main connection, this will automatically synchronize the buffer depth of the other TCP paths, as well.

Multiple Path TCP is accomplished by assigning multiple IP addresses to the air-chain server. In Figure 6 both IP addresses 1.1.1.1 and 2.2.2.2 are assigned to the air-chain server and could either be assigned to two physical Ethernet adapters on separate subnets or both could be assigned to a single Ethernet address. Using the two IP addresses appropriate TCP/IP routing can be established using standard IP practices to have both TCP connections go across separate STLs for all or just part of the entire data path.

The Internet Engineering Task Force (IETF) has approved RFC8684 [11] that shares many design concepts to this implementation using multihomed and multiaddressed hosts:

TCP/IP communication is currently restricted to a single path per connection, yet multiple paths often exist between peers. The **simultaneous use of these multiple paths for a TCP/IP session** would improve resource usage within the network and thus improve user experience through higher throughput and **improved resilience to network failure.**

Multipath TCP provides the ability to simultaneously use multiple paths between peers. This document presents a set of extensions to traditional TCP to support multipath operation. The protocol offers the same type of service to applications as TCP (i.e., a reliable byte stream), and it provides the components necessary to establish and use **multiple TCP flows across potentially disjoint paths.**

The current Nautel implementation uses two separate TCP/IP sessions and sequences the application stream outside of the connection. However, as Multipath TCP matures, adopting this approach and recommending it for standardization of this architecture will be considered if appropriate.

Hot Standby Air-Chain

Hot standby air-chains are fully connected to a backup air-chain and can be placed on air without the need of connection initiation minimizing down time of the on-air broadcast. By the definition of multiple TCP, the same source and same destination are required for all paths which means the air-chain itself is not redundant. A hot standby air-chain differs from multiple TCP in that it connects to independent air-chains as shown on Figure 6. Simultaneous TCP/IP connections are made to both the on-premises and the local backup air-chain. Each connection fills its respective buffer to the target fill level independently using the buffer control algorithm on each connection. The read side of all buffers is synchronized with the FM and exgine modulators such that on an air-chain changeover initiated by the air-chain selector the exgine modulator produces a continuous stream of IBOC symbols aiding in receiver lock acquisition at the symbol level even if a few IBOC symbols are muted on changeover. A synchronous hot standby changeover maintains L1 frame and IBOC symbol timing for fast receiver acquisition of and fast HD lock on the new air chain. The blend function in an HD Radio receiver produces a pleasant cross-fade to the new audio content.

Furthermore, the buffer read side is synchronized such as to dequeue packets from all connections within the same L1 frame sequence number. For example, if the on-premises air-chain is currently on sequence number 45,641 and L1 frames are cyclical with modulus 16 it is currently on the 9th packet within that L1 frame. The local backup air-chain buffer will be advanced until its read packet sequence number is also the 9th packet, for example 11,705. At least 16 packets are maintained in the buffer, such that even on a complete link failure a graceful changeover may be performed on L1 frame boundaries on the first packet within a frame.

While the exgine modulator is kept synchronous, the modulator is reset to flush its internal state on a changeover. It is possible to perform a changeover without loss of HD lock and a seamless cut-in of the HD audio provided all layer 5 audio frames are synchronized across the two air-chains. Until L5 frame alignment can be guaranteed up to two L1 frames may be dropped on a changeover. The FM content is switched in seamlessly while the receiver is still locked to the old HD stream. Once the HD lock is lost, the blend function performs a pleasant cross-fade to the new analog FM audio content on the main channel. Secondary HD channels will exhibit a 3 to 4.5s silence before producing the new audio content but only if the sub-channel exists within the new air-chain. Most receivers will indicate the channel is no longer available if it does not exist in the new air-chain.

Hot standbys are a great way to perform air-chain software updates. Create a new air-chain, update it, configure it, test it to your satisfaction. Bring it up as a hot standby, changeover, retire the old air-chain all with minimal downtime. Of course, both multiple TCP paths or hot standby double the overall bandwidth requirements unless one can either locally source an air-chain or configure TCP/IP routing across different STLs.

Cold Standby Air-Chain

When STL bandwidth is a concern, a cold standby can be configured to quickly serve up a new connection to a backup air-chain but since the buffer is not prefilled as shown in Figure 6 there is a possibility of exhausting the currently active air-chain on a link failure prior to a new connection being established. Unlike an exciter changeover, even on an empty buffer we can maintain an unmodulated RF carrier at the configured power level eliminating any power ramp up delays.

Cold standbys can take on many forms. It can be a clone of the active air-chain without an active connection. However, more sophisticated topologies emerge. Over a fleet of transmitters, a broadcaster may dedicate a few air-chains for emergency use. As the primary air-chain for a given transmitter fails, it connects to a load balancer system that redirects and connects an emergency air-chain to this failing transmitter air-chain. This may involve waking up a virtual air-chain or container and connecting the appropriate ingest streams automatically. All these steps may take some time. It is possible to increase the transmitter's buffer levels to account for all these steps to minimize downtime at the expense of added throughput delay. The proposed client/server architecture that reaches out to a backup air chain allows us to use standard IT components, like load balancers, to handle many disaster recovery use cases via cold standby changeovers.

Legacy UDP

Legacy UDP used by the E2X protocol today in legacy equipment can be supported, since this architecture is based on established standards. However, since the legacy UDP does not support the clock architecture and buffer management described in this paper, over time the legacy UDP buffer will either underflow, if the exporter rate is too slow or overflow, if it is too fast causing HD dropouts. These can be mitigated by GPS synchronizing both the transmitter and exporter, but then what results is essentially a 4th generation architecture with all its limitations.

As described in the preceding sections, earlier FM HD Radio generations do not handle the analog FM component. In the same manner this legacy UDP implementation also only carries the digital IBOC component and must rely on reactive off-air receivers to guarantee FM-HD1 time alignment. It is however possible to decode the HD1 at the exgine level back into a PCM audio stream to be modulated into FM. While the general audio processing that may have been applied prior to the exporter will be preserved, any FM-specific processing will not necessarily be applied (like composite limiting). This method can, in theory, produce good FM-HD1 alignment but because of the sub-standard FM processing may only be appropriate for a last-defense backup audio stream.

Since legacy UDP relies on a downstream listening port, it is not recommended to use this connection method across public networks. This applies both to this architecture and all HD Radio generations.

Constant FM-HD1 Delay with Synchronous Changeover

To illustrate the architecture's superior changeover behavior, two air-chains in AWS were set up. The transmitter output was monitored with an Inovonics Justin 808 to measure the FM-HD1 alignment and an Inovonics Sofia streaming receiver set to split FM/HD mode to be able to plot audio levels on a graph. The Justin output is shown in the top half of Figure 9, the Sofia output is shown in the bottom half. Air-chain #1 was set to process the audio at a loud level, while air-chain #2 was set to bypass at a lower audio level to be able to distinguish the two sources on the audio level graph.

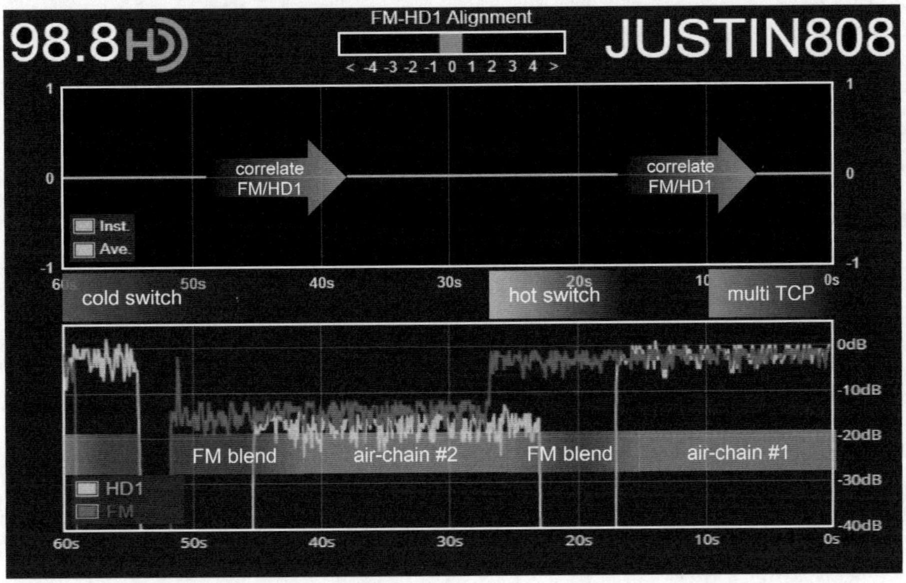

FIGURE 8: CONSISTENT FM-HD1 ALIGNMENT ACROSS CHANGEOVER. A COLD STANDBY CHANGEOVER MAY CAUSE SHORT SILENCE WITHOUT RF CARRIER DROP, A HOT STANDBY CHANGEOVER BLENDS GRACEFULLY TO THE FM CONTENT, A MULTIPLE TCP CHANGEOVER TO THE SAME AIR-CHAIN IS HITLESS.

The transmitter was also outfitted with dual exciters. To establish a baseline, the impact on the broadcast service was measured using standard exciter changeover with legacy UDP. Since the RF carrier is affected in an exciter changeover, the FM service will produce static depending on the received signal level based on the distance to the transmit antenna until the transmitter has completed ramping to full power; typically, 90% of power is reached within 10s. Long periods of HD re-acquisition were noted after an exciter changeover of up to 70s on several receivers. It is assumed that receivers attempt to decode the old IBOC signal until a timeout is hit forcing a new signal acquisition. This timeout may be receiver dependent. This causes an extended HD Radio outage for the station. It may be possible to SFN synchronize both exciters to solve this problem at added cost and complexity.

In contrast, a cold standby, hot standby and multiple TCP changeover all maintain the RF carrier and transmitter power output level. Figure 9 starts with a cold switch initiated manually at the 60s mark. Since there was no other active buffer at the time the transmitter runs out of modulation content silencing the FM audio shown in the red trace. An HD Radio receiver will hang on to the broadcast for another 4.5 seconds, the depth of the IBOC interleaver of 3 L1 frames, before muting its output by blending back to the silent FM. The second air-chain was brought back online using a manual button push simulating the length of connection establishment. If a connection is established prior to buffer depletion and the interleaver an HD Radio receiver may not experience any down time.

A hot standby changeover will be an instant switch over on the FM and a few seconds and the HD Radio receiver will blend to the new analog FM using a pleasant cross fade. When the receiver blends back to the digital simulcast, the experience will be smooth as the audio is perfectly aligned as shown by the time alignment graph in Figure 9. Switching multiple TCP paths is hitless without any impact on the underlying broadcast. Table 3 provides an overview of the various changeover methods.

	Dual Exciter	Cold Standby	Hot Standby	Multiple Path TCP
Backup Air-Chain	Yes duplicate equipment	Yes	Yes	No
RF	1-10s to RF on	Not affected	Not affected	Not affected
FM	Initial static	some silence	Instant switch	Hitless
HD1	FM blend 10s-70s	FM blend (short silence)	3-5s FM blend (blends to new)	Hitless
HD2-4	10s-70s silence	<10s silence	3-5s silence	Hitless
FM-HD1 Alignment	No	Yes	Yes	Yes
Supported	All generations	HD Air-chain G3/4 Manual	HD Air-chain	HD Air-chain Bit splicing

TABLE 3: CHANGEOVER COMPARISON CHART

Changeover methods are not mutually exclusive and can be combined to best suit the station's needs and requirements based on available STL paths. A multiple path TCP implementation can have a concurrent hot standby air-chain, as well, should the main air-chain and not the STL fail itself. A set of two hot standbys can be maintained from a pool of cold standbys to always have a quick changeover.

Conclusion

This paper presents and demonstrated an integrated FM and HD Radio transport architecture that allows for a location- and platform-agnostic air-chain architecture bonding all broadcast services into a single transport stream that ends at the transmitter exciter and originates from software-based air-chains. Software-based air-chain services can be virtualized or containerized allowing for a common implementation regardless of the underlying host platform, whether this is a physical on-site server, an on-premises data center, or even cloud services like AWS.

To maintain consistent timing across the entire air-chain all air-chain services are synchronized to the high-quality crystal in the broadcast transmitter, all the way back to the air-chain ingest in the cloud without the need for GPS synchronization. This makes the main FMHD audio processor a key component of the air-chain. Critical to the architecture also is a network protocol, based on MPX and E2X industry standards, and a buffer management algorithm that allows for multiple concurrent synchronous backup air-chains that always keep the transmitter on-air with cold standby, hot standby and multiple TCP connections. A standardization effort on the network protocol between transmitter and air-chain services will lead to an eco-system of interoperable products from multiple vendors. Future work on integrating MPX compression codecs can widen the applicability and scalability of this architecture.

The cloud connectivity presented in this paper is a proof point that this new architecture can be realized and fielded today because it is built on industry standard protocols like digital composite MPX for the FM and E2X for the HD Radio broadcast. All air-chain components and building blocks, like the Xperi supplied Gen4 encoder and exgine modulator, are available today without modification and continue to guarantee HD Radio receiver interoperability through a common air interface implementation; the blocks just have to be recombined under this new architecture paradigm that is location and platform agnostic. The discussed synchronous buffer management algorithm allows for multiple concurrent synchronous air-chains that always keep the transmitter on-air provides maximum reliability through multiple TCP paths. Adopting an IT standard client-server paradigm not used in today's HD Radio broadcast architecture allows the industry to adopt state-of-the-art security practices such as solid firewall rules and private/public key authentication between transmitter and air-chain services a major leap forward compared to today's feed-forward purpose-built embedded broadcast devices.

Acknowledgements

The author would like to thank the team at The Telos Alliance for their expertise regarding audio processors and the virtual studio, the team at Xperi for their support and expertise on HD Radio system components, Inovonics Broadcast for the measurement equipment used in this paper, and my friends and colleagues at Nautel helping me create this architecture and review this paper.

References

[1] G. Shay, "The Virtual Radio Station in the Cloud," in IEEE BTS Pulse, 2022.

[2] P. Schmid, "E2X Bandwidth and Bit Error Requirements for Ethernet Synchronization," in NAB Broadcast Engineering Conference, Las Vegas, 2007.

[3] National Radio Systems Committee, "HD Radio™ FM Transmission System Specifications," 2016.

[4] P. Schmid, "An Improved Method of Peak-to-Average Power Ratio Reduction for FM+IBOC Broadcast Transmission," Halifax, 2009.

[5] National Radio Systems Committee, NRSC-G203: IBOC Time and Level Alignment Guide, 2017.

[6] National Radio Systems Committee (NRSC), "Transmission Signal Quality for IBOC Signals," 2011.

[7] National Radio Systems Committee, NRSC-5-D: In-band/on-channel Digital Radio Broadcasting Standard, 2017.

[8] Y. Zhang, C. Xu, X. Lin and X. Shen, "Blockchain-Based Public Integrity Verification for Cloud Storage against Procrastinating Auditors," IEEE Transactions on Cloud Computing, pp. 923-937, July 2021.

[9] "UDP flood attack," Cloudflare, 13 March 2022. [Online]. Available: https://www.cloudflare.com/en-ca/learning/ddos/udp-flood-ddos-attack/.

[10] "SYN flood attack," Cloudflare, 13 March 2022. [Online]. Available: https://www.cloudflare.com/learning/ddos/syn-flood-ddos-attack/.

[11] Internet Engineering Task Force (IETF), "RFC8684: TCP Extensions for Multipath Operation with Multiple Addresses," 2020.

[12] P. Schmid, "Radio Air-Chain Innovation Webinar," 2020.

Exploring the Effects of Directional Antenna Pattern Bandwidth on MA3 Transmissions

David Kolesar
Hubbard Radio
Washington, District of Columbia, United States
dkolesar@wtop.com

Mike Raide
Xperi Corporation
Columbia, Maryland, United States
Mike.Raide@xperi.com

Abstract – WWFD (820 kHz, Frederick MD), commenced operations on July 16th, 2018 as the first AM broadcast station to transmit full-time using the HD Radio MA3 all-digital AM mode. For nighttime operation, WWFD utilizes a two-tower directional array, forming a simple pattern with one null. When preparing for MA3 transmissions, the antenna system was modified for improved bandwidth, but also with the goal of reusing as many components as possible in order to reduce digital conversion costs. As a result, the pattern bandwidth in the null direction may not be fully optimized. In this paper, an effort is made to characterize the received signal in and off-axis to the null direction, in order to document the real-world failure conditions of MA3 transmissions. By examining the received signal using a spectrum analyzer and a test receiver that monitors the received signal constellations, the maximum tolerable distortion with regards to amplitude and phase can be characterized. It is hoped that such data will be of use in the design or modification of antenna systems where all-digital operation is contemplated.

The Antenna System

The WWFD nighttime antenna system consists of two towers, 73.5 degrees tall, with 16.5 degrees of top-loading as part of the top level of guy wires. The towers are physically spaced 60 degrees apart, with Tower 2 oriented at an angle of 253 degrees from Tower 1. Tower 1 is the reference, and Tower 2 is driven with a ratio of 0.89 and with 122 degrees of phasing as compared to Tower 1. Power is fed to the antenna system via a simple Ohm's Law power divider [1], with the phase to each tower adjusted via T networks. A cardioid pattern is formed (Figure 1).

The oldest components in the WWFD phasor and Antenna Tuning Units (ATUs) date to WMHI, a 500 watt daytime directional station on 1370 kHz, which first signed on in 1961. In 1988, the towers were reoriented on the property, and the frequency was changed to 820 kHz in order to allow for the current (4.3 kW non-directional daytime, 430 watts directional nighttime) operation. Components from the original antenna system were repurposed with thrift and economy in mind, and in 2018 the same considerations were prominent in the station's conversion to MA3 all-digital operations [2]. As a result, some compromises were unavoidable in the retrofit of the array, such as the pattern linearity and bandwidth in the null direction. Since the null is rather deep, it is instructive to examine how the

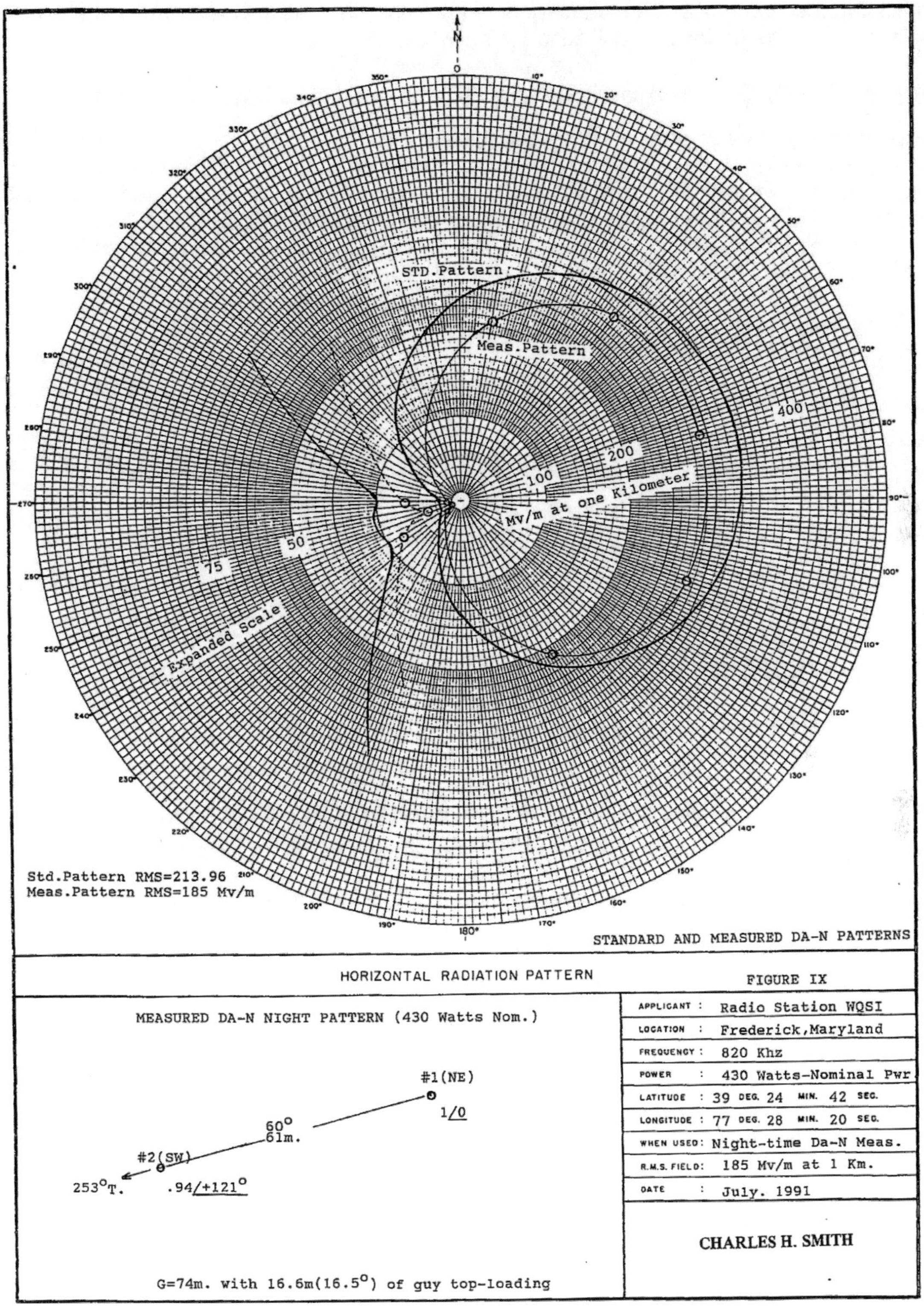

FIGURE 1: THE WWFD NIGHTTIME ANTENNA PATTERN.

station's MA3 transmissions perform on and adjacent to that radial. Such "real world" data from a necessarily imperfect antenna system adds to the knowledge base as to when all-digital MA3 transmissions fail due to inadequate null-fill in the array.

Examining the MA3 Waveform in the Context of the Antenna System

A discussion of the MA3 waveform is available in the literature [3], and a plot of its magnitude versus frequency is given in Figure 2. Because of the functionally random nature of the data points within the signal constellations, the waveform, when viewed using a spectrum analyzer with sufficient video averaging, can easily reveal amplitude nonlinearities within a transmission channel. As a result, the waveform as viewed on a spectrum analyzer can serve to approximate the amplitude nonlinearities of a directional AM antenna system as a function of azimuth.

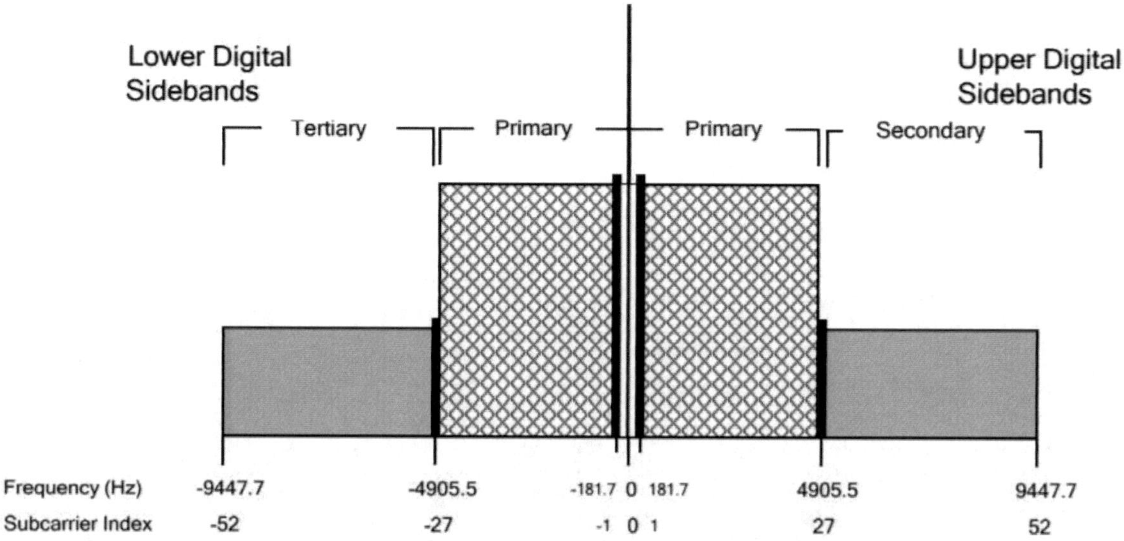

FIGURE 2. THE MA3 WAVEFORM [3]. NOTE THE REFERENCE CARRIER AT 0 FREQUENCY, WHICH AIDS IN RECEIVER SYNCHRONIZATION.

Here, measurements taken along an arc cutting through the system's null, compared to a measurement taken in the major lobe of the array, serve to characterize the approximate in-channel amplitude response of the antenna system. At the same time, an examination of the signal constellations provides insight as to phase distortions that may occur as a function of azimuth, referenced to the signal in the major lobe.

In a typical digital receiver, demodulation involves several processes, for example automatic gain control (AGC), which utilize phase-lock and equalizer loops [4]. Since such circuits provide correction for channel distortions, typical field measurements can only indicate when the entire transmission-reception process (channel corruption plus channel correction) breaks down. By travelling along an arc, noting points of reception failure, and taking these measurements, information as to how much amplitude and phase nonlinearity can be tolerated before system failure can be gained. Such efforts provide experimental data to antenna system designers.

A well-designed directional antenna system will pass MA3 transmissions in its major lobe, but difficulties can arise at the edges of such a lobe and within the null areas. A deep null can create either a ripple or notch in the channel passband, which compromises the digital carriers. The WWFD nighttime antenna system contains one such deep null, and thus provides an opportunity to characterize the impacts of nonlinearities typical in directional AM antenna systems on all-digital transmissions.

Test Procedure

A test vehicle (Figure 3) is outfitted with an omnidirectional, medium wave loop antenna, mounted as close to the center of the roof as possible. This antenna feeds a test receiver capable of depicting the signal constellations, as well as a spectrum analyzer to monitor the amplitude linearity of the received signal (Figure 4). The vehicle's factory stock radio is used to monitor the signal for reception or no reception while in motion.

FIGURE 3. THE TEST VEHICLE.

A test route is chosen that sweeps through the null of the antenna system, starting from the north and proceeding south. The first test point is chosen to be a location to the north and far enough away from the null (on the 253 degree radial) such that reception is strong on the monitor radio. This is determined by the presence of fast receiver acquisition (typically on the order of 1.5 seconds), meaning that the Program Information Data Service (PIDS) carriers and both sets of Primary carriers are being decoded by the receiver. Field strength is then measured with a field intensity meter calibrated for MA3 measurements (a Potomac Instruments FIM-4100) to ensure that at least 0.5 mV of signal is present, which is the minimum threshold for reliable decoding of the Secondary and Tertiary carriers [4].

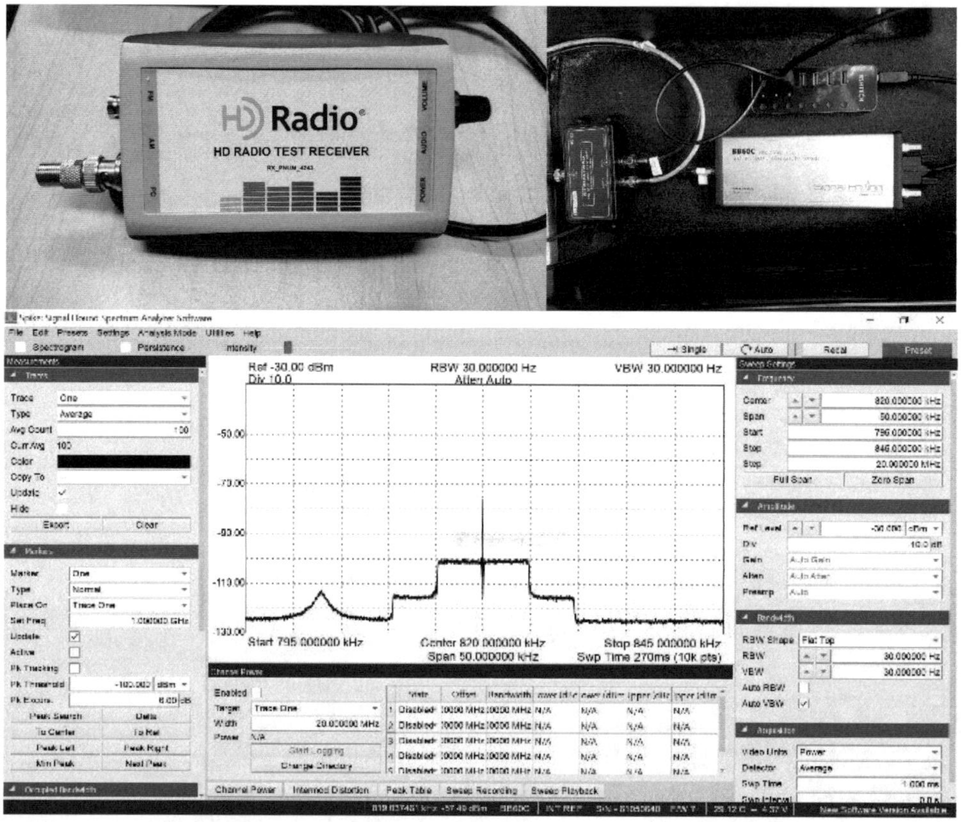

FIGURE 4. HD RADIO TEST RECEIVER (TOP LEFT), SPECTRUM ANALYZER HARDWARE (TOP RIGHT), AND SPECTRUM ANALYZER SCREEN SHOT (BOTTOM).

The vehicle is then driven south and stopped for stationary measurements at several places, including the three designated monitor points, which are along the 268, 253, and 238 degree radials. The vehicle is driven south until reception quality approximates the first point, indicating that the vehicle has travelled through the subtended azimuth angle where reception is impaired by the poor pattern bandwidth and null-fill performance of the antenna system. At each point, reception quality of the monitor radio is noted, and a field strength measurement is taken. A spectrum analyzer screenshot is taken to measure the amplitude ripple of the channel. Signal constellations of both sets of Primary carriers, as well as the Secondary and Tertiary carriers, are examined using the test receiver. The quality of the signal constellations indicate which sets of carriers are being successfully passed through the antenna system and decoded by the receiver. Test points are located in as open of a location as possible, and measurements are taken in the middle of the day, both in order to eliminate variables such as power line noise and skywave interference.

After the data is collected in the null direction, the vehicle is driven east of the tower site to a point in the major lobe. A set of stationary measurements is once again taken, this time to provide a reference to demonstrate the upper limit of signal quality being transmitted from the antenna system. A map of the test points to the west, as well as the reference point to the east, is displayed in Figure 5, as is the nighttime pattern of the antenna (half-NIF contour at 5.4 mV/m).

FIGURE 5. THE TEST POINTS, LABELED TP1-TP8, AS WELL AS THE REFERENCE POINT LABELED MAJOR LOBE 1. THE "HALF NIF" CONTOUR OF 5.4 MV/M IS DISPLAYED AS THE RED LINE.

Test Data

Test Point	LAT	LON	Field Strength (mV/m)	Reception
TP1	39.422695	-77.503557	4.900	Yes
TP2	39.418972	-77.503028	11.500*	Yes
TP3	39.411111	-77.502809	0.725	No
TP4	39.404667	-77.50833	1.530	Marginal
TP5	39.400471	-77.509308	1.230	Marginal
TP6	39.393055	-77.510171	0.606	No
TP7	39.383888	-77.510781	0.826	Marginal
TP8	39.380749	-77.494783	5.170	Yes
Major Lobe 1	39.405084	-77.383833	30.900	Yes

TABLE 1. TEST POINT POSITION, FIELD STRENGTH, AND RECEPTION DATA.
*THE PRESENCE OF A NEARBY TOWER LIKELY CAUSED SOME RERADIATION OF THE WWFD SIGNAL AT THIS POINT, AFFECTING THE MEASUREMENT.

Table 1 shows the test data at each point, indicating position, field strength, and whether there was reception on the stock vehicle radio. Points TP3, TP4, and TP6 correspond to the station's monitor points along the 268, 253, and 238 degree radials, respectively. The Major Lobe 1 point corresponds to a parking lot adjacent to the Frederick Municipal Airport (FDK).

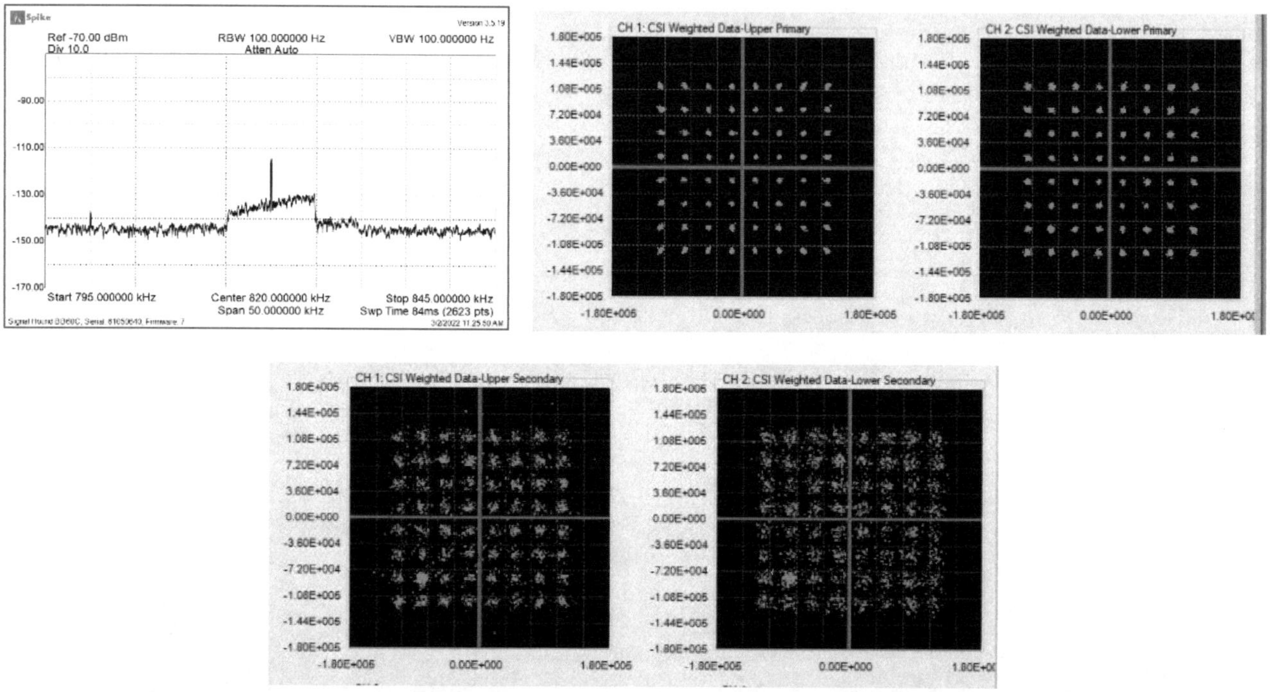

FIGURE 6. TP1: SPECTRUM ANALYZER VIEW (TOP LEFT), PRIMARY UPPER AND LOWER CARRIERS (TOP RIGHT), SECONDARY AND TERTIARY CARRIERS (BOTTOM).

Data collected from the first test point, TP1, shown in Figure 6, is notable in that even though all of the carriers are coherent enough to be decoded by a receiver, the antenna system is distorting the amplitude of the MA3 carriers as a function of frequency. Using the spectrum analyzer's video averaging and markers to make an estimate, the ripple in the Primary carriers appears to be approximately 8 dB across both sets, but is limited to about 4 dB for the upper and lower ones individually.

As the vehicle is driven south, reception becomes solid as the amplitude response smooths out, and all carriers are received solidly (Figure 7). At the 268 degree radial monitor point, however, reception collapses as the Reference carrier is almost completely suppressed (Figure 8). The signal recovers somewhat at the 253 degree radial monitor point (Figure 9), as the upper Primary and Tertiary carriers are linear enough to be decoded. Note that the lower Primary carrier has approximately 8 dB of ripple and a high amplitude relative to the reference carrier, which makes its decoding unlikely. At TP5, some coherence to the lower Primary and the Secondary carriers has returned, as the ripple shifts position slightly (Figure 10). Note the amplitude distortion that creates an "X" pattern within the lower Primary carrier constellation.

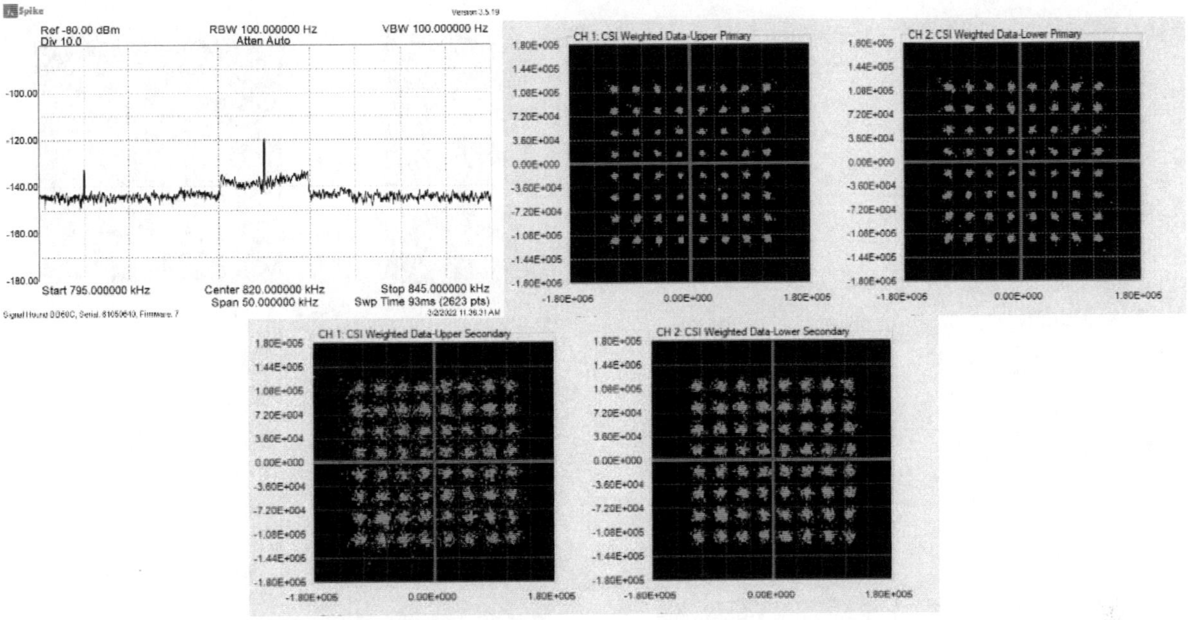

FIGURE 7. TP2: SPECTRUM ANALYZER VIEW (TOP LEFT), PRIMARY UPPER AND LOWER CARRIERS (TOP RIGHT), SECONDARY AND TERTIARY CARRIERS (BOTTOM).

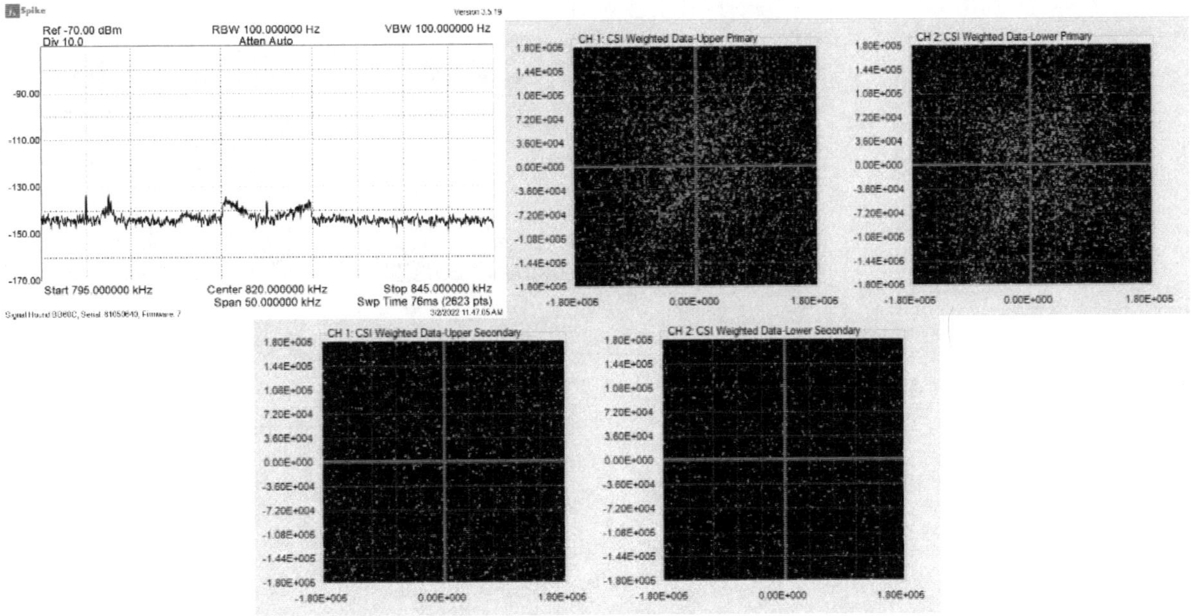

FIGURE 8. TP3: SPECTRUM ANALYZER VIEW (TOP LEFT), PRIMARY UPPER AND LOWER CARRIERS (TOP RIGHT), SECONDARY AND TERTIARY CARRIERS (BOTTOM).

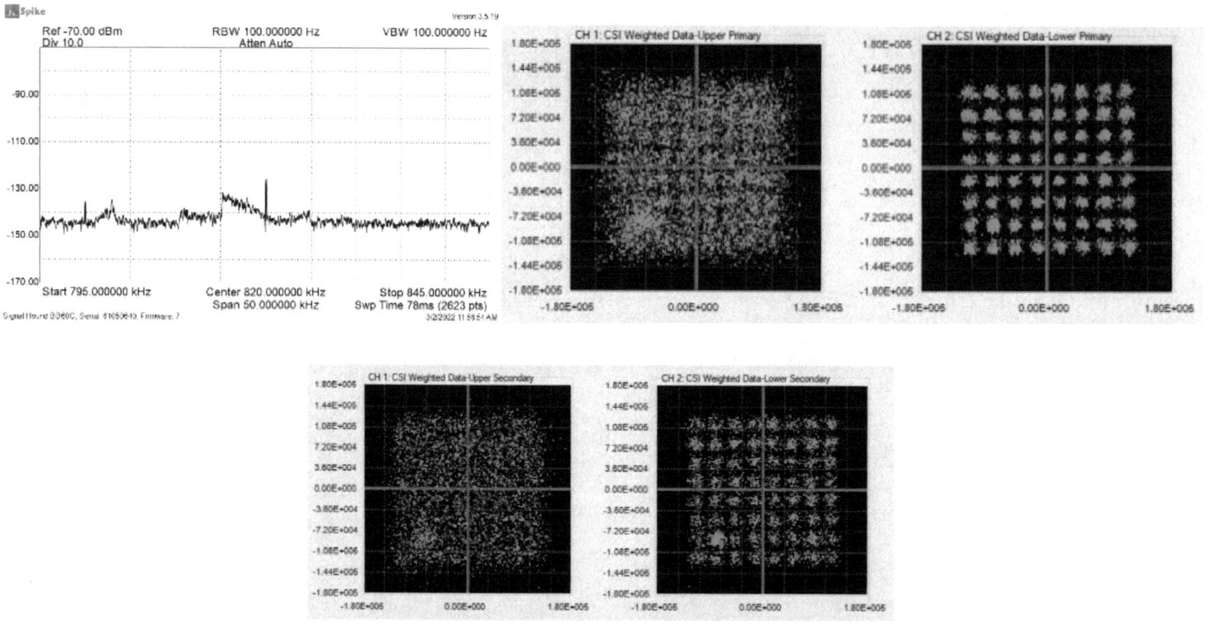

FIGURE 9. TP4: SPECTRUM ANALYZER VIEW (TOP LEFT), PRIMARY UPPER AND LOWER CARRIERS (TOP RIGHT), SECONDARY AND TERTIARY CARRIERS (BOTTOM).

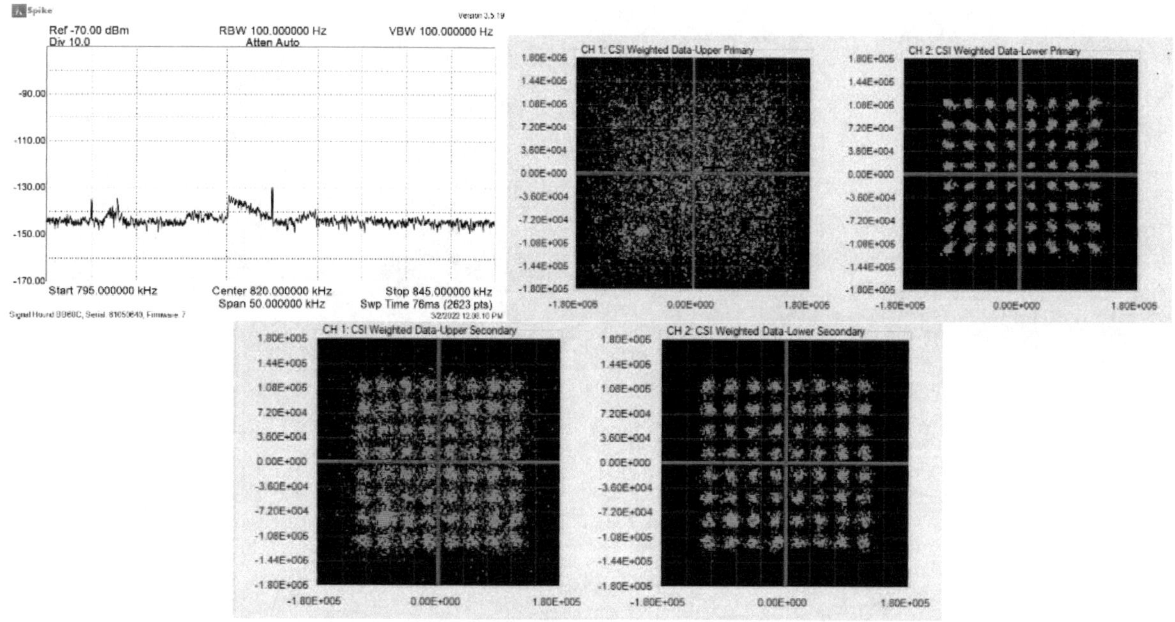

FIGURE 10. TP5: SPECTRUM ANALYZER VIEW (TOP LEFT), PRIMARY UPPER AND LOWER CARRIERS (TOP RIGHT), SECONDARY AND TERTIARY CARRIERS (BOTTOM).

Reception once again collapses at TP6, the 238 degree radial monitor point (Figure 11). Note the rotation and incoherence of the signal constellations as the Reference carrier is suppressed. Reception progressively improves as the vehicle is driven through points TP7 (Figure 12) and TP8, away from the null radial, and as more carriers come into coherence. By TP8 (Figure 13), the Reference carrier has about as little suppression as in TP1.

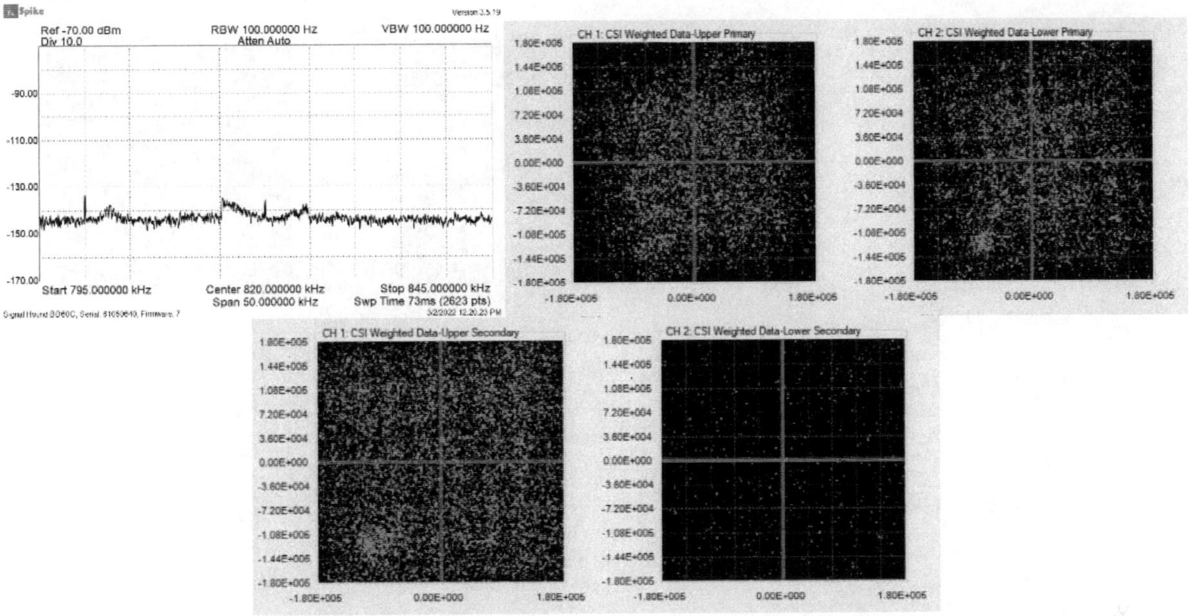

FIGURE 11. TP6: SPECTRUM ANALYZER VIEW (TOP LEFT), PRIMARY UPPER AND LOWER CARRIERS (TOP RIGHT), SECONDARY AND TERTIARY CARRIERS (BOTTOM).

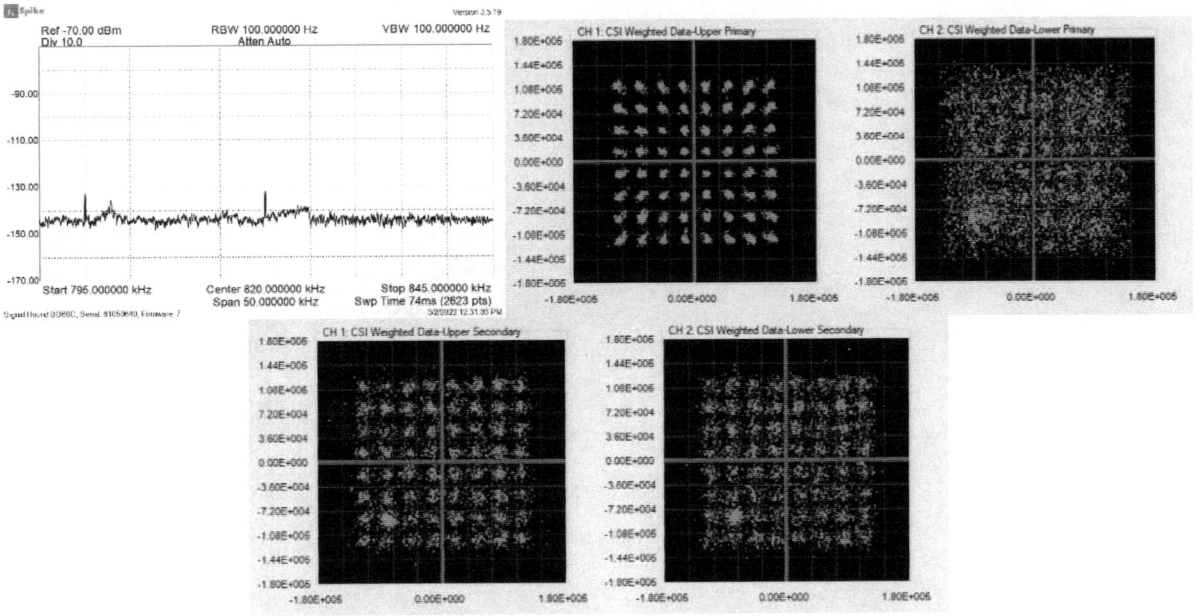

FIGURE 12. TP7: SPECTRUM ANALYZER VIEW (TOP LEFT), PRIMARY UPPER AND LOWER CARRIERS (TOP RIGHT), SECONDARY AND TERTIARY CARRIERS (BOTTOM).

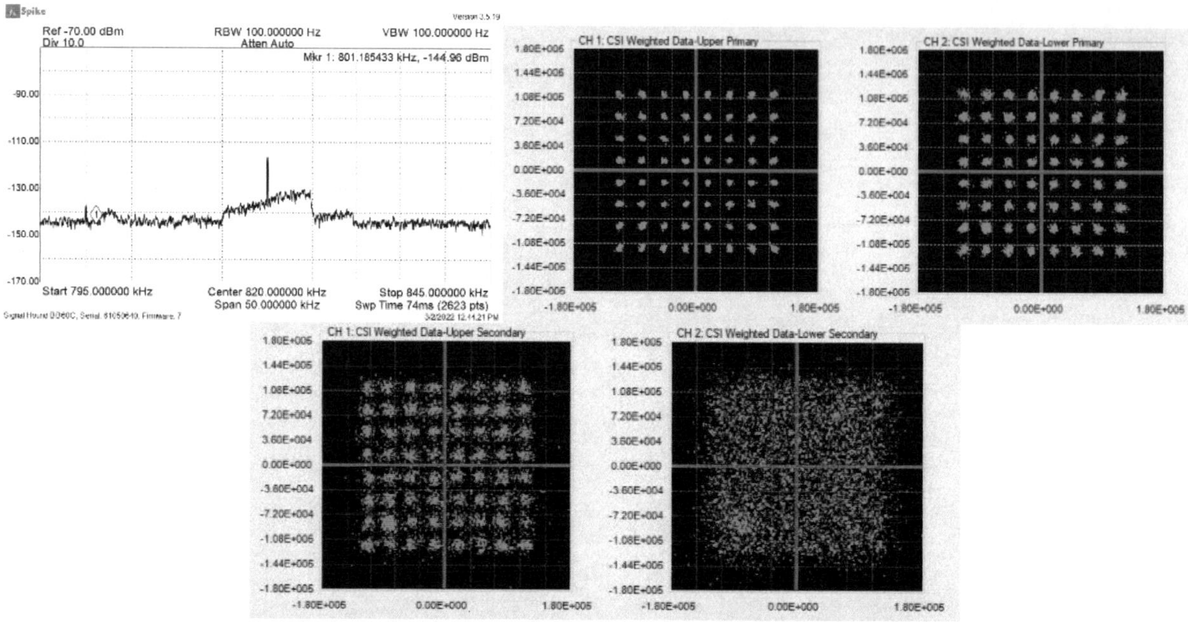

FIGURE 13. TP8: SPECTRUM ANALYZER VIEW (TOP LEFT), PRIMARY UPPER AND LOWER CARRIERS (TOP RIGHT), SECONDARY AND TERTIARY CARRIERS (BOTTOM).

Having driven through the null, a point in the major lobe is chosen for reference, and the data collected is displayed in Figure 14. This point indicates the minimum amplitude and phase distortion of the MA3 signal that is caused by the antenna system.

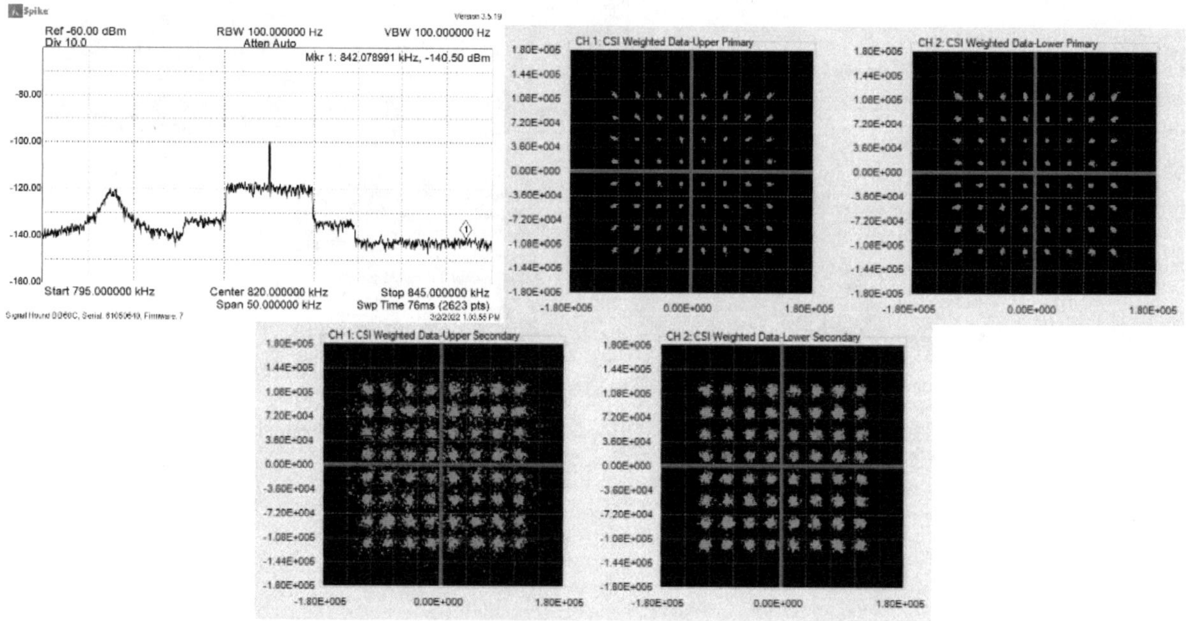

FIGURE 14. MAJOR LOBE: SPECTRUM ANALYZER VIEW (TOP LEFT), PRIMARY UPPER AND LOWER CARRIERS (TOP RIGHT), SECONDARY AND TERTIARY CARRIERS (BOTTOM).

Discussion

		Passband ripple (dB)				Constellations	
Test point	Meas. field strength (mV/m)	Upper Primary carriers (0 to 5 kHz)	Lower Primary carriers (0 to -5 kHz)	Reference carrier level, dB over Upper Primary	Reference carrier level, dB over Lower Primary	Primary Upper	Primary Lower
TP1	4.900	4	4	14	15	Solid and tight	Solid and tight
TP2	11.500	4	4	14	15	Solid and tight	Solid and tight
TP3	0.725	8	8	0	0	Incoherent	Incoherent
TP4	1.530	3	10	14	8	Incoherent	Some noise
TP5	1.230	7	5	5	10	Incoherent	Some noise
TP6	0.606	5	7	1	0	Incoherent	Incoherent
TP7	0.826	4	3	8	10	Solid and tight	Incoherent
TP8	5.170	4	5	14	15	Solid and tight	Some noise
Major Lobe 1	30.900	0	0	20	20	Solid and tight	Solid and tight

TABLE 2. SUMMARY OF TEST POINT DATA. SPECTRUM ANALYZER WAS SET FOR 100 KHZ RBW, AND A VIDEO AVERAGING OF 10.

In examining the spectrum analyzer plots for the various test points, it can be seen that the MA3 signal can be decoded despite fairly adverse channel transmission characteristics. In the WWFD test data, an amplitude ripple of 4 dB within one carrier set seemed to be compensated by the synchronization and equalization processes in the receiver. As the vehicle is moved through the test points, there appears to be a point of maximum suppression as a function of frequency varying within the channel. When this point of maximum suppression lands on the Reference carrier, the receiver cannot lock onto the MA3 signal. It is worth further exploring the effects of the level of the Reference carrier upon the receiver's ability to coherently decode the signal, as has been proposed in other contexts [6]. Where the point of maximum suppression lands also affects the slope (both steepness and positive/negative direction) of the ripple. It is here where the MA3 transmission system compensates well for these channel faults: the Lower and Upper Primary carriers are redundant, and the same applies to the Secondary and Tertiary carriers.

The receiver will still decode the MA3 signal if one set of Primary carriers is impaired. With a directional antenna system, it is entirely plausible that a receiver switches between the Lower and Upper Primary carriers, depending upon channel conditions. It should be noted, however, that if neither set of Primary carriers can be decoded, the receiver will not decode the Secondary or Tertiary carriers, even if coherent. This has implications for the coverage area of audio and data services using the Enhanced carriers, such as Station Logo, Artist Experience, and Secondary Program Service (SPS) channels: they are usable only in a subset of the Core service area.

As an aside, an examination of the signal constellations at the Major Lobe 1 test point reveals an item of note about the Secondary and Tertiary carriers: they are not as well-formed as the Primary carriers. This is not due to the antenna system, as this effect is also observed at the RF monitor port of the transmitter. These carriers are approximately 12 dB lower in amplitude than the Primary carriers. Additionally, the nighttime TPO of WWFD is 460 watts, well below the stated 5 kW capacity of the transmitter. As a result, at nighttime power levels, the Secondary and Tertiary carriers are more affected by the noise floor of the amplifiers within the transmitter than are the Primary carriers. Nighttime power levels must be considered when operating a transmitter in the MA3 mode, and for very low power levels (relative to the stated capacity of the transmitter) it may be necessary to utilize a power divider network with a resistive load in order to operate the transmitter within a range where the Secondary and Tertiary carriers can be formed with an adequate signal-to-noise ratio.

Despite the redundancy built into the MA3 transmission system, antenna system engineers and designers should not overlook the pattern bandwidth and null-fill characteristics of AM directional antenna systems. In the areas of marginal array performance, reception robustness is lost. Ensuring maximum impedance bandwidth as well as pattern bandwidth is a must for any all-digital AM transmission system. Such efforts will pay off by creating the best listener experience by maximizing the useful coverage area of an AM station with a directional antenna system.

Acknowledgements

The authors wish to thank the following individuals for their support and guidance: Joel Oxley, Dave Garner, George Molnar, Ginny Morris, and the entire Corporate Leadership Team at Hubbard Radio; Tom King, Joshua King, and Jim Moser (Kintronic Labs); Philipp Schmid (Nautel), Gary and Cindy Cavell (Cavell, Mertz & Associates); Jeff Baird, Paul Peyla, Ashruf El-Dinary and Russ Mundschenk (Xperi Corporation), and David Layer (National Association of Broadcasters).

References

[1] King, T., Cox, B., & Moser, J., "Antenna Coupling and Phasing Systems," *National Association of Broadcasters Engineering Handbook*, 11th Edition, 2018, p. 1215.

[2] Kolesar, D. and Raide, M., "Facility Upgrades for Full-Time All-Digital HD AM Broadcasting: A Case study," *NAB Broadcast Engineering and Information Technology Conference*, April 2019, pp. 1-7.

[3] iBiquity Digital Corporation, "HD Radio Air Interface Design Description Layer 1 AM," *SY_IDD_1012s,* Rev. G, December 14th, 2016.

[4] Sklar, B. and Harris, F., "Synchronization," *Digital Communications*, 3rd Edition, 2021, pp. 619-673.

[5] Kolesar, D. and Raide, M., "A Case Study in All-Digital HD AM Broadcasting: Refinements, Performance Tests, and Lessons Learned," *NAB Broadcast Engineering and Information Technology Conference*, April 2020, p. 9.

[6] Kolesar, D. and Raide, M., "Incorporating a Supplemental Program Service (SPS) Channel into MA3 Transmissions," *NAB Broadcast Engineering and Information Technology Conference*, October 2021, pp. 7-8.

The Time to Consider All Digital Radio Has Arrived

E. Glynn Walden
CBS Radio (retired)
Marlton, New Jersey, United States
glynn.walden@audacy.com

Abstract – In the absence of available spectrum for the implementation of a new-band digital radio service in the United States and other countries, a consortium of US broadcasters invested in and developed a digital transmission standard for transmitting digital radio within the existing AM and FM spectrum. The technology was called In Band On Channel, IBOC, and the system this consortium developed is now branded HD Radio. The system added digital carriers to the existing analog broadcast channels that provided a hybrid digital-analog service. The system was designed to function with simultaneous analog and digital signals until such time that it became economically more advantageous to turn off the analog signal and transition to all-digital signaling. For AM, that time has arrived.

Background

Radio is the only remaining analog entertainment delivery system and analog AM radio is incapable of providing the quality of audio that modern day digital audio systems provide. As an industry, broadcasters have harvested as much as is possible out of analog delivery AM and FM systems. For radio to remain relevant in the future it will have to transition to a digital delivery system to provide services competitive in a world that has left analog media behind.

The HD Radio system was designed to serve as a transition vehicle for radio using existing AM and FM spectrum. The transition was to occur by using the radio as the transition vehicle rather than new spectrum as was done in the US conversion to HDTV. The TV transition was mandated to occur on a specified date where analog transitions would cease, and all TV stations would begin transmitting with a digital-only signal.

In other countries, new spectrum was made available for radio to be delivered digitally. Having clean, new spectrum would have been an attractive way to implement a digital radio service in the US, however, the spectrum was not available, and broadcasters opposed a digital service in new spectrum as they feared new competition.[1] And systems available at the time would have required 60 MHz of spectrum to accommodate all of the existing AM and FM stations in the largest markets, leaving hundreds of available channels for use in the smaller markets. Additionally, there was no new spectrum available but had there been, it would have likely been auctioned not only to existing broadcasters but new entrants as well.

AM radio as a service is struggling to be relevant in the age of digital audio distribution, but this does not have to be so. With the FCC's authorization of all-digital AM services in October 2020, AM

[1] Digital Audio Broadcasting, DAB (originally known as Eureka 147), was such a service.

This paper is excerpted from the Proceedings of the 2022 NAB Broadcast Engineering and Information Technology (BEIT) Conference, © 2022, National Association of Broadcasters, 1 M Street S.E., Washington, DC 20003 USA.

broadcasters now have a path to a more competitive digital service. There are currently more than 80 million registered cars with HD radios capable of receiving the all-digital AM HD Radio transmissions.[2] Several stations have already transitioned from analog to all-digital AM transmissions providing greater coverage with metadata and stereo audio quality similar to FM radio.

USA Digital Radio, the developer of HD Radio, was formed by a consortium of radio broadcasters (CBS Radio, Group W Radio and Gannett) in 1992 to develop In Band On Channel (IBOC) digital radio, an analog-compatible AM and FM radio system that used the broadcaster's existing spectrum. System designs began in 1992 to test the feasibility. Shown in Figure 1 is a group of engineers involved in the first digital AM transmission in 1994. The AM and FM HD Radio systems went through several design changes prior to the finalized IBOC system in 1998, with a minor change to the AM system to improve AM reception in 2002. These are the systems in use today with additional features incorporating capabilities that were included in the original design.

FIGURE 1: FIRST DIGITAL AM BROADCAST, CINCINNATI, OH AT THE WESTINGHOUSE, XETRON FACILITY, SPRING, 1994. FROM LEFT TO RIGHT: PAUL DONAHUE, RON RACKLEY, TONY MASIELLO, GLYNN WALDEN, (UNKNOWN) AND BARRY CARLIN

[2] 80 million cars as of 12/31/2021. Xperi has more recently stated that it is likely that the number now exceeds 90 million, but those numbers will not be verified until the end of the first quarter of 2022.

The AM design goals were to provide improved, noise-free coverage, stereo FM-like audio quality, and metadata to display station and program-related data. In the early days of AM development, audio codecs were not capable of providing high quality stereo audio, but simultaneously with the development of the RF transmission system, audio codecs became available capable of delivering stereo FM-like quality at bit rates as low as 32 kbps. The AM digital audio broadcasting system approved by the FCC in 2002 used a transmission of 30 kHz bandwidth, whereas at a later time, backward-compatible codec improvements were incorporated at the transmitter that allowed the same quality in a 20 kHz bandwidth.[3]

The system operated in two modes, a hybrid mode with simultaneous analog and digital signaling and an all-digital mode that provides significantly better coverage without an analog component.[4] The hybrid mode, incorporating digital and analog signals was introduced to provide a quality improvement where the signal was strong and to help seed the marketplace with receivers capable of receiving the all-digital mode when broadcasters viewed in their economic best interest to switch to all-digital and leave the analog system behind.

The Technology Behind the All-Digital AM HD Radio System

The HD Radio transmission system uses hundreds of digital carriers for the FM system and more than 50 digital carriers for the AM system grouped into upper and lower digital sidebands. The existing analog AM and FM signals may encounter interference on the upper and lower sidebands and to some extent the digital components will be subject to same interference situations as these operate within the existing channels as authorized by the FCC. To overcome this expected interference, the digital audio is replicated in the upper and lower digital sidebands to provide service even in the presence of first-adjacent channel interference. Co-channel interference is less of a problem as the channels are better protected (by FCC rules) from co-channels than interference arriving from first-adjacent channels.

All-Digital Carriers

The all-digital AM system is a multichannel orthogonal frequency division multiplexing (OFDM) system where the design parameters are optimized to mitigate interference, survive the effects of Grounded Conductive Structures (GCS) and provide a stereo FM-like audio service over an extended service area. There are 54 digital carriers within the all-digital AM system 2 using Binary Phase Shift Keying (BPSK), and 52 digital carriers using 64 Quadrature Amplitude Modulation (QAM).

BPSK carriers have two states, representing either a 1 or a 0, and are capable of delivering a very robust 1 bit per hertz. BPSK carriers are used to provide robust system timing signals needed to recover data from the 64 QAM carriers.

The QAM carriers are used to convey the audio and error correction bits. Each carrier has 64 possible combinations of 1s and 0s or 6 bits of information per Hz. The higher order carriers in each of the sidebands are capable of conveying more bits of information however they are significantly less robust than are the BPSK carriers.

[3] The codec improvements resulted in the reduction of the needed number of bits from 32 kbps to 20 kbps making it possible to eliminate first-adjacent channel interferences when the band transitions to all-digital while still delivering noise-free FM like quality.
[4] Not to be confused with "hybrid radio" that employs both over-the-air and internet connectivity.

Error Correction

While it would be not classically defined as error correction, the power in the two digital sidebands combines for a 3 dB power gain. The error correction per sideband differs in a manner allowing the total error correction when both sidebands are present to deliver a more robust error correction rate.

Each sideband carries the entire 20 kbps audio with a Convolutional Punctured Pair Codes (CPPC)[5] rate 5/6 error correction per sideband. When both sidebands are received, a rate 5/12 error correction is achieved. The robust rate 5/12 provides 12 bits of error correction for each 5 bits of audio data.

64 QAM, while providing more throughput, is significantly more prone to amplitude distortion, phase distortion and noise than is BPSK. The AM channel has fading caused by power lines that can result in extremely fast fading and phase rotation of the digital carriers with similar effects due to destructive self-fading from skywave.[6]

Distortions caused by amplitude and phase variations are reduced by error correction and sophisticated carrier tracking in receivers. The error correction, in addition to the choice of subcarrier timing rates that are much higher than the pulse width of typical noise signals, results in a system that can survive in the noisy AM band.

The reception of OFDM systems operating in the AM band is affected by driving under and beside power lines. The power lines produce a notch in the spectrum of the desired channel. The overhead power line along with the supporting poles and the conductive path through the ground produce a resonant circuit, a notch, that "sucks" out a portion of the band as shown is in Figure 2.[7] These structures are GCS as briefly discussed above. Depending on the "Q" of the notch, the fading characteristics and phase rotation can be extremely rapid. The amplitude changes cannot be met with automatic gain control (AGC) as they are too fast and can affect a number of the OFDM carriers. The receivers, aided by the transmitted reference carriers and rapid responding amplitude and phase corrections of the digital carriers by the receiver, help the system track through nearly 99% of the incidents of GCS-induced distortions. The response of the channel can be seen in Figure 3. Here we can see the effects of a two-lane overpass with open air between the spans.

---

[5] CPPC refers to a code where some of the bit coding on each sideband's error correction can be "punctured", producing a lower coding rate. Different, complementary, coding bits are "punctured" on the other sideband, such that missing bits from each sideband are combined and the resulting code rate is much higher.

[6] Phase distortion causes the individual OFDM carriers to rotate making it more difficult to recover the desired audio bits. Error correction and carrier de-rotation circuits, in the receiver, using embedded reference carriers are effective against these effects.

[7] The readers may have experiences this phenonium when driving under a power line. The analog carrier will be notched by the resonance of the power line. The notching of the carrier causes the AGC to increase the receiver gain, bringing up the background noise level.

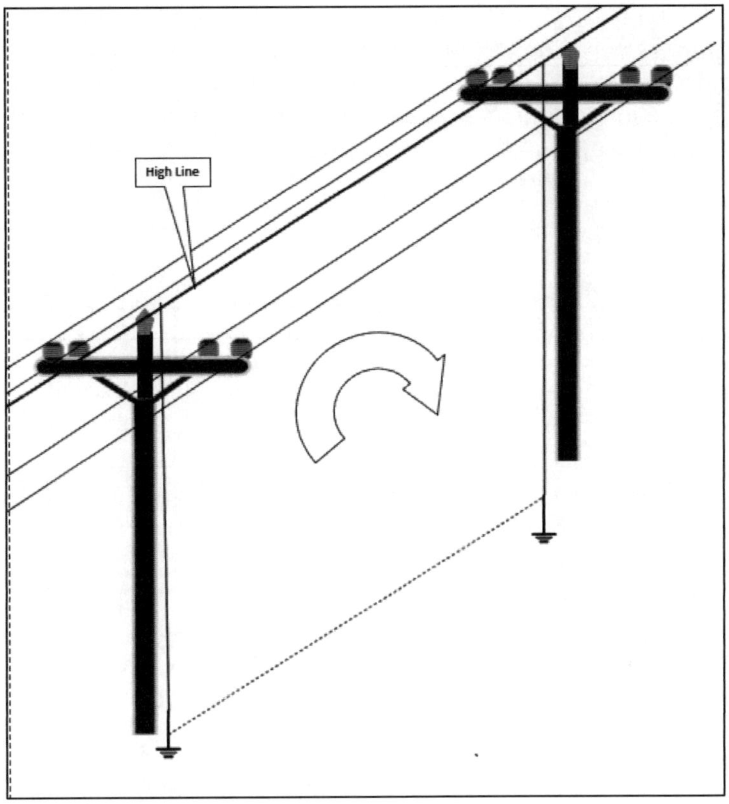

FIGURE 2: SHOWS THE HIGH LINE OF THE POWER DISTRIBUTION NETWORK. THE HIGH LINE IS USUALLY GROUNDED ST EACH POLE AND SERVES TO PROTECT AGAINST LIGHTNING STRIKES. THE HIGH LINE ALONG WITH THE GROUNDING WIRES RUNNING ALONG THE POLES TO GROUND SERVE AS A RESONANT CIRCUIT.

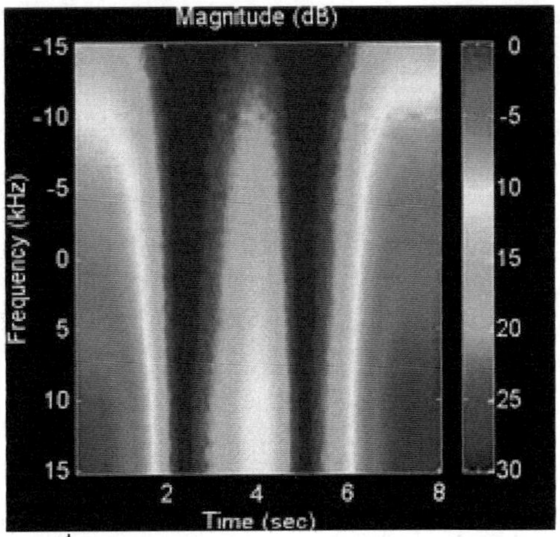

FIGURE 3: SHOWS THE EFFECT OF DRIVING UNDER A DUAL FREEWAY OVERPASS ON THE RECEPTION OF A 740 KHZ CHANNEL, RECORDED AT 27 MPH. THE Y AXIS ON THE LEFT SHOWS THE UPPER AND LOWER SIDEBANDS, THE X AXIS SHOWS THE TIME IN SECONDS AND THE COLOR SCALE ON THE RIGHT SHOWS THE DEPTH OF THE CHANNEL LOSS IN DB

Interleavers

In a digital transmission system, error correction is able to recover data from lost bits of information it there are not too many successive errors. Interleavers are used in the transmission of the data to scramble the data bits and also to "unscramble" or restore the correct order of the bits in the receiver (see Figure 4). Generally, the longer the interleaver the better the error correction performance. Longer interleavers also introduce more system delay and increase access time when tuning to a new station. This is problematic in that audiences are not use to waiting a long time when changing channels.

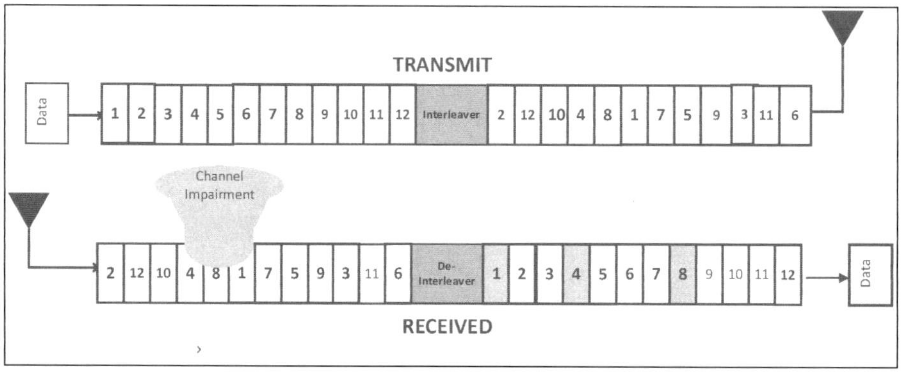

FIGURE 4: SHOWS THE FUNCTION OF AN INTERLEAVER IN PREVENTING SUCCESSIVE LOSSES OF BITS. IN THIS EXAMPLE THERE ARE THREE ADJACENT LOSSES OF BITS 4, 8 AND 1. WHEN THE BITS PASS THROUGH THE DE-INTERLEAVER THE ERRORS ARE SPREAD OUT AND ARE NO LONGER SUCCESSIVE ALLOWING THE ERROR CORRECTION ALGORITHMS TO PROVIDE CONTINUOUS AUDIO.

The delay time when tuning issue is solved in the HD Radio all-digital AM system by employing a main and a backup channel. The main channel has a long interleaver and the backup channel has a short interleaver. The radio initially tunes to the backup channel, with a 1.5 second interleaver, and switches to the main channel, with a 4.5 second interleaver, when the audio is available. This allows for more rapid tuning while simultaneously taking advantage of the more robust performance of the longer interleaver in the main channel.

Time and Frequency Diversity

The AM radio spectrum is a harsh environment where the reception of both analog and digital signals is challenging. The HD Radio system transmit the audio data on main and backup digital channels and simultaneously on the upper and lower digital sidebands. Thus, the system has both time and frequency diversity which Xperi refers to as LUMB, where L refers to the lower sideband, U the upper sideband, M for the main channel and B for the backup channel. Each channel is coded in a complimentary code where each channel is a standalone, independently decodable subset of stronger composite code. The effects of the channel coding gain and the redundant digital sidebands combine for a 3 dB power gain.

Another advantage is that the time difference between the main and backup channels decorrelates outages due to various channel impairments, i.e., going under a bridge, passing through a GCS or selective fading. The radio, after acquisition generally decodes the main channel and seamlessly blends to the backup channel when there is an impairment until the main channel operation is restored (see Figure 5).

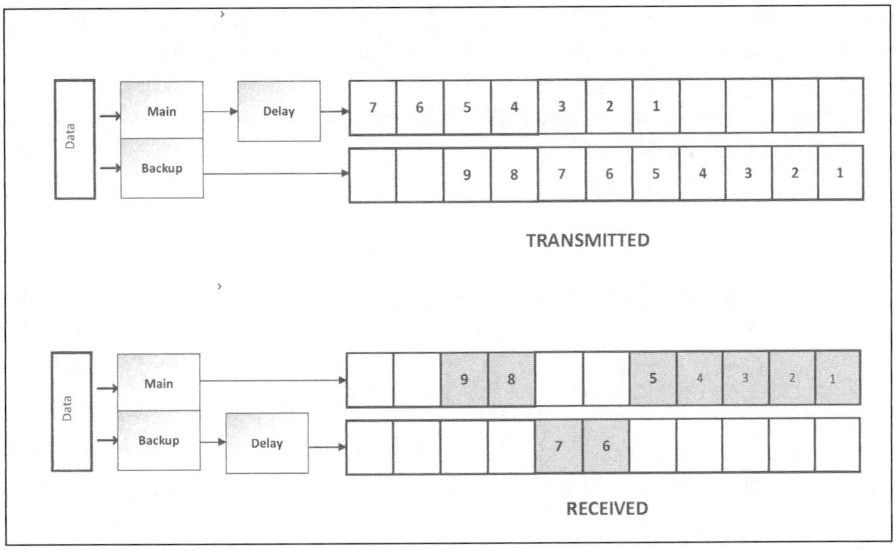

FIGURE 5: SHOWS HOW DECORRELATION BETWEEN THE MAIN AND BACKUP CHANNEL ALLOWS CONTINUITY OF THE AUDIO PROGRAM. IN THIS EXAMPLE SEGMENTS 7 AND 7 IN THE MAIN CHANNEL ARE LOST, HOWEVER, THE RECEIVER BLENDS TO THE BACKUP CHANNEL TO FILL IN THE MISSING AUDIO SEGMENTS.

Transitioning to All-Digital AM

Reception of analog AM radio is difficult due to the noise levels that exist in the band. AM radio has always been subject to degradation of listenability due to RF noise. In recent years noise levels have increased. Listeners accustomed to higher-quality FM radio and digital audio services have abandoned the AM band. Fewer listeners resulted in revenue losses and less investment in programming. The AM band is in a downward spiral due to problems that cannot be solved by broadcasters continuing to broadcast in analog.

The downward spiral of the AM band has resulted in AM stations turning in their licenses at an unprecedented rate and concerns that the automotive manufacturers will not continue to include the AM band in future cars.[8] An increase by radio broadcasters in conversions to all-digital and a sense that they consider digital to be their future, could result more auto manufacturers choosing to keep AM radios in the dash.

There are tools to aid in the transition to all-digital: crossband AM to FM translators, the use of FM HD Radio multicast channels to re-broadcast AM and a large number of existing vehicles with HD Radio receivers that grows with nearly every new car sold.

The FCC has made available the use of crossband translators, allowing the transitioning AM station to continue to serve their audience an analog signal in the FM band. Additionally, the AM station can be re-broadcast on the multicast channel of a co-owned FM station. Thus, the owner of an AM station has the option to transition to all-digital while mitigating the loss of audience.

The AM HD Radio all-digital system was designed to work within the existing AM band with minimal impact on broadcasters continuing to operate with analog. In addition to noise, adjacent channel AM

[8] Some electric vehicle manufacturers have already deleted AM tuners in their vehicles.

analog stations interfere with reception in the AM band.[9] In a future where all stations have transitioned to all-digital HD radio, first adjacent channel interference would be eliminated.

The transition to all-digital AM will allow broadcasters to switch to a noise-free digital radio with quality similar to FM radio over a wider service area.

Conclusion

In addition to more than 80 million registered vehicles on the road with HD Radio receivers, there are tools to aid in the transition to all-digital AM. The FCC has allowed the use of crossband translators to duplicate the AM station's programming on an FM channel and FM HD Radio multicast channels are also capable of duplicating the AM signal on FM HD Radio stations.

The ability to transmit album art and station logos over the all-digital AM signal has already been demonstrated and in the future, there will be the ability to deliver a second audio channel, as well.

AM broadcasters need to be concerned that the car manufacturers will eliminate the AM radio from vehicles. The all-digital AM system is a proven technology that is ready to transition AM stations to noise-free high-quality audio over a larger service area. The time is now for the industry to transition to digital and leave analog broadcasting behind.

[9] In the past, some of the FCC's policies have resulted in overcrowding of the AM band. First adjacent channels are interleaved meaning that first adjacent channels are overlapped in frequency.

CLEAR AI for Segmentation

Harish Bharadwaj
Prime Focus Technologies
Bengaluru, Karnataka, India
harish.bharadwaj@primefocus.com

Abstract – In this paper, we present a solution to perform automated segmentation of videos for Broadcast and Over-the Top (OTT) applications with CLEAR Vision Cloud's AI based Segmentation solution. The Segmentation module analyzes a video, automatically generates physically distinct Technical Segments such as Color Bars, Black Screens, Slates and cinematically distinct Creative Segments like Credits, Teasers, etc. and segregates the Broadcast-ready Content as standalone Content Segments. The physical segments are detected with very high detection accuracy and are frame accurate. Due to the inherent creative nature of the content, it becomes imperative that the system understands new representations and variants of these broad segment classifications and learns to detect the same over time. We introduce 'Auto Learning' feature to optionally consume the feedback from a Quality Check (QC) step which follows the Automatic Segmentation and learn representation of creative cues such as Bumpers, Recaps so as to improve the overall segmentation accuracy. We reinforce the need for such a learning mechanism with certain use cases.

Introduction

Background

The M&E industry has grown leaps and bounds and evolved over decades. Broadcasting, Transmission and Media Delivery standards have evolved in parallel, with significant contribution from Broadcasters themselves and standardization organizations such as EIA, SMPTE, EBR, etc.

However, unlike other industries, a common standard for the preparation and presentation order of content within the media files is nearly impossible to agree upon due to the inherent creative nature of the content. Creative choices are governed by a multitude of factors and thus, even in the same genre of videos, the order and length of the shots, clips and scenes vary significantly. Of late, 'Hard Parting' and 'Soft Parting' features defined in standards such as AMWA's AS-11 are being adopted as part of standard delivery of finished media assets to broadcasters or publishers, thus, bringing in uniform content separators and common formats, which would allow for faster and machine-based segmentation of content. However, even such standards do not mandate the location of creative segments such as Recaps and Opening Titles in the media content.

Besides the creative content, certain 'Technical Segments' are also inserted during filming or during an editing/post processing step to allow recording of asset specific metadata on Slates, transmit information for changing monitor settings to match the recorded content using Color Bars, amongst others. These segments need to be edited out at the receiving broadcaster's end before being actually broadcast. The term 'Segments' is not limited to Technical Segments and could be defined with a huge degree of variability to merge multiple segments under a single segment type.

This paper is excerpted from the Proceedings of the 2022 NAB Broadcast Engineering and Information Technology (BEIT) Conference, © 2022, National Association of Broadcasters, 1 M Street S.E., Washington, DC 20003 USA.

What Are Segments?

Segments are the physically distinguishable cinematic elements in a video. Segments could vary from being made up of a single frame or a single camera shot to as large as a sequence of scenes. Common types of Segments include the following:

- **Content Segments**: These are the segments which are finally broadcast.
- **Black Frames**: Typically accompanied by silence and used as separators between Content segments. They could also indicate Ad Insertion points within lengthy scenes. Blacks with audio are regarded as Creative Blacks and classified as Content Segments.
- **Color Bars**: Color Bars are Technical Segments used for calibration of the broadcast content with the receiving device. They typically follow the SMPTE standards set in ECR 1-1978 and SMPTE RP 219:2002 [1]. Certain Media Houses add Color Bars with static or mobile text blocks depicting their in-house standard Color Bars.
- **Slates**: Slates are Technical Segments generally added at the beginning of a segment and contain metadata regarding the upcoming content such as the series name, episode number, duration of a video. Newly adopted delivery standards such as AMWA's AS-11 standard [2] for PAL content allow for multiple slates to be present in a single video. Each of these slates display information about the upcoming Content Segment.
- **Opening Titles**: Opening Titles are typically a sequence of shots which repeat over episodes of a series. They are usually created as a montage of shots captured across episodes of the series.
- **Credits**: Opening and Closing Credits occur near the beginning and end of the actual content. Rolling Credits and Credits with black background are the most common flavor of Credits and are referred to as Credits on Black. Credits superimposed over actual Content segments are typically seen in Reality shows and classified as Credits on Content/Graphics. The distinction of Credits on Black from Credits on Content/Graphics is an emerging requirement to use the power of 'Picture within Picture' features to display promotional videos of upcoming episodes of the same show or the upcoming shows in the TV channel.
- **Bumpers**: Bumpers are a sequence of shots which are placed at the beginning or end of each Content segments. Some shows prefer a single bumper to be used as Opening Bumper and Closing Bumper across the episodes of an entire season. However, certain shows, create Bumpers by creating a montage of shots from upcoming/past Content segments, thus, having multiple Opening and Closing Bumpers in a single episode.
- **Teasers**: Teasers are indicators of upcoming/past Content. Recaps are typically observed near the beginning of a Content segment and contain excerpts from previous episode of a series. Throws signify the content coming up in the subsequent episode of a series. Some variants include Visual cues (e.g. - Text showing 'Previously On') and Audio cues (e.g. - Voiceover saying 'Previously On'), while some do not contain any cues whatsoever.
- **Textless Elements**: Segments such as Credits and Opening Titles are created with text in one language. To distribute the same media file to regions with linguistic preferences different from the source language, textless versions of such texted segments are typically added at the end of the file. These are known as Textless Elements.
- **Production House Logo and Banners**: Logos and Banners typically occur at the end of Closing Credits and signal the end of Content. Logos are almost always proprietary signatures and copyrighted, thus, necessitating the operators to be knowledgeable about the customer whose files are being segmented.
- **Elements**: These indicate standalone stories within a single episode of a series.

Certain broadcasters also require use of segment types which are customized to their requirements. In some cases, the custom segment types are a combination of one or more of the above segment types. Some such segments are Interstitials, Event Windows and Customer Feedback Windows. Though such elements are usually creative, broadcaster specific rules govern the duration, placement and the characteristics which make them up.

Segmentation

Content Segmentation, or Segmentation, in short, is the process of separating out Content Segments from the other technical and creative segments and preparing for eventual broadcast or sharing. The process of Segmentation is performed using a player on a Non-Linear Editor (NLE). The editor parses through the content, frame by frame, and removes the technical segments to finally generate the 'Broadcast-only' content. The process is based on a set of conventions, specific to each broadcaster, with little to no codification of what needs to be done at boundaries with transitions and effects such as merging or dissolves. The Segmentation process has also been extensively used to mark out Recaps, Opening and Closing Bumpers to help speed up Remastering and Conformance workflows.

Over the years, with increased internet and mobile penetration, there has been a huge increase in demand for newer and trending content. The volume of videos generated has increased manifolds with the onset of 'On-Demand' and Video On-Demand (VOD) ecosystems, where consumers can watch content wherever and whenever they want. This has in turn lead to further increase in creative content being produced and distributed. New VOD-friendly features, such as Skip Intro, Skip Recap, Ad Break Insertion point have further reiterated the need for fast and accurate Segmentation.

Automatic Segmentation

With the increase in volume and ever-increasing demand for content, it becomes imperative to automate most of the rules-based Segmentation workloads. Automatic Segmentation would be cheaper, more accurate and more predictable than a human operator, for technical segments. This could be followed up with a manual overview of the detected segments and corrections, if any, which would almost always be near the boundaries of the detected segments. The manual QC step would also involve marking of any creative segments, which might have gone undetected.

As mentioned earlier, there are no specific standards on the placement of creative content in a media file. With the advent and acceptance of specifications such as AMWA AS-11 for Commercial MXF Delivery, the concept of standard 'Partitions' is gaining traction. The specifications suggest "Hard Partitions", where multi-part programs are separated by Black frame markers in the video. However, the bulk of the content in existence today does not follow the partition specifications on videos. This has resulted in standalone implementations for detection of Technical Segments such as Black Frames, Color Bars and Credits. Computer Vision and Machine Learning based implementations detect these segments and present the same for use in Segmentation workflows.

The Technical Segments, however, constitute only a subset of all the segments which could be present in an asset. Creative Segments, which are highly contextual in nature and are specific to the creative brains of Production Houses and shows, make up the bulk of the unaddressed segments. The lack of detection of Creative Segments reduces the usability of the existing solutions as an operator will need to parse through the entire asset to look for elements such as Opening Titles, Bumpers, Teasers and Logos. Such implementations also ignore the context in which a particular segment is placed within the asset and lead to further misclassifications, thus defeating the entire purpose of adopting an Automatic approach to Segmentation.

All the above factors in the development of an Automatic Segmentation alternative to traditional manual segmentation, lead to the need for a comprehensive solution for Automatic Segmentation which is capable of detecting both Technical and Creative segments while minimizing the external effort necessary to detect the context specific segments.

CLEAR Vision Cloud AI-Based Segmentation

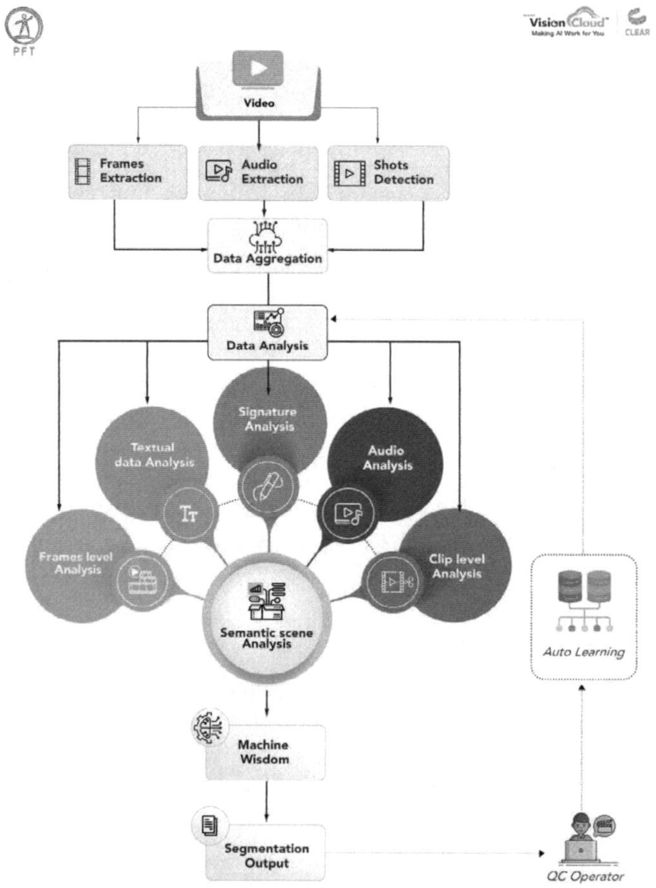

FIGURE 1: CLEAR VISION CLOUD SEGMENTATION

The CLEAR Vision Cloud Segmentation, represented in Figure 1, is an AI-powered solution for the comprehensive detection of segments with emphasis on the semantic dynamics between the elements making up a segment. Due to the high intra-segment variations arising out of creative visualization of certain segments, it becomes imperative to divide the Segmentation workflow into a multi-level, multimodal feature analysis. The data extraction and analysis layers are followed up with a Semantic scene analysis layer and a Machine Wisdom layer, which greatly improves the contextual classification of media files.

Data Extraction and Aggregation

The incoming videos are analyzed for multiple cues - Video, Audio and Textual features. In the initial extraction layer, the following steps are performed as precursor to extracting such features:

- **Frames Extraction**: Frames are the basis of detection for image-based segments, including the Technical Segments of Black frames and Color Bars. Frames also serve as the input for detection of image level text features.
- **Shots Extraction**: A video is made up of one or multiple shots, with each shot representing a sequence of frames in which the camera view remains stable. Abrupt changes in the content of frames over a short duration of time signify shot changes. Camera movements such as pan, tilt and zoom are accounted for in the shots-extraction step. Detection of these shots is also the precursor to classification of cinematic shots such as Long shot, Close-up shot, etc.

Accurate detection of shot boundaries is critical to the frame accuracy of the overall solution. Shots ending with cuts as transitions are the easiest to detect due to abrupt change in content between adjacent frames. Complex transitions such as Fades, Dissolves and Crossfades require analysis of frames over a larger time frame and with necessary cinematic knowledge.

- **Audio Extraction**: A media file could be made up of one or multiple audio tracks, each with one or multiple audio channels. To build a proper representation of the audio content in the file, all the channels of the audio component are extracted. Merging of multiple channels into a single channel to reduce the overall computation complexity is not recommended as channel merging leads to issues with Transcripts and Speaker diarization, which adversely affects the detection accuracy

The extracted data is then passed through a Data Aggregation block where the inputs necessary for subsequent features extraction are combined, if necessary.

Data Analysis

The Data Analysis layer is a collection of feature extraction and analysis engines. These engines are typically Machine Learning based algorithms which analyze a specific modality of data and output features or classifications necessary for subsequent Semantic Analysis of the data.

- **Frame Level Analysis:** The frames extracted in the previous layer are passed through multiple algorithms analyzing the frame level features. Computer Vision algorithms, Statistical Analysis tools and Deep Learning based models are employed to generate classifications with respect to different image characteristics of the frame under consideration. For certain use cases, the classification task is extended to perform detection of objects within the frame.
- **Textual Data Analysis:** Textual cues play an important role in the overall segmentation process. These textual cues can be extracted in a single frame, or across a sequence of frames. On-screen words and their structural properties detected using Object Character Detection and Recognition (OCR) algorithms are major indicators to the presence of absence of certain segments.
- **Signature Analysis:** Certain segments are made up of visual cues which cannot be analyzed at a frame level or using textual data. Such features are extracted in the Signature Analysis section. Computer Vision algorithms to detect and classify parts of frames which act as segment specific signatures are implemented here.
- **Audio Analysis:** Audio is a rich descriptor and indicator of quite a few segment types. For example, Color Bars always have a monotone audio accompanying the visual pattern typical to them. Classifications which confirm the presence or absence of such distinguishing characteristics are implemented in this section. Speech to Text translation, Speaker Identification, Speaker diarization, Audio Segmentation and Classification are some of the vast numbers of algorithms implemented here. Algorithms which perform Joint Classification and Segmentation of Clips using audio and video data are also implemented here.
- **Clip-level Analysis**: Extraction and analysis of clip or shot level features is performed in this section. Spatiotemporal classification of clips involves time series analysis of the frames making up a shot. Algorithms detecting clip level similarities for detecting Bumpers and Titles are also implemented here.

Semantic Scene Analysis

The complex nature of Segments classification requires a bottom-up approach of features detection and aggregation instead of a one-shot clip analysis and classification. This also necessitates the encoding of interactions with the various sets of features and/or their classification results output from the Data Analysis layer. The Semantic Scene Analysis layer performs this specific task.
This layer is built of algorithms which implement classification tasks based on a weighted score of the features extracted earlier and the spatio temporal characteristics of the video under consideration.

These weights are accompanied by a bias value. The combination of these weights and bias values are fixed initially but can be learnt over time to provide a higher flexibility to the system for accurate classification.

Consider the classification of Credit segments into Opening Credits and Closing Credits. Multiple Credits segments can be detected in a single media file. However, the classification is relative to the location of the Credits either at the beginning of the asset or towards the end of it. This positional information of the independently detected segments is incorporated in the Semantic Scene Analysis step, resulting in far more accurate classification of segments.

Machine Wisdom

The Semantic Scene Analysis step outputs Segmentation results governed by a set of encodings which are static or learnt over time. However, the creative nature of the media files could result in the encodings learnt by the Semantic Analysis step to be misinterpreted, resulting in false or missed detections. Such rules could be specific to a Production House or a Broadcaster and can only be implemented as Instructional Learning. This layer of algorithms which implement the Instructional Learning is termed as the Machine Wisdom layer. Machine Wisdom transcends the Artificial Intelligence imbibed in the system by having observed a huge amount of sample data.

To explain the need for Machine Wisdom, consider the detection results for a Creative Black – Frame Level Analysis classifies the sequence of frames as Black frames and the Audio Analysis section classifies this portion of the media file as a non-silent segment. Standalone classification based on frames would have led to misclassification of this segment as valid Black frames. However, due to the incorporation of an overriding Machine Wisdom layer, which encodes the need for Black frames to be accompanied by silence, the frames are correctly identified as Creative Black frames and merged into a Content segment.

Auto Learning

Classification of segments using the standalone Segmentation flow reduce the manual effort of operators by 40-50%. However, this flow is a one-way process where a QC operator consumes the results of Automatic Segmentation and moves on. The system does not benefit from the output of QC process, which is expected to generate a perfectly segmented file. To provide a closure in the loop, increase the predictability and to help the system improve itself for subsequent runs based on the feedback of a QC step, we introduce the Auto Learning layer.

The Auto Learning layer is made up of algorithms which figure out the gaps in the output of the Automatic Segmentation engine and the finalized segments after QC. Any deviation from the manually verified segmentation results is consumed as feedback or shortfall. The feedback is then analyzed and consumed by multiple engines, corresponding to the feature extraction steps necessary for detection of the segment under consideration. The models in the Data Analysis layer are then updated with the parameters learnt after incorporating the feedback into the existing models. For all the files passing through the Segmentation engine after the feedback is incorporated, the updated model is used, thus, ensuring lesser chances of missing the undetected segment or parts of a segment.

As an example, consider an episodic content with a show specific stylized logo being used to represent the beginning and end of a Recap segment. Being a signature specific to the show, the chances of the Data Analysis layer being able to detect, extract features corresponding to the logo and classifying the segment as a Recap segment would be minimal. This would result in the segment being misclassified as part of a Content segment. When the operator performing QC on the file corrects the misclassification and publishes the finalized segmentation boundaries, the Auto Learning engine picks up the cue to learn the missed recap. The algorithm tries to learn and represent the feature specific to the recap. In this case, the presence of a stylized logo is detected by the feature extraction algorithms reporting to the Signature based Analysis section and the model learns the representation corresponding to the same. The prediction model and the weights of the Semantic Scene Analysis layer are also simultaneously updated. When subsequent episodes of the Episodic Content are processed, the updated models in the Data Analysis layer in the prediction flow readily detect the frames and shots where the newly learnt signature appears on screen.

Effectively, with no extra manual effort, the system evolves itself to detect segments based on prior observations. Auto Learning helps in minimizing repeated correction efforts of QC operators and also improves the endpoints of detection by predicting with greater frame accuracy. This leads to a significant reduction in overall manual effort.

Candidates for Automatic Segmentation

Use Case 1: Spots Segmentation

One of the clear-cut use cases of Automatic Segmentation has been Spots Segmentation. Spots are typically less than a minute in duration and made up of segments limited to Black Screens, Color Bars and Slates besides the Content. Usually, spots are made up of only one Content segment which contains the actual advertisement to be broadcast. Operators need to go through hundreds of such spots every day and mark out the Content segment from the rest. The manual segmentation is followed by a manual QC step where the results are reviewed.

Due to the limited creative variations in the structure of the spots, the AI based Segmentation solution provides a straightforward alternative to the manual segmentation step. The Segmentation engine analyzes the spot, eliminates the technical segments and passes on the endpoints of the Content segment which can then be directly reviewed by a QC operator. This allows the QC operator to focus more on the creative technicalities of the spot.

Leveraging on the ever-improving scalability of cloud infra, the horizontally scalable solution for spots can process multiple spots in parallel. This minimizes the idle time of QC operators. In practical deployments, both the detection accuracy and frame accuracy of the segments exceed 99%, and dramatically decreases the overall manual effort involved in the process, by up to 90%. Due to the short processing time which would be necessary for such assets, the additional cost incurred due to the introduction of the Automatic Segmentation flow is also minimal.

Use Case 2: Segmentation of Episodic Shows

Episodic Shows are typically made up of assets longer than a few minutes and extending into hours. They comprise of episodes of sequential or standalone nature, with the content spanning across one or multiple genres. An episode could be made up of one or more Content segments, which are separated by Black Frames or some other visual or audible separators. In certain cases, the Content segments are preceded only by Slates as separators.

Manual segmentation of such Long Form assets is usually performed by speeding up the play-out to 2x or 4x the original frame rate and parsing through the entire asset. Presence of segments which might be a part of a larger Content segment, such as Opening Titles, Teasers and Bumpers necessitates the operator to parse through the file multiple times before actually finalizing the segments. This 'Context Aware Segmentation' results in the segmentation time being directly proportional to the asset length and the number of segments in it, leading to lesser predictability in turn-around time.

CLEAR Vision Cloud's AI based Segmentation reduces this complex process into a much simpler process by detecting the bulk of segments with high accuracy. Technical Segments like Black Frames,

Color Bars, Slates and Credits are detected with more than 99% accuracy and with more than 99% frame level accuracy. However, creative segments such as Teasers, Bumpers and Opening Titles are detected with much lesser recall and precision. The behavior of series specific or show specific Bumpers and Titles are difficult to capture without prior context about the show. This leads to errors at the boundaries of such creative segments and in certain cases, failure to detect entire such segments, bringing down the detection accuracy to about 60-70%.

With the Auto Learning feature enabled, the finalized results of segmentation by a QC operator would be fed back into the system to learn the feature representations of show-specific creative segments. In particular, Opening Titles are learnt based on their first occurrence in any episode of a show. For all the subsequent episodes of the particular show, the Opening Titles are now automatically detected. Teasers, Bumpers and other montages are learnt and detected in a similar manner, thus increasing the overall detection and frame level accuracy of creative segments to well over 90%. The QC operator only needs to adjust the boundaries of such creative segments, thus, minimizing the overall manual effort.

Unlike manual segmentation, our AI based Segmentation analyzes the various features of a video in parallel. This eliminates the need for multiple parses of a file and hence, significantly reduces the time needed for segmenting an asset. Depending on the genre of the Episodic Content, time savings between 50% and 85% can be observed.

Use Case 3: Global Master Creation

Due to the increasing need for creating a media file for delivery across geographies, a regional master is used to synthesize a single global master file, which can be edited at the broadcaster's end as suited to a particular delivery format. The analysis of the regional master requires an operator to manually parse through the file, detect and establish segments which are necessary for generating the corresponding global master. The task is further complicated by the need to replace some or all Texted elements with their Textless versions. After the analysis of regional master, the global master is created by performing 'Lift and Shift' operations on the segmented regional master. In some cases, slates in the regional master are ignored and replaced by a global master equivalent of the slate. This process of manually distinguishing individual segments of a regional master typically consumes more than 80% of an editor's time in the overall Global Mastering process. Processing a regional master through the AI based Segmentation flow, the bulk of the segmentation workload is reduced to a simple QC process. In regional masters with hard partitions, the QC step gets further reduced to a QC check at the very boundaries of the segments. This results in savings of up to 75% manual effort per asset. Further codification of rules in the creation of the global master results in overall reduction of manual effort by up to 90%.

Use Case 4: Preprocessing in Content Conformance

Conforming is the process of replacing lower-quality media in an edited file with the corresponding higher quality media, in most cases, from the camera-original files. As a precursor to the actual conformance process, both the high-resolution file and the edited file need to be segmented and corresponding segments replaced with the high-resolution equivalents.

Automatic Segmentation of the files helps minimize the manual effort necessary for Segmentation in the conformance process by up to 90%. The time saved in the manual segmentation step can be effectively used in the effort intensive conformance step, leading to overall cost reduction.

The solution is also extendable to conformance of standalone audio files or dub tracks and their corresponding caption files.

Conclusion

We have proposed an automatic, cloud-based AI based Segmentation solution to perform frame accurate segmentation of media files. The solution detects Technical and Creative segments with great accuracy and is frame accurate. The automatic generation of segments results in manual efforts being reduced by up to 90% for certain use cases. The incorporation of Auto Learning enables the solution to learn from operator verified segmentation cues and reduce effort on subsequent files.

Scope for future improvements includes detection of Interstitials and burnt-in commercials, which would further reduce the manual effort and cost involved in a manual QC process.

References

[1] https://en.wikipedia.org/wiki/SMPTE_color_bars

[2] https://www.amwa.tv/as-11

Green, AI-Based Video Compression

Xavier Ducloux, Jean-Louis Diascorn, Thierry Fautier
Harmonic Inc
San Jose, California, United States
xavier.ducloux@harmonicinc.com, jean-louis.diascorn@harmonicinc.com, thierry.fautier@harmonicinc.com

Abstract – Artificial intelligence (AI) is often seen as a way to introduce new system features and capabilities, at the expense of a significant increase in power consumption. However, if the usage of heavy processing in an offline machine learning training phase leads to lower energy consumption during the deployment phase of a system, the carbon footprint can be improved at the end. This paper will present concrete AI-based techniques that can be applied to live video compression to reduce CPU power consumption in the headend or to minimize the delivery and storage impact utilizing lower bitrates. It will also provide interoperability test results for each of the techniques discussed.

Introduction

It has been reported that video consumption is playing an increasingly prominent role in carbon emissions, with consumer devices making the biggest impact due to the huge numbers deployed throughout the world. Networks are the next biggest contributor, and with the increase in consumption of VOD content and linear video channels, we believe that bitrate reduction will be critical in minimizing the delivery and storage impact. The datacenters in which video headends are deployed come last on the list. And while reducing CPU power consumption and increasing density have been continuous efforts over the last two decades, the pressure to go further will remain high in the coming years.

Thanks to new tools and system features, artificial intelligence (AI) can provide a way to decrease bitrate without affecting perceived quality – at the expense of a significant increase in power consumption (see example [1]). But it's much less obvious to think of AI as a way to actually decrease global power consumption. However, if the usage of heavy processing in an offline machine learning training phase leads to lower energy consumption during the deployment phase of a system, the carbon footprint can be improved at the end.

In this paper we will describe three AI-based technologies that Harmonic has developed over the last few years:

- The first one, a content-aware encoding technique named EyeQ, reduces the average bitrate significantly with no extra CPU power consumption
- The second one, a dynamic frame rate encoding (DFE) technique, provides significant CPU power savings and some associated bitrate savings
- The third one, a dynamic resolution encoding (DRE) technique, reduces the peak bitrates and provides significant CPU power savings compared to constant high-resolution encoding, while keeping video quality at its best

The first section of this paper will describe how the three technical problems had been addressed until recently. The second section will describe how machine learning was a game changer, allowing

This paper is excerpted from the Proceedings of the 2022 NAB Broadcast Engineering and Information Technology (BEIT) Conference, © 2022, National Association of Broadcasters, 1 M Street S.E., Washington, DC 20003 USA.

Harmonic to build extremely powerful predictions in real time and to divide the required CPU by a factor of 2 or 3. In the third section, we will present objective results for the three technologies. The fourth section will talk about interoperability of the technologies and deployment. The last section will be a discussion of results and will provide an outlook.

New Video Compression Techniques for Bitrate Reduction

The usage of new codecs – from MPEG2 in the 90s to HEVC in the last decade – have provided a strong and powerful engine to reduce bandwidth for the delivery of video content at increasing resolutions. The video compression toolbox was enriched with each new generation, with encoder developers spending an enormous amount of time optimizing the encoding choices at picture and block levels to get the best of these codecs at a well-mastered CPU power consumption level in comparison with their reference models. For further bitrate reduction, developers had to think of innovative encoding strategies on top of their existing codecs. These strategies were first popularized for offline VOD content production, and then fueled the live encoding world over the last decade.

Content-aware encoding techniques were the first to be developed. They became popular by decreasing the average video bitrate by putting bits where they matter the most, through adaptive quantization, and taking the human visual system into account. For that, the quantization of pictures and blocks is increased up to the point where a degradation is perceived. The mechanism often runs in multiple passes, at the expense of a significant increase in CPU power consumption and latency.

Another field of investigation was to play with the resolution. In the broadcast world, the resolution is kept constant for a channel. In the streaming world, players are used to adapt to network conditions by receiving video representations of variable resolutions. Video compression experts all know that when bandwidth is reduced, a good trade-off to preserve quality and limit visible compression artifacts is to reduce the resolution. Of course, the best resolution for a given bitrate highly depends on the video content.

In December 2015, Netflix popularized the concept of variable resolution encoding in its blog "Per-Title Encoding Optimization" [2]. At the time, the best resolution was selected for each VOD content. In the following years, Netflix improved the concept with dynamic resolution selection, applied for each scene [3]. As Netflix's market is VOD, this selection can be made offline, but a visual-based selection would be much too time consuming. To mitigate this issue, Netflix developed an objective video quality (VQ) metric, called VMAF [4], to help in the automation of the resolution selection process. The scenes are encoded at multiple resolutions, VMAF measures are produced for each of these resolutions, and the resolution with the best VMAF score is selected, as shown in Figure 1 below. Thanks to this process, Netflix was able to significantly improve the quality of its VOD content, even in areas where bandwidth resources are scarce.

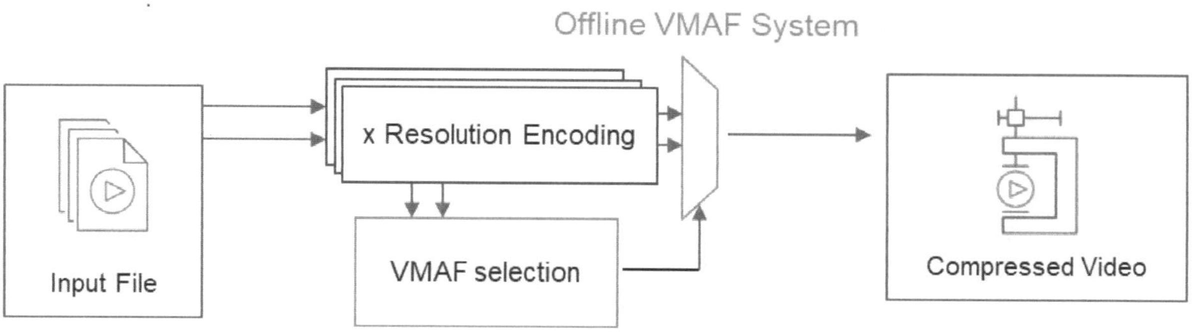

FIGURE 1: OFFLINE, SCENE-BASED DYNAMIC RESOLUTION ENCODING WORKFLOW

The last field of investigation was to play with the frame rate, as represented in Figure 2 below.

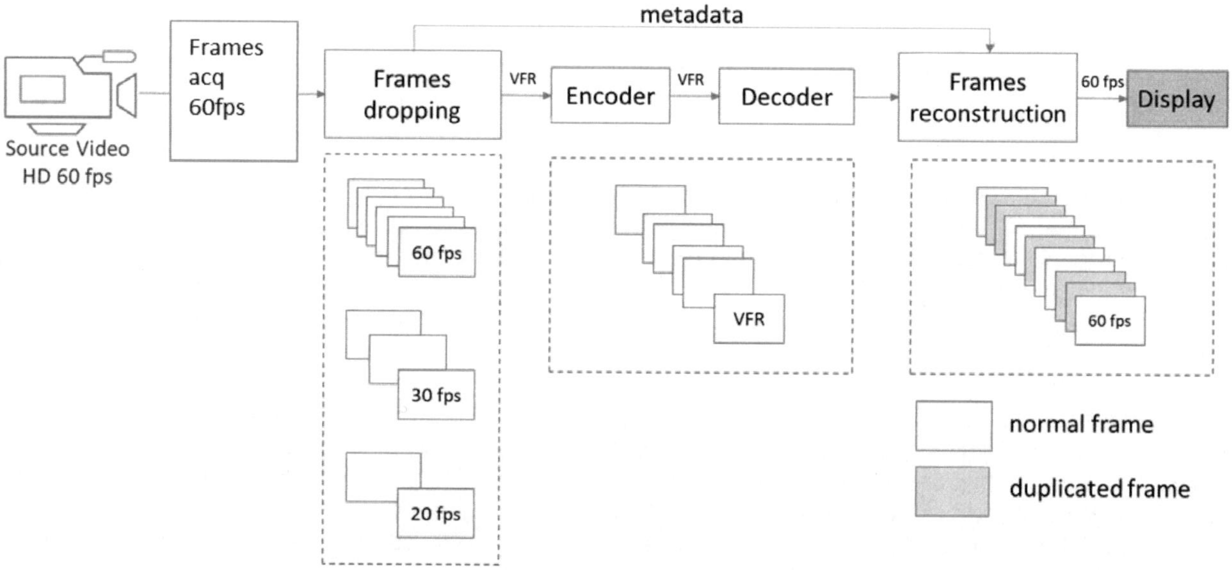

FIGURE 2: DYNAMIC FRAME RATE ENCODING WORKFLOW

Lowering the frame rate of encoding can also lead to bitrate savings. The usage of a lower frame rate for encoding has been a technique since the old days of digital TV on 3:2 pull-down video content (interlaced video at 29.97fps embedding 24fps movie content with duplicated fields). In this case, the duplicated fields of the 29.97fps input signal were removed during encoding to get the native 24fps signal and added back in at the set-top box (STB) or TV during the reconstruction of the interlaced video signal at 29.97 fps.

Here, we aren't talking about duplicated fields or frames, but the possibility of skipping some frames in scenes where the use of a lower frame rate will not affect the motion perception. Any legacy codec (MPEG2, AVC, HEVC) has the appropriate syntax to signal that a decoded frame in a progressive stream needs to be duplicated once (frame doubling) or twice (frame tripling) in the reconstruction. Therefore, for each group of three successive frames, a decision can be taken to skip zero, one, or two frames. The bitrate savings aren't spectacular, since in many cases the skipped frames belong to scenes with large still areas and the video codec is already optimized to benefit from still areas by using skipped blocks with no interprediction and or residual costs.

However, studies show that skipping frames doesn't happen for scenes where a large part is still, but happens more for scenes where the global motion is regular. Studies show that bitrate savings up to 10% can be reached with the variable frame rate technique. Even if the legacy codec had the appropriate syntax to signal the skipped frames for progressive streams from the first MPEG video standard, the usage of a variable frame rate for encoding has remained confidential. The main reason was certainly the risk of creating some visible issues on the motion fluidity if wrong decisions were taken. We will see in the next section that AI helped a lot in building a safe algorithm.

Lowering CPU Consumption With AI

The first AI-based optimization that Harmonic developed in 2016-2018 was for its EyeQ live content-aware encoding technique. The quantization of pictures and blocks was increased up to the point of perceived degradation. The encoding was first optimized through multiple passes of quantization, controlled by an internal VQ metric at the block level that mimics our human visual system. Video experts carefully watched the encoding results, tuned the VQ metric to match the subjective feelings, and once the encoding results were good, the quantization choices were used as a ground truth in our training to learn the rules between quantization choices and input video content characteristics. The learned rules were then tested on a new set of sequences and implemented to drive quantization in one single step. Therefore, the technology is deployed in Harmonic real-time encoders without any extra latency or impact on density.

Compared to multi-pass content-aware encoding techniques deployed for VOD applications, EyeQ technology can consume three times less CPU power. Furthermore, the technique provides significant bitrate savings for OTT streaming compared to constant bitrate encoding techniques. A telco operator deployed EyeQ to relax bandwidth pressure due to Covid19 stress and measured a 50% reduction in backbone traffic and a 30% reduction of CDN peak usage. A tier-1 streaming provider measured an average bitrate savings of 30% across its twelve channels, including three sport channels. EyeQ can also be used for statmux applications and has been successfully deployed at one tier-1 satellite provider, where the number of HD AVC channels has been increased in their transponders.

In 2019-2021, Harmonic made use of AI to develop a real-time DFE technique, in which the number of frames to be encoded per second can be constantly adjusted by skipping input frames. The ground truth was built by encoding groups of three successive pictures with multiple frame-skipping options, from zero to two pictures, producing VQ statistics using a Harmonic VQ metric and all video input characteristics. A frame-skipping model was trained offline using this ground truth. Video experts from Harmonic checked the quality of the prediction model by watching the results on a test based on new content, and once the generalization capability of the model was judged as good enough, the model was implemented in the real-time encoders, as shown in Figure 3 below.

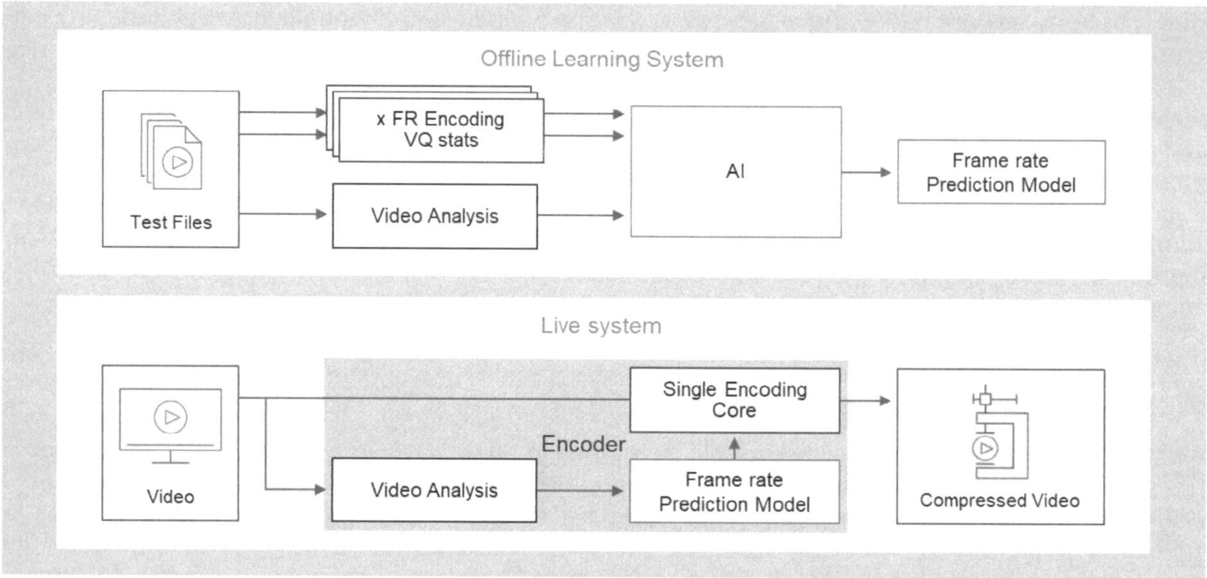

FIGURE 3: OFFLINE LEARNING AND LIVE IMPLEMENTATION OF DFE

It was particularly important to avoid cases where the skip frames could have a visible impact on motion fluidity. The model itself does not represent a huge piece of SW code, and since it makes use of video characteristics that were already computed in the pre-analysis stage of the real-time encoder, the extra CPU power consumption of the frame-skipping-decision stage is quite limited. Then, the technique provides an interesting savings in CPU power in the encoding stage by bypassing further heavy processing elements – like block-based motion estimation – on skipped frames. Consequently, the global CPU power consumption of the encoder is reduced, and our tests show that ~20% in CPU power savings can be achieved on 1080p content with no impact on the perceived quality. It also provides bitrate savings of around 10%, which is lower than the CPU power savings since the skipped frames of still sequences would have had a low cost.

In 2019-2022, Harmonic made use of AI to develop a live DRE. With this technique, a live encoding system is characterized by a limited look at the picture analysis before the encoding stage. Therefore, it isn't realistic to make a decision for a global scene that can be of a variable duration, as Netflix did for their VOD applications. Instead, a very dynamic decision scheme is built with a selection of resolution applied for each video segment of limited duration (typically two to three seconds). Features from the video pre-analysis stage have been used to train an ML-based prediction model, offline, in a supervised learning environment, as shown in Figure 4 below. Each video segment is encoded with various resolutions at a given target bitrate (constant or capped bitrate). At run time, using the already existing pre-analysis stage and the same target bitrate, the live encoder can decide on the best resolution to encode the pictures of the current segment by using the prediction model created offline. The best resolution is the one that provides the best visual quality.

By using lower resolutions on complex scenes and keeping the highest resolution only when needed (i.e., on static scenes, when our eyes have time to appreciate the sharpness of pictures), this technique not only improves the global quality and reduces the peak bitrates, but it also provides CPU power savings compared to a constant high-resolution encoding. This technology can favor a massive 4K deployment in ATSC 3.0 broadcasting or OTT streaming by reducing the delivery bandwidth and the CPU consumption for producing the 4K streams. As for EyeQ, AI-based live DFE and DRE technologies can offer three times less CPU power consumption than the same technologies applied for VOD applications, since only one encoding is used instead of multiple encodings with the different options.

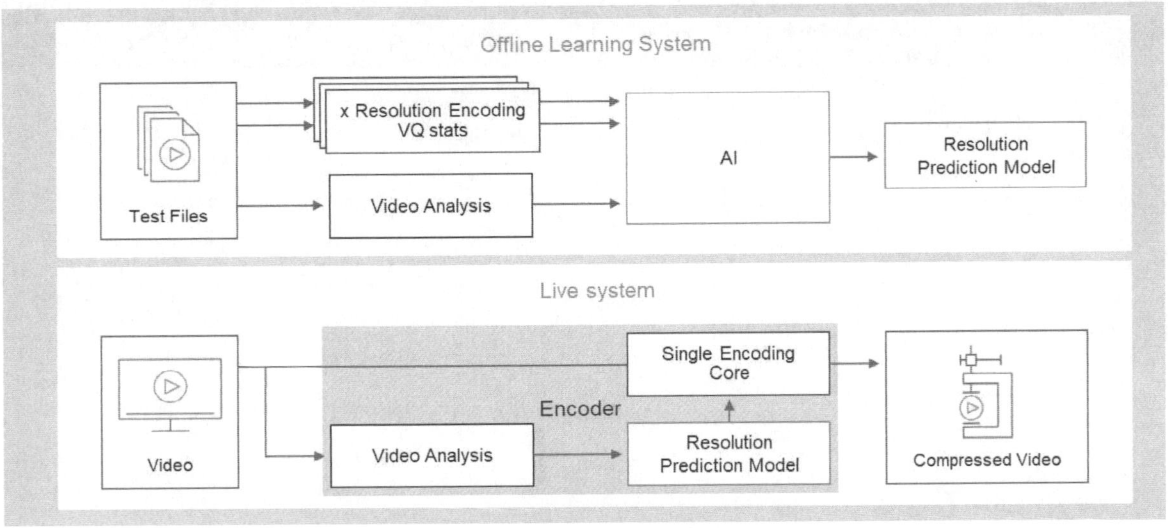

FIGURE 4: OFFLINE LEARNING AND LIVE IMPLEMENTATION OF DRE

CPU or Bitrate Reduction Measurements

EyeQ works without any increase in CPU power consumption or latency compared to the reference AVC or HEVC SW encoder and provides significant average bitrate savings compared to CBR OTT encodings. Our internal measurements show that the savings can be up to 50% on some content and many of our customers measure average savings of 30% to 40% on their channel line-ups.

Live DFE plays on two sides of the greening of video compression and delivery: First, by reducing CPU power consumption at the headend side, and second, by reducing the average bitrate for delivery. Our internal measurements have shown ~20% savings in CPU power consumption. The same savings have been measured globally on OTT ABR channels by the first customer who deployed DFE. In regard to bitrate reduction, a 10% savings was measured in our tests.

Live DRE also plays on two sides of the greening of video compression and delivery: First, by reducing the peak bitrates compared to a constant high-resolution delivery, and second, by reducing CPU power consumption when encoding the most complex scenes. Our internal measurements have shown that when targeting challenging bitrates, savings up to 33% can be achieved on the peak bitrates of the most complex scenes, making DRE a complimentary companion to EyeQ, which provides bitrate savings on content of small or moderate complexity. Table 1 below summarizes the CPU power consumption and bitrate savings of the three technologies, which can be associated for a greater benefit.

	Bitrate Savings	QoE Improvement	Native Density Improvement	Density Improvement vs Legacy Techniques	Interoperability
EyeQ	Up to 50%	NA	NA	3x	TS/IP/HTTP
DRE	~20% - 25%	Yes	15% - 20%	3x - 4x	~~TS~~/IP/HTTP
DFE	~10%	NA	20%	3x	TS/IP/HTTP

TABLE 1: BENEFITS SUMMARY

Interoperability Tests

EyeQ, as a content-aware encoding solution that plays with the quantization of pictures and blocks, produces a fully compliant stream. It has been deployed with success in more than 3,000 OTT channels across every region of the world. DFE also produces a fully compliant stream, but the signaling of skipped frames is limited to progressive content with any codec. It can be used for OTT streaming or broadcast applications making use of progressive formats (720p, 4K).

DRE interoperability is a bit more complex. While the change of picture resolution in a closed-GOP configuration is fully supported by the video decoders of any codec standard, in practice the resolution has never been changed in broadcast applications. Not surprisingly, the tests performed with TS-based STBs and TVs show that the system layers in charge of reconstructing the frames at a constant resolution cannot perform the task seamlessly. A short black (often below 100ms) is perceived, making the use of DRE unacceptable when applied very dynamically.

For segment-based streaming applications, we can be much more confident since the concept has already been deployed by Netflix for VOD applications, and the OTT players – DASH or HLS – are used to adapt to a new resolution seamlessly when changing video representations. Our tests show that reference DASH and HLS players behave well with DRE streams. Tests are ongoing within application SDOs (DVB, ATSC, SBTVD) to validate broad support for players.

For segment-based broadcast applications, like ATSC 3.0 DASH ROUTE, our tests with three major brands have shown that one of them is able to display a DRE channel perfectly well. The other two show visible imperfections at the resolution changes. These artifacts don't come from the video decoder but from the rendering engine. Harmonic is working with these manufacturers to improve the behavior of the rendering engine to present a smooth, seamless up/downscale.

Discussion of Results and Outlook

This paper shows that AI can reduce the carbon footprint of video compression in two aspects:

- By reducing the delivery impact with lower bitrates thanks to new encoding techniques
- By decreasing the global power consumption of a headend, which is much less intuitive

Indeed, the technologies developed by Harmonic for live applications don't increase CPU power consumption and can even lower it by building smarter live encoding strategies after an offline training phase.

EyeQ doesn't deliver a reduction in CPU power consumption but has already demonstrated its benefit by decreasing average OTT bitrates by 30% to 40% in a huge number of channels deployed throughout the world. It was particularly useful during the COVID-19 crisis in relaxing the bandwidth pressure due to an overconsumption of video. Operators needed a solution that could be deployed fast without changing their current infrastructure, and EyeQ, being fully AVC- or HEVC-compliant, was the right answer. Being able to decrease bitrates while keeping the legacy codecs, AVC or HEVC, supported by billions of devices deployed is obviously a much greener approach than switching to a new codec that requires the full replacement of consumer devices.

DFE's main advantage is in increasing the density of video channels in the headend, while at the same time offering the benefits of bitrate reduction. DRE can reinvent live OTT streaming by building content-aware dynamic profiles instead of constant profiles based on average statistics, as is currently done. This will lead to bandwidth savings, better QoE, and storage and CPU power savings. DRE can be deployed with existing codecs like AVC and HEVC, since DASH or HLS players support, by design, the resolution changes. Segment-based IP broadcasts, such as ATSC 3.0 DASH ROUTE, should also be able to support it using the HEVC standard. This requires more work towards interoperability, which will best fit under the CTA umbrella.

In Brazil, the SBTVD Forum is currently considering DRE as a possible enhancement to the VVC-based TV 3.0 standard for its new broadcast system, which will be deployed in 2023. Considering the very limited bandwidth of the targeted terrestrial transponder and the impossibility of sharing bandwidth among multiple channels, as in the past, DRE seems to be a promising solution to trigger up to 4K delivery. The three techniques are fully complementary and can be associated to get the full benefit of CPU power consumption and bitrate reduction.

References

[1] J.L. Diascorn, "AI Technology is Changing the Future of Video Compression," NAB 2019 technology paper, Broadcast Engineering and Information Technology Conference, April 2019.

[2] https://netflixtechblog.com/per-title-encode-optimization-7e99442b62a2, Netflix blog, Dec 2015

[3] https://netflixtechblog.com/optimized-shot-based-encodes-for-4k-now-streaming-47b516b10bbb, Netflix blog, Aug 2020

[4] https://github.com/Netflix/vmaf

Acknowledgments

The authors would like to thank their colleague Patrick Duménil for providing DFE material.

Real-World Use of AI for Better Video Compression

Tony Jones
MediaKind
Southampton, United Kingdom
tony.jones@mediakind.com

Abstract – This paper looks at two specific real-world applications for Artificial Intelligence (AI) within the application area of video compression when implemented in software. It investigates the types of problems where AI may offer better solutions than more traditional algorithmic approaches, evaluating the difference in compute costs with and without AI in those cases and then translates that into potential for better bitrate efficiencies or compute costs. Reducing compute resource usage also has an environmental benefit through the reduced need for energy, as does reducing the bitrate needed for delivery (for example CDN power consumption). The first area relates to optimizing the effectiveness of compute resource allocation between categories of compression tools and the second relates to complex decision-making when there are a large number of potential options.

A Brief Introduction to AI

Artificial Intelligence (AI), or more often (and perhaps more correctly) termed Machine Learning (ML) aims to take an approach analogous to the human brain for learning. While this sounds abstract, in fact there is a basic architecture that is founded on simple principles with learning characteristics which do indeed have similarity to the way networks of neurons learn in a human brain. These building blocks are simply a set of multipliers followed by summation and a non-linearity (or "activation") function and are known as 'Nodes'. Each value input to each node is multiplied by a weighting factor W that is unique to that specific connection for that layer.

Finally, the non-linearity is necessary for the learning process, because otherwise, mathematics tells us that we would be able to collapse the processing into a single layer, with the consequent inability to increase "understanding" at each layer.

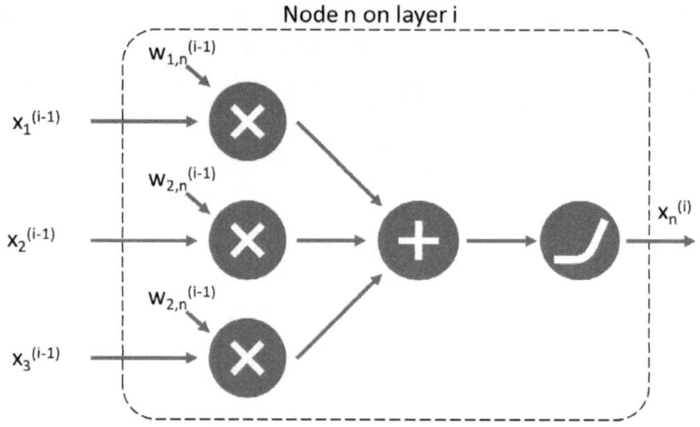

FIGURE 1: BASIC STRUCTURE OF A NEURAL NETWORK NODE

This paper is excerpted from the Proceedings of the 2022 NAB Broadcast Engineering and Information Technology (BEIT) Conference, © 2022, National Association of Broadcasters, 1 M Street S.E., Washington, DC 20003 USA.

Nodes are arranged in layers, with many layers used in complex modeling problems. Nodes on one layer take inputs from the previous layer, so it is easy to think of such layers being stacked. This is known as a Neural Network.

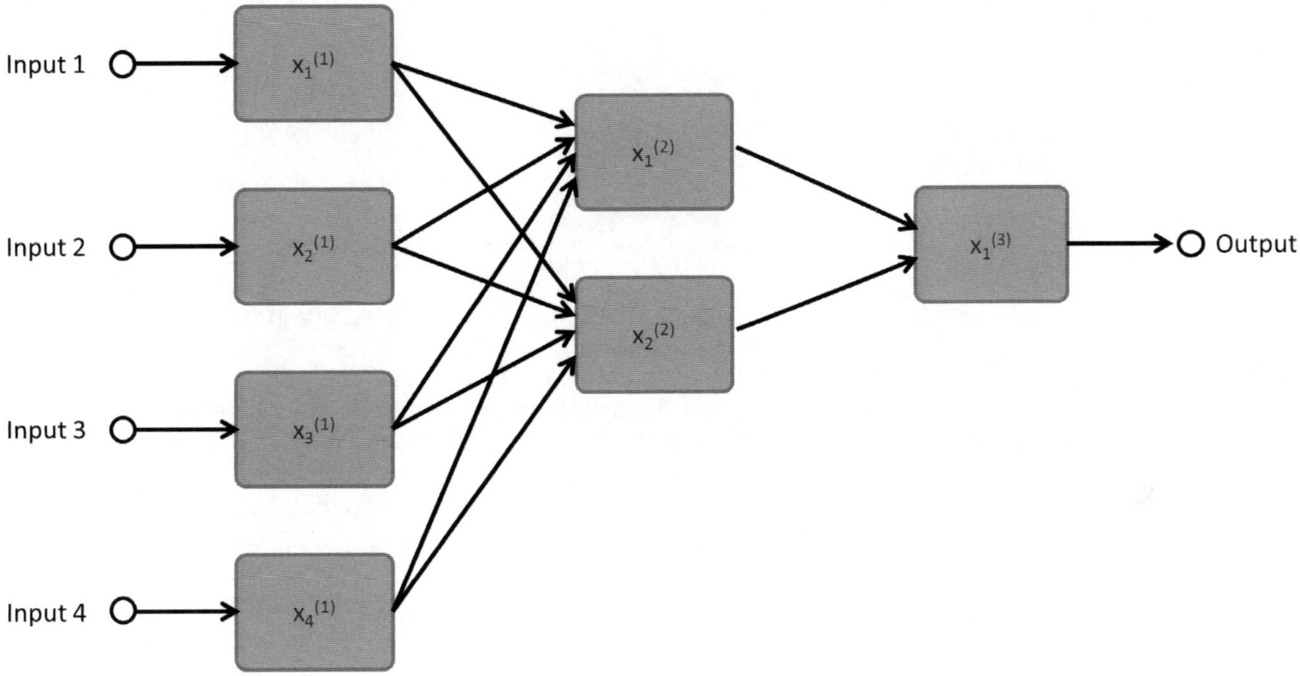

FIGURE 2: ARRANGEMENT OF NODES AND INTERCONNECTS IN A NEURAL NETWORK

As a result of this topology, there are usually very many weighting factors in a neural network.

The set of weighting factors W defines the learned characteristics of the neural network, and these are iteratively adjusted during the training process through back-propagation. Back-propagation feeds the error found when comparing the network's output to "ground truth" back through the network, using the weighting factors again to scale the error feedback to nodes in previous layers.

Overall, this means that Neural Networks are able to determine patterns within large and complex data sets, where the relationship would be difficult to model using a defined algorithm.

There are, in fact, many variations on the exact structure of Neural Networks. Some, such as Convolutional Neural Networks (CNNs) and their close relatives Residual Networks (ResNets), are optimal for extracting information from multi-dimensional data, such as pictures and video sequences. While these can be extremely effective for some tasks, such as up-conversion or object classification, being designed for operation on raw data means they can scale to be very large networks, requiring GPU or AI-specific accelerators to perform the calculation in a reasonable time.

CODECs, Encoders and Complexity

All CODECs offer a range of different mechanisms ("encoding tools") to reduce the data required for delivery. These address various ways in which redundancy exists in complex moving image sequences. Each new generation of CODEC, such as AVC, HEVC and the more recently standardized VVC, include more types and options of encoding tools. Encoders are free to choose any combination of tools and any approach to making decisions about which options to take, as long as the output meets the syntax and constraints defined by the relevant profile and level defined in the standard. Encoders, therefore, benefit from research to continually obtain a lower bitrate for a given visual quality target, and to do that within a constrained compute budget. Enhancements to encoder algorithms improve the cost/benefit relationship, but of course still have the same fundamental tradeoffs within a particular encoder version.

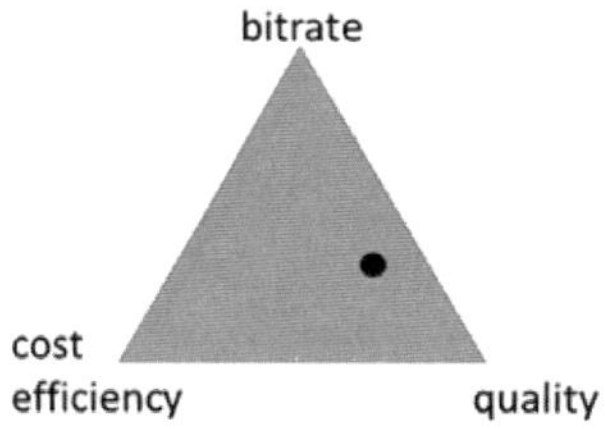

FIGURE 3: ENCODING TRADEOFF BETWEEN COST, BITRATE AND QUALITY

Different applications may benefit from a different balance between these different parameters, depending on factors such as the value of content, cost of delivery and viewing population. So, for example, a television service carrying valuable content to a mass audience might justify high levels of compute cost, in order to reduce the delivery costs. Conversely, a point-to-point link might have a relatively high bitrate capacity, and so the bitrates are high enough to mean that the compute cost is more of a consideration than bitrate efficiency.

As mentioned above, encoder innovation aims to improve the balance between these parameters: lowering the bitrate for the same quality while keeping the compute cost the same, or reducing the compute cost while keeping the quality and bitrate constant, etc.

This paper evaluates the role that AI can play to improve two areas of encoding: one relating to high-level and the other to low-level decision-making. As noted above, neural networks themselves can demand a significant compute cost to execute, so when comparing performance between encoders without and with AI, then the compute cost of the AI itself must be included in the latter.

AI For Improved Management of Encoding at the High Level

Most traditional encoders have multiple encode presets, each offering a different balance between compute requirements and the resulting bitrate vs quality relationship. For example, the open source AVC encoder, x264, has a range of presets, from "ultrafast" at one extreme, through "medium" and to "placebo" at the other, offering a spectrum of options from very low compute cost giving higher bitrates through to very high compute costs and the lowest bitrates for a given quality. With each step up in encoder preset, more tool capabilities are enabled - for example, increasing the number of options evaluated, areas searched, or sophistication of the bit distribution strategy.

Figure 5 shows the same 60-second video clip encoded using different x264 presets with a fixed CPU configuration. The processing cost is indicated via an achieve frames-per-second (fps) figure, with the bitrate efficiency indicated by the resulting file size for the encoded clip.

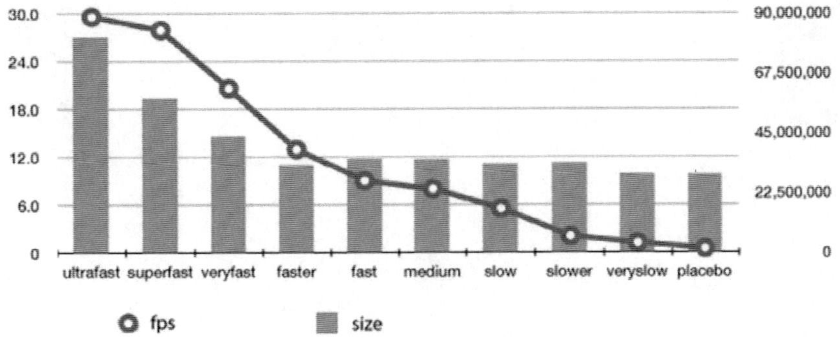

FIGURE 4: BITRATE EFFICIENCY AND COMPUTE COST COMPARISON FOR DIFFERENT X264 PRESETS FOR A 60-SECOND CLIP

These presets are defined a priori and typically allocate an overall compute budget to each of the tool categories, based on historical statistical knowledge. However, we can see from Figure 4 that there is an opportunity to allocate processing more effectively if the distribution is dynamic and adaptive to the characteristics of the incoming content. It is also worth noting that the bitrate curve is not monotonic: the “faster” preset is actually more efficient that the “medium” preset, highlighting the issue that the consequences of increased processing in one tool category might impair the behavior of another area.

As previously mentioned, CODECs contain many tools that help to identify and remove redundancy from video content. There are many tools, but they can be considered as groups of tools, each of which exploits a particular characteristic of video content. In this paper, the tools categories were defined as follows:

Category	Feature description
ME	Motion estimation
MCP	Motion compensation precision
IPS	Intra prediction search
PIPA	Picture partitioning
MD	Mode decision strategy
TQR	Transform and quantization refinement
BA	Bitrate allocation strategy
SEQ	Sequencing
TM	Transition management
PPE	Pre-processing and estimation

TABLE 1: CATEGORIZATION OF ENCODING TOOLS

The effectiveness of each tool category varies depending on the characteristics of the content. An example of how some of these categories vary by content is shown in the diagram below:

FIGURE 5: EXAMPLE ENCODING TOOL CATEGORY EFFECTIVENESS BY CONTENT TYPE

The cartoon content can have highly variable spatial complexity through different areas of the picture, as well as content that shows motion precision errors very clearly, hence spatial allocation and motion precision are particularly important. As expected, the motion estimation tool category is very significant for sport content, as there is a high degree of motion and there are often content characteristics that make matches hard to find, such as occlusions or lighting level changes. Conversely, the news content has relatively little motion, but is composed from multiple areas, requiring more consideration to how bit budgets are distributed within the picture.

Whilst it might be tempting to imagine that AI can solve this by simply applying a neural network (e.g. a CNN) to the input video signal, the reality is that neural networks that operate on source video content can be very large, resulting in high compute cost and also being more difficult to train, because the pixel data patterns for training need to be represent of what might be seen with new content.

Instead, it is possible to take advantage of the fact that many encoders already have look-ahead stages, which are used for some aspects of planning the behavior of the main encoder stage. Usefully, these typically have access to characterization metrics, such as spatial and temporal complex (along with many other parameters), that can be useful to summarize the nature of the content, avoiding the need to use a neural network to repeat that processing.

Neural networks were considered to be a good candidate for evaluating how to best distribute the allocation of processing power to different tool categories, because the relationships are complex and difficult to model accurately with a simple algorithm. Instead, we can use a neural network to learn the relationship between content characteristics and optimal compute allocation. For this application, a fully connected neural network was targeted.

When comparing compute costs, the processing cost of the neural network was included, so that there was a fair comparison.

In order to train the neural network, a selection of content was used with several classes of spatial and temporal complexity, some examples are shown in Figure 6.

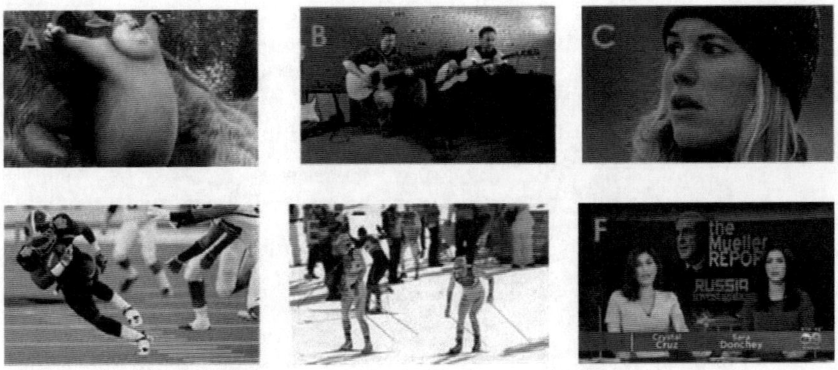

FIGURE 6: TEST CONTENT EXAMPLES

Figure 7 clearly shows how the resource consumption varies between different tool categories for each class of content, for content encoded with a specific preset (VQ preset =1). The overall total varies as expected, but the distribution between tools is also dependent on the content characteristics.

Since the total processing varies between different content, it is necessary to conservatively select a traditional preset based on the most complex content anticipated, which might be more difficult than one used for evaluation, such as content D in Figure 7.

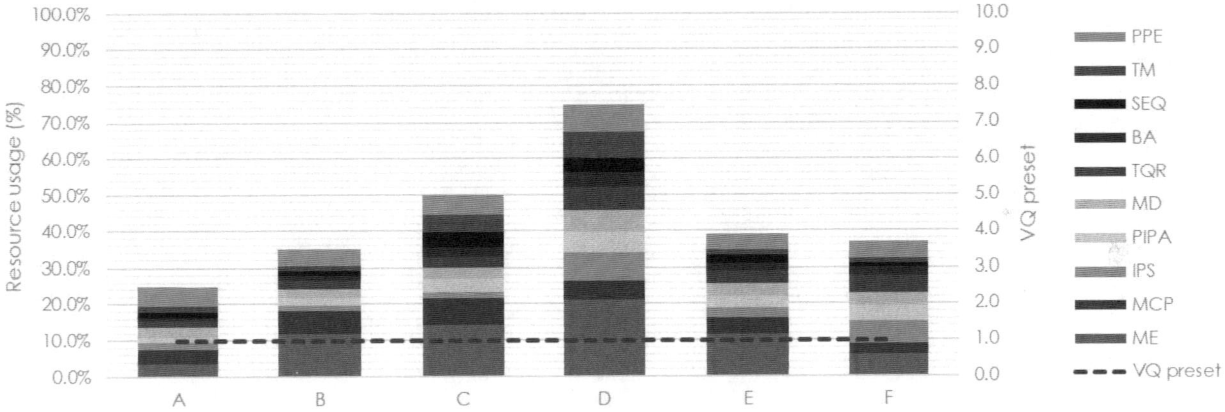

FIGURE 7: RESOURCE CONSUMPTION BY TOOL CATEGORY FOR MULTIPLE CONTENT CLASSES

If the presets were to be chosen dynamically, in order to utilize the compute budget in a more optimal manner (and thereby result in lower bitrates), it would result in adaptive distribution as in Figure 8 below. As can be seen, the preset in use can be a much higher-quality one in many cases, leading to an overall improvement in quality (or conversely the ability to reduce bitrate).

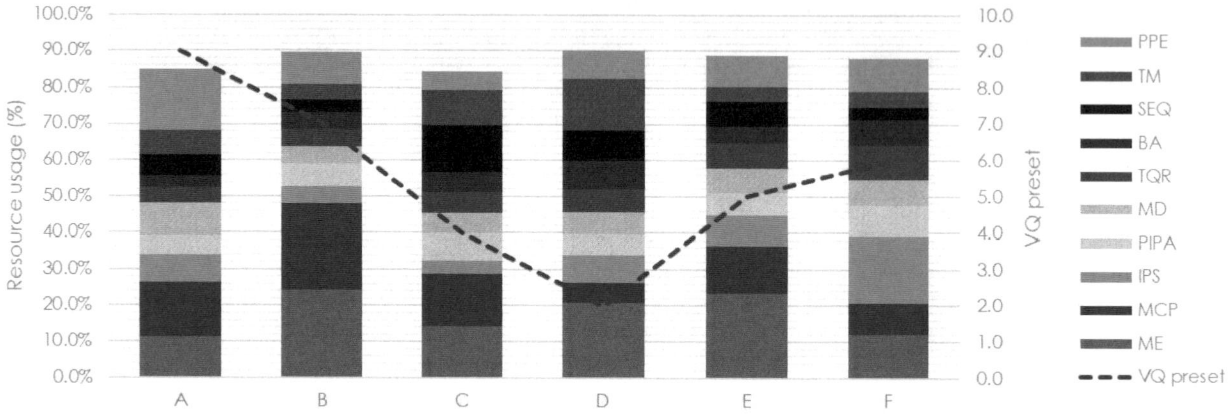

FIGURE 8: RESOURCE USE WITH CONTENT-ADAPTIVE PRESETS

The overall encoder architecture is shown in Figure 9. Input source content feeds the look ahead encoder, producing characteristic metrics C. This data, along with the target bitrate $EncT_T$ and target CPU resource $CpuT_T$ are used by the neural network to set the dynamic preset p. Feeback of the actual bitrate and CPU are provided as EncT and CpuL, which are used by the neural network to make real-time adjustments to ensure compliance with the constraints.

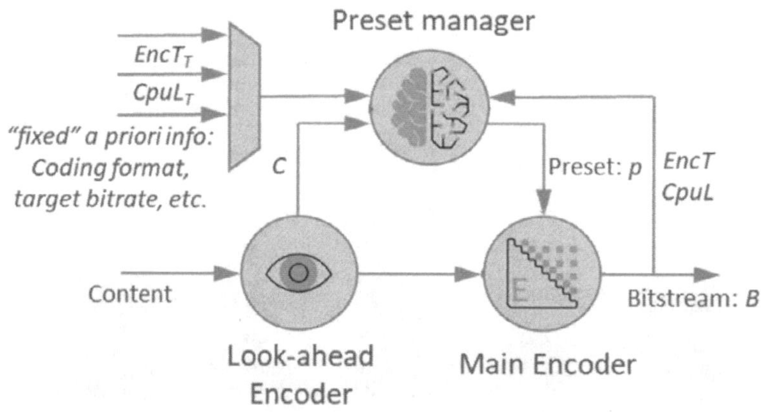

FIGURE 9: ENCODER ARCHITECTURE WITH NEURAL NETWORK FOR HIGH-LEVEL DECISIONS

The neural network was trained by running multiple encodes, with the encoding tools and configuration parameters being adjusted, for a wide range of source content. The neural network was then used to infer in real time the optimal base preset configuration, based on the input characteristic metrics.

This approach was applied and tested for both AVC and HEVC using the same content set, but with tool configuration parameters set appropriately for each codec.

With a fixed budget for compute resources (including the neural network's CPU load in the case of the AI-based approach), the AI-based approach resulted in BD-SSIM gains of 18% and 19% for AVC and HEVC respectively with HD content, versus the preset traditional approach. The reference for comparison was the highest-quality traditional preset that was able to guarantee real-time operation, whereas the AI-based approach adjusted parameters every frame.

AI-Based Improved Decision Making for Encoding at the Low Level

HEVC introduced a hierarchical structure for splitting the basic processing units, known as Coding Tree Units (CTUs), into smaller blocks. CTUs can be 16x16, 32x32, or 64x64 pixels, with the larger sizes being particularly beneficial for high-resolution formats, such as UHD. A CTU is not necessarily encoded as a single coding unit (CU), but can optionally be split into 4 smaller CUs. Each CU can be further split and so on, down to a minimum size of 8x8 blocks. This is illustrated by Figure 10 by way of an example.

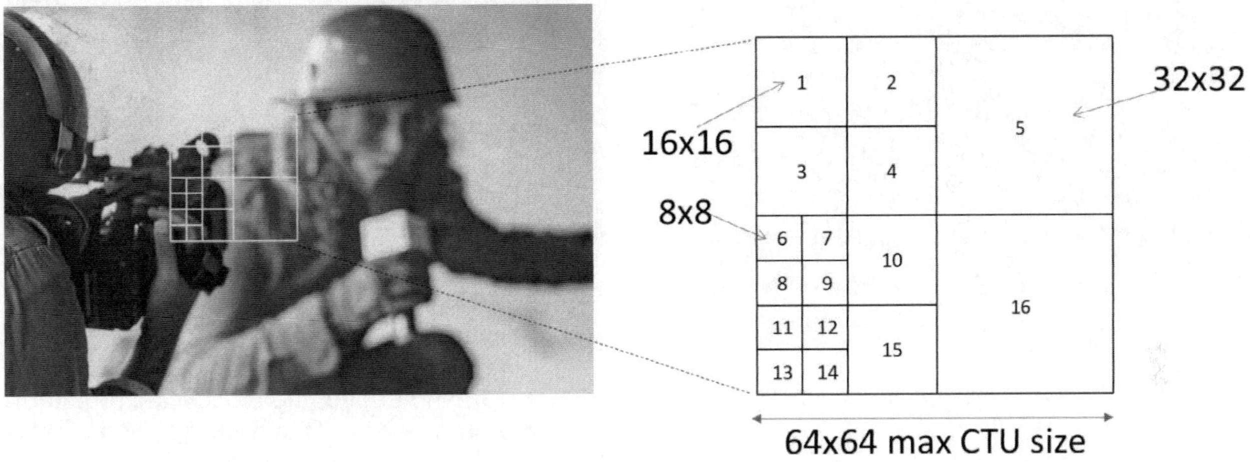

FIGURE 10: HEVC CTU SPLITTING

The options for CTU splitting are useful, because larger blocks tend to be more efficient for relatively low-detailed areas, whereas smaller blocks are useful for edges or fine detail (remembering that this is applied to motion-compensated or intra-predicted residual data).

For a 64x64 sized CTU, there are a total of 85 possible options for coding units if splitting down to 8x8 is completed exhaustively. Each of these potentially could be transformed and quantized, in order to make an optimal choice of split based on rate-distortion (RD) calculations. This requires a significant amount of processing power, and the nature of the problem has characteristics that made an AI-based approach plausible.

The optimal decision is not only dependent on the content, however, as the operating point also affects how the decisions are best made. Figure 11 illustrates how the optimal choice tends to favor larger blocks for lower bitrates (left) and smaller for higher bitrates (right).

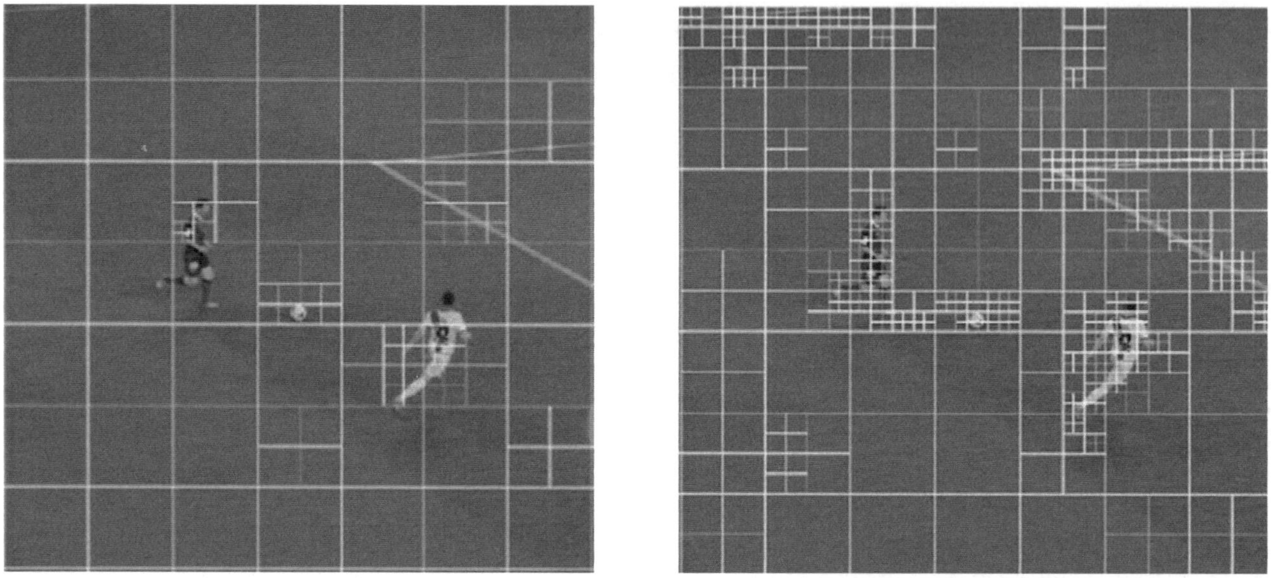

FIGURE 11: OPTIMAL CTU SPLITTING PATTERNS FOR QP=46 (LEFT) AND QP=18 (RIGHT)

As resolutions increase, particularly with 4K UHD (3840x2160 p60) and above, the processing required for bitrate efficient HEVC encoding becomes limited by available processors. Therefore, solutions that can free up inefficiently used compute resources are valuable, as the release compute resources can be applied to other tools and options.

In this CTU-splitting application of AI, a lower-level set of metrics from the same look-ahead encoder were used as input to the neural network, to avoid the need for a large CNN. Metrics used included spatial activity, inter complexity and gradients, using the lower-resolution look-ahead encoder.

The selected neural network used 4 layers, each fully connected, varying from 50 down to 21 nodes per layer. It was able to achieve 92% accuracy compared to an exhaustive evaluation approach. The architecture of the network meant that, unlike CNNs, it did not require GPUs to run in real time and was reasonably efficient using conventional SIMD instructions on standard server processors.

Training for the network was performed in non-real time, using an unconstrained encoder as the reference, using a full RDO approach on all of the 85 options. This was repeated at multiple QP levels and for a wide range of content.

The neural network's output was a probability that the CU should be split, based on the RD training that had been performed. Initially, a single threshold was used whereby the decision making was performed based on a comparison between the neural network's output F(C) for a given set of metrics for content C and a threshold D_1:

- if F(C) < D1, do not split,
- else if F(C) ≥ D1, split

However, near the decision threshold, there is a reasonable probability that the decision will be sub-optimal. As a result, a second threshold D_2 was used, with a revised logic:

- if F(C) < D1, do not split,
- else if D2 > F(C) ≥ D1, evaluate both options
- else if F(C) ≥ D2, split

Introducing the second threshold requires more compute, since some CUs will still require both options to be evaluated but reduces the probability of making a sub-optimal choice. Potentially, the difference between D_2 and D_1 can be adjusted in real-time, based on the actual available compute resources.

Evaluation was performed using SSIM as a quality metric, with the bitrates and compute requirements referenced to the exhaustive approach. In the case of the AI-based approach, the neural network's CPU load is included in the overall CPU cost.

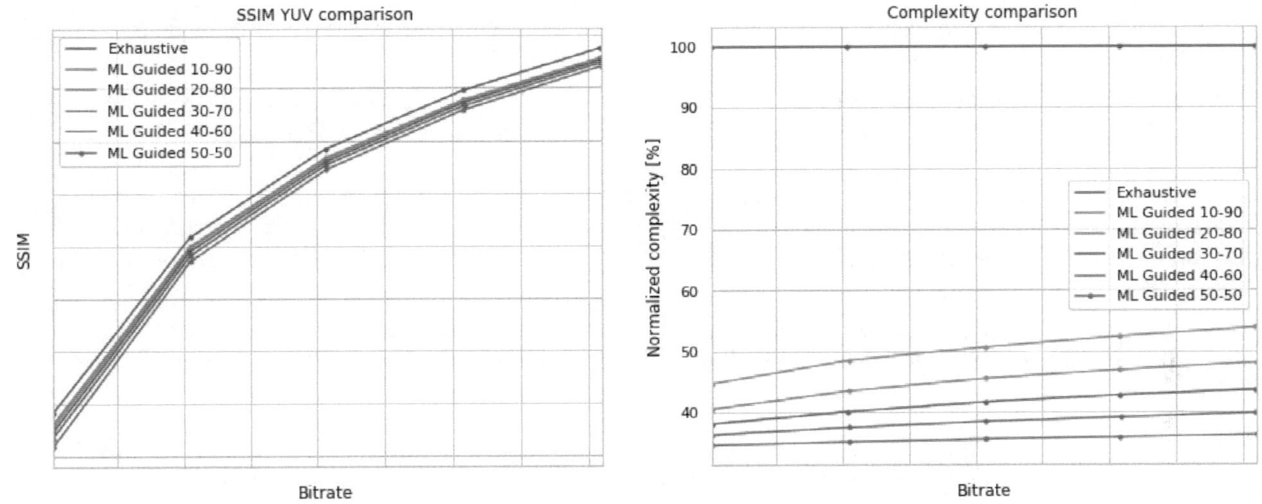

FIGURE 12: SSIM AND RELATIVE COMPUTE COST COMPARISON FOR VARIOUS D_1, D_2 VALUES

Figure 12 shows how quality (left chart) and relative CPU load (right chart) vary with bitrate. The blue lines represent the exhaustive approach and is presented as 100% normalized complexity. From the chart results it is clear that applying the AI processing to make the CU splitting decisions impacts the SSIM score in a relatively limited manner (about 5.5% in BD-SSIM terms), but the CPU load is reduced dramatically, typically saving 50% or more, depending on the D_1 and D_2 thresholds.

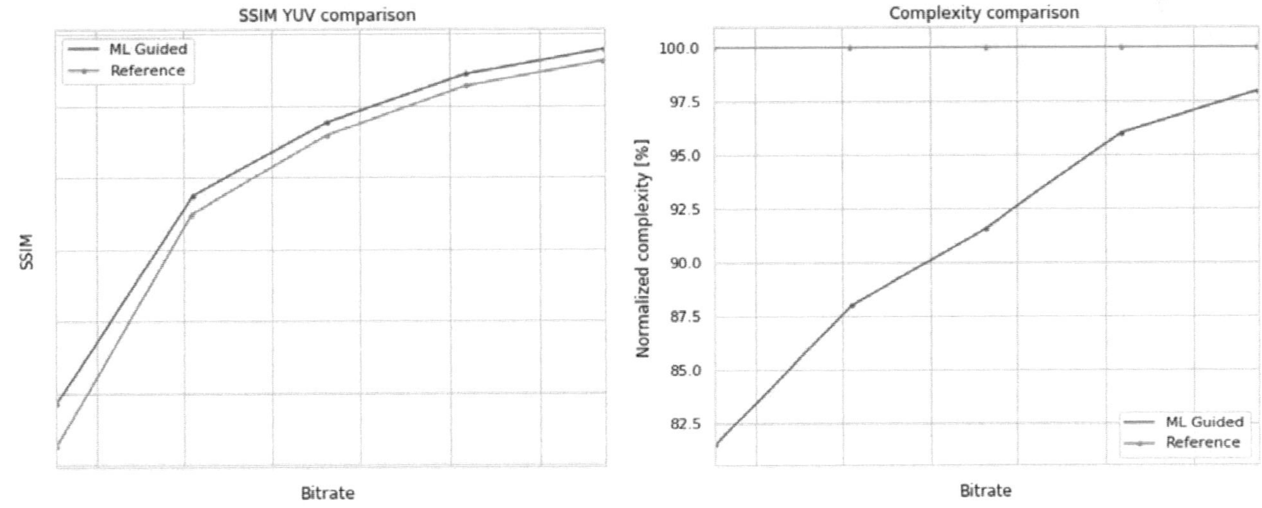

FIGURE 13: COMPARISON OF SSIM RESULTS TO NORMALIZED COMPUTE REQUIREMENTS FOR UHD SEQUENCES

The CPU resource savings resulting from the cheaper decision-making process can be re-applied to enable more encoding tools that were previously disabled to fit into the available CPU. These newly available tools translate into better encoding efficiency, and Figure 13 shows the impact of that on overall encoder performance.

In this case, an improvement in encoder efficiency of over 10% was achieved, while still using a lower overall compute budget.

Conclusion

In this paper, we have shown how AI can be effectively and efficiently applied to two different aspects of a video encoder, improving the relationship between bitrate vs quality and CPU cost.

The two algorithms operate at different levels: one at picture level control, the other for making more efficient decisions at the low level. These have been shown to offer up to 50% in processing power reduction for equivalent encode efficiency, or alternatively to improve encode efficiency by up to 20% within the same compute budget.

AI has been shown to have real-world applicability for video encoding, when used for selected aspects of encoders.

Future work may include a similar approach for the Versatile Video Coding (VVC) CODEC and there remain other decisions within the existing CODECs that may benefit from a similar approach.

References

[1] Okell, A and Jones, T, "Machine Learning Based UHD Up-conversion Using Generative Adversarial Neural Networks," BEIT 2020 Conference Proceedings, 2020.

[2] Bolei, Z et al, "Object detectors emerge in Deep Scene CNNs," International Conference on Learning Representations, 2015.

[3] ITU-T, "H.264: Advanced video coding for generic audiovisual services," 2021.

[4] ITU-T, "H.265: High efficiency video coding," 2021.

[5] ITU-T, "H.266: Versatile video coding," 2020.

Interactive NextGen Broadcast TV

Mike Kralec
Sinclair Broadcast Group
Hunt Valley, Maryland, United States

Abstract – Broadcast TV has traditionally been an experience where viewers channel surf to find something to watch. Today, people are accustomed to searching and selecting content they want to watch or listen to by using an over-the-top (OTT) service on their smart TV or connected device. Advancements present in the ATSC (Advanced Television Systems Committee) 3.0 standard offer broadcasters the ability to evolve broadcast TV into an interactive experience that rivals and can potentially surpass some of the popular OTT services. The NextGen Broadcast Application is a robust solution developed by broadcasters that brings the newsroom to the viewer. It can be delivered via an ATSC 3.0 broadcast signal or loaded via a broadband connection. The NextGen Broadcast Application transforms traditional broadcast TV into a customizable interactive experience where viewers can easily access the latest news, weather, and so much more whenever they want. In addition, EAS (Emergency Alert System) and FEMA (Federal Emergency Management Agency) alerts that come through the DASDEC and BNA (Broadcast News Alert) from the newsroom can be enriched with more information and be updated in real time. This is an open-source solution designed to help all broadcasters fully transition into the NextGen of Broadcast TV. This paper will highlight the NextGen Broadcast Application and its features. We will explore the interactive experiences viewers can use to engage with our newsroom today. We will also unpack the ability for broadcasters to customize the look and feel, incorporate audio/video content feeds, and enrich NextGen Alerts with content from the newsroom, including images, maps, URLs, and even on demand videos that can be updated in real time. Since the NextGen Broadcast Application is already live in many markets, we will look at a current implementation. Additionally, we will explore the possibilities of connecting to the newsroom computer systems to automate certain tasks, monetization opportunities to generate revenue through dynamic ad insertion, premium VOD content, eLearning services, and gaming.

New Consumer Expectations

The vast majority, nearly 90%, of Americans have broadband at home [1] and over 82% have at least one Internet-connected TV device with nearly 40% of adults in U.S. TV households watching TV via these connected devices on a daily basis [2] (Figure 1). These connected devices, including smart TVs, are providing an interface beyond the traditional linear channel experience, setting an expectation for searching and finding content and information on-demand. They are connecting through their device to expand their available options to include the latest shows, sports, movies, news, and weather content. They are consuming this content on the schedule and the medium they want and with the capabilities provided via NextGen TV broadcasters are now empowered to provide this experience for an OTA (over the air) viewer.

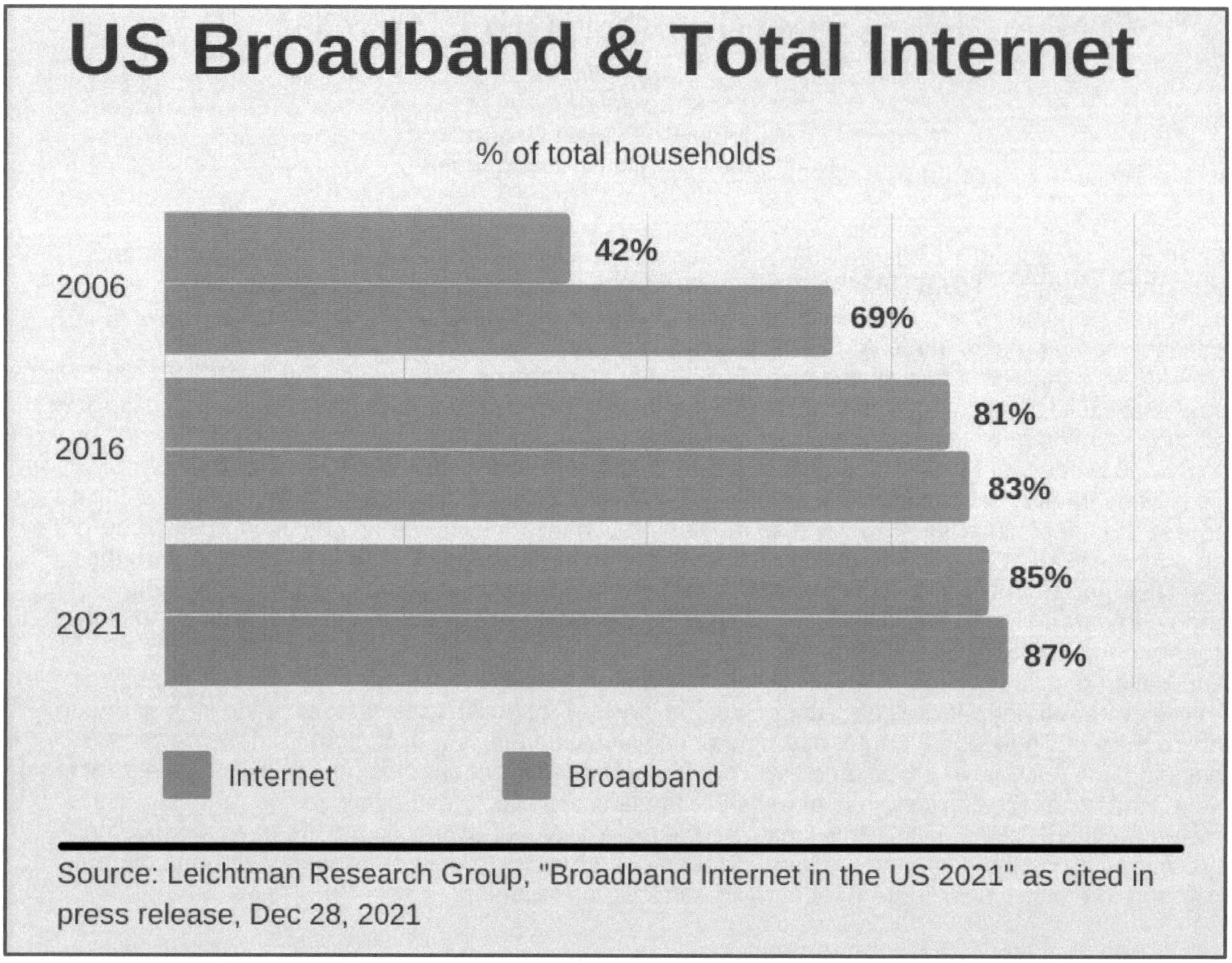

FIGURE 1: HOUSEHOLDS WITH INTERNET SERVICE AND HOUSEHOLDS WITH BROADBAND

This OTA (over the air) viewership is, of course, governed by the penetration of NextGen TV sets and while set penetration is still small, it is growing quickly. Sinclair's own data has shown consistent monthly increases in OTA viewership via 3.0 sets and over the past 6 months alone, 3.0 viewership has doubled. Spending the time now to test, develop, and improve the interactive experience provided by the NextGen Broadcast Application is critical to continued future growth for the ATSC 3.0 / NextGen TV standard and our ability as broadcasters to deliver content in a manner consistent with how our viewers expect.

The NextGen Broadcast Application

Dynamic and Interactive

The NextGen Broadcast Application is not a static, pre-installed application in the traditional sense you might think of a typical OTT (over the top) streaming application. The standard OTT streaming applications are developed specifically for the operating system and platform they are running on like Android TV. The NextGen Broadcast Application on the other hand is a dynamic, interactive environment that is delivered just-in-time to the TV when a viewer tunes to a broadcast channel. This delivery can be via OTA (over the air) broadcast as a package, or it can be delivered via broadband over a traditional CDN (content delivery network). Once delivered, the receiving device loads the

NextGen Broadcast Application and displays a simple call-to-action (CTA) that is unobtrusive and gives the viewer some navigation hints (Figure 2). This CTA is displayed for a a short and configurable time before disappearing, but the NextGen Broadcast Application itself is now loaded and available for user interaction.

FIGURE 2: THE CALL-TO-ACTION (CTA) DISPLAYED ON DELIVERY OF THE OPEN-SOURCE BROADCAST APPLICATION

While the NextGen Broadcast Application is loaded, it is only loaded for the current viewing session. Contrary to being a drawback, this just-in-time nature means that dynamic updates can happen to NextGen Broadcast Application content on a continuous basis, much like your favorite website is updated regularly. This applies to both the application design and the application content. We still need small, persistent, cache to provide the best experience possible, specifically for storing basic user settings, including zip code for location-based alerting and preferences for notification levels, both of which we will discuss later.

After the call-to-action (CTA) a viewer can now open the NextGen Broadcast Application with the click of a button (Figure 3). This action is key because the viewer is consciously switching their consumption from viewing only what channel they were on to now also consuming another stream of information. The existing channel and content being viewed is preserved while the NextGen Broadcast Application squeezes the video back into the same aspect ratio as before but now with interactive content available as well. This interactivity allows for consumption of additional information that would have previously meant the viewer would have had to switch devices or at least stop the current viewing to access, but now, with the NextGen Broadcast Application capability, if the viewer is interested in consuming the news in snack-sized pieces they can load up the latest top-stories; if they are interested in what next Tuesday's weather will be, the seven day forecast is a few remote clicks (Figure 4). This is all done without interrupting the current channel they are tuned to or the video they are currently consuming.

FIGURE 3: THE MAIN INTERFACE OF THE OPEN-SOURCE BROADCAST APPLICATION

FIGURE 4: THE WEATHER INTERFACE OF THE OPEN-SOURCE BROADCAST APPLICATION

This is important because we believe in an improved viewing experience, giving greater access to the content relevant to the viewer while retaining them on the same viewing medium and not distracting from the content they've already been consuming. New, relevant content may be available as an alert, as a news flash or as other streams of OTT (over the top) data or content including sports gaming data or detailed program information beyond what is supplied via the existing guides. For entertainment, our goal is to present one or more catalogs of on demand streaming video and audio content for the user to select from. Some content sources could even require the viewer to perform authentication via website or mobile application, potentially accessed through a unique QR code or URL, like OTT services. These services could be free in nature, but just require authentication like content hosted by a public library or could require a premium subscription for access. To deliver this effectively, we will need to work closely with manufacturers to ensure a positive consumer experience through consistent behavior across sets and NextGen Broadcast Application implementations.

Coming back to a few points we have made earlier; it is important to call out additional information available in the form of notifications and alerting. Advanced Emergency Information (AEI) is a critical component in enhancing the delivery of potentially life-saving information to our viewers (Figure 5). We can enhance traditional EAS (Emergency Alert System) alerts with rich-media or deliver timely and relevant news flashes with low disruption to the viewing experience. Newsrooms can update an existing government-agency-provided alert with media, including graphics, videos or photos that provide significantly more detail and awareness to the viewer. Another option is to deliver data, like URLs or QR codes to, when we absolutely we must, send the viewer to another site, portal, or application to be informed. The newsroom can also create their own BNF (Broadcast News Flash) that details important or critical local-level events or concerns. Automating these Broadcast News Flashes through integration with the traditional Newsroom Computer System will provide an improved content experience without creating an additional process for our newsrooms to handle. While we all know and love the simple text-crawl and tone, it simply cannot provide the contextual relevancy that we now can using the NextGen Broadcast Application.

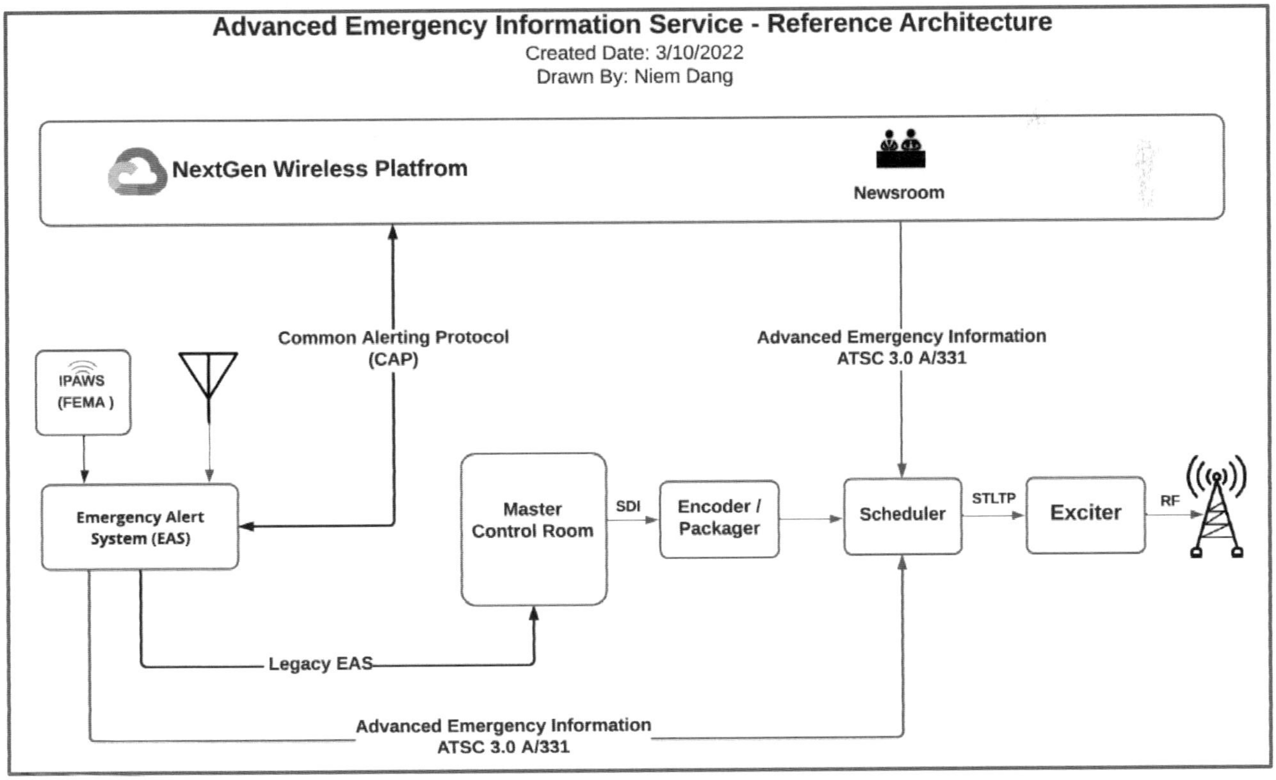

FIGURE 5: SIMPLIFIED, HIGH-LEVEL, DIAGRAM OF THE ENABLEMENT OF RICH-MEDIA ALERTS IN NEXTGEN TV

Open-Source and Available

Fundamentally, we do not believe that NextGen Broadcast Application code ownership and licensing should be a barrier to adoption and use by broadcasters. There has been a lot of discussion about needing one industry NextGen Broadcast Application. One perspective is that a single application supports a single-threaded approach to variations in ATSC (Advanced Television Systems Committee) 3.0 A/344 standards implementation across TV set manufacturers or variation where the standard is not adequate to address emerging needs. While this is true, it is not a critical roadblock and the drawbacks created, including reduced business flexibility, slower feature innovation and a more restrictive creative environment more than offset the perceived benefits to a single, industry wide, NextGen Broadcast Application implementation. We will, however, need consistent alignment on feature development/enablement to maintain a positive consumer experience, just not the same application, codebase, or framework.

To that end, Sinclair Broadcast Group has a well-designed open-source shell we will contribute to the industry with basic instructions for how to incorporate weather, station logos, Google analytics IDs, and basic OTT (over the top) content feeds (Figure 6). We will commit to keeping it updated with the latest code and security updates to support the industry as NextGen Broadcast Application support is added or updated on TVs.

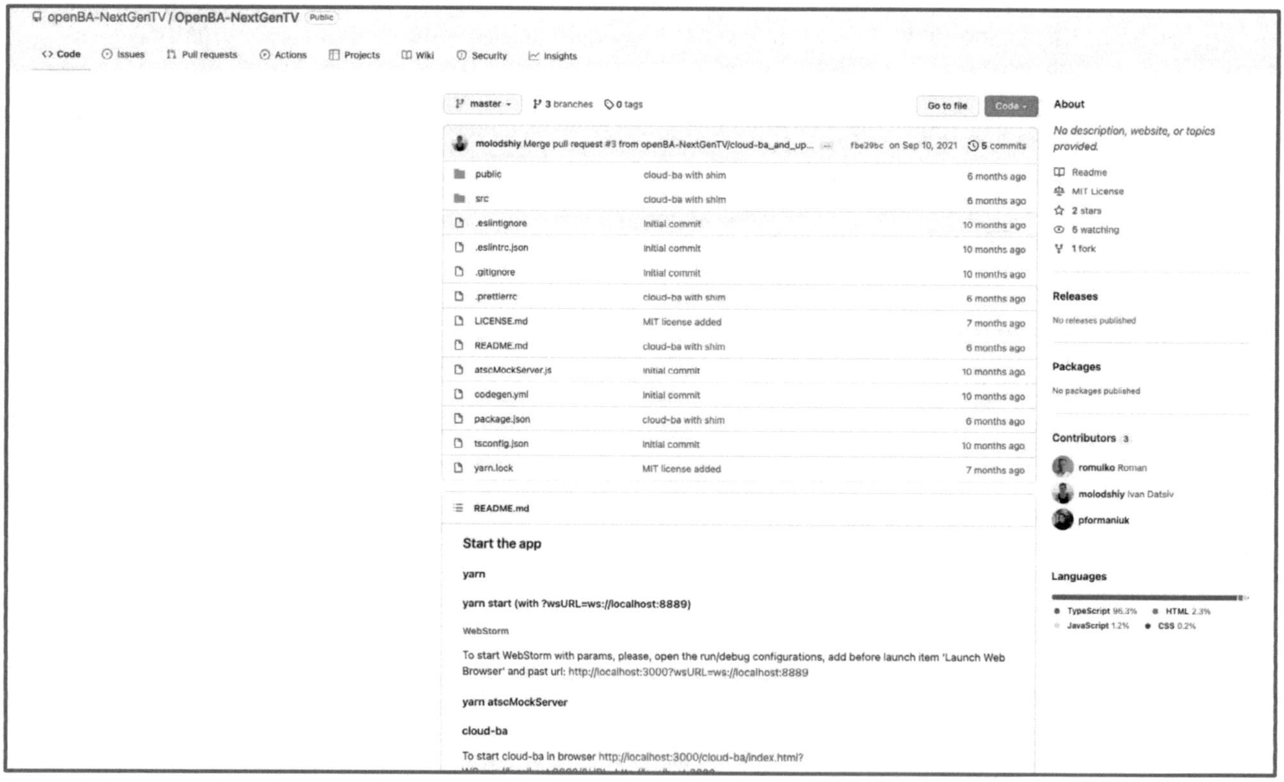

FIGURE 6: THE GITHUB REPOSITORY OF THE OPEN-SOURCE BROADCAST APPLICATION

Customizable

The open-source NextGen broadcast application allows each broadcast station to configure their application to display their station's logo, keep icons and graphics familiar with their viewers by using their current design standards, feature content that they have generated and streaming content libraries they are able to distribute. The design itself is extensible, accommodating additional or reduced content as needed and allowing the navigation menu to expand or contract to handle feature changes.

Monetization Potential / Additional Revenue Models

We believe it is incredibly important to develop revenue models on top of the open-source broadcast application that might follow a path towards improved integration with other existing content systems and platforms, improvements related to data distribution to viewers or students, and improvements critical to robust telemetry and data analysis.

At the most basic level of monetization, having a high-level of interactivity with the viewer and the TV platform increases opportunities for distribution and integration of other types of content valued simply for the scale and low-latency of distribution that broadcasting can achieve. These other types of content might include gaming platforms for both the data feeds and for the gaming itself.

With respect to telemetry and data analysis, the application can be configured to generate a unique and anonymous identifier available for the viewing session. This capability can unlock interactivity outside of the broadcast application to include signing up for access to premium content or content restricted to a specific group like students at a particular school, district, or state. This e-learning content could then be made available by either OTA (over the air) or OTT (over the top) distribution and interaction validated through existing connected data channels. This first-party data on viewer interaction is valuable at even the most basic level to understand viewer behavior. We have the linear program schedule; we know the current date and time and we are already aware that the viewer is tuned to our channel. We can answer then, with our own data, questions related to the efficacy of content, reporting back usage metrics that empower the broadcaster with the awareness of the content or features with the most engagement.

There are also additional ad-related monetization opportunities that can be introduced if we are precise in how we operate. We may be able to link and feature sponsors within the application if we can account for non-conflicting advertiser separation. This extends to effectively handling the business rules required of us by both our content providers and potential advertisers with respect to DAI (dynamic ad insertion) in both live and VOD (video on demand) content and throughout the user interface.

The NextGen Broadcast Application Next Steps

We invite everyone to download the open-source broadcast application at the following QR code, to ask questions, to challenge assumptions, to get creative and contribute to a NextGen Broadcast Application ecosystem that is collaborative and valuable for the entire industry.

References

[1] Leichtman Research Group, "Broadband Internet in the US 2021" as cited in press release, Dec 28, 2021

[2] Leichtman Research Group, "Connected TVs 2021" as cited in press release, June 4, 2021

NextGen TV Trends: Lessons Learned From Pioneering And Ground-Breaking Application Examples

Oliver Botti
Fincons Group
Milan, Italy
oliver.botti@finconsgroup.com

Abstract – The US market has embraced NextGen TV with enthusiasm and it is already possible to identify emerging trends from an applications point of view that can help scale to a wider audience. Both businesses and consumers can benefit from the take-off of these applications. This paper presents a collection of market trends, challenges, opportunities, and lessons learned during the implementation of groundbreaking pilots and compelling production ready ATSC3 applications in collaboration with leading broadcasters and associations in the US. It also integrates the US perspective within direct experiences of the author with European broadcasters, identifying a global move towards a new form of Television.

NextGen TV: TV Re-volution

ATSC 3.0 is the next generation terrestrial broadcast system designed to improve the television viewing experience with higher audio and video quality, more accessibility, and, in particular, with personalization and interactivity. Based on the same Internet Protocol as today's popular streaming media platforms, it was designed to bring together Over-the-Air with Over-the-Top content.

There are over 50 markets where at least one station is broadcasting ATSC 3.0 or NextGen TV signals, and we expect about 75% of the U.S. population to be able to receive services by Q2 2022. One of the latest announcements is that of WNET in NYC, which will serve as the host station for ATSC 3.0 broadcasts for the three major PBS member stations in the New York metropolitan area.[1]

ATSC3 takes the baton from European experience and literally runs with it. Standing strong on the foundations laid by previous experience in Europe, US broadcasters are not only able to avoid falling into the same pitfalls that cost significant time and effort to amend ten years ago but are able to launch their new platforms directly into the latest next generation solutions and in synergy with their latest OTT efforts. Leveraging the synergies between Hybrid TV and OTT remains critical to the future success of broadcasters.

Fincons Group has been instrumental in spreading the HbbTV standard in Europe and has actively contributed to the development of the US ATSC 3.0 standard as well as its promotion together with the National Association of Broadcasters (NAB) since the early days in 2018.Together with leading US broadcasters we have piloted their new business cases and applications and put in production some of the first live ATSC3 broadcaster app implementations.

[1] ATSC, STREETINSIDER: New York City Public TV Plans NextGen TV Launch

Critically, interactive TV adoption is a great opportunity but requires a sound strategy in synergy with the broadcaster's positioning in the market.[2] This whitepaper, providing numerous early examples of NextGen TV applications, helps broadcasters benefit from emerging innovative trends being rolled out across the pond and provides a guide for defining a strategic roadmap for the integration of their NextGen TV initiatives within a renewed TV offering, leveraging innovative technologies into future proof architectures.

The growing adoption of the Advanced Television Systems Committee (ATSC) 3.0 standard is providing an opportunity for over-the-air (OTA) broadcasters to be competitive in the digital space and compete with online content providers.[3]

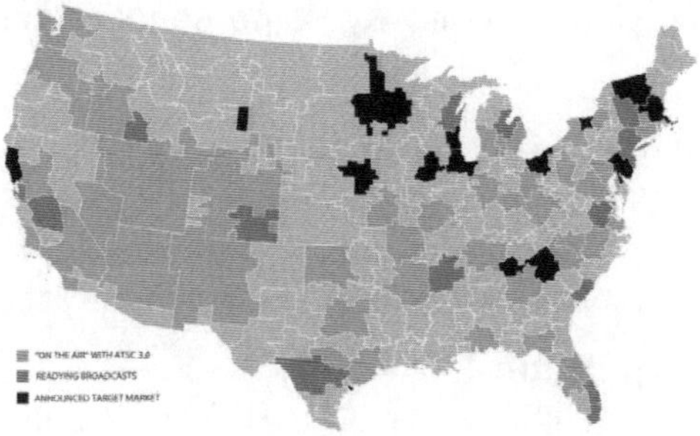

FIGURE 1: MAP OF ATSC 3.0 MARKET COVERAGE[4]

Pioneering Pilots

Among the European HbbTV applications we put in production, I would certainly mention Mediaset in Italy and a tier1 broadcaster in France. The former started a process of hybrid TV launch and continuous evolution in 2017, exploring and actually live testing the market feedback on User Interactivity and content personalization – proposing functionalities such as startover, highlights, multicamera, voting, polls, etc. – as well as new advertising models, such as Interactive and Targeted Ads, with multichannel advertising and attribution, and, more recently, interesting Drive-to-Store and Drive-to-Site campaigns, which are attracting brands from different markets, with Automotive and Food paving the way for others to come.

The tier1 French broadcaster we are working with prepared the grounds for a visionary adoption strategy during 2019-2020, starting with GDPR compliance, covering Live Audience Management and Advanced Advertising Models, as well as "Content Related Convergence" paradigms, to be ready to grasp the opportunities of the French market move, where the SALTO[5], grouping together the main French broadcasters, is giving clear direction to the national market.

Regarding the US market, I think this is bringing in fresh air regarding the different types of NextGen TV applications, scouting monetization and entertainment focused ones, but also expanding to really new services to the citizens, which may provide an incredibly effective scaling factor for the whole ecosystem: as we have seen today, we can move from hyper local news, to education, to weather forecasting, to emergency alerting, to automotive applications for autonomous vehicles, and in-car infotainment, and many more to come. The start with non-monetization driven apps is helping to expand the adoption on a larger scale and to prepare the ground for consistent monetization models. These applications are revolutionizing the way people experience media and entertainment.

---

[2] Rapid TV News, CES 2022: ATSC 3.0 sees "significant" industry momentum,05 January 2022
[3] META online, Technicolor, Sinclair: ATSC 3.0 is Helping to Blur the Lines Between OTT and OTA, 15th December 2021
[4] ATSC.org website, Map of deployments
[5] GroupeM6, Les Groupes France Télévisions, M6 et TF1 annoncent le lancement commun de SALTO

In the next section we introduce the most relevant experiences we had with US market leaders, right from the first ATSC3 pilot app we developed together with the NAB back in 2018, up to the first ATSC 3.0 broadcaster app we put in production with Univision in 2020; showcasing a number of novel services for citizens, ranging from Remote Schooling with the Howard University Middle School of Mathematics and Science to News Literacy with the E.W. Scripps Company, from TV-driven e-commerce with CBS, to the redesign of the Sinclair broadcast app already in operation, in view of its scaling to larger audiences.

All these applications are effective opportunities to enhance user engagement, increasing audience loyalty, but also to create new inventory spaces and monetization models. They are also a precious opportunity to collect data, in a GDPR compliant way, to personalize content and advertising as well as create new services.

Leveraging this huge availability of data, Machine Learning and AI, in combination with Interactive TV standards (HbbTV for Europe and ATSC3 for US) is bringing TV personalization and audience engagement to the next level, moving towards an "Intelligent Content" era, where data are collected to enrich the user experience and to enable new data-driven business models[6].

NAB: The First ATSC3 Pilot App in the US

Starting in 2018, as part of our collaboration on the NAB PILOT[7] initiative, we developed the first Broadcaster App leveraging the new ATSC 3.0 A/344 standard. Showcased for the first time at the NAB 2018 event on experimental TV sets from Samsung, Sony and LG and introducing Channel Info, Channels List, EPG and VOD access on sport content, this early trial clearly highlighted the bright future prospects for this technology.

FIGURE 2: THE FIRST NAB BROADCASTER APP PILOT

CBS: From Sponsorship to TV E-commerce

Also in collaboration with the NAB, in 2019, we developed the first Cooking Show App for the CBS Saturday Morning segment, "The Dish."[8] While the famous guest chef of the show was cooking, the audience was able to download the recipe on mobile phones, share it on social networks, order ingredients on Amazon Fresh, or purchase the latest book published by the chef online.

This was an interesting experiment for TV-driven E-commerce, enabling a Click&Buy approach, with both remote controller and Alexa voice control, introducing the idea of moving from sponsorship to TV e-commerce. It heralded a smart anticipation of a wider move, from Audience to Consumers. A videoclip is available here: https://www.youtube.com/watch?v=gcTUqzH_LRU.

[6] NAB.org, NAB Show Adds 'Intelligent Content' Showcase to 2022 Experience
[7] NAB PILOT
[8] NAB Show Express ATSC3.0 Interactive Application Prototype

FIGURE 3: CBS COOKIE SHOW APP

E.W. SCRIPPS: False News Recognition

In 2021 with E.W. Scripps we worked on a revolutionary "News Literacy App", designed in conjunction with NAB and the News Literacy Project, to help citizens recognize and dismiss false news and avoid misinformation.[9]

Introducing quizzes, polls, and access to online tips and tools to better identify fake news, or reliable information sources, the app leverages TV interactivity and participation to create a new and interactive dialog with the audience on a topic of broad interest. A videoclip is available here: https://www.youtube.com/watch?v=qYyW8Sovsl4.

FIGURE 4: E.W. SCRIPPS NEWS LITERACY APP

Educational Equity with NextGen TV: The Howard University Middle School Prototype

Also in 2021, a year in which COVID created room for running research and innovation investments, together with the NAB and the Howard University Middle School, we developed an ATSC3 Remote Schooling pilot application leveraging ATSC3 datacasting features. It was a first-of-its-kind prototype application to enable students to undertake remote learning via their television screens without broadband.[10] [11]

This application provides the class timetable presented in a TV guide-style with easy navigation and a traffic light color-coded system that indicates to students: work that is outstanding, ongoing and completed. When work is complete, a QR code is generated, allowing students to submit their work to their teacher with a mobile device. This innovative feature allows two-way communication between the school and the students, which is crucial for remote education to be effective.
This was a great opportunity to explore how Remote Schooling can be an effective means towards educational equity, in particular during the pandemic where the non-uniform availability of internet connection at home was widening the digital divide between students with access to internet and those more disadvantaged. A videoclip is available here: https://www.youtube.com/watch?v=ZBLMtC8UT6w.

---

[9] NAB.Amplify, TV News Literacy App Shows the Potential of ATSC 3.0 | NAB Show Premiere Rewind
[10] NAB Amplify, Next Gen TV Prototype Shows How Educational Equity Can Be Achieved for All Students
[11] NAB Amplify, Educational Equity with NextGen TV

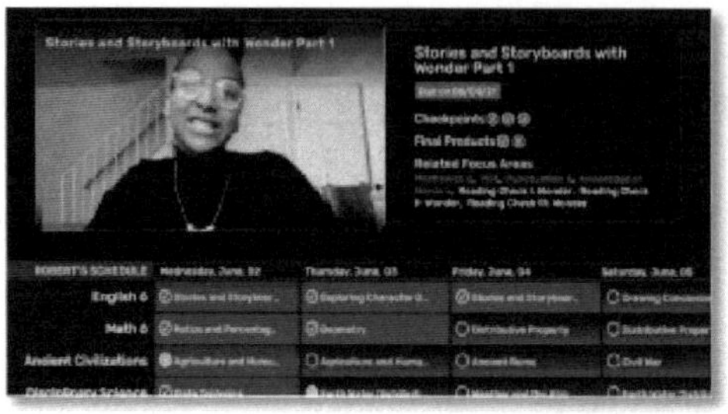

FIGURE 5: HOWARD UNIVERSITY REMOTE SCHOOLING APP

Sinclair: NextGen TV UX

Sinclair is investing a lot in the ATSC3 take-off and is a recognized driver within the US market. Sinclair Broadcast Group and its subsidiary, ONE Media, have been active since early days on multiple NextGen TV levels, from research and development to deployment. "NextGen TV Broadcasting's ability to reach deep into buildings and moving vehicles, and its easy integration with Internet and advanced cell phone service (like 5G), allows supporting multiple new business models in addition to linear TV"[12].

Fincons contributed to the redesign of the Sinclair broadcast app, including Call-To-Action, Emergency Alerting, Weather, Favorites, Categories, Channels, and introducing a new interactive User Experience to prepare the "second-wave" of adoption and usage on a larger scale.

In this direction Sinclair believes that to favor the adoption by broadcasters, the core of a NextGen TV broadcast app should be a flexible open-source, 1) to guarantee a consistent alignment of features UX, 2) to allow the application configuration by each broadcast station maintaining their branding and content offering and 3) to enable new revenue models which can leverage other existing platforms and business rules, benefit of datacasting and of new data measurement and analysis.
Fincons is supporting Sinclair Broadcast Group in the evolution of this open-source approach, putting at disposal its consulting, development and integration skills and experiences accumulated in years of Research and in field application.

FIGURE 6: SINCLAIR OPEN-SOURCE BROADCAST APP UX DESIGN

Hybrid Linear-VOD Binge Watching

2020 was the year of actual launch of the ATSC3 standard, and with a major content distributor we had the opportunity to develop a pilot application for what we can now call "Hybrid binge-watching," i.e., an application promoting Live-To-VOD and VOD-to-Live functionality for Broadcaster's channels to a fragmented audience. While watching their preferred show on linear TV, when the show is going to end and moving to content for a different target, the TV viewer receives on-screen recommendations for similar content to follow in VOD on the same screen and via a simple "click" on the remote. Vice versa,

[12] Sinclair Broadcast Group/ ONE media 3.0, ATSC 3 activities

while watching VOD content, the viewer is alerted about the incoming start of content of his interest on linear programming of a channel. Again, a simple "click" allows viewers to switch to linear.

FIGURE 7: HYBRID BINGE-WATCHING.

Several other ATSC3 trials and actual launches characterized the NextGen TV take-off during the last couple of years, such as the Pearl TV Pilot. [13] [14]

We will proceed in our collection of samples with a deeper dive into a live production case study.

UNIVISION: Hyperlocal News to Start the NextGenTV Roadmap

The Challenge

Univision, a leading American Spanish-language television network, was looking for a flexible and user-friendly Broadcast App to:

- enable personalization of viewer experience and additional choice and content over both broadband-connected and linear TV;
- continue to build loyalty and retention among key viewer demographics;
- enable multi-device viewing and browsing experiences;
- maximize user engagement and advertising opportunities.

The Solution

Fincons' App leverages ATSC 3.0 to provide viewers with dynamic content both via Broadband and Broadcast connections. It enables entirely unprecedented functions for OTA TV such as the delivery of additional information, access to QR-coded external content and dynamic local weather forecasts. The weather section specifically enables two levels of navigation, depending on the TV connection. For OTT viewers, the App also provides access to on-demand local news clips.

From a technology perspective this app, which integrates the A3FA Consortium Framework[15], is one of the first to leverage the ATSC 3.0 standard to deliver enhanced viewing experiences to both connected and unconnected TVs. The App can be deployed across multiple channels with new branding elements and provides user-friendly editorial control so that content can be managed dynamically from the editorial system without the need for third party intervention or additional integrations.

Thanks to its level of innovation put at work in a real environment this app won the NAB Product of the Year Award in 2021. [16] [17]

---

[13] PEARL Phoenix Model Market
[14] NAB PILOT ATSC3 Projects
[15] A3FA Consortium Framework (RUN3TV)
[16] NAB Product of the Year Award 2021
[17] NAB, NAB Announces Winners of Annual Product of the Year Awards, 2021

The Benefits

The dual application for both broadband-connected and broadcast TV, supported by the ATSC 3.0 standard, is revolutionary and ushers in a complete reimagining of viewer experience. Univision can now provide viewers with additional personalization, as well as local and hyper-local content that really speaks to their interests, continuing to build loyalty and retention among viewers, maximizing user engagement and advertising opportunities.

The Sports R-evolution

We dedicate this section to the sports arena, since we think it is going to be a significant driver boosting the overall NextGen TV take-off. The personalization and engagement that new technologies such as Machine Learning and AI, in combination with Interactive TV standards can achieve, are changing the face of the sports industry entirely. Through accurate near-real-time data analysis and prediction capabilities these technologies provide a new take on the sporting action taking place but also critically provide content owners with an unprecedented understanding of their audiences.

During the pandemic we had to deal with the reality of live sports events taking place in an empty stadium and therefore to reinvent the user experience of one of the most consolidated and valuable forms of TV content, introducing a new (virtual) social dimension. This need became an opportunity to revamp revenues via new revenue generating streams.

The world of sports content distribution continues to experience unprecedented disruption as partnerships emerge between rights owners and platform providers like Amazon, Facebook and Netflix, but also between short form video providers, and niche players in longtail content and agencies to deliver DTC (Direct to Consumer). Commentators identify a clear trend towards fragmentation of the content landscape with content owners trialing novel DTC avenues rather than traditional contracts with Virtual Multichannel Video Programming Distributors (vMVPDs). A more direct relationship with the customer through DTC and NextGen TV technologies and greater use of analytics are the culmination of a process that has been developing for years.

Gamification: The Game Within the Game

Data and statistics relating to real and fantasy sports can fuel increased engagement in the game, encouraging fans to place wagers and pit themselves against other fans in their predictions. A more powerful use of data analysis through Machine Learning and AI can inject an even greater level of competition and engagement attracting promising advertising and merchandising opportunities. Contests and leader boards, for example, can create highly engaging and sticky experiences making a strong game within the game, keeping interest active and introducing a new (virtual) social dimension within sport events fruition.

To do this, they rely on interactivity and on information being delivered in real-time and accurately. The use of HbbTV in Europe and ATSC3 in the US, the integration of Gaming and Video Platforms, the combination with AI to gather and interpret data from multiple IoT sources and to automatically analyze content and recognize specific events, can help achieve truly engaging contest experiences for viewers.

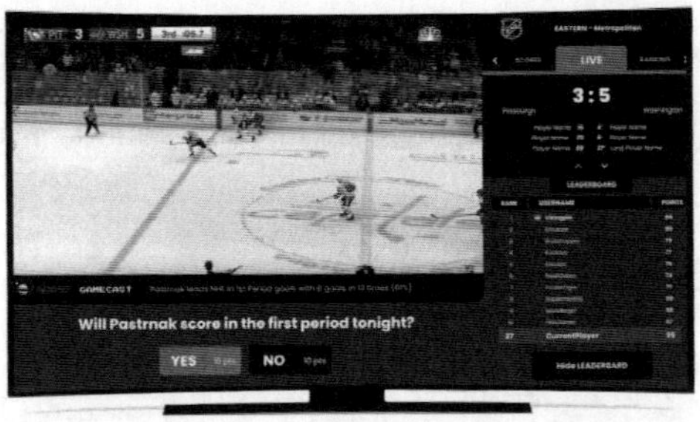

FIGURE 8: SPORT GAMIFICATION APP.

We designed and implemented a visionary prototype early in 2019 with the NESN Boston-based broadcast network, which created a new sport TV format, where commentators of the live event were commenting for both the hockey match and the virtual game, bringing the level of engagement and enthusiasm to the next level. A videoclip is available here: https://www.youtube.com/watch?v=ykdfG7Oj_xc.

Live Sports Betting

Following the NESN experience, Fincons implemented a technological stack to realize a complete sport betting platform on NextGen TV enabling new revenues streams for networks and broadcasters.
It provides an enriched user experience to sports enthusiasts who can enjoy matches on the big screen while being engaged in betting on what will happen during the games.

The solution includes a NextGen TV app for the big screen that is paired with a synchronized mobile application that fans use to authenticate themselves and place bets, on which they will be notified on the big screens while enjoining sports events.

The sport betting platform is based on an open architecture that allows the integration between the core applications powered by Fincons and the systems provided by broadcasters, sports stats providers, and betting companies, the key players to offer this compelling betting experience. The big screen guarantees user engagement; betting is placed on the mobile device and notified on the big screen.

FIGURE 9: SPORTS BETTING APP.

Smart Watching

Machine Learning enables a better understanding of the viewer preferences and the tailoring of his/her experience. When combined with NextGen TV interactivity and applied to sports, it may result for example in what we call "Smart Watching;" interesting moments or actions are automatically identified, i.e., in car racing, and through a smart video player, the user can jump directly to these key events. Not only can specific actions be easily replayed, but personalized highlights can also be extracted.

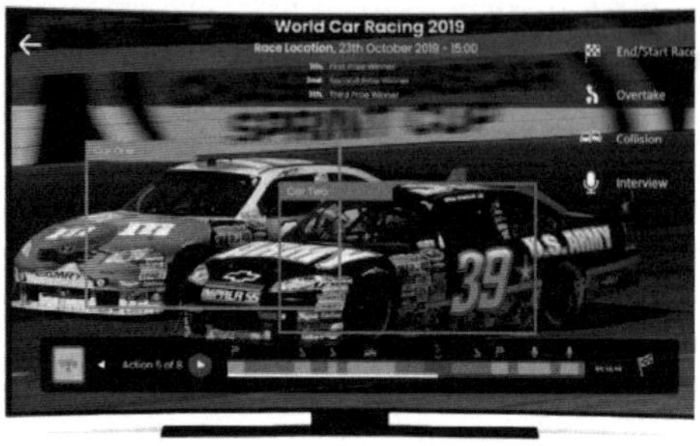

FIGURE 10: SPORT SMART WATCHING.

The ability to, for example, select the video camera from which to view a specific action or the Formula 1 driver to focus on, enhances both live and VOD experience and makes a more efficient use of the content archives that rights owners hold.

The combination of Machine learning and NextGen TV also enables integrating more sophisticated features which can further enrich the user experience, such as augmented overlays, brand monitoring, contextual advertising and shoppable content.[18]

Incoming Innovation for a Bright Future

NextGen TV is a reality and is now ready to scale to business relevant volumes globally, opening new vistas on appealing business cases. On the other side of the ocean, European Hybrid TV services are in a more mature adoption phase and already measuring interesting results enabled by addressable TV advertising paradigms, such as Interactive Display Advertising, Dynamic Advertising Replacement, Cross-channel Advertising Re-targeting and Attribution, up to the latest Drive-to-Store and Drive-to-Site models.[19] [20] European success stories are built with a concurrent launch of new content related services to the citizens, on one side, educating the audience to the new interactive experience and opportunities, and monetization-oriented models, on the other, attracting brands into new valuable investments.

Scaling towards total audience will require other available innovation to be put to work, such as (1) watermarking technologies, to make NextGen TV also applicable in any set-top-box and cable scenarios;[21] (2) Anonymization techniques, to enable a GDPR compliant usage of audience data in a cookie-less scenario; (3) open sourcing of HbbTV/ATSC3 code for core interactive TV functionalities, to favor a rapid and homogeneous spread of the "new language" among TV audiences. Completing the ongoing TV manufacturers onboarding is then the final ingredient of a successful recipe.

Broadcasters and operators should carefully define their strategic roadmap towards the integration of NextGen TV services within their cross-channel proposition, combining TV with online channels and defining the proper mix of new services in accordance with their overall brand positioning.

---

[18] Next Gen Technologies now at bat, 2020
[19] ADD+: Pioneering Innovative Cross-channel Advertising and Attribution Analysis
[20] Broadcast-driven Connected TV
[21] First HbbTV ADB2 Watermarking Implementation

ATSC 3.0 as a Use Case for Public Safety Communications – Development Milestones

Fred Engel CPBE
PBS North Carolina
Research Triangle Park, North Carolina, United States
fengel@pbsnc.org

Red Grasso
North Carolina Department of Information Technology
Raleigh, North Carolina, United States
red.grasso@nc.gov

Chris Lamb
Device Solutions Inc.
Morrisville, North Carolina, United States
clamb@device-solutions.com

Tony Sammarco
Device Solutions Inc.
Research Triangle Park, North Carolina, United States
tsammarco@device-solutions.com

Abstract – Many fire and EMS services across the United States still rely on analog VHF paging technology to communicate emergency incident information to responders. The infrastructure for these paging systems is typically owned, operated, and maintained by the local government or agency to ensure coverage includes as close to 100% of the jurisdiction as possible. This paper proposes the use of datacasting technology to provide a redundant method for critical data distribution over a wide area to serve the paging needs of public safety and uses North Carolina as a test case. This concept could lead to cost-sharing, higher reliability, greater collaboration across jurisdictions, and reduced response times. The public deserve the best possible response from the public safety sector and therefore, public safety deserves the best technology available in order to achieve their mission.

PBS North Carolina, with the leading organizations from the North Carolina Department of Information Technology First Responder Emerging Technologies Program (FirstTech), presented this concept at the 2019 NAB Broadcast Engineering and Information Technology Conference. Much progress has been made since then. Starting in early 2020, a United States Department of Homeland Security Small Business Innovation Research contracted a prototype broadcast system that has been developed including custom ATSC 3.0 paging receiver and miniature antenna, encoder, on a live broadcast in eastern North Carolina. This paper will talk about the overall concept and current progress using ATSC 3.0 to address a critical emergency communications need.

The State of Public Safety Paging

Currently, paging is still widely used in the Fire and EMS disciplines for dispatching emergency calls. This dispatch refers to the transmission of emergency information to the responders in the field from a Public Safety Answering Point (PSAP), which is the industry name for a 9-1-1 Center. The PSAP is the connection point between someone reporting an emergency need and the public safety agencies that will respond. This can be true for both volunteer and career agencies.

Today's voice pagers are tuned to a specific radio channel and messages filtered using a 'selective' call setting that will keep the speaker silent until a trigger (such as a specific set of tones) is heard on that channel. When a trigger is heard, the pager will then alert the user, either with a special beep and/or vibration, and unmute the speaker so that the dispatcher can be heard. There are a number of manufacturers of these voice pagers, each with a number of different features such as audio recording (stored voice), a display screen, customized audio alerts, etc.

The selective call feature allows responders to be alerted only for emergency incidents or for other information that is targeted for a specific group. The group being targeted can be a fire department, a particular station within a department, or even a specific fire truck or officer. The criteria used for determining how many groups is a mutual arrangement between the responding agency and the PSAP that dispatches that agency.

Fire and EMS services have to be assured that this information will be delivered to the responders in the field. It is not viable to rely on commercial paging or cellular services for this type of mission critical communication and industry best practices do not recognize such systems, as they are not controlled by the agency or a governmental partner and may rely on unsecured best-effort methods.

The Challenges with Pagers

The voice pager is based on outdated technology that is slow at delivering emergency information. This type of pager uses an analog radio channel, and the selective call feature relies on an audible set of tones. Each unique group's tone sent from the PSAP can be 2-3 seconds long (depending on setup). When multiple groups need to be paged, all of the tones have to be transmitted sequentially before any of the dispatch information can be delivered. Then, the actual voice dispatch can take 20-40 seconds depending on how much verbal information is provided. During all of this, other emergencies are queued waiting for the paging transmitter to become available.

Understanding Datacasting

In the late 1990's, television stations in the United States began broadcasting a digital transmission service. All analog broadcasts ended in 2009, making broadcast television digital only. This transition to digital television (DTV) uses the Advanced Television Systems Committee (ATSC) standard. DTV allows for more video (in the form of data) to be delivered using the same amount of spectrum as an analog transmission. This data stream can also be used to broadcast many other types of useful information besides video, such as TV program guides, emergency alerts, etc. Any portion of this data stream that is unused is a missed opportunity. Datacasting is a concept to transmit useful data utilizing the unused capacity of the DTV transmission signal. Datacasting is the ability to send data over digital broadcast television signals to specialized receivers. This data can include video streams, audio streams, pictures, documents, and other computer files. The nature of broadcasting is that it is a one-to-many form of communication used to deliver a huge volume of data quickly to many receivers at the same time. It is not a two-way exchange of information.

Television stations use high power transmitters and antennas atop tall towers, buildings, and mountains. Their signals are in the VHF and UHF bands, and the coverage footprint and in-building coverage are unmatched by any other current technology.

An enhancement to the current ATSC digital broadcast system is here. ATSC 3.0, utilizes a different delivery scheme that is far more robust and useful for mobile applications. Often referred to as "NEXT GEN TV," it also has the added benefit of better building penetration, especially when using UHF broadcast television channels. Areas that may not receive a robust signal from the full power transmitter may be candidates for lower power transmitters to "fill in." ATSC 3.0 allows for the development of a Single Frequency Network (SFN) for synchronized, on-channel transmitters to accomplish the fill. The ability of ATSC 3.0 to be reliably received by a device that is moving (mobile) is an added capability.

Using Datacasting for Public Safety Paging

Datacasting may present a perfect solution for the current challenges found with existing analog voice paging. TV infrastructure already exists, and the transmitting equipment, towers, antennas, power, and spectrum is already in use supporting broadcast television. The footprint of this Public Safety Datacast Paging system would be far greater than current paging systems, which would increase interoperability, reliability, and dependability. Similarly, many PSAPs, which provide the information needed by public safety responders, already support the export of such information to their existing paging system. Having a centralized paging system available to several PSAPs will also increase the ease of providing backup dispatch services between jurisdictions.

Datacasting may provide an opportunity to advance public safety paging to a new level for more timely public safety service delivery. The ability to alert multiple responders will only take milliseconds using a datacast digital format, which is literally a thousand times faster than today's analog paging format. Datacasting is a one-to-many broadcast, similar to today's public safety analog paging. The number of receivers is unlimited, unlike a cellular service which can only support a limited number of devices in a given area. By delivering the emergency dispatch information in a digital format over datacasting, the technology can support over 2000 dispatches during the same time frame that it would take an analog system to perform a single dispatch. At that rate of delivery, it may not seem important to prioritize the messages or dispatches, but a Public Safety Datacast Paging service could also support such prioritization.

Datacasting Paging Progress in North Carolina

As a result of evangelization efforts by PBS North Carolina and the North Carolina Department of IT FirstTech Program, the United States Department of Homeland Security authorized a Small Business Innovation Research (SBIR) grant opportunity in 2020. The grant was developed with three phases. The first phase was to identify small businesses who could prove their ability to address the issue. The second phase was to expand that work to develop prototypes to prove the concept. And the third phase is to bring the product to market.

Device Solutions Incorporated, Morrisville, North Carolina engineering firm qualifying as a small business, along with the Wireless Research Center (WRC) of North Carolina, won the Phase 1 SBIR award to describe how they would address this challenge. Device Solutions and the Wireless Research Center advanced on to phase 2 to build a prototypes device and have partnered with PBS-NC and Triveni Digital to demonstrate a working broadcast solution system.

Phase 1 Goals included:

- Provide responders and incident commanders with improved pager coverage and capacity, quicker dispatching, and messaging content for increased situational awareness
- Develop a Proof-of-Concept digital paging system and receiver for emergency responders using public television (Figure 1 below).

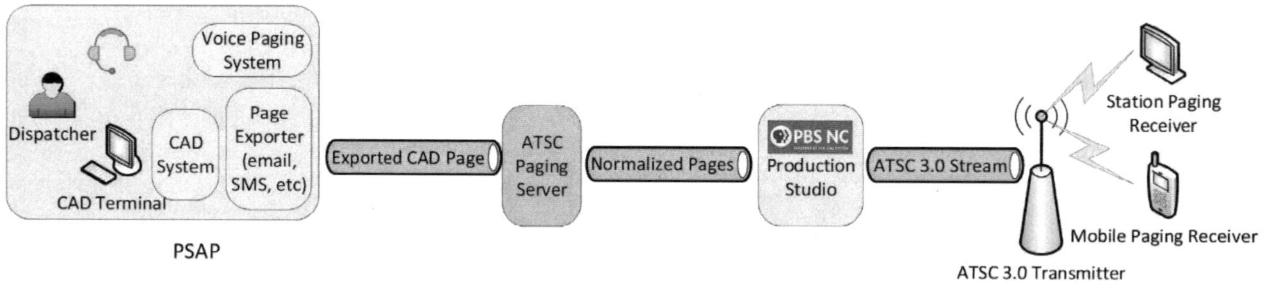

FIGURE 1: PROOF OF CONCEPT

Phase 2 Goals included:

- Develop a prototype ATSC 3.0 paging receiver which displays the CAD information normalized and sent from the ATSC paging server to the ATSC 3.0 transmitter or forwards it to other Bluetooth capable devices
- Optimize ATSC 3.0 delivery chain for delivery of emergency pages
- Deliver results from performance modeling and testing of ATSC 3.0 receptibility in a controlled environment for anticipated paging receiver design (for example, body worn small device on a belt)
- Prototype two different paging receiver designs, one based on a stand-alone model and the other based on a smartphone integration with the ATSC 3.0 information passed along to a smartphone application
- Provide a practical demonstration of the capability with at least 10 receivers located with different first responder organizations from different jurisdictions within a state. The organizations should represent different types of jurisdictions from urban to rural, career to volunteer, mountainous to coastal.

To fully appreciate the benefits and requirements it is helpful to review how emergency calls are handled in many jurisdictions. When someone dials 9-1-1, it is automatically routed to the nearest PSAP or 9-1-1 call center. Once sufficient information is received from the caller, the operator alerts the first responders via a VHF transmitter and belt worn audio pagers (Figure 2 below). The received audio quality is often limited by the low quality of the device speaker, poor use of the microphone by the dispatcher, dispatcher speech accents, local noise at the receiver etc. If the first responder does not clearly hear and remember all the relevant details, the pager may have limited ability to replay the message and the responder may have to use a cell phone or two-way radio to request details from the PSAP. Furthermore, in many jurisdictions, updates are not always transmitted over the paging channel– resulting in delayed responses and responders arriving at the incorrect address.

Most PSAPs utilize a Computer Aided Dispatch software to input all of the details of an emergency and track the status of responding units, among other features. This software is simply referred to as CAD and each PSAP may have their own vendor and instance of CAD in use for their operation. In many cases, the CAD data is also exported and sent, often via email and SMS, directly to users or to third party application servers for delivery to the first responder. Third party application servers work to normalize the data from multiple PSAP/CAD feeds and deliver it in consistent formats, sometimes decreasing the usability of the message. Adding to the complexity of handling these exported CAD messages – each dispatch center formats their exported data uniquely – and therefore for a statewide deployment we propose a normalization function to be integrated into the ATSC paging server to ensure consistent broadcast format and content and potentially augment with additional GIS content. These issues are particularly problematic in rural, volunteer-oriented departments which cannot afford to equip the majority of their responders with modern, digital radios, which can cost $3,000 or more.

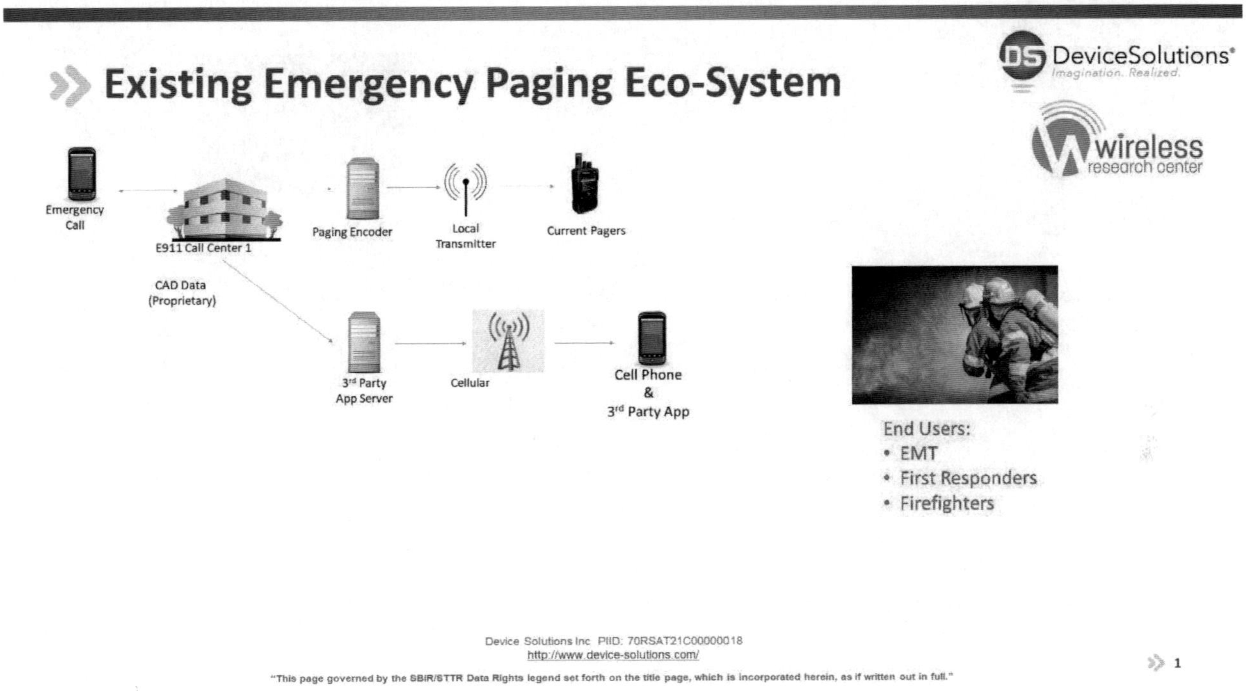

FIGURE 2: EXISTING EMERGENCY PAGING ECO-SYSTEM

In the prototype system a custom page normalization function has been developed as part of the ATSC Paging Server which transfers standardized messages to the ATSC 3.0 broadcast system with a few simple APIs, implemented by Triveni Digital (a business partner), over secure IP connections. (Figure 3 below).

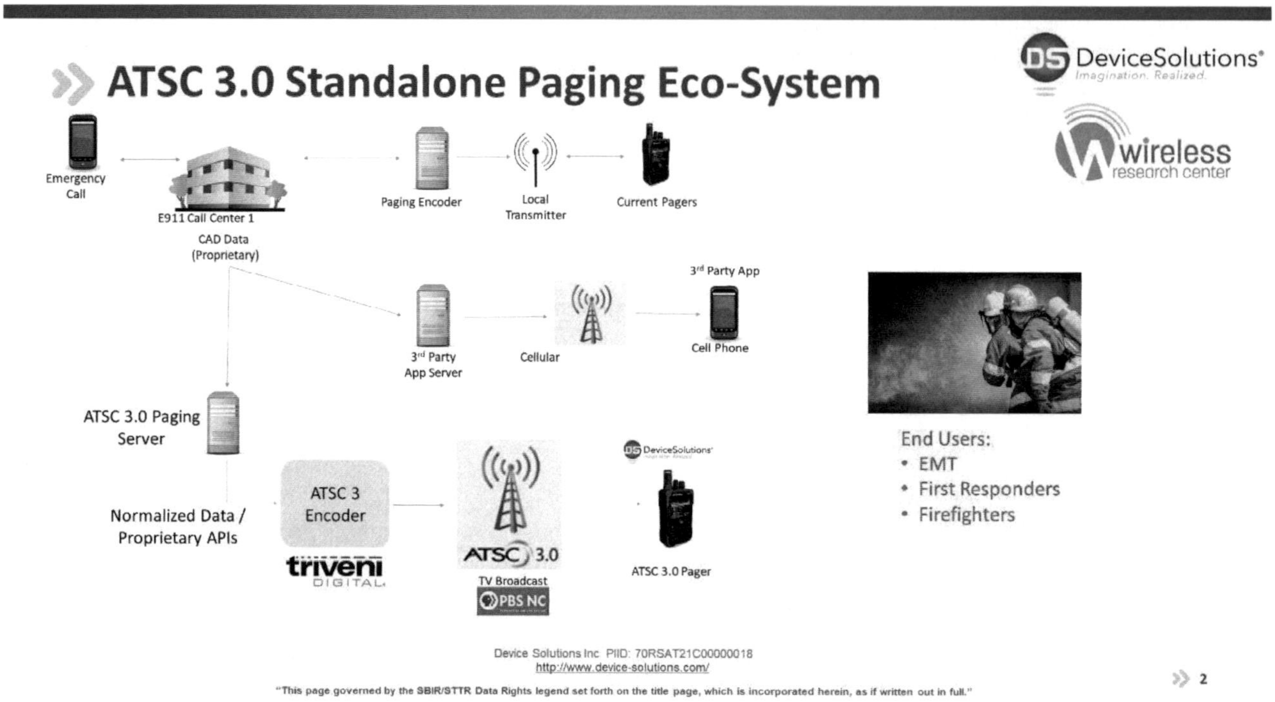

FIGURE 3: ATSC 3.0 STANDALONE PAGING ECO-SYSTEM

Additionally, as shown below, the paging receiver can be further minimized by connecting to a standard cell phone over Bluetooth to provide all the user interface functionality and providing a redundant data path to existing phone applications (Figure 4 below).

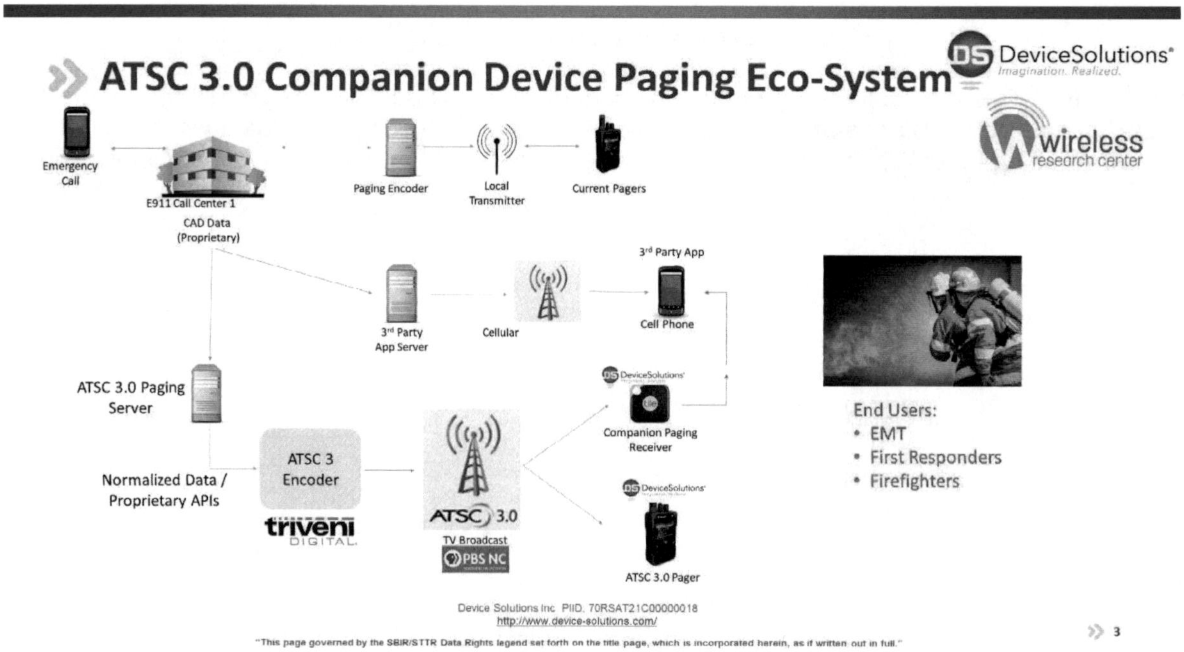

FIGURE 4: ATSC 3.0 COMPANION DEVICE PAGING ECO-SYSTEM

This next section will look at more of the technical details of the ATSC 3.0 broadcast.

The ATSC 3.0 standard is based on IP protocols meaning that all the connections from the video encoders to the transmitter are all IP based. The only coax cable in our lab is used in conjunction with the inputs to the video encoders and the RF output of the exciter modulator.

In Figure 5, going left to right across the diagram, the signal flow starts with video sources feeding an HEVC video encoder system that generates IP video streams. This output, using the DASH protocol, feeds a signaling server.

The signaling server is an IP signal aggregator. It can receive a variety of data feeds from various sources such as the output from the video encoders, the programming guide information, and other data feeds such as those from emergency services, Emergency Alert System (EAS), and other sources. This is where the paging data is input into the transmission path. The signaling server assembles the various IP streams and uses the Route protocol to send that data to the Gateway.

The Gateway then packages the data and creates an IP output using the STL TP protocol that is then used to send the data to the exciter modulator. The STL TP protocol allows several things to happen including the ability to introduce forward error correction to minimize data loss during transport to the transmission site. It also imbeds the mod cod information so the transmitter's exciter can create the RF signal with the desired Physical Layer Pipe (PLP). Security signing is also part of the STL TP protocol. This prevents man-in-the-middle attacks from being successful against the station. In other words, your transmitter will only broadcast what you send it and not something from someone else.

In our lab, the exciter modulator is a transmitter exciter that was donated by GatesAir. The output of that exciter feeds a multi-port RF splitter that feeds a wide variety of receivers as well as other RF test devices.

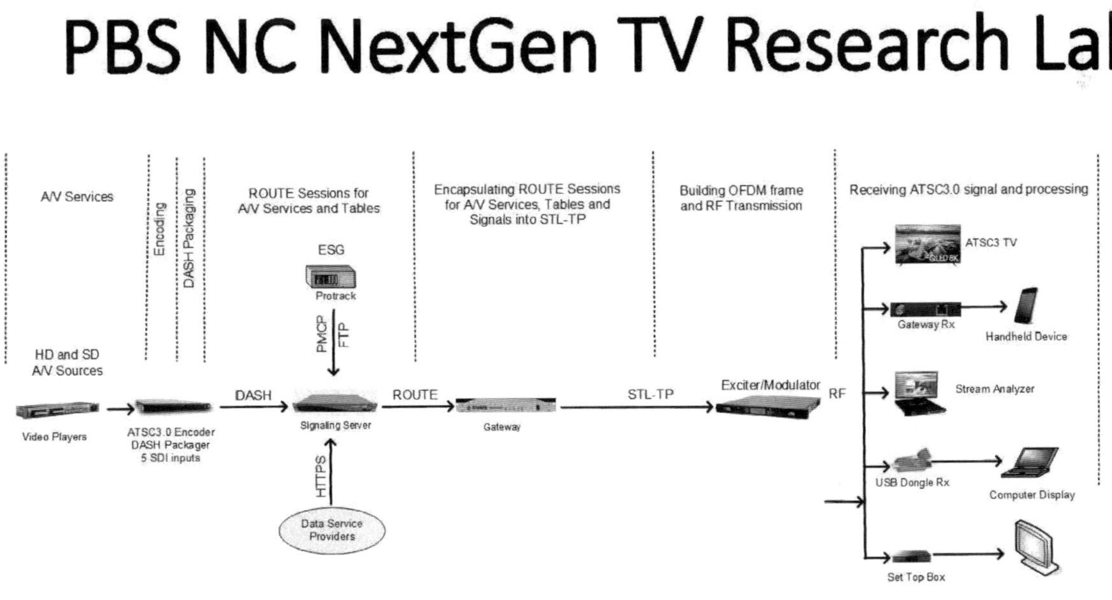

FIGURE 5: PBS NC ATSC 3.0/NEXT GEN TV RESEARCH LAB

PBS North Carolina operates 12 full power, UHF stations (see Figure 6 below). All facilities are ATSC 3.0 capable. All of the transmit antennas are also elliptically polarized. We currently have two stations that are operating with an ATSC 3.0 broadcast signal.

The first station is WUNC-TV Chapel Hill. It began operation as a guest station on Capitol Broadcasting's host station WNGT-CD. This signal is also shared by Capitol's other 2 Raleigh stations WRAL-TV, an NBC affiliate, and Fox 50, WRAZ. The signal is on channel 23 with a power of 15 kW ERP using a circularly polarized directional antenna at a height of 1040 feet and it serves the Raleigh Durham area.

The other station is our over-the-air research lab station, WUNK-TV Greenville North Carolina. There are no guest stations currently sharing the WUNK signal. The station operates on channel 25 with 1000 kilowatts ERP using an elliptically polarized nondirectional antenna. That antenna provides a 500 kilowatt vertically polarized signal as well as the 1000 kilowatt horizontally polarized signal. The antenna height is 1142 feet, and the station serves the Greenville-Washington-New Bern area of eastern North Carolina.

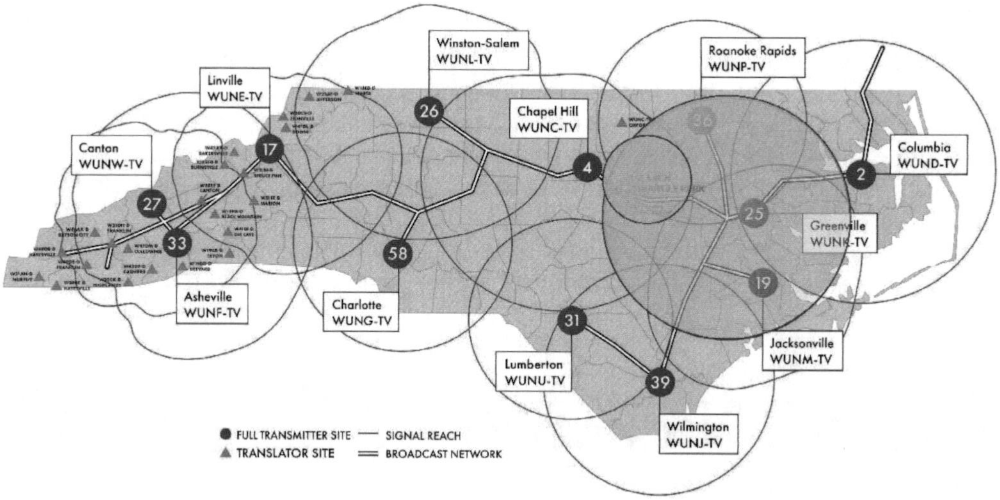

FIGURE 6: WUNK-TV COVERAGE MAP

In cooperation with our partners (WRC, Triveni Digital), Device Solutions and PBS-NC are in the initial phases of field testing with the WUNK transmitter and live dispatches from multiple counties, using second generation prototype paging receivers, shown below. We are continuing to optimize the RF performance and battery life of these devices and survey signal propagation with a dedicated, highly robust PLP. These pagers will be deployed with multiple departments for end user testing later this year (2022).

FIGURE 7: DEVICE SOLUTIONS PROTOTYPE PAGING RECEIVER

Summary

Tone and voice paging has been used by public safety for decades. This technology delivers emergency notification information at a slow pace compared to today's digital world. The advent of datacasting presents a unique opportunity to serve emergency notifications to first responders in a more efficient manner, over a greater distance, and with better coverage than ever before. The timing is perfect for further development of this concept. The following highlights the key ideas presented in this paper:

- Digital delivery of information will greatly increase the speed of reception, thus decreasing response times.
- Datacasting capacity allows for dozens of separate dispatches within seconds.
- A centralized paging system serving a large region will decrease mutual aid requests.
- A larger coverage footprint will allow departments to notify members outside their jurisdiction.
- Transmitting infrastructure is already in place.
- Receivers could also support live audio streaming, video, data files, maps, and sensor data.

Open and Public Knowledge of Datacast Paging

The contributors of this paper acknowledge that this concept is part of the public domain. The concept and further development of such products supporting this concept should be openly available for all to use without formal, informal, implied, or explicit restriction or permission. The desire is to prevent a proprietary implementation which could cause interoperability issues, increase costs, and decrease quality incentives. Regardless of what is developed or where the industry takes this concept, it is time to upgrade the paging and call notification technology for public safety personnel. This should be done as an open standard-based approach that enables the technology to support different manufacturers, eliminating dependency on any single manufacturer.

References

[1] Sadowski, Allan; Grasso, Red; Engel, Fred; Woodlief, Adam; Public Safety Datacast Paging, 2017.02.13.

Building a Core Network to Seamlessly Connect Data Producers to Data Consumers

Azita Manson
OpenZNet Inc.
Mountain View, California, United States
azita@openznet.com

Abstract – With maturity and adoption of Next Gen TV standards, broadcasters are poised to benefit from surplus bandwidth capacity. This poses several questions regarding how this increased capacity can be utilized by the suppliers to target and deliver their content to end-consumer devices. Can an open exchange platform enable seamless connection to a myriad of broadcasters and diverse set of selected equipment vendors? How easily bandwidth can be discovered, reserved, and utilized to deliver the packages? Are there any precedence in such technologies and what are the similarities and differences between them? Can such a platform be scaled nationally and beyond? This white paper addresses some of these questions and describe some fundamental design considerations for a successful deployment of such system.

Introduction

The increased bandwidth capacity generated by the broadcasters can be utilized in a wide range of use cases such as delivering

- Updated maps to vehicles
- Navigational information to drones
- Educational content
- Multimedia content to billboards
- Multimedia content to kiosks and monitors
- Caching of bulk data or multimedia content
- Public and safety alerting

In addition to building mission-driven and profitable business models around such a delivery system, a key aspect of adoption by the content suppliers and broadcasters, is to provide an open and well-defined interface and a developer community to support it. This enables stakeholders to demonstrate new business models and opportunities quickly and efficiently. Creating such a developer community reduces the high cost of development and integration.

To better understand how such a system can be built and operated, we must first define what a broadcast pipeline is and how it compares with other systems in the market.

This paper is excerpted from the Proceedings of the 2022 NAB Broadcast Engineering and Information Technology (BEIT) Conference, © 2022, National Association of Broadcasters, 1 M Street S.E., Washington, DC 20003 USA.

Broadcast Pipeline

A broadcast pipeline works like an oil pipeline, where the pipeline is owned and operated by a different company than supplying the oil. The companies owning the pipeline can then lease pipeline to the suppliers for delivering their content from point A to point B, at which point, it can be picked up by a different delivery system. The similarity ends there, since there is a one-to-one relationship between pipelines owners and the suppliers for the period it needs to transfer the oil, while for the broadcast pipeline, one or more suppliers can share the same broadcast pipeline.

While there are similarities with other technologies on how to utilize and optimize the broadcast pipeline, due to unique and dynamic nature of broadcast delivery system, none of these technologies applies directly; however, some aspects of them can be used and borrowed, while building these systems:

- Ad placement in a broadcast channel
- Oil pipeline reservation and delivery
- Networking Quality of Service (QoS)
- DOCSIS (Cable Data Delivery) channel allocations
- Airline reservation – or any other form of 1:1 reservation

To see how the broadcast pipeline is utilized, we must first define the workflow of such a system.

Workflow

The following diagram shows a simplified workflow for such a delivery system:

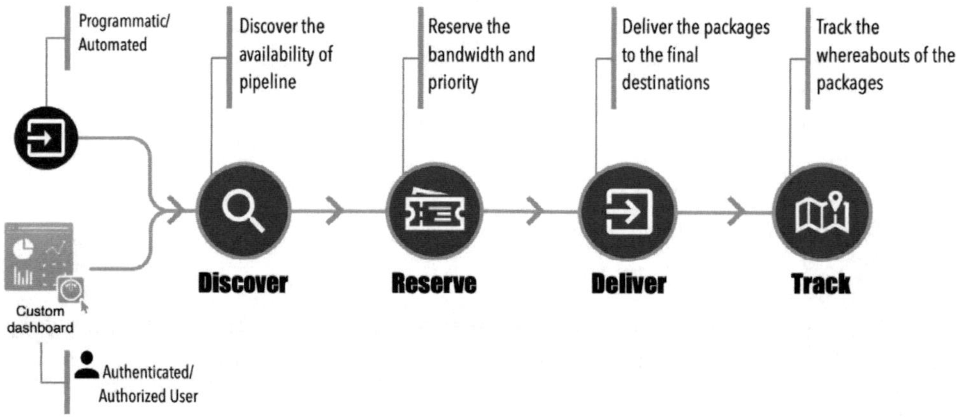

FIGURE 1: SIMPLE WORKFLOW

For a successful adoption of such a system, the system must seamlessly transition between these steps and follow a set of fundamental design principles must be considered:

- Cloud-based architecture handling connectivity from a wide range of systems across different physical locations
- Highly automated and scalable system to satisfy the requests, as the demands grow
- Flexible, configurable, and programmable interfaces to interact with different delivery equipment requirements
- High-level of security for connectivity among the interfaces
- Secure sandboxes accessible to authenticated and authorized users
- Wide system security and health check monitoring

Discovery

For the suppliers to be able to discover the availability of bandwidth across multiple delivery systems, the supplier must interface with the system and be able to discover:

- Participating broadcast station
- Area of coverage
- Availability of desired delivery time window
- Bandwidth availability
- Signal quality and strength
- Cost

Once it is determined the delivery pipeline, the supplier must be to complete the reservation process.

Reservation

Once the discovery process has been completed and broadcast station(s) have been selected, the supplier must be able to easily reserve and schedule the delivery of the packages over the selected broadcast pipelines.

Delivery

Upon successful reservation of bandwidth over the selected broadcast pipelines, the suppliers must easily be able to provide packages to the systems. A successful deployment of such a system includes both programmatic and automated ingest interfaces, as well as an easy-to-use web-based dashboard accessible only by an authenticated and authorized user for sending and monitoring lifecycle of the packages.

To complete the delivery process, the following steps must be taken:

- Ingest
- Verification
- Transformation
- Storage
- Scheduling
- Targeting
- Packetizing
- Transmission
- Reception

Due to diversity of software and systems deployed on both the supplier and broadcast delivery system, the system must provide a set of standardized interfaces and well-defined packaging compressions.

For accurate and proper retrieval of the packages, several steps must be followed:

- Ingest/Create – The packages are ingested either programmatically via an API or created via dashboard by dragging and dropping the package to the system.
- Verification – The content must be verified to meet the requirements of the system.
- Transformation – Once the packages are verified, then will then be normalized and organized into their proper sandboxes.
- Storage – It is then securely stored and only accessible by the authorized users and delivery systems.

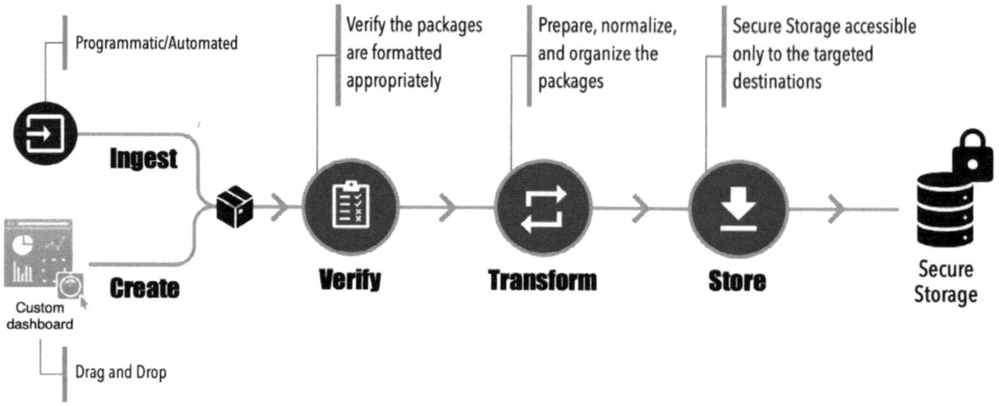

FIGURE 2: PACKAGE RETRIEVAL AND PROCESSING

During the reservation process, a schedule and target destination has been defined for the packages stored in the secure storage. Once the packages are ready to be transmitted, they are then handed off to the specific third-party vendors to be packetized and transmitted over the air.

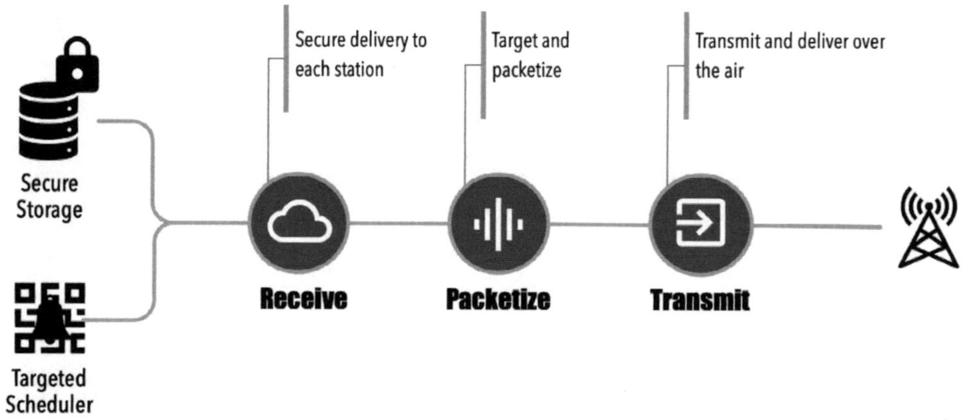

FIGURE 3: PACKETIZING AND TRANSMITTING

If the targeted devices have tuners, they receive, consume, and terminate the content. If the targeted devices are connected to a gateway device with a tuner, it then serves the content to the targeted devices.

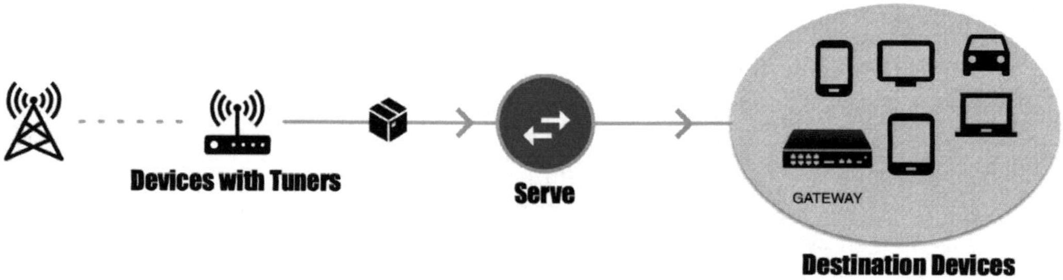

FIGURE 4: RECEPTION

Tracking

Tracking is an important aspect of the system, as it documents the whereabouts and lifecycle of a package once the reservation has been successfully completed. Upon the successful transmission and delivery to end-consumer devices, the billing process can begin. Here are some of the examples of the lifecycle of the packages during its delivery process:

- **Ingested**: Package has been successfully retrieved from the supplier
- **Verified**: The verification process has been successfully completed
- **Scheduled**: Package has been scheduled for transmission
- **Delivered**: Package has been successfully delivered to its end destination; this state is only available, if there is a two-way communication with the end-destination devices
- **Consumed**: Packaged has been consumed by final targeted device; similar to above this state is only available, if there is a two-way communication with the targeted device
- **Expired**: As part of the lifecycle of a package, the package has been expired, as the delivery time-window has been missed.
- **Archived/Deleted**: Once a package is delivered, it might be archived or marked for deletion, depending on the business logic and rules

Conclusion

As the Next Gen TV is being widely adopted and deployed, the broadcasters can benefit from the additional bandwidth capacity to serve either their mission or business ROI. A successful business model is highly dependent on several factors:

- Making it easy for the suppliers to discover and reserve the additional bandwidth
- Building a developer community around such a system to reduce the development and integration costs
- Creating an interoperable system that works with a myriads of vendors

This paper has provided a glimpse into all processes and steps required to deliver content over the broadcast pipeline. For a more in-depth description of our proposal, please see our submission for ATSC 3.0 Core Network. Please contact me with any questions regarding this paper.

Advanced News Workflows

Ernie Ensign
Sinclair Broadcast Group
Hunt Valley, Maryland, United States
eensign@sbgtv.com

Abstract – New camera technologies and workflows now allow us to address three major pain points that have impeded field acquisition of news for decades:

1) little to no metadata associated with field content,
2) delays between field acquisition of media and production/distribution, and
3) much of the source content is lost and cannot be repurposed.

This paper describes how new camera technology can integrate metadata and workflows to overcome these pain points and expose value in the form of, greater speed to distribution and increased time value of news, lower workflow friction enabling greater efficiency, and greater discoverability leading to increased re-use and monetization.

Current State and Past Workflows

In 1996 Bill Gates authored an essay titled 'Content is King.' In it he stated, "Content is where I expect much of the real money will be made on the internet, just as it was in broadcasting" [1]. Gates often gets credit for coining the phrase, but it first appeared in several mediums prior to his essay. Even though the phrase's origins may be hazy, the concept is not. No matter how news is packaged, it always comes down to substance and not the delivery mechanism. With the constant need to feed digital platforms such as Facebook, Twitter, YouTube, TikTok, as well as station-owned websites and over the air broadcasts, the need for delivering more targeted content and increasing engagement is expanding rapidly. Video traffic represents approximately 66% of all mobile data traffic today and is projected to rise to 77% by 2026 [2]. Newsrooms need to be ready to handle the increasing need of news consumers.

These consumers are also searching for expanded content to provide more context on stories. A typical television news story averages around only a minute and a half, yet often there's 30 minutes or more of raw content gathered for the story. There are numerous opportunities to provide extended targeted content on the web whether in the form of raw interviews, full surveillance videos, police bodycam footage, or any other documents or material that may be available on a viral story. As we look to build modern data driven workflows, a review of current and past technology can assist to identify deficiencies to providing content for the future news consumer.

The first fully digital nonlinear editor debuted at NAB in 1989. It would take another 15 years for computer processing power to advance enough for remote editing to be available on laptops in the field. The news gathering and remote field edit process have remained mostly unchanged for nearly two decades. A videographer spends several hours, or more, recording various media clips required for their story. After the video is shot, the operator transfers those files from the camera to the laptop, edits them into a finished package, and then sends the final file via wireless back to the station. It's quite a leap in technology compared to the days of film for news, but the major shortcoming of the process is that much of the content remains remote and on the cutting room floor so to speak. It's not easily available for viewing in a station's edit system or for distribution to any external platforms in a timely manner. In many cases during the gathering process, the first piece of content may not be available on a story for six hours or more. There are of course mechanisms to get content back to the station if urgently needed, but they interrupt the process. A more automated way of moving that content back to the station is needed to meet the needs of the modern newsroom, and it needs to be mostly transparent to those involved with little or no user intervention required.

Many newsrooms may have standard operating procedures to move raw media into editing systems after the videographer returns to the station so it can be used in other places. But with more employees working remotely and the myriad of reasons why the content may not get deposited in the (Production Asset Management) PAM, changes to current workflows need to be made. Not to mention, by the time the material makes it back and made available for distribution, time has passed and numerous viewers and potential revenue opportunities could have been missed.

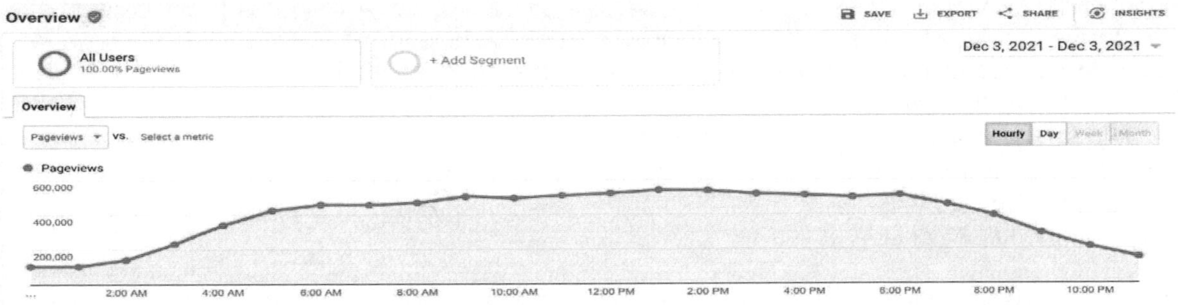

FIGURE 1: DIGITAL PAGE VIEWS SHOWING A TYPICAL DAY OF WEB PAGE TRAFFIC FOR NEWS VIEWING. THE PEAK IS EARLY AFTERNOON. BY EARLY EVENING NEWS VIEWERS START TO TREND DOWNWARD. THE NEED FOR MORE CONTENT WHEN VIEWERS ARE AT THEIR PEAK IS PARAMOUNT.

Traditionally there are three news gathering cycles in TV newsrooms, morning, early evening, and late evening. There's a several hour period of gathering for each of those cycles and then fresh content flows in shortly before the broadcast. With today's ever shifting consumer content demands the shift to acquire and distribute in real time is critical.

Are Newsrooms Ready for the Future?

Are current news workflows ready to meet the future needs of digital content consumers? There has been a seismic shift in engagement on social platforms as the industry has worked to funnel more eyes to websites. However, the fact remains many newsrooms still have strong division between digital and traditional broadcast workflows. Newsrooms have transitioned closer to a digital first philosophy and can quickly post a story to web but it's still a challenge to get those first pictures back and posted quickly. If digital teams need pictures or video to complement the text only version, then they are reliant on a journalist in the field to take some action to receive content. Newsrooms need a better mechanism to automate content acquisition and ingest. The lines need to continue to blur between digital and traditional broadcast workflows to capitalize on the future increase in video consumption on web and mobile. What follows is an exploration into one proof of concept that can aid in supplying a constant flow of video content that can be delivered quickly to news consumers in the future.

Advanced News Workflows

Bonded cellular was reviewed as a means to acquire more content. Its ability to transmit live video from anywhere with a small backpack has transformed the news gathering process and reduced reliability on expensive trucks. However, there are limitations to providing a constant stream of content from every videographer back to the station with this technology. First is the storage consideration presented by not only higher bit rates that would have to be recorded but also the continuous stream coming from the camera capturing an immense amount of material in between shots that would not be useable. Content producers would not have the time to review all that would be recorded. There are cost limitations as well with having to assign a device to every news gatherer across a large organization. Bonded cellular is another live tool that will continue to be used, but the feasibility of an operator being always tethered to a backpack is just not tenable. There had to be a better way.

Since a constant linear stream would not solve providing immediate access to all content from every news gatherer, the focus shifted to file-based workflows directly from the ENG field cameras. With bandwidth and data usage a concern, careful consideration must be taken with what bit rates to use. With social and web platforms typically occupying smaller screens the need for all material to be high resolution isn't necessarily required. Therefore, we can leverage the X-AVC H.264 proxy created at the camera at lower bit rates for these platforms rather than mezzanine formats. Expanding 5G networks can supply the throughput for quick transfers from the cameras to the station. There are four aspects to consider for enhancing news workflows:

- Metadata from the Newsroom Computer system
- Media Object Server Protocol
- Transfer and ingest
- Future workflow considerations

The overarching design goal was to use existing newsroom tools wherever possible as a foundation to building enhanced workflows. The existing newsroom computer system (NRCS) and most importantly the assignment queue was the first building block for the workflow. This queue holds the necessary metadata already collected as part of the daily editorial process. Assignment editors build a list in the NRCS, and through a connection to the Sony NRCS gateway the stories are exposed and pushed to the cameras in the field. The focus was to make that process happen with no additional user intervention.

Event Tim	Slug	Reporter	Crew	5A	6A	5P	6P
	DESK INFO						
	TEST SLUG						
	WJLA STORIES						
	WJLA LIVES						
	REPORTERS						
9AM-5PM	HISPANIC CHAMBER BUSNINESS	SCOTT/ASH	RICH G.			VOSOT	
5PM	LCPS BOARD MEETING	NICK	FRANK			LVOSOT	
	GAS PRICES FOLO	TOM	BEN			LPKG	LPKG
	PG SCHOOLS CEO	BRAD	DALE				LPKG
	THERAPIST RULING	SAM FORD	MATT			PKG	
	DC DIAPER BANK	HEATHER	MIKE V			PKG	
	DC DOG REUNION	CAROLINE					
6AM	RUSSIA/UKRAINE NATIONAL	AHTRA	DC BUREAU		LIVE		

FIGURE 2: TYPICAL DAILY STORY ASSIGNMENT QUEUE. THE METADATA FROM THE NRCS.

The Assignment Queue list is transferred to via the MOS Protocol to a Sony NRCS gateway on the internal network. Currently only the "rostorysend" messaging of the protocol is supported by the Sony NRCS gateway which allows for the <roID>, <storyID>, <storyslug> and <storyNum> tags to be transmitted. Future updates will support additional tags. The workflow required the deployment of an additional MOS gateway to handle the communication from the NRCS to the Sony metadata gateway. There was also minor configuration of the assignment rundown. The Sony NRCS gateway that is receiving the MOS traffic from the NRCS runs as a lightweight service and can run on a virtual machine or PC with low system requirements.

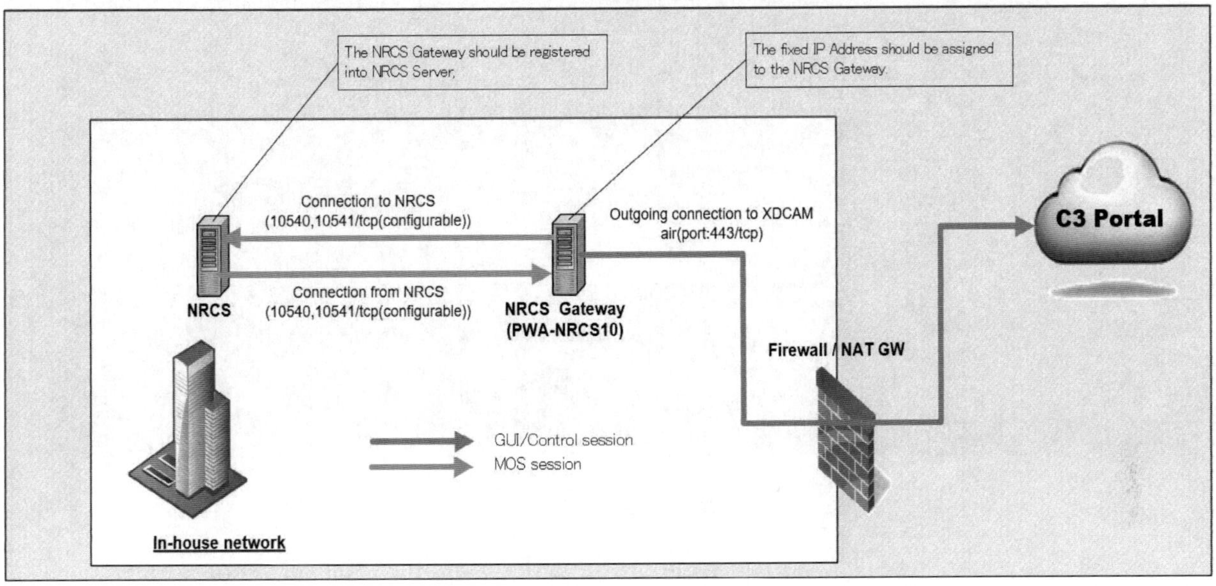

FIGURE 3: NRCS COMMUNICATION WITH GATEWAY AND C3P

Figure 3. shows the MOS traffic communicating over ports 10540 and 10541 to the Sony NRCS gateway. With the NRCS configured and communicating with the Sony gateway, the stories contained in the assignment queue are now forwarded over port 443 to the Sony C3P (Camera, Connect, Cloud) portal. The portal is the broker that communicates with each camera and automatically pushes the NRCS metadata to each camera that is registered in C3P. It is possible to set up groups that contain a subset of cameras that can be isolated to individual NRCS systems.

With configuration between the newsroom system and the cloud complete, there is setup on the camera to enable the automated delivery of the proxy clips via FTP. The process is fairly-straight forward and is set up as follows by:

- Loading a USB WIFI dongle into the camera
- Enabling WIFI on camera and connecting to phone or hotspot
- Configuring FTP delivery location for the clips
- Entering a web address and credentials for C3P connection

Now that the connection to the C3P cloud is complete, the camera is ready to receive metadata from the NRCS. By executing a couple of clicks through the camera menu the photographer can scroll through and view the available stories of the day and select their story assignment.

FIGURE 4: METADATA AVAILABLE TO THE REMOTE FIELD CAMERA

Once the story is selected, each individual media clip recorded from that point forward is labeled with the story name. A sidecar planning metadata XML file with a pointer back to the original NRCS story is also saved on the camera SD media card. This could potentially allow for the original NRCS item and its associated metadata to be extracted and delivered to archive along with the completed story in a future phase.

After the metadata has been loaded for the story, the videographer can begin shooting. As soon as the first proxy file closes it begins to transfer. The clips are then transferred from the WIFI connected camera via FTP directly to the storage location. The media does not flow through the C3 portal. As soon as the files arrive on the file server a transcode engine acquires the clips from the storage location and delivers them into the PAM for editing or digital delivery. The clips arrive typically about two minutes from the time the file closes on the camera. This will vary depending on cell bandwidth available and the length of the clips. There is some retraining that must take place for camera operators surrounding when the record button is started and stopped. Since the files will not transfer until closed operators need to be aware of this and potentially segment clips sooner than they may have traditionally. At this point the content is now available for viewing by the entire newsroom including digital content producers.

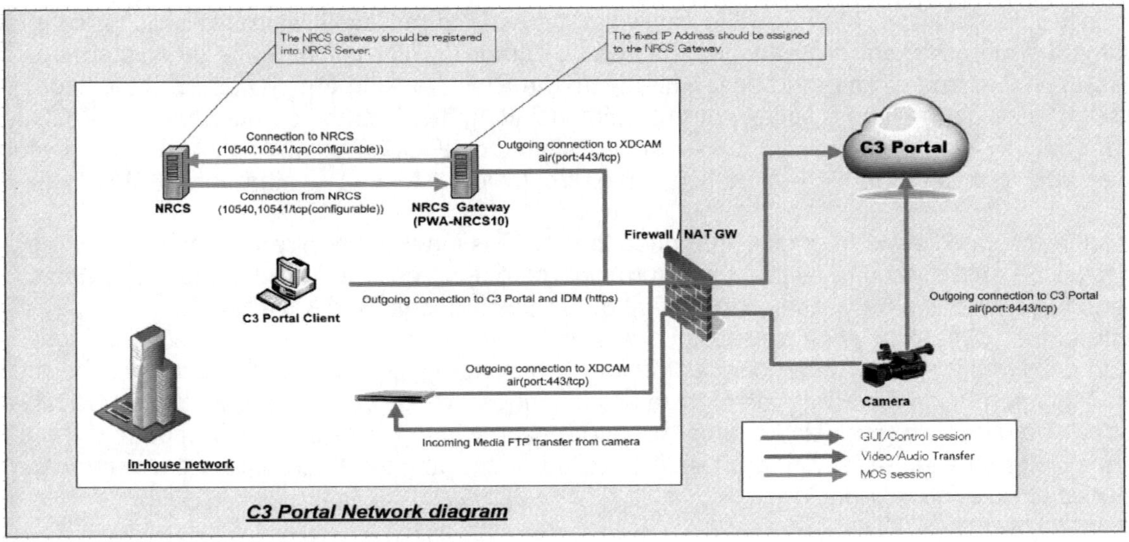

FIGURE 5: END TO END WORKFLOW

Future Considerations

This first phase of the overall workflow provides a grounding point for several divergent future phases. One potential path could be to simply increase the bit rate. As data costs and cloud storage costs decrease and 5G bandwidth increases, that may get the resolution closer to an acceptable quality for on-air material.

A second but albeit more complicated phase two would be to edit in proxy and relink only the high-resolution bits needed directly from the camera. In this manner the need for a videographer to download content to their laptop in the field would be negated. Instead, content would already be available as proxy media in the PAM and immediate remote editing could begin when the gathering process was complete. This would also potentially reduce the need for costlier laptops as processing requirements would be significantly decreased.

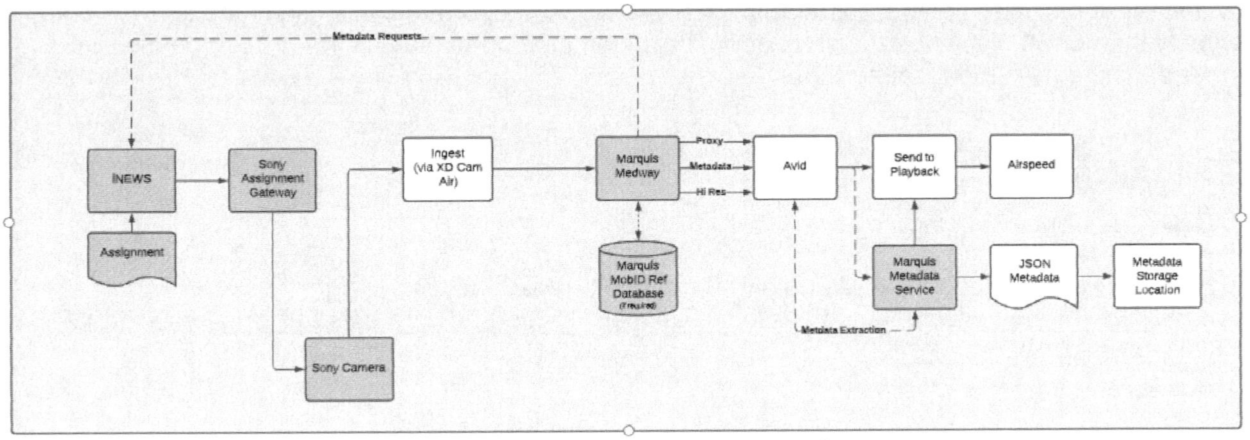

FIGURE 6: POTENTIAL FUTURE WORKFLOW.

In this conceptual workflow, Marquis Medway would be used to retrieve the proxy asset, ingest them into the PAM and track them in a relational database. The proxy files will arrive at the system before the high-resolution files and will need to be ingested into the PAM tracking the unique ID of the clips. A limited set of metadata will be available at this point including the Assignment ID from the NRCS and Geolocation ID. Further metadata will be available within the NRCS. This solution will look to include additional calls to extract the high-resolution video directly from the camera through a C3 API.

A key part of the workflow is to ensure that once the proxy is ingested and registered within the edit system it will be able to recognize that the future high-resolution copy is linked to the proxy and to ingest and register it as a new resolution variant of the same asset. This will allow the editing system to make use of the "Dynamic Relink" capability and switch seamlessly between the proxy and high-resolution copy in the Media Composer. As the Marquis system will know the ID's used for the proxy it will save this information for use in the high-resolution ingest workflow. There are options available for how this will be managed, such as keeping this information within Avid Interplay and performing a query on Interplay when the high-resolution is being ingested or creating an external reference database that can be used to hold the information.

The Marquis Medway system allows proxy content in Avid to be used as a trigger for the restoration and import of partial segments from the high-resolution source media. A sequence can be exported to Medway through a pre-configured Media Composer 'Send To...' target that outputs an AAF describing the sequence. Medway can then show the segments of proxy content in the sequence and use this to trigger a partial restore of the required media (plus configurable handles). The restored segments are then ingested to Avid and registered against the parent asset, allowing the original sequence to be switched to the higher quality media through the 'Dynamic Relink' function of Media Composer. In this case, the high-resolution media will be managed by the Sony system and Medway will be extended to allow it to make the restoration requests on the Sony C3P API.

Conclusion

Early use is promising, and significant implementation hurdles remain for future workflow modifications. But we are optimistic that vendors will address the remaining challenges to realize the vision. All content that is shot can be viewed and used on any platform within minutes of it happening. Newsrooms can see stories as they develop in real time. Speed to social, digital, or air from all crews of any content is multiples of times faster than past workflows. Reporters can log in to the edit system remotely through VPN and log the story as it's happening to improve efficiency. Future phases will further enhance newsroom capabilities.

References

[1] Gates, B "Content is King," p. 1

[2] Ericsson Mobility Report "Mobile data traffic outlook" (2020), p. 13 https://www.ericsson.com/4adc87/assets/local/mobility-report/documents/2020/november-2020-ericsson-mobility-report.pdf

Advanced Security Using a NoCode Media Integration Platform

Julián Fernández-Campón
Tedial
Málaga, Spain
jfcampon@tedial.com

Abstract – Security is one of the hot topics today as many key companies in all sectors has suffered cyber-attacks with a huge impact in their business. While ransomware attacks have been around for many years, there is evidence that organized cybercrime entities are investing heavily as the number of attacks and the sophistication is growing exponentially. Garmin was hacked in July 2021, and that left millions of devices without service for a few days, causing a huge impact in the business [1].

Some companies from the M&E industry have also been affected but these attacks, such as Sinclair Broadcast (Oct 2021) [2] and more recently SIC [3], the third the third terrestrial television station in Portugal.

Media Companies are aware of this situation and security has become a priority but workflows in the M&E industry have specific needs and the standard security policies for the IT word are not sufficient or are not fully tailored for the Media Management challenges. In this paper it will go from the levels of security in the IT world to understand the key principles and challenges, then outline the specific requirements in the M&E Industry and finally how a NoCode Media Integration Platform can provide advanced security policies required in the content production workflows.

Levels of Security: Zero Trust and the VPN Privacy Fallacy

Implementing an efficient security schema can be really challenging. The first step and the most important is the definition of the scope which will determine the systems involved and the associated procedures. And from that point, choose the proper tools and configure all the elements to meet the desired goals.

In addition, security does not affect to a single layer (network, operating systems, applications, etc.) and it can vary from the very basic protection up to really complex and sophisticated mechanisms. It can also be seen from many different angles depending on what elements they focus, the approach or the protection level.

Here is an example of three levels of security based on the protection they offer:

- Level 1. Basic protection. Mainly adopted by small companies, this level focus on providing an 'entry level' of security consisting of just securing the access to the corporate network by a firewall and scanning the connected devices for viruses, malwares, etc. This level is mainly passive and does not cover targeted attacks, such as DoS Denial of Service and neither acts proactively to analyze the different systems/applications for security issues.

This paper is excerpted from the Proceedings of the 2022 NAB Broadcast Engineering and Information Technology (BEIT) Conference, © 2022, National Association of Broadcasters, 1 M Street S.E., Washington, DC 20003 USA.

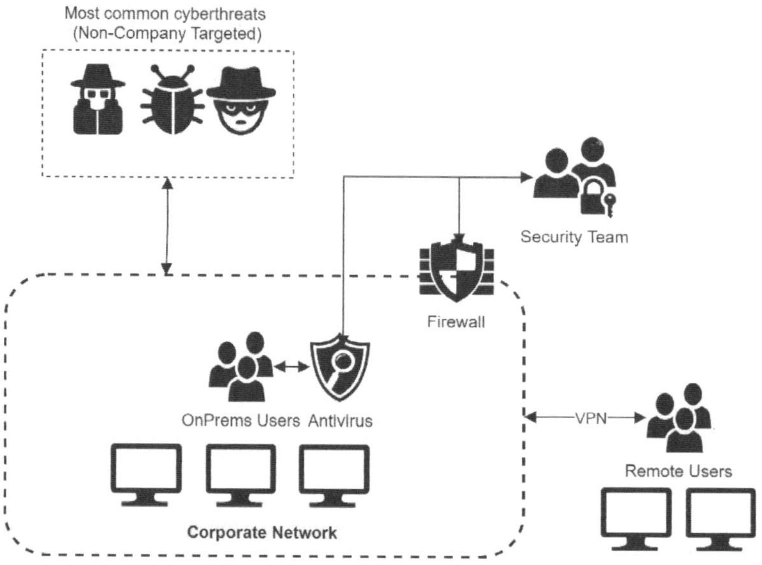

FIGURE 1: BASIC PROTECTION SCHEMA

- Level 2. Medium protection. This level adds more proactive actions such as periodic vulnerability assessments, penetration tests and security improvements in other elements such as email scanning, spam filtering and even adding some IDS (Intrusion Detection System) and IPS (Intrusion Prevention System). More sophisticated firewalls can be configured to isolate the access to each of the individual business units in the company. This approach is usually adopted by midsized companies.

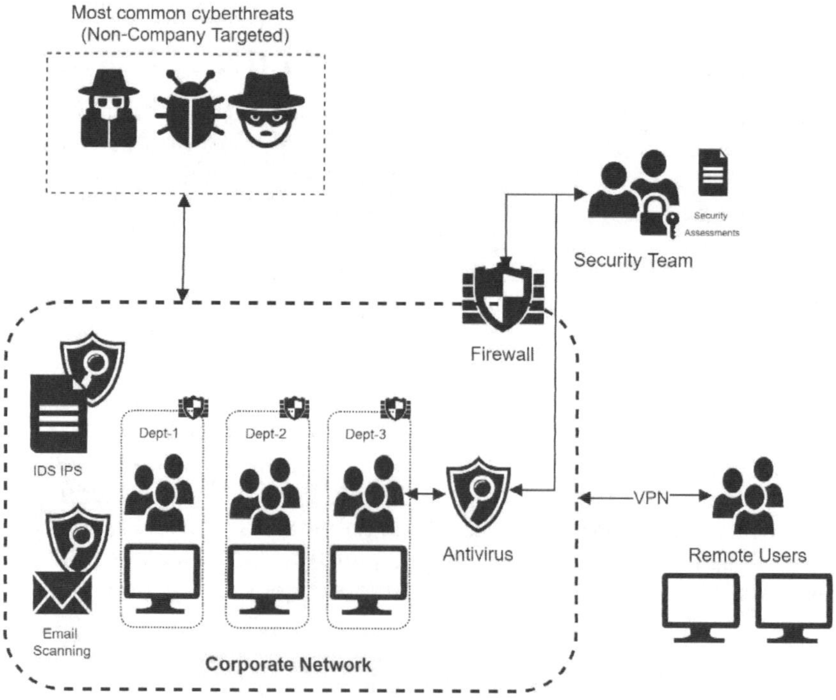

FIGURE 2: MEDIUM PROTECTION SCHEMA

- Level 3. Improved protection. In this level are added more security features such as DLP software (Data Loss Prevention) for sensitive and personal information, SIEM (Security Information and Event Management) and even more proactive and frequent analysis for thread monitoring and quick incidents response. This approach is adopted by large enterprise and regulated industries.

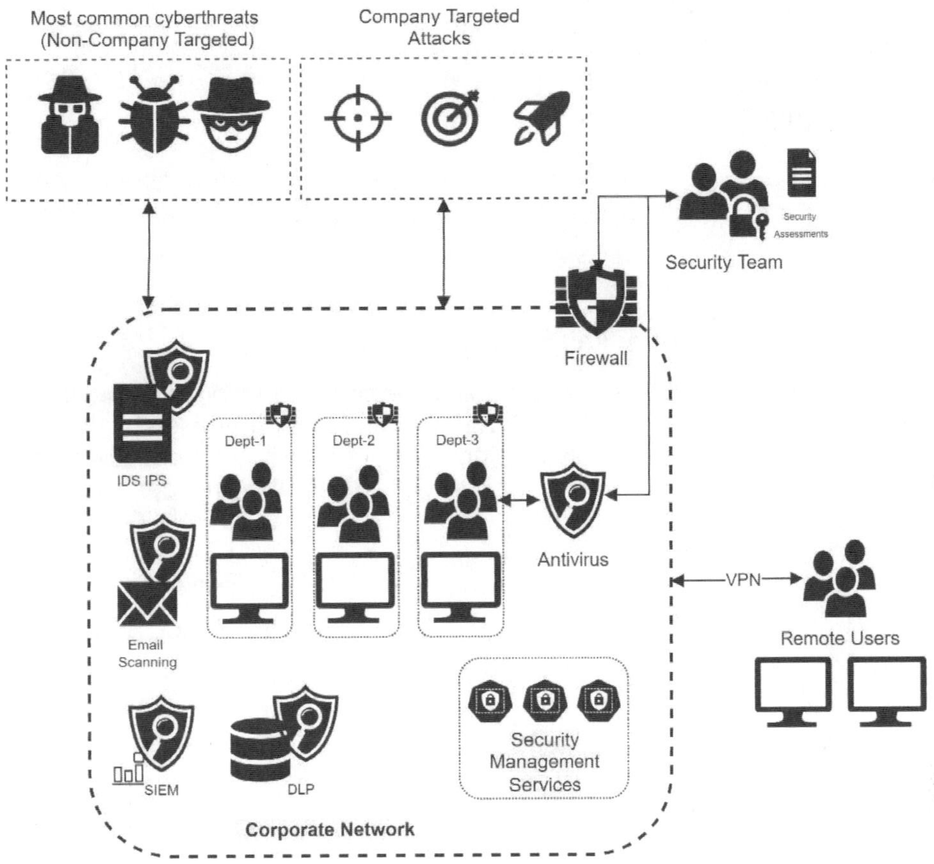

FIGURE 3: IMPROVED PROTECTION SCHEMA

But something to point out is that regardless the approach that is adopted all of them are focus on the IT: they are not covering anything related to Media, and more importantly in many cases is used a VPN (Virtual Private Network) to give access to the corporate network to enable the external operation. The VPN gives a sense of false security as it's equivalent of having the key of a building and once you're in, you can have access in one way or another to the different resources as the security is relaxed. This is also known as the 'VPN Private Fallacy'.

To avoid this, the VPN needs to be wrapped into a Zero Trust security schema, as one of the points to be secured (the external access).

According to Wikipedia [4], *"The zero trust security model (also, zero trust architecture, Zero Trust network architecture, ZTA, ZTNA), sometimes known as perimeterless security, describes an approach to the design and implementation of IT systems. The main concept behind the Zero Trust security model is **"never trust, always verify,"** which means that devices should not be trusted by default,* *even if they are connected to a permissioned network such as a corporate LAN and even if they were previously verified."*

There are many points to be verified in a Zero Trust model, many of them include:

- Segregation of Duties.
- Least Privilege Access
- Business Segmentation
- Multifactor Authentication (MFA)
- Just-in-time Access
- Logging, Auditing

Implementing and maintaining a Zero Trust strategy is mandatory to be protected and secure against cyberthreats, or at least to minimize the impact and quick incidents recovery in case a security breach happens.

Security in IaaS, PaaS and SaaS Models

In the previous section we saw different strategies to secure the platform without defining who is responsible for it. In the case of the traditional system with is fully managed by the organization that is using it, it's clear that the full responsibility relies on them. But in other models where there is some kind of service involved, the responsibility is shared between the service provider and the organization using the service. This is shown in figure [4]

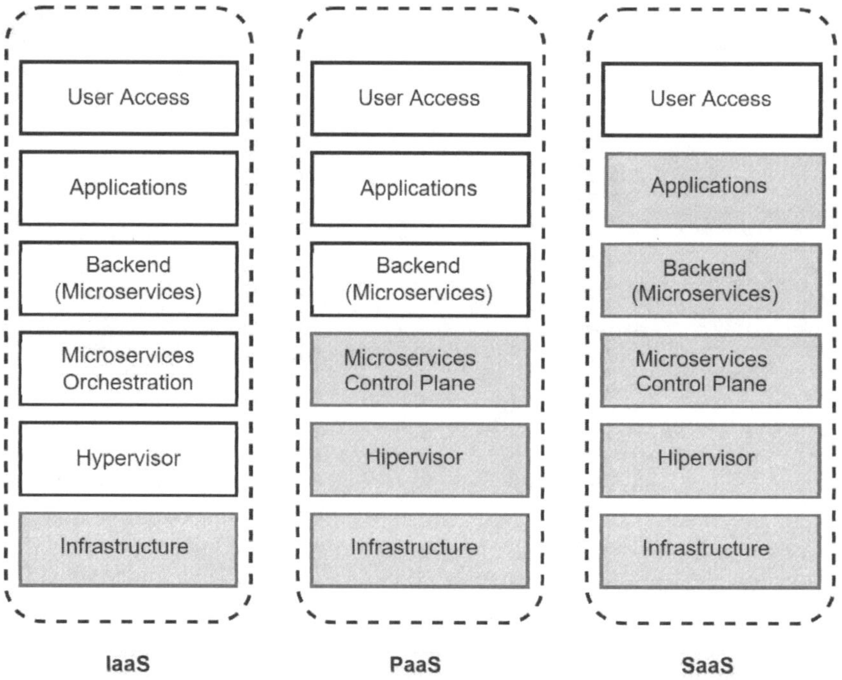

FIGURE 4: SECURITY RESPONSIBILITIES

In the first model, the Infrastructure as a Service (IaaS), the service provider is responsible only of securing the infrastructure. In the Platform as a Service, the service provider needs to secure the Infrastructure and the Microservices Orchestration Service, which is generally Kubernetes, with the different services available in public clouds, EKS in AWS, GKE in Google and AKS in MS Azure and finally in the third level the service provider needs to secure up to the applications.

Security in the M&E Industry

It's clear after reviewing the different security levels and responsibilities that security in the IT world applies in the M&E industry, but there is something else needed to secure the assets and the Content Production. Movielabs in the 2030 Vision [5] has prescribed the way to go as a set of best practices and six principles:

- Security Principle 1: Security is intrinsic to every workflow and does not inhibit the creative process. This states that the workflow needs to be secure by design, but a balance is required for not to limit the creativity of the artists that are producing content.
- Security Principle 2: The Security architecture addresses challenges specific to cloud based workflows. This states that the security applies to any infrastructure, including cloud deployments and is divided in three sub-principles that reinforce it by focusing the security on the workflows, assets and integrity.
    - Principle 2.a. Security is centered on workflows, rather the architecture they run on.
    - Principle 2.b. Security is centered on Assets, rather their storage and transport
    - Principle 2.c. The integrity of assets, processes and workflows is protected.
- Security Principle 3. Production, workflows, processes and assets are secured, even on untrusted infrastructure. Using untrusted infrastructures is part of our everyday operation: Editing Workstations, networking, storage locations and even more now with the need of the remote operation.
- Security Principle 4. The content owner controls security and workflows integrity. This principle empowers the content owner to define the security procedures to adapt it to each production needs/situations.
- Security Principle 5. The security can be scaled to appropriate levels and can integrate with existing security policy and management systems. Once all the principles above are met, security needs to flexible and adaptable depending on the type of workflow, requirement, etc. and more importantly use and integrate with external systems to offer a complete security framework.
- Security Principle 6. The security architecture limits the spread of any breach and is adaptable to the evolving threat and response landscape. And finally, it needs to be future proof, to adapt to any new threads that will come in the future.

The key takeaway from these principles and in general from the 2030 Movielabs vision is that security needs to be applied at a higher level. The IT Infrastructure and all the applications need to be secured but seen as a whole and defined, controlled and managed at the production level, and not the individual elements. This high-level security management will have a reflection and some actions on the different subsystems: network, storage, services, applications, etc., but needs to be abstracted and seen from this angle and not from the IT infrastructure and can be seen as a *"Workflows Defined Security"* which focus on the operation, the content and not where the workflows are physically executed.

The NoCode Media Integration Platform Concept

This is a new paradigm as defines a platform where all the applications are integrated, adds media management capabilities and workflows are defined with a NoCode approach, allowing non-technical people to implement the content supply chain processes and production workflows by themselves, without the support of the IT Team nor programmers.

The NoCode Media Integration Platform is based in three key pillars:

- Common Workspace. Applications go to the media, and the media is in the most suitable and cost-effective location on each site.
- Common Interface. All the applications (systems) integrated present the same methods: Transcoders, Editing Environment, Storage Locations, etc.
- Common Datamodel. The metadata in the platform is standardized so any application can access to the metadata generated for any other without the need to translate it.

And these are some of the key technical benefits:

- One to Many Integrations. Each application is responsible of integrating within the platform, offering same methods for the same operations, eg. Send To, Get From, Transcode, etc. and doing the required transformations from the specific datamodel into the standardized datamodel in the Media Integration Platform.
- Media Location Abstraction. The physical location of the media is abstracted by the platform using a UUID. This makes the workflows 'unaware' of the media location.
- Swappable Components. As the interface and the datamodel is standardized, it's possible to change applications easily without having to recode or reconfigure the workflows.
- Workflows Duplication. Related with the previous point and the media location abstraction, duplicating a workflow to change any integration or to deploy in another location (eg. from OnPrems to the Cloud) is really easy.

A typical simple exchange workflow can be designed with these steps:

- Get From. Move the media from the Inbox to the Common Workspace.
- Analyze. Analyze the media using MediaInfo.
- Transcode. Transform the media using ffmpeg
- Send To. Send the transcoded media to another S3 destination.

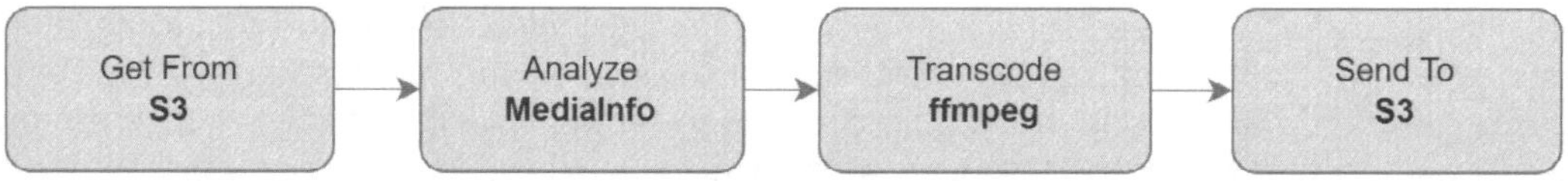

FIGURE 5: SIMPLE EXCHANGE WORKFLOW

Advanced Security using a NoCode Media Integration Platform

In addition to the above-mentioned benefits of the NoCode Media Integration Platform, there are some others not so obvious, but equally important in terms of security that makes it suitable to implement advanced security schemas to meet the most demanding customer needs.

These are the key features in a NoCode Media Integration Platform that add advanced security:

- Common Interface. The common interface is one of the pillars of the platform as it offers the same methods for the same operations, but also protects the applications from the external access offering a single layer to be secured, instead of securing each individual system. These systems can be isolated and protected to prevent attacks.
- Media Abstraction Location. The physical location of the media is not known, it's leaving in a protected storage location and it's given a one time access.
- Infrastructure as a Code [6]. The deployment is adapted to each infrastructure, defined as deployment scripts using tools like Terraform [7] that includes the use of the specific security mechanisms adapted for each target (Kubernetes cluster on prems line OKD [8], AWS, Google, Azure, etc.).
- Zero Trust Approach. Some of the points are achieved naturally by the platform:

- Business Segmentation, Segregation of Duties is provided by the abstraction of the methods provided by the common interface and the workflow defined security that will be explained in the next section.
- One time access, the media location abstraction layer will give access on demand to the specific content as the physical location is abstracted

And others that need to be implemented in the NoCode Media Integration Platform as part of the secure design:

- Least Privilege access. Defining the proper security principles such as Access Control Lists, Roles and User Groups where the access to any resource is denied by default, unless explicitly granted.
- Multi Factor Authentication. Integrating IAM (Identity and Access Management) systems that integrate with tools like Google Authentication, Microsoft Authenticator or more proprietary and/or device dependent tools.
- Logging, Auditing. Registering all the activity in the platform, including anomaly detection, notifications and any other mechanisms to have visibility of all the events, access to the media, applications and services and any other tasks done by the users or any external application.

Implementing a Workflow-Defined Security Schema

Workflows-Defined security consists of defining the security at the workflow level which includes the execution of the individual steps of the workflow but also access to the media content and the protection of the applications that are used. This is a top-down approach where security is defined at the top, attending on the production needs, what access is required on each workflow step and location to what content and application, and that is propagated seamlessly to all the services and IT systems within the platform regardless the physical location.

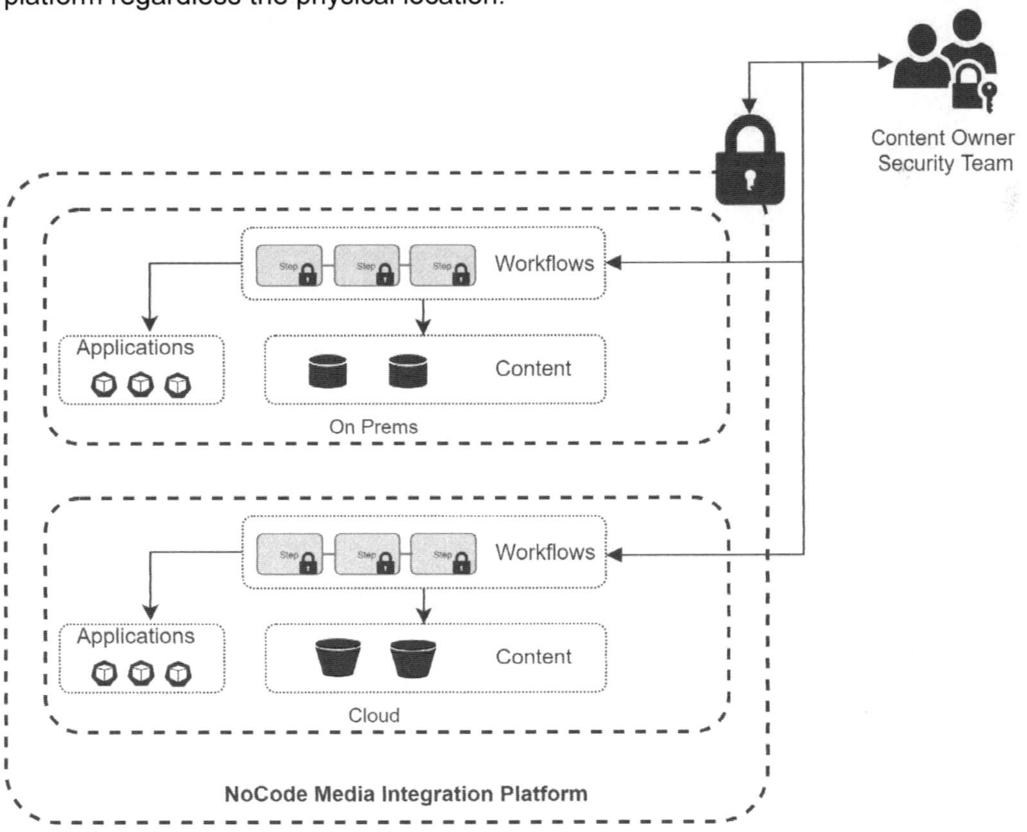

FIGURE 6: WORKFLOW-DEFINED SECURITY

As shown in the previous picture, security is managed globally at the workflow level and these workflows are responsible for giving access to the applications and media involved.

Meeting the Movielabs Security Principles

This section shows at a functional level how the Movielabs security principles are met. This is really key to validate that the NoCode Media Integration Platform is aligned in terms of security for the content production.

1. **Security is intrinsic to every workflow and does not inhibit the creative process**. In a NoCode Media Integration platform workflows are abstracting the users from the internal complexity. It includes adding the security mechanisms needed for each stage without the user being aware of having to add explicit stages to add content protection. In the previous workflow all the stages are secured, eg. In the Get From the microservice executing the operation will interact in this case with the S3 storage service to get the link to the content and move if required to the common workspace. Any of the URIs are known and it's hidden within the platform. The application does not have access to any of this information and the user does not need to care about it. The same applies to the rest of the steps in the workflow when accessing to the media o to the applications that are manipulating it.

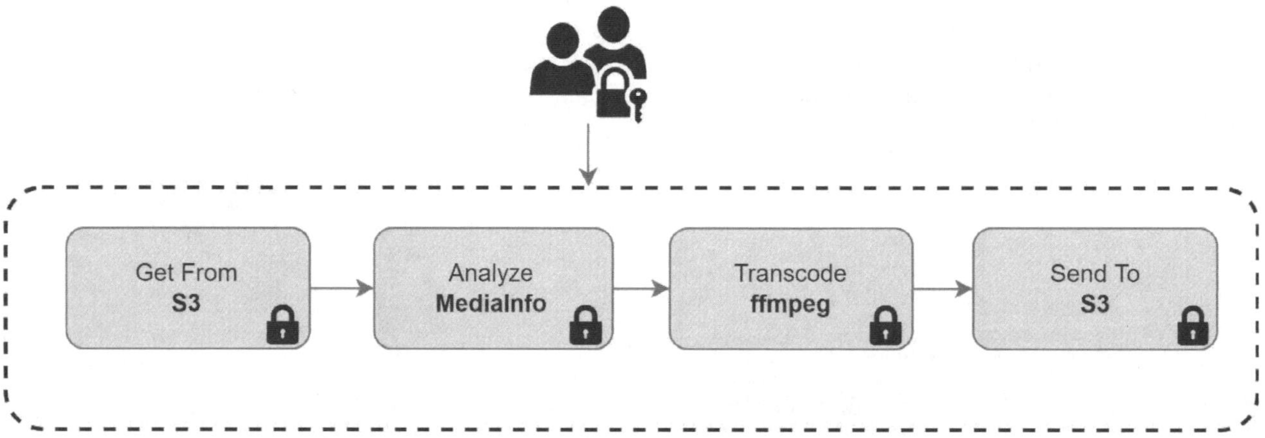

FIGURE 7: SIMPLE EXCHANGE WORKFLOW SECURED

2. **The Security architecture addresses challenges specific to cloud-based workflows**. The deployment needs to take advantage of the security mechanisms and best practices on each cloud at the infrastructure level. In addition, it will add additional security at the workflows and integrations level as each plugin encapsulates all the configuration including the specific API keys, private keys or any other information needed to integrate the applications and run the workflows in the Cloud.
    a. <u>Security is centered on workflows, rather the architecture they run on</u>. The level of abstraction offered by the NoCode Media Integration platform in the deployment (using the Infrastructure as a Code) and in the execution (Media abstraction location) allows the users that are designing the workflows to focus on the permissions for the specific stages of the workflow, by providing a one-time-access to the content only to the specific user(s) that need to execute the task. Figure [8] shows how the access is granted only to specific users for editing and for the QC.

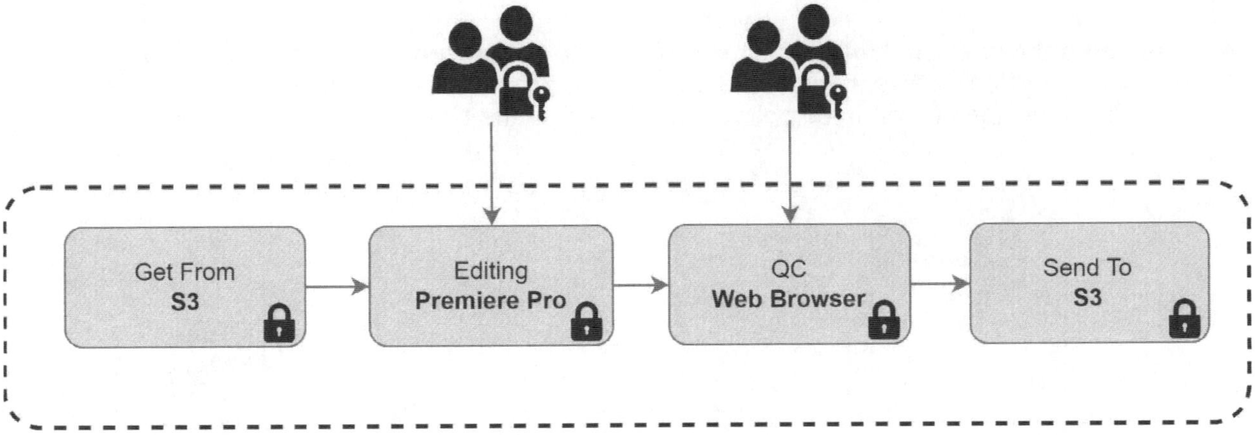

FIGURE 8: EDITING WORKFLOW

b. Security is centered on Assets, rather their storage and transport. Assets are protected and the physical location is not known. It's given a onetime access that will depend on the physical storage and transport, and again, that logic will be implemented by the integration plugin and so abstracted to the end user in the workflows definition.

FIGURE 9: ASSET-FOCUS SECURITY

c. The integrity of assets, processes and workflows is protected. The access to the platform is restricted and verified with advanced security mechanism, such as MFA (Multi Factor Authentication). The visibility and execution of the workflows is controlled by user profiles, as well as the access to the content. There is thus a complete protection at all levels.

3. **Production, workflows, processes and assets are secured, even on untrusted infrastructure**. This is also related with the fact that the security is at the workflow level and there is a zero-trust approach, so even accessing from an untrusted infrastructure will be quite unlikely that a hacker get access to the content or workflows as they are not published and the physical location is unknown and even with temporary access, the platform will be verifying constantly the identity of the user logged in.

4. **The content owner controls security and workflows integrity**. The NoCode Media Integration Platform offers a unified security management schema. The content owner decides and configures the appropriated policies depending on the type of content/operation.

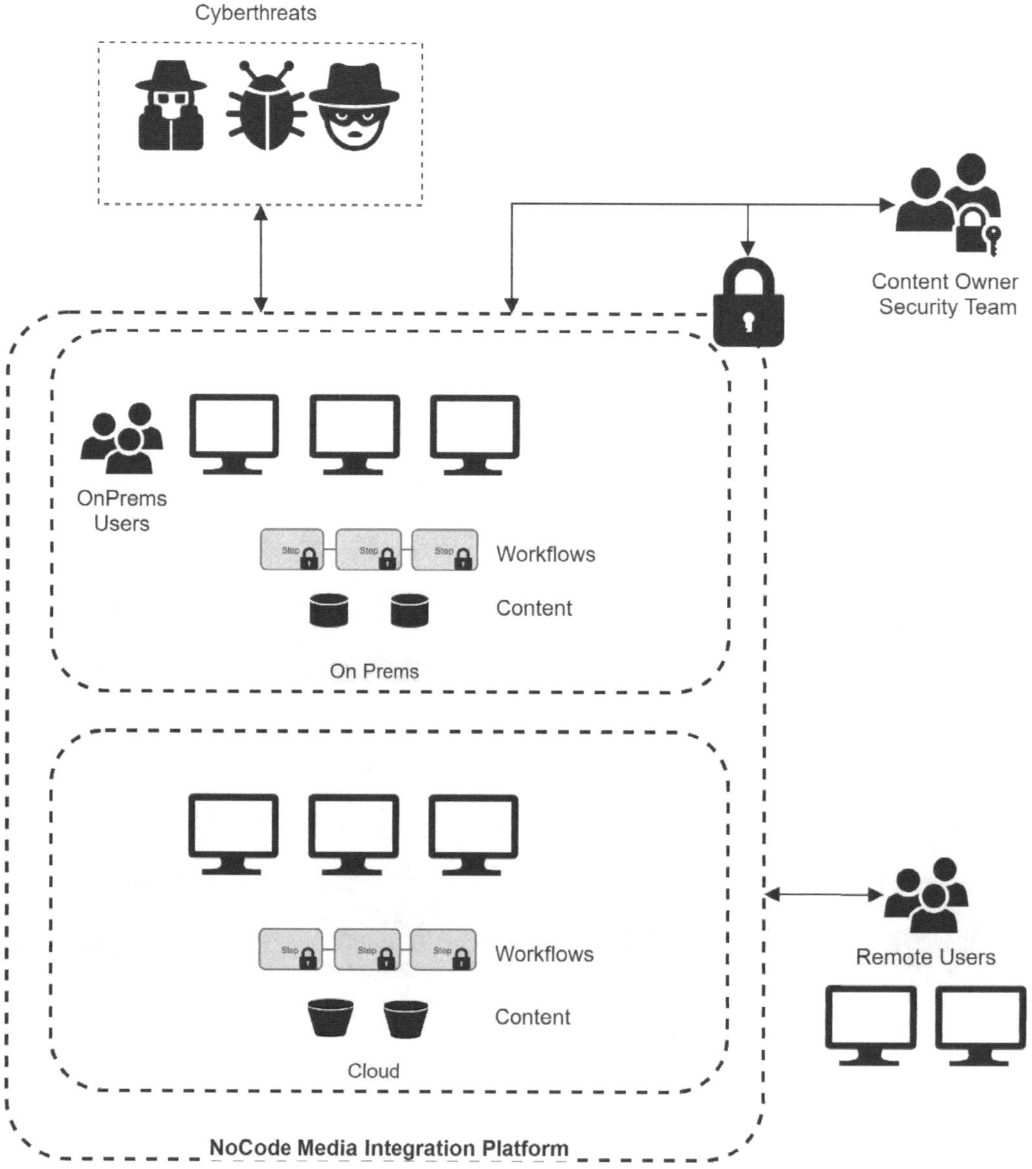

FIGURE 10: GLOBAL SECURITY MANAGEMENT

5. **The security can be scaled to appropriate levels and can integrate with existing security policy and management systems**. This can be achieved as the NoCode Media Integration platform integrates many different applications that can be selected depending on the level of security that needs to be achieved. For small companies it can be sufficient to have simple security policies that will scale up to sophisticated security policies for large organizations that integrate advanced security management systems within the platform and as part of the workflows, seamlessly by the users of the platform.

6. **The security architecture limits the spread of any breach and is adaptable to the evolving threat and response landscape**. This principle is fulfilled as the nature of the NoCode of the Media Integration Platforms is to be future proof. New security systems can be integrated within the platform and be seamlessly available in the workflows as the platform users are not aware of them, this is abstracted by the platform.

Conclusion

Security has become a key priority as there are growing exponentially the number of attacks and the sophistication and resources invested by hackers. The use of cloud services and the remote operation has increased the risk as the platform is more exposed.

Choosing the proper security policies and systems is a real need, but workflows in the M&E industry have several implications regarding media management, systems integrations that requires a different, global, more workflow-oriented approach instead of the IT approach focus on the infrastructure.

In a NoCode Media Integration Platform security can be derived naturally to implement Zero Trust policies and meet the Movielabs Security principles.

References

[1] https://www.cshub.com/attacks/articles/incident-of-the-week-garmin-pays-10-million-to-ransomware-hackers-who-rendered-systems-useless.

[2] https://www.bloomberg.com/news/articles/2021-10-20/sinclair-broadcast-hack-linked-to-notorious-russian-cybergang.

[3] https://www.theportugalnews.com/news/2022-01-02/expresso-and-sic-sites-hacked/64408

[4] https://en.wikipedia.org/wiki/Zero_trust_security_model

[4] Movielabs 2030 Vision and The Evolution of Production Security. https://movielabs.com/prodtech/ML-2030-Vision.pdf and https://movielabs.com/prodtech/security/ML-Securing-the-Vision.pdf

[5] Infrastructure as a Code. Wikipedia. https://en.wikipedia.org/wiki/Infrastructure_as_code#:~:text=Infrastructure%20as%20code%20(IaC)%20is,configuration%20or%20interactive%20configuration%20tools.

[6] Hashicorp Terraform. https://www.terraform.io/

[7] Kubernetes OKD distribution. https://www.okd.io/

NDI in the Master Control Room

Fabio Gattari
Etere Pte Ltd, Singapore
Singapore
marketing@etere.com

Abstract –It's no secret that NDI is the new face of revolution in information transmitting. Capable of higher quality information transfer, broadcast quality videos can be delivered and received in a frame-accurate format. This high-quality transmission makes it an ideal choice for switching in a live production environment within the Master Control room. NDI streams are able to transmit a full frame full resolution version of videos and a lower resolution proxy version that can reduce the load on networks when streaming to multi-viewers, vision mixers and preview screens. Its ability to multicast and switch to full resolution version of video transmissions makes it the ideal choice to use in a Master Control room.

Introduction

This paper discusses the characteristics of NDI, its advantages in a master control room, its respective challenges and how to overcome the challenges effectively. In the inclusive case study, we will explore how Mondo TV in Belgrade, Serbia, integrates NDI technology in the master control room effectively, making it the world's first fully NDI connected system. The station which went live on 28 June 2020 manages 40 playout channels using NDI technology and Etere Ecosystem software. In addition, the station also runs a live internet TV on Mondo TV's online platform as well as on Telecom Serbia's website for the local market.

NDI Compatibility in the Master Control Room

NDI has is known for its reliability. NewTek claims that NDI is an efficient, long-distance transmission capable of simultaneously sending high-quality, low latency videos to multiple sources. NDI enables video and audio sources to be shared bi-directionally across a standard Ethernet local area network, eliminating the need for direct connections, costly cable runs and infrastructure upgrades. Furthermore, Newtek NDI is available royalty free for both developers and users.

These characteristics make NDI the perfect choice for use in broadcasting, its long reach and stability an improvement from the hassle and unreliability of SDI connections. In fact, NDI is already being incorporated into many broadcasting companies around the world. However, SDI being a long-standing information transfer technology is not without its own merits. In this paper, we will explore the extent of NDI's advantages in the Master Control room, its respective challenges and how to overcome them.
In terms of usage in the Master Control room and in fast paced environments, NDI has a few main advantages, namely its flexibility in creating new linkages quickly and its cost efficiency qualities.

This paper is excerpted from the Proceedings of the 2022 NAB Broadcast Engineering and Information Technology (BEIT) Conference, © 2022, National Association of Broadcasters, 1 M Street S.E., Washington, DC 20003 USA.

Broadcast Potential of NDI

The broadcast potential of an IP protocol is the most important aspect when considering usage in the Master Control room. As such, one of NDI's biggest advantages is its ability to run multiple streams simultaneously at no additional costs.

A user can send a large video file to the mixer with low latency, while at the same time, stream it as well as capture it on another network, making it not only flexible, but very useful in a fast-paced environment such as in the Master Control room. NDI is a bi-directional protocol that supports multiple streams of video simultaneously. It supports all resolutions, frame rates and video streams.

Additionally, any generation of NDI is able to work with seamlessly with other generations as NDI is backwards compatible in software. Although NDI's high powered, flexible stream format is what makes the stream so well known, it can also be a hindrance in terms of usage in the Master Control room. The NDI stream does not come equipped with a fixed name, thus creating a disparity in its usage in the Master Control room.

As the master control requires a fixed connection, the NDI protocol cannot be used without additional help. Each signal used must be equipped with a unique identifier in the NDI name. This step takes great importance when linking the signals correctly, for example, two studio signals can be named "Studio 1" and "Studio 2". This step is important, and it requires prior planning, especially when the source signals start to number in the hundreds.

To ensure a continued stable connection, the dynamic list of sources must be periodically checked for conflicts. There is also the issue of the burden on the server, as NDI takes up a bandwidth that increases with the size of the audience. For example, a HD stream may consume up to 200MB, and that number will increase to 800MB if 4 listeners tune in. But this hiccup is not without a remedy. An NDI stream can be kept usable when it is applied with strategic planning in place. The bandwidth needs to be used with proper planning to avoid unnecessary streams and to effectively allocate streaming servers to distribute videos to many locations, similar to SDI distributors.

To eliminate the challenge of manual switching in transmission, the integration of Dynamic Host Configuration Protocol (DHCP) enables an automated and dynamic assignment of IP parameters, IP address, network mask, switch address and name server addressed to each PC/server on the LAN network. In addition, DHCP also automates the assignment of network-parameters to the related network devices.

As a result of the integration, the manual tasks of creating and maintaining of IP address assignments for each client/server is eliminated. The integration of DHCP in Etere IP transmission provides a centralized, server-based setup that reduces the manual tasks of creation and maintenance of IP address assignments for each client/server, the centralized database pools resources for an effective optimization and eliminates duplicate resource assignments. Moreover, DHCP allows operators to automatically upgrade the software on client systems.

Ease of Incorporation in Master Control Room

But is NDI feasible to be used in the Master Control room in terms of its ease of incorporation? The nature of NDI's cost saving and flexible qualities can make the transition from SDI systems to NDI achievable. The move from SDI to a new IP protocol can commonly be seen as a costly change, but with NDI, users are able to use low-cost converters to port over SDI signals to NDI.

NDI is capable of working in tandem with SDI, so the user is able to incorporate NDI for an initial network that links to an SDI endpoint, and switch completely to an NDI endpoint when their budget becomes available. However, an issue with NDI would be that the NDI stream by itself, requires additional software to utilize it to its full potential. For example, the necessity of audio and video monitoring requires an add-on software to be used in the workflow.

With NDI, the signals are not linear, so it can be seen as simple to monitor, but to be truly efficient, the user needs to have an intelligent software to avoid unnecessary bandwidth use. Fortunately, NDI's popularity has continued to extend its support for many software applications in the market today. Popular software programs such as Skype, EasyWorship, and many others offer native NDI support. The requirement to employ additional software programs to use NDI can be seen as an unnecessary expense, but the nature of the software usage is kept scalable, meaning that there is no additional cost to expand the NDI powered systems, unlike with SDI, where the use of hardware increases the expense whenever there are system changes.

NDI's popularity in the software field has ensured that it has many compatible hardware such as NDI enabled cameras from notable companies such as Panasonic, to optimise the Master Control room usage. NDI connects a wide variety of video devices including cameras, converters, video mixers, graphics systems and many other production devices.

Even if the user's initial systems are not compatible with NDI, with the use of an NDI convertor, NDI can be incorporated into the Master Control room. Without expensive high-speed network infrastructures or a major overhaul of existing infrastructure, broadcasters can transition to a versatile IP video facility easily with a NDI setup.

Usage in Master Control Room

For usage in a Master Control room, another important factor to consider would be its ability to preview streams before the content goes on air. Usually in an SDI connected environment, the user will be able to fulfil this with a flip of a switch, but with NDI, a user requires sufficient connection time in order to do the same. This can be offset by using a system that makes use of a preset/program architecture, so that the switch can operate without any glitches. To connect with all NDI signals is not a correct option, the system can have hundreds of NDI signals and connecting to them all could use up all your bandwidth. Thus, an intelligent pre-set must be used to be sure that the next source is always ready.

Cost Saving Quality of NDI

Cost efficiency is one of NDI's biggest advantages. Let us explore the importance of NDI in the master control room and exactly how cost-efficient it is. The broadcast industry is fast-evolving and fast-paced. As the demand for better quality broadcast increases, the need for more adaptable technological tools increases.

There is increasingly demand for both broadcasters and production companies to produce and transmit higher frame rates, leading to higher costs. But with the use of NDI, video feeds can be transmitted with high quality and low latency, at a much lower cost than a conventional SDI setup. In addition, NDI's ability to link multiple inputs is crucial when operating multiple cameras from the Master Control Room.

In contrast, an SDI setup does not allow devices that are connected on a network to communicate with one another.

In addition, by using NDI enabled IP workflows, broadcasters can leverage the benefits of a streamlined IT and IP configuration process for a more cohesive network infrastructure. Newtek also states that NDI is the first ever codec to provide multi-generational stability as once a video signal is compressed, there is no quality loss.

All in all, transitioning to IP does not have to result in higher costs. In fact, moving to IP can be a long-term investment in cost-savings. For one, NDI allows businesses to respond quickly to changes. Unlike NDI, there are limitations in delivering content in more conventional ways such as an SDI setup. For example, the higher costs of scaling can restrict the flexibility and adaptability of the company.

On the contrary, using NDI allows broadcasters to add or manage more content across new media platforms easily. Furthermore, by eliminating the need to invest in new high-speed network infrastructure, costs are kept down while efficiency is maximized. NDI's performance over a GigE network makes it possible for broadcasters to tap on their existing infrastructure using SDI equipment. NDI setup provides the broadcaster with a stable connectivity for users to transmit high quality videos across IP networks in real-time with little to no delay. This provides broadcasters with maximum flexibility and cost-efficiency when moving from a conventional SDI setup to an NDI workflow.

Case Study: Mondo TV Usage of NDI

FIGURE 1: MONDO TV SETUP

One prominent example of live NDI usage would be the Mondo TV systems. A large-scale broadcaster in Belgrade, Serbia, Mondo TV needed to manage 40 playout channels other than 3 recording studios and control room, ingest facility and incoming feeds, plus audio dubbing facilities. During the project initialization phase, Mondo TV decided that an NDI system was the most ideal fit for their business objectives. One of the reasons is that NDI architecture features one to multiple outputs. This allows all the departments at Mondo TV to use a common NDI signal.

The system has been designed without the use of any SDI cables. Etere has outfitted their systems with NDI technology to connect all their software, hardware, and channels together, all without any SDI. Mondo TV is currently one of the world's largest solely NDI powered broadcasting systems. Mondo TV incorporates Etere's integrated end-to-end management software across their software-defined newsroom, transcoding, playout, monitoring, air sales and scheduling modules, allowing them to manage their workflows from a centralized database with complete connectivity across the whole facility.

The system connects three production studios, each equipped with multiple robot camera rigs, three studio control rooms, and three audio dubbing rooms. Each of the functions within the various rooms can be remotely controlled through the master control rooms. The wide array of outputs is kept well optimized and cost-friendly through the use of NDI, which ensures that the Mondo TV connections are constantly stable and fast, even while keeping the overhead costs low.

However, the multiple output sources means that the prearranged 1GB bandwidth reaches its maximum capacity easily. This high bandwidth makes the use of low resolutions options unnecessary. Mondo TV needs to manage their sources and destinations minutely to ensure that their operations run smoothly at all times.

As sending and receiving video streams across an IP network requires applications supporting video to be able to discover the receiving applications that are searching for video, the linkages of the NDI are one of the biggest challenges faced by Mondo TV when switching to a fully NDI based system. Additionally, Mondo TV needed to synchronize all the signals in the system to professional broadcasting standards.

To ensure a seamless connectivity, Mondo TV needed to plan their NDI synchronization before their installation can even begin. The NDI connectivity needs to be sustainable, flexible, and fully realized to ensure no errors when broadcasting began. VPK, as the chief systems designer for Mondo TV, conducted a thorough research to come up with the correct IP design that takes into account the direct and reverse DNS that is hugely beneficial to the NDI discovery and planning. The large number of channels, and fully automated systems amounts to over 150 sole NDI sources that Mondo TV needed to manage. VPK needed to design an appropriate system for a sustainable and easy discovery that will be able to display over 150 NDI sources.

Mondo TV overcomes these challenges with the use of an IP multicast system to create an environment for the discovery of NDI applications, all without any configuration needed. When using IP multicast, the multicast is seen by all the NDI receiving machines on the subnet. Source sends a single copy of data to a single multicast address which is then distributed to an entire group of recipients. This is able to distribute the NDI streams with minimum overload, thus ensuring that the broadcasts run smoothly without any risk of a crash. This method also helps to keep the costs low for Mondo TV, allowing them to reach a much wider audience without too much strain on their finances.

In addition, selecting the network location is an important criterion for the successful discovery and registration of NDI. For example, the domain network location is used for domain networks, such as those at enterprise workplaces. They are typically controlled by the network administrator and changes are usually not allowed. In such instances, the multicast DNS should be allowed at the domain level.

Driven by NDI technology, Mondo TV can stream from satellites, camera feeds, playout devices, local/remote sources and monitor all their feeds on a single dashboard.

Furthermore, being able to integrate into a centrally managed ecosystem allows the tv station to drive workflows across the facility and deliver efficiencies across the capture, production, management and delivery process.

Mondo TV has successfully implemented the world's first fully NDI connected system with a stable connectivity throughout the facility and minimal hardware requirements. It allows the station to do away with the usual master switcher panels, instead requiring only a software to manage their broadcast. This allows them to streamline their workflows and deliver content to market quickly, leading to greater productivity and efficiency.

With the flexibility of NDI, Mondo TV is able to able to fully adapt their environment into a fully IP master control system with precise timing, seamless routing and monitoring. Moreover, the solution does not require any other IP protocols, allowing the station to enjoy greater cost savings while not compromising on the reliability of the broadcast performance.

References

[1] *"NDI Benefits"*, NewTek Knowledge Base https://support.newtek.com/hc/en-us/articles/115001950714-NDI-BENEFITS

[2] Sunter, Liz. "Everything you need to know about NDI." Jigsaw24, 19 September 2018, www.jigsaw24.com/articles/everything-you-need-to-know-about-ndi

[3] Perez, Ann. *"NDI® and NDI|HX for network video production."* Epiphan Video, 4 April 2019, www.epiphan.com/blog/ndi-ndihx-network-video-production/

[4] Baker, Chuck. "Magewell Adds Cost-Saving Encode-Only HDMI- and SDI-to-NDI® Converters." NewTek Studio, 9 May 20019, www.newtek.com/blog/magewell-adds-cost-saving-encode-only-hdmi-and-sdi-to-ndi-converters/

[5] Kota, Sanjeev. *"Broadcasting Industry Embraces Ndi Protocol*

[6] *(While SDI Becomes Archaism)."* Chetu, www.chetu.com/blogs/media-and-broadcasting/broadcasting-industry-embraces-ndi.php

[7] Caliborne, Vickie. *"Video Over IP: Is NDI the Solution?"* PLSN, 4 June 2018, plsn.com/articles/video-digerati/video-over-ip-is-ndi-the-solution/

[8] "NDI Discovery and Registration" NewTek Knowledge Base https://support.newtek.com/hc/en-us/articles/218109477-NDI-Discovery-and-Registration

Optimized Camera Integration in IP-Based Workflows and Infrastructures

Klaus Weber
Grass Valley Germany
Bonn, NRW, Germany

Abstract – The increasing availability of powerful IP infrastructures opens up new application possibilities for system cameras in media and entertainment applications. Additional IP interfaces on camera base stations have enabled initial applications to be covered and experience to be gained in a first step. However, the question arises as to how the integration of cameras in IP infrastructures can be optimized in such a way that an improved workflow can be achieved for almost all use cases. This includes the possibility to adapt the bandwidth requirements of the cameras to the existing IP bandwidths, but also the possibility to do all this without external conversion of the video signals to IP signals. The paper will highlight the various challenges and present possible solutions based on camera systems with fully integrated IP connectivity.

Camera Connectivity

From Baseband to IP

Signal transmission between camera heads and camera base stations or camera control units (CCUs) has continuously evolved [1]. In the 1970s, multicore cables were replaced by triax cables, and more recently, with the introduction of UHD-1 standards, SMPTE hybrid fiber cables and connectors, where all signals except power are connected via two fiber cables, have become the de facto standard for most applications.

At the same time, signals transmitted over camera cables have been converted from analogue to digital, and the most advanced media and entertainment cameras now use IP.

Connectivity between the camera base stations and the rest of the infrastructure was based on multiple baseband signals, and IP interfaces are often used for this in the latest installations. Two different solutions have been developed and specified for the IP signals, one is the SMPTE 2022 standard as a way to use serial digital video signals including embedded audio and ANC data over an IP link, and the other is the SMPTE 2110 standard where all signals are delivered as single essence streams.

Many installations that primarily use IP connectivity still require a certain number of baseband signals to be provided in addition to the IP connection.

An example of a camera base station that provides only baseband signals and a version that provides a combination of baseband and IP connectivity is shown in Figure 1. In the version that provides both baseband and IP connectivity, there is no compromise on the baseband connections and the IP connectivity is provided in addition, allowing the user to choose which of the signals to use and in what format.

This paper is excerpted from the Proceedings of the 2022 NAB Broadcast Engineering and Information Technology (BEIT) Conference, © 2022, National Association of Broadcasters, 1 M Street S.E., Washington, DC 20003 USA.

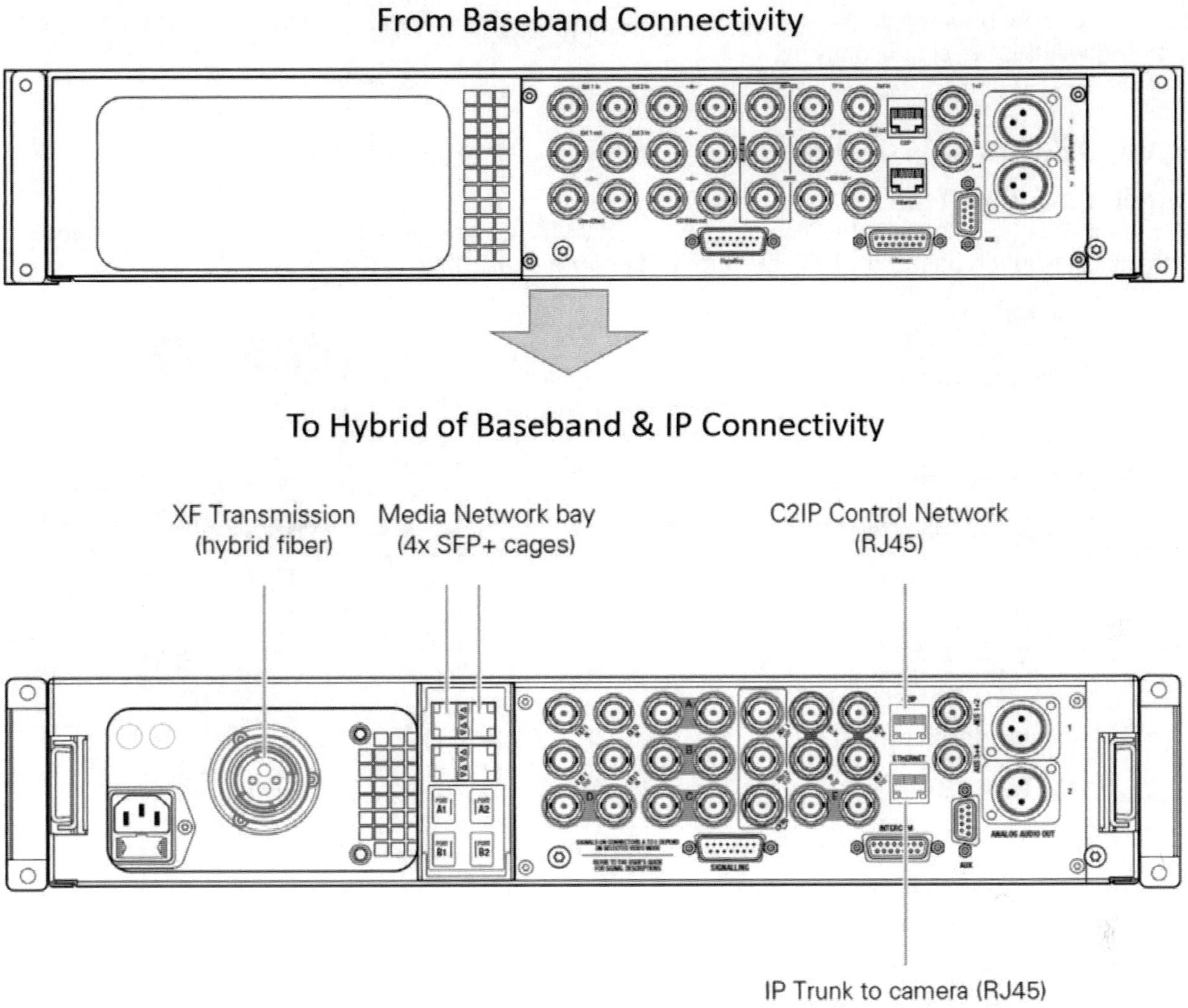

FIGURE 1: FROM BASEBAND TO HYBRID OF BASEBAND & IP CONNECTIVITY

Why Using IP

SDI video, with its recent developments around 12G SDI for single-speed UHD-1 operation, has served the broadcast market well for many years, but more and more limitations are becoming apparent. When moving to full UHD-1 operation, high-speed cameras must also be converted to UHD-1 operation; this requires three or even six times the bandwidth of single-speed operation. In addition, high frame rate (HFR) operation is required for some applications, just as there are initial discussions about 8K UHD operation. 12G SDI would require multiple connections per camera there, which also only support a relatively short cable length. It is clear that the bandwidth requirements for UHD-1 operation beyond single-speed require a more flexible and future-proof solution.

Developments in IP technology have far outpaced developments in broadcast video for many years. Moreover, IP costs per Gbit typically halve every 14 months across all components - for serial digital video they are stagnant at best. And the increasing choice of formats such as 4K, HFR, high-speed operation and the associated requirements to support all these different formats as efficiently as possible are much better managed with format-independent IP solutions. So it is not a question of whether IP will replace SDI video in broadcast applications, but rather when this will happen. It is fair to say that most new broadcast installations are already using IP infrastructures in some form and that the use of SDI will decline significantly.

Camera IP-Based Workflows

Using IP for Signal Transmission

With the introduction of the first HD camera systems with 6x speed in 2014, the first IP-based fiber transmission solution based on 10 GigE (Fig. 2) became available.

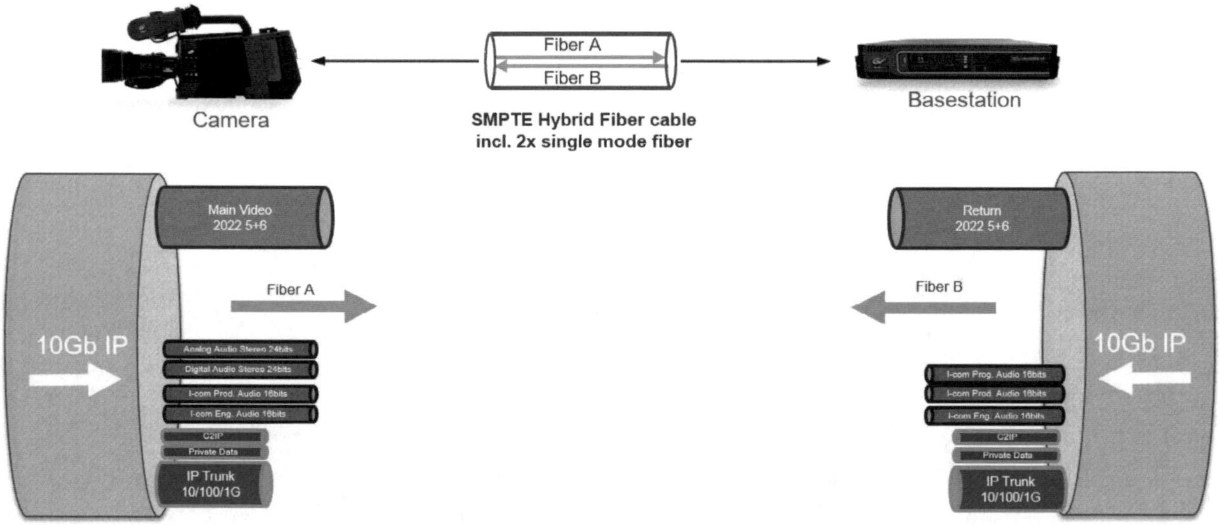

FIGURE 2: CAMERA SIGNAL TRANSMISSION OVER IP

The use of standard IP technology made it possible for the first time to use IP infrastructures to connect camera heads and base stations via DirectIP operation (Fig. 3).

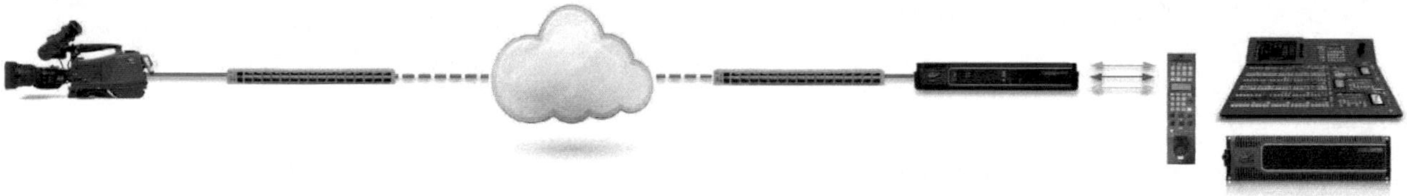

FIGURE 3: DIRECTIP CONNECTION OF CAMERA AND BASE STATION

In DirectIP operation, the camera head is given a unique IP address and all signals are routed to a specific camera base station via an IP network. When setting up the connection, it is not necessary to know to which physical port the devices are connected, as long as they use the same IP domain. For a number of years, there have been several fixed installations worldwide that use this flexible connection of camera systems via IP networks, and the benefits have been proven [2].

In fact, DirectIP was the first application of its kind to utilize existing IP infrastructures for fully integrated remote productions in some of the most demanding broadcast applications.

Since all signals between cameras and base stations are transmitted either uncompressed or visibly lossless compressed with low latency, there is no degradation of image quality or limitation of functionality.

When this IP-based fiber solution was developed, SMPTE ST 2022-6 or AVB were the two options available on the market to provide the required functionality. SMPTE ST 2022-6 was selected as the best solution for the specific requirements and still provides an excellent solution for point-to-point connectivity between cameras and base stations.

The interim introduction of the SMPTE ST 2110 standard now provides a more efficient workflow solution for IP broadcast infrastructures. The camera base station, which receives the camera signals as 2022-6 streams, can now convert them into the new SMPTE ST 2110 compliant streams. In addition to this IP conversion, the base station continues to provide all baseband connectivity, manages the synchronization of all signals and powers the camera in all applications via an SMPTE hybrid fiber cable between the camera head and the base station.

Next Steps to Further Integrate Broadcast Cameras into IP Infrastructures

In a full IP broadcast infrastructure, baseband signals are usually not needed or can be generated via IP gateways if needed. So why still use a camera base station or other hardware to convert the signals from the camera to the required IP standards and not connect the camera directly to the IP infrastructure via commercial-off-the-shelf (COTS) IP hardware (Fig.4)

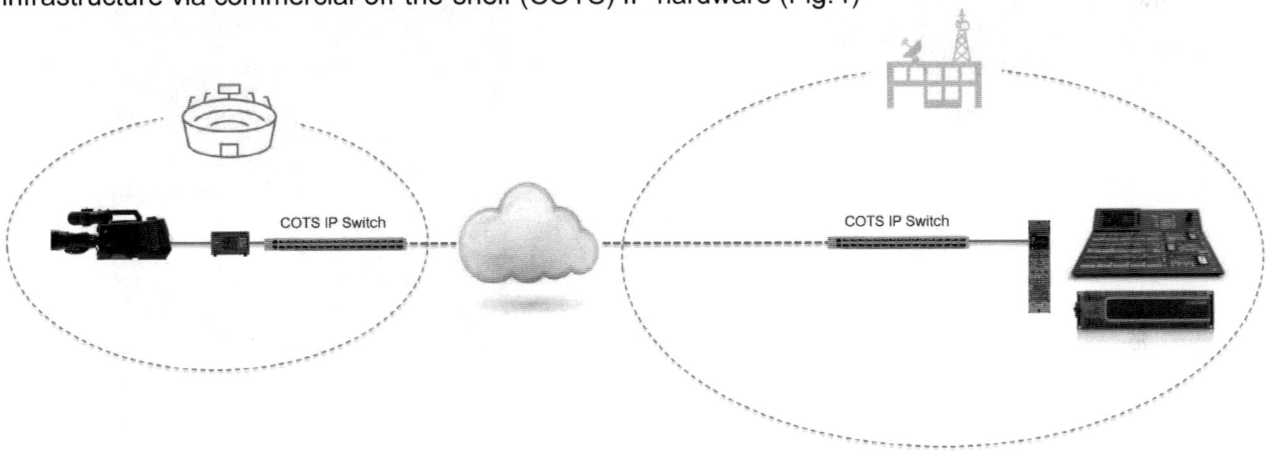

FIGURE 4: NATIVEIP CAMERA CONNECTION TO IP NETWORKS

One of the advantages of an IP infrastructure is that it does not matter where a device is physically located, as long as other devices can identify it by its unique IP address. In a typical broadcast production, the cameras and cameramen need to be in a specific location, such as a stadium or production studio, but the rest of the equipment and operations staff can be anywhere - not even close to the production site. With a native IP connection of the cameras to the IP infrastructure, the camera manages all outgoing and incoming IP streams itself, so no additional active hardware is required other than a local power supply. This drastically reduces potential sources of error and also reduces set-up time.

Another important advantage is that only one interface needs to be upgraded or changed when the bandwidth requirements of the video format or COTS IP infrastructure change. For example, while UHD-1 Single Speed or even UHD-1 HFR can fit into a single 25 Gb/s connection, all UHD-1 High Speed formats would require multiple 25 Gb/s connections or a 40 Gb/s or even 100 Gb/s connection.

Interfacing

The camera's interface to the COTS switch must support the different bandwidth requirements of today's standards, and to be future-proof, the interface must also be flexible to upgrade as requirements change. To meet these requirements, field upgradeable Small Form Factor Pluggable (SFP) or Quad Small Form Factor Pluggable (QSFP) could be used on the camera side, supporting 25 Gb/s, Dual 25 Gb/s or even 100 Gb/s.

An example of such a field upgradeable SFP solution is shown in Figure 5:

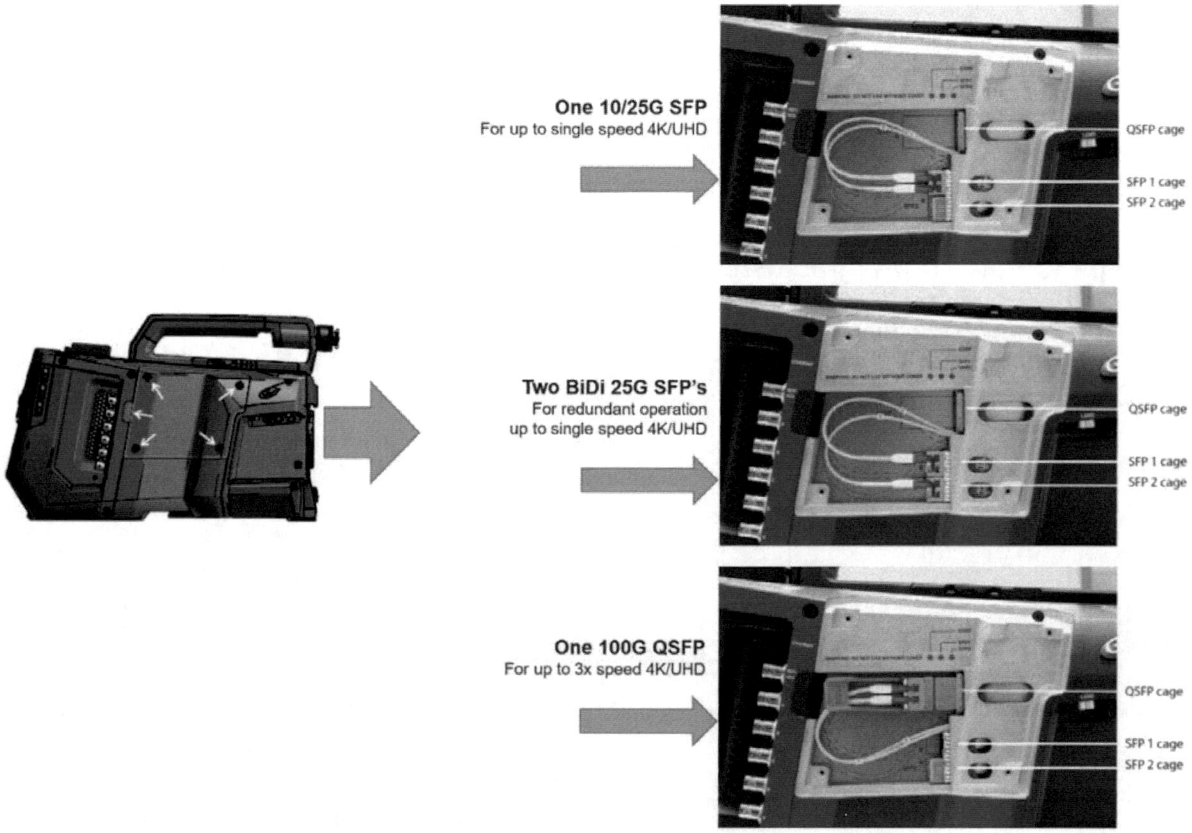

FIGURE 5 – SOLUTION FOR AN UPGRADABLE SFP SOLUTION

A 10G SFP provides backward compatible operation with a camera base station, a 25G SFP supports uncompressed UHD-1 operation even with HFR and a 100G QSFP even supports high-speed operation in native UHD-1 resolution. And by using two bidirectional (BiDi) 25G SFPs, redundant operation from the camera to the IP infrastructure can be realized for all incoming and outgoing IP streams.

Improved Bandwidth Efficiency

Since the bandwidth requirements for uncompressed operation are quite demanding, there will be cases where the available bandwidth does not support uncompressed operation.

However, for live applications, JPEG XS is a widely accepted low-latency video compression codec that delivers visibly lossless image performance up to compression ratios of about 1:8 to 1:10. Multiple in-camera JPEG XS encoders for all outgoing streams and multiple JPEG XS decoders for all incoming streams, without the need for external hardware devices, provide the most flexible and reliable solution for a compressed workflow in live applications.

A signal block diagram of a solution based on JPEG XS compression is shown in Figure 6:

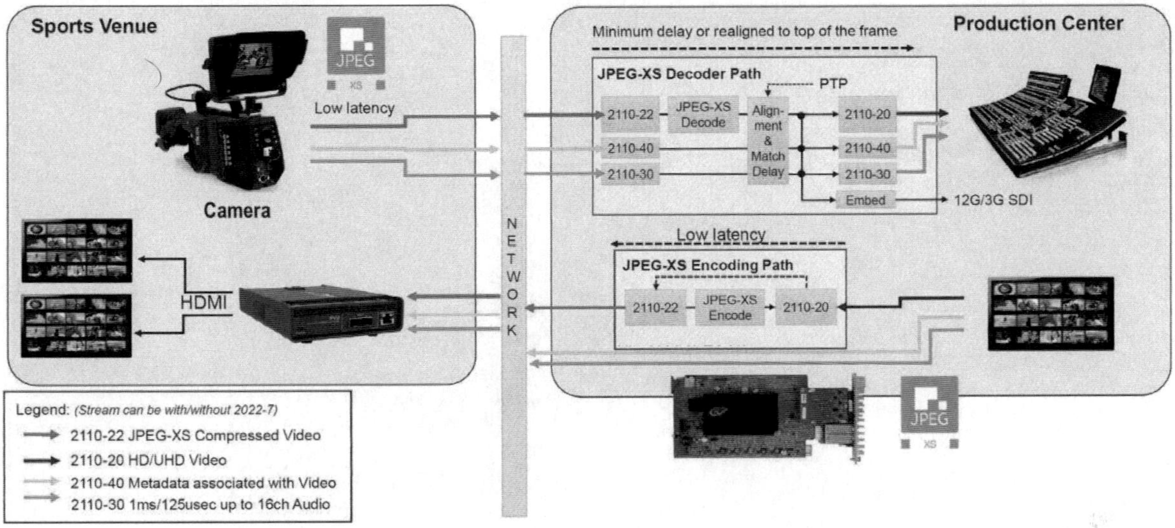

FIGURE 6: JPEG XS BASED WORKFLOW FOR OPTIMIZED BANDWIDTH EFFICIENCY

Workflows With Integrated Proxy Video Streams

In a full IP infrastructure, it may be necessary to use camera signals with an even lower bandwidth than JPEG XS can provide. In most cases, these low-bandwidth proxy video streams are not used to generate the main video signal, but for setup, preview and monitoring purposes. The very low bandwidth of these signals allows them to be distributed not only over the high bandwidth media network, but also over the low bandwidth control network. This allows users to set up, configure and prepare cameras for a production even when the high bandwidth media network is not available. It is important that the proxy videos are generated within the camera head so that they are available without having to pre-configure several different devices with each other first. A typical solution for proxy video is to use H.264 as the compression method, and there are several hardware and software decoders available for these signals from different vendors.

Camera Control Through the Cloud

IP-Based Camera Control

Fully IP-based camera control solutions such as the C2IP camera control system, which use TCP/IP and Ethernet as a basis, have been available for many years. For ease of configuration, these systems are typically based on Layer 2 technology, which does not allow the devices to be interconnected over wide area networks as required for remote production applications [3].

To provide a solution for remote connectivity over a wide area network, name server functionality was developed several years ago. This allows the various components to be connected to each other, even if they are not on the same local network, but are distributed over several different networks. An overview of such a solution is shown in Figure 7.

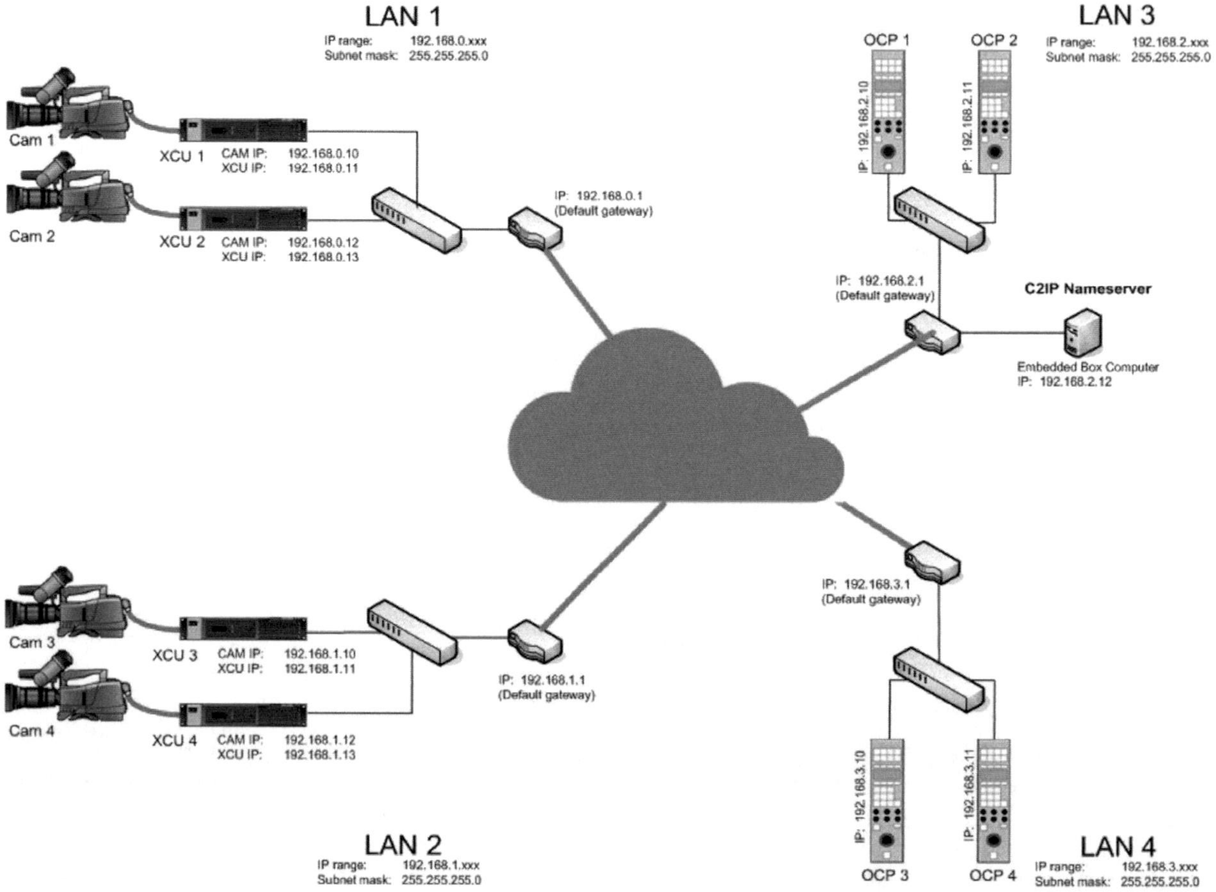

FIGURE 7: CAMERA CONTROL SOLUTION OVER DISTRIBUTED IP NETWORKS

The control connection can be managed by these systems with reasonable effort, but many additional signals and connections are still required for a true remote shading application. Providing these represents an effort that should not be underestimated and typically requires a large lead time, which therefore tends to make flexible use impossible.

Cloud Based Camera Control

Recent developments in cloud-based applications allow for further integration of the camera control solution not only for the control signals, but also for all other signals required for a full remote camera shading application.

An overview of such a potential solution is shown in Figure 8, where cloud services manage and provide not only the control connection, but also all other signals required for the camera shader. These additional signals include a multi-viewer tile with all cameras to be adjusted, but also a selection via the preview function of the camera control panels for a selected high-quality signal. Shading requires not only a video monitor but also a meter that displays luminance video level, RGB color signals, etc.

To avoid additional hardware at the remote camera shading location, this "videoscope" functionality should also be a micro-service provided by the cloud solution.

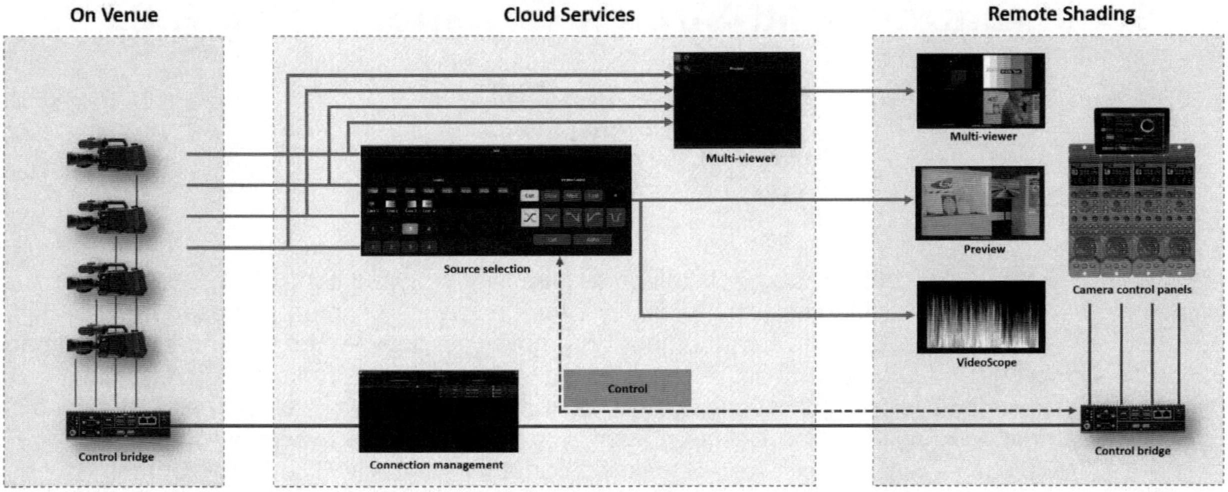

FIGURE 8: CAMERA CONTROL THROUGH CLOUD SERVICES

Summary

The way cameras are connected to the rest of the infrastructure has constantly evolved. Most of today's camera base stations offer an optional IP interface to the transmission infrastructure, but still uses a physical connection between the camera head and the dedicated hardware.

A camera system with NativeIP connectivity to IP infrastructures, offering optional low-latency signal compression and requiring no dedicated hardware other than a local power supply, offers a more flexible and future-proof solution.

The availability of additional proxy video signals with low bandwidth requirements offer enhanced possibilities especially for the configuration and diagnostics of IP infrastructures.

The camera control that is always necessary for live production cameras can be realized very flexibly and completely independent of location using IP network technology in combination with cloud applications.

By combining the various new possibilities offered by IP infrastructures and applications, cameras can be used much more efficiently and effectively in live media and entertainment productions.

References

[1] Weber, K. “IP Connectivity and its impact to camera workflows for live broadcast applications”, SMPTE Media + Entertainment Tech Expo19 Sydney, July 2019

[2] Görner, L., Weber, K., Walker, P. “Live At-Home Production 2.0” NAB BEIT Conference Proceedings, 2018, p. #69-74

[3] Weber, K., van Geel, R. “Creative Grading - Or why a new way of broadcast camera control is needed”, SMPTE 2018 Annual Technical Conference, 22-25 October 2018

Synchronized Multi-Stream Transport Using RIST

Ciro A. Noronha, Ph.D.
Cobalt Digital Inc.
Champaign, Illinois, United States
ciro.noronha@cobaltdigital.com

Abstract – Many broadcast contribution applications require synchronized content decoding. In such applications, there are several video sources (typically cameras), whose content needs to be transported using encoders to an equivalent number of remote decoders. At the decoders, the playback needs to be synchronized – frames that arrive together in the encoders are required to come out together in the decoders. Typical applications are sports and worship, where multiple camera angles are generated and need to be played in lockstep. There are a few products available today in the market that provide such a functionality over IP, using proprietary protocols. The Reliable Internet Stream Transport (RIST) Activity Group is completing the work on TR-06-4 Part 1, which provides an open industry specification for providing synchronized multi-stream transport. This paper provides a technical description of the methods in the Specification, as well as some actual field performance data.

Problem Definition

Synchronized content decoding refers to an application whereby multiple audio/video streams are transported from one location to another and must be displayed at the destination with the same relative synchronization as they had at the source. More specifically, the problem consists of the following elements:

- N video/audio encoders (not necessarily co-located)
- M video/audio decoders (not necessarily co-located), where $M \geq N$
- An IP network (possibly the Internet) connecting the encoders to the decoders.

The requirement is that frames of video that are presented to the encoders at the same time be played back at the decoders at the same time. "At the same time" means within one frame time. It is assumed that audio, if present, is synchronized with the video through the usual means.

Typical Applications

One typical application for synchronized decoding is remote sports production, illustrated in Figure 1. In this application, there are multiple cameras at a sports venue, to capture different angles of the event. If all these camera angles are transported to a remote location for production, the content needs to be synchronized at the playback to allow a director to cut between scenes. In this application, the cameras and decoders are usually all genlocked to a reference.

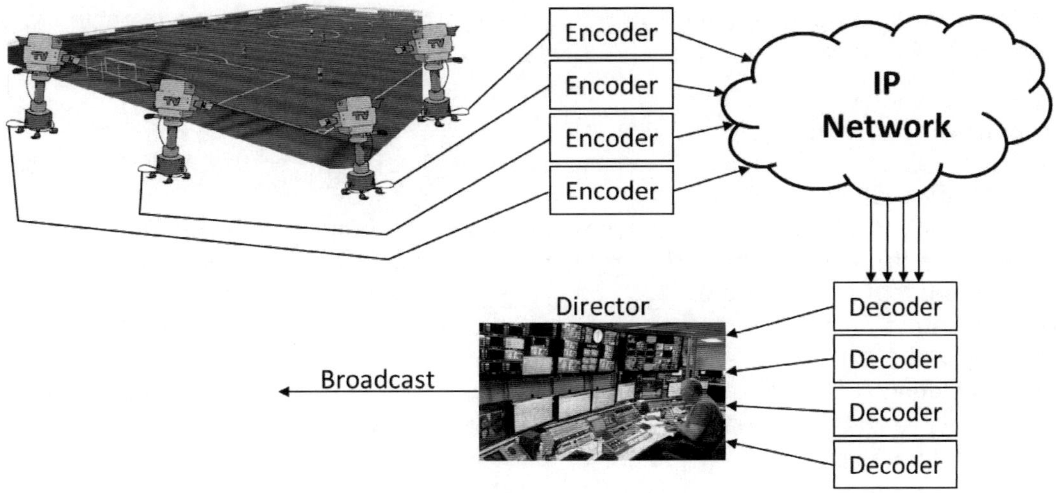

FIGURE 1: REMOTE SPORTS PRODUCTION

Another typical application is a house of worship, illustrated in Figure 2. In this case, there is a main church and a remote church, connected by an IP network. The religious service happens at the main church, and is transmitted to the remote church, which is equipped with large screens. The video between these screens needs to be synchronized as the pastor may move between cameras, and there should be no noticeable lag between them.

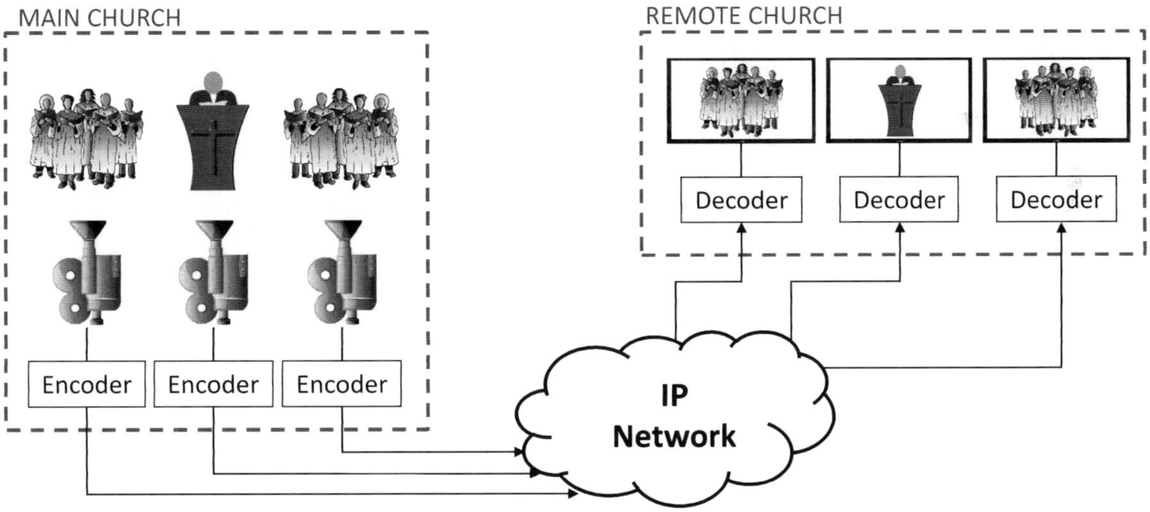

FIGURE 2: HOUSE OF WORSHIP

Using RIST For Decoder Synchronization

The Reliable Internet Stream Transport (RIST) protocol [1] was developed by the Video Services Forum as an open specification for an interoperable low-latency video transport protocol over the Internet. As RIST already provides the reliable transport over an IP network, it is a natural extension to add a decoder synchronization feature to it. The RIST Activity Group (AG) has completed the technical work on this feature. Once approved, the RIST decoder synchronization feature is expected to be published as TR-06-4 Part 1.

Synchronization Algorithm

Figure 3 illustrates the delays from video ingest to playback. The Total End-to-End Delay is composed of the following components:

- **Encoding Delay:** This is the time between the moment a frame of video enters the encoder, and the same frame is transmitted onto the network. This delay is typically fixed and is an intrinsic feature of the encoder.
- **Network Delay:** This is the network propagation delay. This delay can be variable depending on the network traffic.
- **Protocol Delay:** RIST includes some additional delay for ARQ and optional packet reordering.
- **Sync Delay:** Adjustable additional delay to achieve decoder synchronization.
- **Decode Delay:** This is the time it takes the decoder to present the frame once it receives the bitstream.

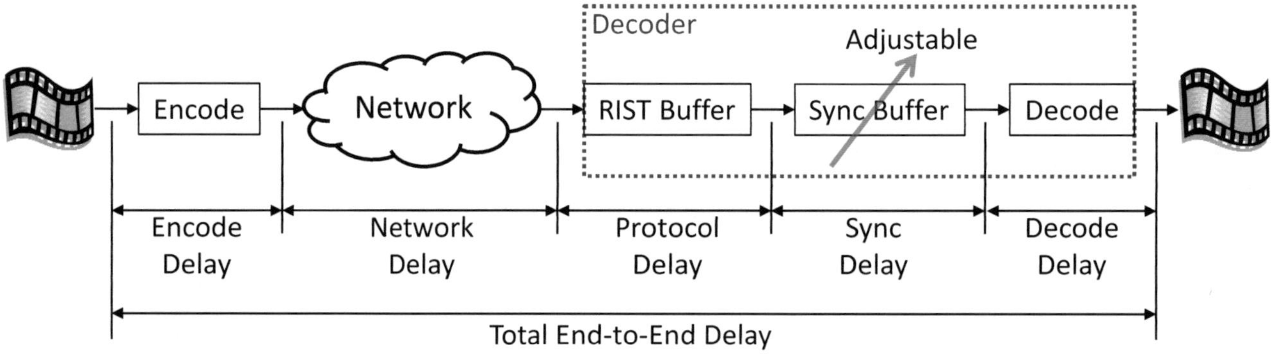

FIGURE 3: END-TO-END DELAY COMPONENTS

The final purpose of the synchronization algorithm is to provide the decoders enough information to dynamically adjust the Sync Buffer in Figure 3 so that the end-to-end delay is the same for every decoder. To achieve this, a common time base is required between encoders and decoders. The RIST AG has selected the Network Time Protocol (NTP) [2] as this common time base. Once there is a common time base, the following high-level algorithm has been selected:

- Encoders will need to provide decoders with the NTP time corresponding to the instant each frame of video has been captured. For efficiency purposes, this does not need to be done for every frame; it can be done periodically, and the decoders will interpolate. Note that the video frame rate clock is not synchronized with NTP, so the information needs to be sent frequently enough to compensate for the clock drift.
- Decoders add a fixed delay to the received NTP time stamp to determine the frame playback time. This is the Total End-to-End Delay in Figure 3. This value must be larger than the sum of Encode Delay, Network Delay, Protocol Delay and Decode Delay. The decoder implements this delay by adjusting the Sync Delay.

Protocol Support

To implement the synchronization algorithm, the timestamps need to be carried from the encoders to the decoders. Fortunately, RIST Simple Profile [1] already includes a suitable mechanism for this communication – the RTCP Sender Report (SR) message, defined in RFC 3550 [3]. RIST Simple Profile uses RTP for data transmission and requires the sender to transmit periodic SR messages every 100 milliseconds to establish state in firewalls so that NACK messages can come back to the sender (see [4] for a detailed explanation). RIST Simple Profile allows for empty SR messages and does not require receivers to process such messages in any way.

The SR messages already include the necessary fields for synchronization, as illustrated in Figure 4. It includes an optional NTP timestamp, and the corresponding RTP timestamp. These two fields are used to inform the recipient that a packet with the indicated RTP timestamp was transmitted at the indicated NTP time. This mechanism is in widespread use to synchronize audio and video for RTSP devices.

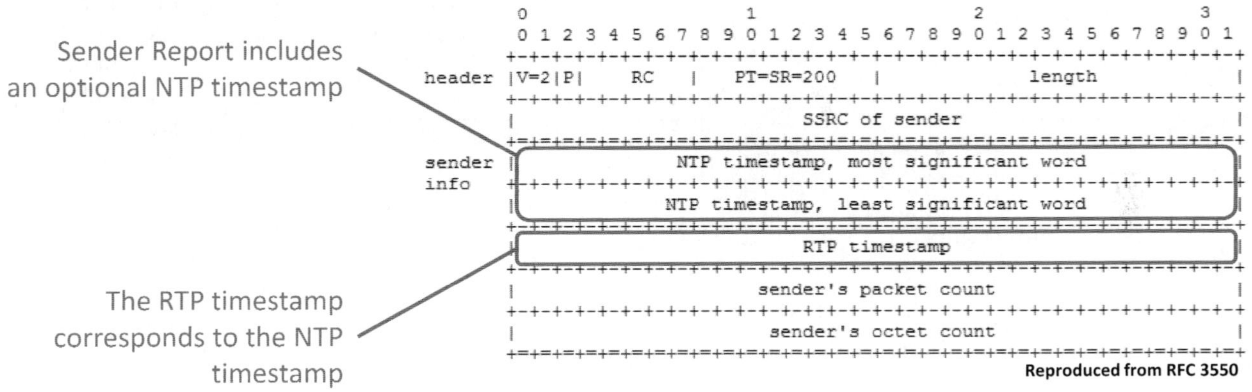

FIGURE 4: SYNCHRONIZATION FIELDS IN THE SR RTCP MESSAGE

To provide decoder synchronization, the RIST AG has made small changes to the interpretation of the two fields above. The changes are summarized in Table 1.

TR-06-4 Part 1	RFC 3550
NTP timestamp is required	NTP timestamp is optional, can be set to zero
NTP timestamp must come from an actual NTP server	NTP timestamp can be device's wall clock
NTP timestamp corresponds to frame capture time	NTP timestamp corresponds to SR message transmission time
RTP timestamp corresponds to timestamp of the packet carrying the frame	RTP timestamp corresponds to the same point in time as the NTP timestamp

TABLE 1: DIFFERENCES BETWEEN TR-06-4 PART 1 AND RFC 3550

Implementation

To fill in the SR message, an encoder will need to tie NTP timestamps obtained when frames are captured to RTP timestamps. The process is illustrated in Figure 5 for an MPEG encoder producing a Transport Stream, and works as follows:

- Every time a frame is captured, the encoder records the value of the System Time Clock[1] (STC) and the corresponding NTP timestamp.
- Every time an RTP packet is prepared for transmission, it is inspected to see if it carries a Program Clock Reference (PCR) timestamp. The PCR is a sample of the STC.
- If the RTP packet carries a PCR, then the value of the PCR is used to interpolate the NTP timestamp from the last STC/NTP capture. This interpolated NTP is now associated with the packet's RTP Timestamp.
- If it is time to send an SR packet, these are the two values used in the packet.

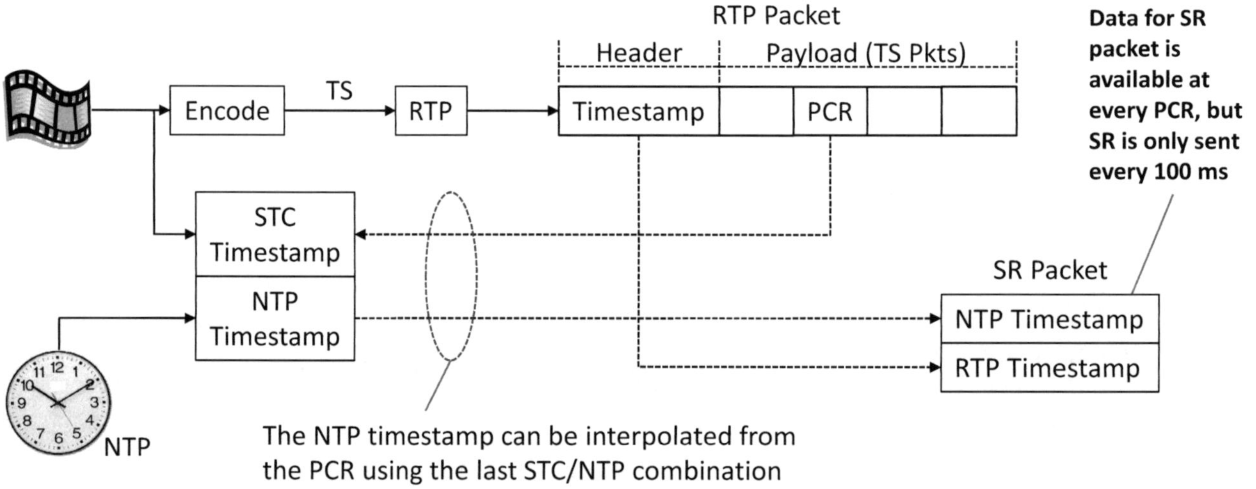

FIGURE 5: SR MESSAGE GENERATION

Actual Field Test Data

We have implemented the proposed algorithm in a set of encoders/decoders and tested the system over the Internet. The test setup is depicted in Figure 6 and includes:

- Two encoders located in Santa Clara, California.
- One video source with burned-in VITC timecode, connected to both encoders, running at 1920x1080i at 29.97 frames/second.
- Two decoders located in Champaign, Illinois, connected to a multi-viewer with output snapshot capability.
- A standard Internet connection between these two locations.

Each encoder transmits a unicast stream over the Internet with RIST to a decoder. RIST Simple Profile is used to recover any lost packets. The multi-viewer can be used to take snapshots of the combined video from both decoders, and the timecode in both screens can be compared to see if the decoders are synchronized.

[1] The System Time Clock for a Transport Stream is a 42-bit counter driven by a 27 MHz clock locked to the video frame rate.

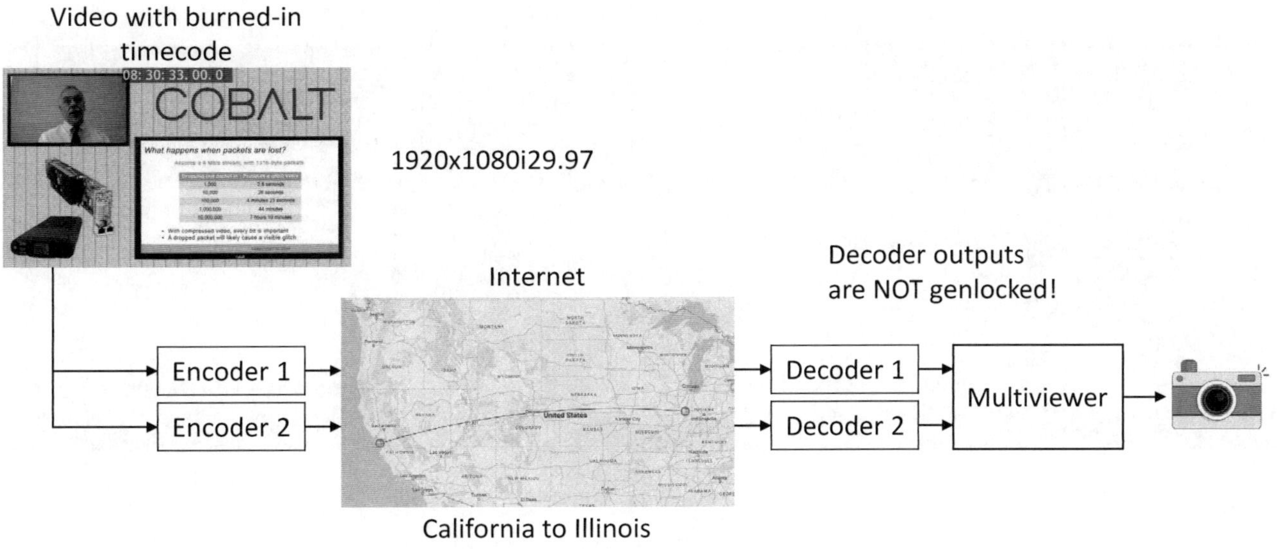

FIGURE 6: TEST SETUP

Test Results

Our first observation is that, when the system starts, the decoders are not quite in alignment. This is because the decoders start with their own version of the STC, which is yet not locked to the incoming stream. Over the course of the first few minutes of operation, the decoders achieve frequency and phase lock with the encoder STC, and the video outputs of the two decoders become aligned. Figure 7 shows the initial lock, a few minutes after the decoders have been started. The video is not completely aligned, Decoder 2 is one field ahead of Decoder 1.

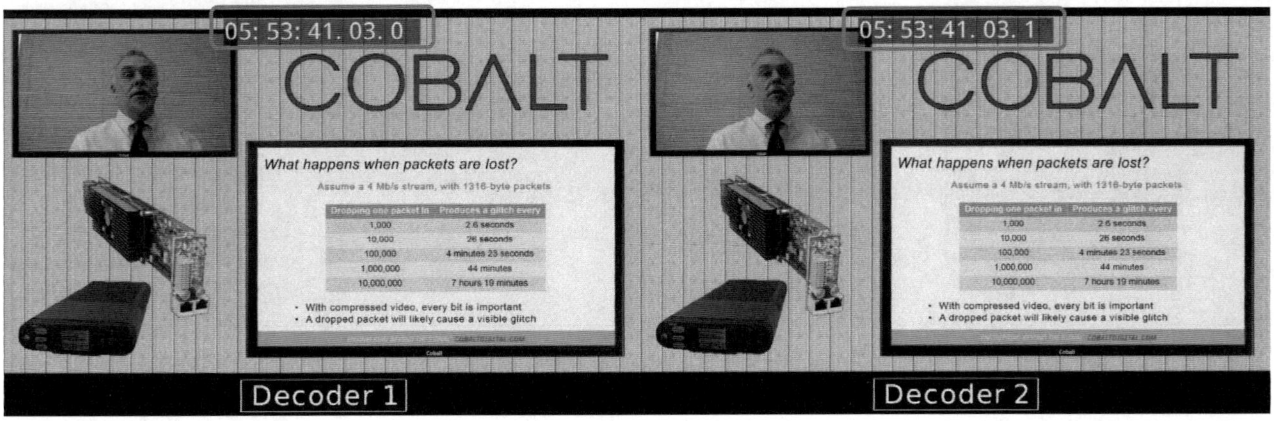

FIGURE 7: INITIAL LOCK

Figure 8 shows the final alignment of the two decoders. This snapshot was taken approximately 12 minutes after the one in Figure 7. As demonstrated by the timecodes, both decoders are fully aligned.

(approximately 12 minutes later)

FIGURE 8: FINAL ALIGNMENT

Figure 9 shows some statistics for this run. It indicates that the round-trip time for the setup is on the order of 75 milliseconds, and even though the Internet dropped packets, RIST recovered them all. Another important measurement is the sync delay, namely the instantaneous difference between the current NTP time and the NTP timestamp in the SR packet, at the time of the SR packet reception. In this case, most of the delay is inside the encoder.

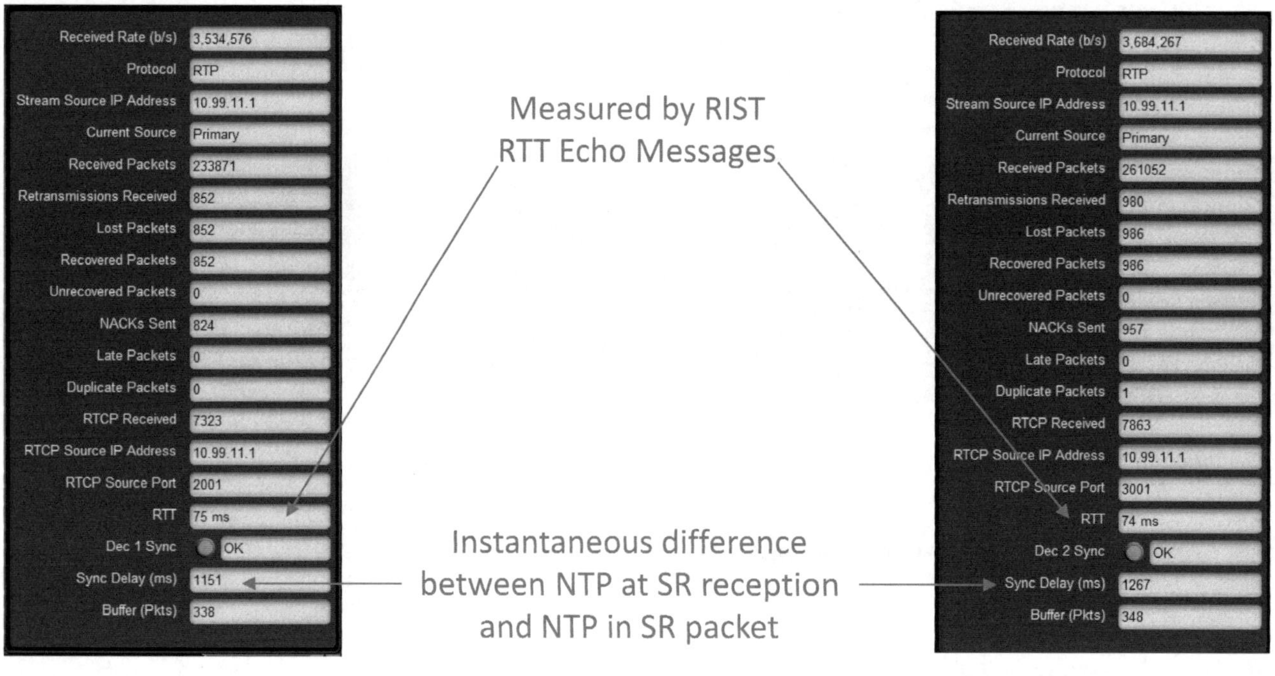

FIGURE 9: DECODER STATISTICS

The results presented above are for non-genlocked decoders. They will play in synchronization, but the video time base will be that of the encoders, recovered by the standard MPEG clock recovery. In many cases, however, it is necessary or desirable to genlock the decoders to a studio reference. The genlock process will occasionally drop or repeat frames as needed to match the video to the reference. Such drop/repeat events are not necessarily synchronized, so multiple genlocked outputs may be one frame off. This is shown in Figure 10, where we have genlocked decoders. The genlock process happens to be in a state where Decoder 2 is one frame ahead of Decoder 1.

FIGURE 10: GENLOCKED DECODERS SHOWING A FRAME DIFFERENCE

Conclusions

We have demonstrated that the method proposed in the upcoming TR-06-4 Part 1 Specification can provide synchronized decoding over the Internet. Decoder clock recovery is a factor, and it may take a while to achieve synchronization – this is dependent on the specific decoder clock recovery. Ideally, the clock recovery should be made a part of the synchronization process, but this is an implementation detail and not related to the RIST Specification.

Another observation has to do with the Total End-to-End Delay setting from Figure 3. This is a value that needs to be manually configured in all the decoders and needs to be large enough to compensate for the worst-case encoder-decoder delay. The RIST Specification has not addressed this issue; it is currently done by manual configuration and could be error prone. More work is needed to automate this setting.

References

[1] Video Services Forum TR-06-1, "Reliable Internet Stream Transport (RIST) Protocol Specification – Simple Profile", 2020-06-25, < https://vsf.tv/download/technical_recommendations/VSF_TR-06-1_2020_06_25.pdf>.

[2] Mills, D., Martin, J., Ed., Burbank, J., and W. Kasch, "Network Time Protocol Version 4: Protocol and Algorithms Specification", *RFC 5905, DOI 10.17487/RFC5905*, June 2010, <https://www.rfc-editor.org/info/rfc5905>.

[3] Schulzrinne, H., Casner, S., Frederick, R., and V. Jacobson, "RTP: A Transport Protocol for Real-Time Applications", *STD 64, RFC 3550, DOI 10.17487/RFC3550*, July 2003, <https://www.rfc-editor.org/info/rfc3550>.

[4] Noronha, C., "A Performance Measurement Study of the Reliable Internet Stream Transport Protocol", *Proceedings of the 2019 NAB Broadcast Engineering and Information Technology Conference.*

Changing the Landscape of FM Broadcast Antenna Technology

John L. Schadler
Dielectric LLC
Raymond, Maine, United States

Abstract – It has been many years since a new game changing technology in FM broadcast antenna design has been introduced to the market. The many advantages of slotted coaxial pylon antenna technology that have benefitted the UHF and high band VHF broadcast community for decades can now be realized in the FM band. Those benefits include smaller size leading to low wind load, less parts and less connections leading to higher reliability and a high degree of both azimuth and elevation pattern flexibility. In most applications, the use of slotted coaxial antennas has been limited to single channel television operation. In this paper, the use of slotted coaxial pylon antenna technology in the FM band is presented. Discussion includes various methods to increase the bandwidth of slotted coaxial antennas. The cumulative effect of the methods can boost the bandwidth to 20% allowing for effective broadband operation at FM frequencies, leading to a new innovative product line of FM broadcast antennas.

Introduction

In 1967 Matti Siukola, RCA Scientist and Unit Manager of Advanced Development for RCA Broadcast Systems, presented his paper "Dual Polarization FM Broadcasting with a Single Antenna" at the NAB symposium (see Figure 1). The concept of radiating circular polarization from a single element revolutionized the FM broadcast industry and is still the basic premise for antenna design today.

FIGURE 1: MATTI SIUKOLA – RCA'S BFC - FIRST DUAL POLARIZED FM ELEMENT.

The BFC was both bandwidth and power limited due to its size. The quality factor (Q) of a circularly polarized antenna element is directly related to the element's volume by equation (1) [1] [8].

This paper is excerpted from the Proceedings of the 2022 NAB Broadcast Engineering and Information Technology (BEIT) Conference, © 2022, National Association of Broadcasters, 1 M Street S.E., Washington, DC 20003 USA.

$$Q = \frac{1}{2}\left[\frac{1}{(\beta a)^3} + \frac{2}{\beta a}\right] \quad (1)$$

Where (a) is the occupied volume radius and $\beta = 2\pi/\lambda$. The fundamental maximum bandwidth bounds of an antenna is given by equation (2) [3].

$$bw = \frac{\pi}{Q ln\left(\frac{VSWR+1}{VSWR-1}\right)} \quad (2)$$

Where the VSWR is the maximum allowable within the passband [1]. It was clear that the one way to increase the bandwidth of the BFC would be to make it larger. Simply making it bigger degraded the circularity, making the azimuth pattern resemble more of a peanut shape then an omni. In 1978, Don Hymas, RCA Unit Manager Antenna Engineering, presented his work at the 1978 IEEE Broadcast Symposium "A New High Power Circularly Polarized FM Antenna", which introduced the industry to the RCA-BFM (see Figure 2).

FIGURE 2: DON HYMAS – RCA'S BFM – HIGH POWER BROADBAND CIRCULARLY POLARIZED FM ELEMENT.

The BFM's quadrupole design was larger for higher bandwidth and filled in the azimuth pattern with its two extra radiators to produce omni directional coverage. This again was a leap in FM technology and is the basis for most FM ring-style antennas today.

The vast majority of UHF broadcast antennas used in the US are slotted cylinder "pylon" designs. Their advantages have been presented and marketed for more than 50 years. It is their simplicity, versatility and low wind load that have made them the antenna of choice. The simplicity was depicted in a witty RCA ad in 1966 shown in Figure 3. The pylon concept has been restricted to the TV bands primarily due to general size and bandwidth limitations. It will be shown in this paper that these limitations can be overcome resulting in a truly innovative game changing antenna design for FM.

FIGURE 3: RCA 1966 AD – JUST NEED A LITTLE PAINT.

Increasing the Bandwidth of a Slotted Coaxial Antenna

The natural bandwidth of a coaxial slot radiator is typically on the order 1% for VSWR operation less than 1.1:1 and is defined as:

$$\%bw = \frac{f_h - f_l}{f_0}(100) \tag{3}$$

The fundamental limitation of a coaxial slot stems from the frequency dependence imposed on the structure by connecting the two sides of the slot together by wrapping the outer conductor to form a cylinder as shown in Figure 4. Even though this fundamental limitation exists, other methods that increase the bandwidth can be applied.

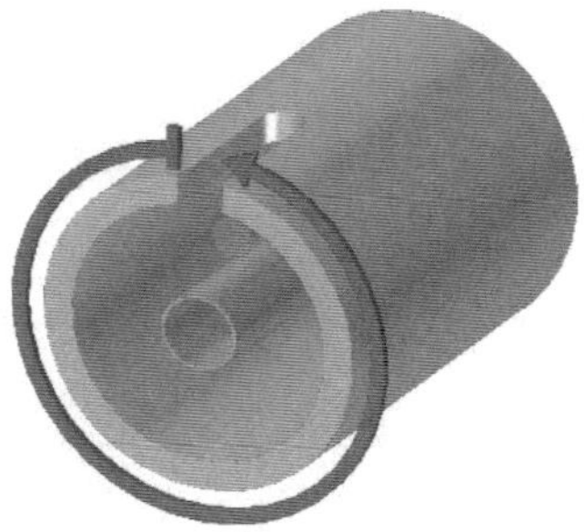

FIGURE 4: CYLINDER CREATES A FREQUENCY DEPENDENCE RESULTING IN NARROW BANDWIDTH.

Techniques to improve bandwidth of an antenna can be classified into two categories: those that lower the quality factor (Q), as seen in equation (2), and those that provide additional phase cancelation outside of the radiating elements. The percent bandwidth needed in order to achieve full band FM operation will need to be on the order of 19%. It must be noted that typical Q values for single slot coaxial antennas range from 30 to 40. In order to achieve 19% bandwidth and considering a maximum allowable VSWR of 1.2:1, the Q must be substantially reduced to approximately 5 to 10, (refer to equation 2). The new pylon design will incorporate two techniques to help achieve the required Q to make full FM band operation achievable.

Reducing the Circuit Capacitance

The Q of a parallel resonant circuit can be expressed as: [5]

$$Q = \omega_0 RC \tag{4}$$

The expression shows direct proportionality between the capacitance C and Q. Reducing the capacitance reduces the Q and in turn will increase the bandwidth as depicted by equation (2). The capacitance of the slot network can be greatly reduced by changing the coaxial inner to a microstrip. The microstrip can be placed near the bottom of the coax outer shell with the slot directly fed with a feed strap. Refer to Figure 5. To quantify the reduction in Q this technique provides, the capacitance of the coaxial line and the capacitance of the microstrip line can be compared. The capacitance of a coaxial line can be calculated using equation 5 [6].

$$C_c = \frac{2\pi\epsilon_0\epsilon_r}{ln\left(\frac{D}{d}\right)} \tag{5}$$

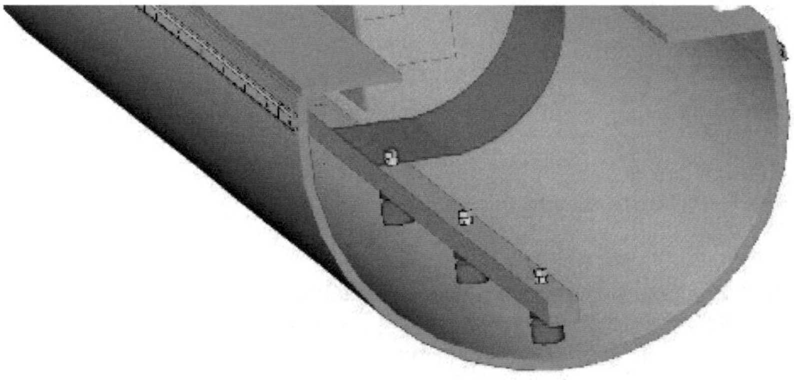

FIGURE 5: MICROSTRIP-FED SLOTTED CAVITY.

Where $\epsilon_0 = 8.854X10^{-12}\ F/m$, (D) is the diameter of the inside of the outer and (d) is the diameter of the inner conductor [5]. The capacitance of microstrip can be found using equation 6 [7].

$$C_m = \frac{\epsilon_r L}{60 v_0 ln\left[\frac{8h}{w}+\frac{w}{4h}\right]} \quad for\ \frac{w}{h} < 1 \tag{6}$$

Where $v_0 = \frac{1}{\sqrt{\mu_0\epsilon_0}} = 299792548\ m/s$, w is width and h the height of the microstrip off the backplane. For a typical coaxial design of near 70 ohms, such as the example shown in Figure 4, compared to a similarly dimensioned microstrip feed design shown in Figure 5, we can see that:

$$C_c \approx 2C_m$$

Since the capacitance and Q are directly related, this means the Q has also been reduced by a factor of 2 when converting the coaxial design to a microstrip fed slot.

Babinet's Principle

Another technique that can be used to provide broadband impedance cancellation and lower the Q of a slot radiator is to place a complementary impedance in the same circuit as the slot. Babinet's principle, put into antenna terms by H.G. Booker in 1946, relates the fields and impedance of an aperture antenna to its dual [4]. The dual of a slot would be a dipole as shown in Figure 6.

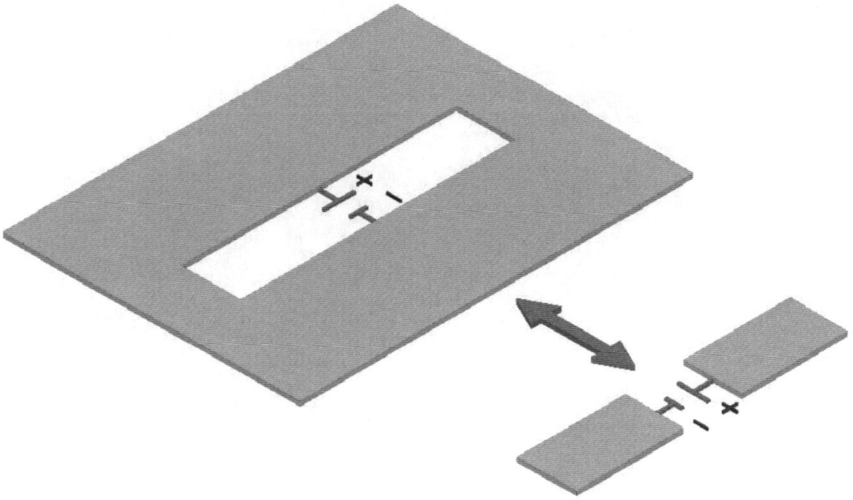

FIGURE 6: DUAL ANTENNAS, (LEFT) SLOT ANTENNA AND (RIGHT) THE DIPOLE ANTENNA.

Babinet's principle relates the impedance of a slot (Z_S) to the impedance of its complementary dipole (Z_D) by the relation:

$$Z_S = \frac{\eta^2}{4Z_D} \tag{7}$$

Where η is the intrinsic impedance of free space and has the value of 377Ω. Since:

$$Z_S Z_D = \frac{1}{4}\eta^2 \text{ represents a real number,}$$

$$(R_D + jX_D)(R_S + jX_S) \text{ is real}$$

$$\Rightarrow R_S X_D = -R_D X_S$$

This implies an inverse relationship and will provide a level of cancelation if the slot and dipole are used in the same circuit. Using a parasitic dipole, which was developed and patented by Dielectric, to add a vertical component to the horizontally polarized signal emanating from the slot as shown in Figure 7, places them in the same circuit. This technique not only provides elliptical or circular polarization, but it also reduces the Q of the radiating combination which provides an overall increase in the operating bandwidth.

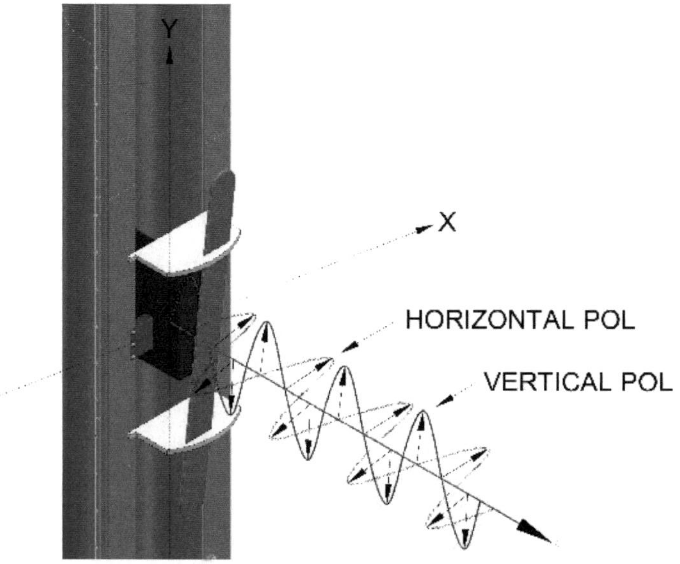

FIGURE 7: PARASITIC DIPOLE PLACED OVER THE SLOT. THE COMBINATION PRODUCES ELLIPTICAL OR CIRCULAR POLARIZATION.

It has been shown that the loaded Q of a coupled slot decrease on the order of 30% to 40% with the complementary addition of a parasitic dipole over the slot. [2].

Simplicity Equals Reliability

As mentioned earlier, an advantage of a slotted pylon antenna is its simplicity. Failure rate is defined as:

$$\lambda = \sum_{i=1}^{n} N_i \lambda_i \pi_{Qi} \tag{8}$$

Where n is the number of part categories, N_i is the quantity of the ith part, λ_i is the failure rate of the ith part and π_{Qi} is the quality factor of ith part [9]. From equation 8, one can conclude that reliability is directly proportional to parts count. The total number of parts in the FM pylon antenna is over 60% less than an equivalent ring style antenna and over 90% less than an equivalent cavity backed panel type antenna used today (see Figure 8).

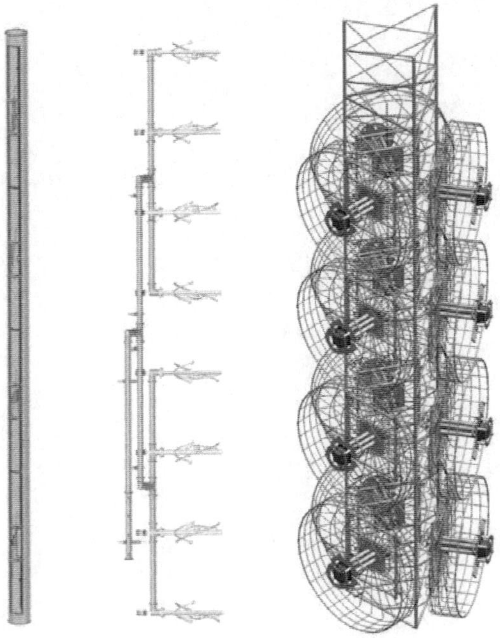

FIGURE 8: FM PYLON ANTENNA (LEFT) COMPARED TO EQUIVALENT RING STYLE (CENTER) AND PANEL (RIGHT) ANTENNAS.

The simplicity of the FM pylon inherently makes it significantly more reliable than any equivalent FM broadcast antenna on the market today.

Improving Polarization Stability

Frequency independence and log periodic theory can be applied to produce a more stable polarization ratio across the FM band. The slot is considered the driven element, but instead of using a single parasitic dipole element to re-radiate the vertical component as shown in Figure 7, multiple elements can be used as shown in Figure 9. Each element is designed uniquely in order to resonate at different frequency slices within the FM band by applying different angles and lengths. A level of frequency independence is achieved by structures which are entirely specified by angles [10]. In doing so, this geometry provides a stable polarization ratio performance across the entire FM band.

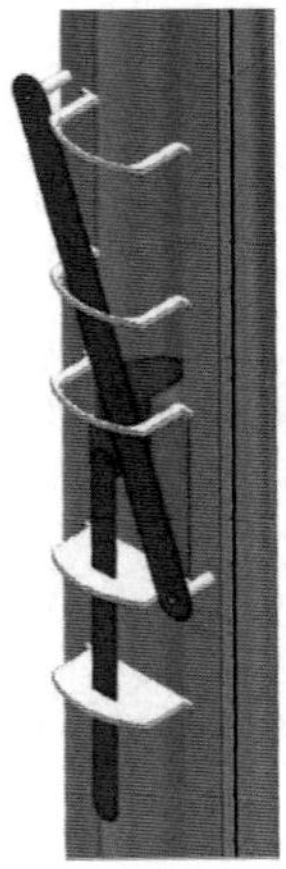

FIGURE 9: FM PYLON USING BROADBAND PARASITIC DIPOLE COMBINATIONS TO IMPROVE THE POLARIZATION STABILITY.

The resulting pattern performance is shown in Figure 10.

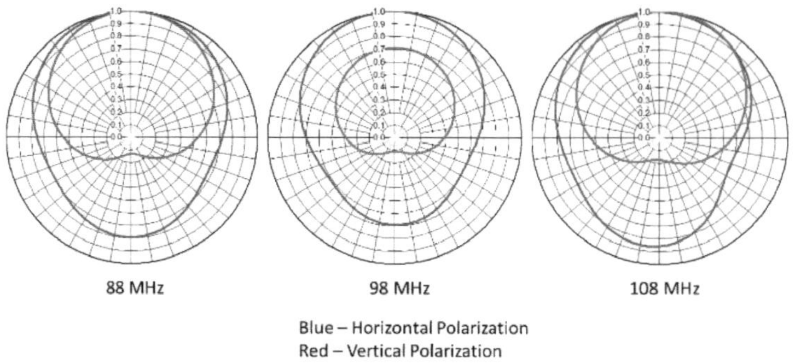

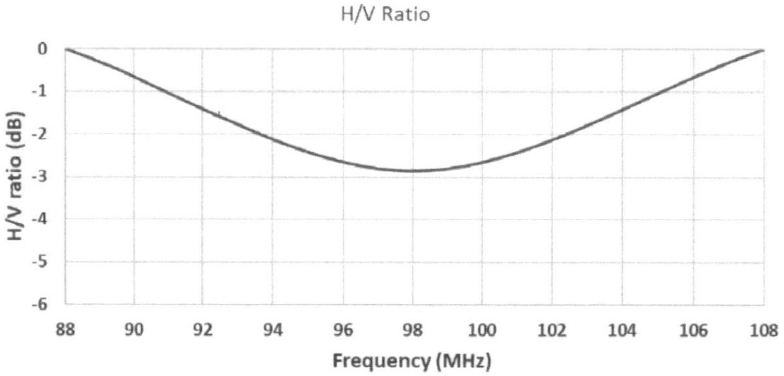

FIGURE 10: FM PYLON PATTERN PERFORMANCE AND POLARIZATION RATIO.

Testing Results

By applying many of the same computer simulation techniques that were developed and refined for TV slot antennas to the new FM pylon, most notably HFSS (High Frequency Structure Simulator), the skills and experience led to the rapid development of a full antenna design. After transferring the virtual design to a final product, testing of a single four bay section of the new FM pylon antenna on a 25-foot trestle proved the performance (see Figure 11).

FIGURE 11: FM PYLON ANTENNA IN TEST ON 25' TRESTLE.

The initial impedance and VSWR vs. frequency are shown in Figure 12 with further improvement expected.

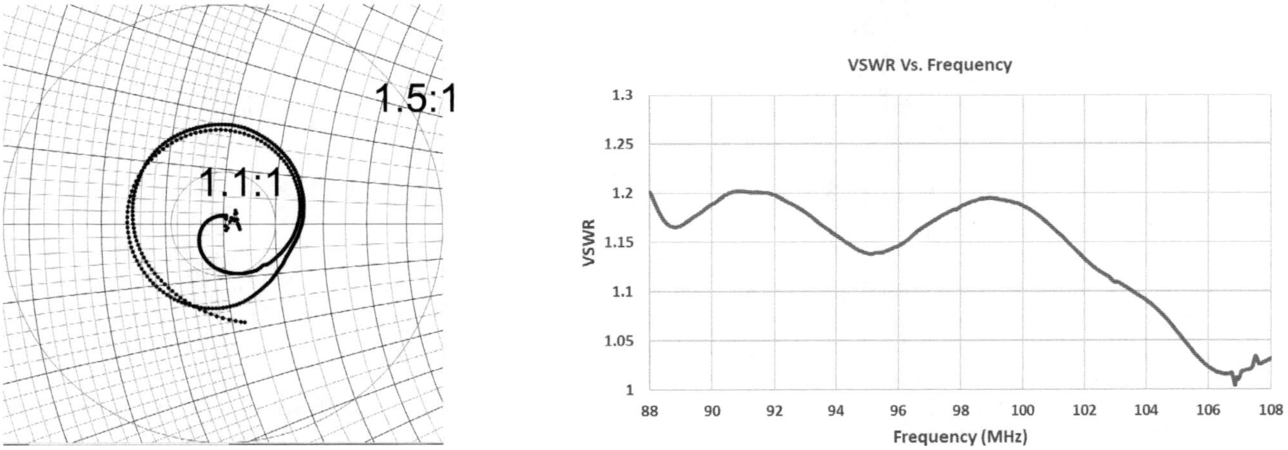

FIGURE 12: FM PYLON PERFORMANCE. IMPEDANCE MEASUREMENT TAKEN 25' ABOVE GROUND ON A WOODEN TRESTLE.

Azimuthal Pattern Flexibility

As seen in the patterns shown in Figure 10, there is a lack of pattern congruency between the horizontal and vertical polarizations of a single FM pylon section in free space. This issue is of little concern since a single section bay will most likely always be side mounted on the tower structure. It is normal for the tower structure to directionalize the patterns with the vertical polarization being affected more than the horizontal polarization. This is due to the tower itself being in the vertical plane. For example, a typical ring style antenna bay will be omni directional in free space for both the horizontal and vertical polarizations. Refer to Figure 13. When adding the transmission line required to feed power into the bay, the vertical polarization begins to directionalize.

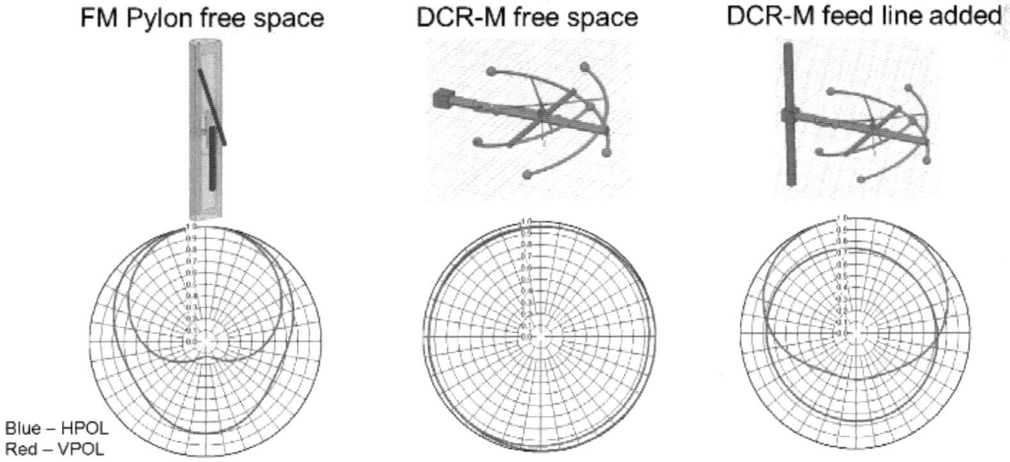

FIGURE 13: COMPARING THE FM PYLON ANTENNA TO A TYPICAL RING STYLE FM BAY IN FREE SPACE AND ALSO WITH THE ADDITION OF A FEEDLINE BEHIND THE BAY USED TO SUPPLY RF POWER.

When including the tower, it can be shown that the resulting patterns of the FM pylon and that of a typical ring style antenna become very similar in nature as shown in Figure 14.

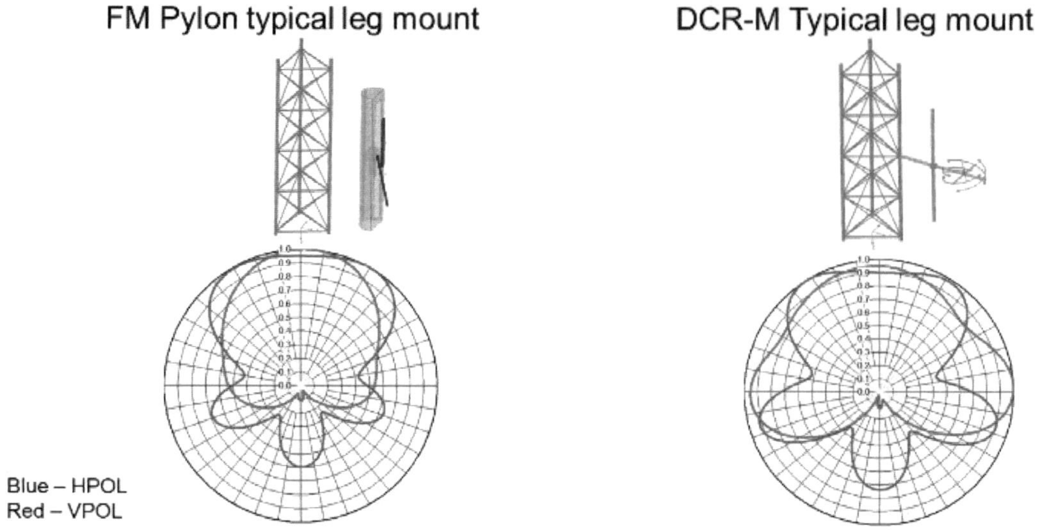

FIGURE 14: COMPARING AZIMUTH PATTERNS OF AN FM PYLON ANTENNA SINGLE BAY AND A TYPICAL RING STYLE BAY SIDE MOUNTED ON A TYPICAL TOWER.

Since the single section of the FM pylon can be used as an array element in both the azimuth and elevation planes, it has the same pattern flexibility as complicated panel antennas. The azimuth pattern can be shaped and optimized to provide desired coverage by placing multiple modules into a support structure. The number of modules around can be 2 to 4 and placed at any orientation with each fed with different amplitudes and phases resulting in a variety of standard pattern shapes as well as an infinite number of unique solutions that can be used for directional applications. The support structure can be either side mounted or top mounted on the tower. Refer to Figure 15.

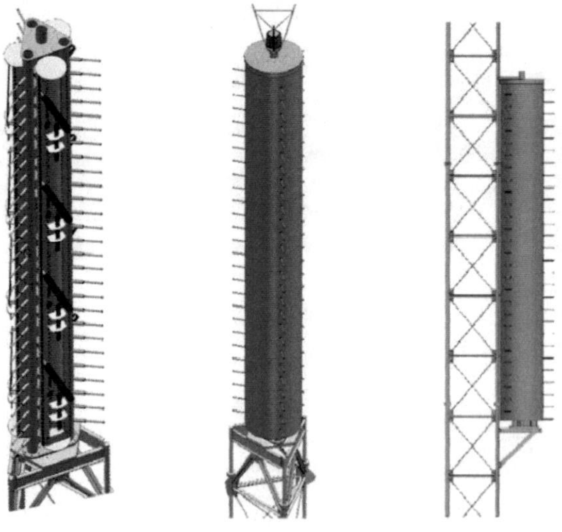

FIGURE 15: FM PYLON ANTENNA MODULES PLACED IN A SUPPORT STRUCTURE TO PROVIDE AZIMUTH PATTERN AND MOUNTING FLEXIBILITY.

Examples of azimuth patterns generated by FM pylon configurations are shown in Figure 16.

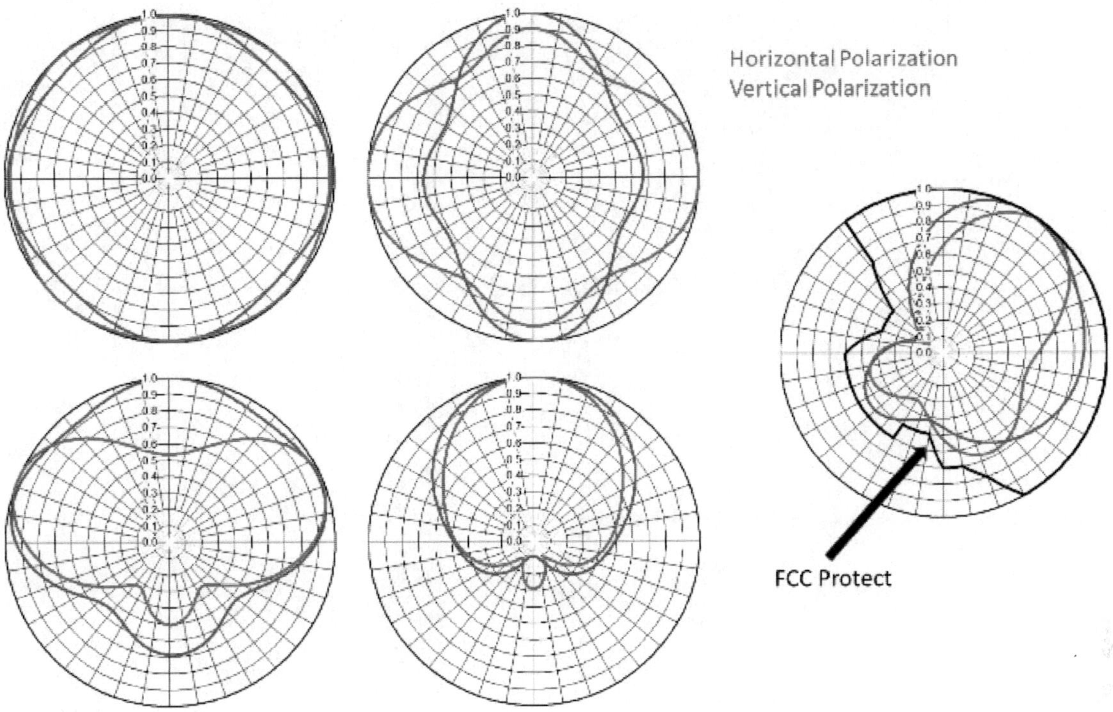

FIGURE 16: EXAMPLES OF AZIMUTH PATTERN FLEXIBILITY BY VARYING THE NUMBER OF BAYS AROUND AND THEIR FEED AMPLITUDES AND PHASES.

Elevation Pattern and Gain Flexibility

The elevation gain can be increased by stacking multiple 4 bay modules into an 8 or 12 bay configuration.

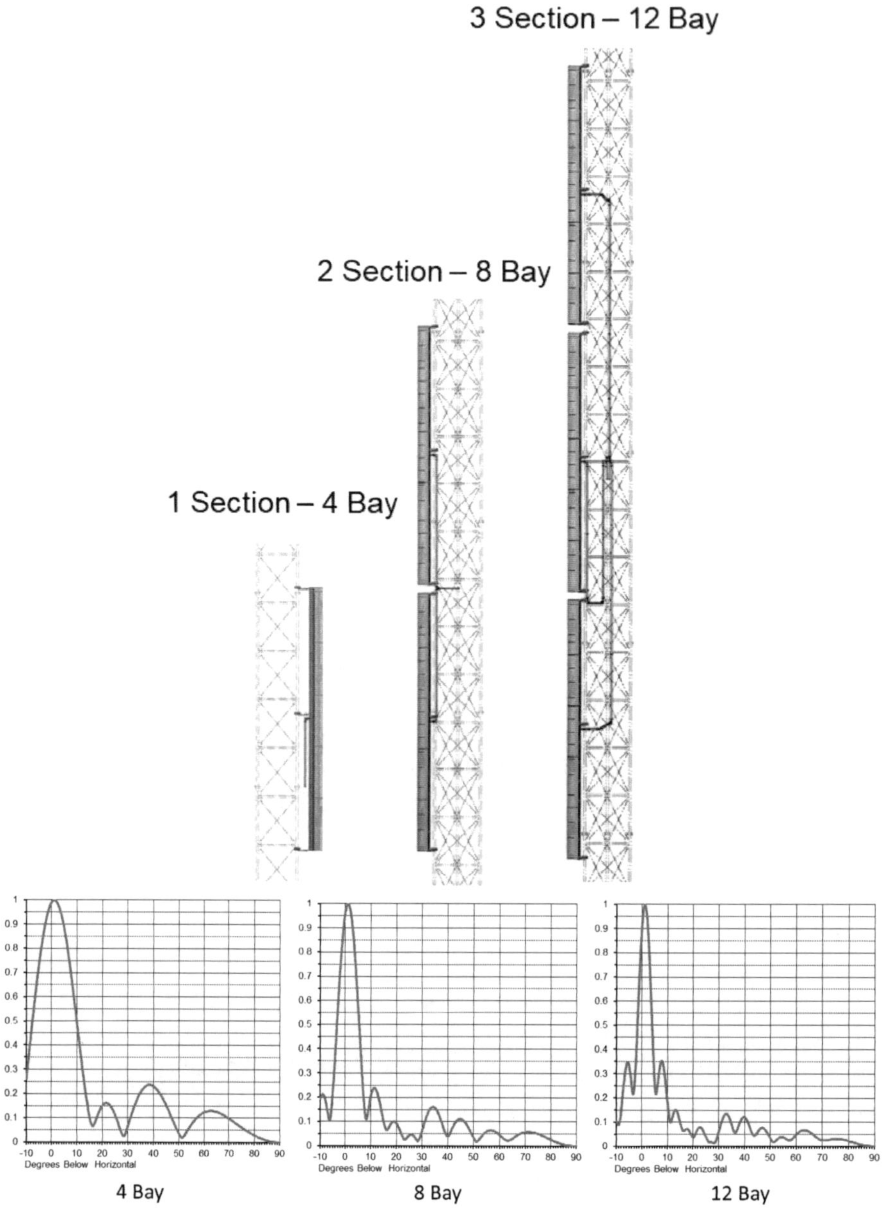

FIGURE 17: FM PYLON 4 BAY ANTENNA MODULES STACKED IN ELEVATION TO INCREASE THE GAIN, CHANGE BEAM TILT AND OPTIMIZE NULL FILL.

Conclusion

The many advantages of slotted coaxial pylon antenna technology that have benefitted the UHF and high band VHF broadcast community for decades can now be realized in the FM band. Those benefits include smaller size leading to low wind load, less parts and less connections leading to higher reliability and a high degree of both azimuth and elevation pattern flexibility. By incorporating techniques to lower the Q of the slot cavity, full FM band VSWR performance can be obtained. The design of a broadband parasitic dipole pair provides a simple, cost-effective solution to stable polarization ratio across the band.

References

[1] Schadler, J. L., “Considerations for -10dBc IBOC Combined Station Side-mount Master FM Antenna Design”, *IEEE Broadcast Symposium*, 2015.

[2] Schadler, J. L., “Broadband Slotted Coaxial Broadcast Antenna Technology”, *White Paper*, Dielectric.com.

[3] Fano, R. M., “Theoretical Limitations on the Broadband Matching of Arbitrary Impedances”, *Journal of the Franklin Institute*, Vol. 249, Jan. 1950

[4] Booker, H. G., “Slot Aerials and Their Relation to Complementary Wire Aerials (Babinet’s Principle)”, *J. IEE, Pt. III-A*, Vol. 93, 1946, pp. 620-626

[5] Pozar, D. M., *Microwave Engineering; 3rd Edition*, 2005.

[6] King, R. W. P., *Transmission-line Theory*, 1955

[7] Paul, C. R., *Analysis of Multiconductor Transmission Lines; 2nd Edition*, 2008

[8] McLean, J. S., “A Re-Examination of the Fundamental Limits on the Radiation Q of Electrically Small Antennas”, *IEEE Transaction on Antennas and Propagation*, VOL 44, No. 5, May 1996, pg.672-675

[9] *MIL-217 Standard*

[10] Rumsey, V., *Frequency Independent Antennas*, 1966

Saving Lives - Rapid Alerts Using RDS for Earthquake and Fire Warnings

Matthew Straeb
Global Security Systems/ALERT FM
Sarasota, Florida, United States
mstraeb@gssnet.us

Abstract – A proven radio broadcast-based emergency notification system has successfully completed the rigorous process to obtain a license to operate with the ShakeAlert® earthquake early warning system for the West coast of the United States and additionally provide tornado, hurricane, fire, and other life-saving alerts. Using satellite connectivity to FM radio stations, this text-based emergency notification system rapidly delivers secure, encrypted ShakeAlert®-powered alerts to residents, schools, hospitals, commercial and industrial facilities that could provide individuals seconds of warning before an earthquake arrives, with demonstrated alert delivery to users in 5 seconds or less. These alerts help save lives and reduce injuries by giving people time to take a protective action like drop, cover, and hold on. The FM radio-based platforms are unique as they deliver alerts based on data from the US Geologic Survey-managed ShakeAlert® system using the existing nationwide FM broadcasting network. These systems provide multiple redundant backup transmitters connected by satellite to deliver secure transmission of single point-to-multipoint messaging, layered by "need to know" groupings without the nodal vulnerability of other communication systems.

Background

As disaster-sensing systems, artificial intelligence and data processing systems improve, it becomes possible to detect, decide, and disseminate life-saving messages rapidly (less than 5 seconds) for disasters such as earthquakes, tornadoes, tsunamis, active shooters, and fire evacuations. The challenge for legacy and switched communications systems is to be able to consume, process, and deliver these messages within a period that allows for the affected to react, potentially saving their lives. Currently, there are two primary communications platforms used to deliver emergency messages: cellular and broadcast (TV and radio). Cellular, while convenient, is a switched network with internet backbone and consequently it is difficult to prioritize rapid alerts. Exhaustive testing by the FCC determined that Wireless Emergency Alerts (WEA, the cellular alerting platform) were not feasible to be deployed for earthquake early warning messages.

TV broadcasting is used by over 85% of the nation to receive emergency information and plays a large role in the decision-making to act or not act. While very useful, it becomes inoperative due to power loss and since TV reception is done primarily using non-mobile devices, is not useful in the event of evacuations. On the other hand, radio broadcasting provides a reliable and mobile solution in the form of both the US government's Emergency Alert System (EAS) and textual emergency information using the Radio Data System (RDS) FM data subcarrier.

This paper is excerpted from the Proceedings of the 2022 NAB Broadcast Engineering and Information Technology (BEIT) Conference, © 2022, National Association of Broadcasters, 1 M Street S.E., Washington, DC 20003 USA.

Rapid Alerting

The objective of rapid alerts such as earthquake early warning systems is to rapidly detect the initiation of an earthquake (or in other cases, weather events such as a tornado), estimate the level of ground shaking (or the tornado path) to be expected, and issue a warning before significant ground shaking (or high wind) starts. If the alerting systems are incapable of delivering messages in rapid fashion the hyper-fast sensing systems will be ineffective in saving lives.

For earthquake warning systems such as ShakeAlert®, a network of seismic sensors (see Figure 1) detects the first energy to radiate from an earthquake (the P-wave energy), and the location and the magnitude of the earthquake is rapidly determined. The anticipated ground shaking across the region to be affected is then estimated. The system can provide warning before the S-wave, which brings the strong shaking that usually causes most of the damage, arrives. ShakeAlert® warnings are distributed to local and state public emergency response officials, critical infrastructure, private businesses, and the public. Earthquake early warning systems have been successfully implemented in some western US states (CA, WA, OR), Japan, Taiwan, Mexico, and other nations with varying degrees of sophistication and coverage.

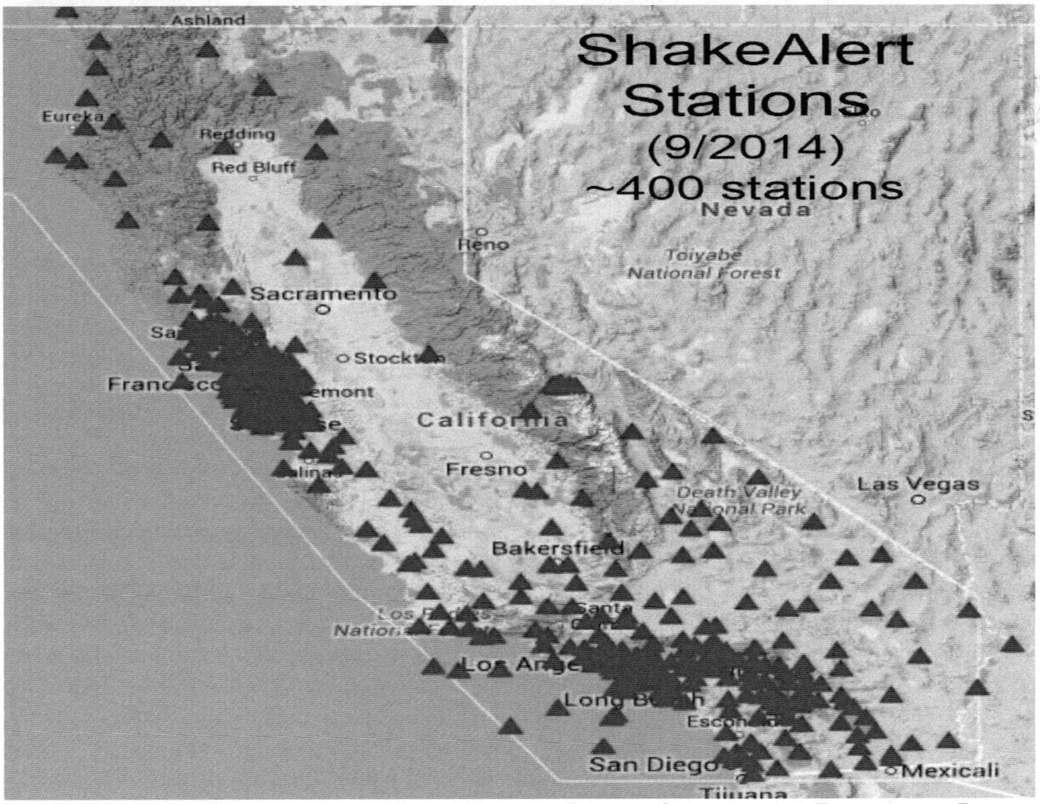

FIGURE 1. SHAKEALERT® EARTHQUAKE EARLY WARNING SENSOR STATIONS FOR RAPID ALERT DETECTION. (SOURCE: U.S. GEOLOGICAL SURVEY, DEPARTMENT OF THE INTERIOR)

ShakeAlert®

ShakeAlert® warning methods provide warning times from a few seconds to a few tens of seconds, depending on the distance to the epicenter of the earthquake. This is enough time to slow and stop trains and taxiing planes, to prevent cars from entering bridges and tunnels, to move away from dangerous machines or chemicals in work environments, to take cover under a desk, or to automatically shut down and isolate industrial systems. However, earthquake-warning notifications must be transmitted without requiring human-review and response action must be automated, as the total warning times are short (see Figure 2).

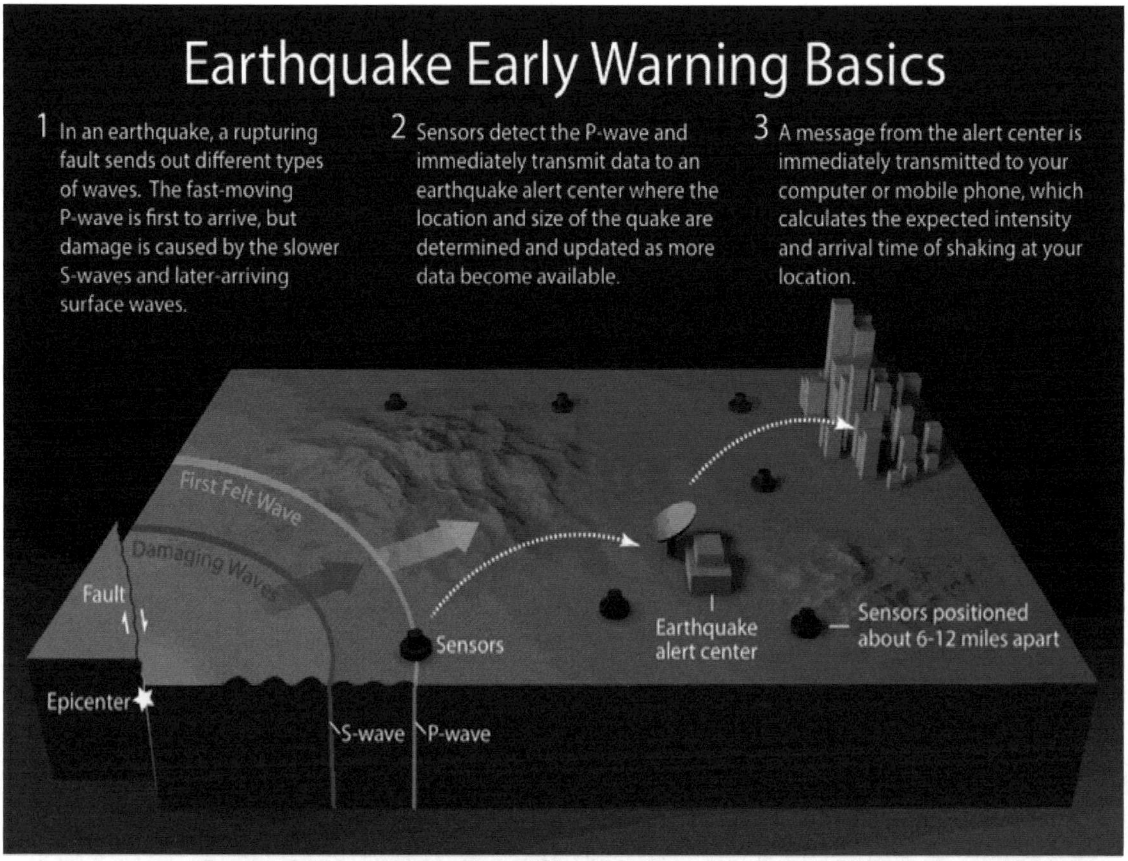

FIGURE 2. EARTHQUAKE EARLY WARNING NETWORK-BASED ALERTS.
(SOURCE: U.S. GEOLOGICAL SURVEY, DEPARTMENT OF THE INTERIOR)

The United States Geological Survey (USGS), in collaboration with university partners, developed ShakeAlert®, an earthquake early warning system for the west coast of the United States. The mission of the USGS Earthquake Hazards Program is to mitigate earthquake losses in the United States. Citizens, emergency responders, and engineers rely on the USGS for accurate and timely information on where an earthquake occurred, how much the ground shook in different locations, and what the likelihood is of future significant ground shaking.

The challenge was to be able to rapidly deliver a ShakeAlert® data payload in less than 5 seconds to meet or exceed the Department of Interior's U.S. Geological Survey (USGS) requirement to obtain a license to operate with ShakeAlert®. The ShakeAlert® system delivers three primary message payloads. The advantage to using contour-based messages is that this allows the processing to be distributed across the FM RDS alert network to achieve rapid alerts of 5 seconds. See Figure 3 showing the primary message engine outputs including a contour map.

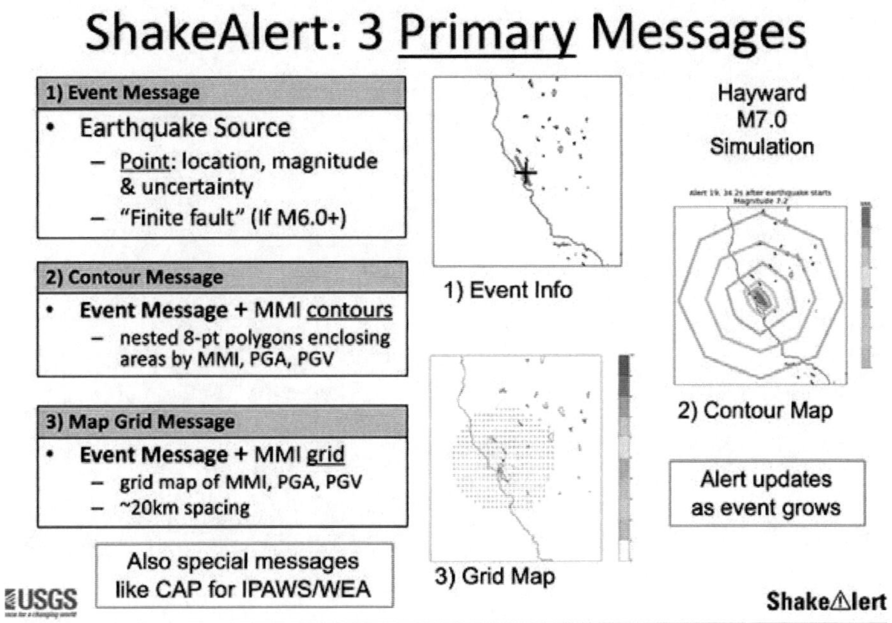

FIGURE 3. SHAKEALERT® PRIMARY MESSAGE ENGINE.
(SOURCE: U.S. GEOLOGICAL SURVEY, DEPARTMENT OF THE INTERIOR)

Figure 4 shows a map with a close-up view of an 8-point polygon contour. Using ShakeAlert® contour map data along with the alert message payload has enabled the use of the FM radio infrastructure to trigger other external devices or systems including devices falling into the "Internet of Things" (IOT) category. These warnings can be distributed using outdoor sirens, two-way radio systems, fire suppression systems, elevators, and generators to name a few.

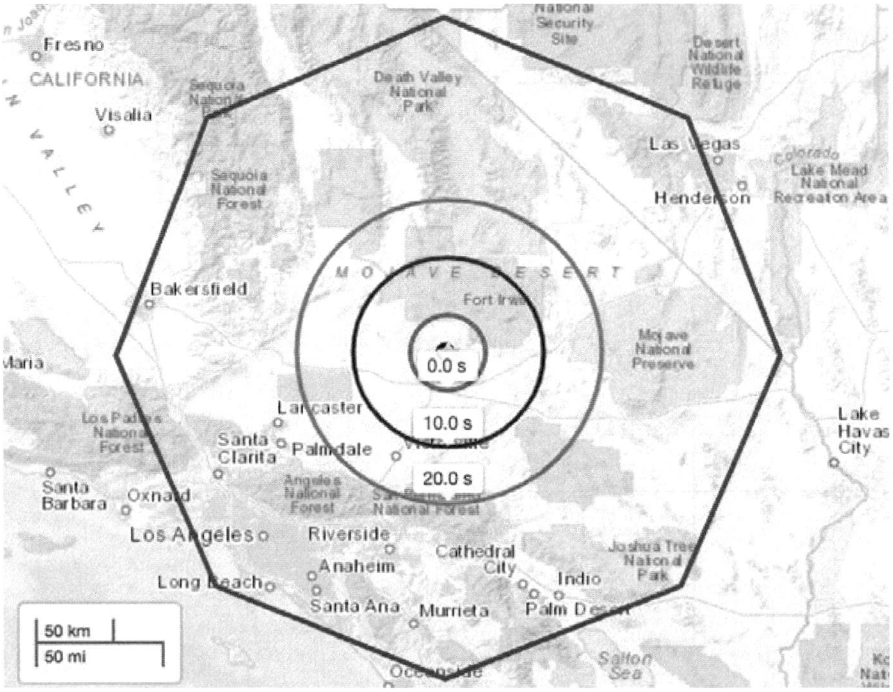

FIGURE 4. SHAKEALERT® CONTOUR MESSAGE 8-PT POLYGON EXAMPLE.
(SOURCE: U.S. GEOLOGICAL SURVEY, DEPARTMENT OF THE INTERIOR)

RDS-Based Alerting

An example of an FM RDS broadcast-based alerting system (see Figure 5) is the Alert FM system. This system is used to deliver the ShakeAlert® polygon data and is satellite-based, wireless and switchless, unencumbered by internet connectivity and switches. This system is used across many southern states for tornado and hurricane alerts and evacuations. ShakeAlert® geo-targeted polygon information is received on addressable portable or fixed receivers that can be programmed for specific groups, counties, or areas. Alert receivers automatically tune to and lock onto the strongest FM signal in the area. No new infrastructure needs to be constructed or deployed. This is in contrast to cellular voice/data alerting systems where new towers typically need to be built, components upgraded, backhaul bandwidth expanded, etc.

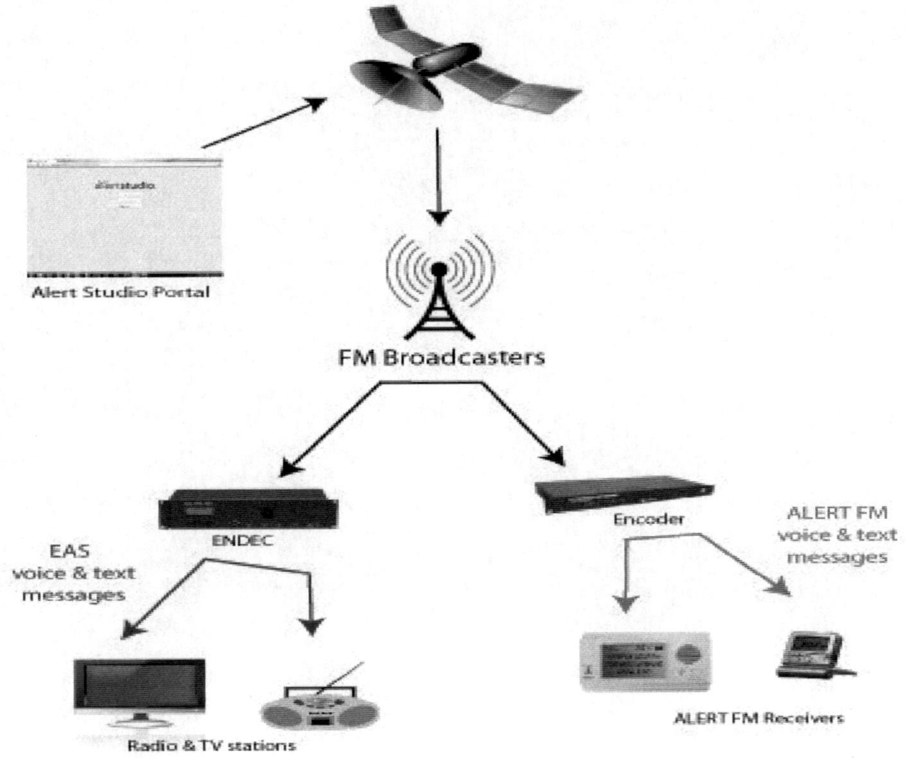

FIGURE 5. AN EXAMPLE OF AN FM-BASED RDS BROADCAST-BASED SYSTEM IS THE ALERT FM SYSTEM. (SOURCE: GLOBAL SECURITY SYSTEMS)

This same FM-based RDS broadcast-based alerting system can send automated polygon-based NOAA weather warnings and targeted state/local emergency information directly from an authorized user or the National Weather Service (NWS). FM-based RDS broadcast-based alerting systems are unique since they operate as dedicated emergency notification systems with the ability to deliver time-committed alerts unlike other cellular, telephone or broadcast systems, which are tied to internet, or telephonic switched systems. These other systems' delivery times are non-committal due to switched networks and lack of prioritization and timing delays because of commercial commitments. Broadcast-based systems using satellite-based wireless and switchless are unencumbered by internet connectivity and switches. Information is received on addressable portable or fixed receivers that can be programmed for specific groups, counties, or areas. Receivers automatically tune to and lock onto the strongest FM signal in the area and display the alert message (example receiver shown in Figure 6).

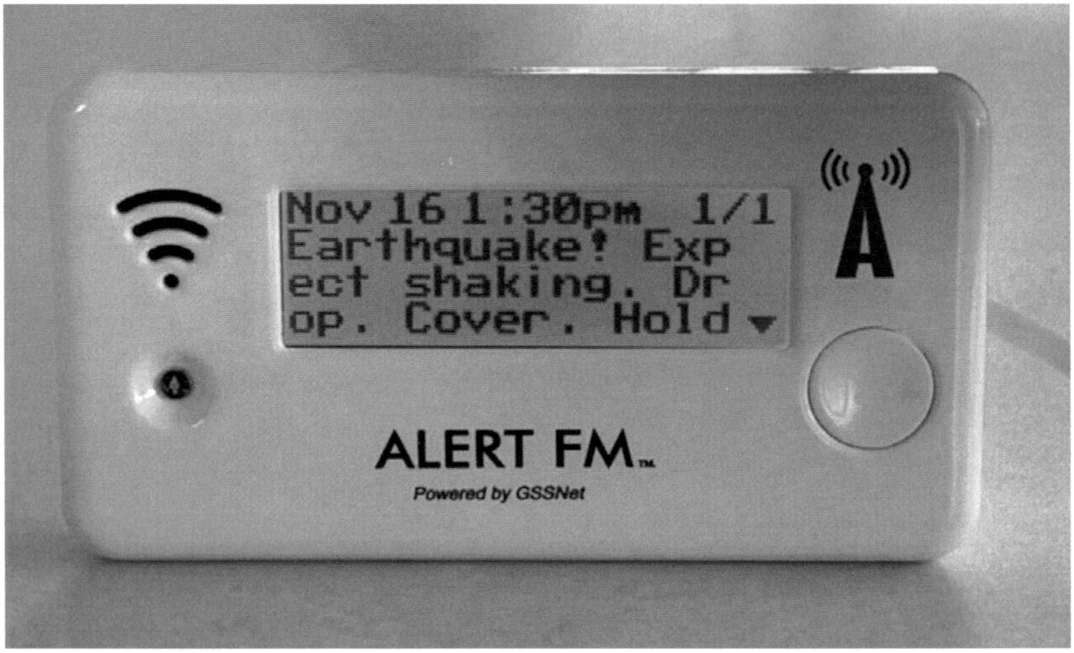

FIGURE 6. A TYPICAL FM-BASED RDS BROADCAST-BASED ALERT RECEIVER USED IN THE ALERT FM SYSTEM. (SOURCE: GLOBAL SECURITY SYSTEMS)

FM-based RDS broadcast-based alerting system warnings are designed as addressable, low-latency, high-value messages that can be received across local, county, state, or nationwide coverage areas, depending upon which broadcasters are sending out the messages. A major design principle for FM-based RDS broadcast-based alerting systems is typically to balance message delivery speed with non-interference to other uses of the RDS subcarrier (for example, delivering song title and artist information), especially considering the limited effective throughput of the RDS data "pipe." FM-based RDS broadcast-based alert systems can be structured to allow implementation of emergency alerting without disabling standard broadcast station transmission of metadata.

FM-based RDS broadcast-based alerting systems that transmit RDS-delivered emergency alerts and information are a complement to the broadcast-based EAS, to WEA cellular telephone-based system, as well as to outdoor warning sirens or telephone-based mass notification systems. Note that the performance of cellular telephone-based systems can be adversely affected by network capacity issues and power outages which occur in emergency situations. By contrast, the FM terrestrial radio stations that are used to transmit RDS-based emergency alerts and information are significantly more robust and have a much greater probability of staying operational during emergency situations.

According to the US Federal Communications Commission (FCC), the US has over 14,000 FCC-licensed radio stations across the US states and territories. Each licensed radio broadcaster is required to carry EAS messages and desires to carry other emergency alert and information messages to citizens. This represents a tremendous opportunity for FM radio to stay relevant and avoid spectrum being re-allocated to non-radio broadcast applications. Part of the strategy is to promote to the consumer electronics industry the value of including emergency alerts in everyday devices (like IOT devices).

The alerting and broadcasting industries need to be actively working with consumer electronics device makers to embed FM radio chips and alert services into various devices with displays if the maximum benefit to the public is to be derived. Devices allowing data entry (for example, on a touch-screen keyboard) would allow for the programming of alert codes into the device which would then support a customized emergency messaging capability. Further, consumer electronics industry companies should be encouraged to integrate FM chips into their products for national distribution based upon a commitment by an alert service provider to deploy a national FM-based RDS broadcast-based alert system. Accelerated adoption by consumer electronics industry and their distributors would be enabled for integration of alerting in alarm clocks, appliances, smoke detectors and other widely used products is dependent on nationwide coverage.

Summary

The needs of the US states and territories for a nationwide FM-based RDS broadcast-based emergency alert and information system can be fulfilled by implementing a proven emergency alerting and information system relying on the world's most stable and robust communications platform, FM radio broadcast.

The Flared-Skirt or Umbrella-Spoke Feed for Grounded Medium Wave Antenna Towers

Benjamin F. Dawson III, P.E.
Hatfield & Dawson Consulting Engineers, LLC
Seattle, Washington, United States
dawson@hatdaw.com

Bobby L. Cox II, PhD
Kintronic Laboratories, Inc.
Bristol, Tennessee, United States
bcox@kintronic.com

Abstract - The increasing use of single antenna systems for multiple frequencies and use of medium wave antenna structures for mounting antennas for other uses has led to the exploration of alternative methods for feeding grounded towers. While the simple skirt feed with multiple parallel wires insulated from the tower is fairly common, other methods such as slant-wire feeds and skirts with other geometries offer substantial advantages. The simple skirt feed has shortcomings that can be eliminated by the use of flared skirts which extend from at or near the tower top to a location near midpoint on a guy wire and then back to a common connection near the tower base. The advantages are that the skirt wires need not add substantial compression load to the tower or be supported by multiple insulators, and that in general their impedance bandwidth is excellent. The flared skirt also has less long-term maintenance concerns and is less obstructive to tower climbers and to installations of other services on the tower. Flared-skirt systems exhibit vertical radiation patterns which are essentially the same as base fed antennas of the same height, and do not generate excessive horizontally polarized radiation.

Antenna Tower Feed Systems

While the base-fed monopole tower has been the most common medium wave antenna since the 1930s, antenna towers grounded at the base have also been employed in many installations. Grounded tower antennas have essentially the same electrical behavior (pattern characteristics) as base fed antennas of the same electrical length.

Straight Wire Skirt Feeds Parallel to Towers

The most common method of feeding the grounded tower employs wires connected to the tower at an elevated location, most commonly a skirt of several wires, roughly parallel to the tower face, as shown in Figure 1.

Traditional skirt feeds have several unfortunate characteristics. The skirt must be kept at a constant spacing from the tower to avoid impedance changes in windy conditions. This can require the use of numerous insulators between the skirt and the tower, or substantial tension on the skirt wire. The wire tension adds additional compression load on the tower legs. The use of insulators adds weight and wind loading and can obstruct other installations on the tower. They can also be a maintenance issue,

This paper is excerpted from the Proceedings of the 2022 NAB Broadcast Engineering and Information Technology (BEIT) Conference, © 2022, National Association of Broadcasters, 1 M Street S.E., Washington, DC 20003 USA.

requiring periodic cleaning, and they can obstruct tower climbing. The spacing of the skirt from the tower and the number of skirt wires are critical for impedance bandwidth. In some cases, the design can result in poor performance because of inappropriate choice of insulator length or tuning stub location. A particular concern often caused by insufficient spacing between the skirt wires and the tower is impedance changes caused by icing. Even a very small skin of ice can result in considerable impedance change under some conditions.

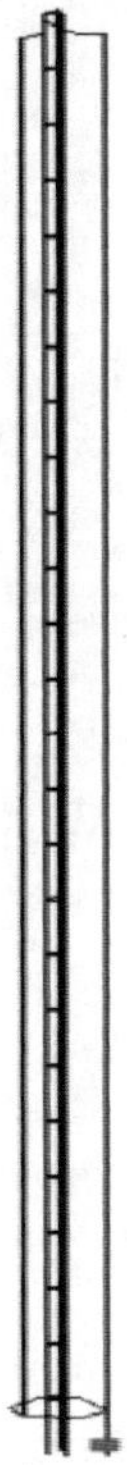

FIGURE 1: TRADITIONAL SKIRT FEED GEOMETRY (NOT TO SCALE OR PROPORTION)

Slant Wire Feeds

Slant wire feeds, which have been used since the 1930s, are a simple feed system solution for grounded towers in the quarter wavelength range. They are simple to install, and structurally minimal. For towers much over 120 degrees in height they result in high angle radiation pattern distortion, however. They also have a ground level high voltage point, at their feed location, distant from the tower base area, as shown in Figure 2. They are the most economical method of feeding a grounded tower. Their only complexity is in high power installations where the slant wire needs to be a ribbon or bundle to reduce surface voltage gradients well below corona levels.

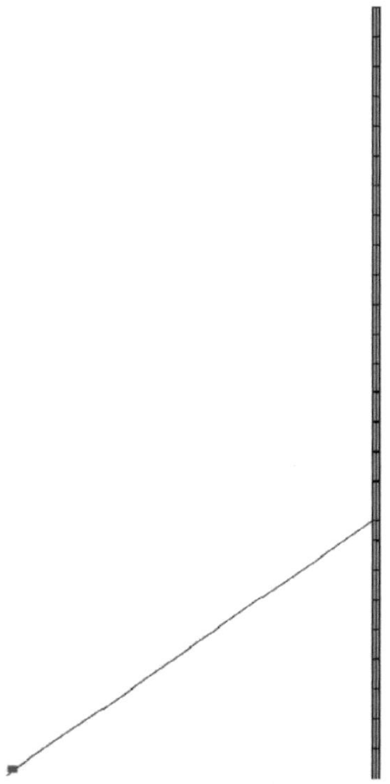

FIGURE 2: SLANT WIRE FEED GEOMETRY (NOT TO SCALE OR PROPORTION)

Single Parallel Wire Feeds

A single wire, extending along the tower structure, connected at the top and insulated from the tower as it descends (like one wire of a conventional skirt), can also be used to drive a grounded tower. It can be visualized as one half of a folded dipole, with unequal diameters. This design can be a good emergency antenna but generally will have relatively narrow bandwidth impedance characteristics.

Single Wire Umbrella-Spoke Feeds

The single wire "umbrella spoke" feed is sometimes used as an emergency or Special Temporary Authority ("STA") antenna and is a good solution for that purpose, such as shown in Figure 3. Examples have also been constructed with the geometry carefully modeled so as to have a purely resistive input impedance. Others have used guy wires on HF curtain antennas or have been supported by grounded FM towers. But this feed arrangement suffers from high angle radiation pattern distortion if used with taller towers and can produce non-circular horizontal radiation patterns.

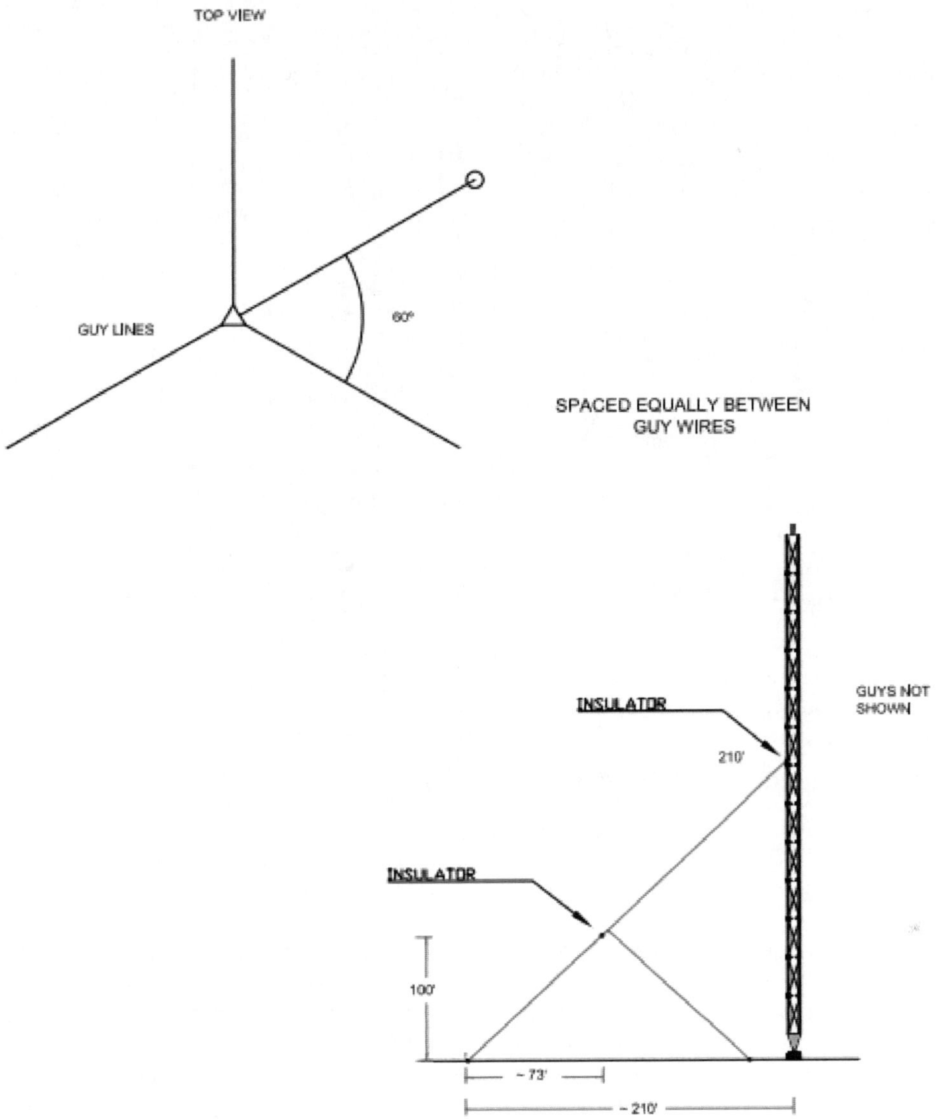

FIGURE 3: STA ANTENNA USING SINGLE UMBRELLA-SPOKE SKIRT WIRE (NOT TO SCALE OR PROPORTION)

Flared Skirt or Umbrella-Spoke Feeds

The flared skirt with multiple wires, usually three for triangular towers and four for square ones, has significant advantages over all other methods of feeding a grounded tower as an efficient wide bandwidth radiator.

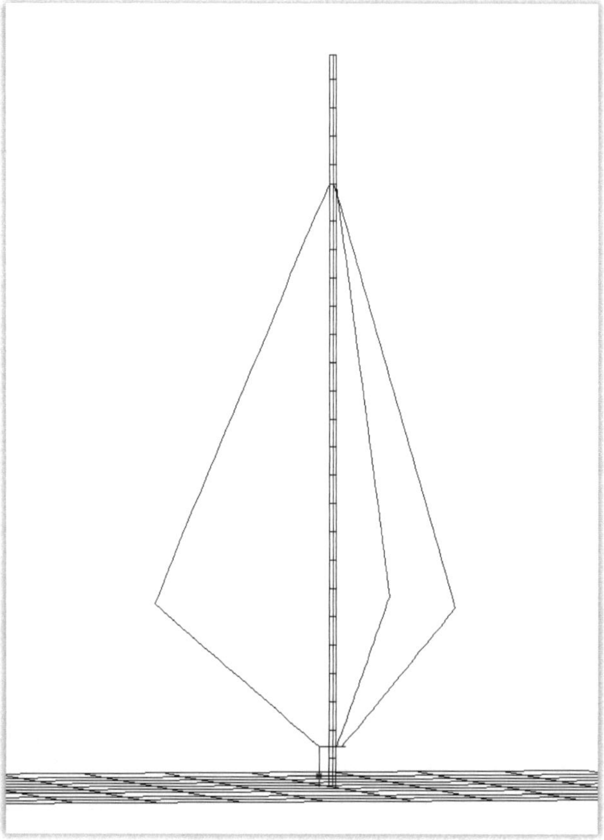

FIGURE 4: THE FLARED SKIRT FEED

The flared skirt, as shown in Figure 4, does not require tower attachment except at its top and (if mechanically convenient) bottom ends. It can be configured so that it's used as part of one of the uppermost guy levels. Its additional structural load is largely just the weight of the necessary cables, with no extra compression load on the tower legs. Because there is no requirement for intermediate support insulators, there is easier access to other antennas and hardware on the tower, and maintenance is reduced. One minor disadvantage is that the skirt wires need to be "clocked" from the primary guy wire directions to avoid contact with the lower guy levels. Intermediate azimuths 60 degrees from the adjacent guy orientations can be used, but much smaller offsets of just a few degrees are also possible. This requires additional anchors, but, unless the skirt support is also used as a primary upper-level guy, this anchor is far less substantial than the anchors for the main guy cables.

Frequency Allocation Considerations

While the RMS efficiency of an MF or LF antenna (directional or non-directional) is a significant characteristic in determining the value of the antenna, the radiation pattern, both vertical and horizontal, is of critical importance in its fit to the allocation requirements for operation.

The horizontal plane circularity of flared skirt antennas is generally well within ±1 dB, which is within the accepted definition of omni-directional operation [see 47 CFR §1.30002(a)]. Vertical pattern characteristics of a flared skirt antenna or of multiple tower directional antennas employing flared skirts are nearly indistinguishable from the patterns of base fed antennas of the same electrical height.

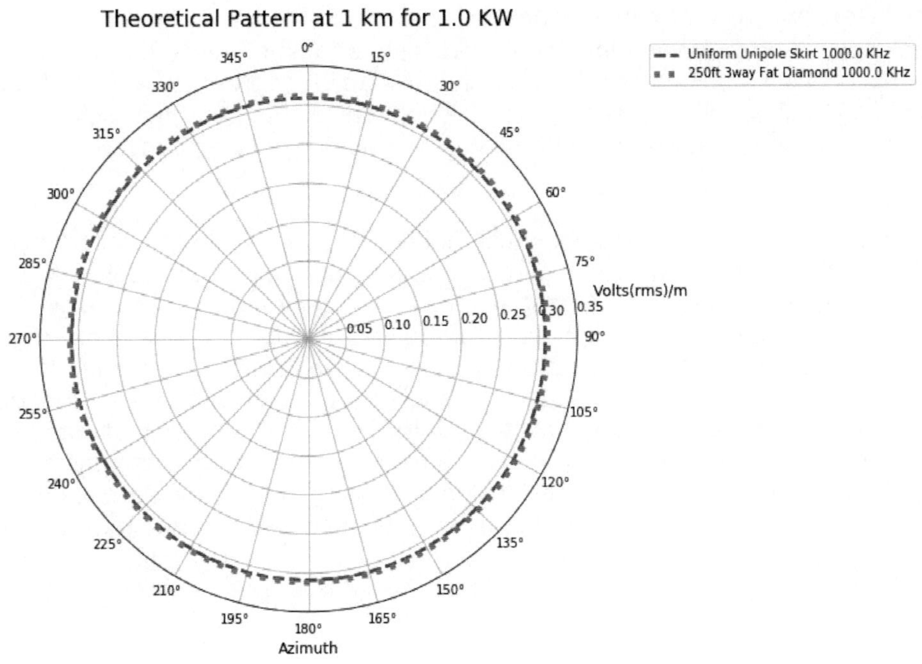

FIGURE 5: HORIZONTAL PLANE PATTERN

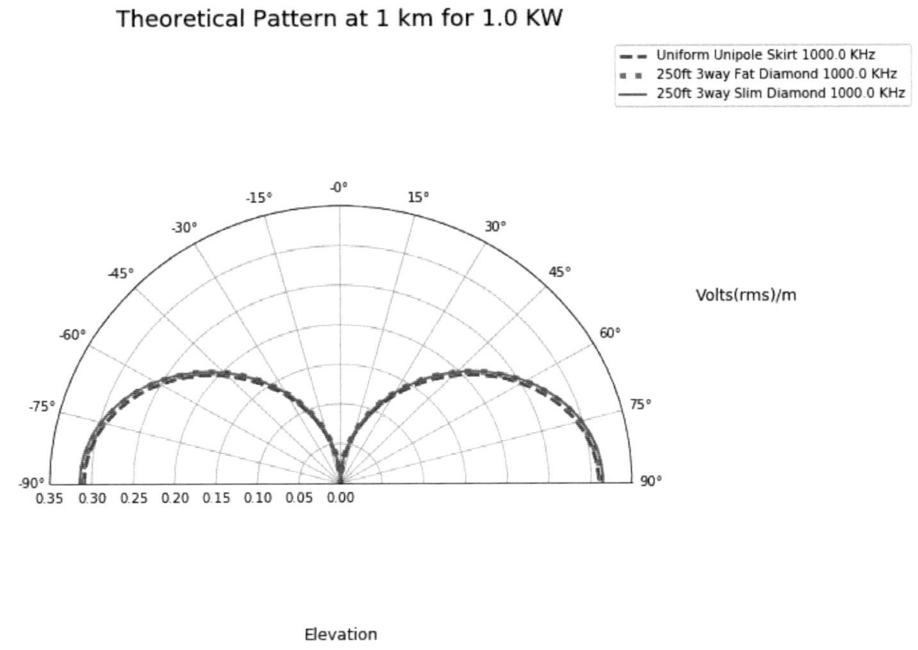

FIGURE 6: VERTICAL PLANE PATTERNS

Impedance and Bandwidth Characteristics

Electrically, the significant advantage of the flared skirt is superior impedance bandwidth characteristics. This is of substantial value for very short (45 to 60 degree) towers, or for use with multiple frequencies. The flared skirt generally has the best bandwidth performance of any feed system for short towers and has significantly better impedance characteristics than conventional vertical wire skirts.

Two examples of flared skirt antennas are shown in Figure 7. The example on the left is a "Slim" flared skirt and the one on the right is a "Fat" flared skirt. The enhanced bandwidth qualities are more pronounced with the wider flared skirt. Note that as the skirt is made more and more slim, the design approaches the case of the traditional straight skirt fed "folded unipole" antenna, and the wideband characteristics diminish significantly. A good proportion for a wide flared skirt antenna is to have the individual folds of the antenna form roughly a 3-4-5 triangle with the tower being the longest length of the triangle, the upper half of the skirt being the "4", and the lower half of the skirt being the "3" of the triangle. This wide flare can be achieved using anchors for the cables that tension the skirt elements placed no further from the tower than the uppermost guy anchors. If this wide flare is not achievable, then the more narrow flare is still a significant improvement in bandwidth characteristics over the traditional skirt fed system.

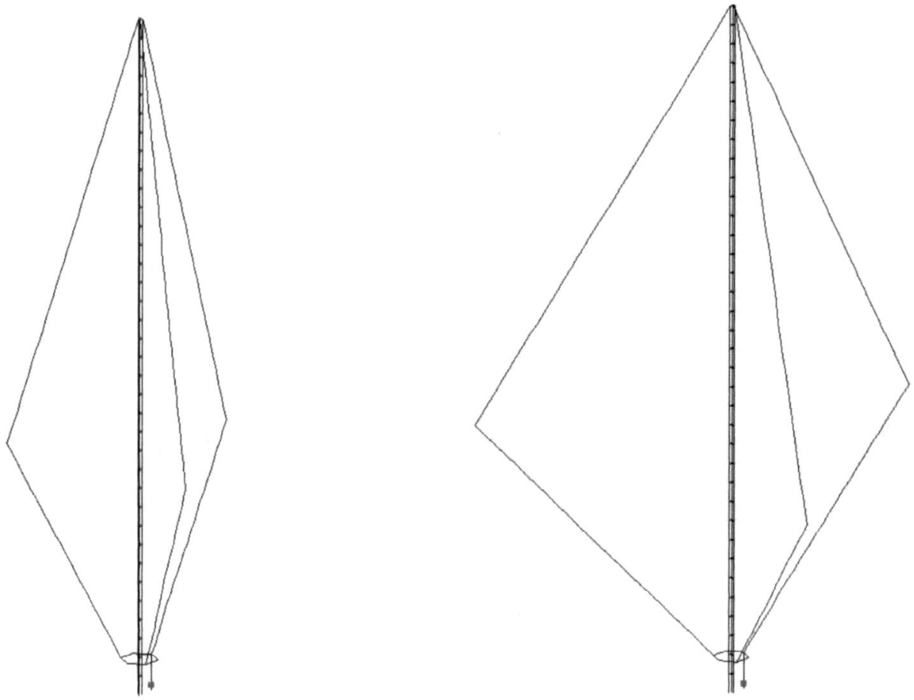

FIGURE 7: SMALL AND LARGE ANGLE DESIGNS OF SKIRT AND TOWER

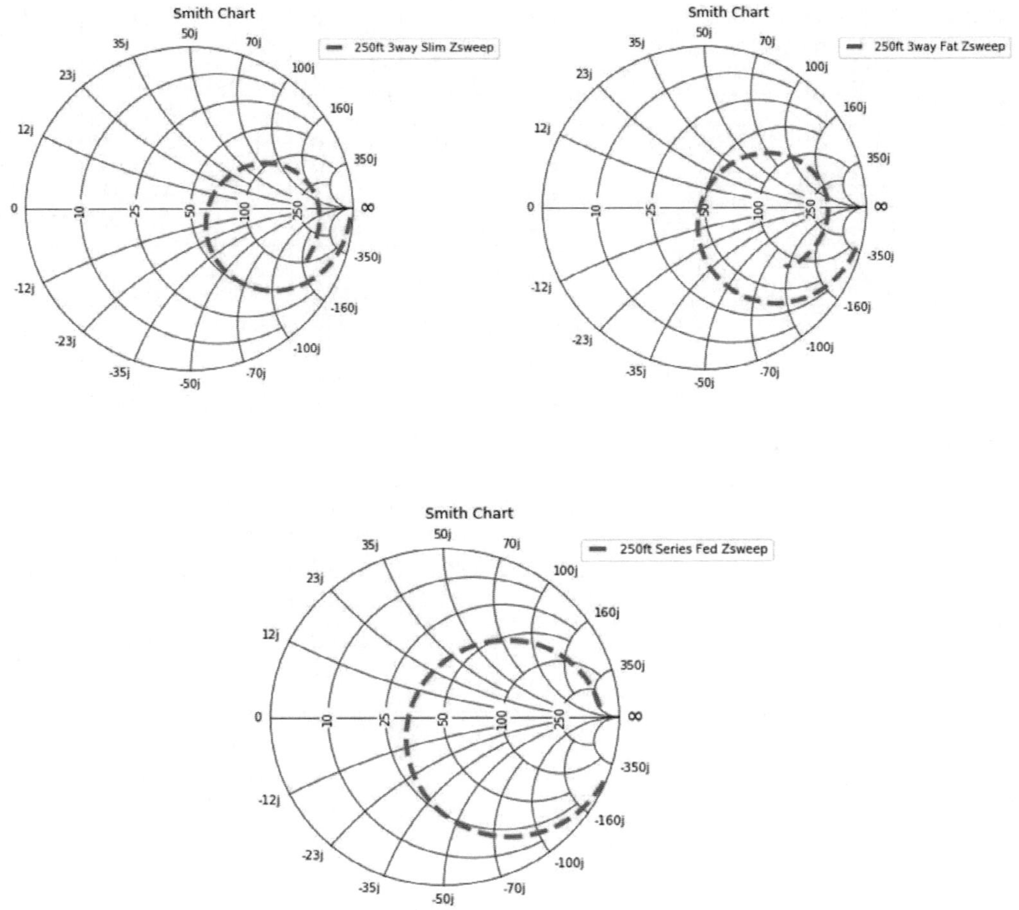

FIGURE 8: 530 KHZ-1695 KHZ IMPEDANCE PLOTS FOR SMALL AND LARGE ANGLE OF SKIRT AND TOWER, AS WELL AS BASE INSULATED AND SERIES FED TOWER; ALL FOR 250 FOOT TOWER HEIGHT

The midband VSWR values for the flared skirt are several percent better at ±10 and ±15 kHz than that of the conventional unipole.

Examples of typical impedances for several feed arrangements are shown in Figures 8 and 9. The fat skirt definitely works well over the full band for the 250-foot tower height used as the example. The example tower's electrical height ranges from 49° to 147.7° over the frequency range. The series fed tower is too short to be desirable at the lower end of the band for that tower height. The slender skirt is a bit in between, but still quite a bit better than the series fed.

The example shows that the usable portion of the band is widest with the fat skirt, and that it has noticeably wider bandwidth than a series fed configuration.

The low resistances of the series fed case on the low end of the band are especially troublesome for multiplexing.

Freq. (kHz)	Series Fed Impedance	VSWR	Slim Flared Skirt Impedance	VSWR	Fat Flared Skirt Impedance)	VSWR
535	7.7 – j 244.4	4.243	350.9 – j 1403	4.600	43.2 – j 359 .0	3.066
540	7.9 – j 240.2	2.694	283.6 – j 1230	2.838	41.8 – j 341.6	2.121
545	8.0 – j 236.1	1.671	236.3 – j 1093	1.693	40.6 – j 325.4	1.453
550	8.2 – j 231.9	1.000	201.6 – j 982.2	1.000	39.5 – j 310.4	1.000
555	8.4 – j 227.9	1.613	175.3 – j 890.6	1.651	38.6 – j 296.4	1.430
560	8.5 – j 223.9	2.523	154.9 – j 813.6	2.595	37.8 – j 283.3	1.992
565	8.7 – j 219.9	3.756	138.7 – j748.0	3.843	37.0 – j 270.9	2.702
885	28.6 – j 22.9	1.319	58.7 – j 12.2	1.181	57.8 + j 34.4	1.159
890	29.1 – j 20.2	1.200	59.5 – j 8.9	1.115	58.9 + j 37.1	1.103
895	29.6 – j 17.6	1.096	60.2 – j 5.7	1.056	60.0 + j 39.8	1.050
900	30.1 – j 14.9	1.000	61.0 – j 2.5	1.000	61.2 + j 42.5	1.000
905	30.6 – j 12.3	1.091	61.8 + j 0.7	1.055	62.3 + j 45.2	1.048
910	31.1 – j 9.7	1.189	62.7 + j 3.8	1.111	63.6 + j 47.9	1.099
915	31.7 – j 7.0	1.297	63.5 + j 6.9	1.169	64.8 + j 50.6	1.151
1235	98.9 + j173.0	1.118	245.3 + j 157.4	1.080	300.3 + j 130.6	1.076
1240	100.8 + j176.2	1.077	251.7 + j 157.3	1.053	306.6 + j 126.6	1.050
1245	102.8 + j179.5	1.037	258.3 + j 156.9	1.026	312.7 + j 122.2	1.025
1250	104.8 + j182.7	1.000	265.0 + j156.4	1.000	318.7 + j117.4	1.000
1255	106.9 + j186.0	1.038	271.8 + j 155.5	1.026	324.6 + j 112.3	1.025
1260	109.0 + j189.3	1.076	278.7 + j 154.4	1.052	330.3 + j 106.7	1.050
1265	111.1 + j192.6	1.115	285.8 + j 152.9	1.080	335.8 + j 100.8	1.076
1585	484.8 + j404.0	1.080	187.4 – j 211.8	1.107	128.4 – j 141.3	1.102
1590	497.5 + j404.2	1.053	181.4 – j 210.3	1.071	124.9 – j 139.3	1.067
1595	510.4 + j404.0	1.026	175.6 – j 208.6	1.035	121.5 – j 137.2	1.033
1600	523.7 + j403.6	1.000	169.9 – j 206.8	1.000	118.2 – j 135.1	1.000
1605	537.3 + j402.7	1.026	164.5 – j 205.0	1.035	115.0 – j 132.9	1.034
1610	551.1 + j401.3	1.053	159.2 – j 203.0	1.071	112.0 – j 130.7	1.068
1615	565.3 + j399.5	1.080	154.1 – j 200.9	1.110	109.0 – j 128.4	1.105

FIGURE 9: COMPARISON OF NORMALIZED IMPEDANCE CHARACTERISTICS FOR 250' TOWER FED WITH THREE METHODS FOR EXAMPLE FREQUENCIES ACROSS THE AM BAND

Comparisons with measured data show that the NEC impedance calculations for the flared skirt antenna are quite accurate. As an example:

Frequency	Calculated Impedance	Measured Impedance
540 kHz	39.3 + J 41.8	43.8 + J 40.8
702 kHz	116.4 + J 83.9	139.8 + J 78.2

FIGURE 10: CALCULATED VS MEASURED IMPEDANCES FOR A TYPICAL FLARED SKIRT ANTENNA

Examples

FIGURE 11: TEMPORARY INSTALLATION (LEFT)
HIGH POWER INSTALLATION (RIGHT)

FIGURE 12: BASE REGION GEOMETRY OF A 6-WIRE FLARED SKIRT (LEFT)
FLARED SKIRT REPLACING CONVENTIONAL SKIRT DUE TO INSTABILITY IN ICING CONDITIONS (RIGHT)

FIGURE 13: FOUR TOWER HIGH POWER DIRECTIONAL ANTENNA WITH FLARED SKIRT FEEDS

Conclusions

The flared or “umbrella-spoke” feed arrangement for grounded towers employed as radiators in medium and long wave antennas is both physically practical and electrically advantageous. Numerous examples of both temporary and permanent installations shown in Figure 11-13 have performed reliably. The vertical and horizontal radiation patterns are essentially the same as conventional parallel skirt fed antennas or base driven antennas. They exhibit drive impedance characteristics that make them very desirable for multiple frequency installations, particularly when the frequency spacing is large. The flared skirt has proven to be a valuable tool to make multiplexed scenarios practical when no other tower feed method would do so. They are no more mechanically complex than conventional skirt feed arrangements and exhibit fewer undesirable effects from adverse weather conditions.

The 99.99% Solution: Four-Nines Reliability from Cloud-Native Television Architectures

Prabu Chelladurai, Jerald Mejarla, Juan Martin
Firstlight Media
Toronto, Ontario, Canada

Abstract – If you watched the Super Bowl in the 1990s, were you ever disappointed because the telecast wouldn't start or played with degraded quality or buffered a lot or threw an error? The answer is "No." It just worked! Why should those issues happen with your OTT service, especially with the way technology has matured over the years? The reason is that OTT technology is intertwined with the other key elements of its enabling ecosystem - the Internet, infrastructure, and devices. While the ecosystem has evolved by leaps and bounds over the past two decades, most OTT platforms have struggled to keep pace with these diverse changes.

This paper discusses a cloud-native technology architecture that can deliver 99.99% reliability for any given OTT service. The paper also details a case study that explains how such a platform has enabled the evolution of live video experience for American sports fans.

Understanding What Changed in OTT

The transition from traditional TV with analog signals to the OTT era of digital, internet-delivered streams has happened over the past three decades. In any discussion of highly-performant, reliable OTT services, it is important to understand how video technology, opportunities, and end viewers' expectations have changed during that time. We will consider four phases of evolution for the purposes of this paper.

Phase 1 – Traditional Analog Broadcast

This is the oldest form of commercial TV service in which only video and audio were broadcast as analog signals using satellites and terrestrial distribution centers. While reliability tended to be strong, these services were limited in terms of content, quality, reach, monetization, and more by their dependence on closed delivery systems, rigid technologies, and reliance on televisions as the sole viewing device.

Phase 2 – Digital Broadcast

The next phase in the evolution of TV services was the shift to video and audio broadcasts via digital signals. Because it was digital, the technology enabled some basic metadata to be sent as well. The actual distribution technology was similar to traditional analog, i.e., satellite and terrestrial distribution centers. Many TV providers continue to use this technology today primarily because of the underlying infrastructure and investments they already have in place.

Phase 3 – IPTV

In this phase, video was compressed to digital formats (MPEG 2 or MPEG 4 converted to MPEG-TS) and multicast over IP networks. This helped multichannel video programming distributors (MVPD) with large network infrastructures that have the originating data center, network infrastructure, and device ecosystem under their control. Advances in video technology, bandwidth, and metadata processing enabled more diversity and quality in viewing experiences; however, viewing remained limited to the television.

Phase 4 – OTT

OTT is the latest incarnation of what a video service can look like: an environment in which high quality video along with rich metadata can be unicast over the Internet to any piece of glass that is connected to the Internet. This creates a wealth of new content, audience, and monetization opportunities for the media industry; the challenge is to deliver them with a reliability that is equal to or greater than that of broadcast.

Figure 1 summarizes the opportunity and potential of these four phases.

VALUE POTENTIAL	Analog Broadcast	Digital Broadcast	IPTV	OTT
Video Quality	Constrained Bandwidth. Basic Quality	Constrained Bandwidth. Basic Quality	Increased Bandwidth High Quality	Increased Bandwidth High Quality
Enriched Metadata	Only Audio & Video	Audio, Video & lite metadata	Audio, Video & Rich Metadata	Audio, Video & Rich Dynamic Metadata
Content Flavors	Live/Linear	Live/Linear	Live/Linear	Live/Linear, Catchup & VOD
Reach	Only TVs (via Satellite)	Only TVs (via STB)	Only TVs (via STB & Hybrid STBs)	Any Device connected to internet
Monetization Potential	Static Ads	Static Ads, PPV Live	Dynamic Ads, PPV Live	Personalized Ads, PPV Live, TVOD
Security	No Security	Conditional Access	Conditional Access, DRM	DRM

FIGURE 1: VALUE POTENTIAL OF DIFFERENT OF TV SERVICES OVER THE YEARS.

The potential value that an OTT service can bring to viewers and businesses easily outclasses the older incarnations of TV services. But this does not come in for free. There are many practical challenges that an OTT service has to overcome in order to deliver a highly available solution.

Firstlight Media Design Principles for High Availability

The Firstlight Media OTT platform pivots on the following three design principles to address the many challenges and deliver a video service with > 99.99% reliability.

FIGURE 2: FIRSTLIGHT'S ARCHITECTURE PRINCIPLES FOR >99.99% RELIABILITY

Below are best practices that enable the Firstlight Media platform to implement the above-mentioned design principles successfully.

VCMS Core

The core of the Firstlight Media platform is based on a microkernel architecture with pluggable components developed as micro-services to facilitate adding/enhancing product features and, at the same time, to support customization. The Firstlight Media micro-kernel provides a web-based Video CMS that can be connected to existing A/V pipelines, subscriber management systems, and web/mobile applications. Plus, it enables an ecosystem of feature extensions.

Modularity

All features are developed as pluggable components to allow individual teams to develop and test independently. Every component is structured as a monorepo consisting of a backend service, a data layer, and a micro-frontend. Each component can be independently validated against a specific version of the micro-kernel and added to a deployment package programmatically.

Automation

Firstlight Media core and plugin components are developed and managed using a proprietary development platform designed for managing core/plugin application code, quality checks, build generation, test automation, and programmatic deployment. The development platform also provides tools for centralized monitoring of all the customer deployments managed by a dedicated team of DevOp and SREs.

Data-Driven

The Firstlight Media platform provides extensible APIs for components to exchange information and modify existing structural data elements, such as state variables. The API supports batch loading and a streaming pipeline to send data in real time. This facilitates centralized data collection, analysis, and dashboard generation.

Security

Security is a top priority of the Firstlight Media platform. All aspects of the platform, components, infrastructure, and human/non-human interaction are treated as equally vulnerable, and all interactions are enforced with principles of least privilege (POLP). All source code (e.g., internal/OSS/3rd party) and binaries (e.g., container images, executables) are scanned for vulnerabilities before deployment.

Ultra-Redundancy

Broadcast TV architecture was path breaking at the time. Yet transport was limited to the power of nature, i.e., radio waves carrying audio/video, which made for light payloads. Services were all but guaranteed to be delivered unless there was bad weather. At the same time, viewers' expectations for quality were modest given that TV as a mode of entertainment was new. With the advent of digital broadcast and subsequently IPTV solutions, expectations increased considerably, and architectural complexity grew. TV providers countered by investing heavily in infrastructure to increase scalability of their end-to-end delivery paths. Redundancy was paid for at a premium.

Today, OTT providers do not have that luxury, thus it is important that performant, yet cost-effective solutions are developed. Firstlight Media has worked out an approach that is:

- **Cloud native** - cloud native and cloud agnostic components eliminate the cost and overhead of setting up and managing multiple redundant instances.
- **Modular** - The modular microservices-based architecture enables different levels of redundancy with various configurations based on load.
- **Automated** - When it comes to maintaining high availability, failover automation is required. Proper telemetry to monitor current and target paths and quick decision-making processes are key.

Along with the above enablers, the Firstlight Media platform has clear guidelines for choosing between Active-Active & Active-Passive redundancy setups.

Solution Area	• Recommended Redundancy	Salient Points
Live Processing	Active-Active	• With this setup, platforms easily operate at >99.99% availability levels. • Recommended for premium live channels. (If cost is a constraint, Active-Passive setup can be considered and will guarantee 99.95% availability.)
VOD Processing	Active-Passive	• Since VOD processing does not incur the high concurrency peaks of live, an active-passive solution typically sufficient
Video Distribution	Active-Active	• The load is logically distributed between sites. • Firstlight Media platform easily scales one of the sites to handle full demand.

TABLE 1: REDUNDANCY RECOMMENDATIONS

Instant Scaling

OTT brought significant technological advancement in the way users watch video content. It opened doors for users to interact with TV, which traditionally had been a one-way communication (broadcast / multicast). Users can request content they like to watch and broadcasters, studios, video distributors, content creators, etc. are able to stream personalized content to any device over the internet. In order to facilitate this two-way communication, the underlying solution needs the ability to scale instantly.

The Firstlight Media platform has solved this scaling need by taking advantage of the evolution of cloud technology. It takes full advantage of cloud native components and serverless computing to tackle this sudden spike in demand. Below are some of the key technologies that are used across various domains of the Firstlight Media OTT platform.

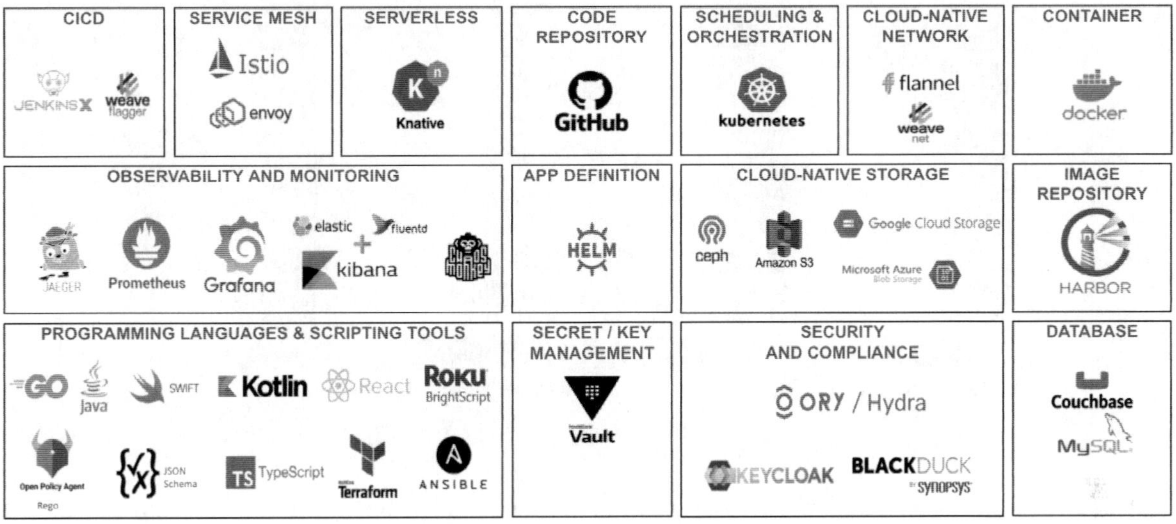

FIGURE 3: FIRSTLIGHT TECHNOLOGY STACK THAT ENABLES INSTANT SCALING

All Firstlight Media components are deployed and managed using cloud managed Kubernetes orchestration. All microservices are deployed as Knative serverless service using Istio service mesh allowing the platform to scale up / down instantly. Istio also allows seamless configuration of traffic shaping, fault tolerance thresholds and dynamic deployment.

Firstlight Media microservices that are developed in Go (as opposed to Java or .Net) not only enable instant start up but also use much lower compute resources thereby keeping the infrastructure spend under check. In figure 4 is a comparison of Java and Go variants of Firstlight Media's playback authorization microservice.

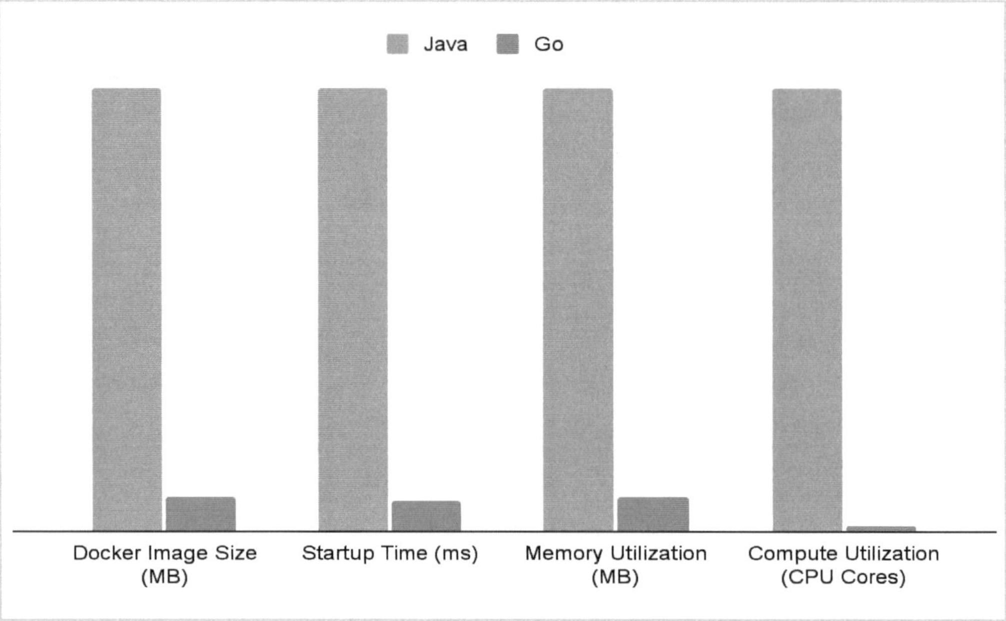

FIGURE 4: MICROSERVICES WRITTEN IN GO LANGUAGE HELP REDUCE INFRASTRUCTURE FOOTPRINT BY ~90%

Experience First Design

OTT services have quite a few moving parts in the form of underlying infrastructure and business constraints, e.g., the need to serve video to audiences with varying internet bandwidths; different device form factors; multi-country distribution; blackout rules, etc. With all these challenges, the approach needs to follow an “Experience First” design, that is placing the user experience as the highest priority.

Picture a high-profile live game starting on a Saturday evening at 7 p.m. and streaming on your favorite OTT service that has 2M+ subscribers. You'll see a vast majority of the viewers (let's say 1M+) spread across different locations on disparate networks rushing into the platform between 6.57 p.m. and 7.02 p.m. (the “flash crowd”). Below are “Experience First” design examples to guarantee a high-quality playback experience.

Circuit Breakers

In Broadcast TV, the game was pushed to TV boxes in a particular region/network and viewers could start watching without additional load to the infrastructure. Comparatively in an OTT service, all 1M+ viewers have to be checked for valid credentials, geo restrictions, and other business rules before they are authorized to watch the game. Most OTT services will struggle to handle this kind of workload, resulting in bad viewing experiences, i.e., timing out, playback not starting, or buffering. Built-in circuit breakers for all load sensitive microservices will defer or distribute out these transactions when predetermined thresholds are hit, while enabling the viewer to watch the stream or blocking viewing a few seconds later if the user is not authorized. This “Experience First” design combined with the platform's ability to auto-scale ensures the best possible experience for the viewer.

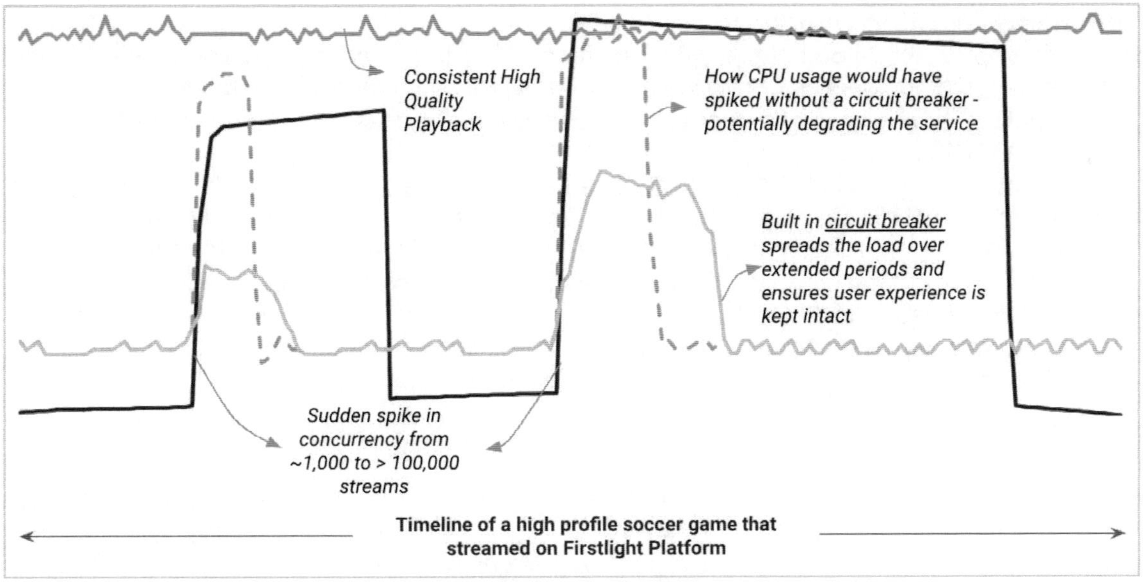

FIGURE 5: HOW FIRSTLIGHT'S PLAYBACK AUTHORIZATION MICROSERVICE TACKLES SUDDEN SPIKE IN DEMAND LEVERAGING IN BUILT CIRCUIT BREAKERS

Degrade Gracefully

Another design tactic that can be employed is to degrade the service gracefully in the event of high concurrency. Let's say a few services are deployed in the same Kubernetes cluster, such as DRM key service, favorites, stream concurrency, or continue watching service. The platform leverages Kubernetes to define fail-last rules based on priority of the services. For example, the DRM key service enables a viewer to watch the video, while the favorites service helps the viewer mark content as a favorite. "Degrading gracefully" ensures successful playback of content first and may defer non-critical features, like the ability to mark content as a favorite. This server-side design should be complemented with the client applications configuration.

Case Study: Evolving Live Video Experiences for American Sports Fans

OTT Provider Overview

A sports video streaming service delivering exclusive premium live games and events from major hockey, baseball, basketball, wrestling, soccer, curling, and auto racing leagues.

- 300+ Monthly Live Events
- 20+ Live Channels
- 500,000 Concurrent Streams
- 10+ Device Platforms

Key Challenges

The service provider had a legacy solution in place that was struggling to meet the requirements and was faced with the below challenges

- Need to set up live events with < 30 mins lead time
- Cloud cost overruns by ~2x
- Overloaded operations team having to manage both on-prem and cloud infrastructure
- No provision to automatically tackle sudden scaling needs
- Frequent outages (<95% Availability)

Firstlight Media Solution Overview

Firstlight Media deployed its cloud native video solution to tackle the video engineering and video distribution demands of the service. A few salient points of the solution are outlined below:

- Live pipeline setup with dual paths for source feeds and processing, providing four viable distribution paths.
- Video Distribution solutions - CMS and Edge services were deployed in two availability regions with an active-active configuration and even load distribution. These services had built-in auto-scaling capabilities, including circuit breakers for services in the critical path of scaling.
- Additional layers of cache between origin and CDN (origin shield) helped reduce the extent of origin scaling needed under high loads.
- The platform was also instrumented with multiple points of telemetry/inspection (source, encoding, distribution) for real-time quality of service monitoring.

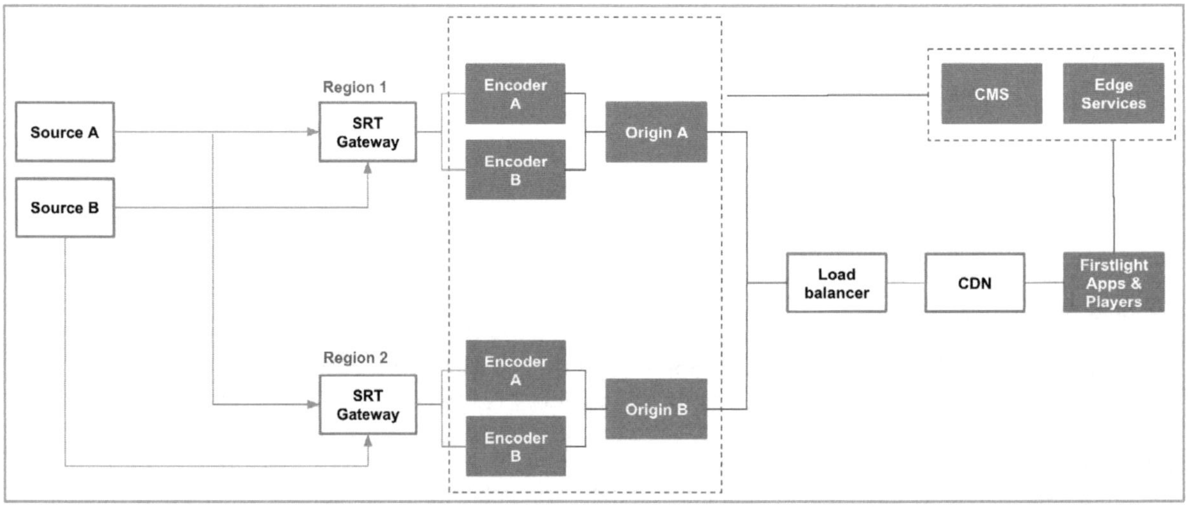

FIGURE 6: FIRSTLIGHT MEDIA'S CLOUD NATIVE VIDEO SOLUTION THAT DELIVERED >99.99% AVAILABILITY

Benefits

- One-Touch deployment for setting up live events in under 15 minutes.
- End-to-end telemetry with control center for live monitoring, resulting in 50% reduction in operational effort.
- Containerized architecture with programmatic orchestration, deploying compute resources only when needed, thus enabling significant reduction of resource consumption.
- Origin servers deployed in an auto-scalable environment combined with an efficient origin cache to meet concurrency needs.
- Dual encoder setup to achieve redundancy both within and across cloud availability regions.

Conclusion

The potential OTT services have in store for businesses and end users is significantly higher than any previous generation of TV. Reaping the benefits hinges on our ability to gain the trust of potential cord-cutters and accelerate the adoption of OTT as the primary mode of content consumption. This directly translates to being able to provide high quality, high performant OTT experiences with >99.99% availability. A cloud native architecture with ultra-redundancy, instant scaling and an experience-first design will deliver on these high expectations.

References

[1] Building sustainable ecosystems for cloud native software, https://www.cncf.io/

[2] Network resilience and circuit breaking with Istio, https://istio.io/latest/docs/concepts/traffic-management/#network-resilience-and-testing , https://developers.redhat.com/blog/2018/03/27/istio-circuit-breaker-when-failure-is-an-option

[3] Knative and Serverless Computing, https://knative.dev/docs/ , https://www.martinfowler.com/articles/serverless.html

[4] Micro-frontends, https://micro-frontends.org/ , https://martinfowler.com/articles/micro-frontends.html

Towards Efficient Multi-Codec Streaming

Yuriy A. Reznik
Brightcove, Inc.
Seattle, Washington, United States
yreznik@brightcove.com

Abstract – One of the biggest challenges in modern-era media delivery systems is the fragmentation of the population of the receiving devices in terms of codec capabilities. For example, modern Apple devices can decode and seamlessly switch between H.264/AVC and HEVC streams. Most new TVs or set-top boxes can also decode HEVC, but they cannot switch between HEVC and H.264/AVC streams in the same streaming session. And there are still plenty of older devices/streaming clients that can only receive and decode H.264/AVC streams. With the arrival of next-generation codecs - such as AV1 and VVC, the fragmentation of codec support across devices becomes even more complex. This situation brings a question - how can we serve such a population of devices most efficiently by using codecs delivering the best performance in all cases yet producing the minimum possible number of streams and such that the overall cost of media delivery is minimal? In this paper, we explain how this problem can be formalized and solved at the stage of dynamic generation of encoding profiles for ABR streaming. The proposed solution effectively generalizes the per-title or context-aware encoding (CAE) class-of techniques, considering multiple sets of renditions generated using each codec and codec usage distributions by the population of the receiving devices. We also discuss additional system-level means (proper manifest generation, HLS and DASH quality annotations, device detection, and edge logic) needed to make the proposed solution practically deployable.

Introduction

During the last decade, most video streams sent over the Internet have been encoded using the ITU-T H.264 / MPEG-4 AVC video codec [1]. Developed in the early 2000s, H.264/AVC has become broadly supported on various devices and platforms. According to the www.caniuse.com analytics website [2], the current reach of H.264 across web platforms is approaching an overwhelming 97.93%.

However, in terms of technology, H.264/AVC codec is pretty old. In recent years, several more advanced codecs have been introduced. The two best-known ones are: the HEVC codec [3] from ISO/ISO MPEG and ITU-T standards committees and AV1 [4] from the Alliance for Open Media. Both technologies claim about 40-50% gain in compression efficiency over the H.264/AVC [6-8]. Even higher gains have been recently reported for an emerging VVC coding standard [5,8,9].

In theory, such gains should lead to a significant reduction in streaming costs. However, in practice, these new codecs can only reach particular subsets of the existing devices or web browsers. For example, for HEVC, www.caniuse.com reports only 18.73% reach, pointing primarily to Apple devices incorporating hardware HEVC support. The AV1's support among web browsers is higher, but notably, it is not supported by Apple devices and most currently deployed set-top box platforms [2,9].

This paper is excerpted from the Proceedings of the 2022 NAB Broadcast Engineering and Information Technology (BEIT) Conference, © 2022, National Association of Broadcasters, 1 M Street S.E., Washington, DC 20003 USA.

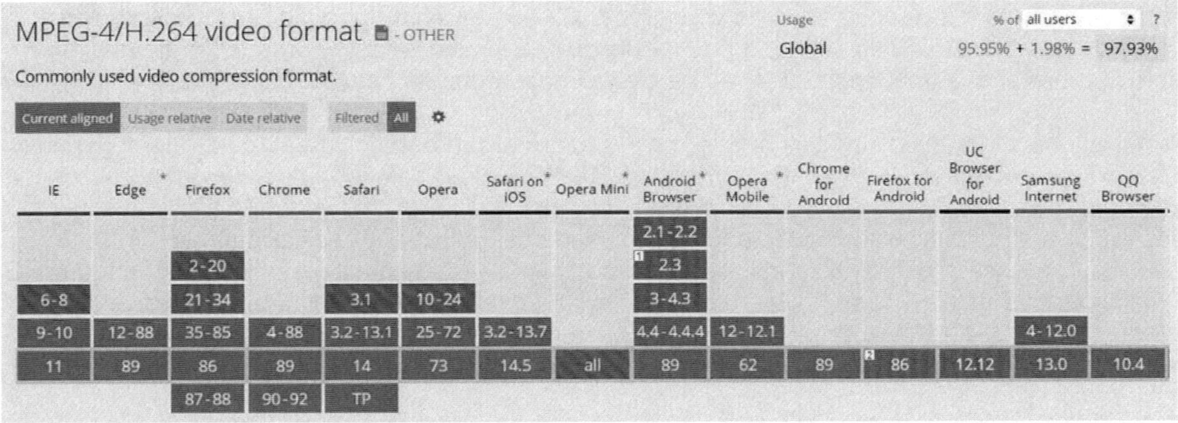

FIGURE 1: SUPPORT OF H.264/AVC VIDEO CODECS ACROSS DIFFERENT PLATFORMS (SOURCE: WWW.CANIUSE.COM [2]).

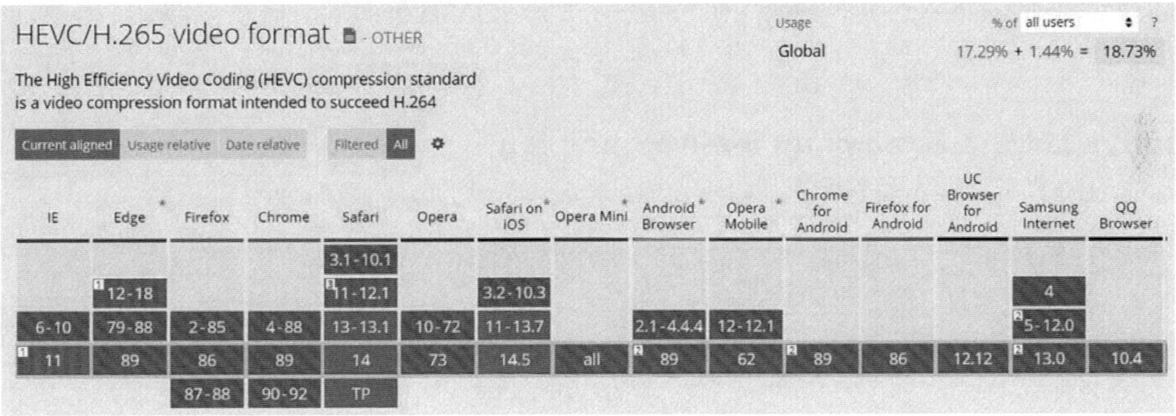

FIGURE 2: SUPPORT OF HEVC VIDEO CODECS ACROSS DIFFERENT PLATFORMS (SOURCE: WWW.CANIUSE.COM [2]).

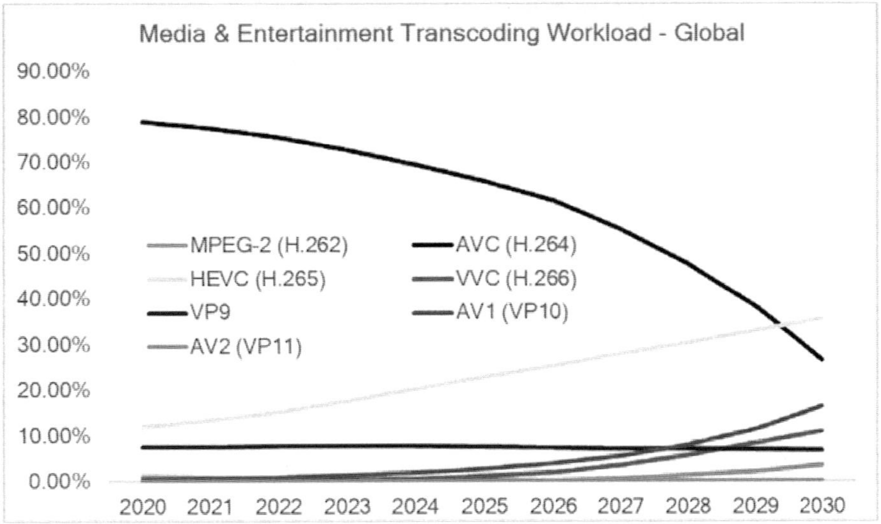

FIGURE 3: PREDICTED USAGE OF VIDEO CODECS IN THE NEXT 10 YEARS (SOURCE: RETHINKTV [9]).

This situation brings a question – how do we serve such a fragmented population of devices most efficiently by using codecs delivering the best performance in all cases, yet producing the minimum possible number of streams, and such that the overall cost of media delivery is minimal?

In this paper, we will explain how this problem can be formalized and solved at the stage of dynamic generation of encoding profiles for ABR streaming. The proposed solution effectively generalizes the per-title or context-aware encoding (CAE) class-of techniques [10-15], considering multiple sets of renditions generated using each codec and codec usage distributions by the population of the receiving devices. The proposed solution also utilizes advanced signaling mechanisms in HLS [16] and MPEG DASH [17], as well as current deployment guidelines and interoperability requirements developed for these standards [18-20]. An example of the practical realization of such a multi-codec streaming system and various additional means for increased robustness and reach will also be described.

This paper is organized as follows. In the first 5 sections, we will provide background information: introduce the concept of ABR streaming, ladders, single-codec and multi-codec operation, etc. Section 6 will define the problem of the optimal design of ABR ladders for multi-codec streaming. Section 7 will explain how to generate multi-codec HLS and DASH manifest files. Additional practical considerations and conclusions will be provided in Sections 8 and 9.

Adaptive Bitrate Streaming: Main Principles

Let us first briefly review the main principles of operation of modern-era Adaptive Bit-Rate (ABR) streaming systems based on HLS [16] or DASH [17] standards. We show a conceptual diagram of such a system in Figure 4. For simplicity, we only consider the VOD delivery case.

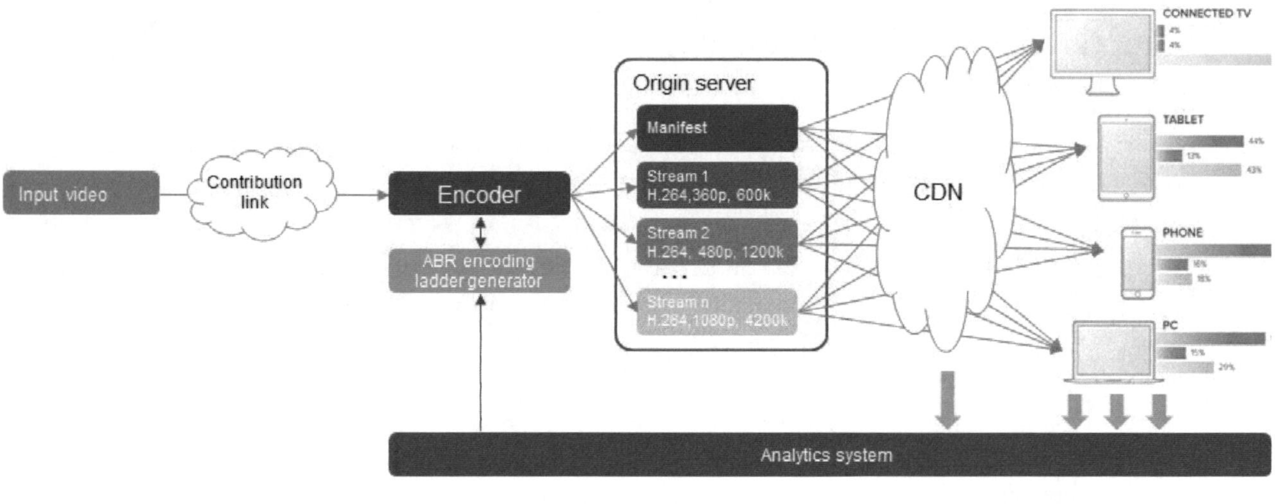

FIGURE 4: TYPICAL ARCHITECTURE OF HTTP-BASED ADAPTIVE BITRATE STREAMING SYSTEM.

As shown in this figure, when an input *video asset* is prepared for ABR streaming, it is typically transcoded into several *renditions* (or *variant streams*). Such renditions typically have different bitrates, resolutions, and other codecs- and presentation-level parameters.

Once all renditions are generated, they are placed on an HTTP web server called the *origin server*. Along with the set of renditions, the origin server also receives *manifest files* describing the properties of the encoded streams. In the HLS streaming standard [16], such manifests are called "playlists," while in the MPEG-DASH standard [17], they are called "media presentation description" or "mpd" files.

The subsequent delivery of the encoded content to user devices is done over HTTP and by using Content Delivery Network (CDN). The use of CDNs ensures the reliability and scalability of the delivery system.

To play the content, user devices use special software called *streaming clients*. In the simplest form, a streaming client can be JavaScript code run by a web browser. It may also be a custom application or a video player supplied by the OS. Regardless of the implementation, most streaming clients include the logic for adaptive selection of streams/renditions during the playback.

For example, if the client notices that the observed network bandwidth is too low to support real-time playback of the current rendition, it may decide to switch to a lower bitrate rendition. This switch prevents buffering. Otherwise, the client may switch to a higher bitrate / higher quality rendition if there is sufficient bandwidth. This switch leads to a better quality of experience. This logic is what makes streaming delivery adaptive. It is also the main reason for multiple (typically 5-10) renditions. For information about the origins of ABR streaming and other benefits of multi-rate design, the reader is referred to publications [21-23].

The system depicted in Figure 4 has two additional components: the *analytics system*, collecting the playback statistics from CDNs and streaming clients, and the ABR *encoding ladder generator*, defining the number of renditions and properties of each rendition to create. For example, in the Brightcove VideoCloud streaming system [24], this block corresponds to Context-Aware Encoding (CAE) [25] module. We will explain the significance of the encoding ladder generation operation next.

Encoding Ladders

Let us now consider an example of an encoding ladder created for streaming. This particular example was created using the Brightcove CAE generator [25] for an action-movie asset.

Rendition	**Codec**	**Resolution**	**Framerate**	**Bitrate** [Kbps]	**Quality** [MOS]
1	H.264	384x216	25	261.59	2.178
2	H.264	512x288	25	513.54	2.719
3	H.264	768x432	25	1024.37	3.408
4	H.264	1280x720	25	2075.71	4.215
5	H.264	1920x1080	25	4203.03	4.769

TABLE 1: EXAMPLE SINGLE-CODEC ABR ENCODING LADDER.

This ladder defines 5 streams, enabling video delivery with resolutions from 216p to 1080p and using from about 260 Kbps to 4200 Kbps in network bandwidth. All streams are encoded using H.264/AVC codec [1]. The last column in this table lists perceived visual quality scores as estimated for playback of these renditions on a PC screen. These values are reported using the standard Mean Opinion Score (MOS) scale [26].

In Figure 5, we plot the (bitrate, quality) points corresponding to all renditions. We also show a trend of the best quality levels achievable by the streaming system with varying network bandwidth. This trend becomes a *step function*, shown in blue.

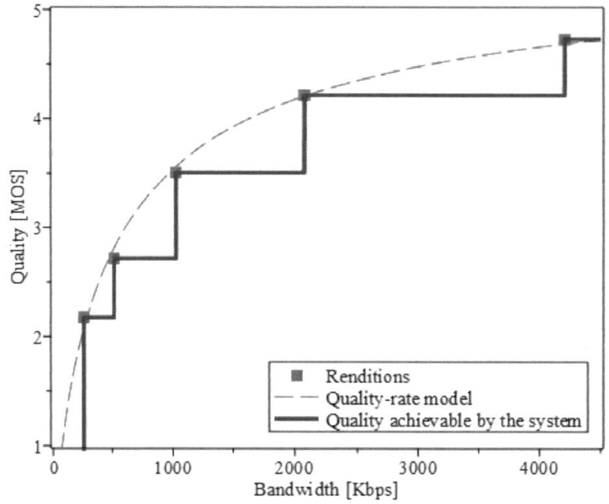

FIGURE 4: BEST QUALITY ACHIEVABLE BY A STREAMING SYSTEM AS A FUNCTION OF NETWORK BANDWIDTH.

Figure 5 also plots the so-called *quality-rate model* function [12-14]. This function describes the quality achievable by encoding the content with the same encoder operating at every possible bitrate point within the same range of bitrates. A dashed red curve shows this function.

As it can be easily grasped, with proper ladder design, the rendition points become a subset of points from the quality-rate model, and the step function describing quality achievable by streaming becomes an approximation of this model. What influences the quality of the streaming system is the number of renditions in the encoding ladder and the placement of renditions along the bandwidth axis. The closer the resulting step function is to the quality-rate model – the better is the quality that the streaming system can deliver.

This example shows that the encoding profiles/ladders for ABR streaming must be carefully designed. This is why most modern streaming systems employ special profile generators to perform this step dynamically by accounting for the properties of the content, networks, and other relevant contexts. Related techniques are known as "per-title," "content-aware," and "context-aware" encoding techniques [10-15].

Multi-Codec Streaming: Ladders and Adaptation Models

Now that we've explained the key concepts, we can turn our attention to multi-codec streaming. To make this presentation more specific, let us again consider an example of an encoding ladder generated by using two codecs: H.264/AVC and HEVC.

Rendition	**Codec**	**Resolution**	**Framerate**	**Bitrate** [Kbps]	**Quality** [MOS]
1	H.264	384x216	25	261.59	2.178
2	HEVC	512x288	25	300	2.529
3	H.264	512x288	25	513.54	2.719
4	HEVC	768x432	25	607.89	3.260
5	H.264	768x432	25	1024.37	3.408
6	HEVC	1024x576	25	1166.03	3.793
7	H.264	1280x720	25	2075.71	4.215
8	HEVC	1600x900	25	2362.74	4.549
9	H.264	1920x1080	25	4203.03	4.769
10	HEVC	1920x1080	25	4203.45	4.915

TABLE 2: EXAMPLE ENCODING LADDER FOR TWO CODECS: H.264 AND HEVC.

The plots of rendition points, quality-rate models, and quality achievable by streaming clients decoding only sets of H.264 and HEVC streams are presented in Figure 6.

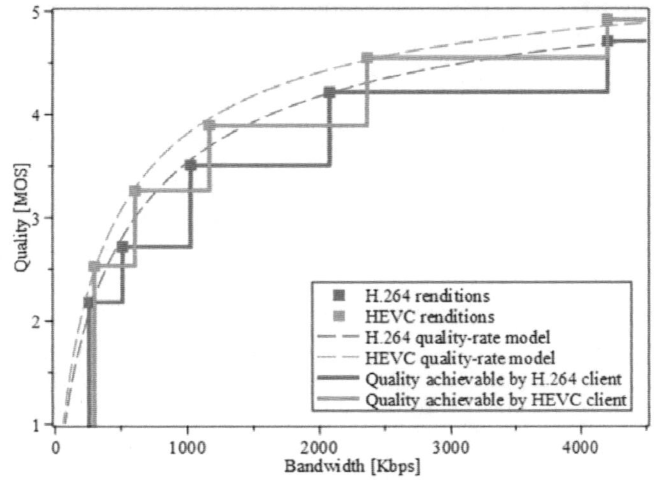

FIGURE 6: BEST QUALITY ACHIEVABLE BY STEAMING SYSTEMS USING H.264 AND HEVC CODECS.

As easily observed, the quality-rate model function for HEVC is consistently better than the quality-rate model for H.264/AVC. By the same token, HEVC renditions should also deliver better quality-rate tradeoffs than renditions encoded using H.264/AVC encoder.

However, considering that there are typically only a few rendition points, and they may be placed sparsely and in an interleaved pattern, this may create regions of bitrates, where H.264/AVC renditions may deliver better quality than the nearest HEVC rendition of smaller or equal bitrate. Such regions in the above figure are seen when step functions for H.264/AVC clients go above the same functions for HEVC clients.

What does this mean? This means that 2-codec ladder decoding of only HEVC-encoded streams does not automatically result in the best possible quality! Even better quality may be achieved by clients that selectively and intelligently switch between H.264/AVC and HEVC streams. We illustrate the quality achievable by such "2-codec clients" in Figure 7.

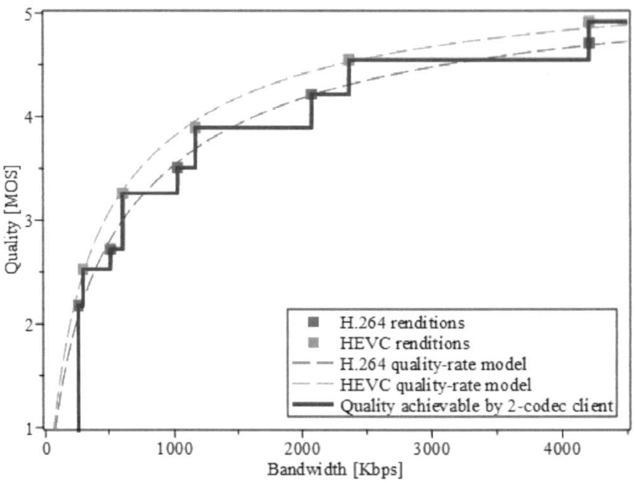

FIGURE 7: BEST QUALITY ACHIEVABLE BY A STEAMING SYSTEM EMPLOYING "2-CODEC CLIENT".

In this example, the 2-codec client can make 9 adaptation steps instead of just 5 in HEVC or H.264-only ladders. This enables better utilization of the available network bandwidth and delivery of better quality overall. This also allows fewer renditions using both H.264 and HEVC codecs to be generated, as both subsets are effectively used for adaptation.

Multi-Codec Support in Existing Streaming Clients

As we just noticed, the ability of the streaming client not only to decode but also intelligently and seamlessly switch between H.264/AVC and HEVC streams is extremely important. This leads to better quality and allows the reduction in the total number of streams, reducing streaming costs.

Perhaps the best-known examples of existing clients supporting codec switching are native players in most new Apple devices: iPhones, iPads, Mac computers, etc. They can decode and seamlessly switch between H.264/AVC and HEVC streams. Recent versions of Chrome and Firefox web browsers have added support for so-called *changeType()* method, which allows JavaScript-based streaming clients to implement switching between codecs. Using this method we may expect most web-browser-based clients to add codec switching capability in the future.

But there are indeed some other platforms, such as some SmartTVs, set-top boxes, etc., that can only decode either H.264/AVC or HEVC streams and won't switch to another codec during a streaming session. And naturally, there are also plenty of legacy devices that can only decode H.264/AVC encoded streams.

This fragmented space of streaming clients and their capabilities must be accounted for at stages of the generation of encoding ladders, properly defining HLS and DASH manifests, and design of the delivery system for multi-codec streaming.

Efficient Multi-Codec ABR Profile Generation

We will next discuss the problem of optimal design of encoding ladders. Our presentation will closely follow the notations and concepts introduced earlier in [12,13].

Definitions

For simplicity, we will consider a case of 2 codecs and 3 clients with a conceptual diagram of the system presented in Figure 8.

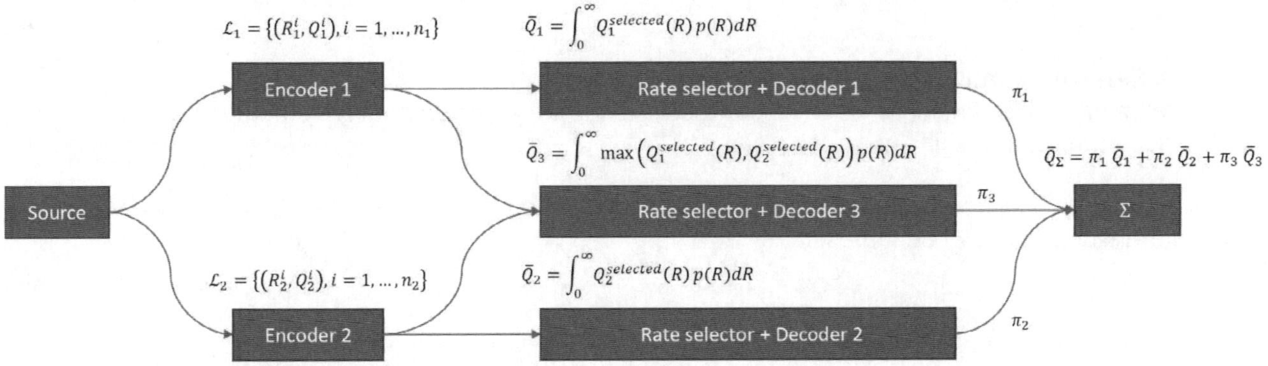

FIGURE 8: CONCEPTUAL DIAGRAM ABR STREAMING SYSTEM WITH 2 ENCODERS AND 3 TYPES OF DECODERS/CLIENTS. DECODER 1 AND 2 CAN DECODE ONLY STREAMS FROM ENCODER 1 AND 2 RESPECTIVELY. DECODER/CLIENT 3 CAN DECODE AND SWITCH BETWEEN STREAMS FROM BOTH ENCODERS.

Translating this to practice, we can think that codec 1 is H.264/AVC, codec 2 is HEVC, client 1 is the one that can only decode H.264/AVC streams, client 2 is the one that can decode HEVC streams, and client 3 is the one that can decode both H.264/AVC or HEVC streams and can switch between them during the streaming session.

By $\mathcal{L}_1$ and $\mathcal{L}_2$ we denote *encoding ladders* produced by using codecs of type 1 and 2 respectively. Mathematically, we will assume that each ladder is presented by a set of (rate, quality) points, corresponding to the bitrate and quality characteristics of its renditions:

$$\mathcal{L}_1 = \{(R_1^i, Q_1^i), i = 1, \dots, n_1\}, \quad \text{and} \quad \mathcal{L}_2 = \{(R_2^i, Q_2^i), i = 1, \dots, n_2\} \tag{1}$$

Here, by R_j^i we denote bitrates and by Q_j^i we denote quality values of each rendition. The sub-indices indicate codec type. The upper indices indicate rendition number in each set. The values $n_1$and n_2 denote the number of renditions in each set, and $n = n_1 + n_2$ denotes the total number of all renditions used for streaming.

As in [12], we further assume that the performance of each codec can be modeled by certain *quality-rate functions*: $Q_1(R)$ and $Q_2(R)$, and that above (quality, rate) points can be understood as samples taken from these functions:

$$Q_1^i = Q_1(R_1^i), i = 1, \dots, n_1, \quad \text{and} \quad Q_2^i = Q_2(R_2^i), i = 1, \dots, n_2. \tag{2}$$

Also, as in [12], the behavior of the *network bandwidth* during streaming session is modeled as a *continuous random variable* R with known (or empirically measured) probability density function $p(R)$.

On the receiver-end, we assume that clients follow *idealized client model* [12], selecting maximum ladder rate R^i that is less or equal than available network bandwidth R:

$$R_1^{selected}(R) = \max_{\substack{i=1,\dots,n_1 \\ R_1^i \le R}} R_1^i, \quad \text{and} \quad R_2^{selected}(R) = \max_{\substack{i=1,\dots,n_2 \\ R_2^i \le R}} R_2^i. \tag{3}$$

Assuming monotonically increasing quality-rate models, this also implies that:

$$Q_1^{selected}(R) = \max_{\substack{i=1,..,n_1 \\ R_1^i \leq R}} Q_1(R_1^i), \quad \text{and} \quad Q_2^{selected}(R) = \max_{\substack{i=1,..,n_2 \\ R_2^i \leq R}} Q_2(R_2^i). \tag{4}$$

Average Quality Achievable by the Streaming System

Next, given all above definitions, we write expressions for the *average quality* values achievable by clients / decoders of each kind.

For instance, the *average quality* achieved by client 1 when working with ladder $\mathcal{L}_1$ and network with bandwidth distribution $p(R)$ becomes:

$$\bar{Q}_1 = \int_0^\infty Q_1^{selected}(R)\, p(R) dR. \tag{5}$$

Similarly, the *average quality* achieved by client 2, working with ladder $\mathcal{L}_2$, becomes:

$$\bar{Q}_2 = \int_0^\infty Q_2^{selected}(R)\, p(R) dR. \tag{6}$$

Finally, for client 3, which is capable of working with both ladders $\mathcal{L}_1$ and $\mathcal{L}_2$, including switching between all such streams, the expression for the average quality becomes:

$$\bar{Q}_3 = \int_0^\infty \max\left(Q_1^{selected}(R), Q_2^{selected}(R)\right) p(R) dR. \tag{7}$$

The max() function in the above expression reflects the capability of a dual-codec client to select best streams across renditions encoded by both codecs.

The average quality achieved by the entire population of clients, becomes:

$$\bar{Q}_\Sigma = \pi_1\, \bar{Q}_1 + \pi_2\, \bar{Q}_2 + \pi_3\, \bar{Q}_3, \tag{8}$$

where π_1, π_2, π_3 denote normalized $(\pi_1 + \pi_2 + \pi_3 = 1)$ population counts of clients of each kind.

Optimal Multi-Codec Ladder Design

By considering all above definitions, and observing that average quality value $\bar{Q}_\Sigma$ can be understood as a function of network bandwidth density $p(R)$, client distribution π, the number of ladder points n_1, n_2, and the sets of rates used in the ladder, we are now ready to define the following ladder optimization problem.

Given:

- the total number of ladder points n,
- limits for all rate points: $R_{\min}$, $R_{\max}$;
- maximum limits for first rate points: $R_{\max}^1$,
- quality-rate functions for both codecs and content $Q_1(R)$, $Q_2(R)$
- network bandwidth density $p(R)$, and
- distribution of clients π,

Find:

- numbers $\hat{n}_1, \hat{n}_2$, such that $\hat{n}_1 + \hat{n}_2 = n$, and
- ladder rates $\hat{R}_1^1, \dots, \hat{R}_1^{\hat{n}_1}$ and $\hat{R}_2^1, \dots, \hat{R}_2^{\hat{n}_2}$

such that overall quality $\bar{Q}_\Sigma$ delivered by the streaming system is maximal:

$$\bar{Q}_\Sigma\left(p,\pi,n,\hat{R}_1^1,\dots,\hat{R}_1^{\hat{n}_1},\hat{R}_2^1,\dots,\hat{R}_2^{\hat{n}_2}\right)=\max_{\substack{n_1+n_2=n\\ R_{\min}\le R_1^1\le\dots\le R_1^{n_1}\le R_{\max}\\ R_{\min}\le R_2^1\le\dots\le R_2^{n_2}\le R_{\max}\\ R_1^1,R_2^1\le R_{\max}^1}}\bar{Q}_\Sigma\left(p,\pi,n,R_1^1,\dots,R_1^{n_1},R_2^1,\dots,R_2^{n_2}\right).\quad(*)\qquad(9)$$

As easily noticed, this problem folds into a class of non-linear constrained optimization problems. The details about the design of a numerical solver for this problem and examples of solutions can be found in [13].

Additional Remarks

We note that all constraints introduced in the problem setting (*) are essential in practice. For example, the maximum rate limit $R_{\max}$ is needed to prevent allocation of bitrates beyond those that are physically achievable. The minimum rate limit $R_{\min}$ is usually related to minimum quality level at which streaming as service is even feasible. The limit on maximum first rate in the ladder $R_{\max}^1$ is typically used to limit start-up time and/or buffering probability of clients, etc. In practice, several additional constraints may also be introduced.

We also note, that while (*) does not explicitly operate with the choices of *video resolutions* for each stream, it is assumed, that the best choices of resolutions are already absorbed in the definition of quality-rate models for each codec. In other words, given a set of allowed resolutions $\mathcal{S}$ and quality-rate models $Q_1(S,R)$, obtained for each specific resolution $S\in\mathcal{S}$, we will assume that final quality rate model $Q_1(R)$ is defined such that

$$Q_1(R)=\sup_{S\in\mathcal{S}}Q_1(S,R).\qquad(10)$$

This way, the ladder optimization problem becomes effectively reduced to the choice of bitrates needed for each rendition.

Practical Implementation

The described mathematical problem and its solution finder form the basis for the design of the profile generator in the Brightcove CAE system [25].

As shown in in Figure 9, the Brightcove CAE system includes several "ingest profiles", with the "Multiplatform Extended HEVC (CAE) mixed-codec" profile corresponding to a mode where both H.264 and HEVC codecs will be used in final generated streams. Our example profiles, shown earlier in Tables 1 and 2 have been generated by using this system.

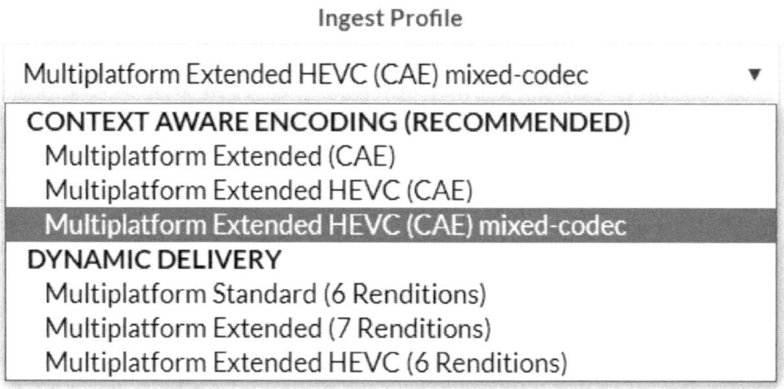

FIGURE 9: MULTI-CODEC STREAMING OPTIONS AVAILABLE IN BRIGHTCOVE VIDEOCLOUD SYSTEM [24,25].

When operating this system, the users can customize some overall ladder parameters – such as the limits on the numbers of renditions, ranges of resolutions and bitrates, assumed network and usage distributions, etc. But the final choices for the number of renditions, and their parameters (resolutions, bitrates, codec HRD controls, etc.) are all done automatically by the CAE system.

Using Multi-Codec Features of HLS and DASH

In designing multi-codec streaming systems, particular attention must also be paid to proper generation of HLS and DASH manifests.

One of the important components of such design is the inclusion of quality attributes that may be needed to better guide selection of renditions by the streaming clients. This is important because in mixed-codec ladders the increase in stream bitrates may no longer mean the increase in quality. In our example ladder in Figure 6, the monotonicity of bitrate-quality relations is preserved by proper choices of codecs and bitrates, but more generally, it may not be the case. An HEVC stream with lower bitrate may have a better quality than H.264/AVC stream using more bits. Hence quality-related attributes are important.

Additionally, there is always the need to make sure manifests are generated in a backwards-compatible fashion such that older generation clients, which can only recognize a subset of declarations, would still operate properly.

And there are also certain new and advanced features of both HLS [16] and DASH [17] standards, as well as limitations imposed by HLS deployment guidelines [18] and DASH-IF interoperability requirements [20], that become important to account in such designs.

To explain some of these nuances, in Figures 10 and 11, we show sketches of the HLS and DASH manifests constructed for a composition of H.264 and HEVC streams from the ABR ladder in Table 2.

```
#EXTM3U
...
#EXT-X-STREAM-INF:BANDWIDTH=267868,CODECS="avc1.4d401e",RESOLUTION=384x216,SCORE=1, ...
Rendition1.m3u8
#EXT-X-STREAM-INF:BANDWIDTH=307200,CODECS="hvc1.1.6.L90.90",RESOLUTION=512x288,SCORE=2, ...
Rendition2.m3u8
#EXT-X-STREAM-INF:BANDWIDTH=525864,CODECS="avc1.4d401e",RESOLUTION=512x288,SCORE=3, ...
Rendition3.m3u8
#EXT-X-STREAM-INF:BANDWIDTH=75378,CODECS="hvc1.1.6.L90.90",RESOLUTION=768x432,SCORE=4, ...
```

```
Rendition4.m3u8
#EXT-X-STREAM-INF:BANDWIDTH=1048954,CODECS="avc1.4d401e",RESOLUTION=768x432,SCORE=5, ...
Rendition5.m3u8
#EXT-X-STREAM-INF:BANDWIDTH=1194014,CODECS="hvc1.1.6.L93.90",RESOLUTION=1024x576,SCORE=6, ...
Rendition6.m3u8
#EXT-X-STREAM-INF:BANDWIDTH=2125527,CODECS="avc1.640028",RESOLUTION=1280x720,SCORE=7, ...
Rendition7.m3u8
#EXT-X-STREAM-INF:BANDWIDTH=2419445,CODECS="hvc1.1.6.L120.90",RESOLUTION=1600x900,SCORE=8, ...
Rendition8.m3u8
#EXT-X-STREAM-INF:BANDWIDTH=4303902,CODECS="avc1.640028",RESOLUTION=1920x1080,SCORE=9, ...
Rendition9.m3u8
#EXT-X-STREAM-INF:BANDWIDTH=4304332,CODECS="hvc1.1.6.L120.90",RESOLUTION=1920x1080,SCORE=10, ...
Rendition10.m3u8
...
```

FIGURE 10: HLS MASTER PLAYLIST (.M3U8) FILE CREATED FOR ABR LADDER FROM TABLE 2.

```
MPD xmlns="urn:mpeg:dash:schema:mpd:2011" minBufferTime="PT1.500S" type="static" ... >
<Period duration="PT0H12M14.167S">
<SupplementalProperty schemeIdUri="urn:mpeg:dash:qr-equivalence:2019" value="1,2" />
<AdaptationSet id="1">
  <SupplementalProperty schemeIdUri="urn:mpeg:dash:adaptation-set-switching:2016" value="2" />
  <Representation id="1" mimeType="video/mp4" codecs="avc1.42001e" bandwidth="267868"  qualityRanking="10" .../>
  <Representation id="2" mimeType="video/mp4" codecs="avc1.42001e" bandwidth="5525864" qualityRanking="8" .../>
  <Representation id="3" mimeType="video/mp4" codecs="avc1.42001e" bandwidth="1048954" qualityRanking="6" .../>
  <Representation id="4" mimeType="video/mp4" codecs="avc1.640028" bandwidth="2125527" qualityRanking="4" .../>
  <Representation id="5" mimeType="video/mp4" codecs="avc1.640028" bandwidth="4303902" qualityRanking="2" .../>
</AdaptationSet>
<AdaptationSet id="2"">
  <SupplementalProperty schemeIdUri="urn:mpeg:dash:adaptation-set-switching:2016" value="1" />
  <Representation id="1" mimeType="video/mp4" codecs="hvc1.1.6.L90.90" bandwidth="307200"  qualityRanking="9" .../>
  <Representation id="2" mimeType="video/mp4" codecs="hvc1.1.6.L90.90" bandwidth="75378"   qualityRanking="7" .../>
  <Representation id="3" mimeType="video/mp4" codecs="hvc1.1.6.L93.90" bandwidth="1194014" qualityRanking="5" .../>
  <Representation id="4" mimeType="video/mp4" codecs="hvc1.1.6.L120.90" bandwidth="2419445" qualityRanking="3" ./>
  <Representation id="5" mimeType="video/mp4" codecs="hvc1.1.6.L120.90" bandwidth="4304332" qualityRanking="1" ./>
</AdaptationSet>
</Period>
</MPD>
```

FIGURE 11: DASH MEDIA PRESENTATION DESCRIPTION (MPD) FILE CREATED FOR ABR LADDER FROM TABLE 2.

As show in in these figures, in the HLS system, all HEVC and H.264/AVC renditions can be included in the natural order in the master playlist. However, in MPEG DASH, they must be listed separately, in different *adaptation sets*, defined independently for each codec. To enable switching between HEVC and AVC renditions, the "adaptation-set-switching:2016" *SupplementalProperty* descriptors must be included in each adaptation set.

Such separate placement of renditions in DASH is needed to improve compatibility with legacy players. It is required by DASH-IF Interoperability Guidelines [19]. This practice also enables conformance with CTA WAVE content specification [20] which defines its media profiles on a per-codec level.

By looking at Figures 10 and 11, we next note that the means for adding quality annotations in HLS and DASH are quite different.

In HLS, quality related parameters are called "SCORE" attributes, with higher values indicating better quality. In MPEG DASH, they are called "qualityRanking" attributes, but now with lower values indicating better quality. Furthermore, since HEVC and AVC renditions in DASH become split across different adaptation sets, the "qualityRanking" attributes should be produced to indicate correct and unique relative rankings values for the entire set of renditions and the "qr-equivalence:2019"

SupplementalProperty descriptor must be included at the period level. This extra descriptor advises client that "qualityRanking" attributes represent correct relative quality values considering the complete set of all renditions.

All other standard content-related requirements and constraints as specified in HLS authoring specification [18] and DASH-IF interoperability guidelines [20] must also be considered in the design of encoding profiles and manifests for multi-codec streaming.

Additional Practical Considerations

While the above-described declarations in HLS and DASH manifest should ensure interoperability across all proper implementations of HLS and DASH clients, in practice, there may still be a risk that some legacy clients may be confused by the presence of extra renditions or manifest descriptors and will not start play of the stream or will not play it well.

Sometimes suboptimal behaviors may also be encountered with newer devices/clients, which attempt to support new codecs or features of HLS or DASH, but their implementations are not yet mature.

To minimize the likelihood of running in such situations, advanced streaming systems may employ *device detection* and *manifest filtering* logic at the edge when processing requests from players to deliver HLS or DASH manifests. Such logic may use the "user_agent" string in HTTP request headers to detect the type of the device, OS, or web browser and then dynamically decide which renditions or attributes to retain in the manifest.

For example, if the client device is classified as one that can only decode H.264/AVC streams, then only H.264/AVC streams can be retained in the manifest and the rest of them are pruned.

Such logic may generally help increase the streaming system's robustness, maintainability, and cross-platform reach. In practice, such extra logic is easily combinable with existing edge-level functions that advanced streaming systems employ for CDN selection, multi-format management, redundancy management, and other advanced delivery functions [15,27].

Conclusions

We considered the problem of fragmentation of codec support across streaming devices. We've shown that it can be practically addressed by creating multi-codec sets of renditions for HLS or DASH streaming systems with specifically optimized design of the encoding profiles, proper generation of manifests, and manifest filtering functions of the streaming platform.

We've also shown several interesting phenomena achievable with multi-codec deployments.
For example, we've demonstrated that devices/clients that can decode and switch between different codecs can deliver better quality of experience than "non-switching" clients even if they use a better codec. Another critical factor is that the total number of streams needed to support the operation of such "switching" clients can be much smaller than for clients operating with just a single codec.

These factors suggest that with growing support for codec-switching functionality in streaming clients, the concept of multi-codec streaming should become increasingly more practical, cost-efficient, and deployable at a mass scale.

References

[1] ISO/IEC 14496-10:2003, "Information technology – Coding of audio-visual objects – Part 10: Advanced Video Coding," *ISO/IEC*, December 2003.

[2] "Can I use" web service, https://caniuse.com/, March 18, 2022.

[3] ISO/IEC 23008-2:2013, "Information technology – High efficiency coding and media delivery in heterogeneous environments – Part 2: High efficiency video coding," *ISO/IEC*, December 2013.

[4] AV1, "AV1 Bitstream and Decoding Process Specification, Version 1.0.0," *Alliance for Open Media*, January 18, 2019.

[5] ISO/IEC 23090-3:2021, "Information technology — Coded representation of immersive media — Part 3: Versatile video coding," ISO/IEC, February 2021.

[6] T. Laude, Y. G. Adhisantoso, J. Voges, M. Munderloh and J. Ostermann, "A Comparison of JEM and AV1 with HEVC: Coding Tools, Coding Efficiency and Complexity," *2018 Picture Coding Symposium (PCS)*, 2018, pp. 36-40.

[7] P. Topiwala, M. Krishnan, and W. Dai, "Performance comparison of VVC, AV1, and HEVC on 8-bit and 10-bit content," *Proc. SPIE 10752, Applications of Digital Image Processing XLI*, September 17 2018.

[8] D. Grois et al., "Performance Comparison of Emerging EVC and VVC Video Coding Standards with HEVC and AV1," SMPTE Motion Imaging *Journal*, vol. 130, no. 4, pp. 1-12, May 2021.

[9] RethinkTV research, "Media & Entertainment Transcoding Workload and Device Royalty Forecast 2020-2030", https://rethinkresearch.biz/reports-category/rethink-tv/#media-entertainment-transcoding-workload-and-device-royalty-forecast-2020-2030, April 30, 2021.

[10] A. Aaron, Z. Li, M. Manohara, J. De Cock, and D. Ronca, "Per-title encode optimization," https://medium.com/netflixtechblog/per-title-encode-optimization-7e99442b62a2, Dec. 15 2015.

[11] C. Chen, Y. Lin, S. Benting, and A. Kokaram, "Optimized transcoding for large scale adaptive streaming using playback statistics," in Proc. IEEE Int. Conf. Image Proc., Oct 2018, pp. 3269-3273.

[12] Y. Reznik, K. O. Lillevold, A. Jagannath, J. Greer, and J. Corley, "Optimal design of encoding profiles for ABR streaming," in Proc. *Packet Video Workshop*, Amsterdam, NL, June 12, 2018, pp. 43-47.

[13] Y. Reznik, X. Li, K. O. Lillevold, A. Jagannath, and J. Greer, "Optimal Multi-Codec Adaptive Bitrate Streaming," in Proc. *IEEE Int. Conf. Multimedia & Expo*, Shanghai, China, 2019, pp. 348-353.

[14] Y. Reznik, "Average Performance of Adaptive Streaming," in Proc. *Data Compression Conference (DCC'21)*, Snowbird, UT, 23-26 March 2021.

[15] Y. Reznik, X. Li, K.O. Lillevold, R. Peck, T. Shutt, and P. Howard, "Optimizing Mass-Scale Multi-Screen Video Delivery," *SMPTE Motion Imaging Journal*, vol. 129, no. 3, pp. 26-38, April 2020.

[16] R. Pantos and W. May, "HTTP live streaming, RFC 8216," IETF, 2017.

[17] ISO/IEC 23009-1:2019, "Information technology - Dynamic adaptive streaming over HTTP (DASH) - Part 1: Media presentation description and segment formats," ISO/IEC, August 2019.

[18] Apple, "HTTP Live Streaming (HLS) Authoring Specification for Apple Devices," https://developer.apple.com/documentation/http_live_streaming/http_live_streaming_hls_authoring_specification_for_apple_devices, Apple, November 12, 2021.

[19] DASH-IF, "DASH-IF Interoperability Guidelines, v.3," https://dashif.org/docs/DASH-IF-IOP-v4.3.pdf, DASH-IF, November 15, 2018.

[20] CTA-5001-A, "Web Application Video Ecosystem – Content Specification", https://cdn.cta.tech/cta/media/media/resources/standards/pdfs/cta-5001-a-final.pdf, CTA, December 2018.

[21] D. Wu, Y.T. Hou, W. Zhu, Y-Q. Zhang, and JM Peha, "Streaming video over the internet: approaches and directions," *IEEE Trans. CSVT*, vol. 11, no. 3, pp. 282-300, 2001.

[22] B. Girod, M. Kalman, Y.J. Liang, and R. Zhang, "Advances in channel-adaptive video streaming," *Wireless Comm. and Mobile Comp.,* vol. 2, no. 6, pp. 573-584, 2002.

[23] G. J. Conklin, G. S. Greenbaum, K. O. Lillevold, A. F. Lippman, and Y. A. Reznik, "Video coding for streaming media delivery on the internet," *IEEE Trans. CSVT*, vol. 11, no. 3, pp. 269-281, 2001.

[24] Brightcove VideoCloud platform, https://www.brightcove.com/en/onlinevideo-platform

[25] Brightcove Context-Aware Encoding, https://apis.support.brightcove.com/general/overview-context-aware-encoding.html

[26] ITU-R Rec. BT.500, "Methodology for the subjective assessment of the quality of television pictures," *ITU-R,* October, 2019.

[27] Y. Reznik, J. Cenzano, B. Zhang, "Transitioning Broadcast to Cloud," Proc. *2020 NAB Broadcast Engineering and Information Technology Conference*, Las Vegas, NV, May 13-14, 2020.

Using Real-Time Data to Drive Engagement and Build Community – Lessons from Gaming

Simon Crownshaw, Brady Woods
Microsoft
Redmond, Washington, United States
simon.crownshaw@microsoft.com, bradywoods@microsoft.com

Abstract – As we move quickly to a service and experience model in Media, we will discuss how LiveOps techniques developed by the gaming (video game) industry when it was faced with similar challenges of audience fragmentation and personalization, can now be selectively applied to streaming media and beyond. Beyond Live Ops as a single solution, the industry will move more towards inclusive digital communities that provide a social fabric of robust engagement tools: providing users the ability to connect their friends and family and carry them to all of a media company's endpoints, creating that friendship familiarity within all of their assets. We also explore the potential future horizons of possibility if we collectively embrace the opportunity.

Games as a Product to Games as a Service

It began with games as singular objects to be created, distributed, and consumed. This chapter of the games industry was dominated by premium, in-home experiences. Players needed dedicated hardware, an expensive piece of software or cartridge, and many hours set aside to focus solely on gaming. The business of games was also tightly linked with retail. The need for shelf space and the pressures of retail sales cycles necessitated a focus on advertising campaigns leading to hotly anticipated game launches. Players and developers were strangers, with no Reddit tantrums or Twitter smear campaigns. For those working on console or non-connected PC games, the distance between developers and the people playing their games was even greater.

As access to high-speed internet expanded and online culture emerged, games changed, and we entered a new chapter: Games as a Service.

Here, a new kind of game made its way into the mainstream: a game as an ongoing service. As games began to focus on player acquisition and funnels instead of retail cycles and ad buys, social and mobile games were in the best position to take full advantage of digital distribution. Developers started to form direct, transactional relationships with their players. But as social media exploded, communication between developers and players became more common, more frequent, and more emotionally charged. The media industry started taking notice.

Now the Games as a Service chapter is evolving, and the next chapter of LiveOps is taking hold, where a frequently connected, and interactive customer expects to earn, compete, and engage with other like-minded customers.

This paper is excerpted from the Proceedings of the 2022 NAB Broadcast Engineering and Information Technology (BEIT) Conference, © 2022, National Association of Broadcasters, 1 M Street S.E., Washington, DC 20003 USA.

Where Did the Concept of LiveOps Come From?

"Live" refers to any game that is not static and has some element of connectivity. This doesn't have to be a multiplayer or competitive game, just any game which is engineered and designed with inevitable change in mind. "Operations" means to take care of something over time. In reference to games, this implies actively managing a game over time. Operations can also refer to processes used to deliver the game. But that is just a definition, let's look more closely at what LiveOps really means for game or media content development.

LiveOps Is a Way of Thinking About Players or Fans in the Media Sense

LiveOps calls on us to think of our players as a community. A complex group of people who come and go, have an evolving relationship with the game, and an evolving relationship with each other. Because LiveOps games build relationships with players over time, they must consider long-tail motivations like the desire for new skills, deeper relationships, and more autonomy. Since players might play a LiveOps game for years, games must consider how they will fit into their players' lives well beyond a singular entertainment experience.

LiveOps Is an Approach to Design and Game Direction

LiveOps is a player-centric approach to game design, but it's also a philosophy. Games as Product tend to be very developer-centric; they seek to deliver a developer's story, a developer's point of view, or a developer's crafted experience. LiveOps games are different. These games are primarily focused on what the player wants, how to deliver opportunities to the player, and satisfying player needs. Not to say that LiveOps games lack design vision, they almost need it even more, as navigating the gap between what players say they want and what pleases them is an endless challenge. The LiveOps approach skews more toward satisfaction (how the player feels after playing) and away from attraction (how excited the player is before they play).

LiveOps Is an Experimentation-Focused Process

LiveOps isn't just a philosophy. It's also a powerful iterative approach to game development and now media content creation. Gamers see players as an ever-changing community, and game design is player centric, LiveOps games are never really done. We must keep experimenting with and evolving the game to please our community. LiveOps achieves this through frequent game updates that test hypotheses about player behavior and evaluate the results with data. This necessitates the ability to push content and other changes frequently; LiveOps games are often architected as modular, independent features that can be iterated on without fear of dependencies. LiveOps games also usually store large amounts of content data on servers instead of in client apps so they can be changed without the need to distribute new client versions.

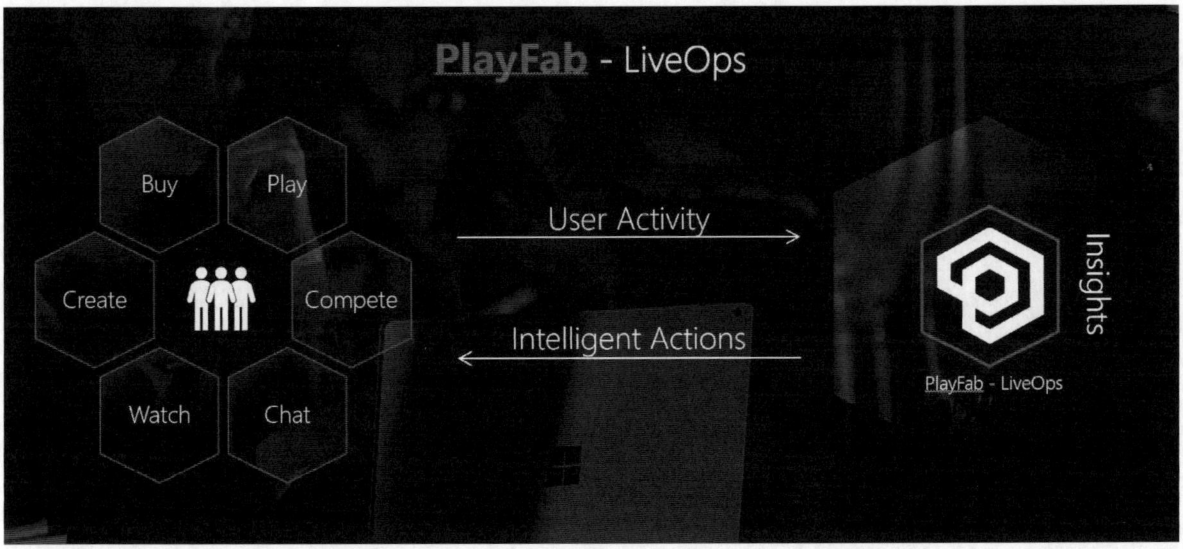

FIGURE 1

Blurring of the Lines Between Media and Gaming

M&E companies will look to create a digital entertainment flywheel with an increased focus on immersive gaming experiences to complement their streaming bundles and reinforce the value of their IP. Over the past 10 years we have seen major media companies put their energy into building direct-to-consumer streaming offerings focused on the development of original content. The next major advancement in this strategy will be to develop a gaming intellectual property (IP) arsenal to enable an interconnected bundle of film/TV media and interactive gaming experiences. There is existing precedent for this as historically, legacy media companies with valuable IP have used amusement parks to foster this intimate and interactive connection between fans and popular characters, often referred to as a "flywheel effect."

The lines have already become blurred and it's accelerating as streaming leaders have emerged as leaders in the race to solidify and integrate the gaming and media ecosystem of the future. These leaders are hiring gaming executives and buying gaming studios. Gaming has become a strategic imperative for media and engagement.

The Future of Media Based on LiveOps

Hopefully we can all agree on the value of LiveOps and its increasingly important role in modern media development. Gaming highlighted that this was a great mechanism to engage in real time with customers, enable their experience and ensure that that right experience is delivered at the right time. As OTT streaming platforms look to reduce or avoid subscriber churn, they can look to LiveOps to increase engagement. Managing churn is part of the story, seizing opportunity is the other. By engaging users with new, interactive, fun, and connected experiences, the media industry can use this transformative moment to capture attention and dramatically increase Lifetime Customer Value.

For the media industry we can think of LiveOps as:

- **Continually evolving** the product in concert with the audience
- **Personal experiences** that are alive, real-time responsive, iterative (not static) yet also connected to a community.

We believe Media organizations can evolve to meet the change in user expectations by adapting and personalizing their streaming interface in real-time and applying gamification. It also needs to be easy to integrate with existing applications and architecture.

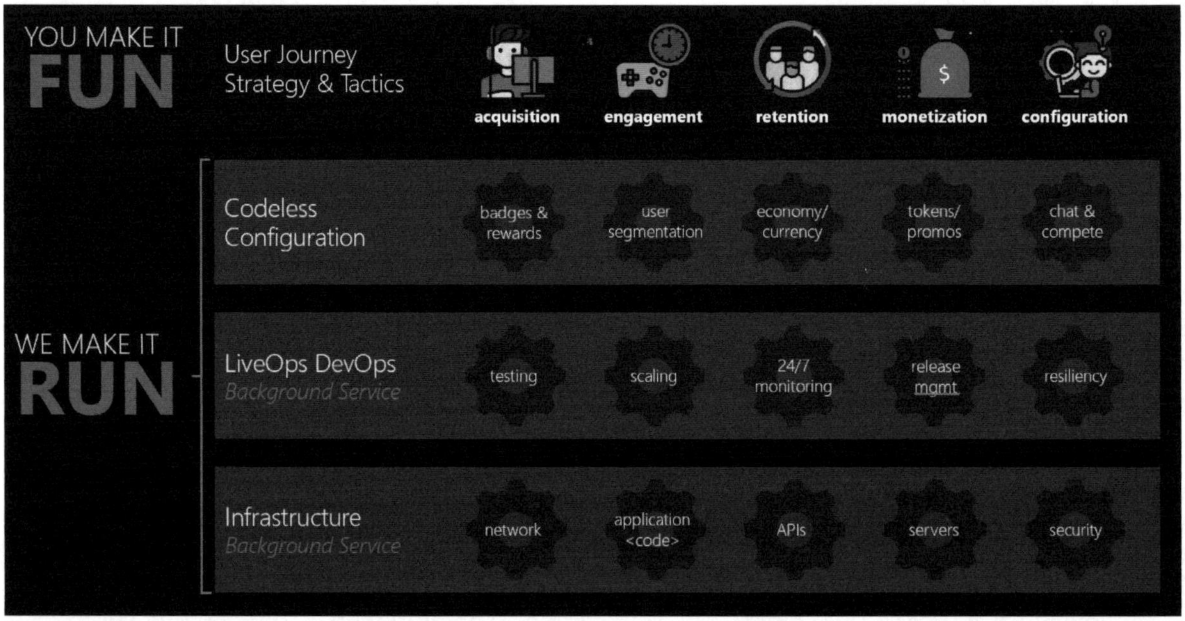

FIGURE 2

LiveOps – A Critical Element of Community-Based Engagement

A customer's or fan's desire to be part of a group or community is now a critical element to the required personalization of experiences. A social fabric of robust engagement tools, providing users the ability to connect their friends and family and carry them to all endpoints, creating that friendship familiarity within all their assets When achieved at scale, community gives users a safe place that fosters a sense of belonging as well as a sense of ownership over their experience. It does this by enabling people to see their friends, know they are online and with them and engage with them over shared interests like media or sports.

These digital communities when integrated across media ecosystems can provide what media organizations desire. The ability to communicate in real time with their members, support live commerce, provide opportunities to connect and interact with other members safely, and help keep the audience's attention across all available end points. It can also be known as a digital utopia for both customers and organizations if done right.

FIGURE 3

Data at the Heart of Engagement

Microsoft has looked to create a frictionless platform across all its products, and it is uniquely positioned to bring both gaming techniques for engagement and data to drive personalization to media. Data will be at the heart of both community and LiveOps for media and beyond. The requirements to understand the customer are greater than ever as we all expect experiences either physical, or digital to be personalized to ourselves. Unification of data across 1st and 3rd party sources will be critical as society increases its focus on identity, privacy, and safety.

Conclusion

For the Media and Entertainment industry or every chief marketing officer the goal is to find inclusive ways to help all customers enjoy their content, making intelligent content a primary area of focus. Ultimately, it's the need to deliver the right content to the right person at the right time on the right device in the language of their choice. Technology enables this and the core elements of gaming are now strategic imperatives to compete for subscribers and experiences. LiveOps presents an opportunity for audiences to engage in real time.

LiveOps is based around leveraging data to the maximum effect to provide meaningful interactive experiences. We know that media organizations have historically not been great at managing data or having centralized data repositories. The faster they can bring unification to their data estate and processes, the more intelligent their content will become. At Microsoft we are looking to build a differentiated ecosystem to enable intelligent content and data-based engagement across Media and Entertainment. Our global ISV network only extends our capabilities. And now, we are looking at how we can support a synthetic society where artificial products will enhance what's natural with products like Microsoft Mesh and HoloLens.

Microsoft will continue to invest in cloud services in a way that enables our customers to get a combination of just-in-time automation, machine learning and data insights that will bring intelligence into their content delivery. We're helping customers deepen their audience engagement with personalized, connected, and immersive experiences across all channels, platforms, and venues to increase audience satisfaction, and drive loyalty. And we're using AI and real-time insights to better understand customer behavior, improve responsiveness, and rapidly connect audiences to relevant content and experiences.

CDNI Metadata Model Extensions

Glenn Goldstein, William Power
Lumen Technologies
Broomfield, Colorado, United States

Alfonso Siloniz
Telefónica
Madrid, Spain

Guillaume Bichot
Broadpeak
Cesson Sevigne, France

Abstract – This paper presents specification work being done within the Streaming Video Alliance (SVA) and the IETF Content Delivery Network Interconnection (CDNI) Working Group to define an industry standard configuration metadata model for CDNs and Open Caching systems. The presentation will focus on the IETF draft titled *CDNI Metadata Model Extension*, a document derived from *Open Caching Configuration Interface Part 2: Extensions to the CDNI Metadata Object Model* (see References for links).

Definitions

- **CDNI (Content Delivery Networks Interconnection)**: An IETF standard that defines a set of interfaces enabling upstream CDNs (uCDNs) to delegate requests to downstream CDNs (dCDNs).
- **Open Caching**: A specific use case of CDNI where the Content Provider or a commercial CDN is typically the uCDN and a caching layer within the ISP is typically the downstream dCDN.
- **CDN Configuration Metadata:** Defines origins, caching directives, authorization rules, and request/response transformations that should occur in the content delivery pipeline.
  - In the Open Caching use case, this metadata can specify request routing method and Open Caching node selection information.
  - The interchange of CDN configuration metadata between the various entities in the delivery ecosystem is essential for efficient interoperability.

Motivational Drivers

CDNs and Open Caching systems have many common requirements for configuration metadata, as they both sit in the delivery pipeline between content providers and their audiences. Key drivers for creating an industry standard include:

- Improving efficiency of integration (standardization & automation).
- Driving interoperability to facilitate multi-CDN and hybrid content delivery scenarios.
- Improving governance & compliance.

This paper is excerpted from the Proceedings of the 2022 NAB Broadcast Engineering and Information Technology (BEIT) Conference, © 2022, National Association of Broadcasters, 1 M Street S.E., Washington, DC 20003 USA.

IETF Draft Excerpt

Following is the Introduction and Scope section excerpted from the IETF *CDNI Metadata Model Extension* draft:

> The Content Delivery Network Interconnection (CDNI) Metadata interface enables interconnected Content Delivery Networks (CDNs) to exchange content distribution metadata in order to enable content acquisition and delivery. To facilitate a wider set of use cases encountered in the commercial CDN and Open Caching ecosystems, this document describes extensions to the CDNI Metadata object model and its associated Capabilities model.
>
> The objectives of this document are:
> - Identify the requirements for extending [RFC8006] and [RFC8008] and specify a set of extensions that realize these requirements.
> - Maintain backward compatibility with [RFC8006] and [RFC8008] by not altering the definitions or semantics of the original object model. All extensions are defined as new GenericMetadata Objects.
> - Define the metadata object model independently of the APIs used to publish and retrieve metadata.
>
> Scope this document ADDRESSES:
> - Define and register CDNI GenericMetadata objects, as defined in section 4 of [RFC8006].
> - Define and register CDNI Payload Types, as defined in section 7.1 of [RFC8006].
> - Define Capabilities Objects that facilitate advertisement of a dCDN's support of these new metadata features, extending definitions in section 5 of [RFC8008].
> - Specification of a Metadata Expression Language Section 3 used within the metadata object model extensions.
> - Provide JSON examples illustrating real-world CDN and Open Caching use cases.
>
> Scope this document DOES NOT ADDRESS:
> - Metadata object model definitions already specified in [RFC8006].
> - Interface API definitions for publishing and retrieving configuration metadata. The Metadata Interface (MI) as defined in [RFC8006] can be used to retrieve metadata. To enable more sophisticated metadata configuration publishing workflows, the Streaming Video Alliance (SVA) Open Caching API [OC-CI], as documented in the SVA Configuration Interface Part 3 (Simple API) and Part 4 (Advanced API) specifications can be used.

References

[1] Goldstein, G., Power, W., Siloniz, A., and Bichot, G., "CDNI Metadata Model Extensions", Version 2, March 2022, https://datatracker.ietf.org/doc/draft-goldstein-cdni-metadata-model-extensions/

[2] The Streaming Video Alliance, "Open Caching Configuration Interface Part 2: Extensions to the CDNI Metadata Object Model", Version 1, February 2022, https://www.streamingvideoalliance.org/project/configuration-interface-api/

[3] Niven-Jenkins, B., Murray, R., Caulfield, M., and K. Ma, "Content Delivery Network Interconnection (CDNI) Metadata", RFC 8006, DOI 10.17487/RFC8006, December 2016, https://www.rfc-editor.org/info/rfc8006

[4] Seedorf, J., Peterson, J., Previdi, S., van Brandenburg, R., and K. Ma, "Content Delivery Network Interconnection (CDNI) Request Routing: Footprint and Capabilities Semantics", RFC 8008, DOI 10.17487/RFC8008, December 2016, https://www.rfc-editor.org/info/rfc8008

Open Caching: An Innovative Way for Content Providers to Serve Customers

Sanjay Mishra, ErinRose Widner, Jeff Budney
Verizon Business Group
Basking Ridge, New Jersey, United States

Abstract - As media companies focus on growing their Direct to Consumer (D2C) businesses, the ecosystem that enables content delivery over IP-based networks continues to evolve and become even more critical. In order to gain efficiencies in the process, media technology providers want to better leverage each component in the content delivery path. Caching popular content at the network edge—making it closer to end users—is a common ISP network management practice that has long been a part of the Internet's architecture. But the new Open Caching standard enables a move away from proprietary systems, while still supporting an environment that leverages content delivery networks, last mile providers and streaming technologies that bring content closer to the consumer. Based on specifications developed by the Streaming Video Alliance (SVA's) Open Caching Working Group, networks are deploying caching servers directly at the edge of the network, instead of servers in cloud data centers located farther away from where customers are engaging with the content. By caching content closer to customers, the data travels a shorter distance over the network, through fewer routers and switches, reducing the time it takes to reach the end device. As a result, consumers are able to decrease time to the first frame of the experience and face fewer potential network events that cause freezing or buffering. This paper highlights a recent field test in which customers throughout the Verizon Fios footprint were able to access select content using Open Caching and experienced faster start times, smoother streaming, and less buffering.

What Traffic is on the Internet?

Cisco's Annual Internet Report [1] predicts that by 2023, there will be 5.3 billion Internet users, up from 3.9 billion in 2018, an increase from 51% to 66% resulting in two-thirds of the world population with access to the Internet. The report also states, "Globally, devices and connections are growing faster (10 percent CAGR) than both the population (1.0 percent CAGR) and the Internet users (6 percent CAGR)."

Overall, various media reports such as streamingmedia.com [2] predict that video as a single entity will constitute about over 80% of the Internet traffic. Improved access to the Internet together with improved connectivity type (broadband speed) for both wireline (Fiber and DOCSIS over Cable) and fixed wireless access even with 4G–and now 5G–have improved overall broadband speeds. The report from Cisco goes on to state "Broadband-speed improvements result in increased consumption and use of high-bandwidth content and applications. The global average broadband speed continues to grow and will more than double from 2018 to 2023, from 45.9 Mbps to 110.4 Mbps."

Additionally, the Cisco report says an Internet enabled TV with just two HD streams over a three hour period generates traffic equivalent to a day's worth of Internet usage for an entire household. And to quote Cisco's report, "Video effect of the devices on traffic is more pronounced because of the

This paper is excerpted from the Proceedings of the 2022 NAB Broadcast Engineering and Information Technology (BEIT) Conference, © 2022, National Association of Broadcasters, 1 M Street S.E., Washington, DC 20003 USA.

introduction of Ultra-High-Definition (UHD), or 4K, video streaming. This technology has such an effect because the bit rate for 4K video at about 15 to 18 Mbps is more than double the HD video bit rate and nine times more than Standard-Definition (SD) video bitrate."

Rise of the Subscription VOD Market

According to Statista.com [3], revenue in the Video-on-Demand segment is projected to reach US$40.7B in 2022 and an annual growth rate (CAGR 2022-2026) of 6.88%, resulting in a projected market volume of US$53B by 2026. The largest segment is Video Streaming (SVOD) with a market volume of US$36.5B in 2022. In the Video-on-Demand segment, the number of users is expected to amount to 237.1m users by 2026, which the report estimates as 69% of user subscription.

In recent years, at least in the US, the SVOD market has really become a major force in content creation and distribution. The once nascent SVOD market, primarily owned by Netflix, has now surpassed the traditional pay TV market. According to Omdia's Media & Technology Digest, December 2021 report [4], "by late 2020, online video subscriptions began overtaking pay TV in key mature markets, and as of year-end 2020, online has finally overtaken traditional pay TV". According to Global Data [5], "the pay TV market in the Americas region lost a combined 24 million subscriptions, reaching 157 million at year end 2020", while at the same time, in the same region the report also states that in North America, SVOD subscriptions rose to 288.5 by end of 2020 and expect to reach 449M by 2025. The report also states that globally, the subscription pay TV market has now stabilized and shall remain steady at over 1 billion subscriptions through 2025. Even with pay TV stabilizing, SVOD and FAST (free ad supported TV) services, on the other hand, will continue to grow. SVOD when compared with Pay TV has redefined viewing experience. The flexibility of time-shifted viewing along with the ability to watch in bulk (aka binge watching, courtesy of Netflix) and with no-ads to interrupt are all game changing. And particularly, this bodes well with younger viewing audiences. So, it comes as no surprise that SVOD providers such as, Disney+, HBO Max, Peacock, Paramount+, and Discovery+ have all recently reported subscriber growth. Additionally, most of the streaming services are looking to scale globally and they are also moving into owning the studios to produce original content. The direction here seems clear, one that the Content Providers (CP) see a substantial revenue opportunity by going global, but also creating original content. In short, a consumer is likely to have multiple VOD subscription services, so the key for SVOD providers is to invest in creating original content to help reduce churn and add new subscribers.

Given substantial opportunities for growing their revenues but in a very crowded SVOD market, it is imperative for the SVOD providers to be able to give their subscribers a reason to stay. This really translates to how does a SVOD provide the best user experience, both in terms of content available and the user's ability to seamlessly access the content (e.g., fast video start-times, zero or near zero video playback failures, zero or near zero buffering, or higher bitrate).

Content Delivery Networks

Traditionally, Content Delivery Networks (CDNs) have provided a platform on which the CPs have relied on to distribute their content (and still do and for good reasons). The CDNs have invested heavily in building out their networks of data centers across the globe to deliver content on behalf of the content providers.

According to a report by Mordor Intelligence [6], "The content delivery network (CDN) market was valued at USD 11.76 billion in 2020, and it is expected to reach a value of USD 49.61 billion by 2026, at a CAGR of 27.30%, over the forecast period (2021-2026). Growing demand for rich video content,

among the increasing online users, and the trend of digitization in organizations across the end-user verticals boost the overall CDN market demand."
The CDN model has become the standard way Content Providers distribute content because of the reach and capacity their network provides. There is almost nothing that a CP needs to do other than having one or more CDNs take on the responsibility of delivering content to their subscribers.

In short, CDNs are a key part in the delivery chain between the Content Providers and their subscribers. But there are additional opportunities. This model can still be further improved with Open Caching to help CPs and CDNs scale the last mile with even better latencies and Time to First Byte (TTFB), and in the end, improve the overall customer quality of experience.

Can ISP Be Part of This Delivery Value Chain?

Can ISP be part of this delivery value chain? According to The Streaming Video Alliance [7] the answer to this question is a resounding yes. SVA is an industry forum open to all within the online video value chain, including content owners, service providers, network operators, infrastructure providers, and streaming video technology companies. The Alliance focuses on the ecosystem, architecture, technologies, and best practices needed to support the future of video in which streaming may deliver the lion's share of worldwide content. Specifically, within SVA, the Open Caching Working Group (OCWG) [8], is focused on leveraging all principals of the online video value chain to revolutionize how video is delivered to the end customer. Its focus is to identify the critical components of a non-proprietary caching system and to build the platform needed to bring together an architecture that allows content to flow seamlessly between different layers of the content delivery value chain. A system that is based on standards such as the Internet Engineering Task Force (IETF) Content Delivery Networks Interconnection (CDNI) working group [9].

Open Caching

Open Caching is a collaborative work within SVA to deliver streaming content at scale while addressing issues for QoE and latency, including time to first byte. The OCWG is focused on developing an open, non-proprietary architecture within the constraints of the CDNI.

Open Caching addresses scale of delivery towards the subscriber-end while lowering end to end latency. The underlying Open Caching architecture relies on the Standards (Request for Comments or RFCs) as defined by Content Delivery Networks Interconnection. The CDNI specifications describe standards on how an upstream entity can delegate content to a downstream entity. What this implies is any CP or a CDN in compliance with CDNI specification can easily add any ISP in its delivery chain as long the ISP also complies with the CDNI specifications.

In a white paper [10] published by the Streaming Video Alliance, the motivation for open caching is laid out as follows:

> "If all the participants in the distribution chain—CPs, CDNs, and ISPs—continue to work independently, the industry will never resolve the scale and quality issues plaguing widespread adoption of streaming video. To truly address the challenges, CPs, CDNs, and ISPs must come together and collaborate to create a new, integrated delivery architecture.
>
> The Streaming Video Alliance has codified such a collaborative approach in the Open Caching Network (OCN). This innovative solution, developed as a series of specifications from the Open Caching Working Group, is an open way that all three constituents can operate seamlessly together. Rather than siloed technologies, the entire ecosystem works together to develop and

share information as part of each request to satisfy the ultimate goal—ensure viewers get the best possible streaming video experience."

Open Caching Network

Open Caching Network is an edge caching architecture that allows Content Providers and Content Delivery Networks to utilize caches deployed by Internet Service Providers at the edge of their networks. In essence, Open Caching allows CP and CDNs to offload content seamlessly in a manner that brings content closer to the user since the Open Caching architecture extends the content delivery infrastructure deep into service provider networks.

Following is a high-level view of an open caching model:

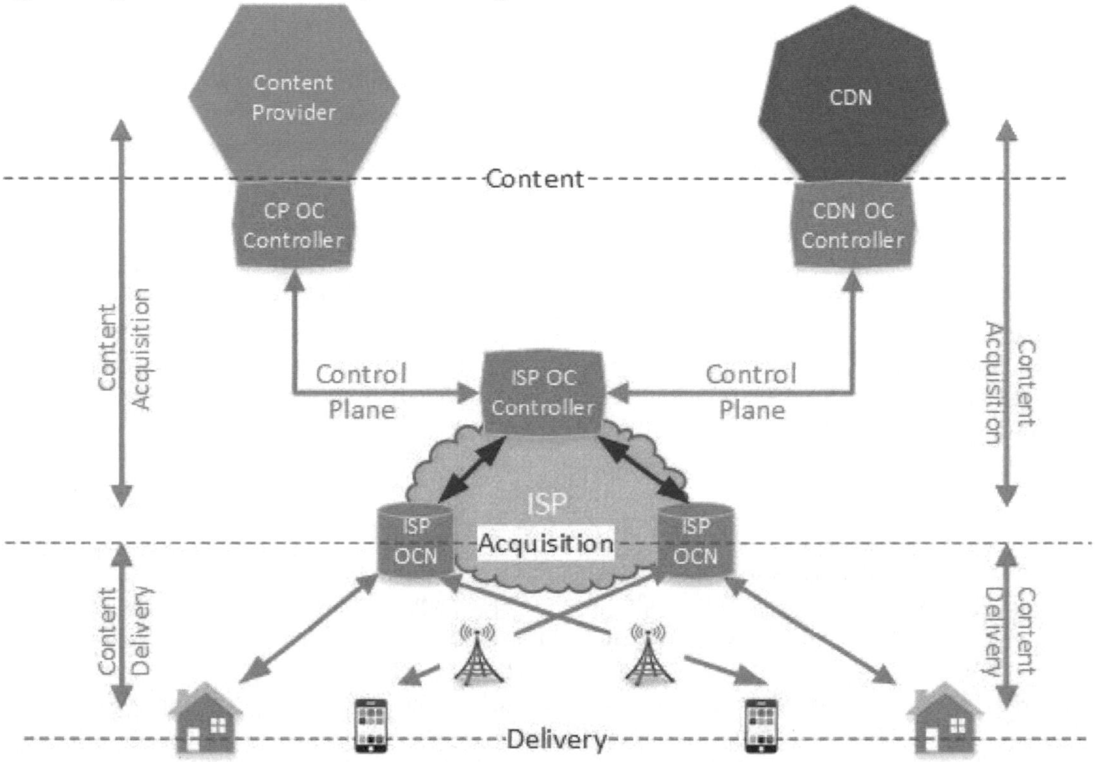

FIGURE 1: OPEN CACHING NETWORK

The Open Caching Working Group identifies three core components that together create the open caching network. The three components are as follows:

- **Open Caching Node (OCN):** A universal multi-tenant cache function deployed and owned by the service provider in close proximity to the users.
- **Content Provider/CDN Open Cache Controller (CP/CDN OCC):** a control function used by delegating Content Provider (CP) and/or a CDN to exchange control plane messages and routing to the open cache resources inside service provider networks.
- **Service Provider Open Cache Controller/Request Router (SP OCC):** a control function used by a service provider with an open caching deployment to interwork with the corresponding instance upstream at the CP/CDN layer and downstream to delegate content to the network of OCNs.

Case Study: Open Caching Delivery

In the following example, we tested a scenario where two streams of content were delivered to a Fios subscriber. The source for one stream originated outside of the ISP caches and the second source was the ISP-hosted caches. For this test, we used Verizon's Fios network with a Fios subscriber that has a 1Gbps service.

Test Setup

- Verizon's Fios Network
- A Verizon subscriber with a 1Gbps using an Alienware Laptop with an Ethernet connection to the Fios Broadband Home Router
- Internet Speed test shows download speed of 947 Mbps and upload speed of 923 Mbps (verizon.com/speedtest/)
- Content played from nearest cache serving the Fios User
- Content also played from content hosted in the Internet Cloud
- Content resolution: 2160p (4K UHD)

Test Methodology and Terminology

- Content initially played simultaneously on split screen from the Origin (CDN) and the ISP hosted open caching network
- Initially, cache did not have the content and it acquired as it played back to the user
- In the example below, a series of content is played multiple times (for the purposes of this report, and for brevity of data, the test shows number of times (5), the test was executed)

The table below shows the Key Performance Indicators (KPI) used for the testing and definition of the KPIs:

	Term	Definition
1	Time to First Byte	The duration from the user or client making a request until the first content byte being received by the client
2	Bandwidth	The measured client throughput from the last segment downloaded
3	Download Time	The download time from the last requested segment. From the first byte being received to the last byte
4	Total Downloaded	The total amount of data downloaded by the client
5	Response Time	The response time for the last requested segment. From request of segment to receipt of first byte
6	Buffer	The duration length of the forward buffer
7	Freeze Events	The count of times where the video had paused for buffering
8	Bitrate	The bitrate of the representation being downloaded
9	Jitter	The standard deviation of bitrate values during this session
10	Quality	The current quality of the video
11	Dropped FPS	The absolute count of frames dropped by the rendering pipeline since play commenced

TABLE 1: KEY PERFORMANCE INDICATOR DEFINITION

The table below captures the raw numbers from the total number of tests executed:

Number of Test Run	Source	Time to First Byte (msec)	Bandwitdh	Download Time (sec)	Total Downloaded (Mbps)	Response Time (msec)	Buffer	Freeze Events	Bitrate	Quality
1	Origin	4.9	50.1	2.57	428	68.1	321	0	35	2160
	Cache	37.4	373	0.21	428	7.3	34.5	0	35	2160
2	Origin	7.8	43.9	2.54	392	66.3	32.1	0	35	2160
	Cache	42.1	422	0.177	410	8	34.6	0	35	2160
3	Origin	13.6	47.4	2.94	177	72	31.6	0	35	2160
	Cache	35.3	362	0.2	177	7.4	34.5	0	35	2160
4	Origin	5	52	2.32	141	72.2	32	0	35	2160
	Cache	31.8	555	0.0266	141	7.8	34.3	0	35	2160
5	Origin	41.4	197	0.0305	126	9.7	31.8	9	35	2160
	Cache	97.9	655	0.029	125	9.5	34.7	0	35	2160

TABLE 2: OPEN CACHING VERSUS ORIGIN SERVER

Observations

The test was conducted on a live network. While the results depict real-time network traffic and constraints, they are limited to performance recorded on a given instance.

In the test that was conducted, the Origin server (hosted on Amazon cloud) performed equally well with ISP hosted local cache in terms of maintaining the bit-rate with no freezing events. However, in other key areas such as video download bandwidth and the time to download, the results show local caches performing extremely well as compared to the Origin server.

- In the graph below, the green and the blue bars represent client throughput (throughput for the last segment downloaded). The green bar corresponds to the Local cache and the blue corresponds to the Origin server respectively. The results show data throughput from Local cache to be at least 6 to 10 times faster (Bursty) than the Origin server.
- Related to above throughput is the time to download. This is plotted as a line graph. The download time from the Local cache (purple line) is in sub millisecond range whereas, the Origin server (red line) has a much wider range between sub millisecond to several seconds.
- Other metrics not plotted on the graph show a similar trend where TTFB and response times are in magnitude of order superior for the Local cache as compared to the Origin server.

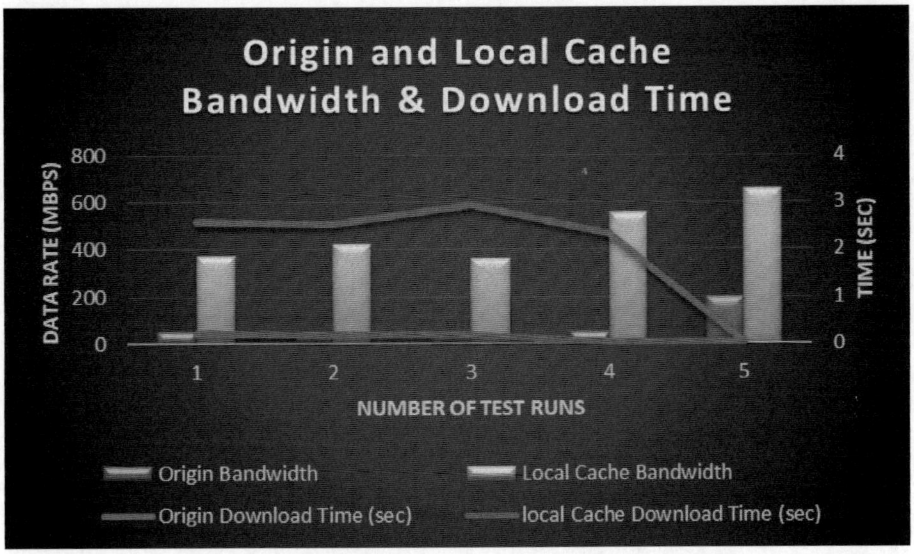

FIGURE 2: CDN AND LOCAL CACHE MEASUREMENT

In summary, following are key observations:

- As the OCN starts to acquire the content it continues to show improving bandwidth (the measured client throughput from the last segment downloaded)
- The local caches show a bandwidth (client throughput) between 373 to 655 Mbps, compared to the Origin (CDN) that ranges from 50 to 197 Mbps.
- Time to download from cache ranges from 0.01 to 0.2 sec versus 0.03 to 2.94 sec.
- The local caches show markedly higher throughput and download time

For this paper, we only kept video on-demand as our focus. However, based on other usage, we see Open Caching performing equally well for live-content and also high bandwidth and low latency applications such as online gaming. Additionally, Open Caching can be used to deliver non-media content closer to the user such as software downloads, pictures and any kind of content that would be at an origin server or a CDN.

Conclusion

The new Open Caching standard enables a move away from proprietary systems, while still supporting an environment that leverages content delivery networks, last mile providers and streaming technologies that bring content closer to the consumer. Content stored closer to customers in this manner travels a shorter distance over the network through fewer routers and switches before reaching the customer. As a result, customers may be able to stream content sooner through fewer network elements with a lower potential for network events that could cause freezing or buffering and improved Quality of Experience for paying customers. Open Caching is standards-based and encourages collaboration between all constituents in the content delivery pipeline including the content providers, the commercial content delivery networks and the last mile ISP.

References

[1] https://www.cisco.com/c/en/us/solutions/executive-perspectives/annual-internet-report/index.html

[2] https://www.streamingmedia.com/Articles/ReadArticle.aspx?ArticleID=144177

[3] https://www.statista.com/outlook/dmo/digital-media/video-on-demand/united-states

[4] Media & Technology Digest, December 2021 (www.omida.com)

[5] Global Data, "Subscription Video on Demand Market Trends and Opportunities in the Americas", June 2021

[6] https://www.mordorintelligence.com/industry-reports/content-delivery-market

[7] https://www.streamingvideoalliance.org/sva-faq/

[8] https://opencaching.streamingvideoalliance.org/

[9] https://datatracker.ietf.org/wg/cdni/about/

[10] https://www.streamingvideoalliance.org/product/optimizing-video-delivery-with-the-open-caching-network/

What the Future Holds for Content Protection with CDN Edge

Gwendal Simon, Lionel Carminati, Gwenaël Doërr, Alain Durand
Synamedia
Rennes, France
gsimon@synamedia.com, lcarminati@synamedia.com, gdoerr@synamedia.com, adurand@synamedia.com

Abstract – Over the past several years, there has been an increased demand for antipiracy solutions and this demand continues to evolve. The most studied method is related to watermarking, with a three-step scheme:

1. the video stream that is legally delivered to every customer is watermarked,
2. the legal service extracts the watermark in the illegal video stream and identifies the pirate,
3. the legal video service stops delivering the legal stream to the pirate, and thus blocks the illegal stream at the root.

The A/B watermarking solution is expected to find a trade-off between CDN scalability and watermark-based personalized delivery. Unfortunately, the A/B watermark solution has three critical limitations:

1. it is resource hungry;
2. it is slow;
3. it requires complex time synchronization between multiple entities.

We introduce in this paper a novel solution for scaling the delivery of unique watermarks. We leverage the concept of edge computing, where the CDN brings more intelligence and more capacities to the edge servers, beyond just being a cache function. We have designed a solution where the edge server is able to modify the video content before delivering it, here to embed the watermark on-the-fly.

Introduction

Context

The business of video content production, whether it is for live events or cinematography, has been built upon the principle that the end-users who consume the video pay the rightsholders, indirectly or directly. The content rightsholders would thus like to limit, ideally annihilate, piracy, which we define here as the act of offering a video stream that has been acquired from a copyrighted video service on another video delivery service. With the development of Over-The-Top (OTT) streaming services, the piracy has been made paradoxically easier, since a pirate receives the video flow on a machine that has processing and storing capabilities. Pirates have developed efficient tools to capture, distort, and forward the video stream. Meanwhile, illegal video streaming platforms aggregate the flows from the pirates and illegally deliver the content without regards to rightsholders. Piracy is thus a serious concern for both content rightsholders and legal video streaming services.

To fight piracy, the legal service providers (content rightsholders and streaming services) have two approaches: shutting down the illegal streaming platforms or identifying the pirate. The former option has proven to be vain, since pirate organizations can quickly create new platforms. Legal service

This paper is excerpted from the Proceedings of the 2022 NAB Broadcast Engineering and Information Technology (BEIT) Conference, providers have thus focused on the second approach: identifying the pirate. In the case of a video that is illegally captured from an OTT streaming system, the pirate is originally a legitimate customer of the streaming service. The idea is thus to stop delivering the video in the legal platform for this specific customer in order to dry up the source of the illegal streaming.

Existing Solutions and Limitations

To identify the pirate, the legal service providers partnered with *watermark* security providers to implement the following scheme:

1. the video stream that is legally delivered to every customer contains a unique watermark for each customer,
2. the legal service extracts the watermark in the illegal video stream (the stream that is delivered on the illegal delivery service). From the extracted watermark, the legal service provider identifies the pirate,
3. the legal service provider stops delivering the legal stream to the pirate, and thus blocks illegal redistribution at the root.

However, the first step of this scheme is hard to scale in practice: to prepare and deliver a different watermarked stream for each customer, the service providers cannot use delivery techniques such as *multicast*. It is however still possible to implement watermarked video delivery in Content Delivery Networks (CDN) with the so-called A/B solution.

The A/B watermarking solution has been developed and implemented in CDNs to find a compromise between the cost of scaling the delivery and the time to identify a unique watermark in the video. Each client is associated with a unique sequence of binary values. The CDN origin server sends two pre-watermarked versions (one A and one B) of the video segments to the CDN edge servers. Then, these edge servers unicast to every user a unique sequence of video segments by switching between the A/B versions of the requested video segments according to the binary sequence assigned to the said user. The video player at the client side displays a unique video stream, which contains a series of A and B pre-watermarked video segments. If this user is a pirate, the stream that is delivered on the illegal video service contains the same sequence; the legal video service knows the identity of the pirate and can take appropriate countermeasures.

Unfortunately, the A/B watermark solution has three critical limitations:

1. it is resource hungry. The solution doubles the bandwidth in the CDN and doubles the memory in the edge servers.
2. the watermark embedding pace is slowed down because a single watermark bit can be embedded per video segment. To fully serve a unique sequence of A/B pre-watermarked videos segments to a population of millions of clients, the CDN may have to deliver several minutes of video content depending on the duration of the video segments.
3. it is somewhat complex to implement since it requires time synchronization between multiple entities (edge server, subscriber management server, video packagers) to guarantee the match between the subscriber identifier and the A/B sequence.

Our Contributions

At Synamedia, we have come to a novel solution for scaling the delivery of unique watermarks. We leverage the concept of edge computing, where the CDN brings more intelligence and more capacities to the edge servers, beyond just being a cache function. We have designed a solution where the edge server is able to modify the video content before delivering it. In our case, we want the edge servers to embed the watermark on-the-fly before unicasting a video segment to the end-user. We separate the watermark *profiling* (the action of determining the location of potential watermark markers in the video bit-stream) and the watermark *embedding* (the action of modifying the video bit-stream to include the watermark). We introduce here the mechanisms that enable watermark embedding in the CDN edge servers.

A noteworthy feature is that our edge solution applies on the compressed and encrypted domain, so the edge server does not have to decode and re-encode the video segments, nor to decrypt and re-encrypt. The solution requires only one version of the video content in the edge, which remedies the A/B resource consumption limitation. To embed the right watermark in the video content, the edge server follows some instructions, which have been incorporated in-band into the video segment. The pipeline is thus simpler to implement and fixes the A/B complexity limitation. Finally, it is possible to embed more information than a single bit (A vs. B) per video segment, so the pirate can be identified faster. This feature fixes the A/B detection time limitation.

Context

Video Packager, Encryption, Encoding

The solution that we introduce in this paper supposes the regular video processes to be implemented in the pipeline backend. The video stream under consideration is divided into frames, which are encoded using a standard video codec, such as one of the popular MPEG formats Advanced Video Coding (AVC) or High-Efficiency Video Coding (HEVC). Then, this series of encoded (or compressed) frames, which is referred to as the video payload, is encapsulated into a video package, which includes the metadata that the different computers in the pipeline may require for streaming and displaying the video. A typical example of a video package is ISOBMFF. For security reasons, it is common practice to encrypt (part of) the video payload using off-the-shelf Digital Rights Management (DRM) techniques. Nowadays, DRMs either rely on AES CTR or AES CBCS encryption to protect video content.

Watermarking, A/B Switcher

Watermarking is a technique that enables content providers to trace delivered data by embedding hidden information in video, image, and other media types so that the authorized copy of the digital content can be uniquely identified. Watermarking systems are typically benchmarked against three fundamental performance metrics:

1. Fidelity. The embedded watermark shall be imperceptible by a human being. In other words, it should be difficult for the users to distinguish watermarked from unwatermarked content.
2. Robustness. It shall be possible to extract the watermark information from watermarked video, even if it has been tempered with by the pirate with operations such as transcoding, screen casting, HDMI stripping, and camcording.
3. Embedding rate. It is desirable to embed the watermark information as quickly as possible in the video content to identify the pirates with video clips that are as short as possible.

Watermarks can be embedded in the video at the client side, just before displaying it in the player. However, this strategy raises significant security concerns, especially with open consumer owned devices such as phones, tablets, and laptops. The pirates can bypass the watermark embedding logic by hacking the video client software. Client-side watermarking also incurs extra processing, which drains the battery of mobile devices faster.

These limitations have motivated content owners and legal streaming operators to shift the trust model to the cloud, where all security critical operations shall be performed. A typical example of such server-side watermark embedding is the A/B watermarking technique, depicted in Figure 1 for the case of an Adaptive Bit-Rate (ABR) streaming system.

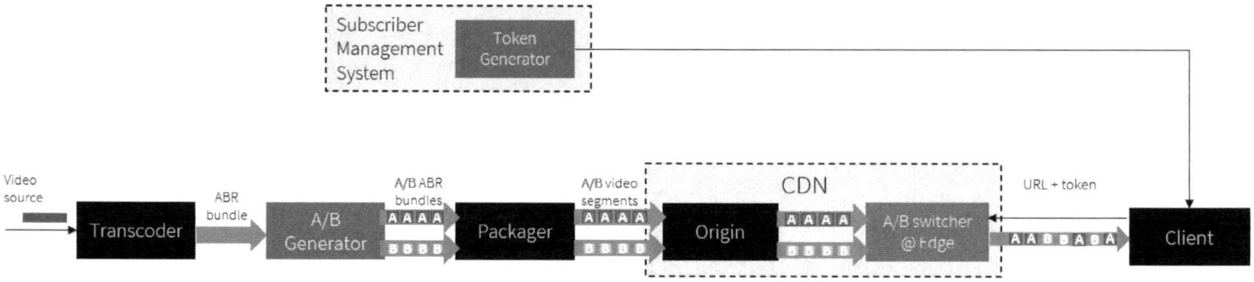

FIGURE 1A/B WATERMARKING: FULL PIPELINE

On the streaming server side, the legal content provider generates two alternate pre-watermarked copies of all video segments (one copy A and one copy B). In the case of ABR, it means that twice the number of video representations transit throughout the CDN and be cached in the edge servers. A/B watermarking then consists in delivering a unique sequence of A and B video segments to the end user. This serialization mechanism usually relies on a watermarking token delivered on the client-side. This watermarking token encodes the unique watermarking sequence assigned to the end user and is forwarded together with request to the CDN so that the response can be individualized accordingly.

Early implementations of A/B watermarking were relying on playlist/manifest manipulation. Using the watermarking token, the CDN is modifying the playlist that declares the list of the video segments that the client device may request so that it points to the (unique) sequence of A/B video segments assigned to the end-user. However, due to limited scalability, poor interoperability with DASH templating mechanism, and security considerations, this approach has been gradually abandoned and the de facto standard in the industry today relies on redirection at the edge, a.k.a. A/B switching. When the client device requests one of the video segments declared in the generic manifest/playlist delivered to all users, the edge server (i) determines which bit of the watermarking sequence is assigned to the requested segment, (ii) select which A or B version of the segment shall be delivered depending on the bit value of said bit in the watermarking token, and (iii) delivers the selected version of the segment to the client device, possibly by escalating the request for the segment version to the CDN if it is not present in cache.

A/B watermarking with redirection at the edge remains a complex pipeline. It requires synchronization between several components of the video delivery pipeline. For instance, the watermark bit assignment process for each video segment is typically based on the filename of the segment, which requires ad-hoc parsing to retrieve some numeral element[1] depending on the Packager provider. It also has shortcomings inherent to A/B watermarking. On one hand, it doubles the footprint at Origin and in the CDN cache which impacts the cache hit ratio. On the other hand, the watermark embedding pace is bridled by design since a single watermarking bit can be embedded per video segment. This requires using longer pirate clips to be able to trace the source of piracy, which may cause issues when the objective is to disrupt the illegal retransmission as soon as possible.

CDN and Edge Processing

The architecture of a CDN can be roughly simplified into two layers: the origin server, which stores the content to be delivered, and the edge servers, which are hardware machines that face the customers and deliver content by using *reverse proxy* techniques. The usual implementation of the delivery scheme in a CDN is a pull-based approach: the end-user triggers the action by requesting a video segment to the edge server it is mapped to. If the edge server has a copy of the segment in its cache,

[1] There is currently a standardization effort in DASH IF Content Protection and Security Task Force to avoid such dependency to file naming conventions.

then it delivers this segment to the requesting end-user. If not, then the edge server requests the segment to the origin, it stores this segment in its cache before delivering it to the end-user.

The performance of the edge server is intrinsically related to the similarities between concurrent requests among the end-users who are mapped to the same edge servers. The more requests for the same video segment, the higher is the Cache Hit-Ratio (CHR) and the more efficient is the CDN. The edge servers have shown very high efficiency (as represented by 0.98+ CHR) for live video streaming since all users watching the same video channel are requesting about the same video segments at the same time. Yet, the concept of A/B watermarking reduces the CHR. Consider two end-users watching the same video. The second end-user has only one chance out of two to get a hit in the cache. To obtain the exact same CHR, the edge server must double the cache storage.

The concept of *Edge Processing* aims at personalizing the delivery to a given user without degrading the cache performances. In comparison to a traditional reverse proxy (get the request, check the cache, extract the asset, send it), a server implementing Edge Processing extracts the asset from cache and then processes it before sending it to the end-user. To personalize the asset as illustrated by the left-hand side red boxes in Figure 2, the edge server implements two main steps: extract information about the client and process the asset to personalize it for this client.

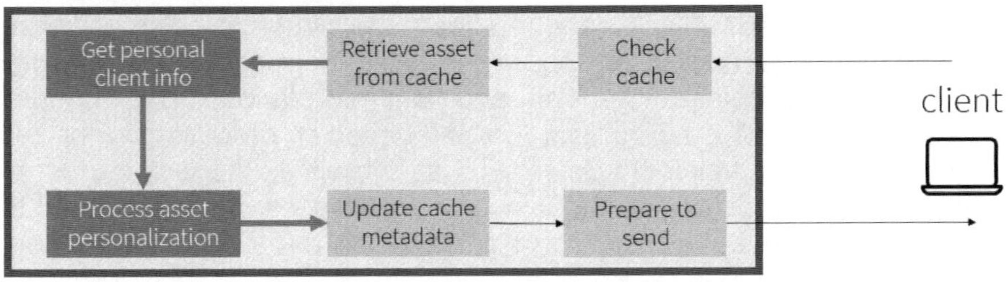

FIGURE 2 EDGE PROCESSING APPLIED TO REVERSE PROXY CDN SERVER

The personalization in Edge Processing can degrade the performance of the cache server in two ways:

1. it introduces latency (from few milliseconds to seconds), which delay the beginning of the asset delivery. The video segments that are not received on time at the client can cause significant degradation of the quality of experience (QoE).
2. it requires processing, which reduces the *density* of the server, i.e. the number of concurrent requests that a given server can process. The CPU can become the bottleneck of the edge server. The risk of degrading the overall performance of the highly scalable edge servers has reduced the popularity of Edge Processing techniques among CDN vendors so far.

2EW: Edge-Embedded Watermark

General Architecture

The main idea behind 2EW is to delay the creations of alternate copies of some video content as much as possible. In A/B watermarking, two A and B pre-watermarked variants of the same video segment are created before entering the CDN. With 2EW, the watermark serialization process occurs at the very last hop of the video delivery pipeline: at the edge. The processing workflow of 2EW is illustrated in Figure 3.

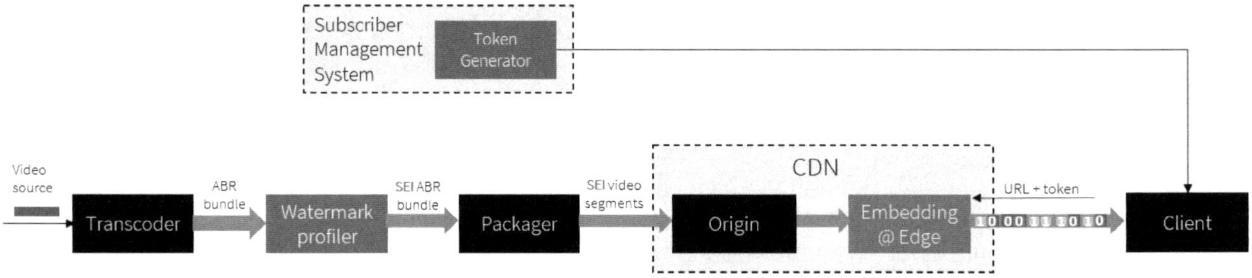

FIGURE 3: 2EW PIPELINE

On the client side, the process remains the same as in the A/B watermarking: the Subscriber Management System generates a unique watermarking token for each client and this token is sent to the edge server when requesting a video segment. 2EW deviates from the generic A/B watermarking blueprint in two main locations.

After transcoding, the *Watermark Profiler* identifies locations in the encoded video bitstream where imperceptible yet robust modifications, a.k.a. markers, can be introduced. In contrast with A/B watermarking, these markers are not embedded immediately to generate two alternate pre-watermarked versions of (part of) the video stream. Instead, the Watermark Profiler seamlessly introduces watermarking metadata in-band with the video payload. In MPEG, such watermarking metadata may be formatted as Supplementary Enhancement Information (SEI). In general, SEI messages contain information which is not required for the decoding process and the reconstruction of the coded video sequence. SEI are helpful to determine features of the coded video sequence that otherwise might be complicated to be derived. In 2EW, SEI messages are constructed to describe the watermarking markers that can be embedded at a later stage. As a result, a single version of each video segment enters the CDN: the original encoded and encrypted video, plus the watermarking metadata that encodes the instructions that can be applied by an embedding engine further downstream in the video delivery pipeline. According to our experiments, the introduction of the 2EW SEI messages usually incur a bandwidth overhead comprised in a 1-10% range depending on the bitrate and resolution of the underlying video content.

At the time of delivery in the edge server, the *Watermark Embedder* recovers the watermark instructions introduced by the Profiler and applies them before delivering the video segment. This process is further detailed below.

Watermark Embedding at the Edge

The operation at the edge server is more complex than a traditional reverse proxy, but we argue that it does not have a large impact on both latency and density of the process. The Edge Processing operation is described in Figure 4.

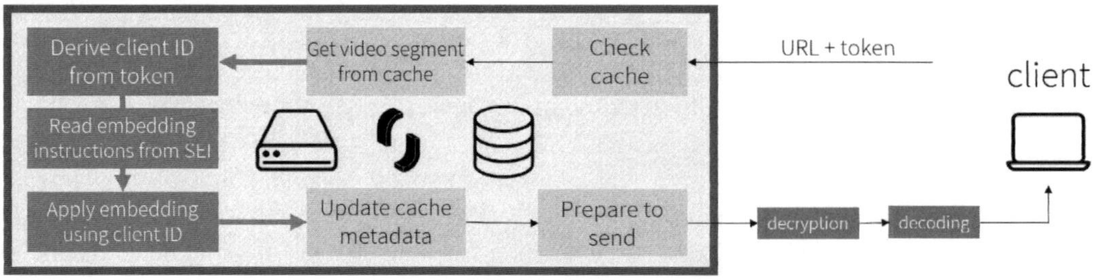

Figure 4: Edge Processing for 2EW

The first step of the edge processing logic extracts the client unique identifier from the watermark token that is included in the video segment request. This action is similar to the unique sequence extraction in the A/B watermarking.

The second step of the edge processing logic consists in extracting the watermark embedding instructions from the 2EW SEIs of the video segment, which can be easily isolated thanks to a unique identifier. It is noteworthy to recall that SEIs are typically left unprotected by conventional DRM systems and are not part of the video payload per se. In other words, the server can extract the watermark embedding instructions without any kind of video decoding nor decryption. Any of these actions would have a prohibitive computational cost for edge processing.

The third step of the edge processing logic applies the watermark embedding instructions to the video payload. The embedding instructions can be divided into two categories:

1. Payload bit entries that instruct the embedding engine to lookup the bit value at a given index in the unique watermark sequence encoded by the watermarking token;
2. Watermark entries that instruct whether or not to perform some modification at a given offset in the bitstream depending on the latest bit value returned by a payload entry. The modification operation reduces to (i) applying a XOR mask to a few bytes at a given offset with AES CTR encryption or (ii) replacing a few bytes at a given offset with AES CBC encryption.

It is important to understand that applying the watermark embedding instructions does not require any decryption and/or decoding of the video payload. As such, it can be done efficiently without significant computing resources. First measurements indicate that the whole embedding logic can be executed end-to-end in order of magnitude tens of milliseconds.

The server applies all instructions to a video segment, which it then transmits to the end-user who requested it. This processing is feasible because the latest advances in edge computing capabilities now grant the ability to modify the binary content of media data. The transmission overhead induced by the watermark serialization process only occurs beyond the CDN, thereby preserving its caching performances.

Impact of 2EW

The advantages of 2EW compared to A/B watermarking are threefold.

First, 2EW is more efficient. Only one version of the video segments is generated and propagated in the video delivery pipeline (packager, origin, CDN). The metadata represents marginal increase of information in comparison to the size of video segments (less than 10% overhead). It halves the number of files and halves the storage requirements for a same CHR in the CDN. Let us take some sample numbers to illustrate the benefits for the CDN. We consider a service provider with 100 video channels. A single video channel accounts for about 700 Mbps due to ultra-high-resolutions (4K) and both ABR formats DASH and HLS with at least half-dozen representations each. We consider edge servers running in containers in servers, such as typically deployed in 5G edge datacenters. These machines have reduced storage capabilities (typically 32 GB RAM) and can serve a thousand clients. We consider a population of 200,000 end-users, who consumes video following a Pareto popularity distribution (where 80% of the requests are for 20% of the video channels). Finally, we consider a lognormal distribution of time-shifting, which means that most end-users watch the content live or with marginal shift against the live, but some users are more significantly shifted. In this configuration, doubling the memory requirements at each edge server due to A/B watermarking makes that, in average, only the 5 latest seconds of the least popular channels are stored in cache, while 70 seconds of the most popular channels. For 2EW, 9 seconds of the unpopular channels and 145 seconds of the most popular channels are stored. The impact on the Cache Hit-Ratio is significant: it goes from 0.54 to 0.68 in each edge server. For a 10 Gbps edge server, it represents 1.3 Gbps traffic reduction per edge server, which accumulates as 259 Gbps in the CDN backhaul for this configuration with a large number of users (200,000) and relatively small edge server instances (10 Gbps, 32 GB RAM).

Second, it is usually possible to embed more than a single watermarking bit per video segment, even if several embedding instructions are allocated per watermarking bit for guarantee some level of robustness. In practice, the number of watermarking bits remains small. Nevertheless, encoding even a few watermarking bits per video segment results in a drastic reduction of the time needed to embed the whole watermarking sequence a unique sequence. For example, five million users can be uniquely identified with 23 segments A/B compared to only 12 segments with two bits per video segment. If two cycles of the sequence are required for reliable detection, with 5 seconds video segments, it takes 3 minutes and 50 seconds to detect the pirate with A/B watermarking and only 2 minutes for 2EW.

Third, the video delivery pipeline does not require component synchronization anymore. While A/B watermarking with redirection at the edge requires the server to infer which bit in the user watermark sequence shall be used based on some ad-hoc segment filename parsing, 2EW only requires the edge server to apply the edge processing logic by following the watermarking embedding instructions extracted from the SEIs. The pipeline is thus significantly simpler, and it is robust to any fast-forward and rewind operations in the video playback, without additional implementation.

Conclusion

In this paper, we have introduced a novel solution for scaling the delivery of unique watermarks. We leverage the concept of edge computing, where the CDN brings more intelligence and more capacities to the edge servers, beyond just being a cache function. We have designed a solution where the edge server is able to modify the video content before delivering it, here to embed the watermark on-the-fly. A noteworthy feature is that our edge solution applies on the compressed and encrypted domain, so the edge server does not have to decode and re-encode the video segments, nor to decrypt and re-encrypt. The solution requires only one version of the video content in the edge, which remedies the resource consumption limitation inherent to A/B watermarking systems. To embed the right watermark on the video content, the edge server follows some instructions, which have been inserted into the video package. The pipeline is thus simpler to implement and fixes the A/B complexity limitation. Finally, it is possible to embed more information than just a single bit per video segment, so the pirate can be identified faster. This feature fixes the A/B detection time limitation.

How to Capitalize on NextGen Targeted Advertising Opportunities With AI and Analytics

Dror Mangel, Guillaume Lossois
Viaccess-Orca
France

Abstract – Video service providers are in a challenging situation, made worse by the COVID-19 pandemic. Service providers are facing an increase in cord cutting, growing competition from agile competitors and SVOD, a rise in content rights prices coupled with the loss of exclusive content, and a decreasing share of viewing time and advertiser revenue. Targeted TV advertising has emerged as a promising solution to reduce churn and increase revenues, with a return rate of about 70% amongst advertisers. But to succeed at targeted advertising, service providers must be able to attain valuable, in-depth insights into viewers' behaviors and preferences. This paper examines how operators can overcome the complexities of the targeted advertising ecosystem and common delivery challenges. In particular, the paper highlights how operators can leverage AI-based targeted advertising systems to take advantage of new revenue opportunities such as the "freemium-to-premium" pipeline, monetization of catch-up content, and ad insertion and replacement in the UI. Powerful, AI-based data analytics and insights optimize the efficiency and scope of operators' target audience segmentation, ensuring highly effective advertising and more personalized television experiences. The paper elaborates on strategies for simplifying the delivery of targeted advertising, along with the significance of AI-based data analytics in fully monetizing targeted TV ads and protecting viewers' data in compliance with privacy-related legislations. Given the new and expanded opportunities of targeted advertising, there is no better time than now for operators to adopt this burgeoning technology. In today's ultra-competitive TV market, AI-based targeted advertising represents a simple way to increase viewer engagement and create additional advertising prospects.

Current Challenges of Service Providers Facing Reduced Monetization

A lot of factors are impacting TV service providers' revenue: subscription prices are decreasing, user profitability is going down, content rights costs are rising, and the loss of their traditional role as home network provider, due to growing cord-cutting and cord-shaving trends, which are expected to further intensify with 5G.

This paper is excerpted from the Proceedings of the 2022 NAB Broadcast Engineering and Information Technology (BEIT) Conference,

FIGURE 1: ESTIMATED AND PROJECTED TRADITIONAL U.S. MULTICHANNEL REVENUES 2012-2025

Even before the COVID-19 crisis began, the TV industry was facing a looming change featuring demolished boundaries between pay-TV operators, OTT providers, and broadcasters. Looking at the pay-TV operators, they are facing a wide range of interlinked challenges from cord-cutting in the U.S. and cord shaving in Europe, to increasing competition from agile competitors and SVOD, a rise in content rights prices coupled with the loss of exclusive content, growing price competition and a decreasing share of viewing time and advertiser revenue. COVID-19 has intensified the pressure, accelerating some trends to the point where it has become difficult to predict the shape of the industry at the end of the year.

Targeted advertising holds a significant monetization opportunity for today's pay-TV operators. TV advertising solutions enable operators to diversify their revenues and launch new services in an effort to mitigate revenue stagnation and cope with the main challenges facing the industry in recent years.

Further challenges include making their data available and relevant in the ad tech ecosystem, privacy compliance, maintaining frame accuracy, establishing connections with multiple advertisers, handling linear peak viewing, and supporting legacy components. To be successful with targeted TV advertising, operators need to choose a solution that fully caters to all these and much more, while also being their bridge between the digital world and their own platform.

When it comes to improving advertising revenues, you can also increase the number of impressions as better personalized TV leads to increased TV usage. All of this makes addressable advertising-driven models seem increasingly more attractive.

Growing Market

Fortunately, it appears that targeted TV advertising may ease at least some of these problems. In 2017, we saw a significant moment where the spending on global digital ads was greater than that of traditional TV advertising. And digital has only grown more influential since.

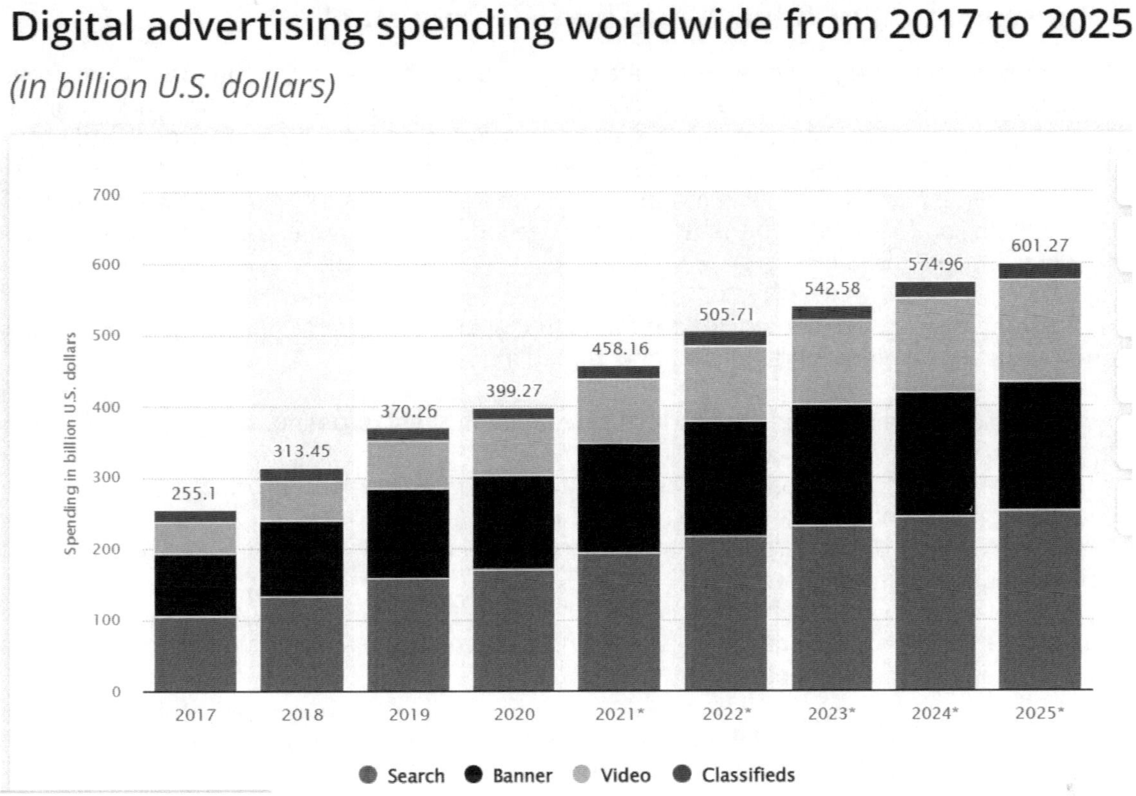

FIGURE 2: WORLDWIDE DIGITAL AD SPEND, 2017-2025 [1]

But with targeted TV advertising, broadcasters and pay-TV operators joining forces can now bring TV advertising back to its glory days, with more efficient and relevant messaging via the superior medium of the larger TV screen. They can welcome onboard new advertisers who are keen to reach the highly segmented audiences that were out of reach via traditional TV advertising and start to get back some of the revenue that has been lost to digital and more.

Is Targeted Advertising the Answer?

There are currently three prime routes for monetization when it comes to pay-TV: transactions, advertising, and data. Targeted advertising optimizes all three of them. The same collection of first-party data that ensures continued customer engagement and helps to reduce churn by offering an increasingly sophisticated amount of personalization in services is also the same data that allows for the increasingly granular segmentation of an audience. Brought together, it results in a powerful offering that simultaneously maximizes viewers' engagement and operators' revenue.

At its core, targeted advertising (TA) is simply the process of serving different adverts to different viewers, based on their interests. Advertisers today can refine the granularity of their audience segmentation to an impressive degree. TV audiences can now be chosen not only by location but by a growing number of attributes such as life stage, pet ownership, household composition, and many more.

Targeted TV advertising increases both the yield and the revenue for the same inventory: Instead of running two commercials in a one-minute break, operators could run, for example, 10 commercials, with each one targeting a different, highly relevant audience, segmented via their own usage data.

When Segmentation in Advertising and TV Data Meet

In traditional media advertising, ad executives make do with aggregate sociodemographic information on media audiences. Paired with the thematic content of the media targeted, this information gives an approximate measurement of the potential interest in the products sold. The main promise of digital targeted advertising is to provide far more accurate forms of targeting by deducing users' interests and intentions from their usage. In short, this means an ad can be directly sent to those interested in a product, without having to go through the filter of age, gender or socio professional category, and therefore allows these to be bypassed.

However, a survey done by an industry leader found that sociodemographic targeting is more effective than interest targeting in internet advertising and in media advertising.

The survey identified three main reasons for this low use of interest targeting:

1. Interest and purchase intention aren't the same.
2. Interests are either very broad and therefore not very effective, or narrow and therefore don't allow a high number of targets to be reached
3. Managing interest-based targeting campaigns means increasing the number of small targets, which is costly for advertisers.

In short, aside from a few exceptions, such as building customer bases for new companies in niche sectors, interest targeting isn't effective.

Another popular form of targeting is the "custom audience," which involves personalized contacting of customer and prospect databases by mail or telephone.

Advertisers' favorite habits involve retargeting people who have started the purchasing process, as well as creating ad-hoc categories based on first-party data. The issue that advertisers face in this method is around the user's attention span as most users are over-folded with emails and intrusive telemarketing. Technically speaking, retargeting mainly involves showing personalized adverts to users identified as customers or potential customers based on personal data. This means combining and crossing advertisers' and TV service providers' first-party data as joint email, which can lead to the same result but with a better user attention span in front of a big-screen TV.

Retargeted audiences have an obvious limitation, that they can't be used to win customers who have never had registered contact with the advertiser. This is why retargeted audiences are periodically combined with another technique: lookalike audiences. This technique involves using a limited user base with a known interest in the advertiser's products, to look for statistical twins of users who have a similar profile and behavior. Once again, combining and crossing advertisers' and TV service providers' first-party data as joint email can lead to the same result but with the user attention span in front of a big-screen TV.

The decision about whether or not to use these tools comes down to weighing their effectiveness versus their intelligibility. Their effectiveness isn't always a given, as shown by lookalike targeting. However, even when these algorithms manage to outperform humans in selecting relevant targets, for example by testing hundreds of targeting items per category and only keeping the most effective ones, using them isn't a given.

How AI Helps Operators Optimize their Service

Focusing on the change underway in the TV service provider ecosystem there is a growing demand for artificial intelligence (AI) techniques and machine learning (ML) to be used on first-party TV data to extract relevant granular segmentation. The headline is, of course, the possibility of ad replacement in linear primetime, which allows operators to increase the number of ad slots without increasing ad load; charge premium rates for them; and decrease churn as viewers have been shown to respond more favorably to targeted ads.

The aggregation of usage data into a holistic overview of users and its transformation into highly specific segments is enabled through ML and AI, which are what empowers providers to interact with the ad-tech ecosystem on premium revenue-share rates.

Concretely actionable insights are based on heavy AI and ML capabilities that we have developed throughout the last decade, while we keep constantly updating our research and algorithms and evolving with the times.

AI can be leveraged to draw insights into the effectiveness of various content sources, enabling personalized and measurable content discovery for maximum user satisfaction and improved content acquisition. All in all, the data-driven AI analysis of usage flows and identifying consumption patterns enables continual performance optimization and effective segmentation, empowering operators to deliver superior user experiences while maximizing their service monetization and boosting their ROI.

Figure 3 shows the way that VO's data scientists visualize data from a single viewing household. The vertical line is time, with each of the 52 lines representing a single week. The horizontal line represents the features of the data: zapping activity and what genres are being consumed. This gives you a viewing profile of a household.

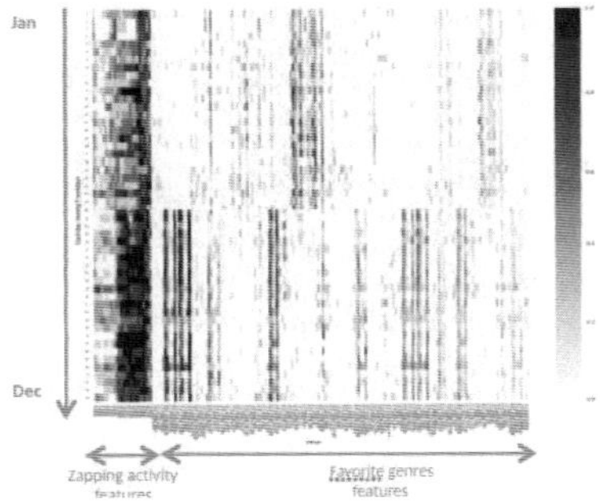

FIGURE 3: VISUALIZATION OF DATA FROM A SINGLE HOUSEHOLD.

When you apply AI techniques to this comparatively raw data you can extract all sorts of information from it starting with user segmentation.

Look at the graph below where our AI has drawn a line across the middle of the data. What it is detecting is a “life moment.” This highlights the fact that there is a change in viewing behavior between the first half of the year and the second half; the genres that are being watched and the viewing activity are both changing with much more peak time content being viewed. This example represents the arrival of a child in the household.

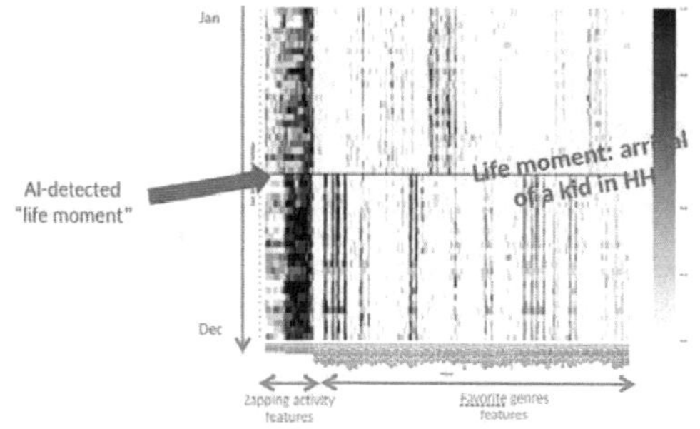

FIGURE 4: AI TRACKS CHANGES IN HOUSEHOLD VIEWING DATA, INDICATING A LIFE MOMENT.

It's a fairly extreme example and the change in viewing pattern is easily detected, but it illustrates the power of AI on TV usage data to provide granular household segmentation from "passive" monitoring of viewer data. More complex techniques, such as deploying neural networks, can lift more complex segmentations from the data and identify when people have retired, for instance.

AI has multiple impacts elsewhere too. When you apply AI to this part of the industry, service providers can start to spot the customers that are about to churn and apply mitigation techniques as well as identify the assets — from entire packages of services to individual movies — that can be potentially upsold to individual consumers. Also, use segmentation can be leveraged to identify consumers that may be more amenable to convert from a freemium model to a full subscription.

Furthermore, utilizing artificial intelligence with TV and first-party data can provide invaluable insights into viewers' preferences, behavior, and household composition, enabling operators to personalize both their content offerings and advertising, thus creating highly engaging, profile-based viewing experiences alongside highly rewarding audience segmentation.

In other words, the AI-based insights help operators gain a better understanding of user behavior and preferences, to not only optimize their ads in real time and target specific and local audiences, but also to create additional opportunities for them to show targeted ads to their increasingly engaged viewers.

The flow chart in Figure 5 helps to define its multipurpose role.

FIGURE 5: THE MULTIPURPOSE ROLE OF AI.

Data Privacy

As with anything related to data, we have to consider data privacy. Protecting viewers' data in compliance with the GDPR and other privacy-related legislation at first seems to be a challenge, but for TV operators is actually an opportunity. As TV is a close and controlled environment, trusted by viewers and advertisers alike, operators have the edge to ensure that no personal data is being shared, keeping operators in full control over data at any given time via the right set of tools.

Moreover, as a result of the GDPR and similar privacy regulations, the value of first-party data has increased tremendously, due to the lack of data availability and accompanying consent management requirements. As such, first-party data is a valuable resource and needs to be kept exclusive for maximum monetization potential.

Therefore, anonymization of the identifiers has a double benefit for operators: it not only creates a walled garden with potentially lucrative and exclusive audiences inside it that cannot be reached outside of the operator environment, but it also ensures easier compliance with regulations. Also, TV operators are both trusted by their users and in a daily communication with the viewers, which enables them to capture consent with relative ease.

To conclude, sociodemographic data is a common language that the entire advertising chain speaks and it is highly available to TV providers. Similarly, interests have the benefit of being immediately interpretable. Algorithms don't describe the criteria used to target a specific audience; neither do they allow you to tell stories or understand a campaign's successes and failures after the fact. As such, sociodemographics still structure campaigns, but the rise of the custom audience and look-a-like models is expected to have a significant impact on TV advertising. Service providers that will adopt AI-based insights will gain a better understanding of user behavior and preferences, to not only optimize their ads in real time and target specific and local audiences, but also to create additional opportunities for them to show targeted ads and improve their offering and customers' yield.

Maximizing Data Usage and Viewer Time

Targeted advertising works both with and without inventory. Operators with existing inventory can offer creative monetization options, enabling them to optimize between their different monetization channels and on top of that use AI-based insights to increase the efficiency and scope of their segmentation. As a result, this boosts reach and revenues. For operators without inventory, an off-the-shelf smart infrastructure enables them to connect with various TV channels and support multi-ad servers. This allows them to leverage their existing first-party usage data to offer attractive segmentation, retargeting, and look-a-like to advertisers, while also supporting and measuring ad insertion.

The key is that beyond the ability to manage it wisely and effectively, operators with or without existing inventory can boost their reach and overall revenues through AI-based insights and analytics. As explained above, it enables them to not only optimize performance but also to actually extend viewing time through the increased engagement afforded by the analytics.

When data and AI are in place, targeted advertising provides multiple new revenue opportunities. The headline is, of course, the possibility of ad replacement in linear primetime, which allows operators to increase the number of ad slots without increasing ad load, charge premium rates for them, and increase satisfaction as viewers have been shown to respond more favorably to targeted ads.

But there are other significant opportunities as well, especially when you consider that, with their first-party data, operators have everything they need to start making money now. Additional opportunities include:

- **Leverage the UI** - Operators can increase inventory still further by serving ads within the UI of their apps. This can be further explored when the user is actively interacting with the UI, such as when browsing content.
- **Catch-up content** - As the amount of time-shifted television watched has increased, the technology behind time-shift has evolved too, from VHS to PVR and now on to cloud PVR solutions. What has not changed is the viewer's desire to use time-shift to skip the commercials in a program nor the loss of revenue to the broadcaster that results in.
- What is new, though, is that there are ways to address the viewer's desire in an enhanced and more elegant solution than simply by pushing the fast-forward button by offering users targeted unskippable ads or a premium rate that will skip the ads for them by introducing an AI and computer vision technology to identify the ads.
- **Event-based ad triggering** - Whenever viewers take certain actions, such as fast forward, pause, resume, etc., it will trigger ad insertion. These have been successfully used by MVPDs such as Hulu, partly as the high CPM promise around event-based advertising comes from the fact that advertisers can be 100% sure that the viewer is in front of the screen.
- **Self-promotion** - With many companies in the OTT sector offering triple-play services and more, TA provides a valuable route to increasing the efficiency of their own promotions, both for additional services and for specific content.

- **Freemium to premium** - Operators can offer free (or almost free) content access, backing it up with significant ad revenues, to increase their market penetration and OTT migration, and create leads that will become premium customers in the future.

Adopting such technology and targeted advertising also allows TV operators to create new business models:

- SVOD/AVOD double play,
- Address the viewers' need to minimize costs in the packed SVOD ecosystem
- Viewers can be offered progressive tiers of declining ad load as they increase their monthly payments, the so-called freemium to premium route.

While increasing revenues, it is critical not to cause user frustration by closely monitoring exaggerated ad load. Indeed, using the addressable TV advertising model enables the reduction of ad loads, which contributes toward higher user satisfaction and reduces churn.

This has been hugely successful, as shown by Hulu for video streaming and by Spotify for audio streaming. The additional benefits that targeted advertising brings to viewers can be illustrated by a five-year-long survey conducted by Sky on its own AdSmart solution's effectiveness which found:

- Reduced channel switching by 48% when addressable adverts were in the first three positions in a break
- Increased ad engagement by 35%

To conclude, data and advertising go together like a horse and carriage. When applying AI and ML techniques that fit TV data, service providers can bring multi-value benefits to their service and increase their customers' yield.

References

[1] https://www.statista.com/statistics/456679/digital-advertising-revenue-format-digital-market-outlook-worldwide/

Hybrid Video on Demand
An intersection of Technology, Media & Economics

Ted Staros
imediat llc
Carlsbad, California, United States
tstaros@ieee.org

Abstract – This paper describes a means to reduce the wasteful bandwidth and infrastructure costs of Subscriber Video on Demand, while improving the operational immediacy that customers require. A multiple thousand-fold improvement in bandwidth utilization and server efficiency can be achieved with the methods described here. Technical drivers including the relevance of IPv6, 5G and ATSC 3.0 are exposed. Economic benefits and barriers are examined. Significant capital and operational cost savings can be achieved for Network Operators & Content Service Providers. Every party within the VoD ecosystem gains advantage or opportunity. The author submits this proposal as an inspirational starting point for a standardization effort to be undertaken by an accredited standards body.

VoD is an Epic Waste

I'm not saying the content itself is a waste, though many might promote this characterization. I'm saying that VoD Distribution is an avoidable, epically wasteful consumer of Bandwidth and Infrastructure. Despite the impressive performance improvements in Video Compression Codecs, VoD remains exceptionally wasteful.

The Scope of VoD

For the foreseeable future, Video on Demand {VoD} is expected to grow in market share and in consumed data bandwidth. We might eventually find out just how much video we, as a society can watch and at what point we'll cry uncle.

Streaming video is by far the top application on the internet. Consumer Internet Video traffic (subscription and otherwise) constitutes >80% of total Internet traffic share. [6] This includes VoD providers Netflix, Amazon Prime, Hulu, Paramount+, Disney+, and Apple TV+, with Comcast's Peacock and AT&T's Warner/Discovery collective vying to further partition the growing pie.

Of this 80%, less than 15% constitutes streams not inclusive of mainstream subscription services. For the purposes of this conversation, this subset is not applicable to VoD, as the use cases are dissimilar, and subscriptions are less common. To be blunt, a significant share of this 15% is short-form disinformation and porn. Not to be distracted by this, True VoD constitutes more than **65%** of the Total Internet Network Traffic share.

The comparative statistics on VoD market share, subscribers, use patterns and revenue is a contradictory collection apples and oranges. It's not instructive to dissect it here. Let's just say for the year 2021 it represented roughly $60B in annual revenue worldwide, half of which is in the USA.

The Growth of VoD

An escalating volume of content offerings, combined with the demand for higher video resolutions, will further the expansion of network bandwidth of streamed video.

The migration from 720 and 1080p video to UHD 4k and higher video resolutions is becoming a dominant Internet traffic accelerant. Cisco estimates that 30% of VoD traffic is currently 4k UHD, accounting for 20% of all Internet Video traffic. The takeaway is that the need for bandwidth and network infrastructure is big and growing.

77% of US household have an VoD service, and almost all households have more than one service. [14] Many households have more than one Set Top Box device. In 2022, the penetration is undoubtably much higher.

The reach of VoD is larger than the subscriptions numbers would imply. Roughly 20% of these subscriptions are shared with others outside of their household. Grandma does not have a Netflix subscription, but she does have a Roku Device. Go figure!

A dominant share of VoD has turning to Original Content from the biggest Content Service Providers. The trend is led by Netflix, Amazon, and HBO. This has been followed aggressively by Disney, Apple, and others. This fresh content plumps up the “Fat Tail” volume, relative to more matured longer tailed offerings.

Derived from Cisco’s 2019 VNI forecast, VoD network traffic delivered to TVs alone will top 83×10^{18} B/month by 2022. [5] The USA represents roughly half of this. It is expected to hold a durable 65% share of Global IP video traffic, itself growing at greater than 30% Compounded Annual Growth Rate {CAGR}.

From this forecast, at aggregate burdened Bandwidth rates of $2,780 /Gbps /month, annual VoD delivery bandwidth costs will be quite significant. Your mileage may vary, scale this up or down if your expectation of burdened bandwidth cost differs. (See Figure 1)

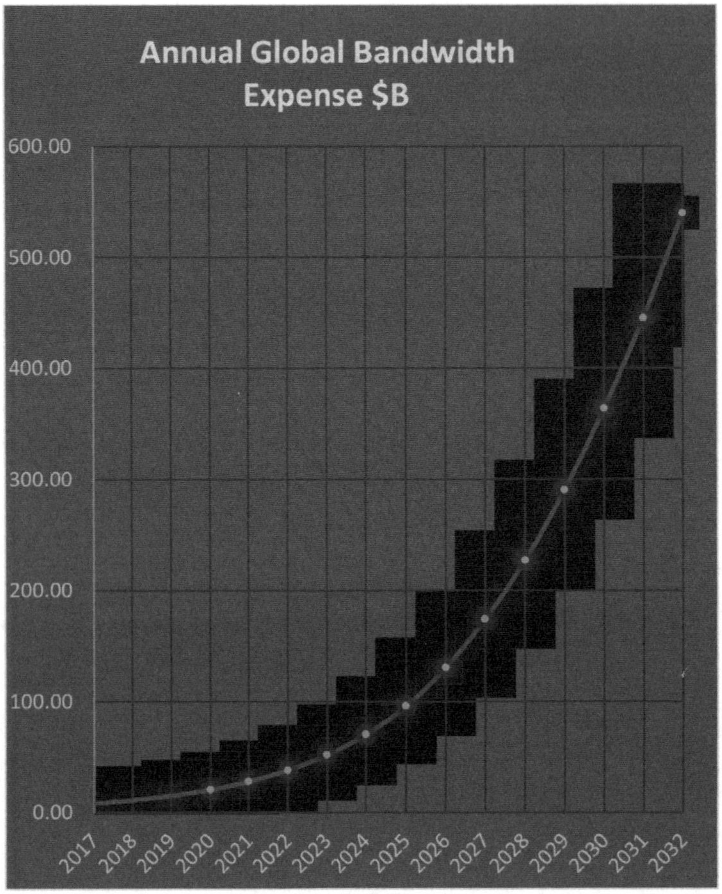

FIGURE 1: ANNUAL GLOBAL BANDWIDTH EXPENSE IN $B.

The Wasteful Nature of VoD

Conventional Internet Protocol {IP} communications allow a content service provider to stream media assets to a subscriber's client device over a network of commercial Internet service providers. The client device is typically a Set-Top-Box {STB}. This is a device specifically crafted to provide a user interface for the selection and playout of the streamed content to a TV or other form of video monitor. The client device may also be an application on a computer, or mobile device.

The content is transported via Unicast Internet Protocol {UIP}. Unicast is a one-to-one communication means. An individual server entity [or software thread] streams the content in near real-time, to each individual subscriber's client device. Video on Demand requires operational immediacy, as the subscriber is free to select, then Start, Pause, Fast-Forward, Rewind, and re-Start a chosen content stream at any time.

The Content Service Provider uses a large plurality of server threads to support the equally large plurality of individual users viewing the content. In between the Server and the STB video rendering device is the Public Internet. For each server thread and its corresponding STB there is a Unicast Internet Protocol stream. The upstream control traffic supporting this session is trivial.

A More Efficient Option

In contrast to Unicast IP described above, I want to describe a misbegotten black sheep of the Internet protocol family; it's called Multicast IP. Multicast is a one-to-many communication means. An individual server entity can deliver content to a group of subscriber STBs concurrently. IP Multicast is a bandwidth conserving means, specifically designed to reduce network traffic by simultaneously delivering a single element of content data, to a plurality of recipients.

Not surprisingly, Multicast is not without its complications, but to be fair, supporting high volumes of unicast isn't exactly a picnic. The quantity of concurrent recipients using Multicast is relatively unbounded, but there are practical implementation limits.

Through the methods described in this document, a single server thread can do the work of thousands. The aggregate network bandwidth consumption is reduced nearly by the same proportion.

Multicast has Failed VoD

VoD has been an epically wasteful distribution medium. Still, Multicast has epically failed too; being thoroughly unsuccessful in gaining adoption.

As a technology, Real time Multicasting is not uncommon for live video distribution within private virtual networks. Despite the considerable reductions in capital and operational expenditures that Multicast allows, it has not lived up to its potential. There are several reasons for this.

- Interdomain Multicast has been poorly supported by all Tiers of ISP networks. The approaching ubiquity of IPv6, in tandem with adjustments to industry-wide best practices changes this. The fruits of Interdomain Multicast are now easily within reach. The topic of Internet evolution is discussed later in this paper.
- Local ISPs never viewed Multicast as an opportunity within an IPv4 landscape. This is in part due to the obstacles presented by residential NAT routers. As I describe later, the availability of IPv6 and its running partner, 5G New Radio, render this obstacle moot.
- For VoD, Multicast fails to provide the operational immediacy required of Video-on-Demand. Multicast is an unsatisfactory means for Video-on-Demand as the subscriber often wishes to pause, Fast-Forward, Rewind and re-start the content. This critical limitation can be overcome with approaches described later in this paper.

AT&T's unsuccessful "Triple-Play" Cable replacement service; *U-verse*, admirably used multicast for Live TV delivery. AT&T sidestepped the interdomain challenges by using a private network delivery system. *U-verse* avoided operational immediacy matters, ceding to wasteful unicast for VoD, and time-shifted catchup content.

Hybrid VoD

This paper proposes a practice the author terms ***Hybrid VoD.*** Hybrid VoD, leverages Multicast opportunities with conventional VoD. Retaining the essential operational immediacy of VoD while gaining the manifest operational efficiencies of Multicast. The goal is to merge two deficient technologies, in order to create a superior one.

Crest Factor Economics

Conventional VoD exhibits what I term a high "**Crest Factor**". I've shamelessly appropriated that term from the telecommunications industry.

In terms of VoD infrastructure, the Crest Factor of content demand determines Server capacity held in reserve, and the buildout of Network infrastructure supporting the peak aggregate bandwidth to all the subscribers.

There are a few dominant factors in VoD crest factor. Time of Day, Day of week, and Blockbuster Content Debut. Demand crests in the evening as subscribers settle down for their evening entertainment. These demand peaks traverse the globe, with the diurnal rhythm of evening twilight. For societal reasons, Sunday night exhibits a more pronounced peak than other days of the week.

The crest factor over the period of a day is pronounced. My original WAG for diurnal Crest Factor was roughly 2. Excluding the Sunday effect. I was wrong. Cisco sets the Crest Factor at 5 today rising to over 6 over the next 2 years. Notably, crest behavior continues to grow more rapidly than average Internet traffic. Cisco's 2019 VNI Forecast [5] estimates that the "busy hour" Internet use will grow at a CAGR of 37%, compared with 30% percent for average Internet traffic.

What if we could somehow flatten out this Crest Factor? For argument's sake let's say that that we use the Pareto Principle. In this case 20% of all content represents 80% of all consumption. Let's not just average out the peaks by time shifting Unicast, let's further shrink that 80% of the consumption by a much larger factor using Multicast.

The Multicast model in this methodology looks to reduce Infrastructure and bandwidth cost of the Fat Tailed assets by a factor of up to 4,000.

Let's be conservative. Let's take only a quarter of that target 4K multiple mentioned above; 1,000 times. Let's apply this approach to the 20/80 Pareto split; 20% of the media assets consumed by 80% of the subscriber population. 80% of the asset downloads can benefit from a 1000-fold efficiency improvement. 20% of the asset downloads remain unaffected. That's a cost reduction of >79%. Applied over a multi-year adoption period, Hybrid VoD could drop capital, and operating expenses to roughly 20% of Conventional VoD expenses.

The simplistic 1st order nature of these estimates aside, this conjecture represents an impressive Capital and Operational cost saving. Accurate statistics regarding the distribution (shape) of the demand tail is closely held by the Content Service Providers. I suspect that the Pareto distribution is under-stated. Looking at how Netflix has apportioned bandwidth vs storage across its devices on their Content Delivery Network {CDN}, it might be closer to a 90/10 spilt. [17]

Nevertheless, the subscriber count for VoD is expected to increase by 100% over the next three years, and double in video resolution over the next 5. This relief can't come soon enough to hold the inevitable cost increases down.

Technological & Media Drivers

The march of technological progress really changes the opportunities, making this proposal not just viable, but possibly unavoidable. A big driver is the cost of memory. It's dropping much faster than the cost of infrastructure, and Network bandwidth. I examine these factors below. (See Figure 2)

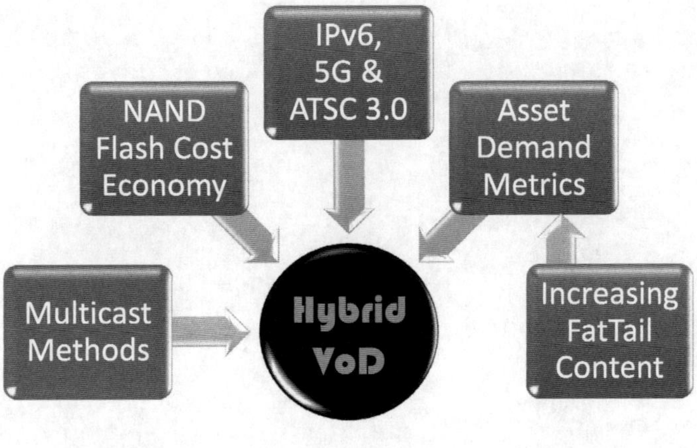

FIGURE 2: TECHNOLOGICAL & MEDIA DRIVERS.

Flash Memory

We have broken the $ 100 per TB Cost point for Flash SSD Drives. 400MB /sec R/W performance across a 6GB/sec Physical interface is typical.

I've recently seen 1TB USB 3.0 Flash memory Drives for $86 on Amazon. These devices can do 400 MB/s R/W operations. That's a retail, single quantity price. You need only a fraction of this to support the cached VoD applications described here. 1TB represents perhaps 200Hrs of 4K video.

This year, I purchased a 256GB device for under $40. It supports >300 MB/s transfer rates. To put this in perspective, 60 MB/s is sufficient for 8k Video use cases.

Over the past few years, the NAND Flash industry has gone through two major shifts in technology:
The movement from 1 to 2 to 3 bits per cell. This directly increases bit density and capacity.
The move from planar flash to variants of 3D stacking.

These architecture changes, along with lithography shrinkage, are clobbering costs, allowing speed and capacity to increase. Figure 3's data is courtesy IDC; DRAM eXchange, Wells Fargo Securities, thru 2012-18. The Cost / TB remains remarkably on-track into 2022, with NAND Spot prices of < $12/TB in January 2022.

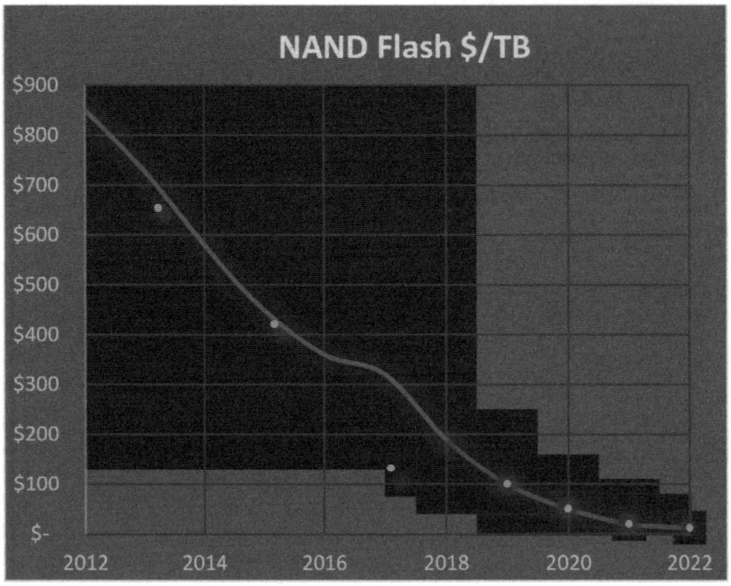

FIGURE 3: NAND FLASH $/TB

Extrapolating the cost trend line implies that the cost of memory will go to zero within a few years. Clearly that can't really happen. Still, given the above, we might reasonably expect the spot price of high speed Flash memory to break $10/TB sooner than we might otherwise expect.

Internet Protocol Version 6

IPv6 is the most recent version of the Internet Protocol (IP). IPv6 was developed to deal with the long-anticipated problem of IPv4 address exhaustion. IPv6 is intended to replace IPv4.

IPv6 theoretically allows 3.4×10^{38} addresses. The total number of possible IPv6 addresses is more than 7.9×10^{28} times as many as IPv4.

Most critically, IPv6 removes the requirement of clumsy Network Address Translation {NAT} practices at residential locations. IPv6 to the residence, permits a barrier free, greenfield path for the last mile for VoD rendering devices. In addition, implementation can be made homogenous across Cable and 5G deployments.

IPv6 provides other technical benefits. Notable to this discussion, IPv6 permits more amenable multicast mechanisms, optimizing the delivery of these services.

So why would an ISP risk effort to provision their IPv4 networks to support Multicast? They wouldn't, it's simply not compelling enough, as the pending IPv6 abundance likely offers more effective, comprehensive, and lasting solutions. The juice is not worth the squeeze, at least during the IPv4 to IPv6 transition period. That's been a significant factor in the meager adoption of Interdomain Multicast.

IPv6 internet access is here today. Inter-Domain connectivity is excellent. IPv6 is everywhere today, on your phones, on your PCs, tablets, door-bell cameras, thermostats. Go ahead, check your equipment, go to https://test-ipv6.com/. In some cases, you might need to check a box on your Residential Router to fully enable it. IPv6 is here now. It's just not being leveraged very well. Yet.

Cisco's 2019 VNI forecast has anticipated that IPv6 connected devices will rise at a Compounded Annual Growth Rate {CAGR} of 26% through 2022. From 6 billion devices to 18 Billion connected devices. [5]

In January 2022, T-Mobile had more than 92% of its traffic going over IPv6, with Verizon Wireless close behind at 83%. Comcast and AT&T have their networks at 70% and 72%, respectively. The unavoidable ubiquity of IPv6 permits the practical deployment of this proposal.

5G "New Radio"

5G NR is a new radio access technology, developed for fifth generation mobile communication. It is designed to be the global standard for the air interface of 5G networks. It promises bandwidth capacity greater than DOCSIS Cable service

5G will be the "Killer Catalyst" that brings IPv6 across the finish line. It's a virtuous symbiotic relationship: IPv6 permits 5G to function, and 5G presses IPv6 into full deployment.

The greatest utility in the immediate future is not just 5G for Phones, but 5G for Fixed Point Customer Presence Equipment. {CPE}. The CPE provides the customer's residence with IPv6 based Wired and Wireless Ethernet.

5G CPE presents a compelling replacement of Cable based ISP service. When 5G CPE deployment become widely available, many more users may choose to cut the cord, and kick the cable company to the curb.

As of January 2022, both T-Mobile and Verizon are offering 5G Home internet service at $50/mo. Verizon boasts 300-980Mb/s download, w/ 50 Mb/s upload. 5G is gearing up for brutal bandwidth battle for the last mile.

5G Wireless Internet, through handheld, and CPE will massively accelerate IPv6 adoption, as 5G has been decoupled from IPv4. In the words of the author William Gibson: *"The future is here, it's just not evenly distributed".*

Asset Demand Metrics

In tight synergy with their established, conventional VoD service, the Content Service Provider would prioritize the distribution of their media assets in highest demand.

Distribution of these assets would be propagated to the subscribers, leveraging a Multicast distribution method. A 3-step process for prioritizing Asset Demand is outlined in a later section of this paper.

The use of Machine Learning techniques is likely already at the service Content Service Providers. Still, even a simple viewing history analysis is likely to provide useful results.

The CSPs are quite possibly doing an aggregate form of predictive modeling today, such as to load balance their server and content storage resources.

This proposal suggests that there are significant gains to be achieved, by giving more granularity to this predictive modeling. In doing so facilitating the creation of meaningful Asset Demand Metrics.

With the Increasing Fat Tailed plumping nature of Original Content Assets being produced by the major CSPs, these Asset Demand Metrics can really leverage the cost saving opportunity of Hybrid VoD.

Economics Drivers

There is a need to examine economics of a transition to Hybrid VoD. (See Figure 4)

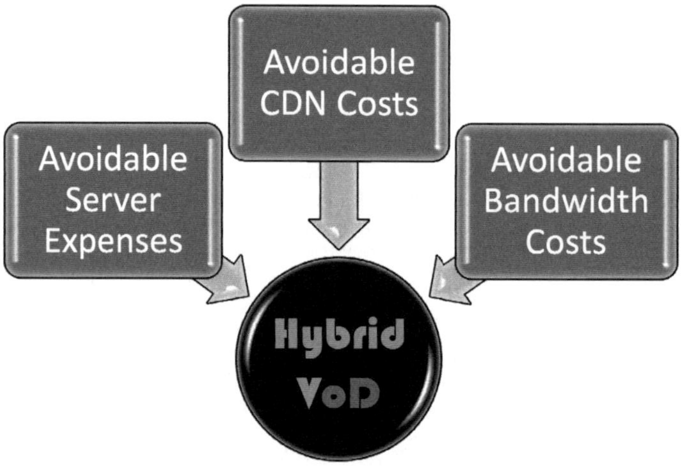

FIGURE 4: ECONOMIC DRIVERS

Content Service Providers

Content Service Providers are a first order winner in an adoption of a Hybrid VoD paradigm. The cost of refactoring their content delivery hardware and software infrastructure are dwarfed by the potential savings.

A concrete example is Netflix. The largest CSP, Netflix owns much of its own edge hardware. Netflix co-locates its hardware at strategic Network Exchange Points {IXP}, and at large ISPs around the world. The Netflix Content Delivery Network {CDN} is known as *Open Connect*. It duplicates its media assets at hundreds of these Open Connect sites, lessening the burden in the Tier1 ISPs, and lessening operational latencies for its customers. Being the largest CSP, Netflix had no choice but to deploy such a large, distributed infrastructure.

With this proposal, server utilization would tend to bifurcate. Some servers would predominantly attend to popular Fat-Tailed Assets with increasing implementation based on Multicast delivery. Longer tailed content would predominate on equipment holding larger asset catalogs via traditional VoD streaming.

The transformation would be gradual and integrated with the anticipated obsolescence schedule of their hardware. This class of hardware is designed for continuous operation of about 4-5 years. Consequently, depreciation schedules on this class of data center gear is on the same order. [19]

Regardless of the mix of delivery mechanisms, the Asset Storage requirements will increase for the foreseeable future. The anticipated performance boosts of Solid State Memory, along with its reduced form-factor, will likely half the required vertical rack real estate. Solid State memory will displace the increasingly quaint rotating media, accelerating the replacement cycle.

The takeaway is that any transformation that includes Multicast methods would be no more transformative than the normal technological replacement cycle, but with very significant strategic cost savings.

ISPs and Independent CDNs

It's instructive to look at Tier1 ISPs separate from their Lower Tier counterparts.

Tier 1 Internet providers provide the backbone of the Internet. They provide traffic to all other Internet providers, but generally not to end users. At least not to VoD subscribers. They connect to each other for mutual benefit, through mutual agreements.

Tier 2 ISP connect to Tier1 ISPs, through bandwidth transit purchase agreements and some peer relationships with other Tier 2 ISPs.

Tier 3 ISPs provide the last mile connection to business and residential customers. Again, connection to a parent Tiers is fee based. The boundary between Tiers 2 & 3 can get a little blurry.

The growth of CDNs is pushing the content delivery out towards the Tier 2 Exchange Points, and Tier 3 ISPs. To a degree, this offsets bandwidth expenditures that would otherwise be incurred, but likely raises other operational costs material to operating the co-located hardware.

To put Centralized Unicast, CDN Unicast, and Multicast into comparative economic perspective, I've borrowed a graphic from my colleague Lenny Giuliano at Juniper Networks. [8] (See Figure 5)

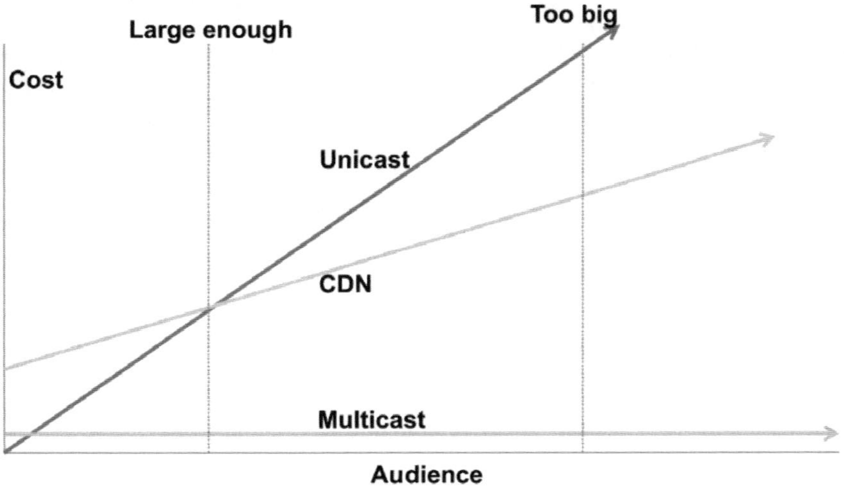

FIGURE 5: CENTRALIZED & CDN UNICAST VS MULTICAST

Centralized Unicast cost scales linearly across audience size. However, at some large audience size, the costs become intolerable.

Comparatively, CDN has a greater upfront cost. Fortunately, at some "Large enough" audience size, the CDN costs drop below that of Centralized Unicast.

Multicast has a low fixed cost, and it tends to remain low, compared to the Unicast alternatives.

As the proposed Multicast methods so significantly relieve bandwidth burden, CSPs might be inclined to reverse the trend towards greater edge server deployment. They might choose to centralize the many fewer Multicast servers, lessening the administrative complexities of CDN operation.

Bandwidth Cost Savings

Using the 80/20 Pareto based examination described earlier in this paper, it might be instructive to see what kind of Bandwidth expense saving might be achievable.

These numbers are predicated on a burdened aggregate $2780 /Gbps /month cost model. Again, cost of burdened bandwidth for each CSP and CDN could vary appreciably. Curiously, some estimates place unburdened bandwidth costs more than an order of magnitude higher than this. [20] [21].

The largest CSPs get better deals. They've also have been moving their network capacity closer to the edge. Roughly a third of all VoD capacity currently bypasses the internet's core; 27% in 2017, growing to 33% in 2022. [5] While this reduces Bandwidth costs, it raises other costs and complexity.

As this market matures further, it is expected that a greater share of VoD assets will be sourced from within each subscriber's ISP. Each CSP "lending" the required hardware to each ISP. Each ISP would house the CSP's co-located gear. This co-opts the ISPs to become a part of the CSP's private CDN. This does not alter the amount of traffic delivered to the subscribers. This is the Netflix model. It's not yet clear if other CSPs will replicate this methodology.

The graph below follows the 30% CAGR until 2022 per the Cisco forecast. I reduced the CAGR estimation in the remaining years to limit expectations. Exponential growth doesn't go on forever.

I've assumed no adoption for 2 years, and a very modest rate for the next 2. As recognition grows and the equipment replacement cycle advances, I imagine a 4% adoption in 5 years. Not adjusted for inflation, the annual savings at that point could reach $11B, and more than a cumulative $300B over a decade.

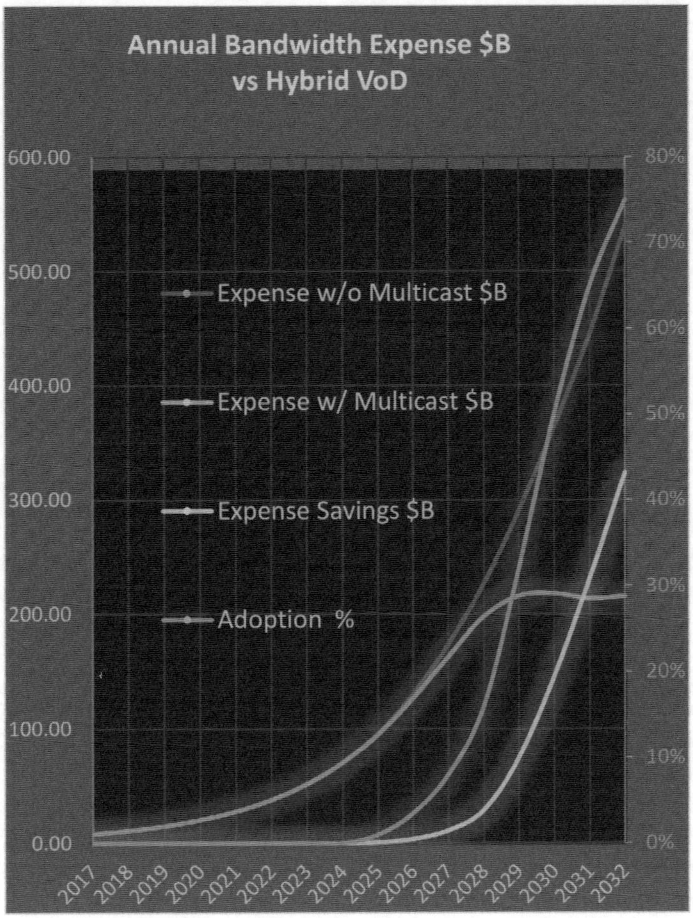

FIGURE 6: ANNUAL WORLDWIDE BANDWIDTH EXPENSE

Figure 6 illustrates Annual Worldwide Bandwidth Expense, projected forward through 2032. The orange curve is the prospective adoption percentage of Hybrid VoD. It is viewed against the right vertical axis. The remaining blue, grey and yellow curves are scaled in Billions of Dollars and are viewed against the left vertical axis.

With these savings, the beneficiaries of this bandwidth expense markdown could easily afford to subsidize the STB replacement cycle, in order to accelerate the adoption curve. In 2025 there will be roughly 1B Internet connected screens in the US, a few might only need a flash drive and a software update.

Don't feel bad for any potential revenue lost by the ISPs and independent CDNs due to this efficiency gain. Their pricing power will remain significant as they continue to be a critical network conduit to the subscriber. These providers will still contend with an exponential demand curve due to IoT, Cloud Gaming, VR & AR, all of which expect to have CAGR in the 50-60% range.

Internet Evolution & Economy

The economy of bandwidth transit across the Internet's "Network of Networks" is complicated. It became this way organically. It continues to adapt to volatile market forces, technology change, and paradigm shifts. The arcane economics of the esoteric "horse trading" of peered bandwidth, and transit pricing packages will likely be the fodder of innumerable doctoral theses. (None of which will get a Nobel Prize.)

The technical landscape of internet bandwidth is ripe with adaptations in performance and efficiency improvements.

Border Gateway Protocol, {BGP} has long been the standard gateway protocol designed to exchange routing and reachability information among "Autonomous Systems" {AS} on the Internet. BGP makes routing decisions based on paths, and network policies. It works, but its limitations are showing.

To Augment BGP, "Segment Routing" made possible by IPv6 {SRv6} is being promoted by networking heavyweight Cisco. [23] A twist on this; SRv6+, is being promoted by Juniper networks. [3] In brief, SRv6 prescribes how IPv6 packets may carry specific instructions of how to route and even add processing to the traffic, as it journeys the network. Various network operators are already jockeying for opportunity in this tumult of evolving network capabilities. [18]

The implementation of Multicast in SRv6 has relevancy to additional use cases, and improved efficiencies. Most recently, two methods for this have been the subject of development. These are Bit Index Explicit Replication {BIER}, and Ingress Replication {IR}, a.k.a. "Spray Multicast".

Can Multicast be the New Rome?

Transitional mechanisms have been promoted to kindle interdomain multicast deployment. This notably includes Automatic Multicast Tunneling {AMT}. [8]. AMT does not depend on a homogeneous end to end network be Multicast compliant. AMT has two components.

- An "AMT Relay", envelops the Multicast content within a Unicast wrapper. It listens for discovery messages from AMT Gateways.
- An "AMT Gateway" initiates connection to one or more AMT Relays with discovery messages. It unwraps and redistributes the Multicast content.

In this manner, AMT facilitates Multicast packet distribution regardless of the undisciplined journey through the Internet. AMT is transitional. As Multicast use increases, Multicast Reluctant Administrative Domains {AD} will see economic motivations to enable native Multicast implementations.

AMT is here today and is very easily provisioned; arguably only "*…one line of config*" away. [9] Mr. Giuliano promotes a broad, egalitarian use of Multicast. His view is that Multicast opens many new and beneficial use cases, many of which we cannot even imagine. AMT is a steppingstone to greater adoption of a fully realized Interdomain Multicast.

An AMT Relay device has been deployed by a High School student. This implementation is instrumental in understanding the tangible accessibility of interdomain Multicast, despite Administrative Domain {AD} non-compliance. [27]

There is activity within the Internet Engineering Task Force {IETF} to formalize Best Current Practices {BCP} to deprecate the burdensome Any Source Multicast {ASM} for Interdomain use. Removing this heavy ASM impediment elevates Source Specific Multicasting {SSM}. SSM is a much easier lift. Importantly SSM represents the substantially greater use-case demand. This putative BCP recommendation is welcome, as this boost for SSM is beneficial for interdomain Hybrid VoD.

A detailed, differential discussion of the AMT, BIER, IR, is worthy of additional attention. Regrettably, it is beyond the scope of this paper. Still, it's relevant to the vitality of the Internet's ongoing evolution. It specifically emphasizes the increasing embrace of Multicast for use cases that require greater economy. Undeniably, for the use case of VoD.

If BIER and IR are not fully applicable to the distribution of VoD, or don't see widespread adoption, progress on interdomain MC won't end there. If future practices are adopted that improve the availability of Interdomain Multicast, it will surely occur within the framework of IPv6. IPv4 not so much.

AMT is here and ready to bridge all interdomain multicast chasms that exist today. No matter the waypoints along the internet evolution highway, it appears that
All roads lead to Rome.

Live Content

VoD presents some challenging issues when it comes to Live content. Live is not just simply wasteful. When dependability matters the most, it's often not up to the task.

The Ephemeral Value of Live

Regardless of medium, Live actualities are most meaningful in the moment, but often fail to retain their value beyond that. Newspapers are the quintessential ephemeral medium. In a matter of a day, the Los Angeles Times becomes the Los Angeles Fish Wrap. Content of a temporal nature is a wasting asset. Its value diminishes as it ages. It's like bread. Desirable as it comes out of the oven, live content holds diminished commercial value with the passage of time. Today's Cinnabon is tomorrow's duck food. The world's most influential media "ecologist"; Marshall McLuhan, has been quoted: "*If it's current, it's currency*".

Temporal content establishes both cultural and tangible currency by being a concurrently shared experience. Live experiences like spectacles or natural disasters are easy to understand in this context. Disasters are not often commercial opportunities. That would be socially reprehensible. Right? Not always. The video medium regularly creates disaster-like opportunities for commercial gain. Three examples come to mind.

- TV news often aligns its coverage to the most blood soaked or politically outrageous footage available. Rather than providing the most useful or informative material, video news provides a mechanism to promote calamity, large and small, for commercial gain.
- Reality TV (a.k.a. "*unscripted*"). It is not a real disaster, but it's promoted as one. Simulated live spectacles with seemingly unscripted social conflict, featuring participants who must compete for the next tier of competition. Outcasts lick their wounds in intimate private confessionals.
- Sports. It's a disaster for roughly half of the spectators. No need for further explanation.

Due to the "spectacular" nature of these programs, it is important to the viewers that they perceptively share the "live" experience. Not surprisingly, the more spectacular the experience, the less intrinsic value it retains over time. This is a good thing. While temporal programming is perishable, its ephemeral nature urges the voracious public to consume their prey warm.

Even relatively small latencies in "spectacular" content is considered a problem. Sports fans don't often appreciate "spoiler" tweets reaching them before they view the winning goal. Viewers are less likely to archive "spectacular" content on their Cloud DVRs and watch it later in the week. They need to consume it live, with its sponsor's commercial messages intact. This temporally enlivened content does not often go into syndication. Once it's aired, it's duck food.

A Live Modality for Hybrid VoD

Live VoD exist today as IPTV. It works about as well as regular VoD does, provided it is not a "Spectacle" event, like a Super Bowl, or a World Cup. If the internet, using Brute Force Unicast {BFU} wishes to keep up, it has material issues of scale that it will need to address. A few stats regarding the TV audience of major events. [10]

- Average NFL game: 15M,
  (A staggering 600 Tb/s at 4k UHD)
- Super Bowl: 100M
- 2015 Cricket World Cup: 200-300M
- 2018 FIFA World Cup Finals: 500M

The trend for Live Streaming appears suitably robust:

- Viewers spend 8X longer with live video than on-demand (5.1 minutes for on-demand vs. 42.8 minutes for live video content). [1]
- Live video is outpacing the growth of other types of online video; a 113% increase in ad growth yearly. [25]

The network's fragility and waste are most in evidence when the spectacle demands critical paths and massive redundant bandwidth. Spectacle Live video will unavoidably trend towards UHD resolutions.

The foremost Content Delivery Network {CDN} is Akamai. Akamai currently sources roughly 20% of the world's total Internet traffic. Akamai's peak delivery via Brute Force Unicast {BFU} is on the order of 70 Tbps. This represents only 1.8M concurrent viewers at 4k UHD. [11] Ominously, that's a tiny fraction of the numbers shown above.

Not surprisingly, Live Super Bowl "broadcast" over the internet has, to-date, been a case study in disappointment. This is where Multicast methods offer the economy, and performance that unicast cannot offer. These methods provide a unique economy for emerging Live video markets. Connected Fitness applications like Peloton come to mind. A Live distribution modality should be integrated into any Hybrid VoD initiative. Given the anticipated demand for live content, it would be irresponsible not to.

Winners and Losers

This is not a Zero Sum game. There are winners, and there some that simply must accommodate change. Some might consider that accommodating change is itself a losing proposition. To quote Dilbert: *"Change is good. You go first."*

In this internet arena, change is a constant, so it's best to embrace it. Fortunately for this change-rich initiative, it's easy to find winners, and hard to pinpoint losers. (See Figure 7) The dominant economic drivers supporting a transition to Hybrid VoD are tied to removing the wasteful dependency of unicast. Two interrelated elements of waste are significantly reduced:

- Substantially less bandwidth is consumed as the redundant servers, and unicast sessions are replaced with multicast methods.
- Significant Crest Factor reduction permits a more efficient infrastructure and strategic planning thereof.

<table>
<tr><th>Stake-Holder</th><th>Loss -------|------Win</th></tr>
<tr><td>Large CSPs</td><td>X</td></tr>
<tr><td>Small CSPs</td><td>X</td></tr>
<tr><td>Tier 1 ISP</td><td>X</td></tr>
<tr><td>Tier 2 ISP</td><td>X</td></tr>
<tr><td>Tier 3 ISP</td><td>X</td></tr>
<tr><td>Indy CDN Operators</td><td>X</td></tr>
<tr><td>ATSC 3.0 Broadcasters</td><td>X</td></tr>
<tr><td>Set Top Box Vendors</td><td>X</td></tr>
<tr><td>Subscribers</td><td>X</td></tr>
</table>

FIGURE 7: STAKE HOLDERS: RELATIVE LOSS & WIN

Large CSPs & w/ proprietary CDNs

These stakeholders can recognize significant reduction the Capital Equipment Expenditures, and on transit charges incurred at IXP sites.

Small CSPs w/ Leased CDNs

These stakeholders can recognize significant reduction the leased CDN Equipment charges, and on transit charges incurred at IXP sites.

Tier 1 ISPs

Tier 1 ISPs don't charge each other for bandwidth exchange, they would however charge Tier 2 for this bandwidth. Most of the large CSP have already moved their largest traffic volumes to Tier 2 IXPs and to Tier 3 ISPs. Consequentially there should be little change in revenue.

Tier 2 ISPs for Transit & IPX hosting

Tier 2 ISPs perform as both conduits to VoD traffic, and as IXP hosts for mid-placed CDNs, their net cash flow for bandwidth that traverses their network would be reduced. Profitability due to moderated VoD traffic should be unaffected.

Tier 3 ISPs & Indy CDN Operators

These stakeholders have a great deal to gain, as their network bandwidth requirements are substantially lessened. Also, as a greater share of edge server capacity is migrating toward these facilities, their CAPX and OPX expenses can be better managed.

ATSC 3.0 Broadcasters

The distribution of Broadband content is a greenfield opportunity for Broadcasters as they adopt the ATSC 3.0 Broadcast standard. Multicast methods are the forte of this new broadband distribution method.

Set Top Box Vendors

The set top box market is likely to achieve saturation before this initiative can mature. This gives STB vendors a beneficial opportunity for a vibrant product replacement cycle.

Subscribers

Subscribers will benefit from a unified operational paradigm of traditional VoD, reliable Live Content and Cached VoD content with greater operational immediacy. Taken together This would yield a higher Quality of Experience {QoE} for the users.

The Importance of the Local ISP

In this schema, the only Administrative Domain that absolutely must be Multicast enabled is the local connection. The local client connection, be it Cable, FTTP, or 5G service must be Multicast enabled. (ATSC 3.0 implementations are Multicast by necessity.) Without the Multicast operation local to the subscriber's administrative domain, the dominant savings of this method simply cannot be achieved. This is probably the most accessible domain in which to make this alteration. It need only be made available for IPv6 connections to clients.

While end users on unicast domains could potentially access multicast content using embedded AMT Gateways, these unicast tunnel connections don't share in the multicast economy. AMT is still a critical interim tool to bridge those pesky upstream Unicast hops. That's ok, the AMT implementations are few, compared to the quantity of end subscribers connected to their local service provider.

Use of AMT to bridge upstream multicast deficiencies is not as elegant as the mythically perfect, homogeneous Multicast Network. Still, it can provide considerable value in facilitating VoD as the Multicast roads remain under construction.

A Common Framework

Adoption of a methodology such as described in this paper requires a well-established common framework; a framework mutually available to all stake holding parties. From CSPs to independent CDN operators, ISP operators of all Tiers, to STB vendors, to TV Manufacturers. All these stake holders have efficiencies to extract and opportunities to exploit.

Such a common framework must provide a method for all participating Content Service Providers to share equal access for multicast transfers to Subscriber Client devices, without favor or advantage to any Content Service Provider. This framework must include constraints to assure equal and isolated access. Included in these constraints should be:

- No CSP would be able to access another CSP's assets, metadata, or other metrics from any subscriber's client device.
- No CSP would have access to client devices without an active customer authorized subscription.
- Each CSP would have equal quantitative, and qualitative access to Client device storage memory resources.

Still, no one stake holder can achieve these gains alone. It must be done in concert with the other stake holders. Leaving any stakeholder out of such a collaboration, intentionally or otherwise, would quickly become a legal matter, with potential charges of restraint of trade.

Collaboration & Standards

Legal protection for collaboration is often facilitated via a Standards Setting or Standards Development Organization [SSO / SDO]. Three such organizations, with a record of involvement in the disciplines described here, are IEEE, SMPTE and the IETF.

There is a new collaborative development process within the Society of Motion Picture and Television Engineers [SMPTE]. It's termed a "Technical Specification". This is a fast-track path to the creation of business driven Technical Specifications and permits elevation to the more traditional, albeit more exacting standards process. This path pledges a rapid start, the necessary legal aegis for collaborative development, and the imprimatur of a well-established standards body. SMPTE offers a promising path.

There are some lesser-known vehicles for collaborative development. Of note is the Joint Development Foundation. [12] Part of the Linux Foundation family, the JDF can provide a corporate and legal infrastructure to rapidly establish and operate lightweight collaborations to develop technical specifications, standards, and source code. JDF projects can then be taken to a larger standards organization when the collaboration achieves maturity.

JDF has sponsored the Alliance for Open Media. The Alliance has the distinction of sponsoring the mutual development of the AV1 Video Codec, a possible successor to H256/HVEC. [2] Not to gratuitously name drop, but Apple, Broadcom, Intel, Microsoft, Netflix, Amazon Prime Video, Cisco, Hulu, YouTube, Vimeo, and many others are contributing members of the Alliance.

There will inevitably be patent holders that have rights that need to be secured. This is truly nothing new in the realm of standards. One of the tasks will be to secure Fair, Reasonable, and Non-Discriminatory [FRAND] commitments from those holders.

The conclusion here is that the only practical path forward to making meaningful cost saving in VoD distribution is to engage the stakeholders with an accredited Standards Setting Organization and make it happen.

Executive Summary - Hybrid VoD

- Annual savings attributable to Hybrid VoD could reach $11B globally within a decade. Cumulative savings could achieve $300B within the same timeframe. This is for Bandwidth expenditures alone. Hardware and other infrastructure saving will add substantially to this figure.
- Demand for VoD Content is growing at significant CAGR, 20-30%. The growing popularity of UHD content will exacerbate this demand.
- Hardware, and Bandwidth burdens are increasing at a rate proportional with this demand.
- Cost of non-volatile memory is rapidly becoming non-consequential.
- The ability of each CSP to infer their subscriber's future viewing choices is already here, albeit in a nascent form.
- The Fat Tail is plumping, bulked up with original content from the major CSPs. This makes viewing inference easier and increases the efficiency of Multicast methods.
- Source Specific Multicast will have a much larger greater opportunity to be fully implemented, as IPv6, 5G and ATSC 3.0 reach their inevitable ubiquity.
- A Means for Live High-Demand content delivery should be integrated into this initiative. This especially includes UHD content.
- Business operations will eventually choose Economy over Waste.
- The above points lead to an unavoidable need for an alteration in the delivery of VoD. Now is time to get in front of this transition.
- Standards will be required to gain the market share benefits, that only a Common Framework can provide.

VoD Integration – 3 Modalities. 3 Use Cases

The utility of this proposal is to provide a means for materially reducing the infrastructure cost and Network burden of established networks of Subscriber VoD services. It does not endeavor to replace VoD. It is a hybrid extension to the current methodology. It does so in a manner that reduces costs by orders of magnitude, targeting the highest volumes of content in an inefficient content delivery system.

The premise of this proposal is to combine conventional VoD with local playout of speculatively cached content delivered by a Multicast means. Multicast delivery of High Demand Live content integrates the functional trio. Hybrid VoD covers these three use cases in a functionally integrated manner. (See Figure 8)

Hybrid VoD provides the following:

- Live, Low latency VoD service.
  Ideal for high demand "Spectacle" content.
- Speculatively Cached VoD service.
  Ideal for high demand "Fat Tail" content.
- Incumbent VoD service.
  Ideal for "Long Tail" content. Essential today, always the fallback service when more efficient means are not available.

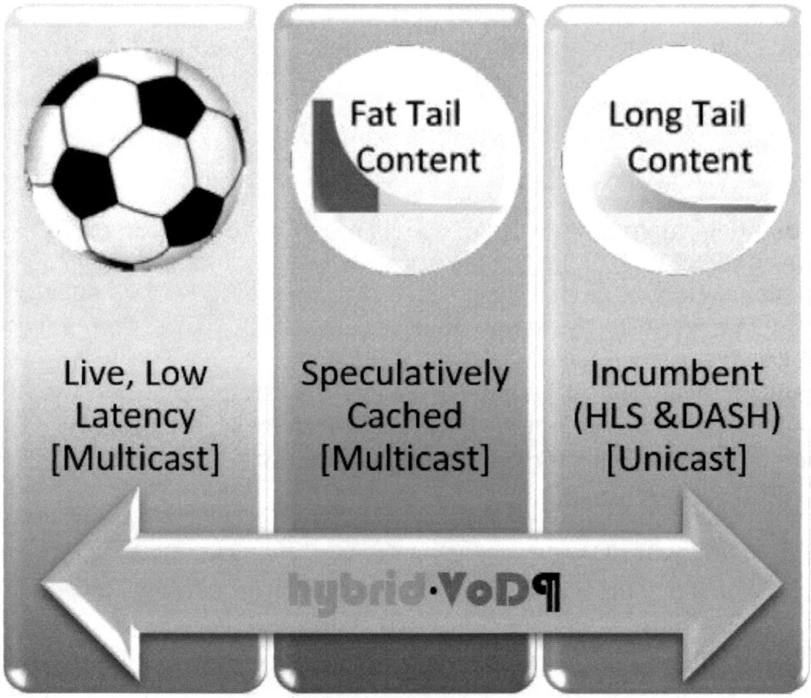

FIGURE 8: THREE MODALITIES, HYBRID VOD

Live and Speculatively Cached content is integrated with the incumbent VoD application. The subscriber is presented a user interface that is not materially different from the familiar VoD experience currently used by the current unicast implementation. A common presentation is desirable as the subscriber need not be concerned with the arcane athletics of the asset delivery.

The Content Service Provider retains their distinctive look, feel and branding that is their distinctive product. The local cached content would be transparently integrated into the viewing experience when it is accessible. The Subscriber would remain largely unaffected by this cost saving hybridization.

There is one important exception that should be noted. The ability for the user to Start, Stop Fast-Forward, Rewind, Skip and Review would be substantially improved for locally cached content. The current VoD operation, with its long round trip network latency, makes these controls at best, user unfriendly. At worst, user antagonistic.

Without this enormous latency in VoD control of these functions, the user experience would be greatly improved.

In the Figure 9 below, VoD Integration can be envisioned in terms similar to OSI abstraction layers. The author offers this model structure, as a starting point for further discussion and improvement. The goal is to use the best means for each layer, in a manner that is appropriate to each of the three dominant use cases of VoD.

While using the right resource for each job, the goal is also to use a common method wherever practically possible. These layers are described, from bottom to top.

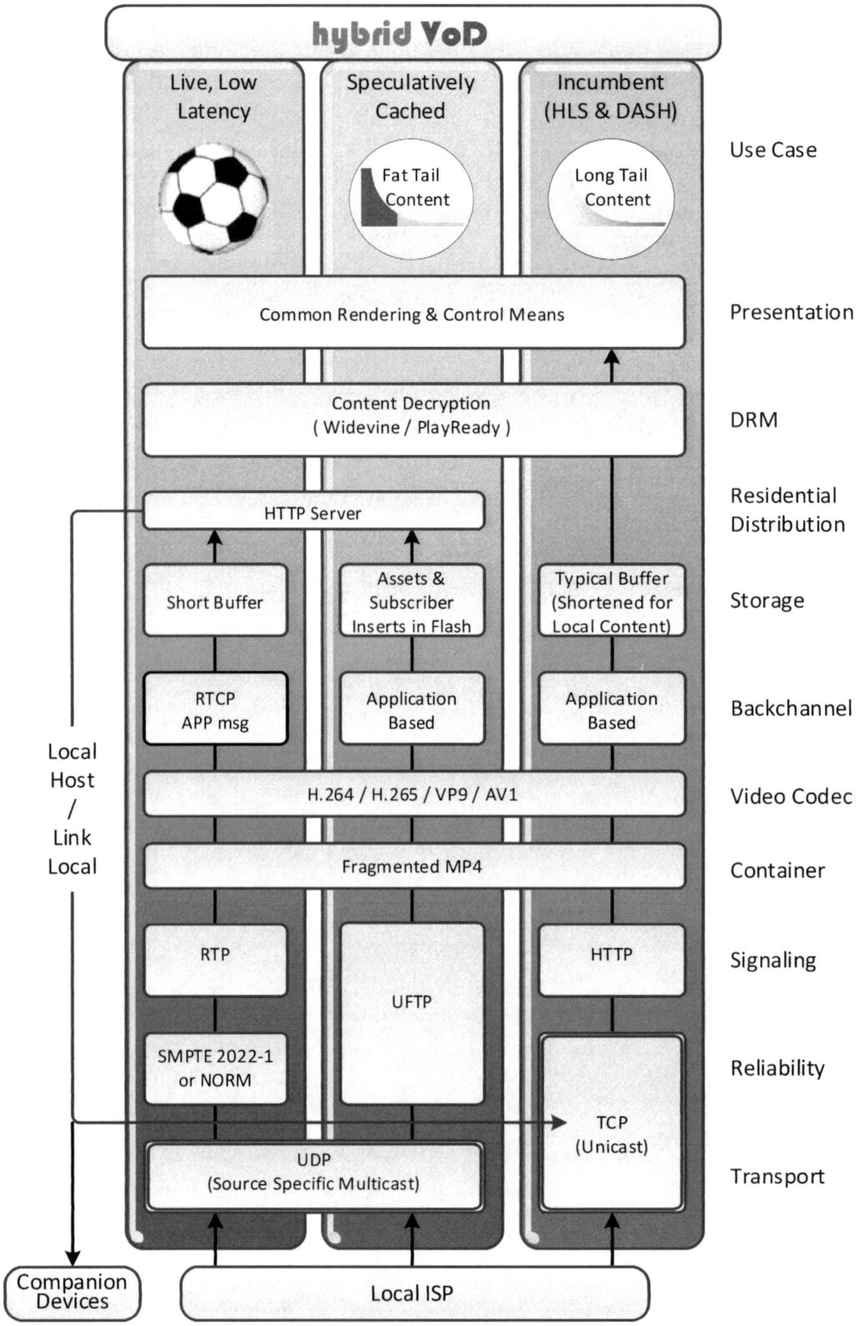

FIGURE 9: OSI ABSTRACTION, HYBRID VOD.

Transport

TCP for the essential and incumbent (HLS & DASH) content delivery. UDP is required for the transport efficiencies of Source Specific Multicast.

Reliability

For Incumbent VoD service TCP provides for reliable, ordered and error checked data. Re-transmission of lost data is managed by TCP.For Speculatively Cached VoD service, UFTP provides its own means for recovery of lost data. For Live VoD service, reliable data delivery is assured via FEC. SMPTE 2022-1 and NORM are contenders for this reliability means.

Signaling

For incumbent VoD service, HTTP is the recognized leading means for content delivery. For Speculatively Cached VoD service, UFTP provides the required constructs for content delivery. For Live VoD service, RTP provides the required constructs for content delivery.

Container

Fragmented MP4 provides a common container means for all three services.

Video Codec

The Video Codec can be whatever is in vogue. It would be beneficial to settle on one of the higher efficiency choices.

Backchannel

The backchannel can be specific to each CSP needs. Still, this is one important area that would benefit from a standardization effort.

Storage

For Incumbent VoD service, typically a large buffer may be required, 30-40 seconds perhaps. For Speculatively Cached VoD service, a large Flash memory is used for holding media assets, and for Subscriber Specific Inserts. Subscriber Specific advertising Inserts are not restricted for playout within Speculatively Cached VoD playout, they would be used for any of the three use cases. For Live VoD service, a rather small buffer is required. A few seconds perhaps, enough to cope with dropped or out of order packets, with recovery through FEC recovery.

Residential Distribution

Speculatively Cached and Live VoD service might both use an internal HTTP Server means to facilitate playout through the Incumbent VoD service TCP/HTTP stack. In this way, Companion Devices within the residence, which only support the Incumbent VoD services, would benefit. Consequently, a Companion Device could be an older vintage set-top box, or any itinerant laptop, tablet, or smart phone. The Incumbent VoD service TCP/HTTP stack would use a significantly shortened Buffer structure for Residentially sourced content.

DRM

DRM by means of Google's Widevine and Microsoft's ReadyPlay are already well established. There is no need for change here.

Presentation

A common presentation and control method is used across all three modalities of Hybrid VoD.

Speculatively Cached Embodiment

The distribution of VoD content starts with the Content Service Provider. In tight synergy with their established, conventional VoD service, the provider would, through a series of steps, prioritize the distribution of their media assets in highest demand. (See Figure 10)

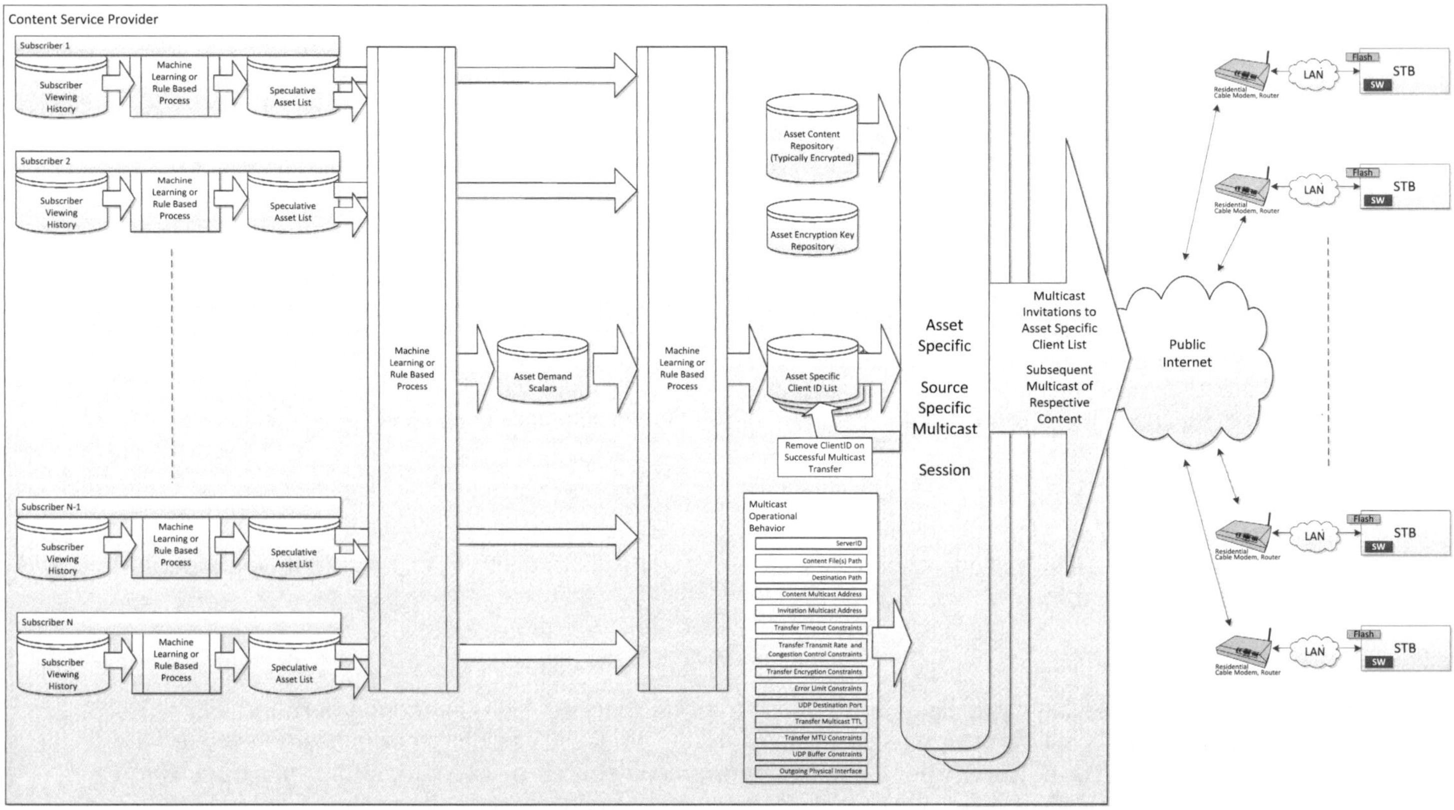

FIGURE 10: SPECULATIVELY CACHED EMBODIMENT

Step 1 – Speculative Asset Lists

A Content Service Provider has a plurality of subscribers within a prescribed distribution region. (HBO in North America, Netflix in Brazil etc.) Each Subscriber has a known viewing history. Each Content Service Provider, through either a simple rule based, or a machine learning process, aggregates a Speculative Asset List.

The Subscriber Specific Speculative Asset Lists would inferentially predict the media content that the subscribers are likely to view in the immediate future.

For example, if a subscriber watched the last 2 episodes of a popular video series, over the last 3 days, that subscriber would likely watch the next episode in the next day or so. If a subscriber has watched to completion, the previous season of a series, and a new season of that series debuts next Sunday, there is a high likelihood that the subscriber will watch that debut. If a subscriber watches a trailer for that new season, perhaps more than once, that viewing history indicates the likelihood that the subscriber will watch that content as soon as it debuts. This is of particular importance for highly popular "Block Buster" content programming where the streaming traffic peaks.

There are many ways in which the Content Service Provider can infer a Speculative Asset List for each subscriber.

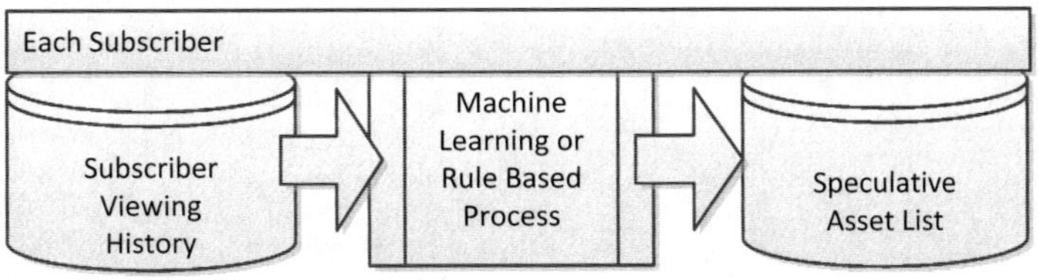

FIGURE 11: SPECULATIVE ASSET LIST

With attention to Figure 11, each Content Service Provider would develop and refine their models for the creation of a Speculative Asset List. These models would be the intellectual proprietary of each Content Service Provider.

Content Service Providers are likely doing an aggregate form of this predictive modeling today, to load balance their server and content storage resources. This proposal suggests that there are additional gains to be achieved.

Step 2 – Asset Demand Scalars

Once a Speculative Asset List for each subscriber has been assembled across a cohort of subscribers, a ranked list of Assets in Demand can be determined.

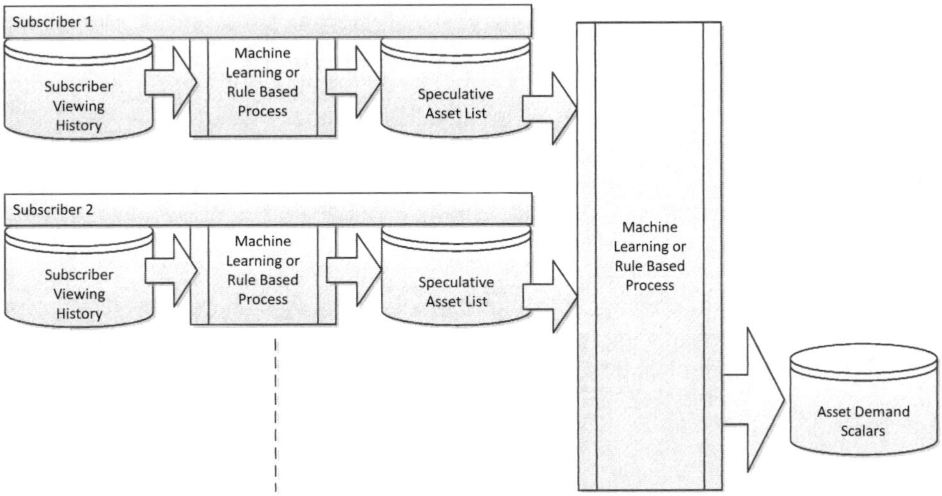

FIGURE 12: ASSET DEMAND SCALARS

With attention to Figure 12, each Asset would be associated with a Scalar value, proportional to the demand for that Asset. The detailed means for this process, either rule or machine learning based, would be retained as the intellectual property of the Content Service Provider. The highest demand Asset for the specified timeframe, would have the highest scalar value. How the scalar is weighted and possibly factored by timeframe is up to the individual Content Service Provider.

Step 3 – Asset Specific ClientID Lists

With attention to Figure 13, matching the individual Speculative Asset Lists with the Asset Demand Scalars produces a list of subscribers for each Asset.

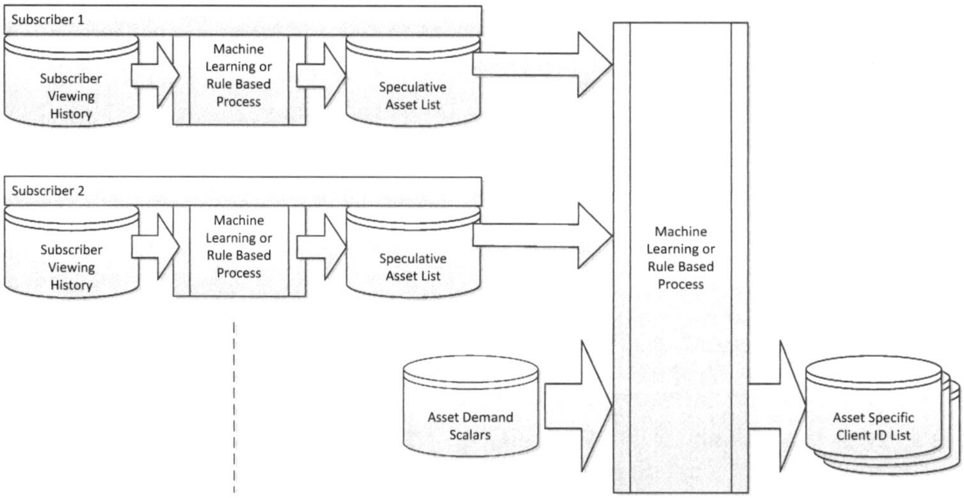

FIGURE 13: ASSET SPECIFIC CLIENT ID LIST

Each Subscriber has a "ClientID" which is associated with their physical Multicast Client receiving device.

For example, Matching of Speculative Asset Lists and Asset Demand Scalars produces a list of individual Assets that have enough demand to warrant multicasting, along with a list of prospective subscribers to each Asset. Each Asset Specific ClientID List contains a list of Subscriber's Multicast ClientIDs. These refer to the Client Devices to which the Multicast of this specific Asset will be applied.

It should be noted that each of the above-described data products is described separately, simply for the purpose of a progressive explanation. The most likely embodiment of the above would involve the ingestion and extraction of the relevant data from an integrated database.

Feedback mechanisms, such as to prune the Subscriber demand lists as content is successfully delivered, are essential to avoid redundantly over serving the multicast delivery process. This would be integral to the database embodiment of this process.

Step 4 – Multicast Process

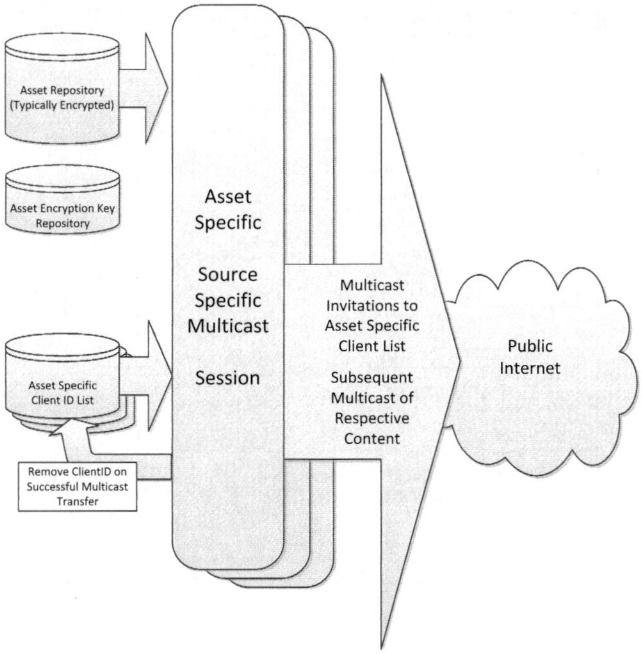

FIGURE 14: MULTICAST DISTRIBUTION

With attention to Figure 14, The Source Specific Multicast process involves the use of the Asset Specific Client List to source the appropriate Asset Content to the appropriate Multicast Client devices across the public internet.

The Asset Content is held in an appropriate repository. Each item of Asset Content is encrypted to safeguard the property rights of that content. Encryption keys are retained for "Just-in-Time" distribution when the Subscriber chooses to view the Content. More on this later.

A Source Specific Multicast {SSM} Session initiates when Asset Specific Client ID list exceeds a threshold set by the Content Service Provider. This might practically be as few as a dozen Clients, or up to thousands.

The mechanism for Source Specific Multicast {SSM} is established art. There are multiple methods to accomplish this. All involve the use of User Datagram Protocol {UDP} and some specific higher layer of abstraction encompassing the use of UDP.

Inclusive of those higher layer abstractions in this embodiment, are NACK-Oriented Reliable Multicast {NORM}, [24] and Unicast File Transfer Protocol {UFTP}. [4] UFTP appears best suited for this embodiment, however all the aforementioned and other practices that share similar attributes might be put in service of this practice. For each of these Multicast abstractions, there is a Server application and a Client application.

Server Side Multicast Session

A Multicast Server session is specific to some Operational Behavior constraints, some of these might be universal to the application in general, some are specific to the needs of the Content Service Provider, and some might be specific to needs of the individual Session. Others might be adaptable to the public network or Client Device performance history. An example of these Server-side Multicast Operational Behavior constraints is shown Figure 15.

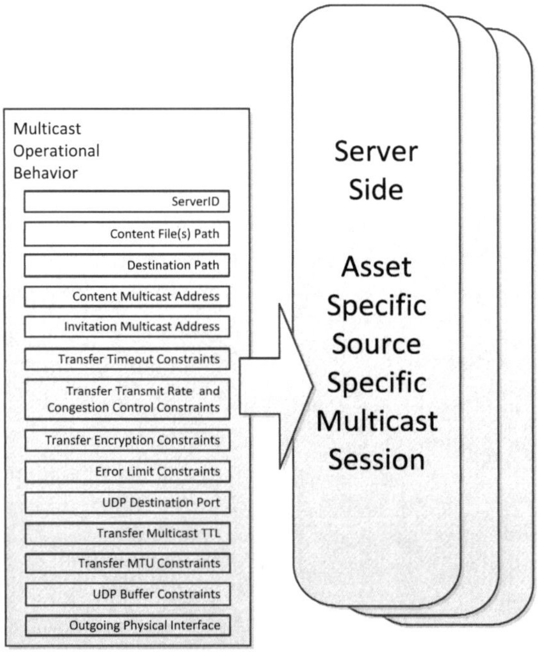

FIGURE 15: SERVER SIDE MULTICAST SESSION

Relevant to the understanding of this embodiment, using UFPT, there are two phases involved in a Multicast session. First an Invitation Phase, followed by a Content Transfer Phase.

Presuming an AMT implementation from the CSPs to the Tier 3 ISPs, the local ISPs might allocate pre-determined Source Specific Multicast addresses for this service, with AMT traffic forwarded to them. The local ISPs, would be free to use the FF3X::8000:0 thru FF3X::FFFF:FFFF address range. Should Source Specific Multicast become fully interdomain, the Internet regulating authorities might offer additional guidelines.

Some of these SSM internet address allocations would be used for Invitation Messages, other addresses would be used for the much larger volume of Content Transfer.

Each Multicast Client would monitor a plurality of Invitation addresses, one Invitation address for each active Content Vendor Subscription.

Client Side Multicast Session

Complementary to the Multicast Server Session, each Multicast Client session has Operational Behavior constraints. An example of these Client Side Multicast Operational Behavior constraints is shown in Figure 16.

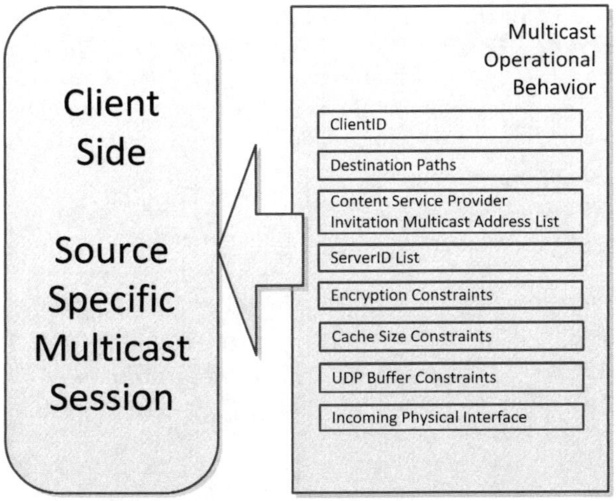

FIGURE 16: CLIENT SIDE MULTICAST SESSION

When not otherwise in service of more crucial activities, the Client device joins a Multicast Session that listens for Invitations from specific Multicast Addresses known for their specific use as Invitation addresses. For additional security, the Client might also only permit operation with ServerIDs on a predetermined ServerID list.

Once a plurality of clients has validated an invitation to a content transfer, the transfer of the Content files commences. The details of the transfer handshaking and the means for assuring reliable transport are not described here, as these details are the domain of the chosen prior art Multicast transport methodology. While many of the transferred content files are typically encrypted, and remain so after transport, the transport mechanism itself may be configured to utilize encryption for the actual transfer. The utility of redundant encryption is worthy of further study. Once the SSM transfer has completed. The transferred files are then held in non-volatile storage on the Client Device.

Subscriber Equipment

As new residential networked devices become available, the features available to Content Service Providers will naturally expand. This proposal highlights how these efficiencies are gained in these expansions. Other than processing performance, a modest number of networking attributes will be required.

- Support for IPv6. This is going to be world-wide-requirement regardless of this proposal.
- Support for Read and Write to local non-volatile memory, Flash Memory or whatever technology supersedes that.
- Support for Read and Write to Local Network Attached Storage.
- Software to support this described capability.

The most ideal embodiment is one which requires the least change in the subscriber's indoctrination to the new environment. This would involve either a Networked Device with integrated Flash memory, or simply the insertion of a small Flash Drive. At this writing, the cost of sufficiently large flash drive (> 100GB) is low and will become vanishingly small in coming years.

A variety of embodiments are illustrated in Figure 17. They range from rapid development embodiments to some more ideal commercial ones. In each embodiment, the host device for the Application is indicated with a {SW} symbol, as is the host device used for the cashed content {Flash}.

The LANs cloud in these illustrations may be wired or wireless, or a combination of the two.

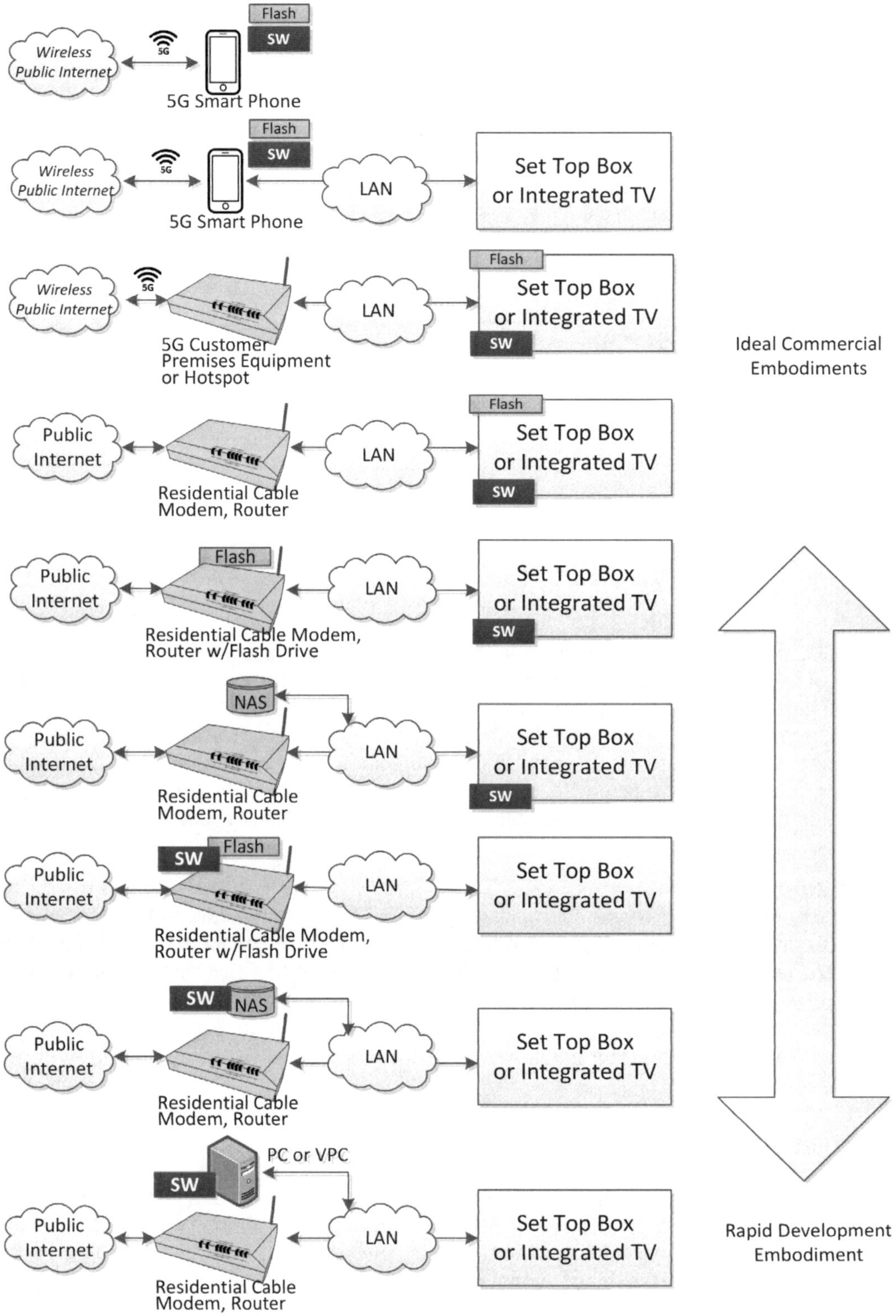

FIGURE 17: SUBSCRIBER EMBODIMENTS

Client Side Economy

It is envisioned that for practical economy of resources, typically one Multicast client thread would run on a Subscriber's client device. It would only typically run when no other viewing activity is active.

Concurrent Content Sessions may be graciously disallowed without harm to the utility of this proposal. As described above, for operational economy, the client might only service one multicast Content Session at a time. Critical to adoption, a responsible client application would support multiple Content Service Providers equally.

If a Multicast Client is in the process of receiving a content from one Multicast agent, and another Multicast agent invites that client to an additional session, the client would, by design, not respond to the second invitation. As this attempted concurrent transfer would not be successful, the Client ID would remain active in the Asset Specific ClientID List. This Asset Specific ClientID List would be accordingly trimmed by means of the successful transfers. As this Asset Specific ClientID List is refreshed, and again reaches its vendor determined demand threshold, a new SSM Session for that Asset would begin.

Similarly, for the purpose of economy of resources, it is envisioned that Clients would refuse Multicast sessions should they be burdened by other more crucial activities, such as actively playing out other VoD content. Clients would be free to abandon transfers in process if it served to optimize the real time user experience. A device that misses an invitation & subsequent Content session, would simply pick it up on the next invited Multicast opportunity.

"Rotted" Client Content

Should Storage space on the Client Device approach a full state, the client could automatically discard excess content, as prescribed by Content vendor specific constraints. These Rotted content constraints would be specific to each Content ID and would be encrypted with the same Key as the Content. These constraints might include Content specific total age duration, age since last viewing, and a prescribed fixed expiration date. Storage Memory on the Client device would allocate equally across all content vendors. No Content Service Provider would be allowed to consume more storage space than any other. The end user always has the option of increasing their total storage allocation, or dropping a subscription, thus allocating more Storage memory to the remaining subscriptions.

Just-In-Time Encryption Key.

Each time a content element is initiated for viewing, a request for the encryption key specific to the content is requested from the vendor. This key persists for a reasonable period and is not requested for each start and stop of the content being viewed. The key is not saved by the Client application. The key would, however, timeout after a reasonable pause duration. The key would be requested again upon resumption of play. When the content viewing has concluded, the key would be discarded, and a message to that effect would be reported to the Content Service Provider. If the content is provided in advance of a particular embargo date/time, a null key would be provided, and the application would politely deny the view, and/or play a clear coded Trailer instead. In more typical usage, the user's interface would simply lack the affordance to view content that is embargoed.

The Transported content files are encrypted files, the file encryption method is largely immaterial to this proposal. The decryption at the client is performed on-the-fly, no intermediary file is generated during playout.

In an economical embodiment, the content files would not be in the form of "selective" video format encryption. In "Selective" encryption, the content files would retain a legitimate video format, but the content would be degraded via encryption in a manner that makes their viewing unviable. The complexities of "selective" encryption is difficult to justify without a compelling rationale. [7] While not critical to this embodiment, it remains a possibility.

Live Content Embodiment

In the illustration below, Live content in AD1 is supplied to a Multicast Reflector. The Reflector in AD2 takes this live content and produces an appropriate UDP Multicast stream. That stream is passed to an AMT Relay which provides tunnels across the Multicast Undependable networks, to Multicast Enabled AD3 and AD4. AD2 can be localized within single integrated device within a Unicast AD.

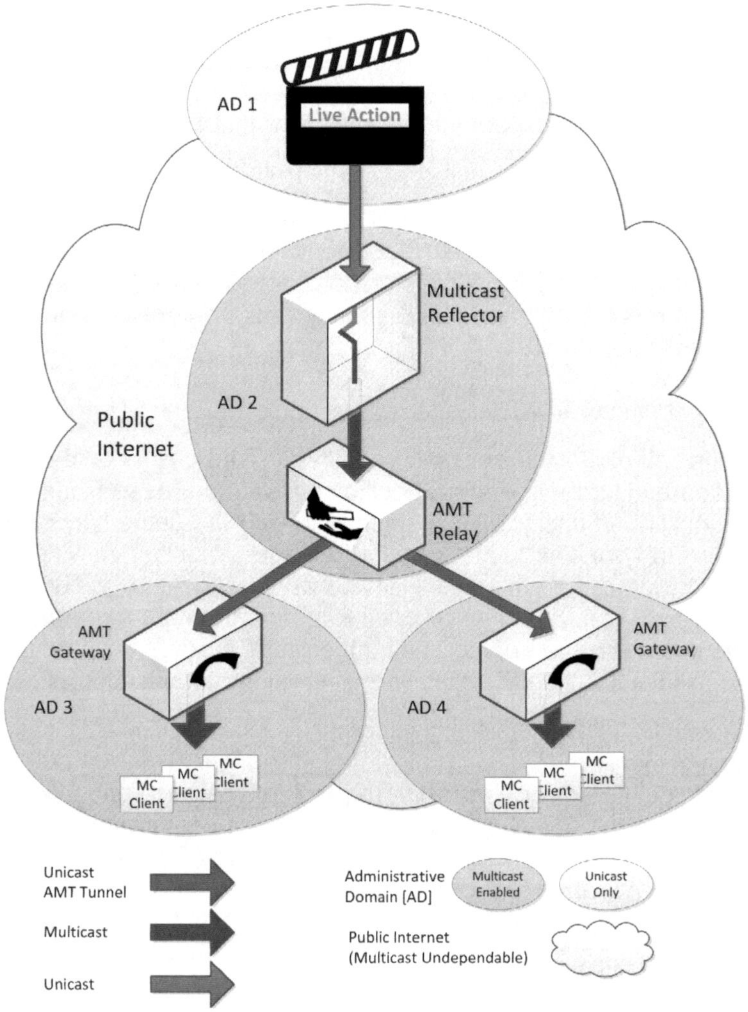

FIGURE 17: LIVE CONTENT EMBODIMENT

To make this a practical reality, other mechanisms are required. Foremost, in a live Multicast transmission It's probably wise to needs to add some features to improve reliability.

Today, Unicast VoD uses TCP/IP to assure replacement of lost packets. This is typically true for both archived and live content. Of the three main streaming methodologies, HTTP, RTSP side-chained with RTP/RTCP, and WebRTC, HTTP is by far the most common. Multicast is a UDP only medium. Lost packets are not recovered. Some other means to enhance the robustness of the Multicast stream is advisable.

The MPEG-TS Container

The customary manner for UDP streaming of content is to encapsulate the Elementary Streams {ES}, within a Transport Stream {TS}. Elementary Streams are the individual elements of the content, Video, Audio, Closed Caption, etc. The Transport Stream puts then together in a composite format.

To package this, the Media packets might be assembled in a manner like:

IP [UDP [RTP [MPEG_TS [ES_v, ES_{a1}, ES_{a2}, ES_{cc}...]]]]

The ES, Elementary Stream(s) could be derived from the codec du jour; H.264, H.265, AV1 etc. Multiple language audio codec streams, and metadata like Closed Caption.

The Fragmented MP4 Container

Instead of using an MPEG_TS container, architectural advantage might be gained by using a container framework more consistent with incumbent TCP / HTTP streaming practices. This alternative provides benefits to both Content Service Providers and Set top Box vendors. The CSPs don't need to create and archive additional files, and STB vendors similarly might deal with one less container format.

Historically, the Fragmented MP4 construct is a derivative of Microsoft's IIS_7 Smooth Streaming initiative. Consequently, the Media packets might be assembled in a manner like so:

IP [UDP [RTP [Fragmented MP4 [moov, moof...moof, mfra, ...]]]]

The Streaming server uses the MPEG-4 Part 14 (ISO/IEC 14496-12) file format as its storage and transport format. Specifically, this method uses an MPEG-4 Movie Fragment (*moof)* and retains it within a MP4 file for retrieval. One MP4 file is expected per each required bitrate. When the client requests a specific source time segment from the host server, the server returns the requested fragment from within the Fragmented MP4 file.

Regardless of the container format, RTCP, the backchannel complement to RTP would be utilized. RTPC would provide delivery metrics and statistical performance. The optional "APP" message within the RTPC provides a means for application specific enrichment.

In this use case, RTCP would report infrequently. Reports from active subscribers would be constrained to be distributed in time, such as to level peak burden on server devices.

Forward Error Correction, FEC

No Network is perfect. As a strawman proposal for Live Multicast Enabled local ISPs, the author believes that an embodiment of a Forward Error Correction {FEC} schema is appropriate. There are a few alternatives to this, SMPTE 2022-1 and NORM are two contenders.

- **SMPTE 2022-1:** Use of this standard is common in Video Content Production communities. [22] ST2022-1 is an extension RFC2733. In SMPTE 2022-1, the Media packets [port N] would be associated with the sidechain FEC packets. These FEC packets are indexed to the Media packet's RTP sequence numbers. The FEC Packets are directed to ports N+2 and optionally to port N+4. The N+2 FEC data allows repair of Burst packet losses, the N+4 allows repair of more random losses. SMPTE 2022-1 typically uses MPEG2 Transport Streams as its container format. The SMPTE 2022-1 FEC mechanism should work equally well for either container format.

- **NORM:** As an alternative to SMTPE 20222-1, NACK-Oriented Reliable Multicast [NORM, RFC5740] transport protocol shows some promise. The proactive FEC enabled Silent Client streaming modalities of NORM appear applicable to Live content. A comparative analysis between NORM and SMPTE2022-1 should prove enlightening.

References

[1] 50Wheel. (2018). The top video live streaming statistics to know in 2018. Retrieved from 50Wheel: https://50wheel.com/the-top-video-live-streaming-statistics-to-know-in-2018/

[2] Alliance for Open Media. (2019). Alliance for Open Media. Retrieved from https://aomedia.org/about/

[3] Alston, A. (2019). SRv6+ Segment Routing Headers - Why We Want Them. Retrieved from Juniper Networks: https://forums.juniper.net/t5/Routing/SRv6-Segment-Routing-Headers-Why-We-Want-Them/ta-p/461964

[4] Bush, D. (2019). UFTP Homepage. Retrieved from UFTP - Encrypted UDP based FTP with multicast: http://uftp-multicast.sourceforge.net/

[5] Cisco. (2019). Cisco Visual Networking Index: Forecast and Trends, 2017–2022 White Paper. Retrieved from www.cisco.com: https://www.cisco.com/c/en/us/solutions/collateral/service-provider/visual-networking-index-vni/white-paper-c11-741490.html

[6] Cisco. (2021). Cisco VNI Forecast Highlights. Retrieved from https://www.cisco.com/c/dam/m/en_us/solutions/service-provider/vni-forecast-highlights

[7] Dubois, Shahid, & Puech. (2013). Selective encryption of images and videos: from JPEG to H.265/HEVC through JPEG2000 and H.264/AVC. Retrieved from Google Scholar: http://bit.ly/2N2eb7k

[8] Giuliano, L. (2014). Retrieved from Archive.NANOG.org: https://archive.nanog.org/sites/default/files/wednesday_giuliano_internetmulticast_62.18.pdf

[9] Giuliano, L. (2019). Multicast to the Grandma (MTTG): It's finally here. Retrieved from IETF104-MBONED-20190328-1050: https://youtu.be/jIDYHFpJYV8?t=3737

[10] Giuliano, L., & Gallo, A. (2019). Multicast for Everyone Else: It’s finally here!

[11] Holland, J. (2019, 7 22). IETF_105_Mops. Retrieved from YouTube Internet Engineering Task Force: https://youtu.be/4G3YBVmn9Eo?t=2991

[12] Joint Development Foundation. (2019). Retrieved from http://www.jointdevelopment.org /

[13] Korte, T. (2019). Over the Top and Through AI to Big Data's House We Go. 2019 NAB BEITC Proceedings.

[14] Liechman Research Group. (2019). Leichtman Research. Retrieved from https://www.leichtmanresearch.com/74-of-u-s-households-have-an-svod-service/

[15] Morales, & Bergstrom. (2017). Did the Super Bowl Kill the Internet? Retrieved from IEEE Xplore: https://ieeexplore.ieee.org/document/7933951

[16] NAB Pilot. (2019). Next Generation TV Home Gateway. Retrieved from NAB Pilot: https://nabpilot.org/next-generation-tv-home-gateway/

[17] NetFlix Open Connect. (2019). Retrieved from https://openconnect.netflix.com/en/appliances/#the-hardware

[18] NOIA Network. (2019). Programmable Internet. Retrieved from NOIA Network: https://drive.google.com/file/d/1aUgWiKiw1c0Xg6ugmWL0FrN5A4d00htv/view

[19] Nolle, T. (2012). Evaluating the useful life of a server. Retrieved from https://www.dell.com/learn/us/en/04/smb/evaluating-the-useful-life-of-a-server

[20] Prince, M. (2014). The Relative Cost of Bandwidth Around the World. Retrieved from Cloudflare: https://blog.cloudflare.com/the-relative-cost-of-bandwidth-around-the-world/

[21] Rao, N. (2016, 8). Cloudflare Blog. Retrieved from Cloudflare: https://blog.cloudflare.com/bandwidth-costs-around-the-world/

[22] SMPTE. (2007). ST2022-1. Retrieved from IEEE Xplore: https://ieeexplore.ieee.org/abstract/document/7291470

[23] Trate, F. (2017). Segment Routing IPv6 – Interoperability demo is already there! Retrieved from Cisco: https://blogs.cisco.com/sp/segment-routing-ipv6-interoperability-demo-is-already-there

[24] US Naval Research Lab. (2019). GitHub. Retrieved from GitHub: https://github.com/USNavalResearchLaboratory/norm/tree/master/doc

[25] Yahoo News. (2016). Retrieved from https://admarketing.yahoo.net/rs/118-OEW-181/images/Yahoo_The%20Live%20Video%20Opportunity_2016.pdf

[26] Zambelli, A. (2009). The Birth of Smooth Streaming. Retrieved from Alex Zambelli's Streaming Media Blog: http://alexzambelli.com/blog/2009/02/04/the-birth-of-smooth-streaming/

[27] Zhang, W. (2017). Public AMT Relay between Internet2 and Commodity Internet. Retrieved from https://www.cs.virginia.edu/~wyz3sp/pub-amt-relay.pdf

Glossary

Any-Source Multicast	ASM	Any-source multicast is a form of multicast where multiple senders can be on the same group/channel, as opposed to source-specific multicast where a single source is specified.
Asset or Media Asset		This term is used by the industry to refer to Media Content which is owned or in care of a Content Service Provider. This term may be used interchangeably with the term “content”
Autonomous System or Administrative Domain	AS or AD	These terms are often synonymous. A network managed by a single entity or organization. An AS presents a clearly defined routing policy to the internet. Taxonomically an AS may be a Tier 1,2 or 3 ISP.

Bit Index Explicit Replication	BIER	An architecture for forwarding multicast traffic. Eschewing multicast forwarding trees, multicast packets are encapsulated into a header and forwarded based on that.
Client		Software that receives or accesses data from a remote service on another computer
Client Device		Hardware Host of the Client software.
ClientID		A unique identification number specific each Client. The ClientID is typically unique to the Client's physical Device.
Content Delivery Network	CDN	A CDN is a network of edge servers, replicating s a CSP's media assets at Tier2 Internet Exchange points, and at some Tier 3 ISP sites. This lessens the burden on Tier1 ISPs.
Content Service Provider	CSP	A provider of Media typically to a subscriber customer base.
Crest Factor	CF	Crest factor is a term to describe the ratio of a peak value to an effective average value. In other words, crest factor indicates how extreme the peaks of demand are, in a plot of demand over time.
Digital Media Adapter	DMA	Another term for Set Top Box
Elementary stream(s)	ES	Typically, the output of an audio or video encoder. Each ES contains only one kind of data (e.g. audio, video, or closed caption). An elementary stream is often referred to as "elementary", "data", "audio", or "video" bitstreams or streams. The format of the elementary stream depends upon the codec or data carried in the stream.
Fat Tail distribution		The antithesis of "Long Tail" distribution, popularized by author Chris Anderson. The idea promoted that in the digital economy, niche products (media content) would find preference to generic, hit products.
Fiber to the Premises	FTTP	Fiber to the Premises
5G, 5G New Radio	5G, 5G New Radio	5G NR is a new radio access technology, developed for the fifth generation mobile network. It is designed to be the global standard for the air interface of 5G networks.
Ingress Replication	IR	A mechanism to deliver IPv6 Multicast traffic across an intermediary unicast network. It's colloquially been termed "Spray Multicast".
Interdomain		Data flow control and interaction between Internet carriers.
Internet Exchange Point	IXP, or IX	A physical infrastructure through which ISPs and CDNs exchange Internet traffic between their networks (Autonomous Systems).
Internet Protocol	IP	Internet Protocol is the principal communications protocol in the Internet protocol suite for relaying datagrams across network boundaries. Its routing function enables internetworking, and essentially establishes the Internet.
Internet Protocol v4	IPv4	Internet Protocol version 4 is the fourth version of the Internet Protocol (IP). It is the predominant networking protocol in use today.
Internet Protocol v6	IPv6	Internet Protocol version 6 is the most recent version of the Internet Protocol (IP). IPv6 was developed to deal with the long-anticipated problem of IPv4 address exhaustion. IPv6 is intended to replace IPv4. IPv6 theoretically allowing 3.4×10^{38}

		addresses. The total number of possible IPv6 addresses is more than 7.9×10^{28} times as many as IPv4. IPv6 removes the requirement of clumsy Network Address Translation practices at premise locations. IPv6 provides other technical benefits. In particular, it permits the more streamlined multicast mechanisms, optimizing the delivery of such services. It should be noted that while IPv4, has expanded to support specifications and resources to support the application of Hybrid VoD across public internet domains. Still, very few networks comply in a uniform manner. The unavoidable ubiquity of IPv6 permits the practical deployment of this initiative.
IP Transit or Transit		The monetary charge levied by a Tier2 or Tier3 ISP for either (not typically both) ingress or egress of IP content.
LAN	LAN	A local area network is a computer network that interconnects computers within a limited area such as a residence or single site business.
Machine Learning		Machine learning is a means to achieve logical objective without using explicit instructions, relying on patterns and inference of predetermined rules. It is a subset of artificial intelligence. Machine learning algorithms build a mathematical model based on sample data, known as "training data", in order to make predictions or decisions without being explicitly programmed to perform the task.
Media		Short for Media Content or Titles.
Multicast, Multicast IP	MC, MC IP	In computer networking, multicast is group communication where data transmission is addressed to a group of destination computers simultaneously. Multicast can be one-to-many or many-to-many distribution.
Network Attached Storage	NAS	Network-attached storage is a file-level computer data storage server connected to a computer network providing data access to a heterogeneous group of clients. It is often manufactured as a computer appliance – a purpose-built specialized computer.
Operational Immediacy		The ability to control a device, at the whim of the user without material latency.
Quality of Experience	QoE	A subjective measure of the quality of subscriber experience. Might include service availability, video stalls, Operational latency, etc.
Real Time Transport Protocol, & RTP Control Protocol	RTP & RTCP	Real-time Transport Protocol (RTP) is a network protocol for delivering audio and video over IP networks. RTP is used in communication and entertainment systems that involve streaming media. RTP typically runs over UDP. RTP is often used in conjunction with the RTP Control Protocol (RTCP). RTCP is used to monitor transmission statistics and quality of service (QoS).
Segment Routing over the IPv6 Data Plane	SRv6	Prescribes how IPv6 packets may carry instructions of how to route and potentially add value to traffic, as it journeys the internet.

Server		A Server is a system that responds to request or programmatically pushes data across a computer network worldwide to provide, or help to provide, a network or data service.
ServerID		A unique identification number specific each Server device.
Set Top Box	STB	A set-top box (STB), is an information appliance device that generally contains means to receive content and displays output to a video monitoring device. Also known as a Digital Media Adapter or DMA.
Source Specific Multicast	SSM	Source-specific multicast is a method of delivering multicast packets in which the only packets that are delivered to a receiver are those originating from a specific source address requested by the receiver. By so limiting the source, SSM reduces demands on the network and improves security.
Speculative Asset List	SAL	A list of media Content elements that a subscriber is inferentially expected to view.
Streaming, Streaming Media		Streaming media is multimedia that is constantly received by and presented to an end-user while being delivered by a provider. The verb "to stream" refers to the process of delivering or obtaining media in this manner; the term refers to the delivery method of the medium, rather than the medium itself. Streaming is the alternative to file downloading, where the end-user obtains the entire file for the content before watching or listening to it.
Subscription-Video-On-Demand, Subscriber-Video-On-Demand Video-On-Demand	SVoD, VoD	Subscription-Video-on-Demand is an entertainment programming model where users pay a monthly fee in exchange for instant access to a streaming library consisting of movies, TV shows, and other media content. Companies like Netflix, Hulu, and Amazon have taken advantage of this new system of media consumption and used the technology to grow their brands into some of the biggest names in the entertainment industry. The demand for their services is only expected to increase from here, with worldwide digital video revenue expected to grow in the coming years and VoD accounting for a larger percentage each year. The number of VoD users worldwide is expected to rise from around 283 million in 2018 to 568 million in 2022. This together with the demand for higher video resolutions is raising the burden on Network bandwidth and other internet connected infrastructures. Video-on-demand is a form of video media distribution that allows users to consume content whenever they choose, instead of having to watch content at a scheduled broadcast time.
Unicast, Unicast IP		In computer networking, unicast refers to a one-to-one transmission from one point in the network to another point; that is, one sender and one receiver, each identified by a network address.

Ultra-High Definition	UHD	A 4K UHD display has 3840 pixels horizontally and 2160 pixels vertically for a total of 8.3 megapixels. An 8K UHD display has 7680 pixels horizontally and 4320 pixels vertically for a total of 33.2 megapixels. 4K UHD has four times as many pixels as conventional HDTV (high-definition television), and 8K UHDTV has 16 times as many pixels as conventional 1080p HDTV.
User Datagram Protocol	UDP	One of the core members of the Internet protocol suite. UDP uses a simple connectionless transmission model with a minimum of protocol mechanisms. It has no handshaking dialogues, and thus exposes the user's data to any unreliability of the underlying network protocol. Damaged packets of data are never received; however, some packets could go missing. If transmission reliability is desired, it must be implemented at a higher layer of abstraction.
Virtual Machine	VM, VPC	A virtual machine is an emulation of a computer system. A computer emulated within a host computer.
Wild Ass Guess	WAG	Engineering nomenclature for an intuitive supposition.
Wide Area Network	WAN	A wide area network generally covers a large geographic distance, the Public Internet is the largest of all WANs.

Adopting New Cloud Workflows and Making Live Happen in this New Normal

Daniel Pisarski
LiveU Inc.
Hackensack, New Jersey, United States
danielp@liveu.tv

Abstract – The COVID-19 pandemic forced producers to think differently about how to deliver quality content. The approach, workflow, gear, budgets, and onsite requirements were drastically different from the traditional way producers "made it happen." Remote monitoring and control in this "work from home" new normal meant producers needed tools and resources to coordinate all the behind-the-scenes moving pieces. This paper discusses cloud solutions for broadcasters and the lessons learned along the way as broadcasters learned to pivot and adapt to working fully remote and "keeping the lights" on for content. In our changed reality, workflows need to be sustainable for everyone in the production process to perform their job from anywhere – ensuring broadcasters can cope with new or unexpected challenges and reduce the environmental impact of shipping equipment or travelling to a studio to get reliable broadcast-grade live video.

Cloud Production: Revolutionizing Content Creation

Outside Broadcast (OB) vans were once the gold standard for any high-quality live sports or news production. However, over the last five years we have seen a gradual shift from this model. Long gone are the days when your production crew had to sit together in one control room at the venue surrounded by expensive hardware. A more flexible approach is fast becoming the norm: one where all or some of your production capabilities – from content creation through to distribution and sharing – are hosted in the cloud. In this white paper, we explore how a production company or broadcaster can leverage the power of the cloud to build a flexible, scalable, and cost-effective production workflow, while delivering high-quality coverage for live broadcasts.

Building A Seamless Cloud-Based Workflow

A cloud-based workflow can encompass all or just some of the four phases outlined below and a hybrid approach may well suit your live news or sports production better than immediately going "all in". Should you go for a turnkey or hybrid cloud production workflow? Here are some questions you need to ask yourself when looking at different workflow options.

Create

- Can my live production benefit from adopting a remote production model?
- Can cloud-based software improve the scalability, flexibility and/or cost- effectiveness of my content creation workflow (e.g., facilitating field-to-studio communication or camera control to reduce staff in the field)?
- What capabilities do I require from a connectivity perspective (the necessary 5G / 4G connection) to support my preferred workflow?

This paper is excerpted from the Proceedings of the 2022 NAB Broadcast Engineering and Information Technology (BEIT) Conference, © 2022, National Association of Broadcasters, 1 M Street S.E., Washington, DC 20003 USA.

Ingest

- What ingest standards (e.g., RTMP, SRT or NDI) should I use to get the best result from a latency and bandwidth perspective when I transfer content to my cloud-based platform?

Produce

- Where can cloud-based software improve the scalability, flexibility and/or cost-effectiveness of my operation in terms of editing, switching, graphics, clipping, publishing and recording?
- How can I further optimize the integration of my solution with other cloud-based solutions to offer an enriched and seamless viewing experience?

Distribute/Share

- How can I take the distribution and sharing of my content to the next level utilizing the latest cloud-based distribution tools (including to platforms like YouTube, Twitch and Facebook)?

The Technology Behind Cloud Production

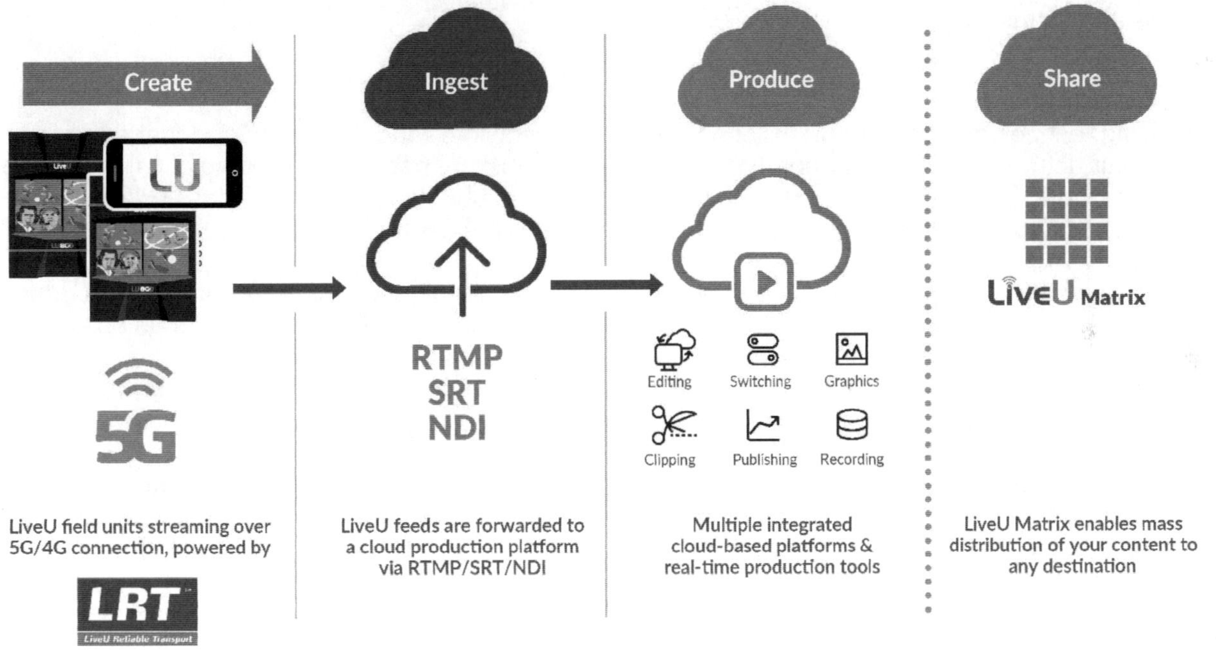

FIGURE 1: A LIVE CONTENT PRODUCTION WORKFLOW IN THE CLOUD, COVERING EACH OF 4 KEY STEPS IN THE CONTENT CREATION CHAIN.

Cloud production tools have developed quickly over recent years to offer an alternative to traditional hardware and can be applied to deliver a turnkey production solution. However, developments in two other areas – remote production and IP bonding – have been equally influential in making cloud-based workflows the future of live broadcasting.

Remote Production

Remote production workflows, also known as REMI (Remote Integration Model) or at-home production, enables crews to bring the cameras and the transmission equipment on-site and send live feeds back to a remote production facility from where the full production can be done. This optimizes resources by reducing the size of the crews you need to send on-site and limits wear and tear on your most expensive equipment.

For broadcasters and production companies, the pandemic has meant new travel and social distancing guidelines. There has also been a need to focus on enhancing the experience for audiences stuck at home. Consequently, remote production has become synonymous not only with cost-effectiveness, but also with a focal point of innovation in the sports and news broadcast sectors.

As one example, the iconic Rocky IV film featuring Rocky Balboa's (Sylvester Stallone) trip to the USSR to defend his title against Ivan Drago (Dolph Lundgren) celebrated its 40th anniversary in 2021. To commemorate the milestone event and the release of the new Ultimate Director's Cut, full-service media company, Broadcast Management Group (BMG) partnered with MGM Studios to produce an eight-camera live program in several locations within the Philadelphia Film Center from its state-of-the-art Las Vegas REMI broadcast production hub. Signals were sent from two LiveU LU800 production-level field units back to the REMI broadcast hub in Las Vegas and then uplinked to more than 700 theaters across the US.

IP Bonding

IP bonding technology enables you to "bring your own bandwidth" and remove your dependency on local infrastructure. It enables the bonding of multiple network connections (including cellular, Wi-Fi and satellite networks) to create the bandwidth necessary to distribute high-quality wireless IP feeds and has empowered broadcasters and production companies to deliver more for less.

IP bonding enables the untethering of cameras which can send fully synced feeds directly to a remote production facility from any location. There was a time when connectivity was regarded as one of the main expenses and one of the main risks of remote production. Advancements in IP bonding technology have changed that. IP bonding has removed the dependence on expensive and inflexible fiber or satellite delivery.

Talking about IP bonding technology, Dave Mazza, Senior Vice President of NBC Olympics Engineering, recently remarked that "this technology gives us ease of use and tremendous mobility, allowing us to transmit while on the move and go live from any venue we wish to on the spur of the moment."

5G is set to amplify many of the intrinsic benefits of IP bonding. 5G isn't only about further improving video and audio capabilities. Lots of work goes into making 3G and even 4G signals reliable from the perspective of total throughput, as well as end-to-end latency and maintaining premium video quality. 5G makes this easier with its greater potential uplink throughput meaning that additional available bandwidth may be allocated, reliably, to other important capabilities. It's not only about transporting premium quality video and audio, it's about having greater throughput to deliver IP-based communication, video return, robotic camera control and control of camera control units (CCUs).

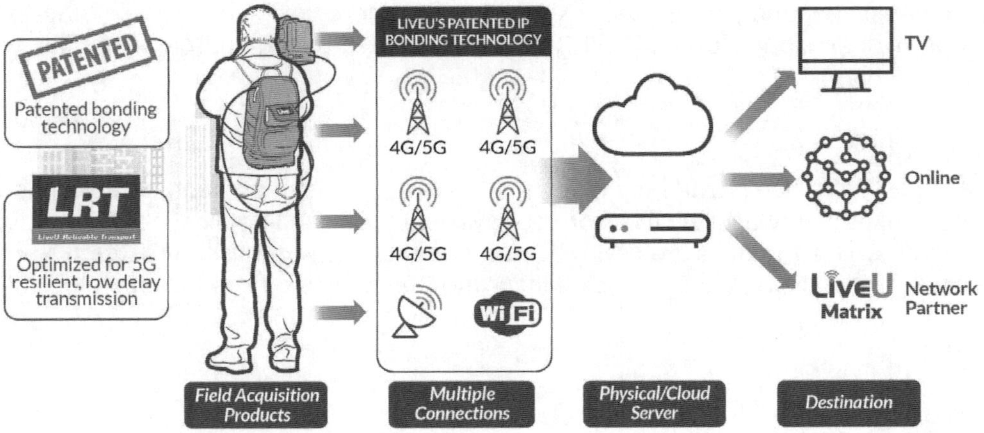

FIGURE 2: A LOOK AT THE CELLULAR-BONDING CONTRIBUTION WORKFLOW, WHERE TECHNOLOGIES SUCH AS 4G AND 5G CAN WORK TOGETHER TO DELIVER RELIABLE, HIGH-QUALITY AND LOW-LATENCY VIDEO FROM ANYWHERE IN THE WORLD.

The Benefits of a Cloud-Based Workflow

Building on remote production and IP bonding, a cloud-based workflow can facilitate everything from the creation of content to the distribution and sharing of content on digital and social media platforms in a way that is more scalable, flexible, and cost-effective than traditional on-site, hardware-dependent workflows.

Scale

It is no longer enough to engage audiences across one or two platforms or to simply increase the amount of content you are pushing out to audiences. Production companies and broadcasters need to ensure that diverse audience segments are properly served, no matter the format, language, device type or platform. The recipe for success to meet the ever-increasing demand for content lies somewhere between scaling vertically (in terms of volume of content) and horizontally (in terms of adapting the content to audience consumption preferences). A cloud-based workflow will afford you this scalability, while reducing or avoiding the upfront costs associated with a traditional on-site and hardware-dependent approach.

Flexibility

Cloud production workflows are software-based and therefore facilitate collaboration, regardless of where you are in the world. They enable broadcasters and production companies to create the "dream team" of replay operators, editors, technical directors, and on-air talent, and leverage the same team for multiple events. This collaborative approach provides consistency, trust, and a high-quality production every time. It also means far higher re-use of technology, further reducing cost. The familiarity with the equipment and workflows can also lead to an acceleration in innovation.

Cost-Effectiveness

One of the most significant benefits of a cloud-based approach is eliminating the need to maintain significant infrastructure assets such as OB vans, equipment rooms, and servers. As a result of the pandemic, the budgets of many broadcasters and production companies are coming under increasing pressure. This is leading many to recognize the benefits of switching from owning their production equipment (a capital expenditure or “CAPEX” model) to a more flexible leasing or “pay-as-you-go” model (an operational expenditure or "OPEX" model). A cloud-based approach can flex with your needs.

Fully Managed

Cloud service providers can provide high levels of security for video content, as well as protection from malware and viruses. They actively monitor your systems and send notifications to alert you about potential incidents. This removes the need for you to manage on-premise infrastructure that requires maintenance and periodic replacement, plus incurring the increasing costs associated with technology obsolescence.

Producing Content That Works for You

As digital channels continue to increase in importance from an audience and commercial perspective, the ability to create content once and reuse it (and re-monetize it) many times over is key. Less is being spent on traditional TV advertising (down 12.5%), while more is being invested in online video advertising (up 30.1%)[1].

A cloud-based workflow can make your content work harder for you without the need for more or additional equipment.

Content Repurposing

Cloud production enables the speedy repurposing of content to adapt to the needs of audiences. For example, a live stream of a sports broadcast can be repurposed for a betting platform, or news content from a national broadcaster can be repurposed for onward distribution to its local affiliates.

Social Media

When there is no time to waste, a cloud-based production workflow gives you the tools to create or repurpose content and distribute it to all major social media platforms with little fuss.

Content Localization

Content produced in the cloud can easily be adapted to cater for local preferences whether they be language, format, device type and/or platform, to ensure the experience is tailored to the audience. For example, for a live sports broadcast that you want to take into new territories, you can add new graphics or a local language commentary.

Second Screen & Supplemental Programming Cloud-based production gives you the flexibility to send content to second screen devices to complement a live sports or news broadcast. This content can be used for other supplementary programming before, during, or after the primary content.

Device Targeting

Cloud production can mitigate the frustrations that audiences experience when trying to view video content across different digital and social platforms on a mobile device, for example, by enabling production teams to deliver content in the optimal aspect ratio.

[1] Fortune.com

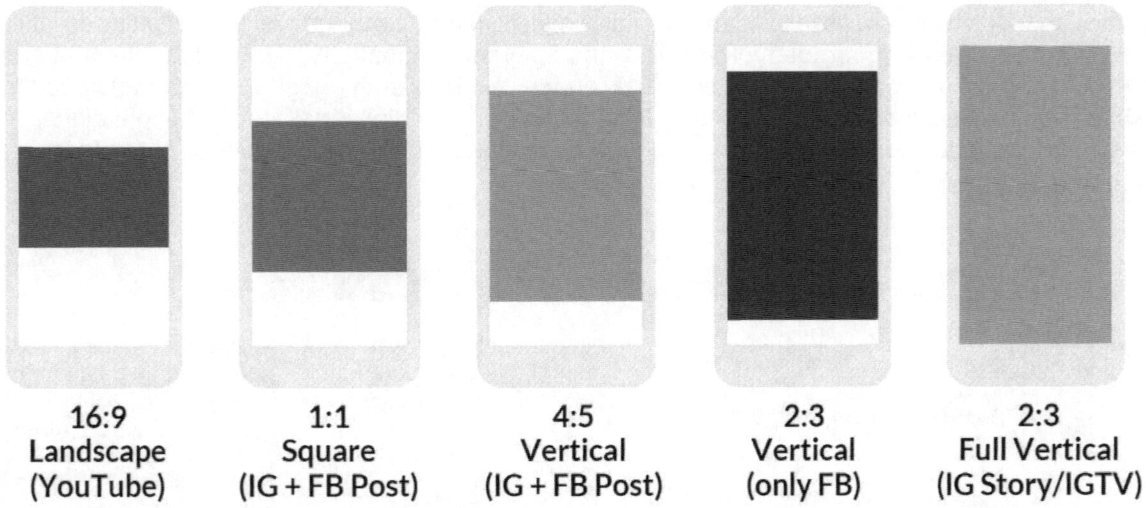

FIGURE 3: SOME ASPECT RATIOS IN USE BY DIFFERENT DELIVERY PLATFORMS. YOUR CONTENT MAY NEED TO SUPPORT SEVERAL DIFFERENT ASPECT RATIOS IN ORDER TO OPTIMIZE FOR DIFFERENT AUDIENCES.

Guest Interviews

Cloud-based production opens the possibility to produce live guest interviews from any location in the world (including from the comfort of their home) without the need to send a crew or be bound by a studio location.

Clipping/Highlights

Cloud production enables content to be tagged instantly with metadata that can deliver clips or highlights in real-time giving the content a longer life span beyond the live broadcast. For example, key moments from your live sports broadcast can be clipped and distributed to your favorite social media platforms.

Example Use Cases

Mediengruppe RTL Deutschland Enhances Election Coverage Via End-to-End Cloud-based Workflow

To enhance their live coverage of the 2021 regional elections in Germany, Mediengruppe RTL Deutschland chose to create, ingest, produce and distribute/share election content using cloud-based workflows. The project was managed by CBC, the production and technology/IT company of Mediengruppe RTL Deutschland.

LiveU customer CBC used the LiveU Matrix IP cloud-based management and distribution platform for dynamic live news content sharing, complementing its existing fleet of LiveU field units. Live feeds were shared from multiple venues (covering the press conferences and interviews with the candidates) and received directly into Matrix's cloud channels with all the incoming feeds recorded in real-time in the cloud. Selected feeds were then distributed to multiple receivers and broadcast on the national news, as well as additional German broadcasters, facilitating a collaborative effort between the broadcasters.

SRT feeds were also ingested into the Matrix platform for the first time. LiveU's network operations center (NOC) provided proactive monitoring of the feeds with dedicated alerts in real-time.

In parallel, the files were accessed in almost real- time using the cloud native editing platform of LiveU's partner, Blackbird. Working remotely, from safe and convenient locations, distributed teams of editors were able to rapidly and collaboratively clip, edit, enrich and publish highlights of the many events. Blackbird then delivered both short and long form high-definition digital assets to multiple digital channels simultaneously including social and web as well as to broadcast media partners for repurposing.

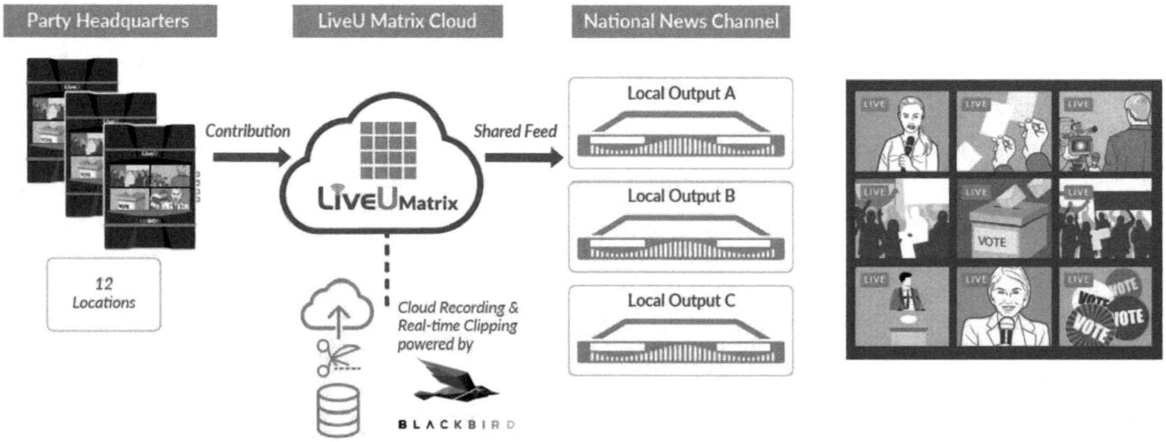

FIGURE 4: THE WORKFLOW USED BY MEDIENGRUPPE RTL DEUTSCHLAND TO PROVIDE NEAR-REAL-TIME CONTENT DURING THE 2021 REGIONAL ELECTIONS IN GERMANY.

J SPORTS Adopts Hybrid Cloud Production Approach to Enhance the Viewer Experience

Japanese broadcaster J SPORTS, together with its production partner Express, wanted to enhance the live viewing experience for matches of the Yokohama DeNA BayStars' baseball team shown on J SPORTS' OTT service (J SPORTS On Demand). To achieve this, they decided to use a multi-camera, remote production solution for all home matches of the 2021 season.

2021 was the first year that J SPORTS offered this live OTT service. The broadcaster initially planned to use only the clean broadcast feed, adding commentary and graphics. However, working closely with Express, expanding the amount of content and increasing viewer engagement became a priority. Moving to remote production was also a long-held Express and J SPORTS ambition.

J SPORTS wanted to transmit multiple camera signals via mobile networks and, of course, it had to be extremely reliable. Originally, they planned to send multiple camera feeds via Ethernet, but demonstrations from LiveU proved that the organization's original ambition was completely possible. They showed us the next level of remote production, with reliable tally light and additional audio functionality via the multi-camera LU800, facilitating bi-directional communications between the field staff and control room."

Conclusion

It is clear that cloud workflows are here to stay. They bring undoubted advantages including enabling you to produce more content and re-use content in infinite ways. You are no longer bound by rack space, available power, availability of specialized hardware, or requiring your entire team to be in one physical space.

Soon, you will see even more computing power and specialized hardware and software leveraged for content production and distribution. AI-assisted layouts, changes, and transformations, machine learning that adapts to your content, and new forms of content such as three-dimensional spatial video and augmented reality will go from cutting-edge to the norm. The cloud workflows that seem cutting-edge today will soon be your everyday.

Perfecting your craft and capability when it comes to cloud production workflows and cloud computing in general will continue to serve well even as content and content creation tools evolve. Cloud is the future of computing and will lead to even more exciting forms of content in the future.

How 5G Technology Simplified Live Remote Broadcasts During the Pandemic

Jim Jachetta
VidOvation Corporation
Anaheim, California, United States
jimj@vidovation.com

Abstract – Broadcasters and production companies adapted to the changing workflows during the pandemic. They were able to save costs using 5G cellular and Public Internet connectivity, producing a live show with multiple untethered handheld cameras using the latest At-home Production and REMI technology. Novel techniques maintained frame-accurate genlock and audio lip-sync across dozens of cameras.

Introduction

There is nothing like a crisis to force advancement in the use of technology to improve the way we do things. It might sound cliché, but that doesn't make it less true – necessity is the mother of invention. So, with the broadcast industry forced to work remotely and with only skeleton crews at locations, broadcasters had to develop new ways to produce and deliver their live event programming.

The truth is that when COVID-19 struck, and most of the world had gone into lockdown, we were very well prepared because we had already solved the problem of at-home production and REMI (remote integration model) and had been doing it for five or six years. Of course, the pandemic forced us to perfect the techniques to make it all work efficiently and reliably, but the technology was all there.

Case Study: First Live Sporting Event After Lockdown

To illustrate the basics of the solutions that have emerged, let's look at how we managed the first major sporting event broadcast live in the US after the lockdowns went into effect. It was a PGA golf event held at the Seminole Golf Club in southeast Florida. The local health authority had put in restrictions that dictated that a maximum of 50 people would be allowed on the course, including the players, officiants, club personnel, camera operators, and other broadcast personnel. No spectators were allowed. The players weren't even allowed caddies and had to carry their own clubs.

Given that the Seminole course is a private club and not a regular venue for PGA events, no telecom or fiber connection was pre-installed for broadcasting. They just weren't equipped. So, a bonded cellular solution capable of 3G, 4G, or 5G connectivity was the only thing that made sense.

The setup out on the course consisted of two cameras in the tee box, two cameras on the fairway, two on the green, and then a couple of POV cameras for beauty shots. The primary cameras were connected to bonded cellular encoder/transmitters that employed eight cellular modems. For the POV

This paper is excerpted from the Proceedings of the 2022 NAB Broadcast Engineering and Information Technology (BEIT) Conference, © 2022, National Association of Broadcasters, 1 M Street S.E., Washington, DC 20003 USA.

cameras capturing shots of the clubhouse and shots of the dunes along the beach, the transmitters were equipped with only two cellular modems – the cellular reception was more than adequate for this.

The camera operators and production team desired encoder/transmitters that mount on the camera. The encoder/transmitter is mounted between the camera and the battery, which is preferred. Most camera operators prefer not to wear a backpack. Production is streamlined as one battery powers both the camera and encoder/transmitter unit.

The bonded cellular encoder/transmitters also featured analog inputs to handle audio. For every video, there could be four to eight audio inputs. For this event, some of the supplemental audio channels used two-modem devices. There were quite a few background microphones and microphones on the talent, microphones on the players, the two commentators walking the course, and parabolic microphones catching the action.

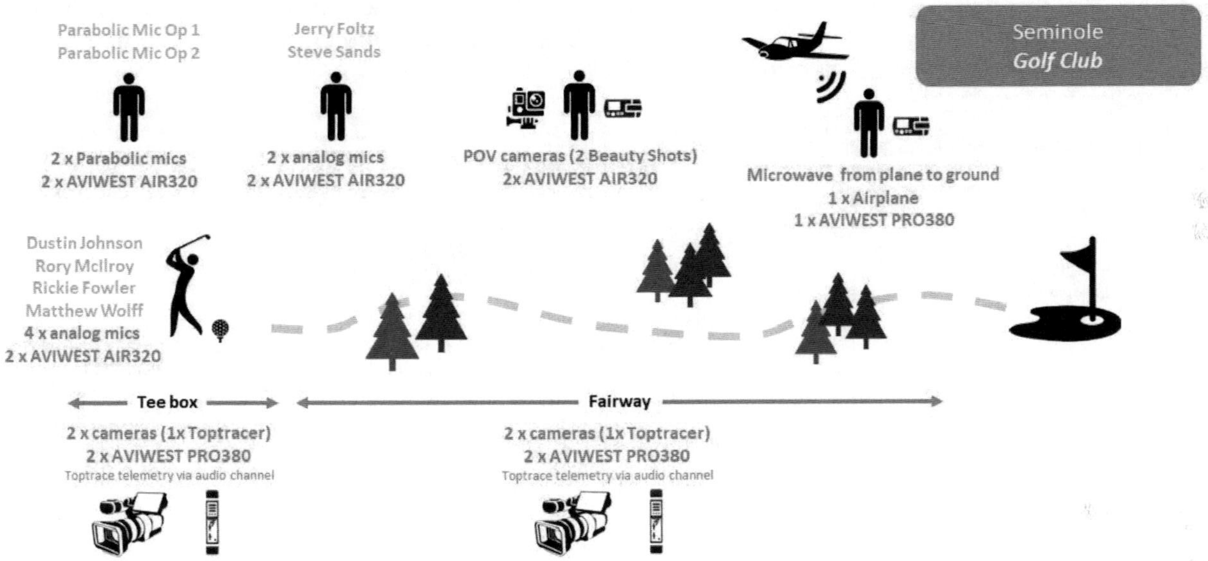

FIGURE 1: CAMERA, AUDIO, AND BONDED CELLULAR CONFIGURATION AT SEMINOLE GOLF CLUB FOR PGA EVENT

Frame-Accurate Video Gen-Lock and Audio Lip Sync

With all the cameras and microphones, it's vital to keep everything in perfect lip-sync; all the cameras in Gen-lock and the technology we used in the bonded cellular devices made this happen. So, all sources going back to the control room in St. Augustine are in perfect sync. If any of these microphones were a little bit out of time, it wouldn't make for a good production.

Frame-accurate video Gen-lock and audio lip-sync across multiple untethered handheld cameras and dozens of microphones covering the entire golf course was critical. The encoder/transmitters typically use unmanaged networks for connectivity, such as the cellular networks and the public Internet. A similar technique to those found on a managed network such as PTP or Precision Time Protocol is utilized over the cellular and public Internet connection. The encoder/transmitters are locked to a GPS reference clock and the cellular network reference clock. A GPS clock is highly accurate. The decoder/receiver sends a timing and reference signal like PTP to keep all the encoder/transmitters in Gen-lock and lip-sync. Any remaining variation in the SDI, NDI, or IP camera video output is corrected via a frame buffer in the decoder/receiver connected to a studio reference signal also derived from a GPS clock.

The traditional way that a PGA event like this would be set up would be to have microwave camera links connected to a truck in the parking lot. However, most of the microwave gear available uses H.264, while the bonded cellular gear we're using is HEVC. So, the actual picture in most cases, looks a lot better than what the PGA producers were used to. Their reaction was typical, along the lines of "Why does the picture look so much better? We've saved a ton of money, we saved on personnel, we saved on travel, and the pictures look better." So, it's been a real win-win for the PGA and others.

From the course in southeast Florida, the bonded cellular uplinks delivered the video and audio to the production facility in St. Augustine in northeast Florida. The show's producer was located along with the play-by-play commentator and two analysts. In addition, there was also another color commentator connected via bonded cellular from his home in Michigan. We must acknowledge that the latency would be near zero if this were done over a fiber link. But going through bonded cellular or the public Internet could result in up to a second of latency. It's not a problem as long as the on-air talent are trained and get used to it, knowing to pause before they speak so as not to talk over one another.

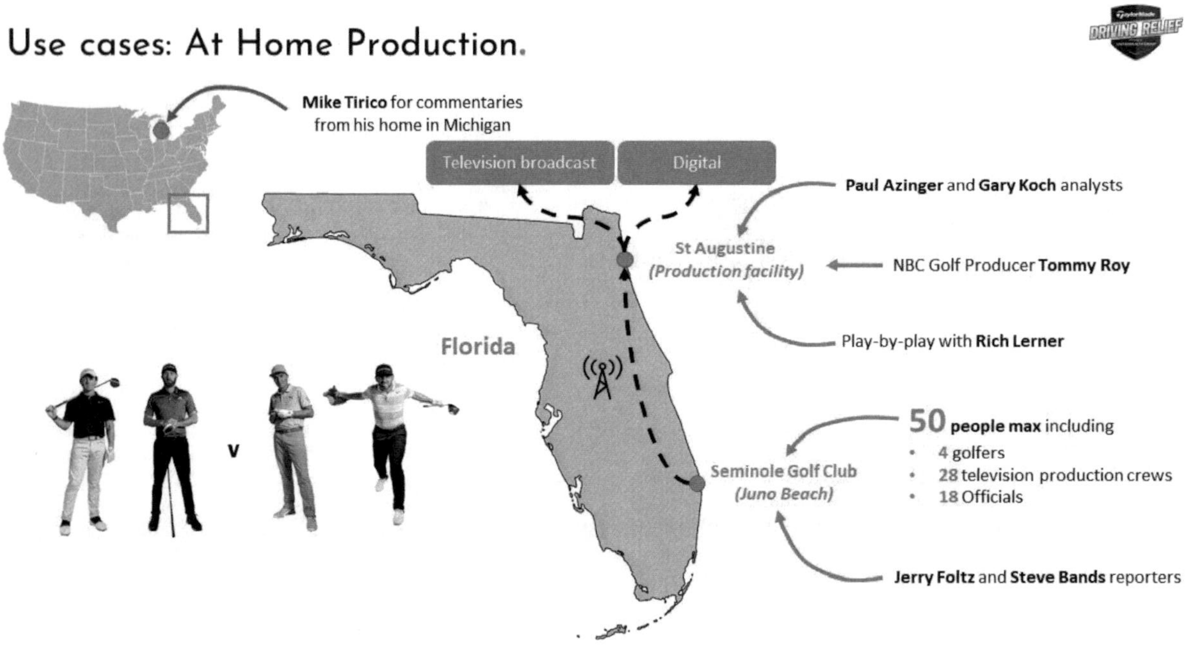

FIGURE 2: PRODUCTION FLOW, INCLUDING CONTRIBUTION FOR REMOTE TALENT

How to accommodate remote talent is another topic all on its own. During the pandemic, sometimes people couldn't travel because of restrictions; sometimes, they wouldn't travel because of their unease. In these cases, the broadcast operators aren't likely to have the resources or ability to send out techs to everyone's homes and set up the equipment for them. So, they're stuck with non-technical people having to set up the gear themselves – they get a shipment with a camera and tripod and a bonded cellular transmitter, and they're left to go it alone. Fortunately, the bonded cellular systems we've been working with are equipped with an "auto live" feature. As soon as the transmitter is powered on (plug it in, throw a switch, attach a battery), the device connects to the cellular network and goes live. So, the talent doesn't have to do anything to make it work, which in most cases is a great relief for everyone.

Another technology that needed to be accommodated for this event was Toptracer, the graphics system that tracks the golf ball in real-time as it flies through the air. Again, this system utilized the analog audio inputs on the bonded cellular devices.

Other Examples

As I stated initially, all of these capabilities and know-how existed before the pandemic struck. They weren't commonly being used for the usual reasons that new technology doesn't gain immediate traction: if your current way of working is working, why change and take the risk? So, before the pandemic, the applications using bonded cellular were those applications that had challenges that couldn't be addressed by traditional means.

A good example is some live reality television shows, where the camera operators must move fast and be flexible, such as some live police shows and shows that follow emergency response teams. The camera operators need to get in and out of vehicles quickly. And you can't have a satellite truck following around police cars and emergency response vehicles, so this bonded cellular technology made these applications -- these kinds of shows -- possible. And for that matter, you can't put a satellite truck on the back of a bass boat either, so fishing tournaments and other events in remote locations become possible to broadcast or at least more cost-effective to broadcast.

Recent Advancements and Conclusion

While most of the tech existed before the pandemic, there has undoubtedly been further development. For example, suppose you have a bonded cellular hub device operating as a receiver, decoder, transcoder, and streaming device by integrating that bonded cellular hub with a cloud service like AWS Elemental MediaConnect. In that case, you have a complete distribution network, enabling quick, easy, and simultaneous sharing of high-quality live content with multiple affiliates or other broadcast facilities. In addition, it provides an all-IP infrastructure with the reliability and security of satellite or fiber services that can be set up in a fraction of the time for a fraction of the cost.

Another significant development is the availability of carrier-agnostic e-SIM cards. This allows bonded cellular devices to connect to the best available cellular network regardless of the provider. Users no longer have to swap out cards if their preferred carrier isn't available at a particular site. The e-SIMS automatically switch over in real-time. These used globally, providing 3G, 4G LTE, and 5G connectivity in 120 countries.

The benefits of bonded cellular productions go beyond just solving problems to cope during a pandemic. Even if the pandemic had not happened, the continued uptake of bonded cellular for live remote production was inevitable. The benefits are numerous and hard to ignore at this point. The amount of time saved in just getting set up is one thing, but the improved efficiency of not having to roll out satellite trucks or ENG vans is enormous. They did not require as many people on site. It all adds up to significant cost savings.

The pandemic gave bonded cellular the chance to be proven, and there's no doubt that it has succeeded.

HDR Challenges and Solutions

Bill Redmann, David Touze, Frederic Plissonneau, Alan Stein
InterDigital
Wilmington, Delaware, United States
bill.redmann@interdigital.com

Guy Ducos
Philips IP&S
Eindhoven, Netherlands

Abstract – Where content producers needed to make drastic choices to allocate the limited contrast and colors in SDR, HDR offers the possibility to show more - meaning greater freedom and flexibility for their storytelling. However, while future-proof, HDR content presents its own challenges, for example, the wide variation in HDR display capabilities and the desire to have any production, HDR or SDR, play optimally on any display, HDR or SDR. The general solution to this issue is tone mapping, whether a tone compression to map from HDR to a lower HDR or SDR luminance, or tone expansion to map from SDR or HDR to a higher HDR luminance. Various techniques of tone mapping, including HLG, static look-up tables, and dynamic metadata, are considered and the relative advantages and performance analyzed.

Introduction

High Dynamic Range (HDR) has only recently been fully deployed into the video ecosystem as a way to capture, produce, distribute, and render images with increased brightness, deeper contrast, and more colors.

HDR has opened a door to content producers' creativity which had been constrained and calibrated to Standard Dynamic Range (SDR) 0.1-100 cd/m^2 limits for the past decades.

While the potential benefits of a higher dynamic range and a wider color gamut are clearly visible to a viewer, a number of challenges have appeared in this new world. Every content producer (post-production, live production…), event (movies, sports…), distribution mechanism (broadcast, streaming…) and consumer device (HDR, SDR TVs, mobile devices) has different constraints, yet all share the same ambition: producing and delivering the best possible image to the end viewer.

What Makes HDR Special?

Originally, HDR was introduced as an *option* for Ultra-High Definition (UHD) TVs, unlike prior video formats, which were mandatory for all TVs. In reality, HDR represents a proposal for *better pixels* [1], which complemented UHD's primary purpose of presenting *more pixels*. Pixel quality and pixel count are orthogonal; each contributes separately to superior image fidelity. Thus, HDR is beneficial to any image size or format, from handheld mobile displays to wall-covering TVs, from resolutions less than HD (< 720p) to UHD1 (4k) and UHD2 (8k).

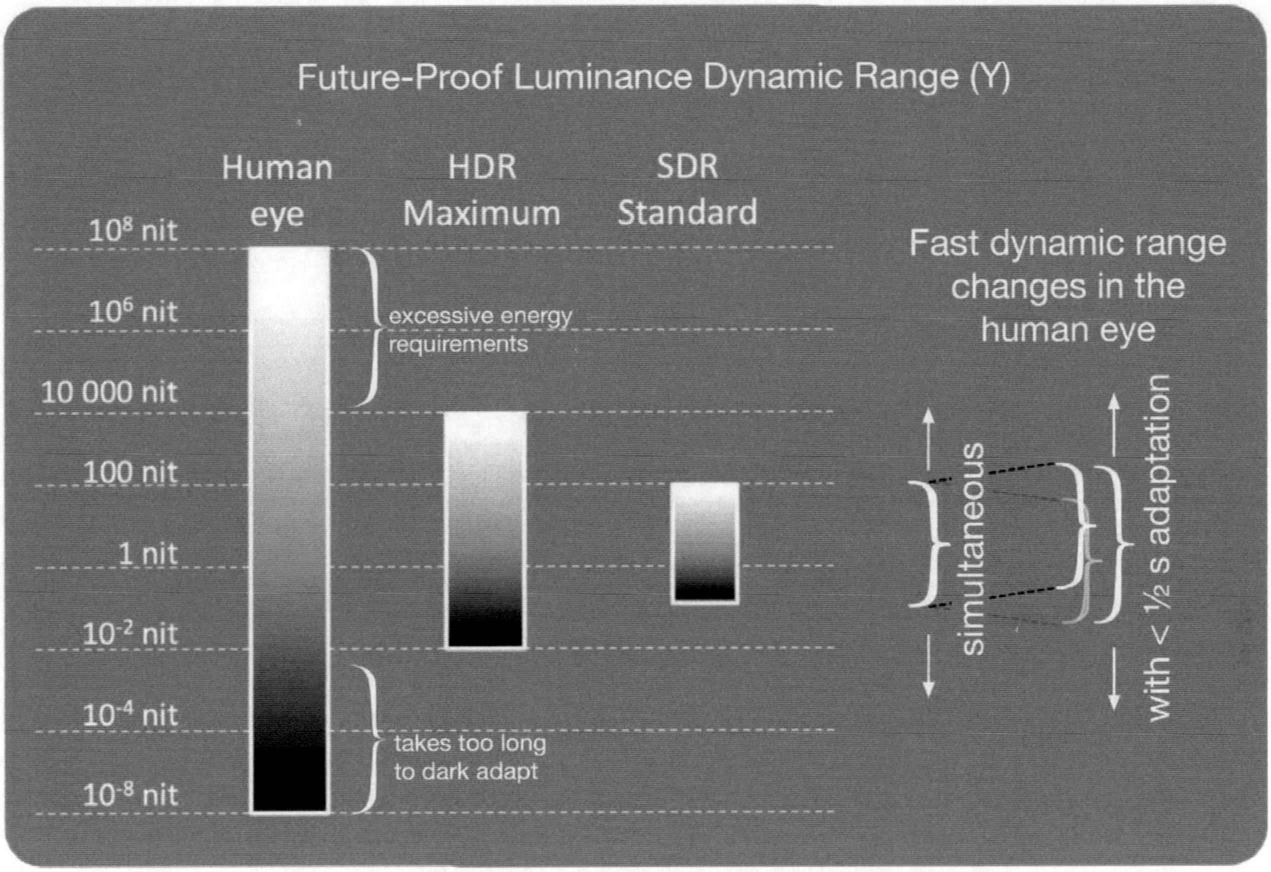

FIGURE 1: A FUTURE-PROOF LUMINANCE DYNAMIC RANGE DERIVES FROM PRACTICAL LIMITATIONS

Indeed, several studies confirm that whatever the display, an HDR image with increased brightness and deeper contrast is clearly adding value as compared to the same image in Standard Dynamic Range (SDR). Figure 1 shows that, while the total dynamic range of human vision extends from glaring sun to dimmer than starlight, the HDR range specified in SMPTE ST 2084 [2] covers a practical, yet future-proof, luminance dynamic range that avoids excessive power and dark adaptation time requirements. The ITU also adopts this scale in BT.2100 [3].

The human eye has a simultaneous luminance contrast range of about 1000:1, wherever in its overall range the eye is adapted. This simultaneous dynamic contrast range is roughly that of SDR's 0.1 to 100 nits, where "nit" is industry jargon for 1 cd/m^2. Typical HDR offers a dynamic range that can require about a half-second of adaptation before the darkest or brightest details can be perceived [4], thereby providing both an experience that is more similar to real world vision in that it requires adaptation at all, and an expanded artistic palette that offers new ways to hide subliminal elements or can engage viewers in a deeper exploration of an image.

Consider that SDR was, until recently, the sole reference for television production, distribution, and rendering, even though SDR is fundamentally directed to the capabilities of cathode ray tube (CRT) TVs, which have become collectors' items [5]. The ambition when introducing HDR was to prepare for devices to become more capable but rely on future-proof formats.

Some HDR formats can represent peak luminances that are 100 times those of SDR formats (up to 10,000 nits, instead of 100). HDR can represent darker blacks, too (1/100th nit, instead of 1/10th). While UHD signals can represent still darker blacks (ST 2084 specifies a lowest luminance value of 0.00004 nits and the UHD Alliance [6] requires black levels as low as 0.0005 nits), these are not practically visible under most consumer viewing conditions in a simultaneous contrast configuration.

Color representation, too, expands to a much wider color gamut: The move in video standards from ITU Rec BT.709 to BT.2100 increased color range by up to 73%, as shown in Figure 2, to cover 57% of the colors humans can perceive, and including nearly all of the colors found in nature.

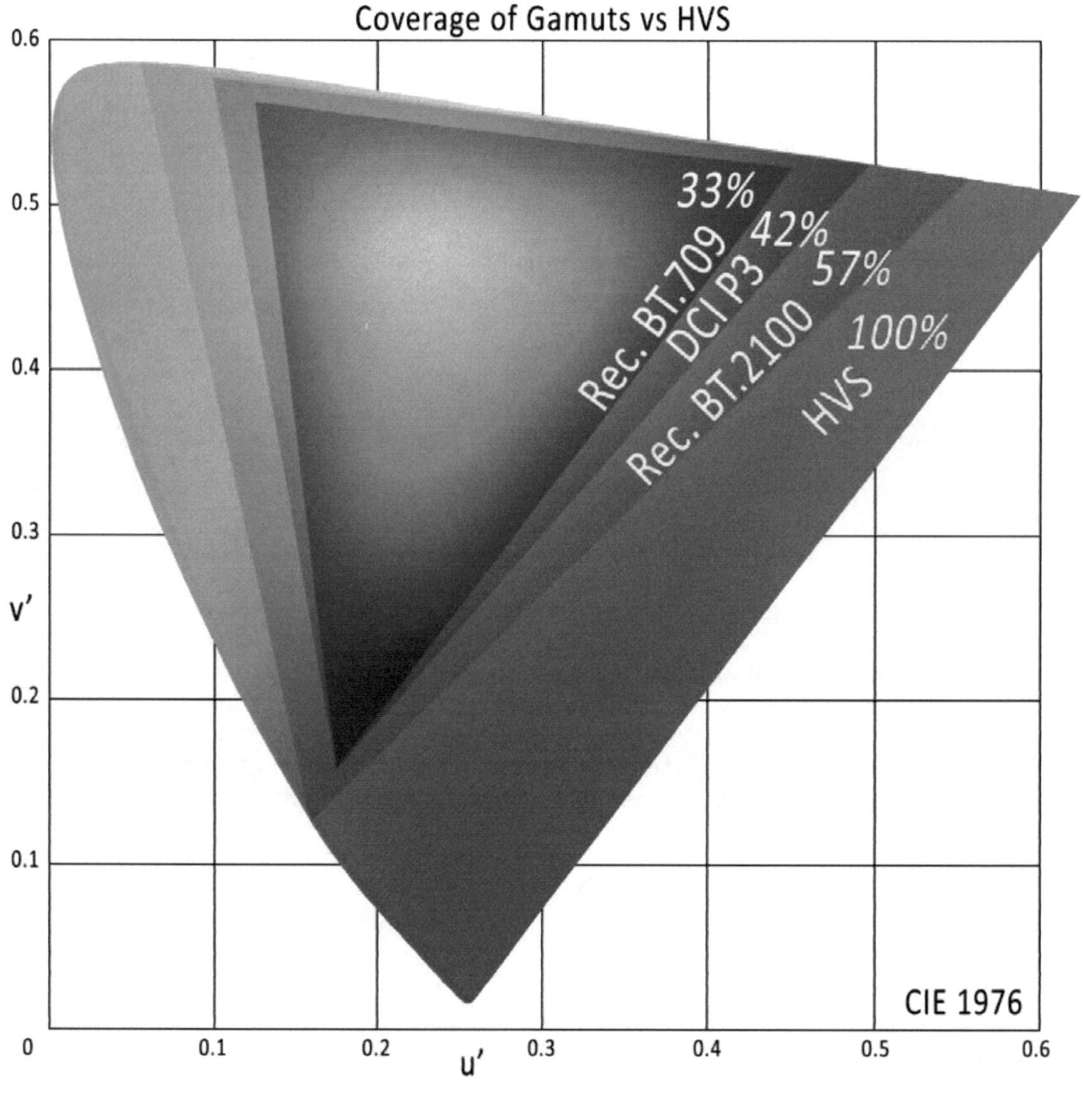

FIGURE 2: STANDARD COLOR GAMUTS AS A FRACTION OF THAT OF THE HUMAN VISUAL SYSTEM.

While no consumer displays can yet take advantage of the full BT.2100 color gamut, there are content production and devices operating under the recommendations of the UHD Alliance [6] that are already achieving increases of 15%-27%, all representing improvements in saturation.

HDR Interest For Content Producers
Drastic choices had always been needed with SDR. Content producers had to allocate the limited available contrast and colors. HDR offers the possibility to show more, meaning greater freedom and flexibility for their storytelling.

FIGURE 3: PHOTOGRAPH OF TWO IDENTICAL LCD TVS, SIDE-BY-SIDE

Just considering whites, in SDR, any bright details or pure graphic whites are clipped at 100 nits. With HDR, a content producer gains the flexibility to capture and retain different "white levels" and can choose whether or not to make bright details and textures visible. Independently, the selection of "diffuse white" offers aesthetic choice in conjunction with the overall image brightness. Figure 3 illustrates how both can be in play simultaneously, while Figure 4 illustrates a presentation where different choices might be appropriate.

FIGURE 4: A BRIGHTER IMAGE IS NOT ALWAYS THE BETTER IMAGE.

The Challenges of HDR

Adapting to change always comes with its share of challenges. While valuable, the introduction of HDR into the media ecosystem is no exception. Talents, skills, infrastructure, devices, and expectations are all stressed.

Mastery of the Capabilities Available
The interplay of whites and overall brightness is just one example of the significant challenges facing those who would create content in HDR: There is a need to develop competencies for how to best exploit these newly available aesthetic choices. These competencies apply to producers, directors, camera operators, engineers, and colorists.

After decades of harmonized, calibrated, SDR production, video engineers and colorists need to be trained for the increased flexibility they can now access. They are going to be called on by others to make their technology perform.

A corresponding challenge exists for manufacturers of display devices, including both TVs and mobile phones, to find the right balance between images that differentiate them from their competition and those that are genuinely immersive.

Initially, industry was treated to HDR demos highlighting the capability to generate much brighter images. While impressive, such images are not ones a consumer would watch with pleasure for a long time on their home TV. Even production crews experience fatigue staring at overly bright images! In a few short years, the industry has come to understand that good HDR images are not necessarily brighter, but rather, images that utilize the dynamic range and color gamut to generate a more appealing, immersive, and pleasant experience.

Luminance Conversion

While HDR is a future-proof way to describe images and enables new artistic options, its whole new range of contrast and color possibilities remains beyond the technical capabilities of many cameras, professional monitors, TVs, and mobile devices to capture and render. After decades of producing, distributing, and rendering against a single SDR calibration, this is yet another challenge introduced by the arrival of HDR.

Consider just the luminance axis, as shown in Figure 5, and focus on only the top portion: The peak luminance capability of different HDR equipment can vary from 4000 nits for a high-end reference monitor, to 1000 nits for a high-end HDR LCD TV, to 600 nits for an OLED TV, and as low as 280 nits for a mainstream HDR LCD TV, which are all higher than the production standard for SDR of 100 nits. Similar issues exist at the bottom portion of the luminance axis.

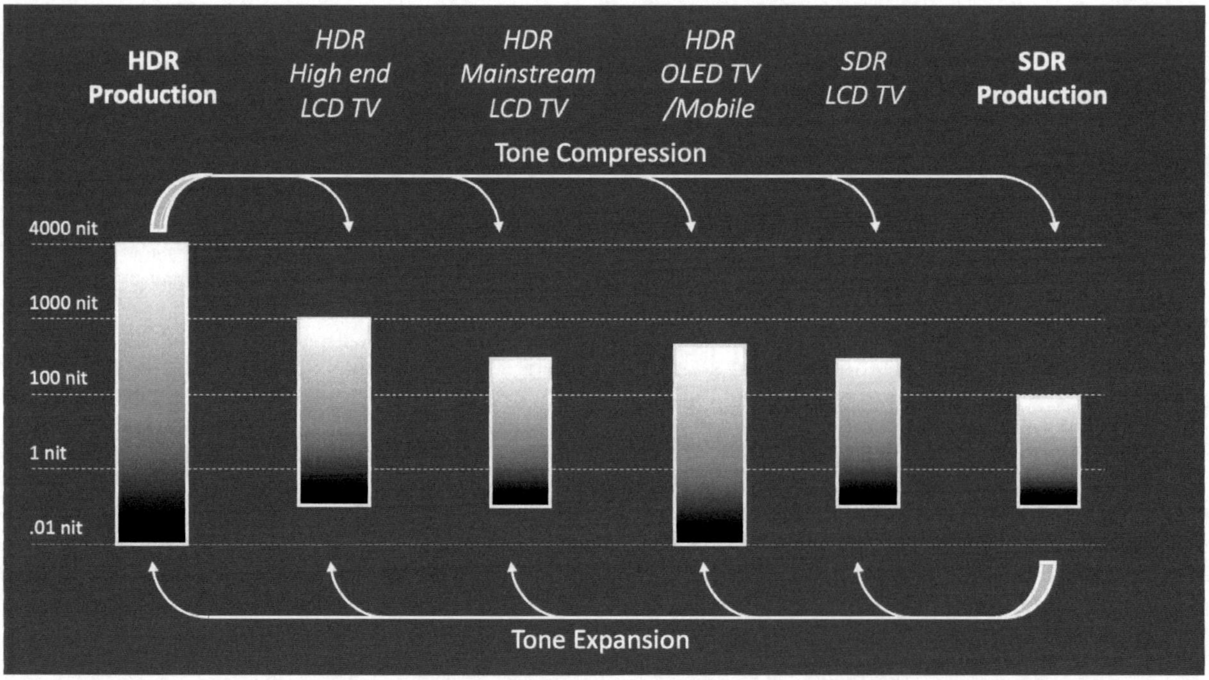

FIGURE 5: THE NEED FOR LUMINANCE CONVERSIONS (TONE MAPPING)

In parallel, SDR is and will remain for some years the dominant share of TVs deployed. Any native HDR production will need to convert down to the ubiquitous 100-nit standard signal if they are to support this SDR install base. Further, because of the diversity of devices, they must support any HDR capability in between.

"Tone mapping" is the formal term for this luminance conversion, whether downward ("tone compression") or upward ("tone expansion"). Tone mapping is a key feature for supporting variations among HDR and SDR devices' peak luminance capabilities.

Such conversions impose choices for how to compress the luminances in an image. The greater the difference between the source and target luminances, the more challenging it is to do tone mapping well.

Perhaps if all images had a uniform luminance distribution, such conversions could be done identically, even mathematically, in a one-size-fits-all fashion. However, real use cases are somewhat more challenging.

The Need for Care in Tone Mapping

Indeed, most video content is a succession of very different images in which, depending on the story and composition of each shot, pertinent details will be found concentrated along varying portions of the luminance axis.

With HDR, as for SDR, this distribution of luminance features depends upon the camera shading and other creative choices that are made.

A worthy concern is that not all the details captured in a 4000-nit HDR creation can be displayed on a 650-nit HDR display, nor maintained in a calibrated 100-nit SDR stream.

The question, then, is how to ensure that details important to storytelling survive as tone mapping is applied, wherever their placement on the luminance axis of the native HDR image happens to be?

Different approaches to tone mapping have been implemented, each attempting to handle this issue. Some solutions are quite simple, others are more elaborate. Many are standardized. To what degree each technique is adequate is a decision for the content creator to consider.

Using HLG in its "SDR Backwards-Compatible" Mode

The first approach for coping with tone mapping from HDR to SDR, was proposed in conjunction with HLG, such that, by keeping an artistic eye focused on SDR production as the primary concern, the production of HDR images having greater dynamic range could be naturally "SDR backwards-compatible," i.e., were an SDR TV to display an HLG-encoded image, the HDR and SDR experiences would be somewhat similar [7][8].

The idea was to exploit the fact that when using HLG as the HDR transfer function, it is substantially similar to the standard transfer function for SDR below about 60 nits. By producing HDR content with only modest enhancements, SDR TVs could indeed display the images without having too drastic an effect.

Practically, while somewhat workable for low brightness images, issues start to appear on images having lots of detail in bright areas.

An additional constraint affecting this technique is that HLG is only standardized using the color space of ITU-R Rec. BT.2100, while conventional SDR, still the dominant distribution and rendering format, uses the less expansive BT.709 color space. As a result, not every attempt to distribute in HLG and rely on this backward compatibility has been successful, running afoul of the many TVs sold before BT.2100 had been adopted [9][10].

Concretely, this means that legacy SDR decoders receiving an HLG signal while expecting a BT.709 SDR signal, will display images with some surprisingly visible hue-shifts, which are hardly acceptable – particularly for sports or advertising, where team uniforms or brand identity would suffer.

In other words, HLG isn't really SDR backwards compatible for distribution. The takeaway is that some deliberate conversion between HDR and SDR is necessary.

Using Static LUTs to Convert Between SDR and HDR

A second approach to provide tone mapping between SDR and HDR relies on 3D-LUTs.

"3D-LUTs are a 'static' conversion method. Essentially, what you are doing is this: a pixel has three coordinates, either (Y, Cb, Cr) or (R, G, B) – these are just different coordinate spaces. A 3D-LUT is a Look-Up Table that converts the three pixel-coordinates together into another set of coordinates. In a nutshell, it maps one pixel color into another. This is done independently for each individual pixel." [11]

To address the challenge of maintaining detail in both HDR and SDR while using 3D-LUTs, two practices have come in place:

- Constrain the HDR being produced, e.g., by limiting "diffuse white" to 203 nits. This provides a reference point about which a LUT is designed to operate but imposes a one-size-fits-all conversion.
- Create different "situationally apropos" LUTs, though this leads to new concerns in that you must make sure the right LUT is being used in every device in the production chain, which could be challenging when you have 25 cameras, etc. Further, downstream, you must know which SDR-to-HDR LUT (or HDR-to-SDR) was used in production, in case you need to reverse the process later in the production chain with the specific inverse LUT to provide a clean "round trip."

These methods have been widely used in 2020 through early 2022 for the production of major sports events, including the Tokyo and Beijing Olympics [12].

Yet there remain professionals who face difficulties when receiving external HDR contribution content, not knowing which LUT to use to down-convert to SDR. Separately, some professionals consider that this constrained HDR does not meet their immersive experience expectations. Marginal satisfaction with LUT-based HDR workflows has led some broadcasters to test dynamic conversions, realizing that the greater flexibility in production provides superior results. Early adopters of static LUTs today agree that to "fully explore the HDR volume…we may prefer to allow a greater exposure latitude in HDR and need to dynamically alter the conversion used to map the HDR to fit in to the SDR colour volume." [13]

Dynamic Tone Mapping to Convert Between SDR and HDR

The utility of dynamic Tone Mapping is being recognized, with the reasons being easily explained: Since the position at which details concentrate along the luminance and color axes will vary, as shown in Figure 6, depending on the image and content, dynamic conversions can provide corresponding mappings between SDR and HDR, preserving details where needed.

In essence, this is what colorists and video engineers have done daily, for decades: Starting from a camera signal that delivers a lot of detail outside the SDR range, the controls and output signals are dynamically optimized to always keep pertinent details safely within the exposure range of SDR.

This changes the emphasis of production. In order to produce great HDR, camera and video engineers, operators and directors should not focus on SDR limitations and constraints, but instead direct their skills and developing expertise to exploiting all the details possible inside the total HDR range of the reference monitor available to shoot and grade their content.

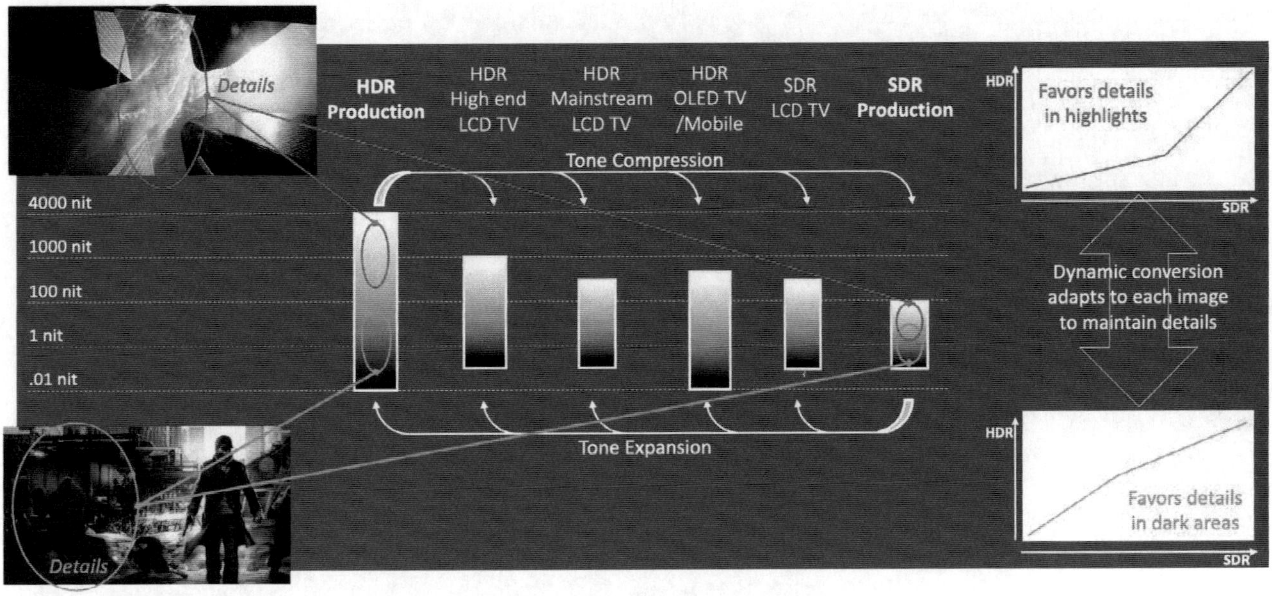

FIGURE 6: DETAILS ARE AT DIFFERENT POSITIONS ALONG THE LUMINANCE AXIS IN DIFFERENT IMAGES. DYNAMIC MAPPING CAN PRESERVE DETAILS WHERE NEEDED.

However, colorists have grading SDR and HDR versions of content for years. Expert decisions are considered and made for perhaps 1500 shots per movie. Such decision-making represents reams of accessible data and where's there's data, there is the opportunity to train a machine learning algorithm, or in the popular vernacular, an artificial intelligence (AI).

While recognizing that tone mapping can be either up or down (as show in Figure 6), depending on the nature of the source content, consider the case of up-converting SDR to HDR. Figure 7 thru Figure 9 are examples of SDR images collectively exhibiting a variety of distributions along the luminance axis and the tone expansion curve that results to produce the HDR image shown for each. Of course, the HDR image, even the SDR image, is far dimmer here than it should be, but the effects of relative degrees of tone expansion within the image can be seen, where details barely visible in the SDR can be more clearly seen in the HDR.

In the tone mapping plot accompanying each figure, the upper diagonal represents a linear mapping of SDR such that 100 nits would appear as 1000 nits in HDR. The lower diagonal represents the linear mapping of the SDR 100 nits to 203 nits, as a first-order approximation of the SDR to HDR conversion Method B described in ITU-R Rep BT.2446 [14] and thus gives an approximate reference along which a properly displayed HDR conversion might appear to be similarly bright when compared against an SDR image presented on a consumer display. Regions of steeper slope represent greater tonal expansion, whereas regions of shallower slope represent lesser tonal expansion. Relatively speaking, regions having a slope less than the slope of the lower diagonal can be consider regions of tonal compression.

The storm clouds in Figure 7 hide the late afternoon sun. While the darkest regions are in the foreground, the storm clouds are represented by dark pixels on the underside, particularly near the rainfall, but near their top they are backlit by diffuse sunlight. The histogram for the SDR image shows the vast majority of pixels are below about 20 nits, and very few are above 50 nits. This is an ideal scenario for conversion to HDR, where the 100-nit peak luminance can be lifted to a full 1000-nits without concern for aggregate power constraints because there are so few bright pixels, and this is the treatment a colorist might reasonably choose when grading/shading an HDR version.

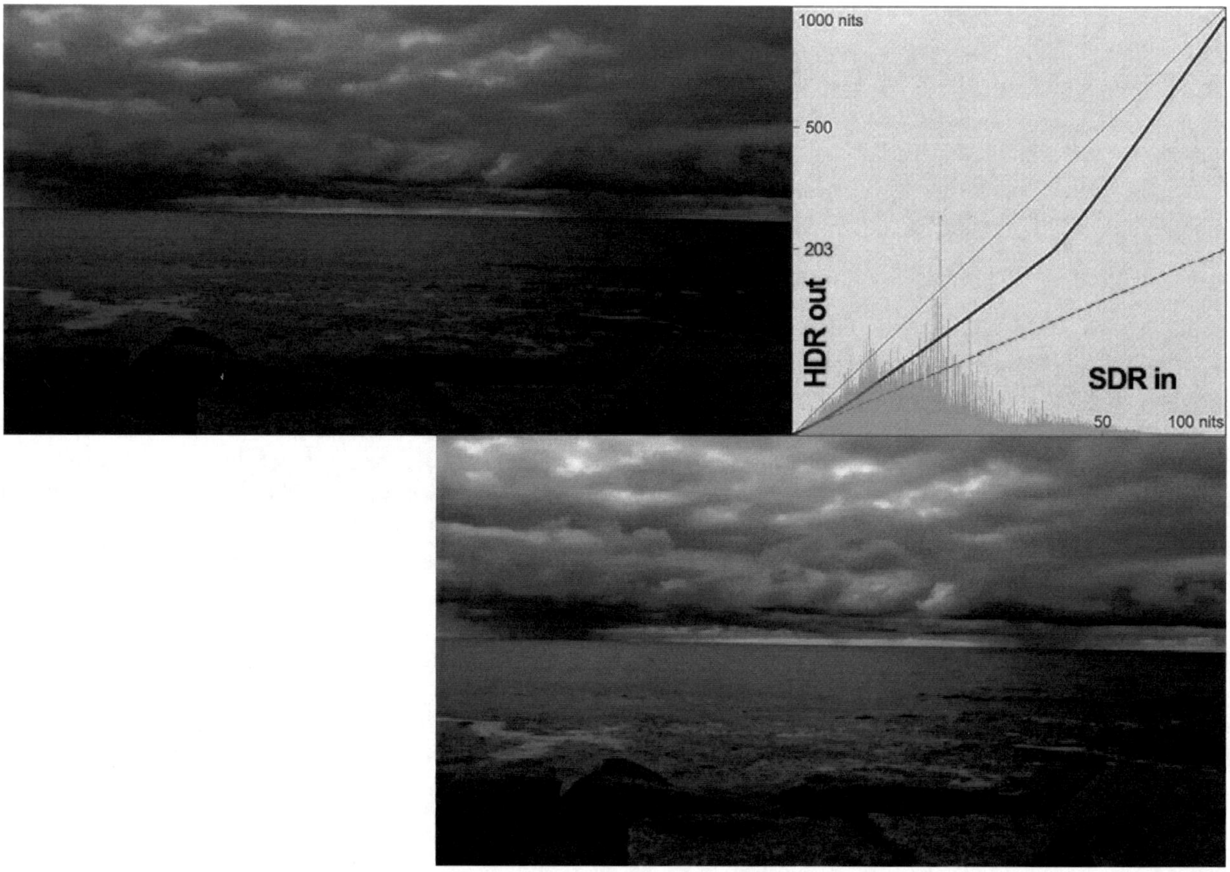

FIGURE 7: STORM CLOUDS IN THE DISTANCE SHOW A FEW SMALL REGIONS THAT ARE BRIGHT.

Figure 8 shows a lamp having an internally illuminated diffuse spherical shade with a number of less diffuse star-shaped regions providing highlights on the surface of the sphere and producing starry projections around the scene. The histogram shows that while many pixels are dim or dark, corresponding to those pixels under the table and representing more distant portions of the wall, there is a non-trivial population that is brighter. Near the 100-nit level, there are two peaks, the larger of the two representing the majority of the lamp's surface, while the narrower one is just a few nits brighter and corresponds to the stars. The peak around 50 nits is from the glossy tabletop. In this case, allowing the 100-nit region of the SDR to scale to 1000-nits would produce an image that is too bright overall, so rather than letting power constraints randomly determine the appearance of the image, the tone expansion at the high end is conservative.

The snowy mountains of Figure 9 are a substantial challenge to an HDR display. A consumer display touting a peak luminance of 1000-nits is not able to present an entire screen at that brightness. In this case, the approach is to increase the contrast primarily in the mid-range luminances, which brings out the texture in the sky. Even more so than for the lamp in Figure 8, the up-conversion is less aggressive with the contrast at the upper end, holding the peak value to about 400 nits.

FIGURE 8: IN THE LAMP, STAR DETAILS ARE CLEARLY VISIBLE AS HIGHLIGHTS IN THE HDR IMAGE (TOP LEFT) BUT WERE ONLY MARGINALLY VISIBLE IN THE ORIGINAL SDR (BOTTOM RIGHT).

From the few examples here, it is clear that differences in conversions between SDR and HDR can be appropriate. Even within the context of a live production of a single event, such differences occur. For example, a golf competition being broadcast presents different backdrop to the action (an open green, bright sand trap, glistening water feature, a gallery sunlit or in shade among the trees, even different skies) and this variety of backgrounds can be encountered from a single camera within a single shot.

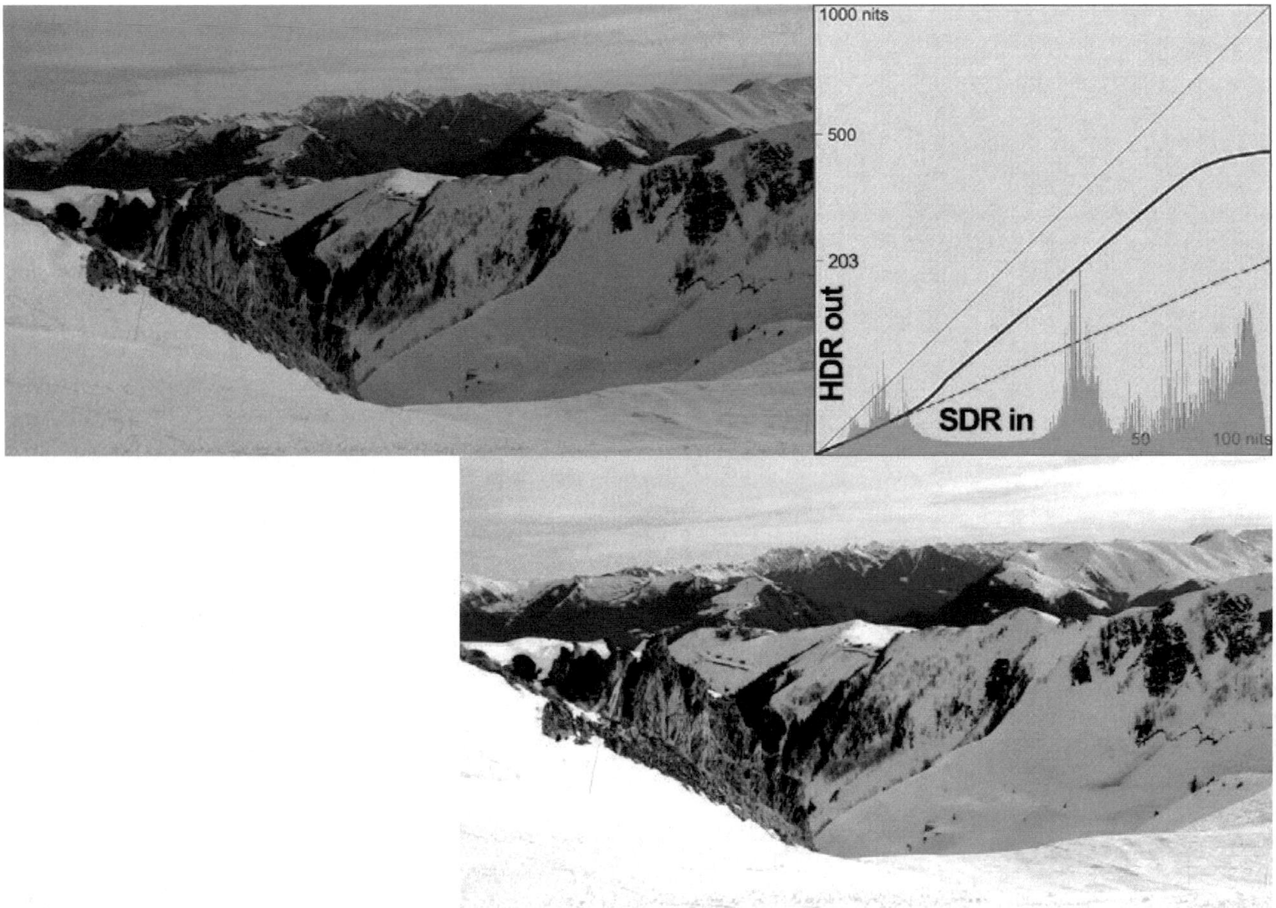

FIGURE 9: THE FOREGROUND SNOW REPRESENTS A SIGNIFICANT PORTION OF THE IMAGE AND IS EXTREMELY BRIGHT.

This evokes a significant question. It is one thing to manage HDR and SDR image production for post-produced content. Colorists have been doing this for years, delivering cinema content according to the motion picture practice of 48 nits, in accordance with SMPTE RP 431-2 and subsequently turning around separate home video grades too: 100 nits for DVDs and variously 650, 1000, 2000, sometimes even 4000 nits for Blu-ray disc; but how is one to perform such dynamic conversions in real time, e.g., for live event production?

Tone Mapping in real time for live production is already done by video engineers. Effectively, this is what occurs when video is shaded either directly on reference displays, or through static conversions, such as with 3D LUTs. However, this means dedicating a video engineer to the conversion and potentially requires adjustments to such tuning at each source change. In some cases, tuning can be reactive, which necessarily comes with some delay, and such a task can be difficult to focus on through a whole live event.

Further, the differences in resulting image quality between what a colorist in post-production can do to an image and what a camera shader can achieve live with a static conversion can achieve over a variety of images must be evaluated and weighed. It is hard to justify one versus the other in terms simplicity because whether a 3D LUT or a dynamic up-conversion is used, the signal must still pass through an up-conversion block.

Artificial Intelligence for Dynamic Tone Mapping in Live Production

Equipping a video engineer with a properly trained AI ally should not only save fatigue, resources, and the related costs, but eliminate latency. An AI in the production environment can analyze each individual image in real time, make adjustments as needed, while requiring little or no supervision.

Such an AI can make the shading choices that a good video engineer or colorist would have and can apply competent aesthetic adjustments that would previously have been made manually. More so, these should be the adjustments that the broadcaster would have wanted to make – had there been time – so that they represent the decisions appropriate for the production at hand.

A key feature that live production needs in a dynamic, real-time, AI-driven conversion between SDR and HDR, is the ability to be tuned, up front, to produce and ensure a consistent "look" that characterizes the particular production and its aesthetic.

Tuning Capabilities to Deliver Aesthetic Intent in Live Production

It is not always the case that tuning a dynamic converter is needed. In large part this will depend upon where in the production and distribution workflow that the conversion is being applied. There is a big difference between the production that takes place in an outside broadcast (OB) van dealing with signals from a mixed bag of cameras and that which takes place in a master control room directing playout from a mix of existing, calibrated contribution sources.

The OB van use case benefits from some care in pre-tuning. One might up-convert the output of a Brand A SDR camera and match the native HDR look produced by a Brand B HDR camera. Such tunings can entail setting the average HDR light (diffuse white), black level, contrast, saturation, and so on.

In a master control room, considering that all the contributions coming in are already calibrated SDR, customized tuning is less critical, and defaults proposed by an unmanned converter might be quite satisfying. Still, a broadcaster might choose different settings, particularly if they wish to manage a different HDR look at the output, for example, depending on whether the content is a movie, live sporting event, or advertising.

In either case, it is important that video engineers have the ability to control the aesthetic choices to be made by an up-front tuning of a converter, after which they are able to rely on the autonomous AI-based system to perform consistently.

Even in a post-production workflow, where real time conversion is not strictly needed, applying the same concepts can represent significant savings in setup time and can accelerate the workflow. Colorists can tune the AI, which can then optimize each shot, providing an efficient starting point, which might even be acceptable as a final grade.

Having the ability to preset a tuning is particularly advantageous when large archives, such as a studio's back catalog, are being processed. Often, all or most episodes of a series can make use of the same tuning, since the look of a series is generally consistent from episode to episode and from season to season.

The Challenge to Enable Great HDR On Any Consumer Device

Once a high-quality HDR program has been produced, including the linear programming that has the HDR program intermixed with additional HDR and SDR sources (e.g., commercials) by leaning on AI-based and tunable converters, a final challenge comes at the far end of the distribution pipelines – How to best render this HDR on all the different HDR consumer devices deployed in the world-wide market?

It is an understatement to say that the UHD/HDR consumer devices available on the market are not homogeneous.

Consider how the market for TVs has developed in recent years:

- Early UHD TVs did not support HDR, they were only SDR BT.709 capable. Some of these are still in use.
- Some more recent HDR TVs only support HDR on an HDMI input (i.e., not on antenna or cable inputs)
- As depicted in Figure 10, about 7 of 8 HDR TVs sold are capable only of less than 500 nits (tagged as “HDR compatible” by Omdia), far below that required by the UHD Association [6].
- Low-brightness HDR TVs often render a worse image when receiving an HDR signal (e.g., due to clipping bright regions in HDR10) than when receiving an SDR signal, leading distributors like Google not to force HDR TVs to take an HDR signal [15].

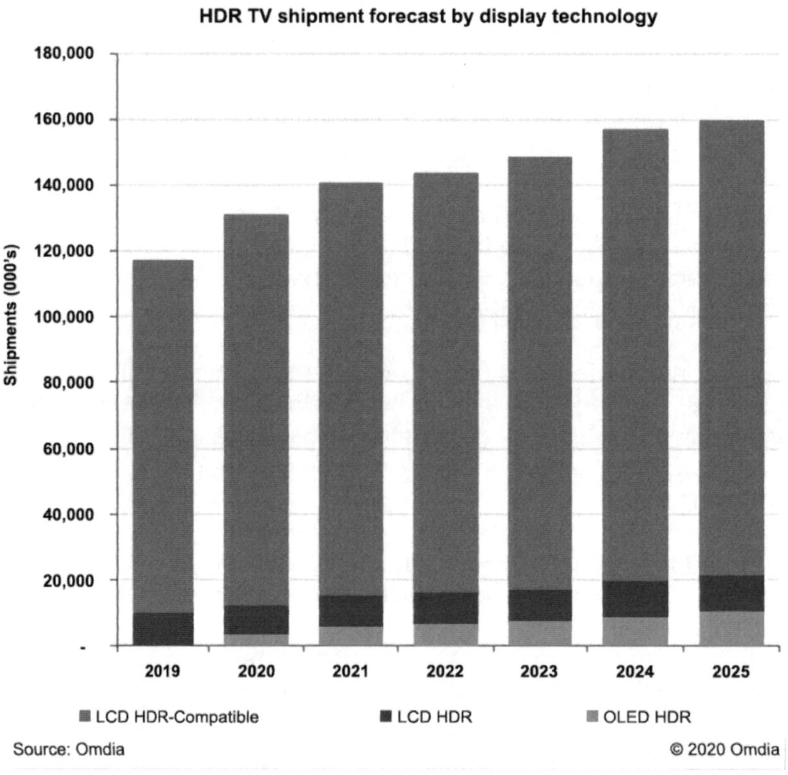

FIGURE 10: HDR TELEVISION SHIPMENT FORECAST.

Thus, a content owner is challenged to deliver programming that offers:

- High-quality images on any device (SDR, BT.709, BT.2020, HDR, 280 nit, 1000 nit, etc.)

- Support for distribution formats already invested in by different broadcasters (SDR, HDR10, or HLG)
- No need for simulcast (for costs and technical reasons…)

Summary of Requirements to Meet HDR Challenges

As presented above, the introduction of HDR has given content producers a greater flexibility and range of aesthetic choices when compared to calibrated SDR, enabling the creation of content that is more immersive.

However, the introduction of different transfer functions, target peak luminances, and color spaces, together with the need to cope with a more diverse range of performance in both production and consumer equipment, presents certain challenges both when producing and distributing HDR content.

The production challenge is to use conversions between SDR and HDR that are:

- Dynamic, to be adaptive to each individual image
- AI-driven, so image analysis and adjustment occur in real time, saving resources and costs
- Tunable, so that video engineers and colorists retain control of the aesthetic choices to be made in conversion.

The distribution challenge is to supply HDR content in a way that produces a satisfying display on any consumer device and, whenever possible, builds on distribution formats in which content distributors have already invested, avoiding the need to simulcast as SDR and HDR. All of this must occur while respecting the varied array of worldwide standards.

These requirements are precisely what has driven the specification and development of the solution that is Advanced HDR by Technicolor.

Advanced HDR by Technicolor

Advanced HDR by Technicolor® is a suite of HDR production, distribution, and display solutions that leverage AI to maximize the image quality of any HDR format, thereby protecting – and enhancing – investments made by industry and consumers in legacy infrastructure and devices.

In the suite, there are two principal tools that can be use individually, or in combination, to support a wide range of use case workflows, both file-based and real-time.

The first of these tools is **Technicolor HDR ITM (Intelligent Tone Mapping**), which is used in production workflows to up-convert SDR camera signals or existing SDR content to the production's preferred HDR format (e.g., SLog3, HLG, PQ). Technicolor HDR ITM is algorithmically complex and relies on professional grade compute resources for its image processing.

The second principal tool is **Technicolor SL-HDR**, which is used for content distribution and thus spans both the professional and consumer domains. On the professional side, HDR content is analyzed, up- or down-converted if needed, and standardized metadata [16][17][18] that parametrically describes that conversion is recorded to accompany the converted signal so that, on the consumer side, the metadata can be applied, if and as needed to reconstruct the original signal and/or adapt that content to specific parameters of the receiving display. The nature of this consumer-side computation is deliberately lightweight to be suitable for implementation on consumer devices. Technicolor SL-HDR enables distribution of a single version of the content, in either SDR or HDR, which will play on any device able to play that single version, but SL-HDR devices will offer the best possible contrast and color their displays can provide.

On the production side, both tools are dynamic systems, with an AI analyzing and optimizing each individual frame. These tools are tunable, to respect content owner preferences. They operate in real time, with low latency (about two frames), which can be masked in its entirety by the multi-frame latency of encoders as they accumulate GOPs. In the professional environment, the conversions are reversible and do not accumulate loss with multiple roundtrips.

Production & Distribution Workflow Overview

Figure 11 does not represent a single workflow, but rather is a conceptual overview of different kinds of production – live and post-produced – and distribution of the content produced. In this case, the productions are shown as being HDR centric, so the producers and directors are looking at HDR images, shading HDR images, and editing HDR images.

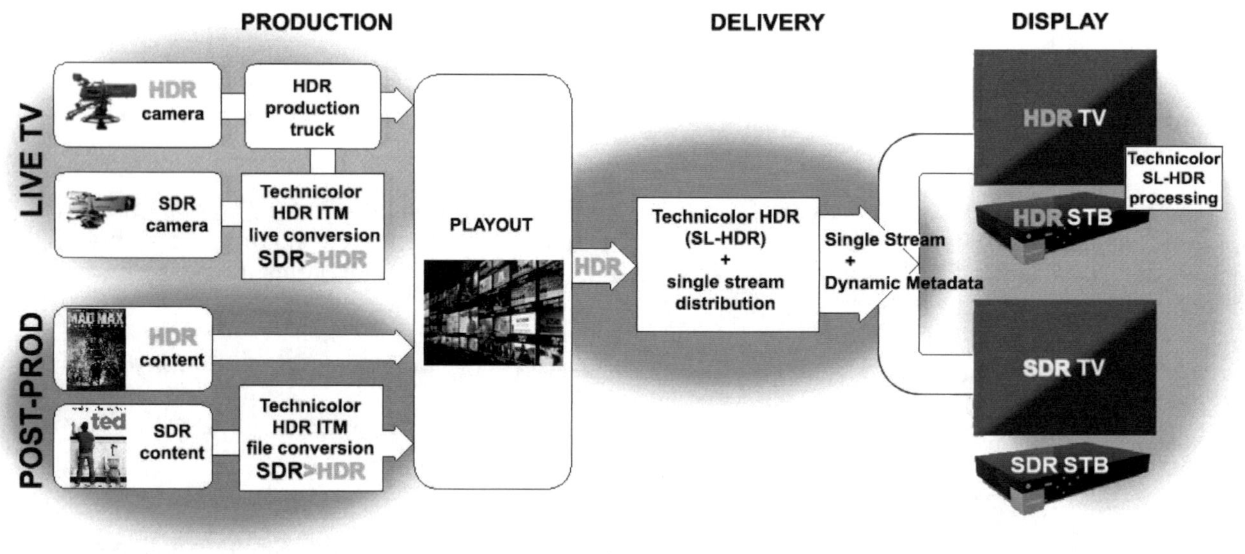

FIGURE 11: SINGLE-STREAM PRODUCTION AND DISTRIBUTION OF HDR.

In general, content sources are produced for HDR playout. If a content source, whether live or not, is received in SDR, Technicolor HDR ITM up-converts the content to HDR. Where the content is already in the production's HDR format, live or not, it can be accepted directly.

The underlying technology is agnostic to the flavor of HDR being used in production and doesn't impose a preference, because computations and analysis are performed on linear light values. Thus, a production can choose to produce HDR in HLG, PQ, SLog3, whether to exploit existing infrastructure or to accommodate a production's aesthetic preferences.

Once the HDR production is ready for delivery, Technicolor SL-HDR delivers an output stream (which can be SDR or HDR) and the corresponding dynamic metadata, for distribution either to consumers, or as a contribution feed (not shown in Figure 11).

Transport of the SL-HDR metadata is standardized in both production [19] and distribution [20][21][22][23][24] environments. However, it is useful to note that SL-HDR metadata isn't typically needed through most of production and is typically created immediately prior to emission or archive. When received as a contribution feed, the metadata is typically applied immediately to provide the content in the receiving facility's preferred HDR format, or it can be ignored, as an SDR-capable affiliate might when receiving a network program, allowing a single contribution feed to be used by HDR- and SDR-capable affiliates alike. As needed, the metadata is regenerated at the point of re-emission, ensuring that it applies to any edits or overlays that have been applied. Of course, a facility has the option of carrying the metadata throughout the production workflow, e.g., if an SDR affiliate were to redistribute to an HDR affiliate downstream, but this is not necessary and not usually done.

Advanced HDR by Technicolor Distribution Standards

As standardized in ETSI, SL-HDR1 [16] uses SDR content and dynamic metadata. SL-HDR2 [17] relies on HDR10 content, while SL-HDR3 [18] is configured to work with HLG content. Each uses only a single layer video (hence the "SL" in SL-HDR).

The reason for three formats (SL-HDR1, 2, or 3) is to best support distributors enhancing their quality of service, whatever previous investments they have made (or not): SDR, HDR10, or HLG.

It is also useful to note the fact that SL-HDR formats are compatible with any existing encoding scheme (8-bit, 10-bit, AVC, HEVC, VVC, AV1, WebM, etc.) and just requires the addition of dynamic metadata (max 60 kb/s) on the existing distribution stream. Even so, there is some evidence that use of SL-HDR1 reduces the net bitrate produced by encoders [25].

On the consumer side, a distribution with native HDR delivery can use either SL-HDR2 metadata (with a PQ transfer function) or SL-HDR3 metadata (with HLG). Upon receipt, an SL-HDR device always enables the display to make the best image of which it is capable.

Content distributed to consumers using SL-HDR1 and native SDR delivery behaves similarly, but has the additional advantage that any legacy device, including TVs, STBs, computers, tablets, mobile devices, etc., can receive the stream, ignore the dynamic metadata, and display high quality SDR. As a true SDR BT.709 stream, this avoids any issues faced by "backwards compatible" formats. Meanwhile, Advanced HDR by Technicolor certified devices reconstruct HDR content and optimize it to their specific display capability (whether 300 nit, 600 nit, 1000 nit, etc.) This is specifically of interest for OTT providers because there is no need to check upfront for HDR device capability and there is no additional file storage. Existing SDR streams are replaced by SDR + dynamic metadata streams, thereby reducing by 1/2 the storage & management requirements for HDR & SDR distribution.

Actual Implementations

Implementations include professional equipment for use in production, system-on-chip (SoC) for device manufacturers, and the manufactured devices themselves. Here are several examples, each a different take on the overview of Figure 11, implementing distinct, user specified workflows.

Sinclair Implementation for ATSC 3.0 Stations

In the U.S., in May 2020, Sinclair Broadcasting Group began deploying ATSC 3.0 stations in HDR using SL-HDR1 metadata. Figure 12 shows a block diagram of the Sinclair infrastructure for the Las Vegas market, one of over twenty regions Sinclair currently serves with over-the-air HD HDR broadcasts. As an NBC affiliate, KSNV Channel 3 receives network content in SDR and also produces local content. In accordance with ATSC 3.0, the broadcast is a 10-bit HEVC encoding. Sinclair has further plans for SHVC (scalable) encoding, while still relying on the SL-HDR1 infrastructure for HDR, to provide robust support mobile devices [26] yet higher resolution to home receivers in a single broadcast.

A list of SL-HDR1 stations is available from the Ultra HD Forum which maintains a publicly accessible Service Tracker on their website [27].

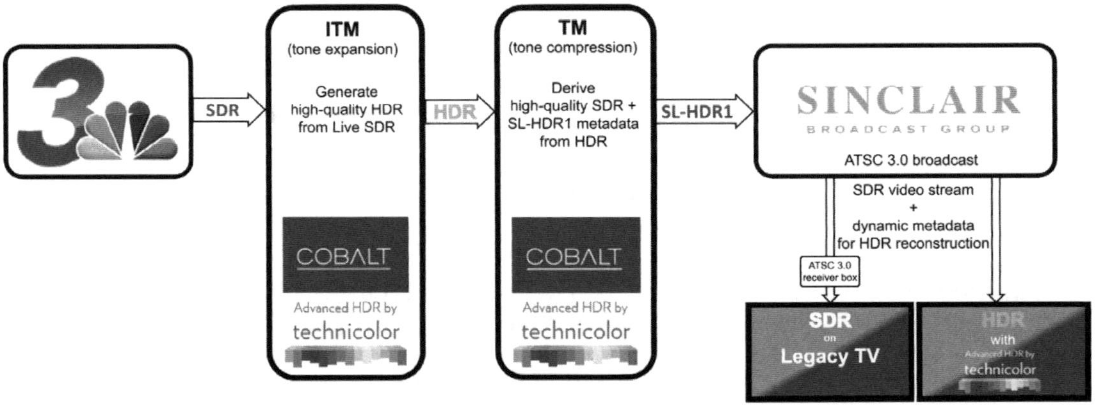

FIGURE 12: BLOCK DIAGRAM SHOWING THE SINCLAIR BROADCAST DISTRIBUTION IN LAS VEGAS MARKET.

ARTE Live HbbTV 2.0 Test Service

In Europe, ARTE, the European culture TV channel has been experimenting with HDR since 2018. [28] Their current deployment [29], shown schematically in Figure 13, makes content available as an or UHD HDR stream using SL-HDR2 for distribution via broadband, while the SDR broadcast is available OTA. The broadcast channel includes HbbTV 2.0 signaling to invite a receiver to switch to the broadband connection for an enhanced experience with greater resolution and HDR.

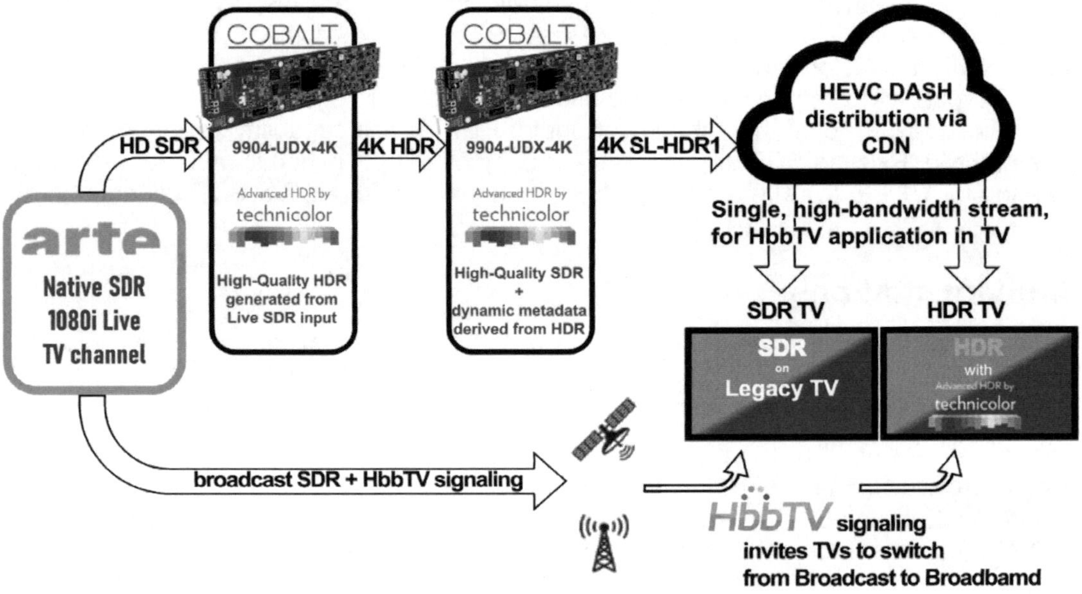

FIGURE 13: BLOCK DIAGRAM SHOWING THE ARTE LIVE HBBTV TEST SERVICE IN EUROPE.

TV Globo Trial in View of Commercial Deployment

In Brazil, TV Globo has conducted broadcast trials over ISDB-Tb according to the TV 2.5 SBTVD standard (AVC 8-bit, BT.709, 1080i) [30] using ITM up-conversion and the SL-HDR1 distribution format. The SBTVD Forum is Brazil's non-profit organization with the mission to "guarantee every Brazilian the right to receive a broadcast with high quality images and sound." The Forum acts as a technical advisory arm of the Brazilian government in matters related to Open Digital TV.

Most notably, the revision to Brazil's television standards remains fully compatible with their only-recently fully deployed Open Digital TV infrastructure ("TV 2.0"), which has been further adopted elsewhere in South America. TV 2.5 also admits HLG, in its SDR backwards compatible mode, discussed at length above. SL-HDR1 is the only dynamic metadata system included in the TV 2.5 standards, specifically because of its intrinsic backwards compatibility to SDR devices. (see [8], Annex H).

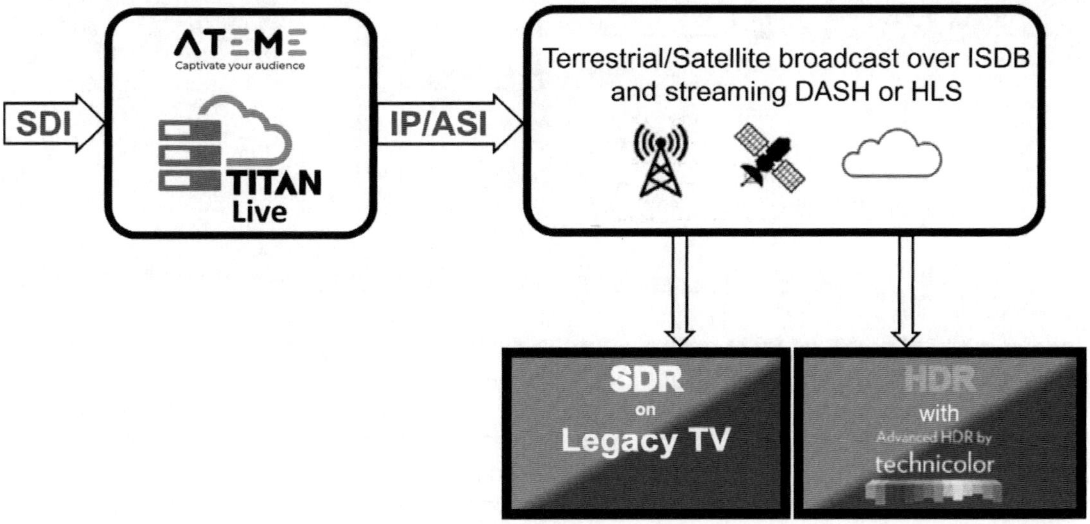

FIGURE 14: BLOCK DIAGRAM OF A TRIAL CONFIGURATION USED BY TV GLOBO FOR BRAZIL'S TV 2.5

Figure 14 shows a block diagram of the later stages of the Globo trial configuration, where the input stage is similar to the two tone-mapping blocks (ITM for tone-expansion and TM for tone-compression) already shown in Figure 12. Here, the HD video broadcast is made available via multiple methods (OTA, satellite, broadband) all carrying the SL-HDR1 metadata. Upon receipt by legacy devices, a quality SDR image is presented, and SL-HDR1 devices will render the more immersive HDR version.

Looking forward to a next generation of broadcast and broadband technologies, SBTVD is writing specifications for TV 3.0 and already includes both SL-HDR1 and SL-HDR2.

Back Catalog Conversions

Many long-time content creators are possessed of enormous back catalogs of legacy content. This includes movies, television series, and specials. Converting such catalogs to HDR would be an obvious way to renew legacy content for today's long tail distribution services.

One pertinent report describing conventional methods for such conversion activities, previously mentioned, is ITU-R REP BT.2446 [14] and its up-conversion Method A, yet we don't see this being done. An explanation for this might be the concern cast over this method by Annex 2 of ITU-R REP BT.2408 [31], which provides an analysis of actual diffuse white levels appearing in broadcast content and finds substantial variation from the mean value. This could, for some images, drastically alter the artistic intent.

Figure 15 illustrates a stunningly simple workflow that employs not only dynamic SDR up-conversion to HDR but an up-scaling to UHD resolution. To support this, sophisticated digital noise filters and film grain removal processes are employed to deliver visually stunning results.

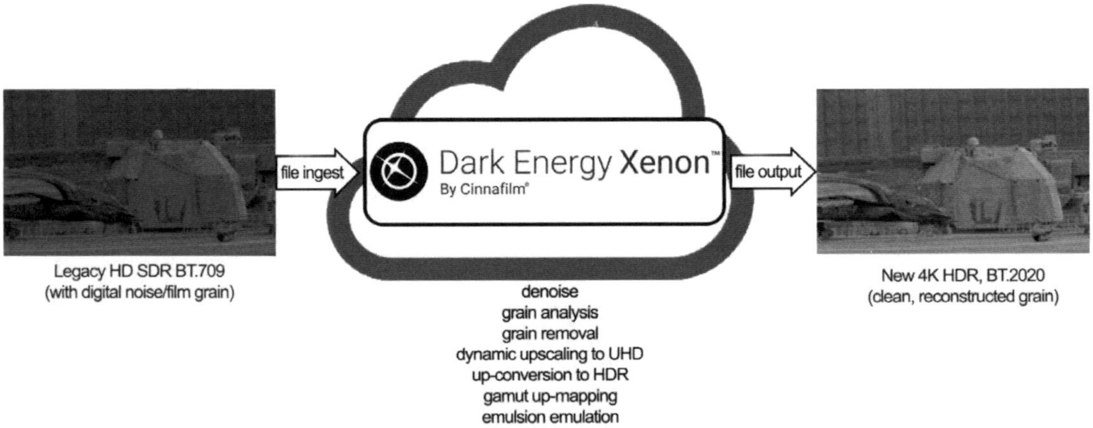

FIGURE 15: REFRESH SDR CONTENT INTO HDR FORMAT

By first removing digital noise and film grain (where it exists), the up-scaling to UHD is particularly clean, leaving the up-conversion to HDR unblemished by artifacts that might have been amplified by the increased resolution. For assets where film grain is a meaningful part of the aesthetic, the original grain structure is analyzed to drive a film emulsion emulation, which can be further manually tuned, before being applied to produce the final result. This process is entirely software-based and thus can run on-premises, given adequate high-end processors, or can be instanced as a service in cloud-based deployments.

Special Live Event Productions

Live performances in UHD represent premium content that can be produced and delivered directly as a live HDR stream. That same content can also be supplied to a far larger audience as an SDR stream, perhaps in lower resolutions, using the techniques discussed above. Figure 16 shows a single-stage workflow and devices that support this function.

FIGURE 16: CROSS-CONVERTING HDR SOURCE INTO OTHER HDR FORMATS, OR DOWN-CONVERTING TO SDR.

This same configuration has been used in OB vans for HD sports productions, where an HDR feed is to be delivered to master control, but contractual requirements demand that an SDR feed be made available to other entities on-site.

Integrated Distribution Appliance

Combining several functions from Figure 11 into a single 1RU device is possible, as shown in Figure 17. Professional content, arriving in HD, UHD, SDR or HDR via SDI or ST 2110 is normalized to the target standard and is provided as SDI or ST 2110, if staying in the professional environment, or if going directly to air or into a CDN for live or on-demand streaming, can be delivered in a variety of compressed formats. SL-HDR metadata ensures that the presentation of the content is optimized regardless of the receiving device.

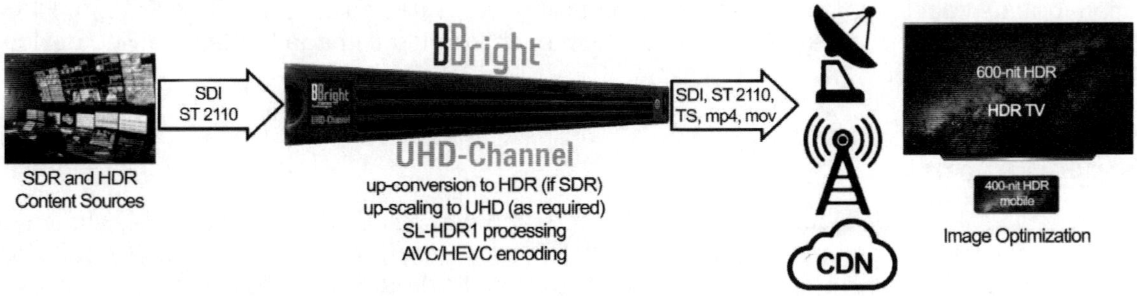

FIGURE 17: STORE AND DISTRIBUTE SDR AND HDR VERSIONS AS A SINGLE-LAYER VIDEO

Summary

Decades of SDR video production targeted exactly one device: The reference monitor. For HDR, there's no such single thing. The diversity of capture and display devices and their widely varying capabilities compel producers, directors, camera operators, engineers, and colorists to grow – to develop competencies for how best to exploit newly available aesthetic choices. Correspondingly, display and camera manufacturers strive to differentiate themselves from the competition yet provide genuinely immersive images. For both camps, the goal is identical: To always produce the best possible image.

Addressing the diversity of cameras, images, and displays comes down to tone mapping. Tone mapping can be done manually. This is the work a colorist performs. Doing that live? Doing that for a 5, 10, 20, 50-year deep back catalog? That would challenge even the most highly skilled and stalwart engineers and operators.

Automatic tone-mapping is widely available in a few readily available forms. The mathematics of HLG provides one form of tone-mapping, though its limitations become too apparent when extended to SDR. Static 3D LUTs offer more control, but either appear in an unmanageable variety, or impose compositional constraints that denature HDR by arbitrarily limiting creative expressiveness, even retroactively, if applied to archival content.

A priori, the best possible solution *must* be dynamic tone mapping, where each image or each shot is treated uniquely, just as colorists have always done. Until the advent of modern AI, untethering that from the unaugmented labor of the artist, engineer, operator has been a profound limitation.

Advanced HDR by Technicolor is a suite of High Dynamic Range (HDR) production, distribution, and display solutions that leverages artificial intelligence to maximize the image quality of any HDR format and applies AI to enable:

- Best picture quality for live-action sports content production and distribution.
- Easy to use, full-picture quality-tuning.

- Fully automated conversion to any target dynamic range (optimizing brightness and color).
- Single video stream distribution to any display.
- Dynamic and tailored adjustment of contrast and colors for any display.

When used in production, Technicolor HDR ITM and Technicolor SL-HDR release content creators from any constraints for producing high quality HDR images while also delivering high quality SDR.

When used in distribution, Advanced HDR by Technicolor can protect -- and enhance -- investments made by industry and consumers in legacy infrastructure and devices. SL-HDR Single Layer HDR distribution formats enable to upgrade any existing distribution video stream (SDR, HDR10, or HLG) to further improve end viewers experience by optimizing each individual image to the receiving device display capabilities.

Acknowledgments

The authors would like to extend thanks to our partners and particularly these individuals, who have contributed invaluably to this paper: **Ateme**: Mickaël Raulet; **Cinnafilm**: Ernie Sanchez; **Cobalt Digital**: Ciro Noronha, Ryan Wallenberg, Chris Shaw, Bob Nicholas; **Philips**: Wiebe de Haan, Joop Talstra, Frank Kamperman, René van der Vleuten; **Sinclair Broadcast Group**: Mark Aitken; and **Technicolor**: Thomas Bohan.

References

[1] Griffis, P., "Next Generation Imaging Formats: More, Faster, and Better Pixels", SMPTE Motion Imaging Journal, Volume 122, Issue 8, November 2013, https://ieeexplore.ieee.org/document/7308250.

[2] "High Dynamic Range Electro- Optical Transfer Function of Mastering Reference Displays", SMPTE, ST 2084, August 16, 2014, https://ieeexplore.ieee.org/document/7291452.

[3] "Image parameter values for high dynamic range television for use in production and international programme exchange", Recommendation ITU-R BT.2100, July 2018, https://www.itu.int/dms_pubrec/itu-r/rec/bt/R-REC-BT.2100-2-201807-I!!PDF-E.pdf.

[4] Kunkel, T., Reinhard, E., "A Reassessment of the Simultaneous Dynamic Range of the Human Visual System", APGV '10: Proceedings of the 7th Symposium on Applied Perception in Graphics and Visualization, July 2010, https://dl.acm.org/doi/10.1145/1836248.1836251.

[5] Moher, A., "Your Grandma's Tube TV Is the Hottest Gaming Tech", Wired, May 27, 2021, https://www.wired.com/story/crt-tube-tv-hot-gaming-tech-retro-games/.

[6] Larsen, R., "UHD Alliance announces 'UHD Premium' specifications & logo", FlatpanelsHD, January 5, 2016, https://www.flatpanelshd.com/news.php?subaction=showfull&id=1452004019.

[7] Borer, T., and Cotton, A., "A 'Display Independent' High Dynamic Range Television System", BBC Research & Development, White Paper WHP 309, September 2015, https://downloads.bbc.co.uk/rd/pubs/whp/whp-pdf-files/WHP309.pdf.

[8] "Ultra HD Forum Guidelines", Ultra HD Forum, version 2.5, November 18, 2021, https://ultrahdforum.org/wp-content/uploads/UHD-Guidelines-V2.5-Fall2021.pdf, section 6.1.9.

[9] Jouinot O., "Rolland Garros 2019L An Ultra HD event channel with MPEG-H Audio", France Télévisions, May 24, 2019, http://idfrancetv.fr/roland-garros-2019-an-ultra-hd-event-channel-with-mpeg-h-audio/.

[10] Paoli-Lebailly, P., "Fransat drops Roland-Garros 4K HDR", Advanced Television, June 5, 2019, https://advanced-television.com/2019/06/05/fransat-drops-roland-garros-4k-hdr/.

[11] Noronha, C., "HDR Format Conversions: Dynamic versus Static", InBroadcast, Vol 11, Issue 8, August 2021, http://europe.nxtbook.com/nxteu/lesommet/inbroadcast_202108/index.php#/p/24.

[12] Kerschbaumer, K., "Live From Tokyo Games: NBC Olympics Team Discusses How HDR Made Leap to Primetime", Sports Video Group, July 28, 2021, https://www.sportsvideo.org/2021/07/28/live-from-tokyo-games-nbc-olympics-team-discusses-how-hdr-made-leap-to-primetime/.

[13] Thompson, S., "Designing UHD HDR for Euro 2020: Islands in the sun", BBC Research & Development, Broadcast and Connected Systems, July 16, 2021, https://www.bbc.co.uk/rd/blog/2021-07-uhd-hdr-television-production-workflow.

[14] "Methods for conversion of high dynamic range content to standard dynamic range content and vice-versa", Report ITU-R BT.2446-1, March 2021, https://www.itu.int/dms_pub/itu-r/opb/rep/R-REP-BT.2446-1-2021-PDF-E.pdf.

[15] Larsen, R., "Chromecast (Google TV) is no longer forcing HDR output", flatpanels**hd**, April 29, 2021, https://www.flatpanelshd.com/news.php?subaction=showfull&id=1619691310.

[16] "High-Performance Single Layer High Dynamic Range (HDR) System for use in Consumer Electronics devices; Part 1: Directly Standard Dynamic Range (SDR) Compatible HDR System (SL-HDR1)", ETSI TS 103 433-1 V1.4.1, August 23, 2021, https://www.etsi.org/deliver/etsi_ts/103400_103499/10343301/01.04.01_60/ts_10343301v010401p.pdf.

[17] "High-Performance Single Layer High Dynamic Range (HDR) System for use in Consumer Electronics devices; Part 2: Enhancements for Perceptual Quantization (PQ) transfer function based High Dynamic Range (HDR) Systems (SL-HDR2)", ETSI TS 103 433-2 V1.3.1, August 23, 2021, https://www.etsi.org/deliver/etsi_ts/103400_103499/10343302/01.03.01_60/ts_10343302v010301p.pdf.

[18] "High-Performance Single Layer High Dynamic Range (HDR) System for use in Consumer Electronics devices; Part 3: Enhancements for Hybrid Log Gamma (HLG) transfer function based High Dynamic Range (HDR) Systems (SL-HDR3)", ETSI TS 103 433-3 V1.2.1, August 23, 2021, https://www.etsi.org/deliver/etsi_ts/103400_103499/10343303/01.02.01_60/ts_10343303v010201p.pdf.

[19] "HDR/WCG Metadata Packing and Signaling in the Vertical Ancillary Data Space", SMPTE ST 2108-1, September 12, 2018, https://ieeexplore.ieee.org/document/8471270.

[20] "Advanced video coding for generic audiovisual services", ITU-T H.264, August 2021, https://www.itu.int/rec/T-REC-H.264.

[21] "High efficiency video coding", ITU-T H.265, August 2021, https://www.itu.int/rec/T-REC-H.265.

[22] "Versatile video coding", ITU-T H.266, August 2020, https://www.itu.int/rec/T-REC-H.266.

[23] "WebM Container Guidelines", The WebM Project, November 28, 2017, https://www.webmproject.org/docs/container/.

[24] "AV1 Bitstream & Decoding Process Specification", Alliance for Open Media, January 18, 2019, http://aomedia.org/av1/specification/.

[25] Noronha, C., Wilken K., Wallenberg R., "Bit-Rate Evaluation of Compressed HDR using SL-HDR1", SVG SportsTechBlog, October 29, 2020 https://www.sportsvideo.org/2020/10/29/svg-tech-insight-bit-rate-evaluation-of-compressed-hdr-using-sl-hdr1/ and (better) The Broadcast Knowledge, March 15, 2021, https://thebroadcastknowledge.com/tag/st-2108/#video150321.

[26] Kurz, P., "ONE Media Testing Demonstrates Viability of 'Mobile First' Strategy", TVTechnology, September 5, 2019, https://www.tvtechnology.com/atsc3/one-media-testing-demonstrates-viability-of-mobile-first-strategy.

[27] Schwarz, B., "UHD Service Tracker B2C", Ultra HD Forum, https://ultrahdforum.org/uhd-service-tracker/.

[28] Briel, R., "Arte launches experimental HDR channel", Broadband TV News, December 10, 2019, https://www.broadbandtvnews.com/2019/12/10/arte-launches-experimental-hdr-channel/.

[29] Ducos, G., "ARTE Launches a New HbbTV 2.0 Test Service for Live UHD Streaming Available to Industry Partners", Ultra HD Forum Newsletter, August 18, 2021, https://ultrahdforum.org/arte-launches-a-new-hbbtv-2-0-test-service-for-live-uhd-streaming-available-to-industry-partners/.

[30] Normas Técnicas – Sistema Brasileiro de TV Digital Terrestre, ABNT NBR 15601-15608, 15610, October 23, 2017, https://forumsbtvd.org.br/legislacao-e-normas-tecnicas/normas-tecnicas-da-tv-digital/.

[31] "Guidance for operational practices in HDR television production", Report ITU-R BT.2408-4, March 2021, https://www.itu.int/dms_pub/itu-r/opb/rep/R-REP-BT.2408-4-2021-PDF-E.pdf.

Live-PSTR: Live Per-Title Encoding for Ultra HD Adaptive Streaming

Vignesh V Menon[1], Hadi Amirpour[1], Christian Feldmann[2], Adithyan Ilangovan[2], Martin Smole[2], Mohammad Ghanbari[1,3], Christian Timmerer[1]
[1]Christian Doppler Laboratory ATHENA, Alpen-Adria-Universität, Klagenfurt, Austria
[2]Bitmovin, Klagenfurt, Austria
[3]School of Computer Science and Electronic Engineering, University of Essex, UK

Abstract – Current per-title encoding schemes encode the same video content at various bitrates and spatial resolutions to find optimal bitrate-resolution pairs (known as bitrate ladder) for each content in Video on Demand (VoD) applications. But in live streaming applications, a fixed bitrate ladder is used for simplicity to avoid the additional latency to find the optimized bitrate-resolution pairs for every video content. However, an optimized bitrate ladder may result in (i) decreased storage or network resources or/and (ii) increased Quality of Experience (QoE). In this paper, a fast and efficient per-title encoding scheme (Live-PSTR) is proposed tailor-made for live Ultra High Definition (UHD) High Framerate (HFR) streaming. It includes a pre-processing step in which Discrete Cosine Transform (DCT)-energy-based low-complexity spatial and temporal features are used to determine the complexity of each video segment, based on which the optimized encoding resolution and framerate for streaming at every target bitrate is determined. Experimental results show that, on average, Live-PSTR yields bitrate savings of 9.46% and 11.99% to maintain the same PSNR and VMAF scores, respectively compared to the HTTP Live Streaming (HLS) bitrate ladder.

Introduction

Motivation

Video on Demand (VoD) and live streaming are widely adopted in video services, and their applications have drawn massive attention in recent years. Since streaming services constantly adapt the video delivery to the end-user's network conditions and device abilities, HTTP Adaptive Streaming (HAS) continues to expand and has become the de-facto standard for providing video over the Internet. In HAS, each video is encoded at a set of bitrate-resolution pairs, referred to as bitrate ladder. Conventionally, a fixed bitrate ladder, e.g., HTTP Live Streaming (HLS) bitrate ladder [1], is used for all video contents. However, due to the extensive variety in video attributes and network conditions, the "one-size-fits-all" can be optimized per title to improve the Quality of Experience (QoE) [2].

Per-title encoding schemes are based on the fact that resolution performs better than others in a specific region for a given bitrate range, and these regions depend on the video content. As shown in Figure 1, for the Bosphorus sequence, the cross-over bitrate between 1080p and 2160p resolutions happens at approx. b_1= 8.0 Mbps, which means at bitrates lower than b_1, 1080p resolution outperforms 2160p, while at bitrates higher than b_1, 2160p resolution outperforms 1080p. For the ShakeNDry sequence, 1080p remains superior at the entire bitrate range, which means 1080p should be selected for the bitrate ladder for the entire bitrate range. This content-dependency to select the optimal bitrate-resolution pairs is the basis of introducing the per-title encoding [2].

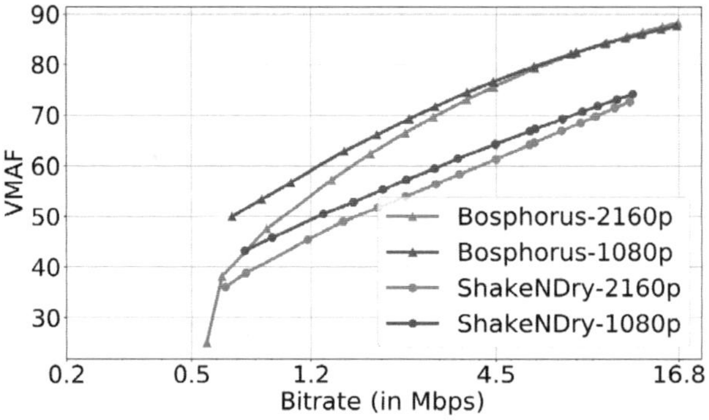

FIGURE 1: RATE-DISTORTION (RD) CURVES OF *BOSPHORUS* AND *SHAKENDRY* SEQUENCES [3] FOR 2160P AND 1080P RESOLUTIONS AT 120FPS.

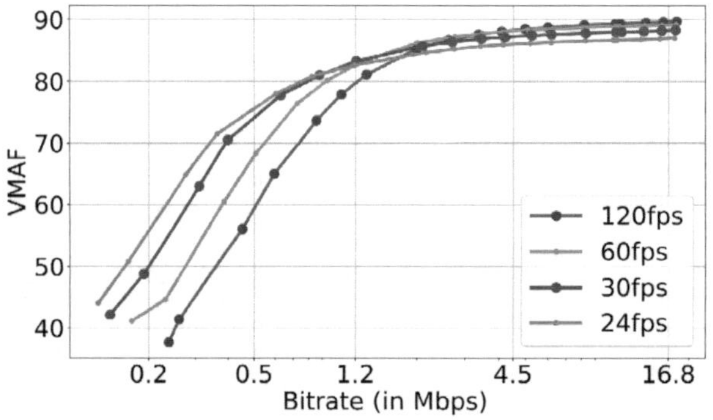

FIGURE 2: RATE-DISTORTION (RD) CURVES OF *HONEYBEE* SEQUENCE [3] AT UHD RESOLUTION AND MULTIPLE FRAMERATES.

In recent years, the spatial resolution of video systems increased to 4K/8K while the temporal resolution mostly remained unchanged [4]. The introduction of HFR videos has stimulated current interest in enriching the viewing experience and visual clarity by increasing the framerate. Several studies show that increasing the framerate reduces temporal artifacts such as flickering, stuttering, and motion blur [5, 6]. However, the main limitation of HFR is a substantial addition in encoding and decoding complexities, which results in increased encoding and decoding times and bitrate overhead compared to low framerate videos [7]. The high bitrate requirement for HFR videos calls for a trade-off between the perceived video quality of *(a)* the compressed video at its original framerate and *(b)* the video compressed at a lower framerate and upscaled in the temporal domain at, *e.g.,* the client [8]. When dropping (some) frames, their bitrate budget is allocated to the remaining frames resulting in a quality improvement of the remaining frames. However, a temporal artifact is added when the video is temporally downscaled. Mackin, et al. [9] showed that higher framerates are advantageous at higher bitrates, particularly in simple sequences with camera motions. However, in terms of encoding efficiency, a lower framerate video performs better at lower bitrates than a higher framerate video. An example UHD (2160p) encoding at various framerates is shown in Figure 2. It reveals that for the *HoneyBee* sequence [3], 24fps is best at 0.2Mbps, 30fps at 1.2Mbps, 120fps at 16.8Mbps. In general, the assumption is that more frames can be dropped in slow-moving videos than fast-moving ones without much noticeable difference in the perceived moving objects' quality [10]. This is the basis for introducing a variable framerate (VFR) coding scheme, depicted in Figure 3. This coding scheme can considerably reduce the bitrate without incurring apparent distortions. Therefore, the bitrate ladder has to be optimized in both spatial and temporal resolutions.

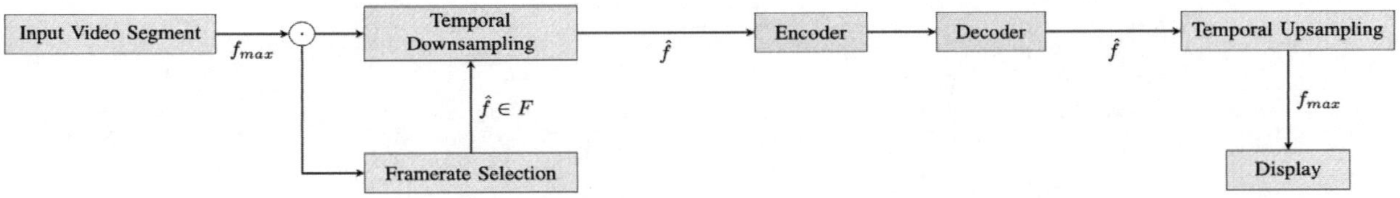

FIGURE 3: BLOCK DIAGRAM OF A VARIABLE FRAME-RATE (VFR) CODING SCHEME [7] IN THE CONTEXT OF VIDEO ENCODING. f_{max} AND $\hat{f}$ DENOTE THE ORIGINAL FRAMERATE OF THE VIDEO AND THE FRAMERATE AT WHICH THE VIDEO IS ENCODED.

Though per-title encoding schemes [2, 8, 11] improve the quality of video delivery, determining the convex-hull is computationally very expensive, which made them suitable only for Video on Demand (VoD) streaming applications. Assuming that the streaming service provider supports r resolutions, f framerates and b bitrates, finding the optimized per-title bitrate ladder requires $r \times f \times b$ encodings [8]. However, some methods pre-analyze the video contents to avoid brute force encoding of all bitrate-resolution pairs [12]. Katsenou et al. [13] introduced a content-gnostic technique that uses machine learning to find the bitrate range for each resolution that transcends the other resolutions. Bhat et al. [14, 15] proposed a Random Forest (RF) classifier to determine which encoding resolution is best suited over different quality ranges and study machine learning based adaptive resolution prediction. Yet, these methods yield latency much higher than the accepted latency in live streaming.

Contributions

This paper presents a low-latency online per-title encoding scheme (Live-PSTR) which improves bitrate ladders for live UHD HFR video streaming applications without any perceptible additional latency. This scheme comprises a resolution prediction algorithm that determines every segment's optimized resolution for a given target bitrate. It also includes a low-latency framerate prediction algorithm which predicts optimized framerate for the predicted resolution and target bitrate for every segment. Content-aware features, i.e., Discrete Cosine Transform (DCT)-energy-based low-complexity spatial and temporal features, are extracted to define video segments' characteristics. Live-PSTR is evaluated using the x265 HEVC open-source encoder [16].

Live-PSTR Scheme

The architecture of the proposed Live-PSTR scheme is shown in Figure 4, according to which the optimized resolution ($\hat{r}$) and the optimized framerate ($\hat{f}$) for every target bitrate for each segment is predicted using the spatial and temporal features (E and h [10, 17, 18]) of the video segment and the set of pre-defined resolutions (R), target bitrates (B) and framerates (F) of the bitrate ladder. The encoding is carried out only for the $(\hat{r}, b, \hat{f})$ tuple for every segment, thereby eliminating the need to encode in all resolutions, bitrates, and framerates to find the optimized $(\hat{r}, b, \hat{f})$ tuples. The convex-hull prediction in Live-PSTR is classified into three steps:

(a) feature extraction,
(b) resolution prediction, and
(c) framerate prediction, respectively.

Feature Extraction

In live streaming applications, selecting low-complexity features is critical to ensure low-latency video streaming without disruptions. In a video segment, two features, *i.e.*, the average texture energy (E) and the average gradient of the texture energy (h), are calculated [10,17–19] as a measure of the spatial and temporal complexity.

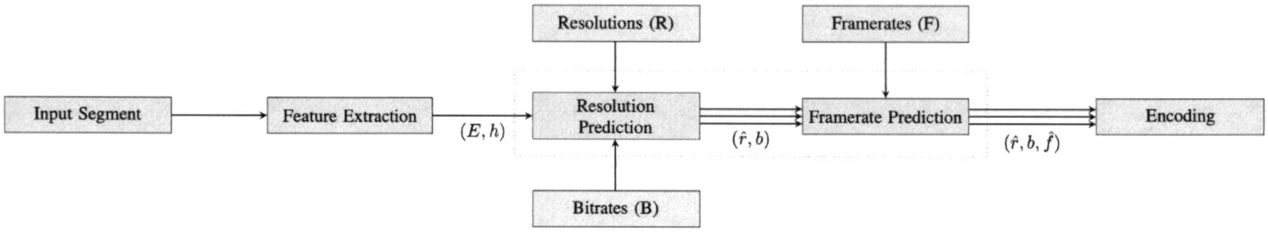

FIGURE 4: *LIVE-PSTR* ARCHITECTURE

Resolution Prediction

Resolution scaling factor (s) is defined as:

$$s = \frac{r}{r_{max}} ;\, r \in R \tag{1}$$

where r_{max} is the maximum resolution in R. In this paper, the optimized resolution scaling factor $\hat{s}$ is determined as a function of the features E and h, and the maximum resolution and framerate. An exponentially decaying (increasing) function is modelled to determine $\hat{s}$ as a function of target bitrate b as shown below:

$$\hat{s}(b) = 1 - s_0 e^{-K_r b} \tag{2}$$

where $s = \frac{r_{min}}{r_{max}}$ (r_{min} denotes the minimum resolution in *R*), K_r determines the rate of decay. The decay rate, K_r, is directly proportional to the temporal characteristics of the segment h and the target bitrate b. At the same time, it is inversely proportional to the spatial characteristics E of the segment. Using this information, K_r is modeled as shown below:

$$K_r = \frac{\Gamma_{MA}(r_{max}, f_{max}) \cdot h}{E} \tag{3}$$

$\Gamma_{MA}(r_{max}, f_{max})$ is the proportion constant named the *Menon Amirpour resolution scaling coefficient*, which depends on the original resolution r_{max} and the original framerate f_{max}. Hence, the final equation for computing the resolution scaling factor is:

$$\hat{s}(b) = 1 - s_0 e^{-\frac{\Gamma_{MA}(r_{max}, f_{max}) \cdot h \cdot b}{E}} \tag{4}$$

To determine $\Gamma_{MA}(r_{max}, f_{max})$, (4) is modified to the form of Y = mX + c as shown below to use linear regression.

$$log\left(\frac{1}{1-\hat{s}}\right) = \frac{\Gamma_{MA}(r_{max}, f_{max}) \cdot h \cdot b}{E} - log(s_0) \tag{5}$$

After determining the optimized resolution scaling factor $\hat{s}$ for any target bitrate, the optimized resolution is determined as:

$$\hat{r} = \hat{s} \cdot r_{max} \tag{6}$$

Framerate Prediction

In this paper, the optimized framerate $\hat{f}$ is determined as a function of the features E and h, the resolution $\hat{r}$ and the maximum framerate f_{max}. An exponential decay (increasing) function is modeled to determine $\hat{f}$ for each segment as shown below:

$$\hat{f} = f_{max}\left(1 - d_0 e^{-K_f \cdot b}\right) \tag{7}$$

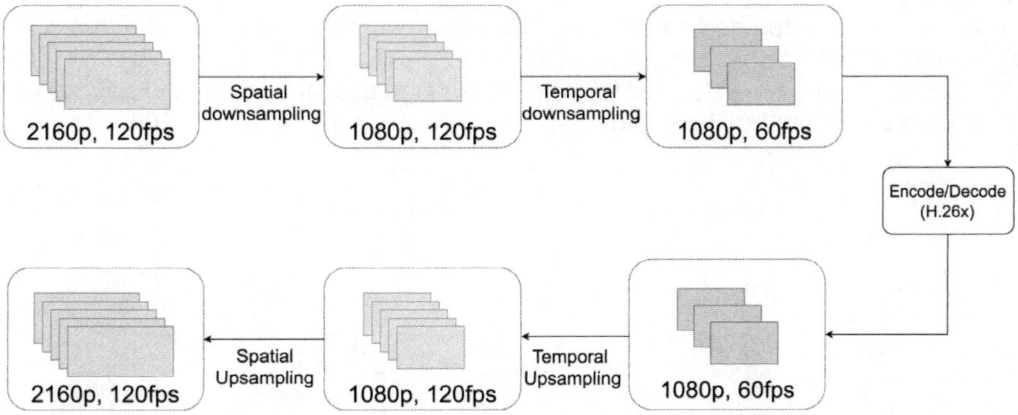

FIGURE 5: THE ORIGINAL VIDEO (2160P, 120FPS) IS DOWNSCALED TO (1080P, 60FPS) AND THEN ENCODED. THE DECODED VIDEO IS UPSCALED BACK TO (2160P, 120FPS) TO MATCH THE ORIGINAL RESOLUTION AND FRAMERATE TO DISPLAY. PLEASE NOTE THAT THE OBJECTIVE METRICS ARE CALCULATED USING THE UPSCALED VIDEO.

where $d_0 = \frac{f_{max} - f_{min}}{f_{max}}$, K_f determines the rate of decay. The decay rate, K_f, is directly proportional to the temporal characteristics of the segment h and the target bitrate b. At the same time, it is inversely proportional to the spatial characteristics E. K_f is thus modeled as:

$$K_f = \frac{\beta_{MA}(\hat{r}, f_{max}) \cdot h}{E} \tag{8}$$

β_{MA} is the proportion constant named the *Menon Amirpour framerate coefficient*, which depends on the video resolution ($\hat{r}$) and the original framerate (f_{max}). Hence, the final equation for computing $\hat{f}$ is:

$$\hat{f} = f_{max}\left(1 - d_0 e^{-\frac{\beta_{MA}(\hat{r}, f_{max}) \cdot h \cdot b}{E}}\right) \tag{9}$$

To determine $\beta_{MA}(\hat{r}, f_{max})$, (9) is modified to the form of Y = mX + c as shown below to use linear regression.

$$log\left(\frac{f_{max}}{f_{max} - \hat{f}}\right) = \frac{\beta_{MA}(\hat{r}, f_{max}) \cdot h \cdot b}{E} - log(d_0) \tag{10}$$

After determining $\beta_{MA}(\hat{r}, f_{max})$, the model predicts $\hat{f}$ for every segment for any given target bitrate and resolution.

On the encoding side, frames are dropped based on the optimized framerate. The video segment is decoded and upscaled in the temporal and spatial domain such that it is displayed at the original resolution (r_{max}) and framerate (f_{max}) as shown in Figure 5. This is because many of the displays do not support VFR coding [7].

Evaluation

Test Methodology

The test sequences are encoded using x265 v3.5 [16] with the ultrafast preset and Video Buffering Verifier (VBV) rate control mode. All experiments are run on a dual-processor server with Intel Xeon Gold 5218R (80 cores, frequency at 2.10GHz). The resolutions specified in Apple HLS authoring specifications [1] are considered in the evaluation, *i.e.*, R = {360, 432, 540, 720, 1080, 1440.

Video Properties				Results				
Dataset	Video	E	h	$\| s_G - \hat{s} \|_2$	$\left\| \frac{f_G - \hat{f}}{f_{max}} \right\|_2$	BDR_P	BDR_V	ΔT
JVET [23]	CatRobot	66.99	12.86	0.01	0.02	-8.95%	-10.43%	-77.62%
	DaylightRoad2	54.78	20.35	0.02	0.03	-9.35%	-13.52%	-76.97%
	FoodMarket4	60.61	22.67	0.02	0.02	-8.74%	-12.11%	-78.01%
UVG [3]	Beauty	37.72	19.34	0.02	0.01	-12.14%	-12.29%	-76.89%
	Bosphorus	23.35	6.33	0.03	0.01	-10.47%	-11.78%	-77.71%
	HoneyBee	40.71	5.29	0.01	0.01	-13.51%	-14.96%	-79.76%
	Jockey	33.79	53.08	0.02	0.01	-7.36%	-11.95%	-76.65%
	Lips	36.96	10.01	0.02	0.01	-6.93%	-9.67%	-76.16%
	ReadySteadyGo	55.40	46.06	0.01	0.03	-5.76%	-10.02%	-76.74%
	ShakeNDry	40.83	10.13	0.03	0.03	-11.31%	-16.02%	-77.67%
	YachtRide	37.72	19.34	0.02	0.03	-6.56%	-9.14%	-77.34%
Average				**0.02**	**0.02**	**-9.46%**	**-11.99%**	**-77.72%**

TABLE 1: RESULTS OF *LIVE-PSTR* AGAINST FIXED BITRATE LADDER APPROACH.

2160}. The lower resolution sources are generated from the original video source by applying bi-cubic scaling using FFmpeg [20]. The set of framerates considered in this paper is F = {20, 24, 30, 45, 60, 90, 120}. The resulting quality in PSNR and VMAF [21], and the achieved bitrate are compared for each test sequence. Since the content is assumed to be displayed on the highest resolution, *i.e.*, 2160p, the encoded content is scaled (bi-cubic) to 2160p resolution, and VMAF and PSNR are calculated. Bjøntegaard delta rates [22] BDR_P and BDR_V refer to the average increase in bitrate of the representations compared with that of the fixed bitrate ladder encoding to maintain the same PSNR and VMAF, respectively. A negative *BDR* indicates a gain in coding efficiency of *Live-PSTR* compared to the fixed bitrate ladder encoding. ΔT represents the cumulative difference in time taken for encoding representations selected using *Live-PSTR* compared to the brute-force approach which encodes in all resolutions, bitrates, and framerates to choose the optimized representations.

Experimental Results

Table 1 summarizes the results of *Live-PSTR*-based encodings using UHD (2160p) resolution and high framerate (60 and 120fps) test sequences from JVET [23] and UVG [3] datasets. The spatio-temporal characteristics of the video are measured using the E and h features [18], which is later used to predict the optimized resolution and framerate for the target encoding bitrates. The optimized resolution scaling factor s_G is determined manually for each target bitrate for every segment which is used as the ground truth. The accuracy of the resolution prediction algorithm is determined by the L_2 norm of the s_G and the selected resolution scaling factor ($\hat{s}$), *i.e.*, $\| s_G - \hat{s} \|_2$. The average $\| s_G - \hat{s} \|_2$ is observed as 0.02. Similarly, the optimized framerate f_G is determined manually for each resolution and target bitrate for every segment which is used as the ground truth. The accuracy of the framerate prediction algorithm is determined by the normalized L_2 norm of f_G. The average speed of the convex-hull prediction for each segment is 370 fps. Hence, *Live-PSTR* introduces no additional latency in streaming. On average, BDR_P and BDR_V of *Live-PSTR* compared to the fixed bitrate ladder approach are -9.46% and -11.99%, respectively. Compared to the brute-force approach to select the optimized resolution and framerate, *Live-PSTR* yields an average time saving of 77.72%.

The improvement in compression efficiency of the encodings of *Beauty* and *HoneyBee* sequences, the predicted optimized resolution and framerates using *Live-PSTR* scheme is depicted in Figure 6.

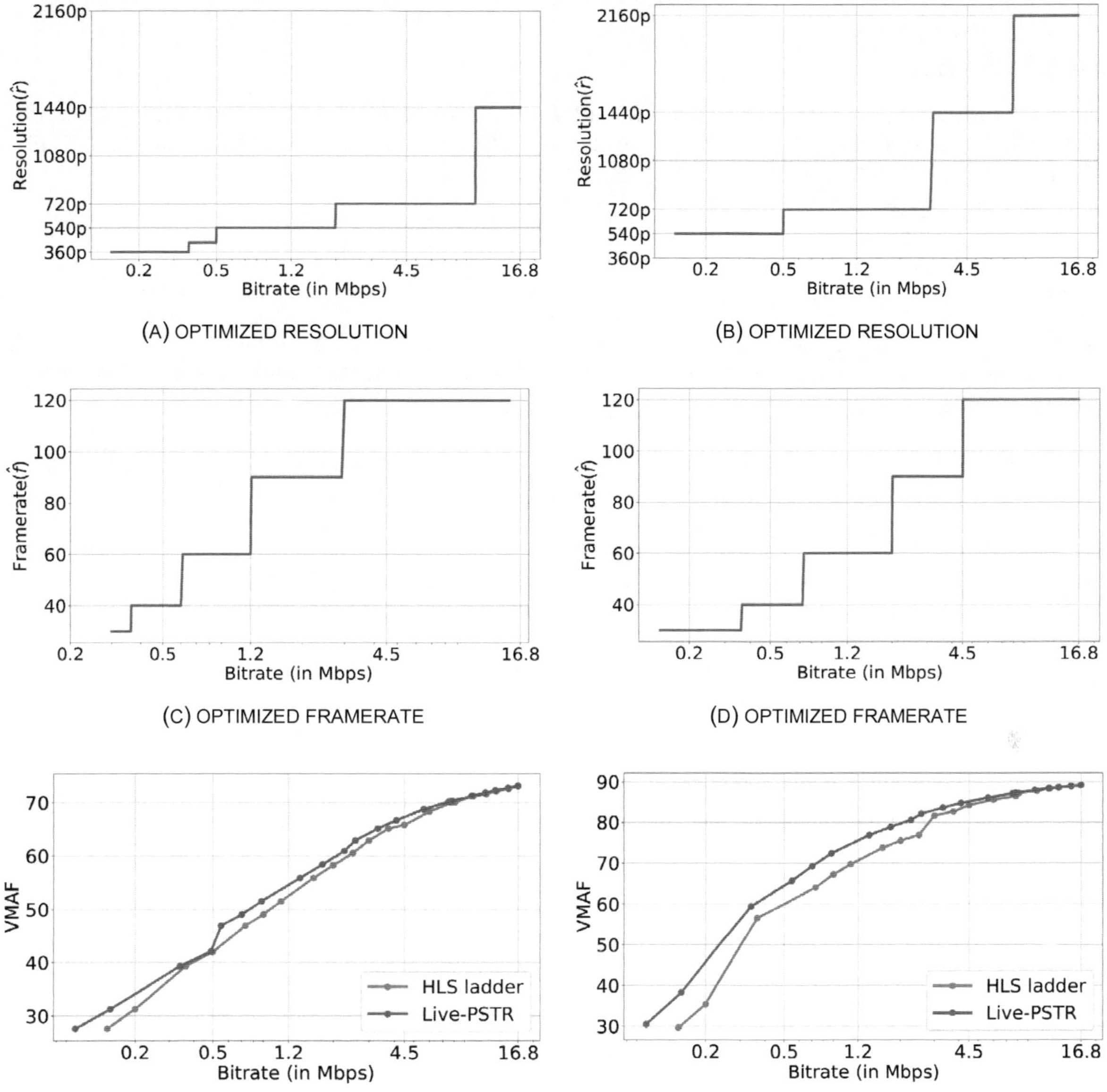

(A) OPTIMIZED RESOLUTION (B) OPTIMIZED RESOLUTION

(C) OPTIMIZED FRAMERATE (D) OPTIMIZED FRAMERATE

(E) RD CURVES (F) RD CURVES

FIGURE 6: THE PREDICTED OPTIMIZED RESOLUTION AND OPTIMIZED FRAMERATE, AND COMPARISON OF RD CURVES OF *BEAUTY* (A,C,E) AND *HONEYBEE* (B,D,F) SEQUENCES USING THE HLS BITRATE LADDER AND *LIVE-PSTR*.

Conclusions

This paper proposed an online per-title encoding scheme with spatial and temporal resolutions (*Live-PSTR*), especially for live streaming of UHD HFR videos. *Live-PSTR* includes a convex-hull prediction algorithm that predicts the optimized resolution and framerate for a given target bitrate for each segment, which helps improve the quality of live streaming. DCT-energy-based features are calculated to determine segments' spatial and temporal complexities, which is fast and effective. It is observed that live streaming using *Live-PSTR* requires 9.46% fewer bits to maintain the same PSNR and 11.99% fewer bits to maintain the same VMAF compared to the HLS bitrate ladder encoding using x265 HEVC encoder.

Acknowledgment

The financial support of the Austrian Federal Ministry for Digital and Economic Affairs, the National Foundation for Research, Technology and Development, and the Christian Doppler Research Association is gratefully acknowledged. Christian Doppler Laboratory ATHENA: https://athena.itec.aau.at/.

References

[1] Apple Inc., "HLS Authoring Specification for Apple Devices," [Online]. Available: https://developer.apple.com/documentation/http_live_streaming/hls_authoring_specification_for_apple_devices.

[2] J. De Cock, Z. Li, M. Manohara, and A. Aaron, "Complexity-based consistent-quality encoding in the cloud," in 2016 IEEE International Conference on Image Processing (ICIP), 2016.

[3] A. Mercat, M. Viitanen, and J. Vanne, UVG Dataset: 50/120fps 4K Sequences for Video Codec Analysis and Development. New York, NY, USA: Association for Computing Machinery, 2020, pp. 297–302. [Online]. Available: https://doi.org/10.1145/3339825.3394937

[4] C. Ge, N. Wang, G. Foster, and M. Wilson, "Toward QoE-Assured 4K Video-on-Demand Delivery Through Mobile Edge Virtualization With Adaptive Prefetching," IEEE Transactions on Multimedia, vol. 19, no. 10, pp. 2222–2237, 2017.

[5] P. C. Madhusudana, X. Yu, N. Birkbeck, Y. Wang, B. Adsumilli, and A. C. Bovik, "Subjective and Objec tive Quality Assessment of High Frame Rate Videos," IEEE Access, vol. 9, pp. 108 069–108 082, 2021.

[6] J. Y. C. Chen and J. E. Thropp, "Review of Low Frame Rate Effects on Human Performance," IEEE Transactions on Systems, Man, and Cybernetics - Part A: Systems and Humans, vol. 37, no. 6, 2007.

[7] G. Herrou, C. Bonnineau, W. Hamidouche, P. Dumenil, J. Fournier, and L. Morin, "Quality- driven Variable Frame-Rate for Green Video Coding in Broadcast Applications," IEEE Transactions on Circuits and Systems for Video Technology, pp. 1–1, 2020.

[8] H. Amirpour, C. Timmerer, and M. Ghanbari, "PSTR: Per-Title Encoding Using Spatio-Temporal Resolutions," in 2021 IEEE International Conference on Multimedia and Expo (ICME), 2021, pp. 1–6.

[9] A. Mackin, F. Zhang, M. A. Papadopoulos, and D. Bull, "Investigating the impact of high frame rates on video compression," in 2017 IEEE International Conference on Image Processing (ICIP), 2017, pp. 295–299.

[10] V. V. Menon, H. Amirpour, M. Ghanbari, and C. Timmerer, "CODA: Content-aware Frame Dropping Algorithm for High Frame-rate Video Streaming," in 2022 Data Compression Conference (DCC), 2022, pp. 475-475.

[11] V. P. K. Malladi, C. Timmerer, and H. Hellwagner, "MiPSO: Multi-Period Per-Scene Optimization For HTTP Adaptive Streaming," in 2020 IEEE International Conference on Multimedia and Expo (ICME), 2020, pp. 1–6.

[12] Bitmovin, "White paper: Per title encoding," 2018. [Online]. Available: https://bitmovin.com/whitepapers/Bitmovin-Per-Title.pdf

[13] A. V. Katsenou, J. Sole, and D. R. Bull, "Content-gnostic bitrate ladder prediction for adaptive video streaming," in 2019 Picture Coding Symposium (PCS), 2019.

[14] M. Bhat, J.-M. Thiesse, and P. L. Callet, "Combining Video Quality Metrics To Select Perceptually Accurate Resolution In A Wide Quality Range: A Case Study," in 2021 IEEE International Conference on Image Processing (ICIP), 2021, pp. 2164–2168.

[15] M. Bhat, J.-M. Thiesse, and P. L. Callet, "A Case Study of Machine Learning Classifiers for Real-Time Adaptive Resolution Prediction in Video Coding," in 2020 IEEE International Conference on Multimedia and Expo (ICME), 2020, pp. 1–6.

[16] MulticoreWare Inc., "x265 HEVC Encoder/H.265 Video Codec." [Online]. Available: http://x265.org/

[17] V. V. Menon, H. Amirpour, M. Ghanbari, and C. Timmerer, "Efficient Content-Adaptive Feature-Based Shot Detection for HTTP Adaptive Streaming," in 2021 IEEE International Conference on Image Processing (ICIP), 2021, pp. 2174–2178.

[18] V. V. Menon, C. Feldmann, H. Amirpour, M. Ghanbari, and C. Timmerer, "VCA," Feb. 2022. [Online]. Available: https://github.com/cd-athena/VCA

[19] M. King, Z. Tauber, and Z.-N. Li, "A New Energy Function for Segmentation and Compression," in 2007 IEEE International Conference on Multimedia and Expo, 2007, pp. 1647–1650.

[20] FFmpeg, "Ffmpeg documentation." [Online]. Available: https://ffmpeg.org/ffmpeg.html

[21] Z. Li, C. Bampis, J. Novak, A. Aaron, K. Swanson, A. Moorthy, and J. Cock, "VMAF: The journey continues," Netflix Technology Blog, vol. 25, 2018.

[22] G. Bjontegaard, "Calculation of average PSNR differences between RD-curves," VCEG-M33, 2001.

[23] J. Boyce, K. Suehring, X. Li, and V. Seregin, "JVET- J1010: JVET common test conditions and software reference configurations," Jul. 2018.

Ground Assault: Obsoleting of Facility Protections

Tom LaBarge, Nancy Swartz, John H. Belk
GroundLinx Technologies, LLC
Blue Ridge, Georgia, United States

Abstract – While broadcast systems adapt to new needs and relatively frequent technical advances, the last line of defense for securing the reliability of facilities full of those new and expensive systems generally suffer from being out-of-sight, out-of-mind. Advances in grounding systems beyond burying a simple rod or plate have been rarely widely adopted beyond Garton's modifying of the surrounding soil (1913), Byrnes' seeping conductive materials into the soil from a pipe electrode (1931), and Ufer's encasing electrodes in modified concrete (1942). New technologies of interest to the broadcast industry have been far more plentiful, and we are seeing the arrival of 5G cellular phones, multiple generations of ATSC, AI, software-defined radios, SVOD, 3D, and vast arrays of power-hungry and data-craving content creation, production and broadcast systems covering transmissions out to at least 30 GHz; all of these systems eventually are electrically grounded to the same old relatively simple variations of a few hunks of metal buried in the yard. Reliable facilities today need their electric current and current faults dissipated quickly and completely in a facility environment that would be barely recognizable even a few years ago. Simple, old-school grounding systems are rapidly becoming obsolete.

Introduction

In the world of broadcasting, digital/electronic advances have completely reshaped the industry, from content acquisition to transmission – and everything in between. Along the way, "traditional" grounding (or earthing) has become completely obsolete and puts entire broadcast plants, from studio to tower, at tremendous operational and financial risk.

Each time a new broadcast technology arrives on the scene, we as an industry focus on the potential benefits of that technology and, for a moment, forget about the infrastructure demands that will need to be faced as a result of adopting new technologies. After a moment of excitement, the industry starts analyzing the real costs of this adoption, leaving the public and our end customers firmly rooted in naïve excitement. This onslaught of new technologies being adopted and considered is huge and littered with acronyms like ATSC, 5G, 6G, WiFi6, AI, SVOD, UX, OTT, TV3.0, UHDTV, DVB-I, and AEA&I, all of which bring with them digital electronics. While the prospects of so many enhancements to entertainment, business and government applications are tantalizing to consider, we as an industry will be called upon at every juncture to be ready with the voice of reason while considering the entire content lifecycle "from creation through consumption" [1].

Cost and Impact

It is hard to overestimate the scale of the equipment at risk when you consider the expected costs of 5G implementations in the United States exceeds $14 million US for a single 50-site millimeter wave and transport core network [2]. Billions of dollars are at stake as we overhaul an already massive digital broadcast environment, and no part of the industry will avoid being transformed.

For critical infrastructure like e911 centers, where costs may be measured more in downtime, the penalties for non-compliance awaiting the operator are steep. For hospitals, where operating costs are balanced against quality of care, the average cost of just their data center downtime was reported as $7,900 per minute during 2016 [3].

Data collected by the Insurance Information Institute indicate that claims for lightning-related damage increased by 77% between 2008 and 2016 and soared 124.6 percent from $920.1 million in 2019 to $2.1 billion in 2020, while lightning-related homeowners insurance-claim costs alone rose 141.3 percent nationally over that same year [4].

What's Changed?

Since Herbert Ufer's invention, a tremendous amount has been learned about lightning, other electrical fault events, grounding efficacy evaluation and improved fault-dissipation strategies. These include:

- Understanding lightning as both AC and DC discharges, containing a cacophony of extremely high frequencies in the AC characteristics of the event.
- Limitations of rod-based grounding in terms of soil impedance mismatch.
- Placement of grounding devices to maximize dissipation and minimize reintroduction of faults.
- Skin-effect depth considerations for grounding system conductors.
- Limitations of using simple low-voltage, low-frequency resistance-to-ground measurements to evaluate high-energy system performance.

Interestingly, very few of the above discoveries and innovations have been incorporated into industry standard designs for traditional grounding systems. As a result, improvements in grounding techniques that could dramatically reduce damage to contemporary equipment and curtail off-air events have been foregone, thus causing per-anomaly losses of tens of thousands of dollars in equipment and revenue. The costs related to relying on outdated grounding systems to protect newer broadcast systems have risen year by year to the point that CEOs are listening with renewed interest to their CFOs' and Chief Engineers' words of concern.

Status Quo: Grounding

A properly designed and installed grounding system is supposed to protect the broadcast facility from electrical faults of all kinds, from internal equipment failures to power company switching faults to lightning strikes. A simple chunk of copper buried in the ground connected via a long solid copper wire or strap simply will neither guarantee reliability nor will it optimize repair and replacement expenses.

Electronic equipment is many times more sensitive to electric-power quality than simple dynamos, power supplies and other analog equipment of the past. In spite of this evolution, grounding methods that are considered industry standards, whether published by professional and safety organizations like IEEE or NFPA, or by equipment manufacturers such as Motorola, have not changed enough to create a grounding environment that protects the expensive, essential equipment and infrastructure now at the heart of every broadcast operation, much less that which is coming. Ground rods and plates as installed and configured simply do not have the storage capacity, bandwidth or efficiency to do all that is being asked of them.

Generally, the health and efficacy of a facility grounding system is about the last thing on a broadcast engineer's mind—right up until the moment a grounding failure burns up critical equipment and/or causes an off-air event. Suddenly, grounding is THE most important subject on the planet, along with how loudly the facility manager is going to scream when he or she gets the news. For most engineers, the mere presence of green wires connecting equipment racks and devices to some mysterious buried wires and rods is good enough: the folks that built the facility had specs in hand and did what they were supposed to do. It's grounded and all is good. Indeed, that may have been the case half a century ago.

Each facility and each company has its own sensitivities to the impact of insufficient grounding infrastructure, of course, but many are shared industry-wide and many are addressable by revisiting their facility infrastructures looking for rats' nests of wires accumulating from years of updates and upgrades, poor grounding in general due to underground corrosion, and inadequate grounding due to newer systems relying more and more on the low-power, low-frequency-handling grounding systems that were originally installed. Clues as to the grounding system being inadequate or seriously obsolete can come from continued lightning-related expenses, event after event, higher electrical noise than desired in all systems, occasional shocks to staff (which often go unreported), or a simple walk around the facility. Any of these can serve as notice that it is time for a professional audit of the facility.

FIGURE 1: ALL TOO COMMON POWER-POLE RESISTANCE-TO-GROUND (RTG) MEASUREMENT.

FIGURE 2: A LOT RIDES ON VERY LITTLE CONTACT.

Traditional grounding is nearly entirely dependent on arrays of ground rods, ground plates, and solid metal wires or straps. The last thing anyone wants is for the grounding system to reject the fault current, sending it into the facility to wreak havoc with the safety of staff and the function of electrical systems. The concept of rod-based grounding as a component of the overall electrical power circuit is more than a century old, developed well before an even rudimentary understanding of lightning characteristics (and other surge/spike events) was known. For standard 50 and 60 Hz electric power, copper-clad ground rods can work quite well, as copper is very suitable for carrying relatively low frequencies.

Advances in grounding systems beyond installing a simple rod or plate have been rarely widely adopted beyond Garton's modifying of the surrounding soil [5], Byrnes' seeping conductive materials into the soil from a pipe electrode [6], and Ufer's encasing electrodes in modified concrete in 1942 [7]. Grounding technology has not measurably changed in more than 75 years. The first line of defense for securing the reliability of broadcast facilities that are now 100% digital, that being the grounding of the broadcast plant, is generally just out-of-sight and out-of-mind—and completely obsolete.

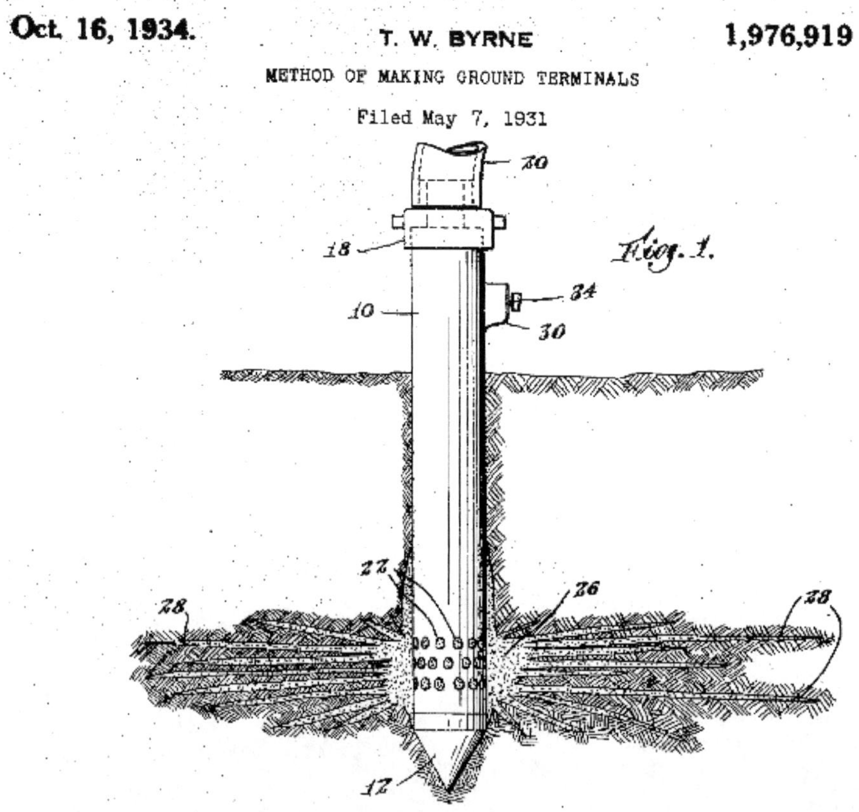

FIGURE 3: BYRNES' POROUS PIPE.

Studies of the corrosion-based frailties of ground rods [8,9] and recommendations by ERICO [10] have not been sufficient to guarantee protection of the electrical grid or facilities in the United States; seriously corroded ground rods are still plentiful.

The more fault current that makes it into the ground, the less that makes it into the building. Copper's electrical conductivity is biased towards low frequencies, but electrical charges occupy different depths from the surface of a conductive rod based on their frequency ("skin effect depth"). Skin depth is calculated as the inverse of the square root of the frequency carried by the ground rod [11]. Therefore, higher frequencies travel at shallower depths, and hence a greater portion of higher frequencies are carried at or near the surface of a ground rod. As such, higher frequencies have greater interaction proportionally with the less-than-desirable properties of soils surrounding a ground rod. The result is a noticeable decrease in the ability of ground rods to carry—and dissipate—high-frequency current.

This is critically important because anomalous surge and spike events, including lightning, are generally filled with a wide range of frequencies, many of which can be in the kilohertz (or greater) range. As an example, a typical 30kA return stroke of lightning can produce electrical current that peaks in 1-10 microseconds, easily introducing frequencies in the 100+ kHz range [12] with a skin-effect depth of less than 1/40 that of household currents. In this situation, right when grounding performance is absolutely necessary, traditional, accepted grounding strategies may be entirely insufficient, if not ineffective, regardless of measured system resistance-to-ground.

What Needs to be New in Grounding

In a facility environment which would be barely recognizable even a few years ago, the need for reconfiguration of protective grounding networks that are truly capable of harnessing and dissipating harmful electric faults of any size and intensity is now entirely obvious. The electronics-destroying components of lightning and electric power supply system transients are well defined. In spite of this, standards and norms for grounding have remained essentially unchanged for many decades. Traditional grounding has become expensively and dangerously obsolete.

Fortunately for the industry, a lot has been learned over the last decades about lightning, other electrical fault events, grounding efficacy evaluation, and improved fault-dissipation strategies. There is indeed also a continuing effort in the industry to explore grounding electrode designs with higher current capacity, increased dissipation efficiency, reduced current back-reflections, broadband absorption, and lower maintenance requirements aimed at various specific applications within broadcast engineering. The next step forward may be for Chief Engineers to rally around increasing the efficiency of their infrastructure protections including grounding systems, and for CFOs to build their business cases for these protections.

References

[1] Exhibits: Go all in on the seriously cool. https://nabshow.com/2022/attend/exhibits, National Association of Broadcasters, 2022.

[2] Supply Chain Reimbursement Program Study, Widelity, FCC DA 21-355, WC Docket No. 18-89, page E-2.

[3] Data Center Performance Benchmark Series: Cost of Data Center Outages, Ponemon Institute LLC, 2016.

[4] Facts + Statistics: Lightning, www.iii.org/fact-statistic/facts-statistics-lightning, Insurance Information Institute, Inc., 2022.foo

[5] Garton, W., Grounding Device, US Patent 1177180A, 1913.

[6] Byrne, T., Method of Making Ground Terminals, US Patent 1976919, 1934.

[7] https://en.wikipedia.org/wiki/Ufer_ground, Wikipedia, 2021.

[8] Romanoff, M., Circular 579: Underground Corrosion, United States Department of Commerce, National Bureau of Standards, 1957.

[9] NFEC, Technical Report R660: Field Testing of Electrical Grounding Rods, Naval Civil Engineering Laboratory, Naval Facilities Engineering Command, 1970.

[10] Rempe, Chris, A Technical Report on The Service Life of Ground Rod Electrodes, ERICO Inc., 1973.

[11] Jordan, Edward Conrad, Electromagnetic Waves and Radiating Systems, Prentice Hall, 1968.

[12] Romero, Carlos, et. al., “A statistical analysis on the risetime of lightning current pulses in negative upward flashes measured at Säntis tower,” International Conference on Lightning Protection, 2012

Thermal Imaging Using Small Unmanned Aircraft Systems (SUAS) for Radio and TV Broadcasters

Paul Shulins
Shulins' Solutions
Wickenburg, Arizona, United States
paul@shulinssolutions.com

Abstract – The advantages of thermal imaging have been well known throughout many industries for decades, as scientists have learned more about electromagnetic radiation and its relationship with detecting heating. Recently, with the advent of digital imaging and small unmanned aircraft systems (drones), broadcasters and others have also realized the value of combining these infra-red (IR) detectors with drones. Reaching places quickly and efficiently with IR cameras mounted on drones can help broadcasters spot anomalies in their transmission systems quickly and, in many cases, prior to damage occurring to the transmission lines and antennas saving many thousands of dollars in lost on-air time and replacement materials and labor. This paper will touch on the theory of thermal imaging as well as some of the practical uses of small, unmanned aircraft systems for visual and thermal tower, transmission line and antenna inspections.

History of Thermal Imaging

Thermal imaging was first discovered in the early 1800's by William Herschel (1738-1822, see Figure 1). Prior to this time the existence of the infrared spectrum was completely unknown. Sir William Herschel was an astronomer, who previously discovered the planet Uranus. While searching for a filter to diminish the sun's glare during solar observations he started testing different colored glass. He noticed that some colored filters passed very little of the sun's heat and others passed significantly more heat. This intrigued him, so he took this experiment a bit further by using a prism and observing the different temperatures of the various colors of the spectrum using a thermometer. When he measured the dark region's temperature beyond the red light, he confirmed that the temperature continued to increase. Herschel named this new portion of the electromagnetic spectrum as the "thermometrical spectrum" and nearly 100 years later the region was named "infrared," the modern term associated with this science.

The usefulness of infrared cameras and detectors became popular in the late 1920's when the military put IR TV cameras to use for anti-aircraft defenses in the UK. Throughout the 1950's and 1960's, development of single element detectors led to the first naval thermal imager used for shipboard firefighting. In the late 1970's, FLIR was founded as a company providing advanced IR Imaging solutions and is still a leader today. [1]

This paper is excerpted from the Proceedings of the 2022 NAB Broadcast Engineering and Information Technology (BEIT) Conference, © 2022, National Association of Broadcasters, 1 M Street S.E., Washington, DC 20003 USA.

FIGURE 1: SIR WILLIAM HERSCHEL.

Thermal imaging hardware devices have come a long way over the past few decades. Today, accessories for smart phones can be purchased inexpensively to adapt IR imaging to the existing hardware contained within the phone, thereby opening up thermal imaging to the masses (an example is shown in Figure 2). However, just capturing thermal images is not enough to be able to diagnose problems. An understanding of how heat is reflected and radiated from different types of objects is generally required. This is referred to as the science of thermography, and different courses and certifications are offered by various companies following the American Society for Non-destructive Testing (ASNT) recommended practice SNT-TC-1A and CP-105. Having a level 1, 2 or 3 certification from this organization is helpful to be able to properly interpret and understand the results of thermal measurements and images. [2]

FIGURE 2: FLIR ONE, AN ACCESSORY TO IPHONE AND ANDROID SMART PHONES.

Infrared is technically classified as electromagnetic radiation longer in wavelength than visible light and is generally invisible to the naked eye. However, there is no hard limit to what is visible to humans as the eye's sensitivity drops off smoothly at 700 nanometers. Sources of light longer than 700 nanometers can be seen if sufficiently bright, creating a danger to eyesight.

Emissivity

Emissivity is a measure of how efficiently an object radiates heat, i.e., how well the surface of an object "tells the truth" about its temperature. Emissivity values range from 0 (a perfect mirror that reflects all energy) to 1 (a theoretical object called a black body) that absorbs and radiates all energy. In general, if the emissivity of an object is less than 0.5 you are unlikely to be able to get an accurate temperature measurement using IR techniques and, in these instances, you may need to find ways to increase your target's emissivity (an example of this is shown in Figure 3). In general, emissivity is one of the more challenging factors to be aware of when making IR thermal measurements. However, if these limitations are understood, it is possible, using the right techniques, to compensate for lower emissivity values.

FIGURE 3: HIGH EMISSIVITY SURFACES LIKE ELECTRICAL TAPE CAN BE USED TO ACCURATELY MEASURE THE TEMPERATURE OF LOW EMISSIVITY SURFACES LIKE SHINY METAL.

Table 1 lists some common materials with corresponding emissivity values:

Copper: polished	**0.05**
Copper: oxidized	**0.65**
Enamel: lacquer	0.90
Fabric: Hessian, green	0.88
Fabric: Hessian, uncoloured	0.87
Fibreglass	0.75
Fibre board: porous, untreated	0.85
Fibre board: hard, untreated	0.85
Filler: white	0.88
Firebrick	0.68
Food & Organic Materials	0.95 - 0.97
Formica	0.94
Galvanized Pipe	0.46

TABLE 1: COMMON MATERIALS WITH CORRESPONDING EMISSIVITY VALUES

There are procedures that allow exact emissivity values to be obtained of specific materials using careful measurements to deduce the values from the readouts of calibrated IR cameras, but in the broadcast industry these are rarely needed, especially since many emissivity values are published for common materials like copper and plastics.

Small Unmanned Aircraft Systems

Small Unmanned Aircraft Systems (SUAS) is the official term the Federal Aviation Administration (FAA) uses to define what are commonly referred to as drones. However, SUAS include several components: the aircraft itself weighing less than 55 pounds (25 kilograms), the remote-control device, and the person operating the controls. The primary use cases for SUAS in the broadcast engineering industry include visual tower inspections, infrared scans for heating, RF signal measurements, and thermal imaging of electrical power panels.

Qualitative vs. Quantitative Thermography

Most all SUAS thermal imaging that is useful to broadcasters is classified as qualitative thermography. The digital images that are captured are radiometric images, JPG images with metadata attached that contain thermal values for each pixel in the image. Unfortunately, these images are usually captured in an uncontrolled environment where wind, relative humidity, and other factors make exact temperature measurements nearly impossible to obtain. Therefore, qualitative examination of the images must be relied upon to determine if there are areas of the antenna or transmission line that appear to have non-uniform heating and are potential problem areas that may need further investigation.

Quantitative thermography, on the other hand, is the science of using specific numbers corresponding to temperatures to determine if a system has changed over time or may have exceeded safe thresholds. These types of measurements are nearly always done in a controlled environment (usually indoors), using calibrated instruments and known emissivity values. Typical quantitative thermography measurements include electrical panels, and RF combiner modules.

Practical and Regulatory Considerations

The FAA has defined a set of rules that cover SUAS operations. The use of an SUAS for commercial purposes is strictly regulated. Today's complex airspace requires pilots of drones, as well as those of commercial and general aviation aircraft to share the airspace in a responsible way.

To aid in this, the FAA has published rules that drone operators must adhere to in order to assure the airspace is safe for all to use. In all cases, a licensed FAA Part 107 Commercial Pilot License is required to operate a drone for commercial purposes. This requires a familiarity with the rules, as well as a test to assure the FAA that the applicant has mastered the knowledge to safely operate in the airspace. In addition, a second person is always required to act as a spotter to maintain visual contact with the aircraft, while the pilot operates the controls to fly the mission and captures the required imagery. It should be noted that depending on the airspace, FAA and local approvals are usually required to fly above 400 feet (122 meters) above ground level.

Additionally, hull insurance and liability insurance are required or are advisable to protect the assets.

Flight Conditions

A large part of the decision as to when it is safe to fly is dependent on the environmental conditions. Many factors need to be taken into consideration. One of the most important factors is the wind speed. Generally, a tolerance is defined by the operator that depends on the equipment being used, the gust factor (sustained wind speed less gusting wind speed), and the skill of the pilot in command.

Other factors include adequate ceiling and visibility so that visual line of sight can be always maintained with the aircraft. In addition, for thermal imaging, it is ideal to fly at dusk or dawn when the sun is several degrees below the horizon to reduce solar loading and maintain a good signal-to-noise ratio. Finally, it should be noted that thermal imaging flights should take place when all the stations on the tower are operational so that maximum thermal effects can be detected.

RTK and RF Interference

Real Time Kinematic (RTK) positioning is highly recommended for drone flights in strong RF fields such as FM and TV transmission towers (see Figure 4). RTK is a technique used to enhance the precision of position-based data derived from satellite-based positioning systems (Global navigation satellite systems, GNSS, GPS, BeiDou, Galileo, and NavIC). The most significant advantage for broadcasters is that RTK can be used to virtually remove the magnetic compass from the aircraft and relocate it to a ground station that is further away from RF interference. In addition, RTK allows for a higher degree of accuracy, lessening the concern about winds, and providing better overall stability for the flight.

FIGURE 4: A TYPICAL RTK OPERATIONAL SETUP.

Challenges and Limitations of an Uncontrolled Environment

Flying a drone outdoors near a tower with high RF, supporting guy wires, and wind presents certain operational challenges. First, it is important to realize that a wind of only 3 miles per hour is enough to cut a temperature reading in half. Considering that the drone's prop wash alone is more than enough to contribute to this, it becomes clear to understand that quantitative measurements of transmission lines and antennas mounted on towers is meaningless. It also becomes clear that the value of thermal imaging is to capture images that can be evaluated in a qualitative way by a skilled thermographer who can interpret the results and point out to the broadcaster areas of concern.

Additionally, it is important for the pilot to maintain a critical angle of acquisition of at least 60 degrees with respect to the target to assure proper readings. Another factor is the emissivity of different components that will result in different image heat contours, that could possibly be misleading. For example, a paper label on a copper transmission line could have a much higher emissivity value than oxidized copper. The results on a thermal image could lead one to believe that the paper label was actually a hot spot on the line. To combat this, a set of RGB (or regular, visual, non-IR images) are useful to identify some of these questionable areas.

The Importance of Spot Size Ratio

Spot size ratio is the ratio of the distance from the camera to the target, compared to the size of the target. This is important to consider for SUAS thermal imaging of a tower and transmission line. It is defined by the focal length of the lens on the IR camera and should be selected to provide acceptable resolution in the final image so that hot spots can be easily seen. Generally, infrared cameras that are gimbal-mounted for use on aircraft have fixed focal length lenses that cannot be changed. For this reason, it is critical to choose an imaging system that is most appropriate for the work being done. For example, a longer focal length lens will allow the operator to obtain high resolution images while maintaining a safe distance from the tower. In contrast, an operator scanning rooftops or solar farms may want to employ a shorter focal length lens to cover more territory. Typically, a focal length of 19 mm is a good choice for tower work (see Figure 5 for typical SSRs).

Lens	9mm	13mm	19mm	25mm
IFOV	1.889	1.308	0.895	0.680
SSR	107:1	155:1	227:1	299:1

FIGURE 5: SPOT SIZE RATIO (SSR) AND INSTANTANEOUS FIELD OF VIEW (IFOV, IN MILLIRADIANS) FOR A VARIETY OF LENSES. AN SUAS WITH A CAMERA USING A 13 MM LENS WILL COVER 12 INCHES FROM 55 FEET (16.7 METERS) DISTANT. IFOV IS OTHERWISE KNOWN AS SPATIAL RESOLUTION.

Typical Flight Deck Preparation

Flying an SUAS is a dangerous undertaking and care must be taken to protect life and property. Some of these aircraft can weigh 10 to 20 pounds (4.5Kg -9.0Kg) and can cause serious damage in a collision. Always set up a safe landing zone area, wear hard hats, and have emergency numbers and a first aid kit on hand in case something goes wrong.

FIGURE 6.: TYPICAL FLIGHT DECK AREA SHOWING CONES MARKING OFF THE LANDING AREA AND THE RTK BASE STATION.

Adjusting the Thermal Span in Post-Processing

There are many good software tools available to manipulate radiometric images which allow the thermographer to more easily detect areas of concern more easily. Most software allows the user to adjust the span of thermal interest in the image. For example, the sky temperature is normally much colder than the tower, and by default, expands the dynamic range of temperatures shown in the image to include the wide range of temperatures the camera captures. However, it's not the sky temperature that is of interest, but mostly the temperatures of the components on the tower such as the transmission lines and antennas. Adjusting the thermal span in post-processing allows for the image to show the maximum detail in the objects of interest as shown in Figure 7.

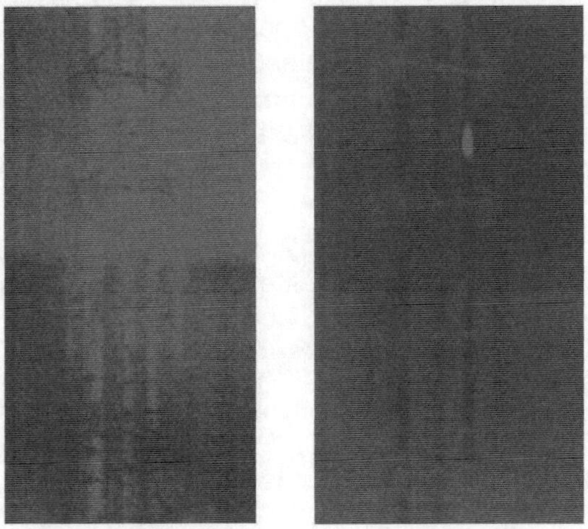

FIGURE 7. THE SAME TOWER IMAGE SHOWN WITH AND WITHOUT POST-PROCESSING IMAGE STRETCH.

Adjusting the Color Palettes in Post-Processing

Different color palettes can be applied in post-processing to help enhance subtle details in the images. Some palettes are more effective for certain applications, but most of the time it is wise to try many different ones to see what is most effective. Changing these colors is non-destructive and will not alter the original image.

The image in Figure 8 shows a transmission lie with a fault that can be recognized easily using different color palettes.

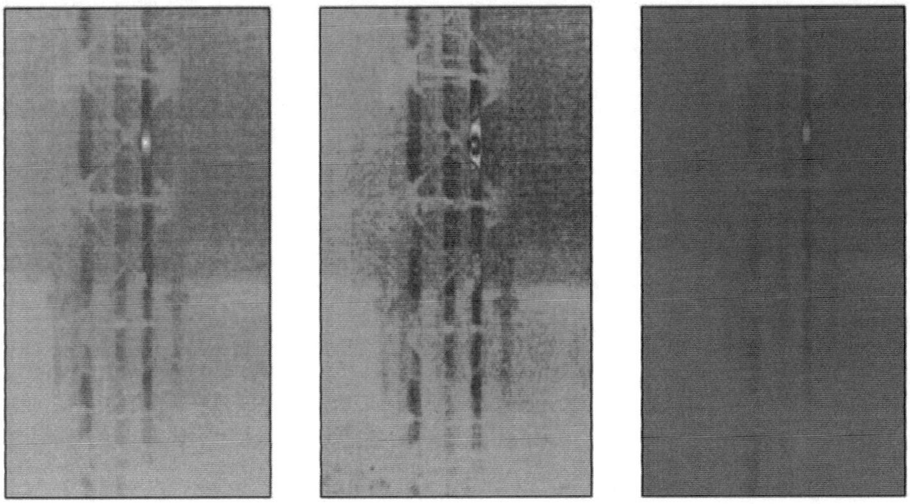

FIGURE 8. THE USE OF DIFFERENT COLOR PALETTES IS DEMONSTRATED HERE. THERE ARE NO RIGHT OR WRONG CHOICES, JUST DIFFERENT WAYS OF PRESENTING THE DATA.

Visual (RGB) Images

In addition to the thermal imaging, as previously noted, RGB images are almost always beneficial to capture, to identify objects such as paper or plastic labels with different emissivity values. These images are also valuable to identify areas on the tower that need attention. While not designed to take the place of a qualified tower climber, locating areas that first need attention before a tower crew arrives can save time and money by directing the crew to exactly where the trouble on the tower is, and having photos of that trouble. The photos in Figure 9 were obtained using a gyroscopically-stabilized camera with a powerful optical zoom.

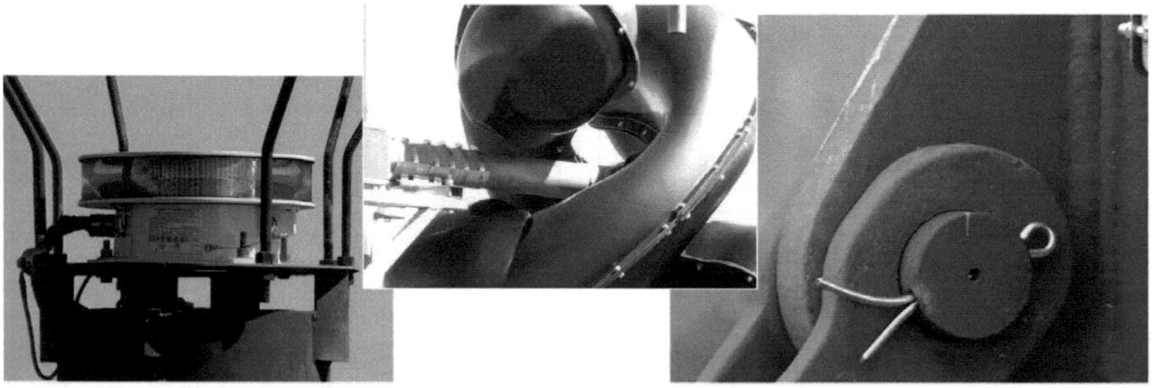

FIGURE 9. SAMPLES OF RGB IMAGES TAKEN WITH A STABILIZED CAMERA FROM AN SUAS WITH A HIGH OPTICAL ZOOM LENS.

Conclusions

Drones can be used in many cases to perform both visual and infrared imaging of broadcast antennas and towers. Proper certification is required (Part 101 FAA license) along with any required FAA airspace waivers. Interpreting the IR imaging requires an understanding of how heat transfer occurs and how IR cameras detect electromagnetic radiation in the IR spectrum. Drones can also provide a unique platform for RF signal measurements. Utilizing drones for intermediate tower inspections will enhance safety, and lower inspection costs.

Acknowledgements

I would like to recognize the following people for their contributions to enhancing the state of the art for thermal imaging as it relates to broadcasting:

FLIR
William Schwahn - Level 3 Thermographer, Instructor
Florida Drone Supply
James Stenberg
Gary and Cindy Cavell
Jim Leifer

References

[1] https://www.flir.com/

[2] https://asntcertification.org/Certification/ASNT_NDT_Landing_Page.aspx